MW00895318

FIFTH EDITION

BUSINESS AND SOCIETY
A Managerial Approach

Heidi Vernon-Wortzel
Northeastern University

IRWIN
Burr Ridge, Illinois
Boston, Massachusetts
Sydney, Australia

IRWIN
Concerned About Our Environment

In recognition of the fact that our company is a large end-user of fragile yet replenishable resources, we at IRWIN can assure you that every effort is made to meet or exceed Environmental Protection Agency (EPA) recommendations and requirements for a "greener" workplace.

To preserve these natural assets, a number of environmental policies, both companywide and department-specific, have been implemented. From the use of 50% recycled paper in our textbooks to the printing of promotional materials with recycled stock and soy inks to our office paper recycling program, we are committed to reducing waste and replacing environmentally unsafe products with safer alternatives.

© RICHARD D. IRWIN, INC., 1977, 1981, 1985, 1990, and 1994

All rights reserved. No part of this publication may be
reproduced, stored in a retrieval system, or transmitted,
in any form or by any means, electronic, mechanical,
photocopying, recording, or otherwise, without the prior
written permission of the publisher.

Senior sponsoring editor: Kurt L. Strand
Senior developmental editor: Libby Rubenstein
Marketing manager: Kurt Messersmith
Project editor: Amy E. Lund
Production manager: Laurie Kersch
Designer: Laurie Entringer
Art manager: Kim Meriwether
Art studio: Graphics Plus
Compositor: University Graphics
Typeface: 10/12 Times Roman
Printer: R. R. Donnelley & Sons Company

Library of Congress Cataloging-in-Publication Data

Vernon-Wortzel, Heidi, 1938–
     Business and society : a managerial approach / Heidi Vernon
-Wortzel. — 5th ed.
       p.   cm.
     Rev. ed. of: Business and society / Frederick D. Sturdivant, Heidi
Vernon-Wortzel. 4th ed. ©1990.
     Includes index.
     ISBN 0-256-11589-3
     1. Industry—Social aspects—United States.   2. Industrial management—United
States.   3. United States—Commerce.   4. Business ethics—United States.   I. Sturdivant,
Frederick D.   Business and society.   II. Title.
HD60.5.U5S88   1994
658.4'08—dc20   93—38861

Printed in the United States of America
1 2 3 4 5 6 7 8 9 0 DO 1 0 9 8 7 6 5 4

To Larry, my
mentor, mate, and
lifetime first
reader.

PREFACE

The fifth edition of *Business and Society: A Managerial Approach* is designed to help future managers confront and deal successfully with the myriad social issues of the middle to late 1990s. This book provides tools and builds skills essential to achieving corporate social goals.

Business and Society is written for upper-level undergraduate and MBA students. Combining academic theory with real hands-on management concerns, it covers a wide range of topics and issues. Each instructor can decide which topics and approaches to emphasize.

With this text as a guide, students learn to identify social issues and their stakeholders, avoid crises whenever possible, and effectively manage those crises that cannot be predicted or avoided. This book will also teach students to integrate social issues and functional business-area strategies.

New Chapters

Four new chapters explore the following topics: crisis management, regulation from an histor-

ical perspective, the current regulatory process, and the international environment.

Crisis Management

Chapter 4 discusses managerial strategies for identifying, handling, and resolving crises. The chapter begins with the Dow Corning and breast implants case, offering models for identifying stages in crisis situations. These models are then tied to three real and very different world events: the Drexel Burnham Lambert junk bond debacle, the Exxon *Valdez* disaster, and the Perrier water contamination scandal. This chapter also makes recommendations for initiating crisis risk analysis and establishing programs to head off potential crises before they arise.

Regulation

Chapter 8, which is the first regulation chapter, examines the development and evolution of regulation from the nineteenth century through Franklin Roosevelt's New Deal. The Interstate Commerce Act and the Sherman Antitrust Act were the first salvos in a twentieth-century barrage of local, state, and federal regulations. This chapter introduces the concept of consumer protection regulations, which are discussed in detail in subsequent chapters. The closing case explores the link between antitrust legislation and foreign competition in the 1980s.

Regulation and Deregulation from the 1960s to the 1990s

Chapter 9 begins with a case on airline deregulation and Air Florida. It goes on to discuss the spate of regulations in the 1960s and 1970s. Beginning with the Carter administration in the late 1970s, the emergence of myriad deregulatory policies had the effect of dismantling, or simply withdrawing resources from, regulatory bodies established only a decade earlier. This chapter presents an in-depth discussion of the effects of deregulation on the airline, bus, trucking, and communications industries. It also examines the regulatory structure of the banking industry during the Reagan and Bush years and the consequences of the savings and loan failures.

Environmental Issues

Chapter 16 focuses on the domestic environment. It begins with a case on the market for the right to pollute, then goes on to explore the effects of the Clean Air Act, the role of the Environmental Protection Agency, and the impact of new clean-air technologies on the automobile industry. Finally, this chapter examines hazardous waste and the evolution of the recycling industry.

International Environment

Chapter 17 deals entirely with the environmental issues that cross national borders. It discusses environmental issues in the European Community, Eastern Europe, the Russian Republic, and Asia. This chapter also looks at the debate over economic development and environmental issues in the developing world. Finally, it focuses on the development of multilateral agreements on the environment.

Additional Topics

This edition includes many new and timely topics:

· Ethics and multinational corporations. Corporations that cross national boundaries have fundamental obligations to the citizens in whose countries they operate. The effects of such voluntary ethics codes as the Sullivan and Valdez Principles are discussed.

· Philanthropy. This topic has been greatly expanded. In addition to a more comprehensive analysis of US charitable giving, this edition takes an international perspective by looking at British and Japanese approaches to the same issue.

· Workplace issues of the 1990s. The impact of technology on employee privacy is examined. New issues include the increase in electronic surveillance and monitoring and the proliferation of workplace violence. Medical issues in the workplace include substance abuse and corporate responses to drug testing. The impact of the Americans with Disabilities Act is a new topic and is discussed in relation to physical disabilities and the AIDS epidemic. The Family Leave bill is also a new topic that is discussed. Family issues in the United States and abroad are discussed. Also addressed are the Clinton health care proposals and their potential impact on corporations.

· Total Quality Management (TQM). TQM is examined as one of the product use issues. The international implications of product quality and American competitiveness in production are also discussed. The growing public concern about the safety of cellular phones and electromagnetic devices is also a new issue.

· Multinational corporations. Multinational corporations and their particular social concerns are addressed more fully. Chapter 18 discusses the problems and opportunities for international tobacco companies and looks at the role of multinational corporations in the North American Free Trade Agreement controversy. The chapter also examines the international legal environment and international codes of conduct, problems of guest laborers in Europe and Japan, and violations of intellectual property rights.

Case Examples

Most chapters in this edition have introductory cases that illustrate real company situations. Students can compare their analyses of these cases before and after they have mastered the analytical tools contained in each chapter.

The Beta Pharmaceutical Company, which is introduced at the end of Chapter 3, continues to be the integrative case. Beta's managers face a variety of new problems in each of the subsequent chapters. Like the introductory cases, Beta episodes are based on concerns real companies face daily. All relevant data are documented and taken from reliable sources. Some situations require that top managers take immediate action, while others allow more time for planning and strategy. In this edition, David Shapiro, vice president and general manager of the Generic Products Division, joins other division heads.

Acknowledgments

Frederick Sturdivant pioneered the managerial approach in the business and society area. Having happily used the first three editions he authored, it was a real pleasure and privilege to carry on his tradition in the fourth, and now the fifth, edition.

I want to thank the following people for their cogent reviews of the fourth edition: Dan Dudley, Tarleton State University; Judith Neal, University of New Haven; and Robert Weight, University of Phoenix. A special acknowledgment is due Robert Giacalone of the University of Richmond for preparing an excellent instructor's manual.

My graduate and undergraduate students tested many of these chapters prior to publication. Their comments contributed to the quality of the book. I particularly appreciate Janet Sutherland's expertise in developing exhibits and her cheerful and fruitful forays into the library stacks.

Heidi Vernon-Wortzel

BRIEF CONTENTS

CONTENTS

I

Strategic Management of Social Issues

In the last few years of the twentieth century, corporations face new economic and social challenges. It is more imperative than ever before that managers meet these challenges with organized, comprehensive, and well-developed strategies. Universities and colleges, recognizing their responsibility to train managers of the future, have begun to incorporate strategies for social issues management into their curricula.

Part I of this book provides models, processes, and tools to help managers handle the social issues their companies encounter daily. The following six chapters analyze the components of social responsiveness, strategy formulation, strategy implementation, crisis management, and ethics. The chapters provide an historic setting for the discussion of social issues and the analytical tools for integrating companies' social issues with their business strategies.

Beta Pharmaceuticals

Beta Pharmaceuticals, introduced in Chapter 3, is the integrative case in this book. The company faces a new dilemma in nearly every subsequent chapter. Each dilemma is related to the issues discussed in that chapter.

Beta's strategic social issues problems are similar to those nearly all large, divisionalized companies face. Although Beta is a fictitious company, the data used in the case and the problems its managers encounter are real.

1 BUSINESS AND SOCIAL RESPONSIVENESS

All corporations have multiple stakeholders. *Stakeholders* are individuals and groups that have an involvement or an investment in the company's decisions and in its social and economic exchanges. The involvement may be direct or indirect. For example, when General Motors decided to close its Willow Run, Michigan, plant and move operations to Arlington, Texas, the owner of the luncheonette across the street anticipated he would lose most of his business. Although he was not employed by the company, he was a stakeholder in GM's decisions as surely as were the supervisor of an assembly process, the union steward, the plant manager, and the nurse in the infirmary.

In the course of doing business, stakeholders judge firms primarily by the quality of their products and services. However, there are additional parameters on which stakeholders assess corporate performance. More and more frequently, stakeholders are evaluating firms based on how well those companies manage social issues.

This book will help current and prospective managers develop the skills they need to respond effectively to their stakeholders' legitimate expectations. When stakeholders raise tough questions about companies' broad societal policies, managers must be prepared with the answers and have in place strategies to meet those expectations.

Even in the absence of specific stakeholder challenges, managers should incorporate social issues management into the strategic planning and implementation processes used to achieve other corporate goals. No corporation is immune to social issues crises any more than it is invulnerable to financial or marketing crises.

Objectives of This Book

This book explores management's role in contemporary society. It encompasses the economic, social, political, legal, and technological factors that affect business. The book has two principal objectives. The first is to enhance managers' understanding of the issues raised by interactions between business and its social, political, and legislative environments. The second is to help managers develop the framework, tools, and procedures that will enable them, systematically and strategically, to become responsible corporate citizens.

Historically free enterprise has always been a dominant institution in the United States. Today free enterprise is a worldwide trend. In the past decade, other countries have turned their large and small government-run corporations back to the private sector. The current international trend away from planned economies toward free enterprise is helping to create a worldwide management culture and foster global interactions among firms.

Regardless of their location, corporations create goods and services. To a great degree, their success depends on their technological progress and the individual growth, development, and creativity of their managers. Companies can and do supply financial opportunities and security for many millions of people around the world.

Yet the production process generates by-products that may harm the environment and society. Along with goods and services, companies create toxic wastes, polluted water, and unhealthy air. In addition, they contribute to unplanned urban sprawl, uneven distribution of wealth, unsafe products, and ethically questionable situations.

Since the 1960s, the debate about what elements constitute a corporation's proper role in society has sharpened. Diverse groups of stakeholders pressure corporations to conform to their view of what corporate behavior should be. Ethnic and racial minorities, environmentalists, consumer advocates, and special-interest lobbyists join regulatory agencies, union leaders, academicians, politicians, and social commentators in demanding that corporations take particular actions. These demands are frequently contradictory and sometimes counterproductive.

The relative power of different groups of stakeholders changes over time. As the issues important to one group dissipate or are resolved, new stakeholder groups take up the banner and respond to new local or national concerns.

The essential issue for every group is the appropriate role of business in an increasingly complex world. Over the past decade, millions of stakeholders in scores of countries have joined the debate. It is incredibly difficult for managers to respond to multiple competing demands on a national basis and even more difficult when stakeholders have global concerns.

Nonetheless, it is essential that social issues management take on global dimensions. The major challenge for corporations, wherever located, is to develop strategies that will help managers work toward a reasonable definition of their appropriate societal role and do an effective job of *implementing* and *managing* social issues.

This chapter begins with a look at the issues of the 1990s and beyond. It discusses linkages between the environment and corporate strategy. The chapter also explores the nature of capitalism and the meaning of responsibility in business, government, and society.

Issues of the 1990s and Beyond

The economy, social climate, physical environment, and composition of the workforce all help determine the mix and scope of social issues corporations and their stakeholders face. Thoughtful managers recognize that they need to address a wide spectrum of national and international economic and social concerns. US stakeholders encounter complex, difficult problems with no easy answers.

The chronicle of recession, job contraction, underemployment, a huge national debt, and ideological malaise that follows may seem dismal. However, companies can formulate and implement strategies to help them survive and thrive into the next century.

Over the remainder of the 1990s, new technologies will necessitate extensive on-the-job training. Ethical issues will take on a new urgency. Companies will face uncertainties in the political and legal environments as the courts change long-standing workplace rules. Every issue will have multiple stakeholders, both proponents and detractors, who are well organized and pursue their own agendas.

To a great extent, managers will be judged by how effectively they identify their stakeholders and then formulate and implement thoughtful, cohesive corporate strategies. Strategic planning will have to incorporate multiple workplace issues such as health care, family care, workplace training, and ethics. Interaction between business and government will likely increase as the courts and agencies churn out new laws and regulations. Global competition will bring international social issues to the fore.

The Economy

Stakeholders in the early 1990s asked many of the same questions stakeholders did in the recession of the early 1980s. They wanted to know why business was not delivering on expectations that American society had always taken for granted. People traditionally expected an expanding employment base with jobs that offered stability, future opportunity, and good pay and benefits.

At a minimum, people believed they should be able to count on business leadership to ensure that American companies were fully competitive with overseas firms. They and their children should have at least as much financial and job security as earlier generations had. Despite these expectations, the number of jobless executives, managers, and administrators continued to grow, jumping 12 percent between December 1988 and December 1989.

In the late 1980s, the gap between the richest and poorest Americans reached its widest point since World War II. Between 1973 and 1989, the ranks of the very rich more than doubled, from 3.1 percent in 1973 to 6.9 percent in 1987. During the same period, the poor got poorer. Children and minorities were hit particularly hard.[1] By 1989, the top 1 percent of American households were worth more than the bottom 90 percent.[2]

Some observers forecast that the number of managers in the 1990s would grow at half the 4 to 5 percent annual rate of the 1980s. Older middle managers found themselves competing with recent college graduates for job openings. For both groups, prospects had dimmed. One college placement officer observed, "there is downward pressure all over . . . [some] college graduates are becoming secretaries and assistants to assistant buyers at K mart."[3]

People wondered what had happened to the American dream. As more Americans found themselves without regular jobs, some had to take part-time work wherever they could find it. Out-of-work families lost benefits, such as health and life insurance, making them far more vulnerable to economic catastrophe.

The 1990s opened with a flood of managerial layoffs. Manufacturing slowed and global competition increased. For the first time, retrenchment took place even in "hot" industries such as advertising and computers.

Most analysts agreed the job situation was not simply a result of a swing in the business cycle similar to the one that occurred in the early 1980s. Restructuring was taking place. America was experiencing a permanent change in the mix of skills, education, and expertise required for industrial competitiveness in the next century.

With the end of the Cold War, defense industries contracted operations. The consequences spilled over into other industries. The computer industry, once the nation's fastest-growing industry, slowed down. Data General cut 1,000 jobs in 1992. CEO Ronald L Skates said, "the industry, as it's generally defined, is a declining work force."[4] Overall, the steel industry lost 10,000 jobs in 1991, mostly among the large producers. The small "mini-mills," on the other hand, developed thriving niche markets.

The effects of downsizing or retrenchment fell heavily on white-collar workers. Insurance companies, banks, department stores, and advertising agencies all cut middle managers and sales associates. In the fall of 1992, the US Bureau of Labor Statistics reported that white-collar workers accounted for 41 percent of people who had become unemployed since the beginning of the recession.[5]

---

[1]L Silk, "Rich and Poor: The Gap Widens," *The New York Times,* May 12, 1989, p. D2.

[2]S Nasar, "Fed Gives New Evidence of 80s Gains by Richest," *The New York Times,* April 21, 1992, p. A1.

[3]B O'Reilly, "The Job Drought," *Fortune,* August 24, 1992, p. 65.

[4]M Mandel, S A Forst, and G McWilliams, "No Help Wanted," *Business Week,* September 21, 1992, p. 28.

[5]R Henkoff, "Where Will the Jobs Come From?," *Fortune,* October 19, 1992, pp. 58–64.

Communities across America suffered as companies let go large numbers of top and middle managers. GE, IBM, Eastman Kodak, Merrill Lynch, and other firms announced massive layoffs and early retirement programs. A prominent management consultant predicted that one in five American companies would engage in downsizing or restructuring each year for the next five years.

Support industries like accounting, consulting, and legal services also cut back personnel. Of the 485,000 people who became unemployed in 1990, 75 percent were managers, professionals, or administrative and technical staff.[6] Although companies adopted different rationales for dismissing managers, the result was the same. Some companies decided to reduce what they perceived as redundant layers of middle management. Others believed top managers should be closer to customers. Still others contracted with outside companies to handle functions, such as data processing, that typically had been done in-house.[7]

Early in 1991, unemployment claims climbed to their highest level since February 1983. The median wage for US workers fell. Many of the white-collar workers laid off in the early 1990s could not find comparable jobs. Jobs with good pension and health care benefits became rarer.

Smaller companies were also hit hard as they lost contracts to supply their large customers. Between December 1991 and September 1992, 100,000 manufacturing jobs disappeared due to cutbacks in defense-related industries such as ordnance, aerospace, shipbuilding, missile manufacturing, communications, and navigation equipment.

In the summer of 1992, the manufacturing sector outlook was bleak. Ninety-seven thousand jobs disappeared in August. Factory employment fell to its lowest point in a decade. California's overall jobless level rose from 9.5 percent in June to 9.8 percent in August. Michigan, a "Rust Belt" state, was close behind with a 9.0 percent unemployment rate.[8] National unemployment hit 7.9 percent, up from 5.3 percent during the growth years of the 1980s. People fell deeper into debt as their incomes lagged. Between 1990 and 1992, household debt rose by 10.2 percent, while aftertax income rose by only 9.4 percent.[9]

Many young adults believed their financial prospects would be limited indefinitely. By mid-1991, the median income of families headed by someone under age 30 was 13 percent lower than in 1973, measured in inflation-adjusted dollars.[10]

---

[6]T F O'Boyle and C Hymowitz, "Layoffs This Time Hit Professional Ranks with Unusual Force," *The Wall Street Journal,* October 4, 1990, p. A1.

[7]T D Schellhardt, "White-Collar Layoffs Open 1990, and May Close It Too," *The Wall Street Journal,* January 15, 1990, p. B1.

[8]R D Hershey, "167,000 Jobs Lost by U.S. Businesses; Fed Cuts Interest," *The New York Times,* September 5, 1992, p. 1.

[9]"The Recovery: Why So Slow?", *Business Week,* July 20, 1992, p. 62.

[10]"What Happened to the American Dream?," *Business Week,* August 19, 1991, p. 80.

High school graduates fared far worse economically than people with college educations. In 1992, high school graduates earned 26.5 percent less in entry-level jobs than they had in 1979. Congress's Joint Economic Committee advised that most young people should get used to the fact that they would have lower lifetime earnings than those of the previous generation.[11]

The graduating college class of 1992 faced the worst employment prospects of any class in the previous 20 years. Between 1989 and 1992, companies eliminated almost one-third of all entry-level positions. The Bureau of Labor Statistics issued a sobering report: Increasing numbers of college graduates were seeking jobs traditionally performed by high school graduates. The bureau predicted that by the year 2005, 30 percent of file clerks and assembly line workers would be college graduates.

Presidential candidates Bush, Clinton, and Perot all touted their economic plans in the 1992 campaign, but the electorate continued to be skeptical and despondent. Polls showed a growing alienation from the government and, above all, from the political process. Large numbers of Americans associated the Republicans with wealth and greed and the Democrats with incompetence.[12]

Bill Clinton's headquarters sported a huge sign saying, "The Economy, Stupid." Clinton won the presidential race largely on his promise to reduce the budget deficit and generate new job opportunities. Even though they voted for Clinton, many people believed something was fundamentally wrong with the American system. There was no doubt that the American economic situation was dismal and that recovery from the recession was not yet in sight.

In the weeks after Bill Clinton's election, the economy showed some improvement. However, the meaning of the new numbers was unclear. The economy had grown at an annual rate of 2.8 percent in 1992, but with no increase in private-sector employment. One explanation was that corporations were simply making workers already in their employ work harder. If recovery was indeed on the way, it was a different recovery than that of the early 1980s. At that time, the workforce was younger and less skilled. The explosion of debt fueled consumer spending, which helped the economy grow and also created more jobs in the service sector.

As 1993 began, retailers were happy with the Christmas sales figures, the manufacturing sector showed some growth, the number of hours worked per week rose, and companies began to invest in equipment. The media made all sorts of predictions about what moves the new administration would make and how effective it would be in reducing the deficit and dealing with soaring health care costs.[13]

---

[11]S Greenhouse, "Income Data Show Years of Erosion for U.S. Workers," *The New York Times,* September 7, 1992, p. 1.

[12]M Oreskes, "Alienation from Government Grows, Poll Finds," *The New York Times,* September 19, 1990, p. A26.

[13]J C Cooper and K Madigan, "This Productivity May Last for Years," *Business Week,* December 21, 1992, p. 21.

In June 1993, companies announced layoffs of 38,669 workers, up from 14,086 in May. However, most economists interpreted the numbers as consistent with a slow, shallow recovery. Total nonfarm payrolls expanded by nearly 1 million jobs between January and August, and small businesses continued to create jobs faster than large companies cut them.

The official national June unemployment rate of 7 percent included everyone 16 years or older who looked for work during May. The figures did not include people who had already given up looking for a new job. As *Fortune* pointed out, US figures looked very good compared to European unemployment statistics, especially if one considered that in 1992, 66 percent of the US population participated in the workforce.[14]

Although the Clinton administration got off to a slow start, by summer 1993 it had made some headway in developing a budget. Internecine battles between Democrats and Republicans over whether new taxes would be part of the economic plan continued. Finally, in August, it appeared Congress had agreed on an economic plan. Although no one thought the plan would do more than slow the rise in debt, it seemed to be the best the administration could wring from legislators.

In this economic climate, even stakeholders committed to social causes began to question whether US firms could afford to concentrate on social issues. They framed social issues in terms of trade-offs: pollution control versus jobs, better health care versus business survival. They argued that restoring the country's economic health and growth should take priority over meeting social goals.

Social Programs

Reagan administration policies quickly eroded social programs in the 1980s. The erosion rate slowed during the Bush years because of administration passivity and neglect rather than proactive changes in social policy.

The appointment of conservative Supreme Court justices caused decisions on civil rights issues to veer sharply to the right. During the Bush years, prospective justices' confirmation hearings drew the public's attention to issues such as sexual harassment, abortion rights, and affirmative action. Many decisions in the early 1990s reflected the court's new composition.

For the first time in nearly two decades, the executive and the judiciary eroded or struck down programs that favored minorities and women. For example, President Bush vetoed the Civil Rights Act of 1990, claiming the bill would compel employers to adopt quotas for hiring. On the other hand, in some areas civil rights legislation and enforcement strengthened. The Americans with Disabilities Act of 1990 went into effect, housing laws were enforced more vigorously, and voting rights were better protected.

In 1993, it appeared the Supreme Court's ideology might begin to tilt the other way. Clinton's appointment of Ruth Bader Ginsburg gave new

---

[14]"Fortune Forecast," *Fortune,* August 9, 1993, pp. 19–20, 22.

strength and encouragement to proponents of issues such as pro-choice, privacy, women's rights, and free speech.

In the late 1980s, some regulatory agencies suffered continuous slashes in budget and personnel, while others modestly increased their activities. Deregulation, vigorously pursued under the Reagan administration, became random and inconsistent under President Bush. The Clinton administration's policies in some areas, such as the environment, were strong and clear, but by mid-1993 no overall regulatory policy or ideology had yet emerged.

The Environment

In 1988, George Bush announced he wanted to be the "environmental president." In retrospect, his administration's record was mixed. During its first two years, the Environmental Protection Agency's budget grew and Congress passed the Clean Air Act of 1990. Environmentalists generally agreed there had been modest gains in environmental protection.

But in 1990, government policy changed. Citing the need to protect jobs, the Bush administration declined to put existing regulations into effect and began to weaken provisions dealing with air quality. The administration drew international criticism when the United States became the only one of 118 participating nations to refuse to sign a treaty on biodiversity. President Bush, reluctant even to attend the Rio de Janeiro Earth Summit, led an industrialized-nation effort to weaken the treaty to combat global warming.[15]

The Clinton administration brought a new commitment to the environment. Vice President Gore told the first substantive meeting of the United Nations Commission on Sustainable Development that "this administration not only supports that commitment [to sustainable development] but we intend to join with all those determined to demonstrate real leadership."[16]

The Changing Workforce

Many managers of the 1980s were no longer in the workforce by the early 1990s. As noted earlier, restructuring and mergers led to upper-level white-collar layoffs. Economic difficulties, global integration and competition, workforce diversity, and regulatory uncertainty have made different and more complex demands on managers of the 1990s.

In the future, managers will lead a workforce composed of large numbers of women, immigrants, minorities, and older people. The Bureau of the

---

[15]K Schneider, "Bush on the Environment: A Record of Contradictions," *The New York Times,* July 4, 1992, p. 1.

[16]W K Stevens, "Gore Promises U.S. Leadership on Sustainable Development Path," *The New York Times,* June 15, 1993, p. C1.

Census reported the minority population has increased twice as fast in the 1990s as it did in the 1980s. Hispanic and Asian populations have grown by more than 50 percent. Immigration from Asia and Latin America has increased, bringing many new highly skilled and well-educated engineers and entrepreneurs into the workforce. A prominent demographer observed that the first universal nation had dawned.[17]

Women entered the workforce in unprecedented numbers in the 1980s and early 1990s. Their paychecks became increasingly important to their families. By 1987, women's earnings accounted for 29 percent of total household income. To increase their earnings, women switched from part-time to full-time jobs.

In 1992, women accounted for 46 percent of the overall labor force. Women with young children entered the workforce at a rising rate. Among women with children under 18, 67.2 percent were in the workforce compared with 67.1 a year earlier.[18] The recession and layoffs of male wage earners increased pressure on women to compensate for lost household income.

Women's income increased much more in wealthier families, rising 34.9 percent among the richest one-fifth of all American families,[19] and women with college educations did best. But despite their gains, women's median income remained far below men's. The average income of unmarried and married women remained only 65 percent of men's.

Even with major changes in government priorities, and the industrial and social structures, American society and enterprise remain firmly rooted in capitalist ideology. In the next section, we discuss the ideology of the capitalist system and the evolution of modern US corporations.

The Nature of Capitalism

Perhaps nothing is more fundamental to an understanding of the relationship between business and American society than the recognition that American ideology is based on capitalism. Essentially a *capitalistic system* is a system in which the means of *production* are privately owned and the *market* operates to guide production and distribute income. Frequently the terms *free enterprise* or *private enterprise* are used interchangeably with *capitalism.* The nature of the system is not easily described, but some basic features are generally accepted.

The classical theory of capitalism is founded on two fundamental assumptions: (1) human beings are rational creatures capable of understanding the natural order of the universe, and (2) the role of government in

[17]F Barringer, "Census Shows Profound Change in Racial Makeup of the Nation," *The New York Times,* March 11, 1991, p. A–3

[18]S Shellenbarger, "Women with Children Increase in Work Force," *The Wall Street Journal,* February 12, 1992, p. B1.

[19]J E Yang, "Women's Pay Is Seen as Key to Households," *The Boston Globe,* September 11, 1990, p. 3.

the economy can and should be limited. The relationship between these two assumptions led classical economists to believe that if all artificial barriers to economic behavior, such as tariffs, monopolies, and wage controls, were removed, labor, capital, and natural resources would all seek their own economic interests. If government or monopolists that enjoyed "unnatural" powers in the marketplace did not interfere, the market would benefit everyone in society.

Exhibit 1–1 shows the essential elements of capitalism: (1) private property, (2) economic incentive in the form of the profit motive, (3) a free market system, and (4) political and economic freedom.

These views were first expressed by Adam Smith in *The Wealth of Nations,* published in 1776. Smith argued that "every individual is continually exerting himself to find out the most advantageous employment for whatever capital he can command. It is his own advantage, indeed, and not that of society, which he has in view. But the study of his own advantage naturally, or rather necessarily, leads him to prefer that employment which is most advantageous to the society."[20]

Ralph Waldo Emerson, a nineteenth century American writer, also emphasized the importance of individualism. He believed societal structures inhibited individual potential; only in an unfettered social and political system could people develop their potential. In his book *The Conduct of Life and Other Essays,* Emerson wrote that people are inclined by their very nature to be productive and to make money.[21]

But it should be noted that free enterprise or capitalistic systems are never pure. In theory, free enterprise requires that an activity return a profit. Every nation in the world has values and goals that place the country on a continuum between free enterprise and a planned economy. No country has

---

[20]A Smith, *The Wealth of Nations,* book 4 (New York: Modern Library, 1937), p. 421.
[21]R W Emerson, *The Conduct of Life and Other Essays* (London: Dent, 1908), pp. 190–213.

EXHIBIT 1–1

The essential elements of capitalism

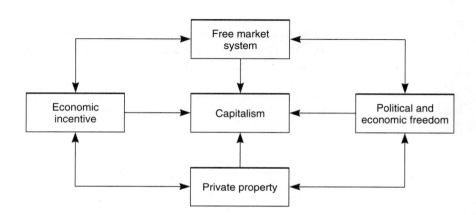

a pure system; each determines where it lies on the continuum by the priority it gives to specific values and goals.

Private Property

The concept of property is an essential and significant element of capitalism. Too often property is thought of only in terms of land. The noted seventeenth century English economist and philosopher John Locke wrote,

> Though the earth and all inferior creatures be common to all men, yet every man has a property in his own person; this nobody has any right to but himself. The labour of his body and the work of his hands, we may say, are properly his. Whatsoever then he removes out of the state that nature hath provided and left in it, he hath mixed his labour with, and joined to it something that is his own, and thereby makes it his property.[22]

In essence, the term *property* refers to the right to exercise the use of one's assets. When one owns property, one has economic power. The classic nineteenth century court case of *Munn* v. *Illinois* clarifies both the meaning of property and the legal struggle that took place to define the legitimacy of the state to control the use of private property.

Because of intense political pressure from farm organizations, the Illinois state legislature passed a law in 1883 allowing the state to fix rates for the storage of grain in elevators. Grain elevator operators challenged the law, and the case eventually went to the Supreme Court. In 1877, the Court found the state did have the right to regulate private property. Chief Justice Waite, in the majority opinion, reasoned that when "one devotes his property to a use in which the public has an interest, he, in effect, grants to the public an interest in that use, and must submit to be controlled by the public for the common good, to the extent of the interest he has thus created."[23] Therefore, the Court rejected the argument that the regulation of grain elevator rates was a deprivation of property rights without due process.

Despite *Munn* v. *Illinois* and subsequent cases that expanded the right of the state to regulate private property, it is clear that in most instances the right to exercise control rests with the owner. People may buy, sell, lease, franchise, and engage in a variety of other contractual arrangements with respect to their assets. These rights are essential to business executives who need to control their tangible and intangible resources.

Economic Incentive

Business executives would probably care very little about property and its control if the management of such resources could not lead to the

---

[22]T I Cook, *Two Treatises of Government by John Locke* (New York: Hafner Publishing, 1947), p. 134.

[23]*Munn* v. *Illinois,* 94 U.S. 113 (1877), p. 125.

accumulation of wealth. Thus, the profit motive represents the fuel for capitalistic machinery. Max Lerner argues, "Men's brains and energy work best when they have no hampering restrictions, and when they see an immediacy of relation between effort and reward."[24]

There is substantial evidence that profit fuels socialist and communist economies as well. In China and the remaining few centrally planned economies left in the world, governments are encouraging managers of factories, farms, and businesses to make a profit. As incentive, a portion of the profit can be kept to augment workers' salaries and to upgrade the business. The prospect of profit appears to motivate managers in every political system.

Free Market System

If business executives, investors, and others are to benefit from the stimulation and rewards of the profit motive, then, according to classical theory, they must have access to free markets. *Free markets* are markets in which people exchange assets for money without outside regulation. Prices are determined by supply and demand, and buyers and sellers gain experience through trial and error. If demand for a given good exceeds supply, prices are forced higher. However, as the profits on that good increase, new suppliers will be attracted into the market, increasing competition and reducing prices.

While a temporary imbalance may exist, the free-flowing nature of the market (with no government regulation and no monopolies) assures suppliers of an opportunity to compete freely. It provides buyers with a variety of alternative sources of goods and services for which there is sufficient demand. The concept, according to classical economists, applies not only to markets for goods but also to labor markets and money markets, in which "buyers" bid for workers and capital.

It is important to note that there has never been a time in which the world operated as a free market. In trade and business, national interests and pragmatism have always prevailed over theory and ideology. Classical theory does not translate fully into practice in any political environment. Since the end of World War II, multilateral negotiations through the General Agreement on Tariffs and Trade have greatly reduced tariffs worldwide. However, trade barriers in many forms still exist.

Political and Economic Freedom

One key to the existence of a free market system is the absence of government regulations. Yet in the United States, most monopolies are dismantled

---

[24]M Lerner, *America as a Civilization,* vol. 1 (New York: Simon and Schuster, 1957), p. 268.

by government regulation. This seems to be a paradox: How can classical economics theorists expect a system to prevent the creation of monopoly power unless the government exercises some control over the economic institutions participating in the system? On a more pragmatic and less theoretical level, how can a government that espouses free market economics pursue deregulation when the result may be a wave of takeovers and mergers that could strangle competition?

Milton Friedman noted this paradox when he wrote, "government is necessary to preserve our freedom; yet by concentrating power in political hands, it is also a threat to freedom."[25] Friedman contended that the dilemma could be solved by recognizing two principles.

First, the scope of the government must be strictly limited. According to Friedman, "Its major functions must be to protect our freedom both from the enemies outside our gates and from our fellow citizens: to preserve law and order, to enforce private contracts, to foster competitive markets."[26]

Second, the power exercised by government must be dispersed. In essence, Friedman argued that government should exercise its limited powers at the level closest to the people involved; that is, local communities should resolve issues involving streets, schools, sewers, and the like. The few problems that could not be solved locally would go to the county, the few that were broader yet would go to the state, and only a limited number of issues would find their way to Washington, DC.

This view of the role of government, especially as it applies to nonintervention in business matters, may be traced directly to Adam Smith. A policy of laissez-faire, under which the government keeps its hands out of economic activities, continues to be central to the debate concerning the role of business in society.

Historically government has played an increasingly active role in economic affairs. But the role the government plays in business changed profoundly in the 1980s and continues to change in the 1990s. Some even assert those changes have put in force mechanisms that will not, in the foreseeable future, allow us to return to the highly regulated environment that existed prior to 1978.

Issues, such as international competitiveness, a huge balance of payments deficit, and foreign investment in American companies and property, have changed some aspects of this country's ideological underpinnings and may change the legal relationships as well. For example, in recent years we have seen a great deal of confusion regarding the government's stand on antitrust. Since 1978, the US government has lifted rules that set prices and controlled entry of new companies. Throughout the mid-1980s, the Justice Department relaxed merger guidelines. To meet foreign competition and

---

[25]M Friedman, *Capitalism and Freedom* (Chicago: University of Chicago Press, 1961), p. 2.

[26]Ibid.

record trade deficits, the Bush and Reagan administrations focused their activities on price fixing and bid rigging rather than on price and territorial arrangements between manufacturers and distributors.[27] We will discuss antitrust and what the future may hold for that issue in much greater detail in Chapters 8 and 9.

While the US economy has moved a long way from the vision of Adam Smith, the concepts of a free enterprise economy are deeply rooted in our culture and continue to influence the definition of business as an institution. Many intellectual conflicts treated later in this book center on challenges to the classical theory of the nature of human beings and the role of government.

The Modern Corporation

The corporation, as a form of business organization, has played a central role in the evolution of capitalism. While sole proprietorships and partnerships significantly outnumber corporations, the sales and assets of the corporation dwarf the other organizational forms. The huge enterprises in the Fortune 500 are almost exclusively corporations.

States charter corporations to engage in specified types of business activity. Corporations enjoy important legal advantages over sole proprietorships and partnerships in that they are characterized by perpetual succession and the personal liability of their owners is limited to the extent of the owners' investment in the corporation. A corporation continues as a legal entity regardless of the physical well-being of its founders and owners. Unlike proprietorships and partnerships, the personal property of the owners is not subject to the claims stemming from liabilities generated by the enterprise.

Another characteristic of the corporation is the relative ease with which ownership interests are transferred. Shares of stock that may be exchanged for cash or other assets represent equity in the corporation. It is easy for individuals or groups to purchase or sell corporate shares through organized stock markets such as the New York and American stock exchanges.

In a sense, the corporation is a fictitious person who has the right to sue and be sued, is protected from claims based on the separate debts of its owners, may own and sell property, and may engage in contracts. In a classic Supreme Court case, *Dartmouth College* v. *Woodward* (1819), which helped confirm the rights of the corporate form of organization, Chief Justice Marshall described the corporation as "an artificial being, invisible, intangible, and existing only in contemplation of law."

Adolph A Berle and Gardiner C Means wrote *The Modern Corporation and Private Property,* an important contribution to our understanding of modern corporations. First published in 1932, this study moved well beyond the legal character of corporations, focusing instead on their political and

---

[27]"Reagan Turns a Cold Eye on Antitrust," *Fortune,* October 14, 1985, p. 31.

social impact. One of the study's principal concerns was the concentration of economic power among the largest corporations and the separation of ownership and control of the corporation. The authors open the book by stating,

> Corporations have ceased to be merely legal devices through which the private business transactions of individuals may be carried on. Though still much used for this purpose, the corporate form has acquired a larger significance. The corporation has, in fact, become both a method of property tenure and a means of organizing economic life. A corporate system has accrued to it a combination of attributes and powers and has attained a degree of prominence entitling it to be dealt with as a major social institution.[28]

Berle and Means's perception of the corporation as a system of organization is even more relevant in the 1990s than it was in the beginning of Roosevelt's New Deal. Today corporations transcend national boundaries and product categories. Their assets, ownership, resources, and power go well beyond the expectations of early scholars and organizational theorists. To a very great degree, corporations as a form of organization touch nearly every part of our daily lives.

The modern corporation has developed stakeholders or, according to Richard Eells and Clarence Walton, a *constellation of interests* that exists not only at the core of the organization but at the periphery as well.[29] Eells and Walton describe the direct claimants on the corporation as security holders (owners of stocks and bonds), employees, customers, and suppliers. The indirect claimants include competitors, local communities, the general public, and governments. Because of its economic power and the scope of its influence on almost every facet of the lives of individuals in our society, one serious student of business has concluded that "the great corporation *is* our way of life."[30]

The corporation and its stakeholders play a central role in our study of business and society. We will focus on the interaction of large corporations with the business environment. We will look at companies that are professionally managed, are publicly owned, and have multiple profit centers. Generally these companies wield great power and influence and are most often the subject of controversy regarding their role in society.

Top managers of large companies are directly concerned with issues related to the social responsibility of business. While their companies may not necessarily be better or more responsive corporate citizens, these managers have a greater vested interest in developing methods of improving their strategic management skills in this area of their firms' operations.

---

[28]A A Berle and G C Means *The Modern Corporation and Private Property,* rev. ed. (New York: Harcourt Brace Jovanovich, 1967), p. 3.

[29]R Eells and C Walton, *Conceptual Foundations of Business* (Homewood, IL: Richard D. Irwin, 1961), pp. 147–63.

[30]D Votaw, *Modern Corporations* (Englewood Cliffs, NJ: Prentice-Hall, 1965), p. 2.

The Linkage Between Strategy and the Economic, Social, and Political Environments

Managers of the 1990s should continue to heed Peter F Drucker's 1980 statement that "... performance in management ... means in large measure doing a good job of preparing today's business for the future."[31] Effective managers must deal with threats and opportunities in the future. Businesses must arrange their employees, financial resources, innovativeness, and strategies in ways that will best ensure their success. To develop and maintain the perspective or scope of vision necessary to achieve that end, they would do well to adopt two axioms.

First, *business is not isolated from other institutions nor does it serve a single purpose or a single constituency.* Business organizations are linked to a broader social system made up of groups of stakeholders. As we discussed earlier, stakeholders include customers, competitors, suppliers, employees, government, regulatory agencies, legislative bodies, political parties, social activist groups, labor unions, trade associations, educational institutions, shareholders, investors, and the news media. These institutions and components of society are each part of a global network.

American business leaders can no longer assume that the geographical boundaries of the United States provide an invisible barrier to competition from Japan, the former Soviet Union, the Middle East, the advanced economies of Western Europe, and the burgeoning markets of Asia. In fact, the North American Free Trade Agreement deliberately eliminates trade barriers between the United States and its neighbors to the north and south. Managers also cannot ignore the problems and opportunities in developing-country economies.

Second, *the major threats and opportunities business faces are environmental.* Well-managed companies must deal effectively with the social, political, and legal dynamics of their environment as well as with the more traditional product- and market-focused variables in the economic and technological environments.

Social performance demands that managers recognize that business is a component of broad and constantly changing social systems. It is within these dynamic environments that managers need to initiate change and modify their firms' policies, practices, and strategies. Fundamentally, companies' attention to social responsiveness will enhance their long-run economic performance and profits.

Social Responsiveness Management

Igor Ansoff describes management as "the creative and error correcting activity that gives the firm its purpose, its cohesion, and assures satisfactory return on investment."[32] In Ansoff's view, managers meet the challenge of

---

[31] P F Drucker, *Managing in Turbulent Times* (New York: Harper & Row, 1980), p. 68.

[32] H I Ansoff, "The Changing Shape of the Strategic Problem," in *Strategic Management: A View of Business Policy and Planning,* ed. D E Schendel and C W Hofer (Boston: Little, Brown, 1979), p. 30.

the environment by using strategy to transform their enterprises. He argues that a firm must have strategies to deal with "sociopolitical variables" as well as "product/market/technology-focused strategies."[33]

Corporate social responsiveness should be an integral component of a company's overall strategy. It is that element of the company's strategy designed to solve the firm's problems or grasp opportunities related to the social, political, and legal environments. Table 1–1 describes the key elements of social responsiveness management.

The segments of the environment, strategy formulation, strategy implementation, and performance evaluation will be covered thoroughly in Chapters 2 and 3. A brief overview of these topics follows.

The Environment

Managers study the environment to identify problems or strategic issues important to the firm. Environmental forces are both internal and external to the company. The most basic organizational resource of a company is its people, who in turn affect the success of the strategy identified by top management. While this book focuses principally on the social, political, and legal and regulatory arenas internal and external to the firm, it also includes related strategic social issues in the economic and technological environments.

Strategy Formulation

Strategy is the linking mechanism between most organizations and their environments as they seek to achieve their missions, goals, and objectives. An effective strategy and a realistic appraisal of the company's strengths and

---

[33]Ibid., p. 43.

TABLE 1–1   Strategic Components of Social Responsiveness Management

Environment	*Strategy Formulation*	*Strategy Implementation*	*Performance Evaluation*
What problems or strategic issues do we need to deal with in the social/ political/legal arenas? Are there related problems in the economic and technological environments?	Who are we, and what are our goals? What are our capabilities and limitations? Which strategic issues are of greatest relevance? What strategy should we pursue?	What operational plans do we need? How should we organize? What information and controls do we need to ensure the strategy is implemented?	What results are we getting? How have organizational units and people performed?

limitations are management's keys to formulating a clear understanding of those missions, goals, and objectives.

Managers need to assess the environment and determine which issues have the greatest relevance to the company. Once they identify the most important problems or strategic issues, they must adopt a variety of means to achieve the end they have defined. In other words, managers must determine how best to organize and use the firm's resources to achieve the goals they have set. *Strategic choice* is the process of deciding which approach is best and selecting among the alternatives available.

Strategy Implementation

Merely developing a strategy is not sufficient. To reach a strategic objective, managers must make it happen. Top management must create an implementation plan and assign responsibility for its execution to individuals and units of the organization. The firm will also need to create a formal or informal information and control system, if one is not already in place, to monitor the implementation of the strategy. An effective control system keeps track of actual accomplishments and provides an early warning system to detect potential problems.

Performance Evaluation

A strategy has little meaning if no one cares about results. Someone must care whether or not the company is getting the job done and how well the strategy is being implemented by those responsible for doing so. Managers need to know their performances are being evaluated and how the results they achieve will be reflected in the company's reward system. This process will be discussed in greater detail in subsequent chapters.

The Business and Society Responsibility Debate

In recent years, managers have begun to think of corporate social performance as a basic functional area of management. One important reason may be new elements in the business and society responsibility dialog.

The role of business in American society has long been the subject of great debate, analysis, and emotion. Even in the colonial period, Puritan ministers exhorted their parishioners to work hard. Wealth and position were seen as signs of God's favor. The framers of the Constitution and other notable thinkers of the time debated the proper roles of business and society.

Alexander Hamilton's goal was to foster a strong economy based on commerce, manufacturing, and finance. Hamilton viewed government's role as supporting an environment of order and stability in which business could grow and prosper. Thomas Jefferson, on the other hand, wanted people to remain on the land to produce the basic elements of clothing, shelter, and food. He abhorred the idea of putting people to work in urban factories. Government's proper role, in his view, was to respond to the will of a responsible electorate.

As business became an increasingly large and powerful force throughout the nineteenth century, concern with defining and shaping its role intensified. *The Education of Henry Adams* provides a remarkably insightful discussion of the seriousness of the matter.[34] This autobiography of the great-grandson of John Adams and the grandson of John Quincy Adams was published in 1918, the year of Henry Adams's death.

Adams viewed with alarm—even horror—the impact of industrialization on the political process and the values of society: "The work of domestic progress is done by masses of mechanical power—steam, electric, furnace, or other—which have to be controlled by a score or two of individuals who have shown the capacity to manage it. The work of internal government has become the task of controlling these men."[35]

Adams had little faith that "these men" could or would be controlled. Although they were supposed to be trustees for the public, Adams was convinced they would "control society without appeal" just as they controlled the workers in their factories. He concluded this point by arguing that "modern politics is, at bottom, a struggle not of men but of forces. The men become every year more and more creatures of force, massed about central power-houses."[36]

The debate continued into the twentieth century. In *The Limits of Corporate Power,* Ira M Millstein and Salem M Katsh observed, "The central issue is corporate control: those forces which operate to constrain the discretionary acts of business corporations—especially, but not exclusively, large corporations. There are those for whom no amount of corporate control is enough; and there are those for whom no amount of corporate control is too much."[37]

David Vogel made some interesting observations about public control over large business corporations in the 1980s.[38] He noted that the public-interest movement of the 1960s dissipated in the 1970s. As deregulatory forces gathered steam during the late 1970s and early 1980s, business interests began to dominate public policy and corporate forces pressured for economic and tax reform.

---

[34]H Adams, *The Education of Henry Adams* (New York: Modern Library, 1931).
[35]Ibid., p. 421.
[36]Ibid., p. 423.
[37]I M Millstein and S M Katsh, *The Limits of Corporate Power: Existing Constraints in the Exercise of Corporate Discretion* (New York: Macmillan, 1981), p. ix.
[38]D Vogel, "The Inadequacy of Contemporary Opposition to Business," *Daedalus* (Summer 1980), pp. 47–51.

Vogel believed business became politically successful because the public deemed the historically liberal tradition of the United States inadequate: "The whole tone of the political agenda has shifted from a focus on corporate abuses to a preoccupation with reforming the regulations enacted to curb these abuses."[39]

A somewhat related point was made by Graham K Wilson, who noted that under the Reagan administration, business became more active and more successful politically than in the previous decade. He asserted that the public shifted its concern from social goals to prices and American competitiveness. This was a change from the 1970s, when public-interest groups seemed likely to alter the very nature of business–government relations.[40]

While some scholars deliberated over the proper balance of business, government, and interest groups, others, like Clarence C Walton, summarized the conservative argument and took a *negative* view of the broad responsibilities of business. Walton asserted, "the expansion of private power into the public domain will upset the already uneasy balance existing in our society to a point where corporation executives will assume too much power or will be so effectively challenged as to lose their existing freedom of action."[41]

Milton Friedman is the major contemporary proponent of a limited—and strictly economic—role for business. Friedman's fundamental argument is that business involvement in the social and political arenas is a threat to freedom. He argues, "if economic power is joined to political power, concentration seems almost inevitable. On the other hand, if economic power is kept in separate hands from political power, it can serve as a check and a counter to political power."[42] Friedman and others who see business as having a central but limited role in society contend that the business of business is business, not social issues or politics.

Those who view the role of business more broadly or more positively disagree with Friedman's position. They contend that social responsibility is also the business of business. For example, Peter F Drucker wrote, "Friedman's 'pure' position—to eschew all social responsibility—is not tenable . . . Business and other institutions of our society . . . cannot be pure, however desirable that may be. Their own self-interest alone forces them to be concerned with society and community and to be predisposed to shoulder responsibility beyond their own main areas of task and responsibility."[43]

---

[39]Ibid., p. 49.

[40]G K Wilson, *Business and Politics* (Chatham, NJ: Chatham House Publishers, 1985), pp. 42–43.

[41]C C Walton, *Corporate Social Responsibilities* (Belmont, CA: Wadsworth, 1967), pp. 57–58.

[42]Friedman, *Capitalism and Freedom,* p. 16.

[43]P F Drucker, *Management: Tasks, Responsibilities, Practices* (New York: Harper & Row, 1974), p. 349.

R Edward Freeman and Jeanne Liedka, two leading scholars in the field of business and society, argue that the idea of corporate social responsibility is outmoded.[44] Their rationale—which could not differ more dramatically from Friedman's—is unique and as yet outside the mainstream. Nevertheless, their ideas are creative and thought provoking. They offer seven reasons to abandon the concept of corporate social responsibility, given in Table 1–2.

Freeman and Liedka suggest that managers should undertake an "ongoing conversation about corporations and the good life." In their view, corporations should be conceptualized as "a network of relationships [making possible] a social world in which 'caring' has primary significance." In place of social responsibility, they offer "Three Propositions for New Conversation":

> **"Proposition 1: Corporations are connected networks of stakeholder interests.**
> This proposition expands the conversation to include suppliers, employees, and customers, among others, making them legitimate partners in the dialogue.
>
> **Proposition 2: Corporations are places in which both individual human beings and human communities engage in caring activities that are aimed at mutual support and unparalleled human achievement.** This proposition pushes us beyond the language of rights and responsibilities to a focus on the ethics of care, which recognizes needs and affirms the self and its linkage with others.

---

[44]R E Freeman and J Liedka, "Corporate Social Responsibility: A Critical Approach," *Business Horizons* (July/August 1991), pp. 92–98.

TABLE 1–2   Seven Reasons to Abandon the Concept of Corporate Social Responsibility

1. The origins of the concept are suspect, as they derive primarily from the field of economics, and fail to include, among others, history, religion, and culture.
2. The different models of corporate social responsibility all accept the terms of the debate as set forth by Milton Friedman's argument that sees corporations only as profit maximizers.
3. Corporate social responsibility accepts the prevailing business rhetoric of "capitalism: love it or leave it."
4. Corporate social responsibility is inherently conservative—it starts with the standard received wisdom and then attempts to "fix" its unintended consequences.
5. Corporate social responsibility promotes incompetence by leading managers to involve themselves in areas beyond their expertise—that is, repairing society's ills.
6. Corporate social responsibility accepts a view of business and society as separable from each other, each with a distinct ethic, linked by a set of responsibilities.
7. The language of rights and responsibilities is, itself, both limiting and often irrelevant to the world of the practicing manager.

SOURCE: R E Freeman and J Liedka, "Corporate Social Responsibility: A Critical Approach," *Business Horizons* (July/August 1991), p. 93.

Proposition 3: Corporations are mere means through which human beings are able to create and recreate, describe and redescribe, their visions of self and community. This proposition urges us to see the projects of 'self creation' and 'community creation' as two sides of the same coin, and see in institutions many possibilities for different ways of living together to pursue the joint ends of individual and collective good."[45]

William C Frederick takes a balanced view of corporate social responsibility. He points out that disruptions of the ethical, social, and legal fabrics arise within the business system; they are not imposed on business from outside: "The issues and problems that have been at the heart of the social responsibility debate are a natural consequence of the institutionalized quest for profits normally sought through the free market. They represent the raw edge of business values rubbing against the social values of human communities and the ecosystems that sustain those communities."[46]

Debate about business responsibility is both important and understandable when viewed on an aggregate or institutional level. Conservative commentator Irving Kristol suggests that had business been such a large and powerful institution in the late 18th century, the founders would have provided bounds for it in the Constitution. Instead, they concentrated on government responsibility, because they knew about and feared oppressive central states.

Notwithstanding the restrictive nature of the Constitution vis-à-vis the federal government, the appropriate role of government has been the subject of serious and ongoing debate. There is, however, general agreement about what constitutes individual responsibility or responsiveness. By definition, public servants and the government organizations for which they work are expected to serve the public good and not act selfishly.

Professionals are presumed to behave responsibly. "To assure performance," according to Wilbert E Moore, "professionals are obliged to regulate their own conduct by adherence to ethical codes."[47] Writing on the same topic, Everett C Hughes observed that a "central feature . . . of all professions is the motto—not used in this form, so far as I know—*credat emptor*[48] ["let the buyer trust"]. Alan H Goldman noted, "The special knowledge of those within each profession relates to a central, even vital, value for their society and the other individuals in it."[49]

---

[45]Ibid., p. 96.

[46]W C Frederick, "Corporate Social Responsibility in the Reagan Era and Beyond," *California Management Review,* 25 (Spring 1983), p. 147.

[47]W E Moore, *The Professions: Roles and Rules* (New York: Russell Sage Foundation, 1970), p. 14.

[48]E C Hughes, "Professions," in *The Professions in America,* ed. K S Lynn (Boston: Houghton Mifflin, 1965), p. 3.

[49]A H Goldman, "Professional Values and the Problem of Regulation," *Business and Professional Ethics Journal,* 5 (Winter, 1986) p. 48.

One can debate whether managers are any more or less "professional" than lawyers, doctors, architects, or engineers, but nearly everyone agrees that trust in business relationships is important. In fact, a strong case can be made that trust is essential to the long-term survival of any business enterprise.

Therefore, it seems the notion of individual responsibility on the part of managers is fairly clear-cut; individual responsibility is a characteristic of a professional. However, the nature and scope of the responsible behavior are hard to define. Does it mean a business should be run like a social welfare agency? Does it mean corporate managers need merely to obey the law?

The Scope of Business Responsibility

Global Imperatives.   In the 1990s, the business and society debate has taken on a global perspective. In a recent article, Donna J Wood and Philip L Cochran discuss business and society in transition. They assert the global economy requires managers to abandon a narrow domestic perspective. International trade, global stakeholders, and multicultural social and political issues all affect business and necessitate new approaches to balancing stakeholder demands.[50]

In another article, Wood points out that multinationals, by their very structure, largely escape national controls.[51] Except for some local operations within national boundaries, multinational corporations govern themselves.

Wood has no easy answers as to how multinationals can be held to norms of social responsibility. One partial solution is to develop bilateral and multilateral agreements and regulations among nations to deal with common issues concerning business activities. As Wood notes, negotiation is time consuming and difficult, and monitoring and enforcing those agreements are even more so.

Wood rejects the notion of world government or comprehensive treaties as solutions to global social responsibility. In her view, the discussion that will lead to global social responsibility is just beginning. She recommends better training in intercultural management, more research on comparative definitions of corporate social responsibility, greater attention to collaborative social problem solving, less aggressive posturing, and more listening.

These recommendations may seem too general and inadequate to deal with global issues and the problems of controlling corporations that operate outside a framework of law and regulation. But the issue is not whether managers and their firms, wherever they are located, *should* behave responsibly.

[50]D J Wood and P L Cochran, "Business and Society in Transition," *Business and Society* (Spring 1992), pp. 1–17.

[51]D J Wood, "Toward Improving Corporate Social Performance," *Business Horizons* (July/August 1991), pp. 66–69.

Legal and Economic Imperatives.   According to Peter F Drucker, limits to social responsibility are imposed on business by (1) economic realities: "Whenever a business has disregarded the limitation of economic performance and has assumed social responsibilities which it could not support economically it has gotten into trouble";[52] (2) the limits of competence: "To take on tasks for which one lacks competence is irresponsible behavior. It is also cruel. It raises expectations which will then be disappointed";[53] and (3) authority: "The most important limitation on social responsibility is the limitation of authority . . . Where business . . . is asked to assume social responsibility for one of the problems or ills of society and community, management needs to think through whether the authority implied in the responsibility is legitimate. Otherwise it is usurpation and irresponsible."[54]

In their comments on the limits of corporate responsibility, none of these observers suggests that obeying the law is sufficient. All agree it is simplistic to suggest that the law provides answers and guidelines in dealing with every social and political issue. The nature of social change is such that the law often lags behind social norms and expectations. Long before the federal law was passed barring former executive branch employees from lobbying the government on a "particular matter" in which they "personally and substantially participated" while in office, those lobbyists reaped the rewards of decisions they made while working in government.

In some cases, the law is just beginning to be written. For example, biotechnological advances are so new and are proliferating so rapidly that the legal system is lagging behind. Issues include the legal implications for business and the health care industry of genetic testing. If, for example, a prospective parent chooses to continue a pregnancy knowing the child will have serious, expensive medical problems, should the parent's employer have to bear the financial responsibility through the company medical plan? Can business require prospective parents to have genetic testing to uncover potentially expensive problems?

Business, government, and society will all have a major stake in the way legislation is drawn up. If we look at the past as predictive, laws will continue to lag behind issues. Social norms and expectations are changing rapidly, far more rapidly than legislators and lawyers can provide even baseline answers. In short, obeying the law is *necessary* for a socially responsible executive, but probably it is not *sufficient* in the eyes of most observers of corporate policy and practice.

---

[52]Drucker, *Management,* p. 345.
[53]Ibid.
[54]Ibid., pp. 347–48.

CASE   *A H Robins and the Dalkon Shield*

In the early 1970s, reports of illness among Dalkon Shield users began to surface. A H Robins Company, the manufacturer, maintained its interuterine contraceptive device (IUD) was no more dangerous than any other, similar device. In 1974, the Food and Drug Administration, concerned about negative reports, asked Robins to stop selling the shield, but it did not issue a recall.

The company complied but treated the issue as a matter of litigation rather than as a public health problem. More than 13,000 women who used the device continued to complain about a variety of ailments, including uterine perforation, pelvic inflammatory disease, sterility, and miscarriage. Robins asserted the responsibility for the problems lay with the doctors who had inserted the IUDs. After a crescendo of complaints by users, 5,100 lawsuits were filed against A H Robins by 38 personal-injury lawyers.

The company then employed a variety of stalling tactics to defer settlement of the claims. Company lawyers cross-examined claimants about minute details of their character and their sex lives. Plaintiffs' lawyers were denied access to potentially damaging company records. In 1984, the attorney who had managed the Dalkon Shield defense in the early 1970s for Robins even admitted he had destroyed sensitive documents concerning the device.

As the company stonewalled, the costs of settling the claims escalated. Between 1974 and 1984, Robins's legal bills added $107 million to its Dalkon Shield costs. During that period, Robins settled more than 9,000 cases out of court for $378.3 million. In October 1984, the company paid about $1.6 million for doctors to remove the devices from 4,500 women. The company paid an additional $4.5 million to promote the removal program, but still refused to pay the claims.

In August 1985, Robins filed for Chapter 11 bankruptcy protection. To the claimants, this move was yet another means of forestalling payment. Judge Miles W Lord, who had heard the case in federal court the year before and chastised Robins officials for "corporate irresponsibility at its meanest," was quoted as saying he hoped the bankruptcy was not yet another company ploy to avoid settling claims.[55]

The court ordered Robins to come up with a reorganization plan by June 1986. By all accounts, the company's legal affairs were in complete disarray. Robins fired its legal counsel right after filing for bankruptcy and, without court authorization, paid more than $7 million to former executives and trade creditors. The federal judge handling the case ordered the company to recover the money and hire outside bankruptcy counsel or be placed under the supervision of a court-appointed trustee. Throughout June 1986, Robins's legal troubles continued to mount. Federal investigators accused Robins of spending $22 million without court approval since filing for bankruptcy, and the federal judge found Robins in contempt of court for making the illegal payments.

Finally, in April 1987, Robins came up with a reorganization plan. The plan allotted $1.75 billion to an independent settlement trust fund for the women who

---

[55]F Schwadel, "Robins and Plaintiffs Face Uncertain Future," *The Wall Street Journal,* August 23, 1985, p. 4.

claimed injury. The company planned to finance the trust with $300 million of its own and up to $800 million of debt through Drexel Burnham Lambert and Shearson Lehman Brothers. Claimants immediately labeled the fund as "stingy and deceptive."[56]

By August 1987, Robins had come up with a new reorganization plan in response to criticisms of its previous plan. By this time only 200 of the 3,100 cases remained unsettled, but claimants still deemed the proposed payments inadequate. Under the new plan, Robins would merge with Rorer Group, Inc. Robins's stockholders would be protected because they would be issued Rorer stock.

A committee representing women who had used the Dalkon Shield determined that claims would amount to at least $4 billion and could go as high as $7 billion—about four times what the company had offered. The court case dragged on through the summer and fall of 1987. Finally, on December 14, 1987, the federal court ruled that Robins must set aside $2.48 billion for claimants.

While one set of stakeholders, the injured women, was somewhat satisfied, other stakeholder groups faced a new uncertainty. Companies seeking bankruptcy as a way to avoid personal-injury litigation would have to deal with the fact that their responsibility would not disappear. Insurance companies named as codefendants in such suits would have to decide how to handle their situation. Robins's shareholders faced uncertainty about the value of their stock. Would they reap the benefits of the merger with Rorer, or would the settlement fund come out of their assets?

Robins's legal maneuverings did not stop with the judge's decision. In January 1988, Robins decided to consider takeover bids by the French pharmaceutical maker Sanofi SA and by American Home Products Corporation. Both shareholders and outside claimants were required to vote on any acquisition proposal. The fourth reorganization plan, filed in February 1988, accepted American Home Products' bid. But there were still outstanding criminal indictments against a doctor who had lied about safety tests of the Dalkon Shield in 1983 and continued perjury charges against the former attorney who had destroyed documents.

In April 1988, American Home Products' bid was accepted and a committee of five was established to run the $2.47 billion trust fund. Almost immediately claimants, lawyers, and consumer and health advocacy groups formed a coalition to vote against the reorganization plan. Ballots were sent to the claimants, two-thirds of whom had to approve the plan. The plan was approved, but disputes between claimants and trust fund officials continued through 1989.

In 1989, Michael M Sheppard was appointed to disburse the monies in the trust. He quickly paid $725 or less to 101,000 claimants with minimal proof they had been injured by the Dalkon Shield. An undisclosed number of claimants with slightly stronger proof received $5,500 each.

By 1991, the easy cases had been settled. Many remaining claimants charged their cases were being unreasonably delayed. Between 25 and 40 percent of the trust's offers were rejected as being too low. If a woman rejected an offer, her next step was to seek a second review and, if that did not work, to seek a settlement conference. To

---

[56]P M Barrett, "Robins Proposes Reorganization Plan," *The Wall Street Journal,* August 24, 1987, p. 4.

the dismay of many claimants, settlement conferences often resulted in offers even lower than those originally made.[57]

By 1993 more than 147,000 claimants had settled their suits, most for less than $5,500. Of the more than 44,000 remaining claimants, 2,500 rejected offers and more than 22,000 were still in negotiations with the trust. Trust officials tried to encourage arbitration by allowing claimants to bypass settlement conferences if they agreed to cap their potential damages at $10,000. But many claimants chose to go to trial. The trust's current chairperson said the trust did not have exact figures but maintained that claimants, on average, were likely to receive bigger damage awards through arbitration or trial than through settlement. However, she warned, "There is significant risk the claimant will walk away with less or nothing."[58]

It is interesting to speculate whether the gigantic expenditures of money, time, and energy were necessary to protect the claimants and the company. Lawyers estimate that had Robins chosen to recall the product in 1974, the company's costs would have totaled $50 million.

Summary

This chapter discussed the importance of social issues management to the overall task of managing a modern corporation. It began with a discussion of the economic, political, and social issues that confront today's managers. The chapter examined capitalism as the fundamental concept underlying the American economic system. The modern corporation emerged from that system and is ideologically molded by the unique political and legal system developed by the framers of the Constitution.

Today's managers are central players in the ongoing philosophical debate over the nature of corporate social responsibility. Many economists, historians, organizational behaviorists, and even practicing managers have failed to recognize the importance of this debate to corporations worldwide. Only recently have academicians and practitioners tried to establish a more rigorous and manageable set of criteria for defining the scope of business responsibility.

Social responsiveness management focuses on a company's management as it relates to the social, political, and legal environments. One of this book's central objectives is to help managers develop an analytical framework and the tools that will enable them to manage corporate social responsibility more effectively and systematically. Any such analytical framework must be based on a solid foundation.

---

[57]M Geyelin, "Dalkon Shield Trust Hailed as Innovative, Stirs a Lot of Discord, *The Wall Street Journal,* June 3, 1991, p. A1.

[58]M Geyelin, "Dalkon Shield Victims Who Spurn Settlements Take on Big Risks," *The Wall Street Journal,* April 30, 1993, p. B6.

The chapter reviewed some of the issues managers face in the 1990s. It then looked at the linkage between the environment and company strategy and reviewed the business-government responsibility debate.

The A H Robins case brought out many of the issues covered in this chapter and emphasized the complexities of doing business in a dynamic, often unpredictable environment. The case also pointed to the importance of company strategy and of the implementation tools needed to meet the demands of stakeholders.

Questions

1. Using two daily newspapers and one popular weekly newsmagazine, list and discuss some of the critical social issues corporations face in the 1990s.
2. If you were the CEO of a large corporation, how would you resolve the corporate social responsibility debate? Be prepared to argue that a company should not get involved in social issues unless it can make a profit on the transaction. Also, be prepared to define the social responsibilities every corporation has toward its stakeholders.
3. What are the two fundamental assumptions on which capitalism is based? What four essential elements derive from those assumptions?
4. What are the major legal characteristics of a corporation? How do they differ from the characteristics of a sole proprietorship or a partnership?
5. Had you been the CEO of A H Robins Company, what strategy would you have developed to deal with the claims against the company?
6. How would you feel about working in a company that espoused the three propositions put forth by Freeman and Liedka on pages 23 and 24? Why?

2

STRATEGY FORMULATION

Good Idea to outline chapters

This chapter focuses on decision processes that help managers formulate strategies to achieve social goals and other business objectives. Before we discuss strategy formulation and its components, we must define corporate strategy. Kenneth R Andrews's classic definition says *corporate strategy* is "the pattern of decisions in a company that determines and reveals its objectives, purposes, or goals, produces the principal policies and plans for achieving those goals, and defines the range of business the company is to pursue"[1]

CASE *Gillette Company*

Early History

King Camp Gillette, the inventor of the Gillette razor, started his career as a salesperson in a hardware store. By the mid-1890s, he had received a number of patents for plumbing products and was hoping to invent an object that "when used once, is thrown away and the customer comes back for more, and with every additional customer you get, you are building a permanent foundation of profit."[2]

Gillette cast about for ideas that would meet these criteria. Suddenly, in 1895, he had an almost mystic experience. As he described it, he was standing in front of a mirror, stropping his straight razor, when "the Gillette razor was born . . . All this [the design] came more in pictures than in thought as though the razor was already a finished thing and held before my eyes. I stood there in a trance of joy at what I saw."[3]

---

[1] K R Andrews, *The Concept of Corporate Strategy* (Homewood, IL: Richard D Irwin, 1980), p. 18.

[2] H Vernon-Wortzel, "The Gillette Corporation: The Formative Years," unpublished paper delivered at the Academy of Management, August 1983. Research for this paper was based largely on reports in *The Gillette Blade*, the company magazine published between 1917 and 1929.

[3] Ibid.

Gillette worked with several friends and acquaintances to form a company, which in 1901 they incorporated as American Safety Razor Company of Maine. The following year, at Gillette's insistence, the company's name was changed to Gillette Safety Razor Company of Maine. Although Gillette, as president, was the only paid employee, the company quickly fell into debt. "In fact," Gillette later reminisced, "we were busted and apparently done for."[4]

Desperate, the owners turned to a group of New York investors, who demanded 51 percent of the stock. Gillette, reluctant to give control of the stock to outsiders, forced the board to reject the New York offer.

After the meeting at which the offer was turned down, Gillette went to his favorite Boston restaurant for lunch. As luck would have it, he met John Joyce, a local financier who had financed some of Gillette's earlier unsuccessful inventions. Gillette had given Joyce a sample razor and 1,000 shares of worthless Gillette stock. Joyce, hoping to recoup some of his investment, offered the despondent Gillette small but regular infusions of cash in exchange for bonds and a substantial, but not controlling, share in the firm.

Overjoyed, Gillette returned to the office, where he called an impromptu board meeting. The directors quickly approved the Joyce offer. From that moment on, the fledgling company had few major financial problems, although its management had serious managerial and strategic disagreements. Gillette and his board frequently quarreled over strategy and control. Gillette became so contentious that top management tried desperately to force him out of the company.

In 1912, the old Maine corporation was reorganized as Gillette Safety Razor Company of Massachusetts. By this time, Gillette had signed over his patents to the company in exchange for a five-year contract and had virtually no part in running the company.

Symbolically as well as managerially, it was the end of an era. The company, which by now was very large and growing, had business worldwide. Professional managers developed and implemented strategy. It is doubtful that anyone could have predicted Gillette Company's phenomenal success or conceived of the strategy that would take the company into the twenty-first century.[5]

Gillette Today

In 1992 Gillette's revenue totaled $5.2 billion, with operating profits of $967 million. More than two-thirds of these totals were earned outside the United States; the bulk of overseas sales and profits came from Western Europe.

Gillette has developed a new strategy to take it into the next century. The strategy combines penetrating new markets and continuously developing better shaving products. Between 1991 and 1993, Gillette proposed or entered new projects and joint ventures in underdeveloped markets. When the Sensor razor was introduced, American and European men abandoned their Trac II and Atra twin-bladed cartridge razors. Gillette refurbished the previous-generation machines used to make these products, installed them in joint venture factories—many of which already made a version of the double-edge safety razor—and tapped new local markets.

---

[4]Ibid.
[5]Ibid.

Among the company's projects was a joint venture formed in St. Petersburg, Russia, in 1991. Gillette planned to develop a factory there with a capacity of 750 million units a year. Between 1991 and 1993, Gillette bought out Turkey's biggest blade maker, Permasharp. It established additional joint ventures or made acquisitions in India, Egypt, Pakistan, and Poland.

Perhaps the operation with the greatest potential was begun in 1992. Gillette and Shanghai Razor Blade Factory, China's leading blade maker, agreed to form Gillette Shanghai Ltd., 70 percent of which would be owned by Gillette. For an initial investment of $45 million, the Chinese venture boosted Gillette's market share from 10 to 70 percent of China's rapidly growing billion-blade market.[6]

Questions

1. Did the original managers of Gillette Company have a specific strategy? If so, what was it?
2. How important was strategic planning in the early days?
3. How important is strategic planning today?
4. What aspects of the economic, social, legal/political, and technological environments have changed since the early twentieth century? How have these changes affected the formulation of Gillette's strategy?
5. What social issues should Gillette's current strategy address?

The Environment of Strategy Formulation

Managers often find they have more difficulty formulating social issues strategy than they do functional area strategies. In both cases, they use many of the same approaches: They study the environment, assess their firms' particular strengths and weaknesses, and analyze the information they have gathered. However, the choices they confront in managing social issues are often more difficult to assess and measure. In fact, many top managers admit they do not even try to deal with social issues strategically. They simply allocate a budget for social issues and address problems as they arise. They make no organized attempt to set goals and priorities to maximize the use of resources. They do not follow up to assess results. As we discussed in the previous chapter, a nonstrategic or ad hoc approach to social issues management is becoming increasingly unfeasible in the environment business firms face.

The strategy problem for managers is to establish which among many social issues to address. They must identify those issues with potentially high impact on their firms and plan how to deal with them in the future. A first step is to understand the environment in which their companies operate.

This chapter begins with a general discussion of environmental analysis and an overview of four basic environmental sectors: (1) economic, (2)

---

[6]F M Biddle, "The Sun Never Sets," *The Boston Globe,* June 27, 1993, p. 51.

EXHIBIT 2-1

Environmental forces affecting social issues strategy

✗ apply this to an issue

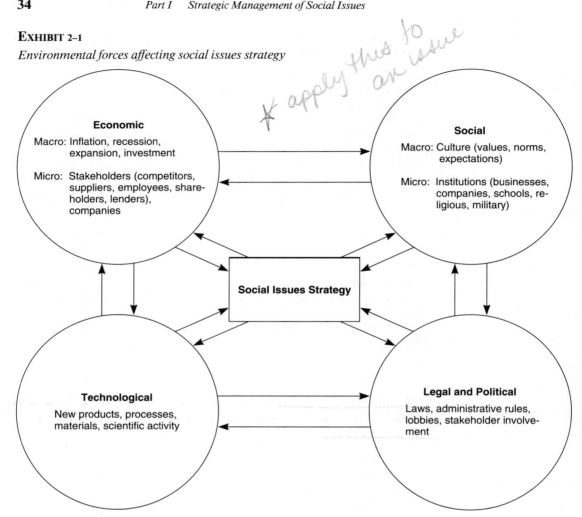

Economic

Macro: Inflation, recession, expansion, investment

Micro: Stakeholders (competitors, suppliers, employees, shareholders, lenders), companies

Social

Macro: Culture (values, norms, expectations)

Micro: Institutions (businesses, companies, schools, religious, military)

Social Issues Strategy

Technological

New products, processes, materials, scientific activity

Legal and Political

Laws, administrative rules, lobbies, stakeholder involvement

SOURCE: Adapted from V K Narayanan and L Fahey, "Environmental Analysis for Strategy Formulation," in *Strategic Planning and Management Handbook,* ed. W R King and D I Cleland (New York: Van Nostrand Reinhold, 1987), p. 155.

social, (3) legal and political, and (4) technological. As we see in Exhibit 2–1, all of these sectors have a potential impact on social as well as business issues.

Elements of the Environment

The Economic Environment

On a macroeconomic level, the economic environment includes broad, sweeping forces such as inflation, recession, and waves of rapid expansion. It also incorporates systemic problems such as uneven income distribution, balance of payments, unemployment, and the rates of saving and capital investment.

These economic forces are highly significant for any business, but they are essentially *given.* Any company, regardless of its size and scope, can do little to alter these forces. They affect all industries and all companies within an industry. General economic conditions influence the mood of the public, the nature of the issues likely to receive attention from activist groups, and acts of government.

At a microeconomic level, the company's environment consists of stakeholders, such as competitors, suppliers, employees, lenders, and shareholders. Managers try to be sensitive to their microeconomic environments. Yet many managers get caught by surprise in their own markets even when forces for change have been highly visible for some time. When macro- and microeconomic forces combine, the effect on industry can be profound.

The Japanese Example.   For years, US industry has looked at the Japanese economic juggernaut with amazement, apprehension, and often not a little envy. But Japan's success was compromised by a serious recession beginning in 1991. The value of the yen soared, making Japanese goods less competitive. Economic growth slowed dramatically, and Japanese productivity fell. By mid-1993, Japanese productivity ranked in the bottom half of the industrialized nations, well below the rankings of the United States and many European Community countries.[7]

In January 1993, Pioneer Electronics announced that 35 middle managers would have one month to retire from the company "voluntarily." If they did not retire, they would be dismissed. This move would have been barely noticed in the United States, but the Japanese public was horrified. The action seemed to be the harbinger of a significant change in Japanese corporate culture, which could in turn bring about equally unsettling changes in Japanese society.

With Japan in a severe economic slump, Japanese companies began to search for ways to minimize the chronic underutilization of their own resources that had reduced corporate earnings. Most companies planned to reduce hiring, offer voluntary retirement, or transfer employees to subsidiaries or suppliers. The spokesperson for Pioneer Electronics observed, "In the old traditional system, you work long and are eventually promoted to manager. That system can no longer work because we're moving into a severe economic situation."[8]

In March there came a single moment that "seemed to shake the national psyche and mark the end of a chapter in the postwar era." The manager of Nissan Motor Company's Zama plant announced to the entire assembly of 2,500 workers that the plant would be shut down over the next

---

[7]E Thompson, "Japan's Struggle to Restructure," *Fortune,* June 28, 1993, p. 84.

[8]A Pollack, "Shock in a Land of Lifetime Jobs: 35 Managers Dismissed in Japan," *The New York Times,* January 9, 1993, p. A1.

two years. A senior auto executive observed that "for Japanese workers the closing of a plant is something completely alien. It is something that happens in the U.S., or on the other side of the earth. And now they are finding themselves stunned."[9]

Even Nippon Telegraph and Telephone, one of the world's largest corporations, announced in March 1993 that it was eliminating 30,000 jobs over the next several years. No longer, it seemed, would people be kept through good times and bad—and no one was exempt. Japanese managers dreaded the *kata tataki,* or "tap on the shoulder." Even top executives were caught in the maelstrom. Under pressure from the Matsushita family, Matsushita's president resigned. The entire corporate leadership of Showa Shell Sekiyu KK, Shell Oil's Japanese subsidiary, resigned after revelations that management had lost $1 billion in bad currency trades.[10]

Major changes in the macro- and microeconomic environments often alter fundamental stakeholder relationships and expectations. Japanese and American stakeholders may have different concerns and assumptions about their corporations' responsibility to employees and to society. However, economic changes can shake those expectations to the core.

American corporations are finally beginning to meet and adjust to changes in both the macro- and microeconomic environments. Increased competition from foreign companies on the United States's own playing field signals a turbulent economic environment. For more than a decade, the opponents' jerseys have read The Netherlands, Great Britain, Japan, Canada, and West Germany. Today, American corporations are meeting the challenge and searching globally for their own opportunities.

The Social Environment

The social environment affects social issues management most directly. As was true in our discussion of the economic environment, it is useful to think of the social environment at both the macro and micro levels. The broad and pervasive influences of culture are most obvious at the macro level. Yet we tend to discount the importance of culture, because it is so deeply ingrained and subtle that we are unaware of its importance in daily life. The classic definition of *culture* is "that complex whole which includes knowledge, belief, art, morals, law, custom, and any other capabilities and habits acquired by man [or woman] as a member of society."[11]

To understand culture, therefore, it is essential to understand the major attributes of a given society. Culture provides a common framework and

---

[9]D E Sanger, "Layoffs and Factory Closings Shaking the Japanese Psyche," *The New York Times,* March 3, 1993, p. A1.

[10]Ibid., p. D5.

[11]E B Tyler, *Primitive Culture,* 3rd Eng. ed. (London: John Murray Publishers, 1891), p. 1.

acts as a social bond. "Bonds," according to the philosopher Ralph Ross, "may restrain, like chains on a slave, or they may sustain, like the climber's rope."[12] Cultures do both. They do not, however, respond to environmental forces uniformly. The diversity of cultures, regardless of similarities or dis- similarities in the physical environment, may be explained by the fact that "culture acts as a set of blinders, or a series of lenses, through which men [and women] view their environments."[13]

We are all aware of the numerous cultures that can exist even within small geographic areas. For example, people on the French side of the Alps have a different language, as well as different political, social, and economic institutions, than their Italian neighbors. Two African tribes within a five- mile radius may have different languages, dress, customs, and hierarchical structures.

Despite its subtle nature, culture may provide a great deal of stability and guidance for a society. A society's body of knowledge, laws, beliefs, and habits result in what Geert Hofstede calls "a collective programming of the human mind that distinguishes the members of one human group from those of another."[14] Although some writers comment on radical changes, "megatrends," and "future shock" in American society, the social fabric has proven remarkably durable and elastic.[15] While society is often flexible and dynamic in nature, its basic cultural traits endure.

A society's value system is a source of underlying stability. Thomas A Petit notes, "Chief among the determinants of the particular shape which an economic system takes are the dominant social values of the society of which the economy is a part. In every society there is a more or less continuous interaction between social values and . . . institutions."[16]

The role institutions play is an essential element of understanding cul- ture and value systems. Institutions are microcultures that include religious organizations, the military, government, businesses, and schools. People create institutions to gain security, generate a sense of purpose and direction, and accomplish certain tasks that are best undertaken as a group. In effect, they bring the individual values they learned early in their lives to the col- lective values of an institution.

However, as Exhibit 2–2 shows, the transfer of values from individual to institution is not a one-way process. Richard T Pascale observes that

---

[12]R Ross, *Symbols and Civilizations* (New York: Harcourt Brace Jovanovich, 1957), p. 172.

[13]C Kluckhohn and H A Murray. *Personality in Nature, Society, and Culture* (New York: Alfred A Knopf, 1949), p. 45.

[14]G Hofstede, "Culture and Organizations," in *International Studies of Man & Organization,* vol. 10, no. 4 (M E Sharpe. Inc., 1981), p. 24.

[15]See best-sellers by A Toffler, *Future Shock* (New York: Random House, 1970), and J Naisbitt, *Megatrends* (New York: Warner Books, 1982, 1984).

[16]T A Petit, *Freedom in the American Economy* (Homewood, IL: Richard D Irwin, 1964), p. 1.

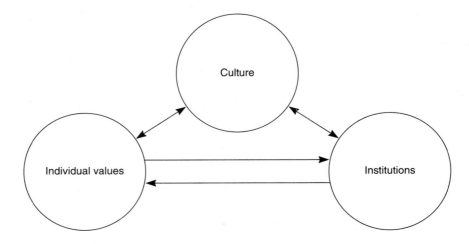

many corporations deliberately socialize new members in the values of the company. In this way, the firm perpetuates a distinct microculture of its own by passing it on to new employees. Pascale notes the value systems of some prospective employees are incompatible with the culture of the firm and suggests these individuals be screened out before they are hired.[17]

The reciprocal transfer of values from individual to institution and from institution to individual carries an expectation that both will realize a return on their "investment." For example, people expect the military to provide defense as well as victories in foreign ventures. In return, the military expects patriotism from citizens and operating funds from the government. Organized religions provide moral guidance and, to some, the promise of eternal life. In return, parishioners volunteer their time and financial support. Some even try to follow the moral guidelines their religions set down.

Likewise, consumers expect businesses to offer fair value in products and services, provide employment, contribute to economic growth, and act responsibly. They also expect products to be safe and of good quality. Employees expect compensation commensurate with their services and working conditions that support their tasks and respect their rights as human beings.

Institutions are remarkably stable, but if they repeatedly fail to deliver on these expectations, they can experience the equivalent of a run on the bank. A withdrawal of values and support can lead to social movements that weaken institutions. In a technical sense, *social movements* have been defined as "large-scale, widespread, and continuing elementary collective action in pursuit of an objective that affects and shapes the social order in

---

[17]R T Pascale, "The Paradox of 'Corporate Culture': Reconciling Ourselves to Socialism," *California Management Review* 28 (Winter 1985), pp. 26–41.

some fundamental aspect."[18] Clearly social movements must be compatible with dominant societal values if they are to affect the social order in some fundamental way. Institutions that do not reflect those values and lose public confidence are particularly vulnerable to attack.

As we mentioned in the previous chapter, many Americans are highly skeptical of the ability of the political system to deal with social problems. President Clinton's popularity ratings, the lowest of any president in history so early in his term, seem to reflect this sentiment. Regardless of Clinton's initiatives and policies, there appears to be a widespread conviction that social movements do not enjoy public confidence and fail to reflect the dominant values of the day.

Social values are not merely free-floating, vague concerns about public confidence in institutions. As they change over time, social values can have an impact on corporate policies and can drastically affect entire industries. The tobacco industry is a case in point.

The Social Environment and the Tobacco Industry. Stakeholders are attacking the tobacco industry from every quarter. Between World War II and the early 1980s, the issue of whether to smoke or not to smoke changed from a question of health and habit to one of civil rights and social etiquette. Our culture changed from "smoking permitted" to "no smoking allowed." The right to smoke versus the right to live in a smoke-free environment became a burning issue. Table 2–1 highlights the key elements in the tobacco controversy.

Throughout Chapter Know this

To counter changing attitudes toward smoking, Philip Morris and R J Reynolds Industries, Inc., formulated and implemented strategies to promote prosmoking issues. Reynolds did a direct mailing in a few states to encourage people to oppose possible increases on cigarette taxes. Philip Morris published a magazine to "influence people and make them feel good and warm about Philip Morris."[19]

In 1988, Philip Morris began a national advertising campaign that stressed the economic and political power of smokers. As Guy Smith IV, Philip Morris's vice president for corporate affairs put it, "Let the politicians take note. You're not just talking special interest group. You're talking swing vote."[20]

But the antismoking trend was clear. By 1988, more than half of American companies had restricted smoking on the job, the Federal Aviation Administration had prohibited smoking on domestic air flights of two hours

---

[18]K Land and G E Lang, *Collective Dynamics* (New York: Thomas Y Crowell, 1961), p. 490.

[19]T Hall, "Philip Morris Cos. Magazine Promotes Pro-Smoking Issues," *The Wall Street Journal,* July 24, 1985, p. 7.

[20]R Rothenberg, "New Ads by Philip Morris Stress Power of Smokers," *The New York Times,* June 29, 1988, p. 1.

TABLE 2–1 **Key Events in the Tobacco Controversy**

1955	The first Federal Trade Commission (FTC) published advertising guildelines.
1964	The surgeon general's report demonstrated a link between cigarette smoking and cancer.
1965	The FTC advertising code passed, requiring a warning label on cigarette packages.
1967	A Federal Communications Commission (FCC) ruling required equal antismoking advertising time on broadcast media.
1970	Legislation passed banning cigarette advertising from all broadcast media.
1971	The Interstate Commerce Commission (ICC) banned smoking in all interstate buses except for the last five rows of seats.
1972	Health warnings were made mandatory in all cigarette advertising.
1972	All airlines volunteered to establish no-smoking sections.
1983	The Senate Labor and Human Resources Committee voted to require tobacco companies to place a harsh health warning on cigarette packages.
1987	Cambridge, Massachusetts, passed a bill making it illegal to smoke in public places and in private businesses.
1988	The Federal Aviation Administration (FAA) prohibited smoking on flights of two hours or less.
1988	Northwest Airlines prohibited smoking on all its North American flights.
1990	Complete ban on smoking on all domestic flights.
1993	Los Angeles banned smoking in restaurants.

---

or less, and Northwest Airlines had advertised that it prohibited smoking on all domestic flights. No-smoking sections in restaurants and no-smoking rooms in hotels became the norm.

In a landmark case in June 1988, a federal jury awarded $400,000 in damages to plaintiff Antonio Cipollone, whose wife died of lung cancer. The jury found that Liggett Group Inc. should have warned customers about the dangers of smoking in its ads prior to 1966.

The societal sanctions against smoking escalated in 1993, when the Environmental Protection Agency (EPA) reported that secondhand smoke caused about 3,000 nonsmokers to die from lung cancer each year in the United States. The report also asserted that environmental tobacco smoke raised the risk of asthma in normal children and increased the severity of attacks in asthma-prone children.

Antismoking groups immediately used the EPA report to demand more restrictions on smoking in public places. To avoid liability, shopping malls, restaurants, businesses, and even sports stadiums banned or severely restricted smoking. Philip Morris and RJR Nabisco sued the EPA, claiming the report was unscientific, arbitrary, and capricious. They accused the EPA of manipulating data and failing to follow basic statistical principles.[21]

---

[21]N Tait, "US Tobacco Groups Sue Over Report," *Financial Times,* June 23, 1993, p. 6.

Whether the suits succeed or fail is almost beside the point. Basic cultural values have changed in the United States. Cigarette smoking is no longer socially acceptable in public places. The Los Angeles City Council may have set a precedent for urban governments across the United States. In August 1993, the council passed a law that totally banned cigarette smoking in restaurants. A group of restaurant and hotel owners, backed by the tobacco industry, gathered almost 98,000 signatures opposing the measure. But the council was not swayed; the ban became legal immediately. A patron who lights up faces a fine of between $50 and $250. A restaurant owner who is convicted of allowing smoking can be fined up to $1,000 and jailed for six months.[22]

In economic terms, smoking costs society about $65 billion annually in health care bills and lost productivity. Who should pay for these costs to society? Should smokers shoulder this burden in the form of excise taxes? Should the political and legal environment change to pass regulations forcing the tobacco industry to lower the amount of tar and nicotine in cigarettes? Should tobacco companies adopt a strategy of technological change in which they put R&D funds into "safe" tobacco or other cigarette substitutes? Finally, should small businesses lose revenue from patrons who want to smoke while they dine?

The Clinton administration is eager to take advantage of this cultural change. It would have liked to impose a hefty tax on cigarettes to help reduce the budget deficit and pay for the new health care plan and other programs. However, the still powerful tobacco lobby would have influenced enough votes to sink the entire economic plan.

The Clinton economic package, passed in August 1993, included $225 billion in spending cuts and $241 billion in tax hikes. The bill also imposed a 4.3-cents-per-gallon tax on gasoline and all other transportation fuels. In principle, a user tax on cigarettes is no different from a user tax on gasoline. A decade ago, it would have been unthinkable to even consider a tax on tobacco products. Today such a tax is not only possible but, within the foreseeable future, may be part of a total economic package.

The Legal and Political Environment

Many cultural conflicts are acted out and sometimes resolved in the legal and political sphere. Social activists may try to accomplish their goals by pressing for the passage of legislation. Each culture develops its own legal and regulatory systems. From culture to culture, these systems will vary considerably, from government controlled to theocratic. We will discuss the process by which laws and legislation are developed and passed in the United States in Chapters 7, 8, and 9.

---

[22]"Smoking Banned in LA eateries as Protest Petition Falls Short," *The Boston Globe,* August 3, 1993, p. 11.

The Technological Environment

Even within the last decade, technological advances have been staggering in their number and their societal impact. Technology affects and interacts with every aspect of the cultural, political, and legal environments. Throughout this book, we will address issues of changing technology and developments in new processes, products, and materials. We will also discuss the impact scientific activity has had on the management of corporate social issues.

Generally, "the technological segment is concerned with the technological progress or advancement taking place in a society. New products, processes, or materials; general scientific activity; and advances in fundamental science . . . are the key concern in this area."[23] Developments such as product innovations (videocassette recorders, fax machines, laptop computers) and process innovations (mass merchandising and telemarketing) are examples of events in the technological environment. The technological environment also is linked to the economic, social, and legal/political environments.

When videocassette recorders became household fixtures in the late 1980s, moviemakers and sports promoters began to realize they were not receiving their full potential measure of royalties. Viewers freely copied movies from commercial cassettes or taped restricted sports programs from pay cable stations. Producers and promoters formed lobbying groups to press for laws ensuring they would earn royalties every time the films and sportscasts were shown.

The proliferation of video rental stores created a new competitive arena, thus affecting the economic environment. Videocassette supermarkets using new merchandising techniques quickly grabbed the rental business from the local drugstore. During the 1980s, many local movie theaters closed because they had lost customers who had discovered a new form of inexpensive entertainment.

The entertainment industry went to court to prevent pirating and to ensure that every rental cassette carried a warning from the FBI about illegal copying. Culturally, the idea of what constituted entertainment also changed. Stores in every small town and major city in America rented videocassettes for weekend amusement. People sat at home in front of television sets instead of going to the local movie theater. Further technological advances, such as high-definition television (HDTV) and satellite transmission, will change the entertainment industry even more profoundly.

Mass merchandising is another technological innovation. In the 1920s, the growth of chain stores began to pose a threat to independent retail businesses. Because chain stores enjoyed relative efficiency by taking advantage

---

[23]V K Narayanan and L Fahey, "Environmental Analysis for Strategy Formulation," in W R King and D I Cleland, eds., *Strategic Planning and Management Handbook* (New York: Van Nostrand Reinhold, 1987), p. 154.

of scale economies, they presented tough competition for traditional retailers. In the late 1920s and early 1930s, as a result of pressure from local merchants' groups, over 30 states passed laws imposing discriminatory taxes on chains.[24] The family-owned drugstore, also a victim of mass merchandising, has virtually disappeared over the past 30 years. Large chains replaced the independent pharmacy, and the pharmacist became a dispenser of medication in a chain store rather than a store manager and entrepreneur.

Controversial technologies are by no means a thing of the past. A couple can donate an egg and a sperm to form an embryo, which is then frozen. A host mother, who has no genetic link to the child she carries, can be "rented" to carry the embryo to term. In theory, a woman could give birth to her own great-aunt or uncle, or even a sibling, years after the embryo was frozen. At present, the body of law and regulation covering this new industry is just being developed, and the ethical implications are only beginning to be explored.

What seemed like science fiction 20 years ago is scientifically feasible and even commonplace today. With new technology proliferating, one cannot even imagine how the biological sciences will develop in the future and what new industries may emerge.

Strategic Management and Organizational Culture

In every case, the business that attempts to plan strategically must consider the interactions of the four sectors that make up its total environment. As our cursory overview suggests, the environment is complex and hard to define. Therefore, if the firm is not going to proceed blindly, managers must identify and deal with those particular environmental forces linked most closely to the firm's truly strategic issues.

Managers have a critical responsibility to assess their firm's organizational culture in addition to the external environment. People within an organization select which issues they will address and what tools they will use to achieve their objectives. We will look next at some of the factors that affect these decisions. Top management especially determines the elements and process of strategy formulation.

Values and Leadership

A key issue for general managers (CEO, chairperson of the board, senior vice presidents) is to understand the company's sociocultural environment and determine how and where social issues fit into the firm's overall strategy. There is no doubt the personal values and leadership styles of the firm's top managers play a major role in this determination. Chester I Barnard, an experienced "captain" and former president of New Jersey Bell Telephone

---

[24]J C Palamountain, Jr., *The Politics of Distribution* (Cambridge, MA: Harvard University Press, 1955).

Company, wrote a book in 1938 that anticipated a number of today's business problems.[25]

Barnard observed that the endurance of organizations "depends upon the quality of leadership; and that quality derives from the breadth of the morality upon which it rests." He went on to explain that executive responsibility is "that capacity of leaders by which, reflecting attitudes, ideals, hopes, derived largely from without themselves, they are compelled to bind the wills of men to the accomplishment of purposes beyond their immediate ends, beyond their times."[26] In essence, Barnard was pointing to the importance of scope of vision and the ability to create an organization of people capable of responding thoughtfully and purposefully to the world around them.

Kenneth R Andrews points out that general managers function as "communicators of purpose and policy."[27] Their values and what they want to do often form the basis for their choice of alternatives. Unless the CEO identifies a social issue as critical, institutes mechanisms for dealing with it, and communicates the importance of doing so, middle managers will ignore the issue.

There are many examples of activist CEOs whose values and influence in the management of social issues persist well after they have retired or moved on. The founder of Polaroid Corporation, Edwin Land—who still enjoys a semimythical status within the company—left a legacy of strong community involvement. Polaroid began a minority-training project called Inner City in 1968, well before stakeholder pressure for such a program existed. The project is now profit making and has trained hundreds of employees for Polaroid and other companies. Polaroid gives financial, administrative, and technical assistance to hundreds of nonprofit institutions in the Greater Boston area and other areas in which Polaroid facilities are located. It offers employees a huge range of courses in career development, information systems, math and science, communication, and management. Land's personal values continue to influence the strategy of the current group of general managers decades after his retirement.

George A Steiner asserts, "the values of top managers are reflected in the network of aims of an enterprise. Whether written or not, these values have the profoundest impact on the direction in which a firm moves and the way it operates."[28] Gerald F Cavanagh notes that while strategic planning is essential to business success, *values* are the criteria by which managers make their important decisions.[29] In effect, the personal values of senior managers

---

[25]C I Barnard, *Functions of the Executive* (Cambridge, MA: Harvard University Press, 1960).

[26]Ibid., pp. 282–83.

[27]Andrews, *The Concept of Corporate Strategy,* p. 7.

[28]G A Steiner, *Top Management Planning* (New York: Macmillan, 1969), p. 144.

[29]G F Cavanagh, *American Business Values,* 2nd ed. (Englewood Cliffs, NJ: Prentice-Hall, 1984), pp. 1, 206.

serve as a filter through which these executives view the world and pilot their firms.

Adaptability to Change

The general manager's assessment of the environment and his or her adaptability to change are among the principal factors in determining how personal values influence the direction of a company. H Igor Ansoff notes that one of the primary difficulties of strategic issue management is top management's refusal to accept new and unfamiliar issues as relevant.[30]

Attitude toward change is the key issue here—the company's willingness to recognize environmental change, adapt to it, or, in some instances, even generate change from within. If managing change is central to an organization's effectiveness in adapting to its turbulent environment, managerial resistance to change, or conservatism, limits the company's vision.

Resistance to change also helps explain why managers do or do not take action. In recent years, American business leaders have been criticized for their lack of innovativeness and risk taking. William R Boulton observes that organizations that have operated in a stable environment over a long period of time find it very difficult to change, and it may even take an impending crisis to make a manager change.[31]

In one extensive study of senior managers' values, conservatism was negatively associated with firms' social responsiveness: The more conservative the values of the senior management team, the less socially responsive the company. This study also found that certain measures of financial performance suffered when the managers' values were conservative.[32]

In sum, it is essential that a company's leaders understand and even welcome change rather than perceive it as a threat. They must build an organizational culture in which people are encouraged to try new ideas and approaches to problems. They must view a dynamic environment as a source of challenge and excitement, not something to be ignored in the hope it will go away. If a firm's strategic planning process fails to anticipate change, the firm will likely be unable to set a strategically sound and socially responsive course.

It is worth noting that social change often engenders economic change. Consider the potential economic changes resulting from our diminishing smoking culture. As tobacco farmers' incomes fall, farmers sell off their land and enter other occupations. Community solidarity and stability disappear. Farmland is developed to support other industries, and generations of tradition are lost. As tobacco manufacturers lose markets in the United States,

---

[30]H I Ansoff, "Strategic Issue Management," *Strategic Management Journal* 1 (April–June 1980), pp. 131–48.

[31]W R Boulton, *Business Policy: The Art of Strategic Management* (New York: Macmillan, 1984), pp. 204–205.

[32]F D Sturdivant, J L Ginter, and A G Sawyer, "Managers' Conservatism and Corporate Performance," *Strategic Management Journal* 5 (October–December 1984).

they begin to acquire new, nontobacco-based companies. They also enter joint ventures with developing-country governments and firms to generate new populations of cigarette smokers abroad. Finally, US consumers who are trying to quit smoking buy nicotine patches, chew nicotine gum, and enter behavior modification seminars. All these activities create new economic opportunities, change established markets, and have major societal implications.

A Framework for Strategy Formulation

In *Competitive Strategy,* Michael E Porter stresses, "The essence of formulating competitive strategy is relating a company to its environment."[33] If a company aligns itself with its environment, it must fit its strategy to the realities of that environment. A company's ability to achieve a strategic fit between itself and its environment depends on management's ability to identify, define, and assess the organization's mission, major objectives, and internal capabilities. Top management must scan and analyze its environment and choose an effective strategy from among a number of options.[34]

We will next develop more fully those aspects of the strategy formulation process most directly related to the management of corporate social responsiveness.

The Mission Statement

In spelling out a company's mission or purpose, top management needs to define the company's product or market boundaries and also provide its people with a sense of direction and purpose. In *A Sense of Mission: Defining Direction for the Large Corporation,* Andrew Campbell and Laura Nash found that in the ideal situation, the sense of mission is established by a company's founders and is revised and extended as the company grows.[35]

In short, the mission statement should answer the following questions:

· Who are we?
· What business are we in?
· What do we stand for?

---

[33] M E Porter, *Competitive Strategy: Techniques for Analyzing Industries and Competitors* (New York: The Free Press, 1980), p. 3.

[34] See, for example, Boulton, *Business Policy;* L G Hrebiniak and W F Joyce, *Implementing Strategy* (New York: Macmillan, 1984); P Lorange and R F Vancil, *Strategic Planning Systems* (Englewood Cliffs, NJ: Prentice-Hall, 1977); D E Schendel and C W Hofer, eds., *Strategic Management* (Boston: Little, Brown, 1979); B Yavitz and W H Newman, *Strategy in Action* (New York: The Free Press, 1982); and H I Ansoff, *The New Corporate Strategy* (New York: John Wiley & Sons, 1988).

[35] J A Kurtzman, "Mission Statements," *Harvard Business Review* (March/April 1993), p. 10.

According to John A Pearce II, the company mission is "a broadly
defined but enduring statement of purpose that distinguishes a business
from other firms of its type and identifies the scope of its operations in product and market terms."[36] James C Collins and Jerry I Porras define the mission statement as "a clear and compelling goal that serves to unify an organization's efforts . . . [It] must stretch and challenge the organization, yet be
achievable. It translates the abstractness of philosophy into a tangible, ener-
gizing, highly focused goal that draws the organization forward."[37]

Some companies restrict their mission statement to a discussion of the
economic mission of the enterprise and supplement it with a separate company credo or ethics statement. Others incorporate their basic beliefs or credos into the text of the mission statement. The company generally benefits
from defining its commitment to good corporate citizenship whether it uses
joint or separate statements.

For example, most observers agree that Johnson & Johnson's (J&J)
credo served the company especially well during the Tylenol crisis. In 1982,
several Chicago-area residents died of cyanide poisoning after taking
Tylenol, a leading over-the-counter pain remedy produced by one of J&J's
divisions. Both employees and customers understood J&J's public position when the firm struggled with the aftermath of the deaths. J&J's mission statement shows the intertwining of economic and social goals (see
Exhibit 2–3).

Some mission statements, such as J&J's, define relevant stakeholders
broadly. In its 1987 *Annual Report,* Polaroid Corporation enumerated the
company's areas of social responsibility. The report clearly addressed both
the firm's philosophy and its objectives. The report discussed personnel
issues, including affirmative action and equal opportunity. It also delineated
the company's strategy with regard to health, safety, and environmental
issues and to the social needs of the community.[38] Even a casual reader could
understand Polaroid's concern for employees and the community Exhibit
2–4 shows Polaroid Corporation's statement of values.

In the late 1980s, managers incorporated ethical codes into their companies's mission statements more frequently. Scandals involving insider
trading and collusion between the defense industry and government officials
over multimillion-dollar contracts rocked the corporate world. Corporations rushed to adopt codes of ethics. The Business Roundtable recommended that top managers implement written codes that explicitly communicate the expectations of top management, develop programs to

---

[36] J A Pearce II, "The Company Mission as a Strategic Tool," *Sloan Management Review*
23 (Spring 1982), p. 15.

[37] J C Collins and J I Porras, "Organizational Vision and Visionary Organizations,"
California Management Review 34 (Fall 1991), p. 42.

[38] Polaroid Corporation, 1987 *Annual Report,* pp. 10–14.

EXHIBIT 2-3

Johnson & Johnson's mission statement

Johnson&Johnson

Our Credo

We believe our first responsibility is to the doctors, nurses and
patients, to mothers and all others who use our products and services.
In meeting their needs everything we do must be of high quality.
We must constantly strive to reduce our costs in order to maintain
reasonable prices.
Customers' orders must be serviced promptly and accurately.
Our suppliers and distributors must have an opportunity
to make a fair profit.

We are responsible to our employees, the men and women who
work with us throughout the world.
Everyone must be considered as an individual.
We must respect their dignity and recognize their merit.
They must have a sense of security in their jobs.
Compensation must be fair and adequate, and working conditions
clean, orderly and safe.
Employees must feel free to make suggestions and complaints.
There must be equal opportunity for employment, development and
advancement for those qualified.
We must provide competent management, and their actions
must be just and ethical.

We are responsible to the communities in which we live and work
and to the world community as well.

We must be good citizens—support good works and charities
and bear our fair share of taxes.
We must encourage civic improvements and better health and education.
We must maintain in good order the property we are privileged to use,
protecting the environment and natural resources.

Our final responsibilty is to our stockholders.
Business must make a sound profit.
We must experiment with new ideas.
Research must be carried on, innovative programs
developed and mistakes paid for.
New equipment must be purchased, new facilities provided
and new products launched.
Reserves must be created to provide for adverse times.
When we operate according to these principles, the stockholders
should realize a fair return.

SOURCE: Johnson & Johnson, 1982 *Annual Report.*

EXHIBIT 2–4

*Polaroid
Corporation's
statement of values*

OUR VALUES

■ **Respect.**
We believe in the dignity of every
individual in the Company.

■ **Ownership.**
Each of us is responsible for knowing
what our business goals are and each
of us is responsible for doing all we
can to achieve them.

■ **Excellence.**
We employ excellent people and we
expect excellent performance; in
return, we enjoy excellent pay and
benefits.

■ **Innovation.**
We seek innovation in all aspects of
our business: human relations, product development, manufacturing,
administration and marketing.

SOURCE: Polaroid Courses, Fall 1988, p. 5.

implement guidelines, and conduct surveys to monitor compliance.[39] We
will discuss codes of ethics more fully in Chapter 5.

If the company's mission changes, or if a new mission statement says
one thing while employees are experiencing something else, employees and
other stakeholders may perceive a gap between the company's stated values
and its observable behavior. In such cases, stakeholders are likely to ignore
the social values proclaimed by the mission statement.

The Stride Rite Example.   Stride Rite Corporation's recent decisions point
out how wide that gap can be for both management and workers. The
Cambridge, Massachusetts–based company, under its former chairperson
Arnold Hiatt, became a model of socially responsible behavior. A pioneer
in inner-city employment programs, Stride Rite's corporate headquarters
and adjacent factory and distribution center in Roxbury, Massachusetts

---

[39]J A Byrne, "Businesses Are Signing Up for Ethics 101," *Business Week,* February 15,
1988, pp. 56–57.

(part of Boston's inner city), once employed 2,500 people. In 1971, Hiatt opened a model day care center in the Roxbury plant. In 1981, headquarters moved to nearby Cambridge, and in 1984, Stride Rite ceased manufacturing in Roxbury. In May 1993, Stride Rite announced it would lay off the remaining 179 employees who worked in the plant's distribution center.

While closing the inner-city plant, Stride Rite shifted production to Asia and moved distribution to the US Midwest. During this time, Stride Rite continued its philanthropic activities. The company contributed heavily to charity, allocating 5 percent of pretax profits to the Stride Rite Charitable Foundation. It gave scholarships to inner-city youth, paid graduate students to work in Cambodian refugee camps, and set up tutoring projects on company time.

But to many inner-city residents, Stride Rite's actions belied its stated mission and reputation. Donald Gillis, executive director of Boston's Economic Development and Industrial Corporation, remarked, "the most socially responsible thing a company can do is to give a person a job." Stride Rite's actions were all the more devastating because Ames Department Stores and Digital Equipment Corporation both closed down their Roxbury operations in April 1993. As one local resident put it, "It is like back-to-back grand slams by the opposing team."

Stride Rite's top management claimed the company had no choice if it wished to remain profitable. By using Asian contract manufacturers and consolidating its distribution, Stride Rite saved millions of dollars each year. The present chairperson, Ervin Shames, noted, "Putting jobs into places where it doesn't make economic sense is a dilution of corporate and community wealth." Even Hiatt, who is now retired, acknowledged that if staying in the city will hurt the company, it should not be done. "I think you can't forget that your primary responsibility is to your stockholder," he said.[40]

The Stride Rite example points out the close tie between the economic and social environments and the mission of the firm. Mission statements and public perceptions of firms both change over time. It remains to be seen whether Stride Rite will continue to garner public service awards as it did in the past.

Corporate Objectives

Organizations have a hierarchy of objectives. *Strategic objectives* are those objectives that cover the broadest scope of organizational activities and require the greatest commitment and risk to resources. The companies that seem most successful in achieving their goals are those that have a limited

---

[40]J Pereira, "Social Responsibility and Need for Low Cost Clash at Stride Rite," *The Wall Street Journal,* May 28, 1993, p. A1.

number of crisply defined and well-understood strategic objectives. For example, if diversification is a major objective, the scope of the firm can delineate the diversification effort (compatible with its mission statement) and quantify the objective (e.g., "No more than 20 percent of our revenues is to be derived from any single product line"). Above all, managers should use the process of objective setting to transform broad directions into *concrete, measurable action commitments.*[41]

Corporate social responsiveness objectives need to be specific, avoid apple-pie-and-parenthood statements, and, as difficult as it may seem, be quantifiable whenever possible. For example, Polaroid's statement of objectives in environmental affairs notes the company uses state-of-the-art methods to reduce the amount of waste generated per unit of production. The company commits itself to reducing the toxicity volume per unit of production and the level of emissions to all environmental media.[42] These goals are measurable and clearly understandable to both employees and shareholders in the same way that goals related to financial or market share objectives are.

Internal Assessment

To a considerable extent, the organization's strengths and weaknesses have a direct impact on the strategic choices the firm makes after assessing its environment. A company's strengths lie in its core competencies or capabilities (what it does especially well).

Some companies's capabilities may be based on their management of technology. For example, Corning Glass Works is often cited as a company whose success is due to its lead in glass-making technology. Some 15 patents provided Corning with a distinct edge for over 100 years.[43]

In contrast, a number of observers have argued that IBM's past dominance in computers came less from technology, where it tended to be more of a follower than a leader, and more from its marketing prowess. However, this marketing prowess focused on large, mainframe computers. IBM did not recognize and react to the growing trend toward workstations and microcomputer networks. In 1993, the company was making a monumental effort to refocus and rebuild its core competencies and capabilities to accommodate environmental changes.

The Body Shop Example.   Anita Roddick, founder of The Body Shop, sees her company's competency as combining good business with socially

---

[41]A A Thompson, Jr., and A J Strickland III, *Strategy Formulation and Implementation* (Dallas: Business Publications, 1980), p. 8.

[42]Polaroid Corporation, 1987 *Annual Report,* p. 12.

[43]R F Vancil, "Corning Glass Works: Tom MacAvoy," in *Implementing Strategy: The Role of Top Management* (Boston: Harvard Business School Division of Research, 1982), pp. 21–36.

responsible behavior. She bases her company's success on its ability to offer high-quality products and assure purchasers that part of the profit is being used to "trade honorably with indigenous communities in disadvantaged areas."[44] She observes that customers come into The Body Shop to buy hair conditioner and find a story about how The Body Shop helped the Brazilian Xingu reserve and the Kayapo Indians. In that case, she relates, the company showed the Kayapos how to extract oil from the Brazil nut, which in turn raised the value of the raw ingredients the company uses. The Body Shop pays the Kayapos more, which gives them an alternative to logging—and less logging means less destruction of the rain forests. See Table 2–2 for the Body Shop approach to trade.

Organizational Weaknesses

Weaknesses of companies tend to center around two major areas: (1) resources, both managerial and financial, and (2) negative social issues visibility. When products or top management are highly visible in a negative way, the company becomes more vulnerable to stakeholders' challenges.

---

[44]"Do You Know Me?," advertisement for American Express, *Fortune,* August 9, 1993, pp. 58–59.

TABLE 2–2   The Body Shop Approach

Trade Not Aid
The Body Shop believes trade—not—aid offers a positive solution to the economic hardship in the developing world. Rather than giving hand-outs, we prefer to help communities acquire the tools and resources they need to support themselves. That way, they retain the power to determine their own futures. We believe such self-determination is a basic human right.
A New Business Ethic. The Body Shop started its first Trade Not Aid project in 1987. We had always been curious about other cultures, so it was natural for us to look for raw materials in other countries.
The challenge with every fair trading arrangement is not locating unusual ideas or ingredients, but creating small scale projects that are economically viable without disrupting the traditional way of life and local customs.
Trade Not Aid is not simply about generating income. If it were, The Body Shop would purchase products or ingredients on the international market. Instead we are creating a new business ethic, basing our projects on mutual need, mutual benefit, fairness, respect and trust between the trading partners. And every project must utilize natural resources in a sustainable manner and guarantee a regular income.

SOURCE: The text in this exhibit is taken from one of the many pamphlets displayed in The Body Shop retail stores.

Managerial and Financial Resources.   Frequently managerial talent is a limited resource. Some companies lack sufficient talented people to sustain certain types of strategies. A company may have a great idea for a new product line but lack the managerial resources or competencies needed to take advantage of the idea. Inadequate financial resources are another major limitation. Good ideas and good people are essential to success, but the financial strength to carry out a strategy is equally important.

The Northern Telecom Example.   In January 1992, Canada's phone equipment giant, Northern Telecom Ltd., announced record profits. Northern Telecom had stolen US market share from its American competitor, AT&T, and also established itself as a major player in emerging Asian markets. CEO and chairperson Paul G Stern, a former IBM executive, announced his determination to make Northern Telecom the world's biggest telecommunications equipment supplier by the year 2000.

Within weeks, Stern announced he was resigning to pursue other interests. The new CEO, Jean C Monty, a career Bell Canada executive, dropped a bombshell in June: He announced that Northern Telecom would post a second-quarter loss. On July 21, 1993, shareholders were shocked to discover the company was in the red by $1.03 billion. The company blamed the loss on layoffs and plant consolidations.

What happened at Northern Telecom? This company, famous for high-quality products, had sold some of its US customers shoddy goods. At the same time, it focused on overseas expansion. With the company's attention diverted to foreign markets, top managers delayed making a decision about whether to revamp its very complex, trouble-ridden phone switch software.

The software problem was not new. US "Baby Bells" that had bought the software experienced problems in the Northern Telecom phone switches that directed calls at their central offices. They had complained to Northern Telecom, but their complaints were ignored.

Some of the phone companies that had new switches and software upgrades on order delayed accepting the merchandise. When Northern Telecom finally began fixing the old software, it held up new versions until the old ones were running properly.

Former CEO Stern argued that switch software always had bugs to be worked out and denied customer service had suffered during his tenure. He asserted the problems arose because the company lost momentum and customer focus during a spate of executive changes.

Monty's version differed. Northern Telecom's board had installed him as president and chief operating officer in October 1992, bypassing Stern's protégé, Edward E Lucente, a former IBM colleague. The board did not consult Stern prior to Monty's appointment, ostensibly because the Bell Canada parent company, BCE, did not like his blunt management style.

Although Northern Telecom had talented people who could carry out its strategy, the destructive interaction between board members and the company's top two managers created a problem in terms of managerial resources and potentially catastrophic financial losses.

Northern Telecom estimated it would cost $158 million to rewrite the faulty software. New software will not be available until 1995. With Northern Telecom's overseas ventures under way and impatient customers threatening to look elsewhere, there is some question whether the company will be able to solve its managerial and financial problems in time.[45]

Social Issues Visibility and Vulnerability.   While distinctive competencies and resources are important in an internal assessment of a company's social responsiveness strategy, two additional dimensions are at least equally important. Management must also assess the firm's visibility with respect to social issues.

Visibility is a double-edged sword. A highly visible company that undertakes a project that reflects cultural values gets rewarded. On the other hand, a company is punished if it acts in a way that is considered wrong or insensitive in terms of those values. Management must consider objectively the firm's vulnerability to stakeholder pressure.

There is a relationship among the three elements of visibility, vulnerability, and social responsiveness. Social activists and others seeking change are likely to target highly visible firms that are close to the consumer. Financially weak firms operating in an intensely competitive environment are also vulnerable to challenges focused on social responsibility.

Company visibility depends on several factors: the firm's size, the nature of its products, the services it offers, the customers it serves, and the personalities of key members of its management. As a result of their sheer size and market position, companies such as Exxon (and most of the other major petroleum companies), Procter & Gamble, McDonald's, American Telephone & Telegraph (at least before the breakup), and Citicorp are subject to especially close scrutiny by the media, government agencies, and social activist groups. Those that serve consumers directly are the most visible.

The PepsiCo Example.   In mid-June 1993, PepsiCo faced a potentially catastrophic problem. In the course of a week, more than 50 people claimed they had found syringes in Pepsi-Cola cans. Despite the fact that it would be nearly impossible to insert a syringe into a can during the canning process, panicky reports came in from consumers around the country.

PepsiCo executives appeared on news shows, talk shows, and anywhere else they could get airtime to refute the allegations. Food and Drug Administration (FDA) commissioner David Kessler immediately called PepsiCo's North American CEO, Craig Weatherup, to discuss the problem. The two

---

[45]"What Really Happened at Northern Telecom," *Business Week,* August 9, 1993, pp. 27–28.

agreed that as long as consumers poured their Pepsi into a glass before drinking it, there was no public health problem.

Weatherup quickly ordered a video demonstrating the safety of the canning process and sent the footage by satellite to television stations. Many TV stations broadcast the video. Within several days, the FBI arrested four people for making false claims about product tampering.

But PepsiCo management still felt vulnerable. Weatherup worked 20 hours a day and spoke to PepsiCo's Chairperson, D Wayne Calloway, several times daily. PepsiCo faxed updates to bottlers twice a day. Employees fielded calls from concerned consumers and bottlers. Some local bottlers invited the local television stations into their plants to demonstrate how difficult it was to tamper with the canning process.

By the beginning of July, the crisis was at an end. None of the tampering allegations were real. The FDA and Dr. David Kessler basked in a public outpouring of approval at their handling of the situation. PepsiCo ran full-page ads in 12 national newspapers telling readers the stories were a hoax. Ultimately PepsiCo got a great deal of free positive publicity and profited from the ordeal.[46]

Had even one of the allegations turned out to be true, PepsiCo could have suffered a great deal of adverse publicity and resultant huge financial losses. This incident points out the vulnerability of companies that are highly visible and close to the consumer.

Examples of social issues visibility and vulnerability abound throughout the remainder of this book. Hardly a week passes without some company attracting unwanted publicity. Such notoriety is not necessarily linked to a faulty or contaminated product. It can result from a well-placed rumor or hoax.

The Sears, Roebuck and Company Example.   On June 14, 1992, Sears, Roebuck and Company ran a full-page open letter to customers in *The New York Times* and other national newspapers. Sears referred to charges made on June 11 by the California Bureau of Automotive Repair. CEO and chairperson Edward Brennan admitted that "mistakes may have occurred," but rejected any suggestion that Sears had intentionally recommended unneeded car repairs. Sears had, however, instituted an incentive program for its mechanics two years earlier as part of a companywide reorganization effort to cut costs and raise revenue. Mechanics earned commissions based on parts and labor used on the cars they serviced.

California's Consumer Affairs Department had accused Sears of systematically overcharging for auto repairs. A year-long investigation revealed that at 38 Sears service centers, employees had recommended unneeded repairs to 90 percent of the autos they serviced.

---

[46]"The Right Moves, Baby," *Business Week,* July 5, 1993, p. 30.

Sears's lawyers, speaking for top management, immediately called the accusations politically motivated and denied any fraud. Sears also charged the Consumer Affairs Department with trying to gain public support because it faced a budget crisis. In response to Sears's hostility and total denial of culpability, the California attorney general's office began preparing papers to close down all 72 Sears auto centers in the state.

Within several days, the New Jersey Division of Consumer Affairs announced it had conducted an undercover examination of six New Jersey Sears auto centers and found that all had recommended unnecessary repairs. New Jersey's attorney general also began to prepare papers for legal action.

This controversy occurred at a time when Sears was experiencing a great deal of pressure on sales and profits. At its annual meeting in May, Sears had faced a shareholder revolt against what shareholder activists called an example of a big company run by entrenched managers who put their own interests ahead of the shareholders'. Dissident shareholders demanded that the company change its style of doing business and proposed that directors and top managers become more responsive to shareholder concerns.

On June 16, Sears directors stepped into the fray. The directors announced they had adopted new corporate governance measures. For the first time, they assured full confidentiality in shareholder voting, required directors to buy and hold at least 1,000 shares of Sears common stock, and claimed that members of the board's nominating committee would be composed of outside directors. Sears chairperson Edward Brennan added to the directors' announcement, saying, "We believe these changes, coupled with existing policies, give Sears a more forward-looking position on the key governance issues."[47] However, Brennan, unlike other crisis-ridden CEOs, stayed in his Chicago office, declining to appear publicly to explain what had happened.[48]

As the furor mounted and investigations began in other states, pressure on Brennan and other top Sears executives mounted. In the nearly two weeks the controversy had been raging, Brennan had steadfastly denied an incentive compensation program even existed. Finally, on June 22, Brennan accepted personal responsibility for the troubles and admitted that Sears employees, whose job was to advise customers on repairs, were compensated solely on the costs of repairs that customers authorized. He announced the company was eliminating its incentive compensation program. Brennan also claimed Sears would discontinue its program requiring service advisers to meet sales quotas on specific auto parts.[49]

---

[47]"Sears Adopts New Rules," *The Boston Globe,* June 16, 1992, p. 46.

[48]R W Stevenson, "Sears's Crisis: How Did It Do?," *The New York Times,* June 17, 1992, p. D1.

[49]G A Patterson, "Sears's Brennan Accepts Blame for Auto Flap," *The Wall Street Journal,* June 23, 1992, p. B1.

In September, Sears agreed to pay $15 million to settle the charges. The settlement included agreements with California and 41 other states, in addition to resolution of 19 class-action lawsuits. Under the terms of the agreement, Sears agreed to refund $50 to consumers for each of five repair services its auto centers performed between August 1, 1990, and January 31, 1991. The refund program covered more than 933,000 transactions. Sears also agreed to pay California $3.5 million to reimburse the state for legal fees and investigative costs. Finally, Sears earmarked $1.5 million for auto repair training programs in California's community college system.[50]

Most crisis management experts doubted anyone could assess the additional long-term damage to Sears's reputation. They agreed the company had made a major blunder by stonewalling, denying the existence of its compensation programs, and accusing the California Consumer Affairs Department of discrimination. Indeed, many observers could not understand why Sears had ever implemented a compensation program based on such a fundamental conflict of interest. Surely, they argued, a company with Sears's experience in auto service would have anticipated the problems that occurred.

Stakeholders hold companies that rely on a high level of consumer trust, such as PepsiCo and Sears, Roebuck, to especially rigorous standards. Both the public and the media react particularly strongly when large numbers of lives are at risk or when a company appears to have deliberately betrayed the public trust. Falling short of that standard ensures a great deal of negative publicity and costly litigation. We will discuss crisis management techniques more fully in Chapter 4.

Top managers' visibility or absence of involvement can either help defuse or help exacerbate a crisis. As we see from the above examples, Craig Weatherup's immediate and candid explanation of PepsiCo's procedures dampened public concern. Even if a syringe had been found in a Pepsi can, public opinion would not have turned against the company so virulently. Edward Brennan's position, on the other hand, diminished consumers' trust in Sears and made them question whether Sears had additional problems it had not yet disclosed.

Environmental Scanning and Analysis

At some time, all companies face uncertainties in the environment and become vulnerable to stakeholder pressure. Managers can use tools such as scanning to minimize vulnerability to stakeholder pressure and maximize their options. Companies use scanning to alert them to potential changes that might constrain their strategic options.

---

[50]G A Patterson, "Sears Will Pay $15 Million, Settling Cases," *The Wall Street Journal,* September 2, 1992, p. A4.

John E Fleming describes environmental scanning and analysis as "a process designed to obtain, analyze, and report information relating to issues in the social and political environments."[51] Companies use scanning techniques try to identify indicators of change in the economic, social, legal/political, and technological environments before they occur. Companies gain time to work out their strategic options before stakeholders apply pressure on them to change. The earlier steps of determining the company's mission, defining its strategic objectives, and assessing its internal strengths and weaknesses are essential prerequisites for an effective scanning and analysis of the firm's environment.

When companies perform these steps properly, they can identify the particular areas of the environment that need to be monitored most closely. The values of senior management and the organization's culture also influence the selection of relevant variables from the environment. Some writers have argued that "systematic and continuous environmental scanning within a comprehensive framework is an essential activity for an ongoing managerial organization . . . comparable to annual budget preparation and review or the preparation of regular operating statements."[52]

The scanning and analysis process consists of four basic elements. Companies must ask:

1. How can we gather the best and most useful information about the environment?
2. What is the competitive environment of the firm?
3. Which participants have the greatest stake in a given issue or management decision?
4. How can we classify the issues into subsets, and how can we manage those issues and evaluate our performance?

Social issues opportunities and threats exist in the environment outside the corporation as well as within the structure of the company itself. The company should gather as much data as possible on external issues such as government regulation, consumerism, pollution, energy sources and costs, and taxation. Internally, the company should amass information on compensation and benefit trends, hiring and firing practices, safety, employee stress, and ethics.

A manager can draw on many sources of information. For example, some individuals and organizations identify themselves as "futurists" and provide broad perspectives on major trends and new forces for change. Their views of the future may appear in book form or in periodic publications. Alvin Toffler, for example, published *Future Shock* in 1970. The book

---

[51]J E Fleming, "Public Issues Scanning," in *Corporate Social Performance and Policy,* ed. L E Preston (Greenwich, CT: JAI Press, 1981), p. 156.

[52]L E Preston and J E Post, *Private Management and Public Policy* (Englewood Cliffs, NJ: Prentice-Hall, 1975), p. 107.

received considerable attention at a time when many people were perplexed by what they saw as a period of dramatic change in social values.

More recently John Naisbitt, author of *Megatrends,* identified "10 new directions transforming our lives." Naisbitt had been publishing *The Trend Report* three times a year for 12 years before writing his best-selling book. Subscribers to his report series paid $15,000 per year for his service. The Yankelovich Group, the Opinion Research Corporation, the Roper Organization, the Survey Research Center at the University of Michigan, the Harris Poll, and many other commercial and academic organizations provided potentially helpful environmental studies and trend analyses.

These and other organizations also conduct specialized studies for specific companies. In some industries, trade associations undertake ongoing studies of social issues and member activities. For example, the American Council of Life Insurance and the Health Insurance Association of America created the Center for Corporate Public Involvement. Since 1973, the center has published an annual report identifying a number of areas of social concern (e.g., equal employment opportunity, contributions, and environmental issues) and provides a summary of the activities and efforts of 250 member companies. Volunteers scan specific publications for particular kinds of issues and events, and each volunteer writes a summary of the relevant item stating what is important. These abstracts go to a committee, which looks for emerging trends.

As we will discuss in the next chapter, the scanning and analysis effort must be systematic and manageable. If the scanning effort is to contribute to improved company performance, it must be an integral part of the firm's overall social reponsiveness management process.

Strategic Choice

Having identified and analyzed the issues and parties that have the strongest possible consequences for the firm, management must make strategic decisions about how best to adapt or respond. The process is one of strategic choice. According to Robert H Miles,

> This view emphasizes the role of learning and choice in the process of organizational adaptation, and observes not only that complex organizations have the ability to alter themselves to conform to the contingencies—constraints and opportunities—posed by their environment, but that they may exercise considerable influence on the environments in which they operate. Indeed, these choices may range from the manipulation of environmental features to make them more accommodative of organizational goals, strategies, and structures, to the actual choice of the environments in which an organization wishes to operate.[53]

---

[53]R H Miles, *Coffin Nails and Corporate Strategies* (Englewood Cliffs, NJ: Prentice-Hall, 1982), p. 11.

The literature on corporate social responsiveness identifies two strategic approaches to stakeholder pressure: proactive and reactive. A *proactive* company attempts to anticipate strategic issues and devise approaches to prevent problems from developing. If the anticipatory effort is not successful and a problem develops, the company attempts to respond as quickly and effectively as possible. In short, the company strives to be on top of situations and take constructive steps to be a positive force for desirable change. For example, the anticipatory activities of Johnson & Johnson's management have allowed the company to handle crises such as the Tylenol scare expertly.

A *reactive* company deals with problems only after they have developed. Its posture is often defensive. When the firm is required to act, such as following litigation or the passage of new legislation, the initial response is minimal: "We do what the law requires—nothing more, nothing less." The A H Robins Dalkon Shield case in Chapter 1 and the Sears, Roebuck incident described earlier in this chapter are classic examples of reactive behavior. These companies acted only when they were forced to. They dragged their heels as long as possible and denied responsibility long after it became obvious they were responsible for the problems. As a result, they suffered more than they needed to.

In practice, companies rarely respond in a purely proactive or a purely reactive way. Most companies make reactive responses to some issues and proactive responses to others. For example, a company may institute a training program for minorities that costs a considerable amount of money and managerial time but refuse to address the needs of its workers with disabilities.

In the 1970s, Polaroid Corporation, which was widely regarded as an extremely proactive company in social issues, had to be forced by a government compliance officer to respond to the issue of equal employment opportunities for women. Why were women's rights a problem for Polaroid? James E Post and Marilyn Mellis speculate that in most companies, the response process for a single issue may vary in its pattern. Since affirmative action necessitated a high-cost structural change within the organization, Polaroid was more reluctant to behave proactively than it would have been if the issue were low cost and had a low organizational impact. In addition, Post and Mellis conclude that commitment is not "a unitary concept" and that each organization learns how far it has to go to satisfy a particular stakeholder without reorganizing priorities.[54]

There is some evidence that the public values the performances of proactive companies for their expenditure of time, money, and creativity in dealing with social issues. Peter Arlow and Martin J Gannon conclude that

---

[54]J E Post and M Mellis, "Corporate Responsiveness and Organizational Learning," *California Management Review* 22 (Spring 1978), pp. 57–63.

Bea Subject Matter ex pert
or a consultant

businesses do recognize the importance of social responsiveness and try to adapt to the concerns of stakeholders. However, they do not find a strong relationship between a firm's social responsiveness and its economic performance. Most firms subordinate social responsiveness to corporate economic goals.[55]

Strategic budgetary and economic considerations appear to weigh extremely heavily in companies' decisions about which social issues to tackle. The possibility of public approval does not always guide expenditures. In Chapter 3, we will look in depth at how companies implement social goals based on the formulation of strategy most appropriate for them.

Summary

This chapter concentrated on developing a framework for strategy formulation. It examined the relationship between elements of the corporate environment and a company's social responsiveness. The major sources of change and turbulence flow from a company's economic, social, legal/political, and technological segments of the environment. While formulating strategy, a company interprets environmental forces and issues based on the values of top management. The extent of the firm's response is influenced significantly by the culture of the organization.

In formulating its strategic response, a company must consider its mission and its strategic objectives. It must assess its internal strengths and weaknesses, scan and analyze its objectives, and then make choices among strategic alternatives. Most companies adopt a mixed proactive and reactive response to issues depending on the particular circumstances with which they must deal.

Project

Pick a Fortune 500 firm and ask its public relations department about the company's social issues agenda. Try to assess the environmental forces affecting its social issues strategy. Also, try to identify the major issues in each of the four types of environment.

Questions

1. What are the major elements of the American macroculture? Is there one identifiable American business culture? If so, what are its elements?

---

[55]P Arlow and M J Gannon, "Social Responsiveness, Corporate Structure, and Economic Performance," *Academy of Management Review* 7 (April 1982), pp. 235–41.

2. Suppose you are the CEO of a large, divisionalized company that makes canned food products.
   a. What statements would you put into the company's mission statement?
   b. A consumer complains that a can of your company's string beans was not properly sealed. What guiding concept tells you how to deal with this situation?
   c. How would you go about scanning for social issues that your company should address?
3. What responses should Sears, Roebuck have made to the California attorney general's charges?

3

STRATEGY
IMPLEMENTATION
AND EVALUATION

Strategy implementation and formulation are highly interrelated activities. The concepts and recommendations discussed in Chapter 2 and the issues addressed in this chapter are both fundamental to accomplishing corporate goals. This chapter examines the key elements of the process that move the company from analysis toward getting the job done and evaluating the results.

Environmental scanning and analysis, introduced in the previous chapter, links strategy formulation and implementation with evaluation. Once the company has collected the best and most useful information about the economic, social, legal/political, and technological environments, managers must be able to identify the stakeholders and the issues that directly and indirectly influence the firm.

Stakeholder Analysis

In their book *Strategy in Action,* Boris Yavitz and William H Newman note that "success and, indeed, survival of every business depends on either obtaining the support or neutralizing the attacks of key actors in its environment."[1] They go on to explain that "we live in a highly interdependent world. To steer a course through this ever changing structure, we need a keen insight into the behavior of those actors who affect our fate."[2] We call these key actors *stakeholders.* A stakeholder is any individual or group who believes it has a stake in the consequences of management's decisions and has the power to influence current or future decisions. Even before managers begin the environmental scanning and analysis process, they should ask,

---

[1] B Yavitz and W H Newman, *Strategy in Action* (New York: The Free Press, 1982), p. 74.
[2] Ibid.

"Who are the actors or players who have the greatest stake in a given issue or management decision?"

Stakeholders may be religious groups, employees, unions, environmentalists, or consumerists. They include government agencies (e.g., the Occupational Safety and Health Administration, the Equal Employment Opportunity Commission, the Securities and Exchange Commission), local chambers of commerce, Mothers Against Drunk Driving (MAAD), the National Association for the Advancement of Colored People (NAACP), and the Gray Panthers. They may also include the traditional industry participants who affect the fate of companies such as suppliers, buyers, and competitors. Stakeholders are also you, me, our families, and our neighbors.

The stakeholder influence map (SIM) in Exhibit 3–1 provides a conceptual framework for understanding the roles and influence of various stakeholders and issues. This map does not include every player in every circumstance, but it creates a foundation for categorizing people and organizations involved in implementing and evaluating the firm's social responsiveness strategy.

Stakeholders hold widely varying expectations and opinions about particular issues. Some stakeholders represent the views of large numbers of people; others speak for just a few; still others speak only for themselves. The amount of power and influence stakeholders wield also runs a wide range, as does the intensity of their feelings about any given issue. Stakeholders may be actively involved in one set of issues and relatively passive in their reactions to another.

EXHIBIT 3–1

Stakeholder influence map (SIM)

		Direct	Indirect
External		Suppliers Customers Competitors Potential entrants Government	Social activist groups Religious institutions Regulators Local community members Media Trade associations Lobbies and PACs
Internal		Board of directors Employees	Unions Shareholders

(handwritten annotations: "very impt" "know this" "apply to a case" "Merk or Tobbacco" "secondary stakeholders per Bowon" "Primary Stakeholders" "Primary Stakeholders")

Stakeholders play a central role in determining whether or not a company achieves its strategic objectives. All firms face major challenges in balancing the legitimate claims of groups ranging from suppliers to employees to environmentalists. This chapter analyzes stakeholder activities according to their position inside or outside the firm, their vested interests in a particular issue, the depth of their involvement, and their power to affect company strategy.

The Stakeholder Influence Map

Exhibit 3–1 classifies stakeholders into four groups along two dimensions. The dimensions are:

- *Location:* whether stakeholders are internal (work inside the firm's structure) or external (work outside the firm).
- *Influence:* the way they exert this influence on the firm, either directly or indirectly.

For example, the upper left quadrant of the SIM includes suppliers, customers, and competitors, which are external to the firm and exert their power directly. Much of their ability to influence the firm comes from their economic power—the power to offset competition within an industry or industries. Employees and the board of directors occupy the lower left quadrant. They are internal to the company and directly affect its policies. In the upper right quadrant are a variety of stakeholders external to the firm whose influence varies from issue to issue. In the lower right quadrant are unions and shareholders. These groups are part of the company "family" and exert power over the firm intermittently and less directly than the company's employees do.

In Exhibit 3–2 R Edward Freeman combines stakeholder analysis with Michael E Porter's five variables (discussed shortly) and refers to the combination as the "six forces that shape strategy."[3] To control the strategy formulation and implementation process, management must build a coalition of diverse stakeholders. The process requires considerable analysis, negotiation, persuasion, and exercise of power. If a company hopes to continue achieving its objectives, its stakeholder management effort must be continuous. According to Yavitz and Newman, "shaping external alignments is a never-ending task. Even with the most thorough analysis of each key actor and the wisest choice of relationship, tomorrow will present new problems."[4]

---

[3] R E Freeman, *Strategic Management: A Stakeholder Approach* (Boston: Pitman Publishing, 1984), p. 78.

[4] Yavits and Newman, *Strategy in Action,* p. 85.

EXHIBIT 3-2

Six forces that shape competitive strategy

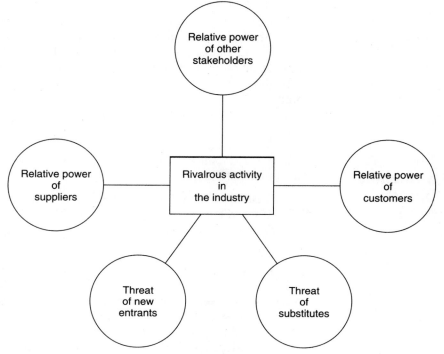

SOURCE: R E Freeman, *Strategic Management: A Stakeholder Approach* (Boston: Pitman Publishing, 1984), p. 78.

Effective Stakeholder Management

Freeman suggests that organizations with high stakeholder management capability are likely to possess the following attributes:

- They design and implement communication processes with multiple stakeholders.
- They actively negotiate with stakeholders on critical issues and seek voluntary agreements.
- They take a marketing approach to serving multiple stakeholders. They spend heavily on understanding stakeholder needs and use marketing research techniques to segment stakeholders and understand their needs and aspirations.
- In formulating strategy, they draw on members of their management teams who are knowledgeable about stakeholders.
- They take a proactive stance, attempt to anticipate stakeholder concerns, and try to influence their stakeholder environment.

- They allocate resources in a manner consistent with stakeholder analysis.
- Their managers think in "stakeholder-serving" terms.[5]

External Direct Forces

Michael E Porter's analytical framework helps managers analyze the impact of these external direct stakeholders.[6] Exhibit 3–3 shows the forces that drive industry competition and play a central role in determining the company's profitability. In the following discussion, we will see how these stakeholders influence telecommunications companies in the United States and abroad.

New or Potential Entrants.   New or potential entrants to an industry present current players with all kinds of problems and opportunities. Sometimes new entrants bring substantial resources and have the power to change

---

[5]Ibid., pp. 78–80.

[6]M E Porter, *Competitive Strategy: Techniques for Analyzing Industries and Competitors* (New York: The Free Press, 1980), p. x.

EXHIBIT 3-3

External direct forces

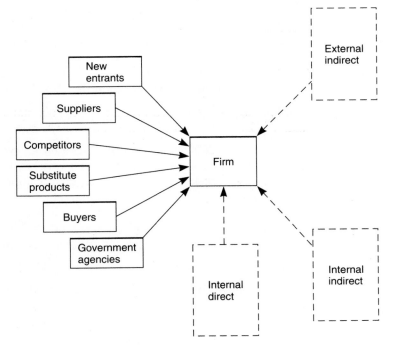

the "rules of the game." For example, those who add capacity cut prices to utilize their capacity efficiently and increase their market share.

In the 1990s, deregulation of the telecommunications industry across Europe weakened traditional national monopolies. The British government decided to grant licenses to a number of new entrants. In the spring of 1993, potential international competitors challenged British Telecommunications (BT) and its smaller rival, Mercury Communications, with a wide range of problems, opportunities, and choices in international calling.

In April 1993, AT&T applied to the British government for permission to start telephone services. AT&T was the latest of 18 companies to apply for various kinds of basic telephone service licenses. Other participants included Sprint International, a unit of US-based Sprint Corporation, the Australian and Swedish phone companies, and Nationwide Linkline Europe, an eight-employee company that planned to offer specialized discounted services such as voice mail and fax.

As deregulation gained momentum, experts expected BT's share of Britain's telecommunications service market to drop from 95 to 83 percent by 1998. They also expected a decline in phone rates as companies competed for customers. What strategy would BT and Mercury Communications adopt to meet these external direct forces?[7]

Intensity of Rivalry among Existing Competitors.   If a number of powerful, aggressive, and well-entrenched competitors exist in an industry, the rivalry is likely to be very intense. Such fierce rivalry characterized the Canadian telecommunications industry as Stentor, Unitel, MCI, and AT&T battled for the long-distance telephone market. For years, Stentor, a consortium of Canadian utilities, held a monopoly on domestic trunk services. In 1992 Unitel, the former telegraph service of the Canadian Pacific and Canadian national railways, received government permission to break Stentor's grip. Immediately the Canadian companies developed new alliances for a major battle.

Unitel sold a 20 percent stake (the highest stake permitted by Canadian law) to AT&T. It received access to AT&T's switches, transmission facilities, and other network technologies. Unitel also obtained the right to adapt AT&T's US products to the Canadian market.

Stentor formed a consortium with MCI, a Washington-based firm that held 17 percent of the US long-distance market. Stentor was attracted by MCI's low costs, sophisticated telecommunications software, and aggressive corporate culture.

Canada's communications minister predicted these alliances would foster fierce competition that would bring new products and services to tele-

---

[7]R L Hudson, "BT Faces a Line of Potential International Competitors," *The Wall Street Journal,* April 29, 1993, p. B4.

phone users and stimulate Canada's "premier high-tech industry." In addition, the cross-border partnerships would foster closer integration of telephone services between the United States and Canada.[8]

Substitute Products.   Products that may be substituted for the offerings of a given industry place a ceiling on the potential returns of an industry. Perhaps the greatest environmental threat any industry faces is the prospect that someone will develop a product or service that will render the industry's traditional offerings obsolete. This happened to rotary dial phones when their Touch-Tone replacements were integrated into new, worldwide telecommunications systems.

In July 1993, AT&T began marketing a hand-held computer called the Personal Communicator 440. The $3,000 machine was part computer and part cellular telephone. Users could send faxes and electronic mail by writing on a small display screen with a special pen. The computer could make cellular telephone calls in addition to transmitting and storing voice messages.

In August, Apple Computer unveiled the Newton, its own version of a similar machine. When the Newton was presented at the MAC exposition in Boston, it was an immediate and fabulous success. Industry observers predicted it would turn around Apple's recent decline.[9] The miniaturization and flexibility of products like the Newton threaten to make larger, single-purpose devices obsolete.

Bargaining Power of Buyers.   According to Porter, "Buyers compete with the industry by forcing down prices, bargaining for higher quality or more services, and playing competitors against one another—all at the expense of industry profitability."[10] Buyers are in a powerful position if they are large in size, are limited in number, and account for a large percentage of industry participants' total revenues. A buyer's position may be even more powerful if the firm is partially integrated or is capable of integrating backward. Buyers' bargaining power extends to consumers, wholesalers, and retailers. For example, a large retailer of consumer electronics can negotiate better terms with suppliers than a small, independent retailer can.

Bargaining Power of Suppliers.   Powerful suppliers are in a position to charge higher prices or offer lower levels of service or quality of goods. Weak suppliers, in contrast, must deliver more for less and thus allow industry participants to enjoy higher profits.

---

[8]B Simon, "Unlikely Allies Fight Canada's Telephone War," *Financial Times,* February 25, 1993, p. 15.

[9]T McCarroll, "How AT&T Plans to Reach Out and Touch Everyone," *Time,* July 5, 1993, pp. 44–46.

[10]Porter, *Competitive Strategy,* p. 24.

AT&T's top management vowed to become the world's telecommunications "global outsourcer." In May 1993, AT&T launched World Source, a set of customized international business telecom services. The goal was to become a "one-stop shop" for 2,500 multinational corporations. World Source was designed to manage and integrate international networks and offer the latest in data and voice facilities through a single point of contact. To facilitate this integration, AT&T planned to develop partnerships with several other international carriers.

British Telecom promoted its own global outsourcing venture, Syncordia, in 1991.[11] At first, BT decided to go it alone. But in June 1993, BT formed an alliance with MCI Communications to bolster its strength.

Although Robert Allen, AT&T's CEO, declared, "A partnership like World Source has better opportunities than a single alliance," it remains to be seen which supplier will be most successful.[12] Which of these giants will determine the base line for prices, quality, and service?

Government Agencies.   The government can directly influence a company's competitive position in two ways. First, as a large-scale purchaser or supplier, it affects the competitive position of firms from which it buys or to which it sells. Its purchases thus indirectly affect the positions of all the other firms in the industry. Second, government can alter the position of a firm or industry by providing subsidies or imposing regulations.

The role of national governments in the telecom industry is just beginning to wane. In recent years, deregulation has opened up telecom markets worldwide. Even Japan's Nippon Telegraph and Telephone Company, two-thirds of which is owned by the Japanese government, lowered its barriers to competition. After years of trade friction over telephone equipment between the United States and Japan, NTT agreed to buy a dozen advanced central office telephone switches from AT&T. This transaction probably would not have taken place had the US government not pressured Japan to increase its purchases from non-Japanese suppliers.

The announcement of the NTT purchase coincided with the Clinton administration's review of the issue of classifying imported minivans and sport-utility vehicles as trucks instead of cars. If they were classified as minivans or sport-utility vehicles, the tariff would go up by 25 percent, a move that would protect Detroit automakers while hurting Japanese producers.

The Japanese government has a long record of making concessions on contracts at politically opportune times. However, both the Japanese and US governments preferred not to link the situations publicly. AT&T's vice chairperson said simply that officials at the State Department and other

---

[11]"AT&T Targets Telecom Needs of Multinationals," *Financial Times,* May 27, 1993, p. 23.
[12]"AT&T Seeks Partners to Help It Enter European Market," *The Wall Street Journal,* July 8, 1993, p. B3.

agencies "have certainly been helpful to us in engineering, as nearly as they could, a level playing field."[13] Japan's economic minister contended the deal had nothing to do with political pressure because NTT had been increasing its purchases since the early 1980s.[14] Despite the disclaimers, even the casual observer can readily understand the power the US and Japanese governments exercised on their industries' behalf.

Internal Direct Forces

Employees.   As Exhibit 3–4 shows, employees at every level exert internal direct force on corporate decision making. Their stakeholder force is both economic and noneconomic. Economic issues that overlap with social issues are comparable worth, equal pay for equal work, and compensation through benefits such as retirement, maternity policies, and medical benefits. Additional issues that directly involve employees include safety and stress in the workplace, privacy, sexual harassment, equal access to training programs, and hiring and firing practices. Employees who abuse drugs and alcohol cost companies in terms of absenteeism, sick leave, poor-quality

---

[13]K Bradsher, "AT&T in a Deal in Japan," *The New York Times,* April 27, 1993, p. D1.
[14]Ibid.

Exhibit 3–4

Internal direct forces

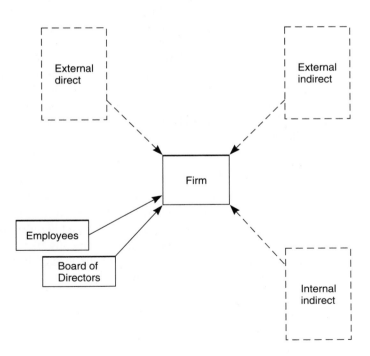

work, and potential danger to co-workers or the public. Co-workers who are not abusers pay in both monetary and psychological terms for those who are. Abusers can make nonabusers subject to drug testing and invasion of privacy.

Boards of Directors.   The other group of internal direct stakeholders, boards of directors, set policy for their firms and are responsible for the companies' financial well-being. They are often involved in the establishment of social issues programs and may even take leadership in this area. In fact, it would be virtually impossible for a company to formulate a social issues agenda without the approval and participation of its board.

Walter J Salmon wrote in the *Harvard Business Review* that boards have a role in crisis prevention.[15] Board composition and oversight have improved significantly since the 1970s. Salmon points to surveys showing the typical board today consists of nine outside directors and three inside directors, as opposed to five inside and eight outside directors 20 years ago. In Salmon's view, the only insiders who belong on boards are the CEO, the chief operating officer (COO), and the chief financial officer (CFO). The CEO should routinely initiate discussions between board members and senior managers.

A properly informed board should be able to spot problems early. Although directors should not micromanage (become overly involved with) issues, they have a responsibility to get involved in long-range planning and identify areas of concern. Effective directors speak their minds, engage in constructive discussion, make tough decisions, and exhibit impeccable personal integrity.

Board members of large corporations often receive retainers of $25,000 and a variety of additional perks such as meetings in posh resorts, gifts of company products, and pension plans. They should *earn* this generous compensation. Each board member's activities should be regularly assessed and evaluated. If a particular member is not fulfilling the oversight obligation, she should be replaced.[16]

External Indirect Forces

Exhibit 3–5 shows the groups of stakeholders in the upper right quadrant. They are external to the firm and wield varying degrees of indirect influence. External indirect stakeholders include social activist groups; some government agencies (especially those not specifically tied to the firm's economic position in the industry); members of the local community; industry trade associations; and religious organizations, lobbies, and PACs.

---

[15]W J Salmon, "Crisis Prevention: How to Gear Up Your Board," *Harvard Business Review* (January/February 1993), pp. 68–75.

[16]Ibid.

EXHIBIT 3–5

External indirect forces

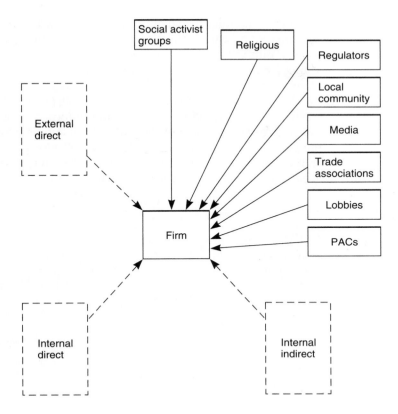

Companies and communities need to coordinate their programs to satisfy all of these stakeholders. If, for example, 25 percent of the workforce in a given company needs child care, this need can have profound implications for stakeholders in the local community. If a child care center is located on company property, local providers may lose their livelihood. If it is located in the community, local government agencies may be asked to participate or religious institutions may be chosen as sites. Teachers may need both local and state certification. School-age children may need transportation to the child care center.

Communities often benefit from corporate perquisites that extend to family members. For instance, AT&T sponsors the US Chamber of Commerce ConSern Loans for Education program. All employees and family members are eligible for student loans to secondary schools, accredited colleges, and universities. Family includes children, grandchildren, siblings, spouses, and even nephews and nieces. Qualified applicants can receive low-interest loans for up to $25,000 per year for tuition, room and board, and books. They may even receive $3,000 for a personal computer.

AT&T has huge installations in central New Jersey. The flow of money into area educational institutions will have an extremely beneficial effect on local communities. Indirect benefits include continued employment of school faculty, support staff, and administrators. Local businesses prosper by offering goods and services to students and school employees.

Access to these loans may make the difference between an employee staying at AT&T, and contributing to the local tax base, or leaving for a more lucrative position elsewhere. Extended families that take advantage of the program but are not employed by AT&T also contribute to their local communities.[17] A ripple effect occurs as these external indirect stakeholders affect and are affected by company policies.

Internal Indirect Forces

As Exhibit 3–6 shows, unions and shareholders belong in the lower right quadrant of the stakeholder influence map. They are part of the company but do not always influence it directly. Unions may work with management to develop programs or take an adversarial approach by making demands management is unwilling to consider. Indirectly, union demands affect

---

[17]"Student Loans Available for Family Members," *Focus: For and about the People of AT&T,* July/August 1993, p. 41.

EXHIBIT 3–6

Internal indirect forces

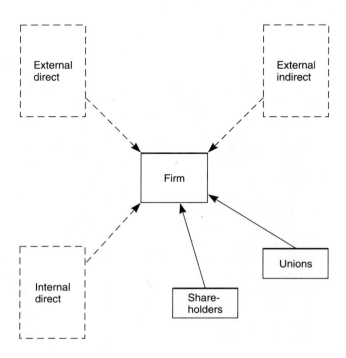

external competition if workers strike or gain concessions. Unions can also affect the quality of work life within the firm. We will discuss union activity in greater detail in Chapter 13.

The US telecommunications industry is only partly unionized. Neither MCI nor Sprint has a union, nor do the US-based subsidiaries of Canada's Northern Telecom or Germany's Siemens. AT&T is, in fact, the only major unionized US telecom company. Between the 1984 breakup of AT&T and 1993, AT&T halved its hourly workforce. As a result of the cutbacks and other issues, the company was hit by strikes in 1986 and 1989.

Instead of perpetuating an adversarial relationship, AT&T decided to give the unions a larger role in worker participation and consult with top union officials on a range of issues. The 1992–1995 labor contract contained a promise by AT&T and its two biggest unions, the Communications Workers of America (CWA) and the International Brotherhood of Electrical Workers (IBEW), to create a "workplace of the future." Business-unit planning councils bring together top managers of strategic business units and local presidents and top officials of unions several times a year. The purpose of the meetings is to set future business strategy. The new relationship between AT&T and its unions is in its early stages. It remains to be seen how much power these internal indirect stakeholders will exercise.[18]

Traditionally most shareholders have been content to sign over their voting proxies to corporate appointees. But in recent years, a new kind of shareholder has emerged. Today some shareholders, primarily large institutional investors, such as pension funds, are taking a real interest in the companies in which they have invested. They are asking tough questions of boards of directors and are not automatically assigning voting proxies for the stock they own. This interaction, called *relationship investing,* usually concentrates on profits and governance. The US Council on Competitiveness, the congressionally sponsored Competitiveness Policy Council, and the Twentieth Century Fund have all endorsed the idea of relationship investing.

There is no structural reason to exclude social issues from relationship-investing concerns. In fact, the close ties between corporations and these large investors should provide an ideal climate for defining and implementing a social issues strategy.

Corporate Partners, a major mutual fund, is an affiliate of Lazard Frères & Company. Since 1989, it has made big stock purchases in seven companies and sits on their boards of directors. Corporate Partners invests in companies in which its capital and management expertise will help the firms solve problems. It always investigates management expertise before making the investment. It also insists on having a board seat to monitor management's progress against a mutually agreed-on strategy.

---

[18]"Rocking the Boat," *The Economist,* May 8, 1993, p. 71.

Supporters of relationship investing point to two major advantages: long-term investing and increased management accountability. Relationship investors provide "patient" capital that focuses on long-term goals. In theory, top managers should be freer to concentrate on productivity and prospects without the pressure of quarterly returns.

Supporters declare this new breed of large shareholder holds the CEO to account. The board of directors can no longer automatically rubber-stamp decisions made by an "imperial" leader. In fact, studies show few CEOs are deposed by activist shareholders. A *Wall Street Journal* study determined that large companies are fairly unresponsive to shareholder threats of bad publicity or proxy fights. According to a University of Rochester study, small and mid-size companies are much more likely to react to shareholder criticism and their CEOs are slightly more likely to lose their jobs than are those at larger firms.[19] Relationship investing is still a new idea, and its effectiveness and influence have yet to be fully felt and assessed.

Stakeholders's Power to Affect Firm Affairs

R Edward Freeman and Daniel R Gilbert, Jr., point out that "power is an interesting concept . . . because it signifies that those who have it control those who do not.[20] Seemingly powerless stakeholders can, if aroused, exert considerable power. Most stakeholders tend to be fairly passive toward a company's affairs unless they see themselves as personally threatened or potentially benefited by the company's actions.

For example, women who used the Dalkon Shield first were threatened by the product's damaging effects but later saw great potential benefit in bringing suit against the company. As individuals they wielded little power, but when organized into a class action group they gained considerable power. As another example, stakeholders who lived near nuclear power plants marshaled their forces after the Three Mile Island incident. In both cases, groups of stakeholders successfully wielded influence through the media and the courts. They took action at the point at which they perceived they *could* affect company strategy. Unless top managers can anticipate the activity and potential power of stakeholders, they may find themselves simply reacting rather than formulating and implementing a well-thought-out strategy.

---

[19]"Relationship Investing," *Business Week,* March 15, 1993, pp. 68–75; J Kim, "Companies to Activists: Let's Make a Deal," *USA Today,* March 23, 1993; S Mieher, "Shareholder Activism, Despite Hoopla, Leaves Most CEOs Unscathed," *The Wall Street Journal,* May 24, 1993, p. A1.

[20]R E Freeman and D R Gilbert, Jr., *Corporate Strategy and the Search for Ethics* (Englewood Cliffs, NJ: Prentice-Hall, 1988), p. 172.

Stakeholders's Resources

Porter perceives power differently than Freeman and Gilbert do. Porter points out that in economic terms, stakeholders possess power only if their resources influence the elements of return on investment (ROI).[21] When social issues are a concern, stakeholders can affect a firm's financial results through the pressure they apply to its buyers, suppliers, and customers.

After the Exxon *Valdez* disaster, activists tried to organize a boycott of Exxon. The boycott failed for several reasons. The boycotters had few resources compared to the giant oil company. There was no loss of human life, the oil spill was in a remote area, and most observers realized they could not meaningfully affect Exxon's ROI.

In contrast, INFACT's boycott against Nestlé was very successful and sufficiently powerful to interfere with Nestlé's buyer and customer relations. Helpless babies' lives were at stake, the moral outrage was sustainable, and a dedicated group of stakeholder activists pursued the issue over a long period of time.

Selection of Alternatives

Managers must understand whether they or stakeholders control the selection of alternative courses of action. The power struggle between stakeholders and managers often revolves around this selection. Active stakeholders try to control management actions and preempt management's choice of alternatives by publicly displaying their particular viewpoints. These stakeholders use common tools such as picket lines, demonstrations, and effective use of the media.

The debate over whether nuclear energy is a societally acceptable source of energy provides a graphic example of how stakeholders have used their power to dictate management and industry policy. Exhibit 3–7 shows a partial list of nuclear energy stakeholders.

The fiasco at Three Mile Island turned passive stakeholders into active opponents of the development of nuclear energy resources. In 1986, the disaster at the Chernobyl plant in the USSR further strengthened the position of antinuclear energy forces, particularly those in the United States. The nuclear energy industry was forced to seriously consider the concerns of a variety of stakeholders. It could not escape nightly television broadcasts of demonstrators locked to chain-link fences that surrounded nuclear plants. Utility companies, in full view of television cameras, authorized police to drag demonstrators to jail.

Public-interest groups went to the courts to prevent plants from coming "on-line." State politicians refused to file evacuation plans, further stalling

---

[21]M E Porter, *Competitive Advantage,* (New York: The Free Press, 1985), p. 5.

EXHIBIT 3–7

*Stakeholder influence
map: nuclear energy
issue—partial list of
stakeholders*

	Direct	Indirect
External	Alternative energy suppliers Nuclear Regulatory Commission Banks Creditors Commercial and residential customers	Local governments State governments Media Public interest groups Industry lobbyists Citizens' groups Other environmental groups
Internal	Employees at operating plants Boards of directors of utilities	Unions Construction companies

the start-up process. Public-interest groups made sure antinuclear energy questions were put on state and local ballots. Stakeholders generated both financial and humanpower resources to constrain the industry's selection of alternative actions. As a result, nuclear power companies became increasingly unwilling to commit to ordering new nuclear facilities.

In addition to the public's concerns about radioactive leaks and potential cancer epidemics, reports of unsafe operations inside a number of nuclear plants proliferated. The Critical Mass Energy Project of Public Citizen, a stakeholder group that published an annual compilation of NRC reports, cited 2,810 accidents in commercial nuclear power plants in 1987. Employee error caused many of those accidents.

Unsafe operating practices continued despite adverse publicity. The Nuclear Regulatory Commission reported the New York Power Authority failed to ensure that certain backup systems were operating properly at its Indian Point 3 plant. Between May 1992 and July 1993, the power authority paid $762,500 in fines for safety violations at Indian Point 3 and an additional $300,000 in fines for problems at the Fitzpatrick nuclear power plant in Scriba, New York.[22]

Industry inertia led to widespread personnel problems and poor managerial practices in other states as well. One stakeholder group, the Institute of Nuclear Power Operations, referred to Philadelphia's Peach Bottom plant

---

[22]"Nuclear Regulators Propose $300,000 Fine for New York Plant," *The Wall Street Journal,* July 23, 1993, p. B5B.

as "an embarrassment to the industry and to the nation." The Nuclear Regulatory Commission eventually closed the Peach Bottom plant because workers were sleeping on the job.[23]

In addition to the stakeholders already mentioned, active players included state and other government officials, local town and city officials, and an assortment of citizens' groups. All had huge stakes in the consequences of managements' decisions about whether to bring new plants online, rehabilitate old ones, or abandon nuclear energy altogether.

By 1993, the US nuclear industry was on its way to extinction. Even plants that were still operating were struggling with radioactive waste disposal problems. The Department of Energy, which was supposed to build a permanent storage facility in Nevada in 1988, had not yet done so. Most nuclear facilities stored tons of waste on site but were running out of room. Portland General Electric, for example, decided to close down its Trojan plant 20 years early rather than deal with the estimated cost of tearing the plant down and disposing of 20 additional years of nuclear waste.[24]

Company management of substance abuse in the workplace is another issue in which firms can take many alternative actions. This issue involves stakeholders in all quadrants of the stakeholder influence map. Approximately 25 percent of an average workforce suffers from abuse of either drugs or alcohol.[25]

Companies must address several issues. Should they carry out involuntary testing, voluntary testing, or no testing at all? Should they begin a formal program to help alcohol or drug abusers? How should they address employee concerns about confidentiality or job security? Should supervisors be given the responsibility of identifying and reporting abusers? Should managers have to use their operating budgets for rehabilitation programs? How should managers integrate the firm's activities with the community? Finally, how, if at all, will the strategy the firm adopts affect its competitive position in its industry?

Each of these questions has several defensible answers. But before a company can formulate and implement a strategy to deal with substance abuse, it must correctly assess the power different stakeholders hold and the degree to which each is actively or passively involved in the issue. The company can be sure that as this issue continues to evolve, it will receive input from stakeholders who are both external and internal to the firm and are involved both directly and indirectly.

---

[23]M L Wald, "The Peach Bottom Syndrome," *The New York Times,* March 27, 1988, p. F1.

[24]M L Wald, "Nuclear Power Plants Take Early Retirement," *The New York Times,* August 16, 1992, p. E7.

[25]J T Wrich, "Beyond Testing: Coping with Drugs at Work," *Harvard Business Review* (January/February 1988), p. 120.

Managing for Social Responsiveness

Obviously companies cannot attend to all issues, and not all stakeholders care equally about particular issues. To deal systematically and effectively with its complex environment, a firm must answer four questions:

- How can managers identify relevant issues?
- How can they classify issues?
- How can these issues be managed?
- How can managers evaluate performance on the issues?

Peter F Drucker stresses that "social impacts and social responsibilities are areas in which business—and not only big business—has to think through its role, has to set objectives, has to perform. Social impacts and social responsibilities have to be managed."[26]

Classification of Major Social Issues

After completing its environmental scanning and analysis, the company needs to classify the major social issues it confronts into meaningful subjects. Five major categories cover most of the significant issues even large, diverse enterprises face:

- *Community and political responsiveness:* the effectiveness with which the company manages its affairs in the political and legal environment and responds to the economic and other expectations of the domestic and international communities in which it operates (e.g., job creation, philanthropy).
- *Human investment:* the provision for the physical, psychological, and economic welfare of present, potential, and retired employees. Also includes the creation of an environment in which people are treated fairly and are given an opportunity to grow, meet challenges, and enjoy satisfaction.
- *Openness of the system:* the company's willingness to communicate honestly and openly with its employees and external stakeholders, including the news media, to establish an effective governance system and to assure employees of due process and protection of their rights.
- *Consumer welfare:* the provision of quality products and services to prospective buyers in an honest and comprehensive manner to reasonably assure their safety, well-being, and satisfaction.
- *Ecology and energy:* the company's efforts to minimize the negative impact of its operations on the natural environment (water, air, plants, wildlife, microorganisms) and the structural environment (buildings, farms, homes) and to conserve natural resources such as energy.

---

[26]P F Drucker, *Management: Tasks, Responsibilities, Practices* (New York: Harper & Row, 1974), p. 325.

Determine Priorities and Collect Data

Table 3–1 combines these five categories, a few selected issues, and several concerned stakeholder groups. Just as a company sets priorities for expenditures in functional areas, it must rank social issues in their importance to the firm. Some firms may decide to consider only issues for which reliable data exist or for which they can generate good data.

However, not all social issues are data oriented. For example, it is almost impossible to measure the benefit of a contribution to a symphony orchestra or the benefit of hosting a fund-raising gala. Likewise, it is difficult to measure employee satisfaction and greater productivity due to a company-sponsored child care program. Data on such an issue are elusive at best.

In reality, most companies do not even care about measuring benefit. Key managers are simply committed to the cause. Top management determines the relative urgency of corporate priorities. As is often the case in other management decision-making areas, management must make trade-offs in targeting certain social issues. If management decides it is critical to improve the company's record for equal employment opportunity, it may postpone its attention to one or more other issues, just as it may delay introducing a second new product until it is sure its first entrant will succeed. The social assessment system (SAS) we will introduce later seems to have its greatest impact on improving a company's social performance when it selects four to six *key indicators* for attention and corrective action.

Select a Plan or Policy

If possible, companies should measure their current performance before they act. Creativity and cooperation are important to the SAS process in developing sound measures. Three types of measures exist for the quantification of social performance: (1) actual performance, (2) level of effort, and (3) surrogates (substitutes that appear to approximate the underlying phenomenon). Measures of actual performance are possible in certain areas, such as the frequency of disabling injuries or the number of product recalls.

Managers must be careful when developing measures of actual performance. The data must be consistent in definition and truly represent performance on the underlying issue. For example, minority employment is an area for which actual performance measures are available.

Where actual performance may not be readily quantifiable in commonly understood terms, companies may measure the effort expended in dealing with a given problem. For example, annual expenditures for pollution control equipment would be a measure of level of effort.

The third type of measure utilizes surrogates of performance. Employee satisfaction is an example of an important issue that is not readily measurable. Management may use absenteeism, turnover, and measures of worker output as appropriate surrogate indicators of employee satisfaction.

TABLE 3-1 Matrix of Issues with Social Consequences and the Affected Stakeholders

Social Issues	Stock-holders	Non-management Employees	Managers	Retired Management and Non-management Employees	Customers	Suppliers	Lenders	Competitors	Government	Neighbors or Local Communities	Activist Groups
Stakeholders											
Community and political responsiveness											
1. Relations with regulatory agencies											
2. Corporate giving											
3. Support of minority-owned business											
Human investment											
1. Minority participation											
2. Health and safety											
3. Treatment of retired workers											

Openness of the system
1. Relations with the news media

2. Composition of the board of directors

3. Financial disclosure

Consumer welfare
1. Handling of customer complaints

2. Customer satisfaction

3. Product recalls

Ecology and energy
1. Pollution abatement

2. Energy conservation

Implementation (Action)

Even when managers have satisfactory measures of performance, they may find that achieving the desired result is not easy. Internal company politics can and do distort both the process by which the policy is put into effect and the outcome.[27]

However, there are ways to maximize the probability that the organization will actually carry out the plan. The plan should be "sold" to lower levels of management with enthusiasm, excitement, and goodwill. Lower-level managers should have the opportunity to ask questions and help move the process forward.

As we discussed in Chapter 2, organizations resist change. Managers must think of social change as a problem-solving mechanism. If all levels of the company accept new social goals as a remedy for an existing problem, implementation is likely to be more successful. Top management should closely relate important social goals to the company mission. If managers regard a plan as a fringe activity, the plan will encounter organizational resistance.

Money and human resources are critical to social goal implementation. It is not sufficient—and is often counterproductive—to make budgetary increases or assign people to new tasks without ensuring they are used effectively.

Top management support must be ongoing. Top managers must direct resources and legitimate the efforts of those implementing the change. Top managers should not be involved in the day-to-day tasks of implementation. In fact, middle managers in charge of implementation may resent interference from above and may even sabotage top management's efforts.

Control and Measure Performance

If management is to incorporate goals into the firm's operations, it must develop and measure success and control for deviations in the plan. These measures can be both objective and subjective. As noted above, companies prefer to rely on hard data such as costs, quotas, and industry averages. Ideally members of an industry should gather as much data as possible to generate a data bank of industry averages. In practice, this sort of participation rarely occurs unless a government agency or a trade association collects statistics. A social assessment system can help greatly in measuring and controlling performance.

---

[27]R Wernham, "Implementation: The Things That Matter," in W R King and D I Cleland, eds., *Strategic Planning and Management Handbook* (New York: Van Nostrand Reinhold, 1987), pp. 439–55.

The Social Assessment System.   Creative management information systems offer the most constructive mechanisms for assessing corporate social performance. These systems are designed to keep management informed about the company's performance in areas of social concern. They are potential control mechanisms, providing management with a basis on which to make decisions about corporate conduct.

Because much of the data a firm gathers are confidential, the company cannot hire an outside organization to evaluate its social performance. Companies differ in how they define the categories of information they gather and analyze. The information may be industry or company specific, but the process of generating the needed information involves similar steps.

The *social assessment system (SAS)* is one form of management information system. It is by no means the only approach, and it is not without limitations. However, it is a straightforward system that many large companies use in their efforts to manage social responsiveness.

Unlike financial reporting systems, the SAS disaggregates performance so that no bottom line of "social profit" or "net increase in social assets" is reported to provide an overall grade or score. Instead, the company develops key indicators for those policies and practices that have important social consequences and evaluates them against standards management or outside agencies consider appropriate. The SAS uses existing data or data generated from corporate records. Therefore, management has discretion regarding whether or not to report social performance externally.

Obviously certain social issues related to business are beyond management's control. Hence, issues concerning inflation, poverty, or reducing terrorism are not classified as relevant stimuli. The SAS recognizes that while literally hundreds of social issues may be relevant to a given corporation, it is feasible to focus on only a relatively limited number.

A particular company may decide it wants to lead, be equal to, or lag behind industry averages in responding to a given issue. However, with or without industry data, management should assess its own performance over time with regular, periodic analyses. Sometimes external direct or indirect stakeholders impose standards. For example, state or federal agencies, such as the Environmental Protection Agency or the Equal Employment Opportunity Commission, or even community groups, may dictate standards.

In summary, the social assessment system is useful as a confidential management tool. The company identifies the major social issues it considers of greatest relevance. It collects data on present performance and formulates a plan. It sets up objective and subjective performance measures to enable management to periodically measure social performance. Management may then determine whether performance is acceptable and, if not, which corrective steps it should initiate.

The Three-Stage Implementation Pattern

Robert W Ackerman observed that many corporations move through a remarkably similar three-stage implementation pattern over a period of six to eight years.[28]

Stage 1. In stage 1, the chief executive identifies an issue important to him or her and to the company. Usually the CEO considers the choice an issue of corporate responsibility or corporate self-interest.

The CEO begins to talk about the issue to external stakeholders who are either directly or indirectly affected by the issue, and may even commit company resources to the issue. Soon the CEO decides the issues should be incorporated into company policy and assigns the responsibility for implementation to the operating units.

Perhaps to the CEO's surprise, little or no action is taken because the company has no established measures of success and no penalties for failure. Also, it is not clear to operating managers that the corporation is seriously committed to the cause. This phase may last for months or even years.

Stage 2. The president or CEO appoints a staff executive to report on and coordinate the company's efforts. This staff member usually has the title of vice president or director of environmental affairs or consumer affairs. The specialist might even be a lawyer or an outside consultant. This specialist collects data, assesses stakeholder interest, and mediates among the operating divisions and the external stakeholders. His or her role is to crystallize the issue for top management.

Middle managers may still balk at implementation because they support their senior line executives rather than the staff member. They know the CEO usually supports senior line executives before staff members, regardless of the issue.

Stage 3. Organizational involvement is the third stage of implementation. The CEO recognizes that if the social goal is to be implemented, she must involve the whole organization and institutionalize policy. A critical task is to work the issue into the company's resource allocation and reward systems.

The Social Audit

In the early to mid-1970s, managers and academics developed the concept of the *corporate social audit,* a "report card" on the company's social performance. Using material from their 1972 book *The Corporate Social Audit,*

---

[28]R W Ackerman, "How Companies Respond to Social Demands," *Harvard Business Review* (July/August 1973), pp. 88–98.

Raymond A Bauer and Dan H Fenn, Jr., wrote a seminal article in the *Harvard Business Review* the following year. They defined a social audit as "a commitment to systematic assessment of and reporting on some meaningful, definable domain of a company's activities that have social impact."[29]

The article's purpose was to help managers answer questions about what activities they should audit, what measures they should use, and against what standards they should measure performance. The authors were quick to point out that any audit must be an ongoing process of collecting data on issues that have been defined as an "explicit corporate policy involving a meaningful level of resource commitment."[30]

John J Corson and George A Steiner discussed major issues related to the social audit. In their article *Measuring Business's Social Performance: The Corporate Social Audit,* they asked whether the social audit was simply a fad that would be abandoned. They concluded that if companies used the proper model in conducting the audit, the resulting social report could be a credible measure of a corporation's commitment to social goals.[31]

The most difficult problem for managers was not data collection but developing methods to measure accomplishment. The early efforts to develop measurement techniques drew heavily on traditional accounting tools. The concepts of the "social balance sheet and social income statement"[32] and the "Socio-Economic Operating Statement"[33] appealed to managers.

However, it is clear that relatively few companies found conventional accounting theory to be an adequate base for developing a social audit. Even Abt Associates, one of the most enthusiastic proponents of the social audit, dropped the procedure in the early 1980s.

Daniel H Gray of Arthur D Little, Inc., explains that ADL examined and rejected the notion. Gray said, "those social problems that disturb us most lie outside the realm of transactions . . . Accounting . . . owes its rigor to what it excludes. To try to stretch it to measure all social costs and benefits is to violate its very foundation."[34] Neil C Churchill of the Harvard Business School and Arthur B Toan, Jr., a retired partner of Price Waterhouse and

---

[29]R A Bauer and D H Fenn, Jr., "What *Is* a Corporate Social Audit?," *Harvard Business Review* (January/February 1973), p. 38.

[30]Ibid., p. 44.

[31]J J Corson and G A Steiner, *Measuring Business's Social Performance: The Corporate Social Audit* (New York: Committee for Economic Development, 1974), pp. 18–20, 40–41, 49–52, 59–63.

[32]Abt Associates, Inc., had been the major advocate of this approach. However, the firm had little success in selling its concept.

[33]D F Linowes, *Strategies for Survival* (New York: AMACOM, 1973), pp. 166–78.

[34]D H Gray, "Methodology: One Approach to the Corporate Social Audit," in *The Unstable Ground: Corporate Policy in a Dynamic Society* (Los Angeles: Melville Publishing, 1974), pp. 92–93.

Company who served as co-chair of the American Institute of Certified Public Accountants Committee on Social Measurement, recommended a non-accounting approach.[35]

A few firms did try to separate economic issues from social performance through the social audit system. International Paper Company, for example, developed a method of setting nonfinancial goals for managers and measuring performance against them.[36] In another experiment, Norton Simon's board of directors requested regular reports on actions to meet social responsibility goals and gave substantial cash bonuses to managers who met the targets.[37] Nevertheless, techniques such as the social audit and social accounting were never widely adopted, and most experiments were dropped within a short period of time.

Companies continue to struggle with a variety of organizational devices to implement social policies. They frequently rely on task forces composed of line and staff people from a number of different areas within the organization. Some companies form permanent committees, and others even create board-level committees to oversee social performance.

Clearly implementation is a difficult and complex process. An effective evaluation and reward process for middle managers may not fall within tidy, quantifiable borders. However, Ackerman observes that "through the creative and persistent leadership of top management, the barriers to incorporating social change in the decentralized company can be overcome."[38]

Summary

This chapter dealt with strategy implementation and evaluation. The degree of social responsiveness and the company's ability to incorporate it into everyday operations depend to a great extent on the power various stakeholders have in the outcome. The stakeholder influence map (SIM) furnishes a model for identifying stakeholders and their importance to the firm. Companies that manage stakeholder demands effectively have common attributes. Their major strength is their ability to build a coalition of diverse stakeholders.

---

[35]N C Churchill and A B Toan, Jr., "Reporting on Corporate Social Responsibility: A Progress Report," *Journal of Contemporary Business* 7 (Winter 1978), p. 8.

[36]D P Brennan, "Establishing and Measuring Management's Non-Financial Performance," in S E Goodman, ed., *Business, Government and Society: An Environmental Analysis* (Lexington, MA: Ginn Custom Publishing, 1980), pp. 144–46.

[37]D Clutterbuck, "Bonus Pay-outs Linked to Social Responsibility," in S E Goodman, ed., *Business, Government and Society: An Environmental Analysis* (Lexington, MA: Ginn Custom Publishing, 1980), p. 154.

[38]Ackerman, "How Companies Respond," p. 97.

Top managers cannot deal with all stakeholder issues and therefore must devise a classification and evaluation scheme. One alternative is the social assessment system (SAS), a form of management information system that organizes social issues into major categories. Using this scheme, managers determine priorities and collect data. Then they select a policy of corrective action and develop measures of actual performance. After the company has taken action to correct the problem, managers evaluate and measure its performance.

Social implementation proceeds in corporations in a distinct pattern. In stage 1, the top executive selects an issue. In stage 2, a specialist assumes the burden of transmitting the message to middle managers. In stage 3, the whole organization becomes involved in implementation.

Nearly all companies find implementation of social goals a very difficult task. For the most part, the usual reward and evaluation procedures are not designed to deal with social issues.

Projects

1. Choose a social issue and use the stakeholder influence map to identify stakeholders.
2. Using the stakeholder influence map, implement the social assessment system for setting social goals for a company of your choice.
3. The class divides into groups or task forces. Each task force is assigned to a particular stakeholder concern. Each group must argue for resources to implement a program to deal with that social goal. Make sure financial issues are taken into account.
4. Examine the annual reports of several publicly owned companies. To what extent does each report mention social issues or describe the company's response to social issues? What issues does each report mention? What do you conclude from your examination?

Questions

1. Give several examples of current social issues that could be classified within each element of the social assessment system.
2. Why is consumer welfare an especially difficult area in which to develop reliable measures of corporate performance?
3. What is the relationship among industry/competitor analysis, social issues analysis, and the management of corporate social responsiveness?

BETA PHARMACEUTICALS: INTRODUCTION

Beta Pharmaceuticals, Inc., is the integrative case that illustrates some of the issues and problems managers encounter as they formulate and implement social issues strategy. The case can be used segment by segment in conjunction with individual chapters. It can also stand alone as a multipart case that deals with a wide range of social issues that affect stakeholders both within and external to the firm.

BETA CASE 1
STRATEGY IMPLEMENTATION

The Economic Environment

Beta Pharmaceuticals, Inc., is a large, multidivisional pharmaceutical company headquartered in Detroit. In 1992, Beta's sales totaled $10.6 billion. In the first quarter of 1993, sales were up nearly 12 percent to $2.48 billion. Although US sales rose only 2.5 percent, international sales were very strong, rising more than 25 percent. Between 1989 and 1993, Beta's profits increased steadily at around 12 percent per year.

In 1993, a congressional study by the Office of Technology Assessment examined pharmaceutical product development in the United States. The study concluded that drug companies were making excessive profits. According to the study, drug companies' average profits were in the range of 13 to 14 percent of sales, and some companies realized profits as high as 25 percent. Other high-technology, high-risk industries dependent on scientific research had profits two to three percentage points lower.

Beta and other drug companies faced a changing economic environment. The Clinton administration's health care reform package promised to have a major (but still unclear) impact on the pharmaceutical industry for years to come. Insurers, health maintenance organizations, and big buying groups were no longer willing to pay whatever the drug companies demanded. Now they told pharmaceutical manufacturers what they *would* pay.

Some drug companies admitted they should have heeded the market forces that drove consolidation of medical supply companies in 1992 as a harbinger of things to come in their own industry. Merck and

Company, an industry leader, was the first major company to respond dramatically to the changing economic environment. On July 20, 1993, Merck announced it was setting aside $775 million for restructuring and was paying more than 2,000 employees to take early retirement. Eight days later, Merck announced it would pay $6 billion in stock and cash for Medco Containment Services, Inc., a prescription mail order seller and discounter.

Beta's top management and board of directors concluded that a new era of mergers, acquisitions, and consolidation was at hand. Some executives speculated that within a few years, only a few large pharmaceutical makers would survive. The rest would fall to declining drug profits, cost containment measures, killing competition, and a trickle of new drugs in the research pipeline.

Beta's Social Environment

Like other companies in the industry, Beta had to deal with the areas of social concern common to most US businesses. These issues included equal employment opportunity, worker safety and privacy, job creation, and product safety. Environmental issues, such as waste disposal, clean air, and clear water requirements, had always been a major concern. As an international company, Beta worried about its overseas subsidiaries and their environmental requirements.

In the mid-1990s, the pharmaceutical industry in general, and Beta in particular, faced a number of unique social issues, including AIDS research and drug development, fetal research, biotechnological advances, rampant patent infringements, orphan drugs (drugs used in the treatment of a disease affecting 5,000 or fewer people), and supervision of controlled substances.

Beta's Corporate Organization

Before 1987, Beta had six operating divisions: ethical products, hospital products, consumer products, diagnostics, therapeutics, and pediatrics. Table 3–2 shows the company's organization chart.

Late in 1987, Beta concluded negotiations to acquire Intac, Inc., a biotechnology company specializing in gene splicing and genetically engineered drugs. Manufacturing operations for the original divisions and the new biotech division were located in 20 states and eight other countries.

In 1990, Beta began a new generic drug division. The company hired David Shapiro, the vice president

of a small, successful generic drug company in New Jersey, to head the division. Like other pharmaceutical companies, Beta had scorned low-priced generic imitators, holding to the industry line that the copies were not as reliable as the originals. But the opportunities for profit were simply too seductive and the penalty for late entry too great. Beta, like Merck, Marion Merrill Dow, and others, decided to grab a piece of the multibillion-dollar-a-year generic market.

Beta hurried its move into generics because more than 60 important drugs with combined American sales of $8 billion per year had patents that would expire over the next 36 months. A few of Beta's managers suggested that selling a product at a price much lower than that of an identical prototype might kill the market for the more expensive drug. Others argued that doctors often continued to prescribe the brand-name drug. They also noted that although pharmacists could provide a generic unless the doctor specifically forbade it, customers whose drugs were

TABLE 3-2   Beta Pharmaceuticals Organization Chart

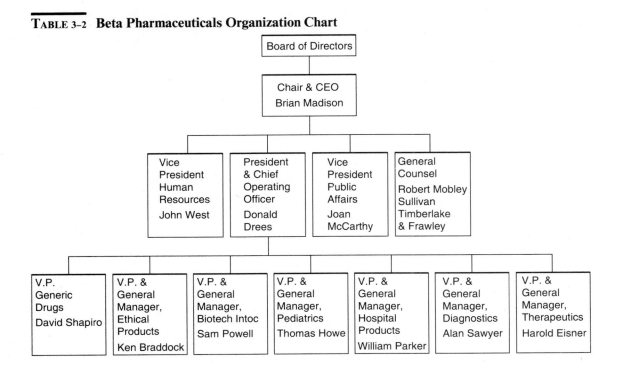

covered by insurance often requested the more expensive versions.[39]

Brian Madison, the chairperson and chief executive of Beta Pharmaceuticals, was strongly committed to social responsiveness. Shortly after being named CEO in 1986, Madison hired Joan McCarthy, who had been working for a competitor, and asked her to create a public affairs department to manage Beta's social responsiveness program. McCarthy was one of three executives who reported directly to Madison. She decided her first task was to identify and classify all of Beta's stakeholders.

McCarthy and her staff put together a public affairs department to begin scanning the internal and external environments for social issues. McCarthy appointed an internal task force, taking one middle management representative from each division. The task force's first assignment was to generate a list of social issues relevant to the company and identify the specific stakeholder groups concerned with each issue.

After they compiled the list, the task force disbanded and the public affairs department assumed the job of setting priorities to determine the importance of each issue. McCarthy met occasionally with Madison to discuss developing management performance measures. Madison believed it was very important to add the selected issues to the firm's planning and evaluation process. He and McCarthy had

a number of inconclusive discussions about how they should undertake this process, and implementation proceeded very slowly.

During the late 1980s and early 1990s, division vice presidents developed yearly and long-range objectives for improving performance in each of the designated areas. Vice presidents told lower-level managers their evaluations would be based in part on their ability to meet those objectives. In practice, financial goals were still the single most important criterion of performance. McCarthy and other members of her department were concerned about the economic pressures on Beta, particularly since the uncertainties of the economic climate were even more acute than in previous years.

The task force identified a number of employee issues. As the internal direct stakeholder group most directly involved with the firm, many employee issues were of particular concern. For example, a review of Beta Pharmaceuticals' employment record (see Table 3–3) revealed women were chronically and substantially underrepresented in the ranks of top management and professionals (category 1). In fact, Joan McCarthy was the only vice president on the corporate or general manager level. Women were also underrepresented among craftspeople, operatives, laborers, and service workers (category 3). Indeed, the only category in which women were fully represented was category 2, with its tradition of "women's jobs" such as office and clerical workers. These traditional employment patterns prevailed during Beta's most successful growth period. McCarthy had been working on this issue for several years and had some success in recruiting women for cate-

---

[39]M Freudenheim, "Now the Big Drug Makers Are Imitating Their Imitators," *The New York Times,* September 20, 1992, p. F5.

TABLE 3–3 **Beta Pharmaceuticals, Inc.: Percentage of Employees Who Are Female**

	1977	*1978*	*1980*	*1993*
Category 1 (officials, managers, professionals)	1.64% ($n = 72$)	2.1% (116)	3.66% (177)	4.12% (373)
Category 2 (technicians, sales workers, office and clerical workers)	51.39% (1,886)	51.71% (2,219)	51.22% (2,557)	53.62% (2,833)
Category 3 (craftspeople, operatives, laborers, service workers)	4.83% (1,335)	4.84% (1,424)	7.20% (2,231)	11.65% (3,438)

gory 3 jobs. However, she was far from satisfied with the company's progress in bringing women into top management positions.

The public affairs department also had to handle the demands of external indirect stakeholders. McCarthy was concerned about the increasing tendency of the media to report that drug companies were claiming exorbitant costs to research and market new drugs. Press coverage was often intensely critical. President Clinton himself had taken the industry to task for high drug prices. Competitors like Pfizer ran full-page advertisements in major newspapers telling consumers the firm was responding to their price concerns.

Members of the public affairs division discussed what the impact would be now that the Clinton administration had lifted the government directive against the use of fetal tissue in research. Would stakeholders seize this issue and inhibit the company's research opportunities?

Beta's management was concerned about potential criticism of the composition of the board of directors, another direct internal stakeholder. Beta had no women or minorities on its board, and most of the directors were inside managers. The company's law

firm had a banker and a senior partner, but there were no executives of other companies, no members of trade organizations, no union representatives, and no participants from the Detroit community.

Shareholders were pressuring Beta to change the board's composition to reflect society's and to increase the representation of independent, outside directors on boards. McCarthy and Madison met frequently to discuss the qualifications and numbers of outsiders who should be brought onto the board.

While McCarthy and her staff agreed they could set objectives for hiring women and minorities and could develop strategies to achieve this goal, they were less sure about their ability to set objectives for many of the other issues. They were particularly concerned about developing measures to evaluate middle and lower-level managers on implementation in nonquantifiable areas. Madison had clearly exhibited his commitment to social goals when he established McCarthy's public relations department and gave the charge to the task force. But the public affairs department was left with unclear goals and an unknown degree of institutional resistance to change. On the other hand, the company's commitment to social responsiveness had generally met with enthusiasm.

CHAPTER

4 | CRISIS MANAGEMENT

The preceding three chapters discuss how companies manage the routine issues of strategy formulation and implementation and how they assess a variety of economic, technological, social, and political issues. The Dow Corning case presented in this chapter demonstrates the difficulties companies face when unexpected and nonroutine events trigger a crisis. Using the Drexel Burnham Lambert and Exxon *Valdez* crises as additional illustrations, this chapter examines the unique managerial strategies, skills, and activities a company must mobilize when confronted with a crisis.

Issues management and crisis management are related activities, but they must be handled differently. Archie B Carroll defines *issues management* as "a process by which organizations identify issues in the environment, analyze and prioritize these issues in terms of their relevance to the organization, plan responses to these issues, and then evaluate and monitor the results."[1] Effective issues management contributes to strategic planning and helps avoid the need for crisis management.

However, even the most foresighted firms confront crises. According to Webster's Ninth New Collegiate Dictionary, a *crisis* is "an unstable or crucial time or state of affairs whose outcome will make a decisive difference for better or worse." For corporations, *crisis management* is the process by which firms manage "disasters precipitated by people, organizations, organizational structures, economics, and/or technology that cause extensive damage to human life, and natural and social environments."[2]

---

[1] A B Carroll, *Business & Society: Ethics & Stakeholder Management* (Cincinnati: South-Western Publishing, 1989), p. 476.
[2] I I Mitroff, P Shrivastava, and F Udwadia, "Effective Crisis Management," *Academy of Management Executive* 1, no. 3 (1987), p. 283.

Many crises develop because companies do not sufficiently monitor or manage internal activities. When such crises arise internally, they can affect the firm's external stakeholders as well as its internal stakeholders.

Sometimes crises are sparked by unforeseen events in the social or physical environment. These too can affect both internal and external stakeholders.

CASE   *Dow Corning and Breast Implants*

On January 7, 1992, the Food and Drug Administration (FDA) called on manufacturers to halt the sale of breast implants pending review of new data. Commissioner David Kessler requested all plastic surgeons to stop using silicone implants. The FDA noted that it had obtained many documents that raised "substantial concerns" about the safety of Dow Corning silicone implants manufactured between 1975 and 1985. The FDA's concerns were exacerbated by a federal court decision in December 1991 that ordered Dow Corning to pay a woman $7.3 million in damages for concealing evidence linking implant ruptures to immune system disorders. Other suits were pending.

The FDA's announcement focused the nation's attention on Dow Corning and added fuel to the already blazing controversy over the safety of breast implants. Dow Corning faced a potentially devastating crisis. Crisis management experts compared Dow Corning's situation to Exxon's dilemma with the *Valdez* oil spill and A H Robins's tribulations with the Dalkon Shield IUD. Would Dow Corning's top executives prove more effective crisis managers?

Two weeks after announcing the ban, the FDA ordered Dow Corning to make public 90 company documents. The chief FDA official in charge of medical devices wrote a letter to Lawrence A Reed, president of Dow Corning, declaring "these memoranda reflect a lack of appropriate safety and performance data . . ." Dow Corning's spokesperson replied that "this is a true travesty, a media circus instead of a true and impartial scientific review."[3]

On March 19, 1992, Dow Corning announced it would stop making breast implants. Barbara Carmichael, vice president of corporate communications, said the decision was "business-driven" and was not tied to the public controversy or pending litigation. In any event, she noted, the business had not been profitable since 1986.[4]

What was the chronology of events that led Dow Corning to abandon the product? Could Dow Corning have avoided the crisis? The firm had manufactured the implants for over 30 years and had had ample warning that a crisis might occur.

Silicone is a long, flexible polymer made up of repeating molecules of oxygen and silicon. Scientists discovered it in the 1930s. But silicone was not used commercially until the 1940s, when the US military asked Dow Chemical Company and Corning Glass Works to form a joint company to develop products using the

---

[3]P J Hilts, "F.D.A. Tells Company to Release Implant Data," *The New York Times,* January 21, 1992, p. C7.

[4]"Dow Corning Charts Communications After Leaving Implant Business," *PR News,* March 30, 1992, p. 3.

material. Since silicone is not altered by extremes of temperature, it made an excellent coolant, sealant, and lubricant for Navy ships.

Silicone was first used to augment breast tissue soon after World War II. Japanese cosmetologists, concluding that large-breasted prostitutes were more attractive to American soldiers occupying Japan, injected the substance directly into the women's breasts. The American medical community heard rumors of this practice but declined to follow the Japanese example of direct injection.

In the 1960s, Dow Corning scientists developed a product that seemed to offer a much safer method of breast enlargement. Although Japanese researchers warned that silicone might cause inflammatory immune diseases, Dow Corning paid little heed. Its scientists, intrigued with silicone's potential, manufactured implants of liquid silicone enclosed in a silicone envelope. The implants appeared to be inert and nonreactive to acids or alkalis. In addition, they were both soft and flexible.

In 1972, McGhan Medical Corporation, a Dow Corning competitor, began to market a silicone-gel implant that was much softer than the Dow Corning product. McGhan quickly gained a substantial share of the breast implant market, putting Dow Corning under pressure to develop its own gel product.

In January 1975, Dow Corning officials formed a Mammary Task Force. The task force was in charge of making the gel, filling the silicone envelopes, and carrying out the engineering, chemical, medical, and quality control tasks necessary to get the product onto the market. Dow Corning officials estimated worldwide demand at 52,000 implants a year.

Although there were no initial data indicating potential dangers, the chairperson of the task force was concerned about potential "bleeding" of the silicone envelope. The technical staff assured him that tests showed no problem. Clinical testing on women began in February 1975, even before animal testing results were reported. Within a week after the first human implants, tests on rabbits showed the animals had a "mild to acute inflammatory reaction." Evidence mounted that the new gel caused further inflammation as it migrated through the rabbits' bodies.

Within the first year after humans received the implants, Dow Corning received complaints from doctors who saw acute inflammatory reactions in their patients. Doctors also reported instances of granulomas and siliconmae, masses associated with leaking implants. As with the rabbits, escaping gel migrated through the patients' bodies.

In 1976, Congress passed a law requiring the FDA to approve the safety and effectiveness of medical devices. Silicone implants were exempted because they were already on the market. Two years later, a further attempt to regulate implants occurred. FDA staff proposed putting breast implants into a category requiring very rigorous safety tests. Plastic surgeons and manufacturers opposed the measure and finally won when the FDA Commissioner overrode his staff's recommendation. In 1982, the FDA again tried to reclassify implants and again failed.

In 1985, Dow Corning became concerned about what one executive called "an ominous shift" in the FDA to require more and stricter lifetime animal tests. In an internal memo, he acknowledged that the company could be in trouble because all its data were based on two-year studies of dogs. Lifetime dog studies had to be of seven years' duration.

Dow Corning began to warn women and doctors about two major problems with the implants: scar tissue could form around the implants, and in cases in which the implants leaked, women could suffer inflammatory reactions. In 1988, the FDA finally reclassified implants and notified implant makers that they would be required to provide safety data within 30 months.[5]

In April 1991, the FDA responded to inquiries from women who were worried about the safety of their implants. It asked all manufacturers to submit scientific data demonstrating their products' safety and effectiveness. The FDA refused to evaluate the safety and effectiveness of silicone-gel implants made by Bristol-Myers Squibb, Bioplasty, and a private physician in California. The FDA asserted that the companies had not submitted sufficient evidence to conduct a review.

However, the FDA agreed to review seven other types of implants made by McGhan Medical, Mentor, and Dow Corning, as well as an alternative model made by Bioplasty. In late July, the FDA ordered US marshals to seize 800 Bioplasty inflatable implant kits. The agency said the company lacked FDA marketing authorization and had made false and misleading claims about the product.[6]

Shortly thereafter, the FDA began to consider banning most or all use of silicone breast implants, noting that the makers had not submitted adequate safety data. As Commissioner David Kessler remarked, "It is as hard, as complicated, as emotional as any issue we've faced since I got here."[7]

Breast implant recipients were divided. Of the 2 million cases of breast implants since the early 1960s, about 80 percent were done for cosmetic reasons and the remaining 20 percent for reconstructive surgery following mastectomy. Some women believed breast implants had changed their lives for the better; others claimed their health had been permanently impaired. In November 1991, the FDA convened a panel to determine whether implants were safe. Two days later, the panel voted to keep breast implants on the market and urged the FDA to set strict rules for continued marketing. It also voted unanimously to reject Dow Corning's safety data.

Managing the Crisis

From Dow Chemical's and Corning Glass Works's perspectives, the FDA ruling was a disaster. Their businesses and managerial responsibilities clearly overlapped in the joint venture association. Officers of both companies sat on Dow Corning's board of directors. Five Corning representatives, including Corning's chairperson, were members of Dow Corning's 14-member board. Dow Chemical also had five representatives on the board. The remaining four directors were Dow Corning managers. Even though the parent companies, Corning and Dow, were not involved in implant research and were not liable for potential damages, they stood to lose a large portion of earnings if Dow Corning's revenues suffered.[8]

Dow Corning and other implant manufacturers took a series of steps between early February and May 1992.

- February 18: Dow Corning continued to withhold hundreds of internal documents addressing safety issues:

---

[5]P J Hilts, "Maker of Implants Balked at Tests, Its Records Show," *The New York Times,* January 13, 1992, p. A1.

[6]B Ingersoll, "FDA Refuses to Evaluate Data Submitted by 3 Manufacturers of Breast Implants," *The Wall Street Journal,* August 26, 1991, p. B3.

[7]P J Hilts, "Amid Heavy Lobbying, U.S. Weighs Breast Implant Ban," *The New York Times,* October 21, 1991, p. A1.

[8]J E Rigdon, "Corning Is Feeling the Heat in Breast Implant Debacle," *The Wall Street Journal,* January 29, 1992, p. B4.

- February 20: Dow Corning promised to carry out 15 more safety tests on implants and establish a patient tracking registry.
- March 2: Dow Corning explored the possibility of seeking bankruptcy under Chapter 11. This action could temporarily halt private litigation and resolve all claims simultaneously.
- March 19: Dow Corning, following the lead of Bristol-Myers Squibb and Bioplasty, announced it would get out of the implant business.
- November 4: Five hundred plastic surgeons signed up to take part in clinical studies of silicone breast implants. Under FDA rules, implants would be available to women only if they enrolled in the study.[9]

Gerald C Meyers, a crisis management consultant, called Dow Corning's activities "a textbook case of crisis mismanagement."[10] Other consultants agreed Dow Corning had a valid argument when it insisted there was little scientific evidence to support injury claims. However, consultants pointed to three major points in handling health care crises:

1. Even a small number of people who believe they were injured or deceived can create a major uproar.
2. The numbers involved in defective or dangerous product cases frequently are higher than initial estimates.
3. Consumers get very upset when they think they have been deceived.[11]

Questions

1. Did Dow Corning handle the crisis effectively? Should top managers have taken a different role?
2. Should management have been more outspoken earlier? Some newspaper and magazine articles compared Dow Corning's performance to Exxon Corporation's response to the Exxon *Valdez* disaster and A H Robin's handling of the Dalkon Shield IUD controversy. Is that comparison fair?
3. Should Dow Corning have stopped making implants?
4. Develop a plan for handling this crisis. What choices would you make?

Internally Generated Crises

Internally generated crises are crises that affect a company or even an industry. Many crises have no direct impact on the external physical environment. Stakeholders in the internal and external direct quadrants of the stakeholder influence map may suffer, but there is no threat to water, air, or land. Internal crises stem from a variety of organizational problems related to management's inadequate organizational structures and controls.

---

[9]"Silicone-Gel Breast Implants Resume with Restrictions," *The Boston Globe,* November 4, 1992, p. 17.

[10]B J Feder, "P.R. Mistake Seen in Breast-Implant Case," *The New York Times,* January 29, 1992, p. D1.

[11]Ibid.

Organizational problems include poor company culture, ineffective information dissemination systems, and unclear punishments and rewards. Additional organizational difficulties arise when planning procedures are not responsive to events or when employees make errors that are not identified and corrected. These inadequacies may lead to production and control problems that go undetected or unanalyzed. They may also be responsible for faulty design and product defects that contribute to the problem.

Drexel Burnham Lambert and Manville Corporation are two companies whose inadequate internal monitoring systems resulted in devastating crises that affected a wide range of direct and indirect stakeholders. At Drexel, Michael Milken and others issued and manipulated the prices of junk bonds, making millions of dollars for the company and for themselves. Milken and his colleagues reaped the profits until the Securities and Exchange Commission (SEC) filed charges and the media were alerted. The crisis had erupted. Investigators concluded that top management failed to monitor and evaluate the impact of its employees' actions. We will examine the Drexel crisis in detail later in this chapter.

Manville's problems with asbestos-related claims is another example of an internally generated crisis. For decades, Manville's top management deliberately concealed data documenting asbestos-related deaths and disabilities. The situation became a crisis when stakeholders brought legal action.

In 1986, Manville filed for bankruptcy under Chapter 11 to protect itself from claims. In 1988, the company agreed to set up a $2.5 billion trust to pay health claims from victims of asbestos-related diseases. Manville emerged from bankruptcy court protection in November 1988. However, litigation dragged on as the trust fund repeatedly ran out of money and fund overseers were charged with mismanagement.

In the early 1990s, Manville's management struggled to overcome the constant drain on the firm's financial resources and create a new, environmentally friendly image. According to image makers, "this kind of aggressive environmental makeover is the only way to reinvent a company whose name has become synonymous with health problems."[12]

Manville's troubles are not yet over. Payments to claimants drag on and on, and observers do not expect the fund to complete payments until after the year 2000.[13] In December 1992, a federal appeals court overturned a two-year-old reorganization plan of the Manville Personal Injury Trust, putting the issue back in the lower courts and stalling settlement indefinitely.

Occasionally a company is plunged into a crisis through no fault of its own. This kind of crisis is generated by external, uncontrollable events. Johnson & Johnson's management of the 1982 Tylenol poisonings illus-

[12]M Charlier, "Manville Tries to Build New Identity as a Firm Keen on Environment," *The Wall Street Journal,* May 31, 1990, p. A1.

[13]J M Moses, "Manville Dispute with U.S. May Force Asbestos Claimants to Compete for Funds," *The Wall Street Journal,* November 14, 1991, p. B6A.

trates how effective crisis management can minimize the negative consequences, especially when the company is clearly not culpable.

The crisis at Johnson & Johnson erupted in September 1982, when several Chicago-area residents died after taking cyanide-laced Tylenol. Tylenol was a leading over-the-counter pain remedy produced by one of Johnson & Johnson's divisions. In the aftermath, top management expertly articulated Johnson & Johnson's public position and company philosophy to consumers and employees. The company convinced the public that it was as much a victim as the people who died. Johnson & Johnson also demonstrated concern for its customers by immediately recalling the product and quickly taking steps to make the Tylenol package tamperproof. Its actions are often cited as a model of effective crisis management. Even more than a decade later, the company's expert handling of the Tylenol crisis continues to enhance Johnson & Johnson's image.

Environmental Crises: A Special Situation

Environmental crises affect the external physical environment as well as specific stakeholder groups. These crises include such events as nuclear accidents, chemical or oil spills, and other industrial catastrophes. Like internal crises, they often have their genesis in the firm's managerial systems. Unless the crisis was caused by uncontrollable external forces, such as actions by terrorists, criminals, or saboteurs, corporate policies and procedures are often responsible. Technical monitoring and backup systems that are inadequate or do not work as designed precipitate crises. Employees who are not properly trained and systems that are not in place to catch mistakes also cause crises.

Increasingly, industrial disasters such as Union Carbide's Bhopal incident and the Exxon *Valdez* oil spill focus national and international attention on company responses. It is very difficult for a company to manage environmental disasters, because media attention is so intense and so many stakeholders are involved. The public's perception of the company's contribution to the crisis often rests on the severity of the crisis and the degree to which innocent stakeholders suffer. Prompt and appropriate responses by management can mitigate public perceptions of culpability. Delayed or inappropriate responses can enhance such perceptions.

When the Exxon *Valdez* spilled oil into the pristine Alaskan waters, the company's reaction was slow, confused, and, some charged, deliberately obtuse. Exxon's top management appeared so disorganized that *The Wall Street Journal* ran the following subheading a week after the spill: "Out of Control: How Lack of Readiness by Exxon and Others Turned Oil Spill into Ecological Debacle."[14] We will discuss the details of the Exxon spill later in this chapter.

---

[14]K Wells, "How Unpreparedness Turned the Alaska Spill into Ecological Debacle," *The Wall Street Journal,* April 3, 1989, p. A1.

A Model for Crisis Management

Regardless of whether a situation is generated internally or externally, top management can identify an impending crisis by the symptoms before the crisis erupts and can predict the likelihood that the issue will become a crisis. A company can adopt models for assessing the potential severity of crises and devising strategies to limit damage to the firm and its reputation. No matter how bad the situation is for the company, even the worst catastrophes can be managed to minimize negative consequences.

Mitroff, Shrivastava, and Udwadia present a useful and creative crisis management model[15] (see Exhibit 4–1). The model can be entered and exited at any point, and the company can take action either clockwise or counterclockwise. The model uses the following sequence:

· *Point I: Detection.* A crisis is detected through the company's early warning systems. The systems include computerized process control systems, plant monitoring systems, management information systems, and internal and external environmental scans. Between the detection (point I) and crisis periods (point II), the company should use simulations and mock crisis exercises to prepare for the real thing as effectively as possible.

· *Point II: Crisis.* No organization can consistently escape the circumstances that cause crises. If the company has done its proactive prevention and preparation well, it can deal more effectively with actual crises when they occur. Prevention and preparation entail developing such items as safety policies, maintenance procedures, environmental-impact plans, crisis audits, and worker-training programs.

· *Point III: Repair.* The company must isolate and contain crises before it can repair the damage. The specific strategies for repairing a crisis will depend on the nature and scope of the problem. For example, Johnson & Johnson immediately recalled Tylenol, changed the seal on the package, and embarked on an expertly devised remedial advertising campaign. A company that does not have such repair mechanisms in place may never recover from the aftereffects.

· *Point IV: Assessment.* In the final step of the crisis cycle model, the company evaluates what it has learned from the crisis. A new cycle begins as the firm develops better crisis prevention and detection systems as a result of its crisis experience.

For example, in the post-Bhopal period, Union Carbide should have examined points I through III step by step and put in place policies to prevent a similar accident from occurring in its factories elsewhere in the world. This process would have enabled Union Carbide to heed early warning signs in the detection stage that would allow the company to behave proactively. Effective routine company procedures can pick up safety

---

[15]Mitroff, Shrivastava, and Udwadia, "Effective Crisis Management," p. 284.

Knowthis

EXHIBIT 4-1

A model of crisis management

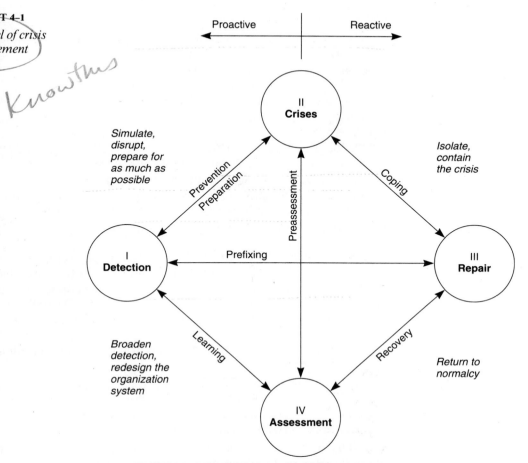

SOURCE: I I Mitroff, P Shrivastara, and F Udwadia, "Effective Crisis Management," *Academy of Management Executive* 1, no. 3 (1987), p. 284.

problems before they become crises and before the company loses control of events.

Anatomy of a Major Crisis

Crises erupt in stages. Gerald C Meyers identifies three specific periods in the course of a crisis: precrisis, crisis, and postcrisis.[16] These stages correspond to Mitroff et al.'s model in Exhibit 4–1.

---

[16]G C Meyers with J Holusha, *When It Hits the Fan: Managing the Nine Crises of Business* (Boston: Houghton Mifflin, 1986), pp. 4–22.

The Precrisis or Prodromal Stage

The term *prodromal* means a crisis is looming. This phase is a warning stage, comparable to the aura that precedes a migraine headache. The prodromal stage fits in the upper left-hand quadrant of Exhibit 4–1. Something is wrong, but the company is unable to pin it down. The symptom is that some person or group within the company is not performing. For example, production quotas are not being met, creating customer delivery problems. Perhaps intermediate goods are not being delivered on time to manufacturers, the product defect rate is increasing, or budgets are missing their targets. Every company experiences one or more of these situations, but many fail to take them as warning signs of an impending crisis.

Typically, as the problem grows, management realizes employees are becoming increasingly uncertain about what actions they should take. Relationships with one another and with top management become dysfunctional.

For example, in the early 1990s, high-technology companies suffered huge losses that threw them into internal turmoil. Yet the public had very little warning of the devastating layoff and downsizing announcements that were to come. At Union Carbide, managers discussed safety problems in the Bhopal plant two years before the crisis, but could not decide who should be responsible.

A company can determine whether it is in a precrisis or prodromal stage by assessing five specific risks:

1. The likelihood that the situation or issue will escalate in intensity.
2. The likelihood that the situation or issue will come under intense scrutiny by government or the media.
3. The likelihood that the situation or issue will interfere with the company's normal business operations.
4. The likelihood that the situation or issue will harm the company's or management's positive image.
5. The likelihood that the company's bottom line will be damaged.[17]

If any or all of these risks escalate into developments, the situation is likely to worsen. In looking for prodromes, or symptoms, a company should base its strategy on the old dictum that it is easier—and far less expensive—to treat a cold than to tackle life-threatening pneumonia. The important thing is to treat the symptoms early. A good detection system will permit the firm to assess all of these risks.

---

[17]S Fink, *Crisis Management* (New York: AMACOM, 1986), pp. 15–16.

The Crisis Stage

In the crisis period, the "world caves in." This period is depicted in the top center portion of Exhibit 4–1. It is an extremely painful time for a company. Managers are blamed, the company loses money, and the problems consume executives' energies. Stakeholders in all quadrants of the stakeholder influence map may be deeply affected. Meyers declares that the harshest reactions to a company's crisis come from creditors and lending institutions worried about financial uncertainty. He also notes that the attention the company wants *least* comes from the government and regulators. If the company cannot manage a major crisis effectively, there is a real possibility that it will eventually collapse.[18] Both Manville and A H Robins are examples of companies that went bankrupt while trying to deal with almost unmanageable crises.

Postcrisis Stage

The postcrisis stage—the right-hand bottom quadrant of Exhibit 4–1—is marked by radical changes that affect the entire company or even other companies in the same industry. During the postcrisis repair process, new players may gain control of the firm. Huge amounts of money may have to be allocated to battling lawsuits, fines, or remedial publicity. Crisis management experts agree that the bottom line is *always* adversely affected. Inevitably the news media will make invidious comparisons between a company that has suffered through a crisis and subsequent situations with any degree of similarity. As Fink points out, ". . . the sad and frightening truth is, the only thing that will make the media stop comparing chemical plant accidents to Union Carbide's is to have a *worse* accident take place.[19]

The public measures all nuclear accidents against Three Mile Island and Chernobyl. Dow and dioxin are linked in the Times Beach contamination, Beech-Nut is associated with adulterated baby food, and Morton Thiakol always brings to mind the crash of the Challenger spacecraft.

Drexel Burnham Lambert: An Internally Generated Crisis

Drexel Burnham Lambert perhaps best epitomizes the meteoric rise and fall of the Wall Street financial moguls and junk bond dealers who financed a huge range of other business activities. Junk bonds are bonds that bear high-interest coupons but are considered risky by buyers. During the late 1970s and 1980s, Drexel's phenomenal success in issuing and selling these bonds made it one of the largest and most powerful firms on Wall Street.

---

[18]Meyers, "When It Hits the Fan," p. 20.
[19]Fink, *Crisis Management*, pp. 89–90.

Working out of Drexel's Beverly Hills, California, office, Michael Milken built the junk bond market into a major force in American finance. But despite Drexel's success and power, the firm became enmeshed in a profound crisis that led to its bankruptcy. Could Drexel have better anticipated this crisis and managed it more effectively? Did Drexel go through the stages of crisis, and were the five risk factors apparent? How well did the company fit into the model of crisis management?

Precrisis or Prodromal Stage

If we look at events at Drexel Burnham Lambert, we can readily see that the company was in a prodromal situation for some time before the crisis erupted. The precrisis period apparently was marked by *overwhelmingly* good performance. Perhaps Drexel's top management should have been more wary of the enormous profits and huge earnings generated and enjoyed by so few individuals. In retrospect, all the risk factors were present, making a full-blown crisis virtually inevitable.

Risk 1. The first risk, the likelihood that the issue would escalate in intensity, was extremely high at Drexel. The first glimmerings of trouble dated back to May 1986, when the Securities and Exchange Commission (SEC) accused Drexel's Dennis B Levine of having made more than $12 million on insider trading. Within weeks, Levine implicated arbitrageur Ivan Boesky. In September, Boesky signed a plea bargain with the government. He agreed to record telephone calls and secretly tape personal conversations with colleagues. In December 1987, Boesky was sentenced to three years in jail.

In January 1988, the SEC concluded a 15-month investigation. It notified Drexel that the SEC staff was about to recommend civil charges of major securities law violations against Drexel, Michael Milken, and other employees. According to the SEC, Boesky's company was a front behind which Drexel purchased stock in a company about which it had nonpublic knowledge. In one case, Drexel bought stock in National Gypsum Company during the period in which National Gypsum was the target of a tender offer by a Drexel client. The SEC charges covered a variety of allegedly illegal transactions connecting Drexel and Boesky. These charges included insider trading, stock manipulation, illegally concealing ownership, margin violations, and fraud in offering materials.[20]

From the beginning, Milken had an unorthodox relationship with Drexel. He insulated himself from supervision by choosing to work in California—a continent away from the New York City headquarters. He was

---

[20]K Eichenwald, "Drexel Burnham Fights Back," *The New York Times,* September 11, 1988, pp. F1, F8.

extremely private about the particulars of his business deals and transactions. He selected subordinates who also operated independently of headquarters surveillance and were loyal to him rather than to Drexel. Milken's highest-paid associate, Peter Ackerman, remained a mystery to other Drexel employees. Ackerman reportedly never even allowed Drexel to publish his photograph. Milken's brother Lowell was another loyalist player in the Beverly Hills office.

Risk 2. Drexel clearly faced the second risk—that it would come under the intense scrutiny of the media and the government. The Drexel situation had all the elements of high drama. By the time the SEC filed charges, Boesky had pleaded guilty to insider trading and was serving his time in a minimum-security prison. Boesky fingered Milken, whom the press quickly dubbed the "Junk Bond King."

In 1987, *Forbes* estimated that Milken was worth about $600 million. By 1988, his net worth totaled nearly $1 billion, all earned while at Drexel. Regardless of the technical aspects of the case, the activities of this cast of characters seemed to epitomize to the American public the quintessential "yuppie" greed of the 1980s. To millions of Americans, the daily unfolding of new details was as compelling as daytime soap opera. Even *The New York Times* contributed to the media hype in describing Milken: "self-effacing and modest in appearance . . . favors sport coats over suits and wears a less than subtle toupee, providing a thatch of dark hair over his boyish face and deep-set dark eyes."[21]

The media watched the regulators and government closely, incorporating their assessment of the government and regulatory agency strategy into the daily reports about Milken and his associates at Drexel. They speculated endlessly over whether charges would stick.

Risk 3. The third risk—that the crisis would interfere with the company's normal operations—became a reality even before the SEC filed charges. Beginning with Levine's arrest, Drexel had to contend with rumors and leaks. By 1988, top management believed it was ready for what *The New York Times* characterized as "all-out war." The myriad hours spent fighting the charges diverted executives from the primary tasks of the company. Executives spent much of their time meeting with lawyers, public relations experts, and other constituents instead of servicing customers and developing new business.

Risk 4. Drexel's CEO, Frederick H Joseph, was well aware of the fourth risk. He knew the company's image was at stake. He had to keep up morale within the company and at the same time reassure customers that Drexel was in good financial and managerial shape.

---

[21]S Labaton, "Drexel Concedes Guilt on Trading; to Pay $650 Million," *The New York Times,* December 22, 1988, p. D4.

Drexel's most important asset was its reputation for successfully managing junk bond offerings. At the time the charges were filed, Drexel held 30 percent of all outstanding high-yield bonds. Even though Drexel had pioneered the junk bond market, competitors such as First Boston Inc., Morgan Stanley & Company, and Goldman, Sachs & Company were beginning to make major moves in the industry. Drexel's position in junk bonds depended on the public's continued confidence in the company's management and solvency.

Risk 5. Drexel's solvency, the fifth risk, was in question. In 1984, Drexel held 68 percent of the market for new public junk bond issues. By 1987, its share had slipped to 40 percent.

If we examine the model of crisis management, we readily see that Drexel did too little about point I: detecting, preparing, and preventing the crisis. During its heyday, Drexel allowed certain practices that made it vulnerable to criticism when the investigations began. For example, Drexel allowed its own employees to purchase parts of the firm's own debt issues. In May 1988, the House Energy and Commerce oversight and investigations subcommittee charged that Drexel had ignored the interests of the firm's clients by selling new issues of junk bonds to its own investment partnerships, including about 150 Drexel officials. The partnerships quickly sold the bonds for substantial profits. In some cases, employees made higher profits than outside clients did.[22]

By permitting this and similar practices, Drexel created a climate that put its ethical standards into question. Although the company ended the practice after the congressional hearings, the media had gotten a whiff of blood, and the feeding frenzy began. Had Drexel been more sensitive to stakeholders' perceptions earlier, it might have lessened public criticism. It appears that Drexel drastically underestimated the magnitude of the crisis and its potentially devastating effects.

Crisis Stage

At the moment the government filed charges, Drexel was plunged into a full-blown crisis. Drexel hired teams of image consultants, lawyers, and public relations experts. The firm had already spent more than $140 million in the two years before the charges became public. It paid Arthur Andersen & Company $46 million just to copy and collate the 1.5 million pages of documents the government requested.

Drexel divided its activities into two distinct components. One part tried to conduct business as usual; the other was devoted entirely to fighting government charges. Employees were demoralized. The committee assigned to work on the government charges grew from 4 to 20 members.

---

[22]T E Ricks, "Drexel Stops Staff Purchases of Its New Debt," *The Wall Street Journal,* May 5, 1988, pp. 1, 3.

Executive committees were organized to plan and implement crisis strategy. Drexel faced the need to practice both crisis management and issues management at the same time.

Drexel sent out more than 15,000 letters to its employees and clients explaining its version of the situation. Employees received T-shirts with booster slogans. Top executives personally called valued clients to reassure them that the company was performing well.[23] Despite Drexel's efforts, however, regulators and lawyers took control of events. Nothing Fred Joseph or other top managers did could divert their efforts.

In December 1988, Drexel agreed to plead guilty and pay $650 million in fines and restitution. In February 1990, the company began selling its securities and businesses, and on the evening of February 13, the directors approved a filing for Chapter 11 bankruptcy protection.[24]

Top management tried to contain the crisis. Following recommendations in point II of the model, Drexel drew up and implemented emergency management plans. It developed and carried out an aggressive public relations agenda. Crisis management teams swung into action. But it was too late. By this time, Drexel's actions were, as the model suggests, reactive rather than proactive. The government and the media determined the course of events. Having ignored warning signals and failed to recognize its vulnerability in the detection stage (point I), Drexel became a hostage to events that eventually destroyed its reputation and its ability to survive.

Postcrisis Stage

In October 1990, *U.S. News & World Report* chronicled the tribulations of the junk bond industry. Prices for junk bonds fell sharply through the autumn of 1990. Between January and September 1990, $8.4 billion in high-yield securities defaulted. Drexel's bankruptcy contributed to huge losses in the savings and loan industry. S&Ls, frequently at Drexel's urging, had invested heavily in junk bonds. Resolution Trust Corporation joined the Federal Deposit Insurance Corporation in a suit claiming that Drexel had plundered S&Ls through "bribery, coercion, extortion, fraud and other illegal means." They charged that junk bond losses for failed thrifts had reached $2 billion.[25]

Eventually thrift regulators and others filed 170 suits asserting that Milken had helped cause the failure of 200 S&Ls and insurance companies by manipulating the junk bond market. Milken denied the charges, but in March 1992 a federal judge finally approved a $1.3 billion settlement against

---

[23]Eichenwald, "Drexel Burnham Fights Back."

[24]K Eichenwald, "Drexel, Symbol of a Wall St. Era, Starts Liquidating after a Default," *The New York Times,* February 14, 1990, p. A1.

[25]P Thomas and W Lambert, "S&L Regulators Are Seeking $6.8 Billion in Drexel Burnham Bankruptcy Case," *The Wall Street Journal,* November 15, 1990, p. A4.

EXHIBIT 4–2

*Stakeholder influence
map: Drexel
Burnham Lambert*

	Direct	Indirect
External	Competitors Government Regulators	Media The public S&Ls Other institutional shareholders
Internal	Employees Top managers Board of directors	Shareholders

him. According to the settlement, Milken would pay $500 million to the government to reimburse it for the damages caused to S&Ls. The courts approved a reorganization plan that permitted a small company called New Street Capital to manage a $400 million portfolio for the benefit of Drexel creditors.[26] Drexel was unable to repair the damage (point III) and return to normalcy. It lost its opportunity to assess the crisis and to redesign the organization to anticipate new crises (point IV).

The Drexel crisis affected all quadrants of the stakeholder influence map (see Exhibit 4–2). The media concentrated on the huge sums lost by big institutional clients. However, thousands of small shareholders in the internal indirect quadrant lost their entire investment.

More than 5,000 employees in the internal direct quadrant lost their jobs. Nearly 1,000 Drexel employees owned stock in the company, and those who counted on cashing in stock for retirement lost everything. A former Drexel broker commented, "I've never seen anything so depressing in my life . . . People were wandering around, so sad, so bitter." Another manager said, "We had no idea it would end in bankruptcy."[27]

The Exxon *Valdez:* A Major Environmental Accident

The potential for industrially caused environmental disasters has increased dramatically in the second half of the twentieth century. As African, Asian, Middle Eastern, and Latin American nations developed economically after World War II, multinationals set up local factories, raw material processing plants, and low-cost labor operations. Indigenous companies acquired

---

[26]J M Moses, "Judge Approves Milken Accord of $1.3 Billion," *The Wall Street Journal,* March 10, 1992, p. A3.

[27]"Did Drexel Get What It Deserved?," *Fortune,* March 12, 1990, pp. 87–88.

industrialized-country technology, which they often used under less than ideal conditions.

When companies use potentially dangerous substances and adopt new technologies, environmental crises are inevitable. Critics of multinationals frequently point to the Bhopal incident as an example of a crisis that developed when poorly trained workers operated inadequately safeguarded technology. It is true that Union Carbide might have averted the Bhopal accident by correcting safety violations identified two years earlier. It also might have managed the aftermath of Bhopal differently or perhaps better. Everyone agrees that companies should adopt systems to diminish the likelihood of disasters. But there is no way for companies to guard against every environmental accident. Once an accident occurs, a company should have a strategy for dealing with it and should develop its own internal systems to avoid similar occurrences in the future.

A broad coalition of environmentalists, government officials, regulators, and industry officials point to the grounding of the Exxon *Valdez* oil tanker as an example of an avoidable environmental disaster. (see Exhibit 4-3.) Should Exxon have acted proactively, that is, developed systems that identified and eliminated the particular problems that led to this crisis? Did Exxon manage the crisis as effectively as possible?

The Precrisis or Prodromal Stage

Environmental disasters do not necessarily present clear warning signs. However, major oil companies *always* face the five major risk factors. Their products and technologies make them ripe for ecological accidents. Some external indirect stakeholders, such as environmental lobbying groups, neighboring community groups, and even foreign country nationals, are skeptical about oil companies' commitment to corporate social responsibility.

These stakeholders note that oil companies are vast corporations with worldwide operations. The companies deal in a nonrenewable resource and, some critics say, have a history of exploitation and arrogance. These characteristics make them particularly vulnerable to media attention. In this age of instant communication and satellite surveillance, it is virtually impossible to hide information about an oil spill, fire, or other accident.

In the case of the Exxon *Valdez,* Captain Joseph Hazelwood's history of drunkenness was a clear prodrome. Hazelwood was convicted of drunken driving only six months before the spill, and his driver's license had been revoked three times in the previous five years. In 1985, Exxon put Hazelwood through an alcohol detoxification program but did not follow up to ascertain whether it succeeded. In hindsight, had Exxon had a system in place to track known substance abusers, it might have averted the spill. At least, Exxon could have removed Captain Hazelwood from command of the tanker, thereby reducing the chances that a prodromal situation would turn into a crisis.

EXHIBIT 4–3

*Model of Crisis
Management: the
Exxon* Valdez

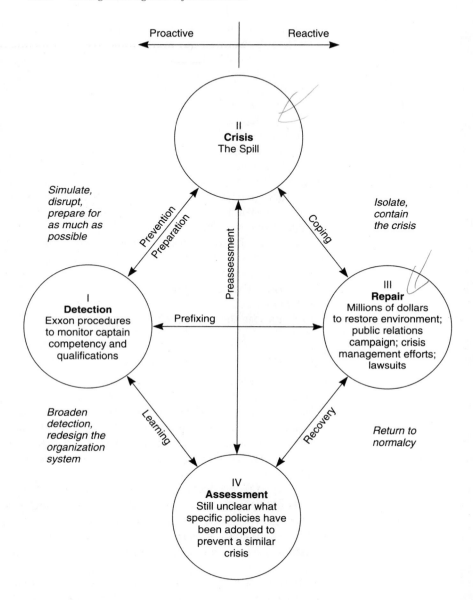

The Crisis Stage

If events trigger a full-blown crisis, it is already too late to avoid public scrutiny. But even at this stage, the company has some control over how, and under what conditions, the crisis develops. Once the oil spilled from the Exxon *Valdez* into Prince William Sound in March 1989, the company lost the option of deciding *whether* to respond. Nevertheless, it still had choices concerning *how* to respond.

Critics charged that Exxon should have prepared more effectively for a disaster. They pointed out that it took Alyeska Pipeline Service Company, the consortium that was supposed to handle oil spills, 35 hours to encircle the tanker with barrier booms. Exxon had a crisis management plan designed to contain an oil spill in five hours, but the plan had never been tested. Oil dispersants were inadequate, personnel were disorganized, and radio systems lacked the power to reach some of the containment vessels. Exxon rejected the criticisms, however, maintaining that its efforts to handle the spill were impeded by state and Coast Guard meddling.

Initially Exxon's top managers refused to comment on the spill. Then they attempted to shift responsibility for the slow response to others. Chairperson and CEO Lawrence G Rawl told the media that his company "got a bad rap" for delays in dealing with the spill, and President Lee Raymond blamed the Coast Guard for reacting slowly.[28] Exxon did little or nothing to mollify angry fishers who saw their livelihoods threatened. Nor did the company immediately respond to the concerns of environmentalists who struggled to save thousands of oil-covered marine animals, birds, and fish.

Critics further charged that Exxon deliberately misled the press and local residents in the early days of the spill when it assured them that beach cleanups and containment were under way. In fact, an Exxon spokesperson later admitted that beach cleanup had not begun and only one boat had been sent out to assess the problem.[29]

Crisis management experts agreed that Exxon's mishandling of the acute stage of the crisis heightened public outrage. When Rawl sent lower-level executives to Alaska to observe the spill rather than going himself, he created the impression that the company thought the pollution problem was trivial. Exxon's reaction, or lack thereof, heightened the public's perception that Exxon was not responding fully to the disaster.

Experts also criticized Exxon's handling of public relations. Valdez, Alaska, the town where news briefings were held, had limited communications facilities. Complaining reporters were told they had to go to Valdez or they would get no information at all. In addition, the company often gave conflicting information in its public statements. One Exxon spokesperson told the media the spill was minor, while another acknowledged it was massive. Crisis management experts concluded that Exxon had made a mistake by refusing to take responsibility for the spill in the advertisement it ran in national newspapers.

Management consultant Gerald C Meyers remarked that "what we have here, in my opinion, is a classic unmanaged crisis . . . As phony as it sounds, sending the chairman to the scene would have shown genuine concern for what happened there."[30]

---

[28]Wells, "How Unpreparedness Turned the Alaska Spill into Ecological Debacle."
[29]"The Big Spill," *Time,* April 10, 1989, pp. 37–41.
[30]J Holusha, "Exxon's Public-Relations Problem," *The New York Times,* April 21, 1989, p. D1.

Postcrisis Stage

Fink calls the postcrisis stage the stage in which "the carcass gets picked clean."[31] Hundreds of lawsuits were filed in the aftermath of the *Valdez* oil spill. The conflicts among local residents, Native Americans, environmentalists, state and government officials, and Exxon dragged on and on.

External indirect stakeholders called for action. For example, consumer and environmental groups demanded a national boycott of all Exxon products, asserting the company was "a polluter without equal."[32] Residents of an Aleut fishing village charged that fish and wildlife pollution threatened their entire cash income.

Internal direct and indirect stakeholders became intensely involved. Exxon union leaders objected to changes the company made to its alcohol and drug abuse rehabilitation policies after the spill. Two thousand Exxon shareholders bombarded Chairperson Rawl with questions at the company's annual meeting. For four-and-one-half hours they discussed the spill. Some even demanded Rawl's resignation. At the end of the meeting, however, it became clear that management's control prevailed. Rawl was reelected.[33]

In October 1991, a federal judge accepted a $1 billion package of criminal and civil settlements to end the state and federal cases against Exxon. The criminal penalty was set at $125 million, $100 million of which was designated for restitution of the polluted area. Chairperson Rawl personally pleaded guilty to one misdemeanor charge of killing migratory waterfowl. The Justice Department reported that with this settlement, Exxon had paid $3.5 billion for cleanup, claims, and the settlement.[34] The criminal charges against Captain Hazelwood were overturned in July 1992, when he was cleared of all criminal responsibility. The only charge that remained against him was a misdemeanor for negligently discharging oil. Hazelwood's license was restored, and he took a new job as an instructor at the New York State University Maritime College.[35]

It is impossible to assess the total costs of the Exxon *Valdez* accident. Although Hazelwood went through some trying times, he never served a prison sentence and is now gainfully employed. He is even qualified to pilot another supertanker. Years of cleanup and millions of dollars have helped restore Prince William Sound, but some damage remains. Exxon's profits

---

[31]Fink, *Crisis Management,* p. 23.

[32]P Shabecoff, "Six Groups Urge Boycott of Exxon," *The New York Times,* May 3, 1989, p. A17.

[33]A Sullivan, "Exxon's Holders Assail Chairman Rawl over Firm's Handling of Alaska Oil Spill," *The Wall Street Journal,* May 19, 1989, p. A3.

[34]"Judge Accepts Exxon Pact, Ending Suits on *Valdez* Spill," *The New York Times,* October 9, 1991, p. A14.

[35]C McCoy, "Criminal Charges in Exxon *Valdez* Spill Are Reversed," *The Wall Street Journal,* July 13, 1992, p. A4.

were depressed in the fourth quarter after the spill, but the company's resources are so vast that the penalty was merely an annoyance. There is no way to estimate the opportunity costs to Exxon of top management's complete preoccupation with crisis management.

In his book *The First 24 Hours,* Dieudonnee ten Berge analyzes Exxon's handling of the crisis. He concludes that Exxon was completely surprised by the disaster. Top management panicked and became paranoid. Finally, he says, "if Exxon did anything efficiently, it was to keep things covered up."[36] While other observers are less critical, they point out that at the very least Exxon might well have spent the equivalent of cleanup costs on prevention. Although Exxon absorbed the monetary losses with little trouble, its credibility remains in question. If Exxon encounters any new environmental problems, public opinion will turn against the company much more quickly than it did before the spill.

Routine Crises	Every day companies deal with crises that have the potential to be catastrophic but, for a variety of reasons, do not cause serious long-term damage. Earnings may be affected in the short run, the media may pay attention for awhile and then lose interest, or a simple mistake may be rectified. In any event, these cases are far more common than the crises we already discussed. Many companies routinely handle and resolve crises that never become catastrophes.

Perrier: A Routine Crisis that Fizzled

The Perrier Company faced a crisis that some observers initially thought could turn into a corporate debacle. It didn't.

In 1990, the Perrier Group of North America, a subsidiary of Source Perrier, S.A., faced a crisis of potentially international proportions. During the 1980s, Perrier and other sparkling waters established themselves as the yuppie alternative to alcoholic drinks. In the United States particularly, tastes changed. Many young affluent adults, now more interested in physical fitness, eschewed alcohol. Perrier, in its distinctive green, pear-shaped bottle, epitomized purity, clarity, wholesomeness, and sophistication. Perrier drinkers were as much a part of the after-work "fern bar" scene as alcoholic beverage consumers were.

In February 1990, regulators accidently discovered small amounts of benzene in some Perrier bottled at the North Carolina bottling plant. The Mecklenburg County Environmental Protection Department routinely

---

[36]Dieudonnee ten Berge, *The First 24 Hours* (Cambridge, MN: Basil Blackwell, 1990), p. 186.

bought Perrier in a supermarket to use as a component in its tests of local surface and underground water. The staff considered Perrier an excellent source of water free of organic matter. This time, however, one of the biologists detected some odd data but thought it was a problem with the spectrometer or the utensils. It took several days for regulators to suspect that the Perrier water itself was contaminated.

The department director notified North Carolina authorities, who retested the Perrier, got the same results, and immediately notified Perrier Group. The company quickly discovered that 13 of its bottles contained traces of benzene, a clear solvent used to remove grease from bottling machinery.[37] Perrier Group announced a recall of 72 million bottles from 750,000 North American outlets.[38] On February 15 the parent company, Source Perrier, expanded the recall worldwide.

In its initial response, Source Perrier asserted that one North Carolina worker had carelessly used a benzene-soaked rag to clean machinery. Management noted that no one was harmed and that the company did not anticipate making any changes in the product or its packaging. Why, then, was this event a crisis for Perrier? What was the potential damage, and how serious were the consequences likely to be?

Source Perrier's spokespeople could not get the story straight. At a Paris conference, Source Perrier's President, Frederik Zimmer, said the initial report of worker contamination was incorrect. He stated that Perrier water naturally contains small amounts of gases, including benzene, and these were usually filtered out with charcoal. Unfortunately, he said, the company had forgotten to replace the filters on schedule. The company had known for several months that Perrier water in other locations also contained traces of benzene. Eventually the company admitted the benzene came from carbon dioxide that bottlers used to augment Perrier water's natural fizz. This admission destroyed the perception Perrier had tried to foster that it bottled the product just as it came out of the earth.

Although the Mecklenburg discovery was the prodrome in this case, the conflicting statements of company officials greatly exacerbated the potential for the five major risks. A confusing series of statements and news conferences heightened the likelihood that the issue would escalate and that government and media attention would intensify. In this case, scrutiny would take on international dimensions. There was no question that the situation would interfere with the company's normal operations and the situation would hurt Perrier's image. It was unclear how much bottom-line profits would suffer.

Despite these risk factors and a bumbling response by top management,

---

[37]"Discovery in a Carolina County Lab: Perrier Taint," *The New York Times,* February 12, 1990, p. A18.

[38]A Ramirez, "Perrier Recall: How Damaging Is It?," *The New York Times,* February 13, 1990, p. D1.

this crisis did not turn into a disaster. There are several reasons Perrier's crisis had relatively minor consequences. Most important, no one was injured. The French government quickly reassured consumers that Perrier was safe. Food experts in the United States and abroad corroborated the company's safety assertions, noting that benzene occurs naturally in several foods.[39]

Other reasons were market related. As we saw in the other crises, the external direct quadrant of the stakeholder influence map is very important. Competition and diversification strongly affect how serious a particular crisis will become. At the time of the Perrier scare, Perrier water represented only 11 percent of Source Perrier's total sales. The company, which controlled 24 percent of the US bottled-water business, had spread its risk across brands very effectively.

The American bottled-water market was huge and growing. It included two price categories, both dominated by Perrier Group. The 2-billion-gallon low-priced market was sourced domestically and packaged for supermarkets and convenience stores. Poland Spring, one of Perrier's popular domestic subsidiary companies, charged less than $1 per gallon for noncarbonated water. Even Poland Spring's carbonated water was fairly cheap. Supermarkets charged about $1.10 for 64 ounces of this domestically produced carbonated water.

The foreign waters were usually packaged in much smaller units, and each unit or serving was much more expensive. Restaurants and bars charged almost the same price for a bottle of water that they charged for a glass of wine or a beer. For example, patrons paid about $2.50 for an 11-ounce bottle of Perrier. As the marketing manager for a competitor remarked, "People don't drink Perrier for drinking water . . . They buy it as an aperitif. You don't boil spaghetti in Perrier."[40]

Evian, the number two foreign-made water in the United States, sold one-third as much water as Perrier. Many observers predicted that none of Perrier's rivals would be able to move quickly enough to seriously hurt its market. John Trout, head of a marketing strategy firm, noted, "The bottled-water market tends to be like concrete . . . it just doesn't change dramatically."[41]

On February 27, Source Perrier announced the recall cost about $70 million and the company was beginning a worldwide reintroduction of newly labeled bottles. Experts confirmed there was no health hazard and the source was completely pure.

Interestingly, some American consumers filed lawsuits against Perrier charging fraud, misrepresentation, and racketeering. They asserted they had suffered economic harm by paying high prices for Perrier in the belief they

---

[39]"Perrier Expands North American Recall to Rest of Globe," *The Wall Street Journal,* February 15, 1990, p. B1.

[40]Ramirez, "Perrier Recall: How Damaging Is It?," p. D1.

[41]Ibid., p. D7.

were purchasing pure, unprocessed mineral water.[42] Eventually the lawsuits were dropped.

Perrier ran into some unexpected glitches as it planned its comeback in May 1990. The US Food and Drug Administration forced bottlers to drop the words "naturally sparkling" from the labels. New York State health officials concluded Perrier contained too much sodium to be labeled "sodium free."[43] Nevertheless, Perrier was not unduly worried. Americans seemed to have some concerns about benzene, but consumer surveys indicated that 84 percent of Perrier's US drinkers intended to buy the product when it became available. As *Fortune* pointed out, "Perrier's very problems underline the enormous inherent value of an established global brand."[44]

There is no doubt that Perrier had not developed the proactive policies necessary to avoid a public relations embarrassment. The company was not particularly effective in dealing with the crisis, but certain aspects of the situation worked against a catastrophe. As mentioned before, no one was physically harmed, and the contamination was limited to only a few units. The company had other brands that were not clearly identified with Perrier. Until the crisis was over, these brands filled supermarket shelf space normally allocated to Perrier. Bars and restaurants also offered Perrier-owned alternative brands.

It might be tempting to conclude there is no great benefit to being prepared and implementing expensive systems to identify risk factors before crises occur. After all, looking at Perrier, one could argue that the company did not suffer greatly despite top managers' fumbling explanations.

Crisis management consultants, however, agree that this view is short-sighted and wrong-headed. Companies should have teams and systems that are always ready to deal with the unexpected. Companies can never predict the eventual consequences. What if a US court *had* awarded damages to consumers charging Perrier with racketeering?

Perrier might have avoided the entire controversy had it heeded early warning flags, acted immediately to eliminate the problem, and been prepared to handle the media honestly and frankly.

Effective Crisis Management

As we have seen, effective crisis management is a skill that companies can and should acquire. All companies, regardless of size, eventually face unanticipated events. A company's survival may well depend on how effectively a particular crisis is managed. Sometimes poor or inadequate managerial

---

[42]A S Hayes and A D Marcus, "Lawsuit by Perrier Drinkers," *The Wall Street Journal,* February 26, 1990, p. B6.

[43]T R King, "For Perrier, New Woes Spring Up," *The Wall Street Journal,* April 26, 1990, p. B1.

[44]P Sellers, "Perrier Plots Its Comeback," *Fortune,* April 23, 1990, pp. 277–78.

oversight leads to a crisis. When events within the firm are not adequately monitored, internal problems may smolder for a long time before they explode into crises. Manville's asbestos crisis and Drexel Burnham Lambert's junk bond scandal are examples of these kinds of crises.

The Team Approach

Crisis consultant Robert Littlejohn suggests that effective crisis management "provides an organization with a systematic, orderly response to crisis situations."[45] This means companies should have mechanisms in place that "audit" or identify risk factors and prodromes. He recommends the six-step process in Exhibit 4–4.

Step 1: Design the organizational structure. In many cases, an effective crisis management system should adopt a matrix structure. This multiple reporting system allows a permanent crisis unit to quickly call on the expertise of different functional divisions. Its managers can tap the corporate skills most appropriate for handling a particular situation.

Step 2. Select the crisis team. In choosing personnel, the company should decide whether to compose the team of full-time or part-time participants. The team should be made up of senior executives, led by the CEO. The heads of the functional company divisions, including legal, financial,

---

[45]R F Littlejohn, *Crisis Management: A Team Approach* (New York: American Management Association, 1983), p. 11.

EXHIBIT 4–4

Crisis management model.

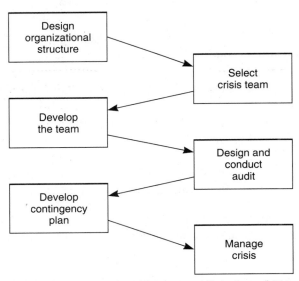

SOURCE: R F LittleJohn, *Crisis Management: A Team Approach* (New York: American Management Association, 1983), p. 14.

personnel, and operations, also should participate.[46] The company should also consider whether a problem requires top-, middle-, or lower-level managerial expertise. Finally, it should decide which additional functional divisions should be represented on a case-by-case basis.

Step 3. Develop the team. The crisis unit manager's task is to develop the unit into a cohesive and effective team. The team's major task is to handle the crisis so that day-to-day operations go on undisturbed. In the Drexel case, Fred Joseph adopted this model, but the crisis was so overwhelming that daily operations were deeply affected. In most cases, however, this model works well. The team leader should help the team analyze its goals, decide what role each member will take, and organize the process of handling the crisis.

Step 4. Design and conduct a crisis audit. The *crisis audit* is a data-gathering process that begins with considering the probability that a particular event will occur. It is imperative that the data be comprehensive and reliable. The audit also assesses the impact the event would have on the company.

Next, the team formulates priorities in the event of a crisis and integrates them into the organizational objectives. The company's goal is to *integrate* issues management and crisis management systems *before* a crisis actually occurs. The team must make sure crisis objectives facilitate the organization's goals at a minimum cost. Bottom-line considerations should be an extremely important but not overriding factor in determining crisis objectives. The CEO or top manager must approve the objectives and be ready to implement them if necessary.

Step 5. Develop a contingency plan. The contingency plan for managing the crisis consists of five steps:

1. *Introduction:* This is the overview of the situation. In the Exxon crisis, the introduction would have been a company statement announcing that the spill occurred and assessing its magnitude. The statement should identify the concerned parties and the major issues.

2. *Objectives:* The team manager articulates the plan's objectives as clearly and specifically as possible.

3. *Basic assumptions:* The team generates a list of realistic situations that the company cannot control but could cause major problems if they occurred.

4. *Trigger for action:* The trigger is an alarm mechanism that activates the plan. The mechanism should be carefully considered ahead of time so that once the plan swings into action, the corporate

---

[46]J Bernstein, "The 10 Steps of Crisis Management," *Security Management,* March 1990, p. 75.

response is measured and incremental. The plan should be tested to ensure that it really works. Had Exxon tested its containment plan prior to the spill, the incident might have been trivial.

5. *Action:* The team implements the plan.

Step 6: Managing the crisis. Should the CEO always take over crisis management? That depends on the seriousness of the situation and the importance the crisis team attaches to events. It is useful for the team to place priorities on the crisis issues. The team should work toward determining whether the crisis represents a significant threat to the organization as a whole. If a threat to the organization exists, the CEO must participate fully in resolving the situation.[47] If not, lower-level executives can handle the problem.

Crises and the Media	Throughout this chapter, we have discussed the dangers media attention poses to a company in crisis. The Dow Corning, Manville, Drexel, and Exxon cases demonstrate the importance of the media to the outcome of a crisis. Media often become the most important players in the external indirect quadrant of the stakeholder influence map and can greatly influence other stakeholder groups' perceptions of crisis events.

As we pointed out, major crises nearly always require the involvement of the CEO or a high-level spokesperson. Perceptions of the company will be determined by the dexterity and expertise with which this person handles the press and television reporters—and a company spokesperson can count on facing television reporters within minutes of a breaking story.

Few people will forget the televised spectacle of Warren Anderson, chairperson of Union Carbide, dashing to India to handle the Bhopal tragedy. He was mobbed, arrested, and put in jail at a time when the company needed him to assert control. Crisis management experts agree that Anderson would have been far more effective by controlling events at headquarters until he had carefully assessed the magnitude of the tragedy. He would have avoided being seen as undignified, out of touch with headquarters, and a hostage to foreign interests.

Exxon's Lawrence Rawl, on the other hand, might have been more effective had he spoken from the scene in Alaska. Many people recall Exxon's April 3, 1988, belated advertisement responding to the disaster. Rawl signed a paid statement titled "An Open Letter to the Public." He noted that the tanker had lost 240,000 barrels of oil, but asserted:

> We believe that Exxon has moved swiftly and competently to minimize the effect this oil will have on the environment, fish, and other wildlife. Further, I

---

[47]Littlejohn, *Crisis Management: A Team Approach,* pp. 7–54.

hope you know we have already committed several hundred people to work on the cleanup . . . Finally, and most importantly, I want to tell you how sorry I am that this accident took place. We at Exxon are especially sympathetic to the residents of Valdez and the people of the State of Alaska . . . I can assure you that since March 24, the accident has been receiving our full attention and will continue to do so.[48]

The ad was carried on the same day television broadcasts showed the death struggles of birds and baby sea otters. Slicker-clad people roamed the beaches using rags to wipe oil off endless numbers of rocks. Rawl later appeared on "CBS This Morning" to tell the public it was not his job to know the technical aspects of the cleanup, and furthermore the Coast Guard and the government, not Exxon, were causing the delays. Most important, Rawl refused to take responsibility and admit Exxon had made mistakes that led to the disaster.

Stratford P Sherman suggests that CEOs and other spokespersons develop and stick to guidelines for handling the press. He observes that in many cases, the CEO should be responsible for press relations and should speak for the corporation. When the CEO does not speak, she should delegate real authority to the public relations spokesperson. The cardinal rule of press relations is that the CEO or surrogate should be truthful. Sherman says if the company has made a mistake, it should not try to hide it and should never lie.

Jonathan Bernstein recommends that every spokesperson be professionally trained in media relations. He suggests that companies contact their local chapter of the Public Relations Society of America or the International Association of Business Communicators.[49] These organizations offer expertise and training.

In *advance* of crisis, Sherman advises companies to get to know reporters who write stories about them. They should educate the reporters and give them reasons to respect the company and its management. Robert Dilenschneider, CEO of Hill and Knowlton, concurs. He advises companies to talk to the press *after* a crisis is over and ask how they could have handled it better.[50]

In general, the spokesperson should be very wary of presenting views on television unless the presentation can be done in organized, carefully worded, 10-second sound bites. A few notable exceptions to this rule exist. Johnson & Johnson used television brilliantly in the Tylenol situation. The chairperson appeared on the "Phil Donahue Show" and also allowed Mike Wallace and "60 Minutes" to tape a strategy session. When the "60 Min-

---

[48]L Rawl, "An Open Letter to the Public," *The Boston Globe,* April 3, 1988, p. 18.

[49]J Bernstein, "The 10 Steps of Crisis Management," p. 75.

[50]"The King of Public Relations Talks Damage Control," *Business Marketing,* September, 1990, p. 86–87.

utes" segment aired in December 1982, the public's response was overwhelmingly positive.[51]

Companies should ensure that their side of the story gets reported. They should not appear before the media and then stonewall. That tactic forces reporters to go to less sympathetic sources for their information. It is wise to make distinctions among the different media and among publications within one medium. Some newspapers, magazines, and television reporters have particular biases, and a small number of reporters should not be cultivated or trusted. However, most reporters are neither friends nor enemies. They simply convey information to the public. Sometimes the company will be portrayed favorably, and sometimes it won't.[52]

Summary

More and more frequently, companies have to deal with crises that can have catastrophic consequences for them and their stakeholders. The eventual outcome of a crisis may rest heavily on stakeholders' perceptions of the company's culpability and on the public response by its top management. Exxon management's inept response to the grounding of the *Valdez* points out the importance of implementing crisis management systems before the problem occurs.

Crisis evolve through three basic stages. During the first period, the precrisis or prodromal stage, companies should be aware of the five major risks. Often potential crises can be avoided if these warnings are heeded. If the situation goes unremedied, the second stage—the crisis stage—occurs, at which point it is too late to avoid public scrutiny. In the third, or postcrisis stage lawsuits, government intervention, and monetary losses may threaten the company's survival. In all these stages, management has some control over how events will unfold. The degree of control is tied to the strength of stakeholders in each quadrant of the stakeholder influence map.

Companies can put in place systems to enhance the chances that they will recover from their crises and minimize financial consequences. A six-step team approach helps a company meet a crisis in an orderly and systematic way.

Expert media management often makes the difference between a successful presentation of the company's position and a bumbling, damaging interaction. All companies should train spokespeople to discriminate among media, learn presentation techniques, and maximize the likelihood that the company's activities will be shown in the best possible light.

---

[51]Mitchell Leen, "Tylenol Fights Back," *Public Relations Journal,* March, 1989, pp. 10–12.

[52]S P Sherman, "Smart Ways to Handle the Press," *Fortune,* June 19, 1989, pp. 69–75.

Questions

1. What are differences between issues management and crisis management?
2. What are the three stages of a crisis?
3. Discuss the five risk factors that signal a potential crisis.
4. What steps can companies take to handle potential crises? Which organizational structures are most effective in dealing with crisis management?
5. Should companies deliberately foster relationships with media representatives? If so, what kinds of interactions are most appropriate?

BETA CASE 4
CRISIS MANAGEMENT

Don Drees and Brian Madison stowed their garment bags in the airplane's overhead compartment, buckled their seat belts, and gratefully accepted the flight attendant's offer of orange juice. They were on their way to a meeting of top managers of major pharmaceutical firms in Seattle. As the plane sat on the runway, heat shimmered off the cement, making the cabin uncomfortably warm. Drees and Madison agreed they would rather have been almost anywhere else this sticky July morning.

Yesterday's events had put them both into a thoroughly irritable frame of mind. Their moods did not improve as they scanned their *Wall Street Journals*. The lead article in the second section reported on yesterday's charges by a consumer advocate group. Dr. Hayes Adams, president of Citizens for Informed Healthcare (CFIH), asked Dr. David Kessler, the commissioner of the Food and Drug Administration (FDA), to open an immediate investigation of Beta.

Adams charged that Beta had criminally withheld crucial safety data about its anesthetic drug, Beltane. Adams told *The Wall Street Journal,* "If justice prevails, the investigation will result in the criminal conviction of Beta for violation of the laws concerning the timely reporting to the FDA of drug safety problems."

He referred to a memorandum from two doctors in Wisconsin who wrote they were no longer using the drug because they could not easily control the dose they gave their patients. "In some cases," they wrote, "we have found that the initial strength allowed oversedation too easily."

Beltane had been approved for marketing in 1987 as an injectable anesthetic. Surgeons and dentists used Beltane for uncomfortable procedures like gum surgery and bronchoscopy. Patients under the anesthetic were not really unconscious; rather, they were in a sort of "twilight sleep."

Drees and Madison were aware that some doctors saw problems in Beltane's concentration levels. Since the drug was used for "conscious sedation" in the doctor's office, an anethesiologist usually was not present. In a few cases, doctors and dentists reported that patients had gone into cardiac arrest and could not be resuscitated.

When these reports started coming in a year earlier, Joan McCarthy had issued a statement that Beta had every reason to believe the drug was safe and that its concentration levels were appropriate for its use. McCarthy denied any direct causality links between Beltane and the deaths. She noted that the drug had passed all of the FDA's clinical and safety tests.

Today's headlines presented a different and much more serious problem, Drees and Madison concluded. The newspaper attention was potentially very harmful. Even worse was Adams's assertion that Beta had suppressed internal documents acknowledging the problem. Although they knew the leaked memo had come from a disgruntled employee who had been fired for incompetence, they were really worried. What response should Beta make to this latest charge? They had to have their strategy in place by the time they arrived in Seattle.

5

ETHICS

Of the myriad decisions managers make every day, decisions involving ethical issues are often among the most difficult and puzzling. As we noted in Chapter 2, the firm is a microculture operating in a social environment within a national culture or macroculture. The macro- and microcultures can follow different ethical standards.

Each firm or organization has a distinctive internal microculture. In one country, and even in one city, companies in the same industry have different ideas of what constitutes ethical behavior. One firm may allow its buyers to accept personal gifts from suppliers, while another strongly prohibits such behavior.

Some companies consider it ethical to make products they know are shoddy or potentially harmful as long as those products are profitable and meet legal requirements. Other companies refuse to manufacture such products. Some companies consider only legal standards. In the personal care products industry, for example, some companies allow testing on animals; other companies consider animal testing unethical, even though it is legal.

Macrocultures, combined with managers' unique personal sets of values, create the ethical and legal contexts for decision making. Each macroculture has its own norms and values concerning right and wrong. The concepts of fairness, honesty, truth, and proper behavior vary from region to region and from country to country. Likewise, various cultures impose different legal sanctions and penalties on companies that violate ethical standards.

For example, in some countries the highest ethical imperative is to ensure that every member of one's extended family has a job, regardless of those individuals' abilities. In another culture, hiring one's relatives is considered nepotism and is unethical, if not illegal. Within each macroculture are subcultures of religion, family tradition, and ethnic origin that further define an individual's values, beliefs, and behavior.

CASE   *Phar-Mor Inc.*

In 1981, Michael Monus was vice president of Tamarkin Company, a family-owned grocery chain and distribution company. The same year the Shapira family, owners of Giant Eagle Inc., bought Tamarkin. Giant Eagle, headquartered in Pittsburgh, was a 50-store supermarket chain with sales of $1.5 billion.

David Shapira and Michael Monus decided to develop a chain of discount drug-stores using Giant Eagle to bankroll the enterprise. In exchange for backing the project, Giant Eagle received 50 percent of the action. By 1987, Phar-Mor had 68 stores. In July 1992, the company opened store number 300 and its sales reached $3 billion. The huge Phar-Mor stores sold clothing, office supplies, and automotive parts in addition to drugstore items.

On the surface, Phar-Mor was a phenomenally successful venture. But under-neath, this enterprise was in desperate trouble. During the decade of Phar-Mor's growth, few investors questioned the actions of president "Mickey" Monus, chief executive officer David Shapira, or chief financial officer Patrick B Finn. In July 1992, Shapira accused Monus, Finn, and several other executives of planning a three-year, $350 million fraud scheme designed to embezzle $10 million in cash and overvalue the company's inventory and earnings. Monus was fired and promptly disappeared.

As investigators discovered, Monus had other passions that had nothing to do with drugstores. In 1987, Monus cofounded and retained 60 percent of the World Basketball League. Two years later, he sponsored two golf tournaments that cost more than $1 million a year. In 1990, he invested in the Colorado Rockies baseball team. Monus's plan was to package the sports events through a teleproductions com-pany in which he was a partner. The World Basketball League was the greatest finan-cial drain. According to Shapira, Monus had funneled at least $10 million from Phar-Mor into the losing WBL.

Monus had other money worries too. In 1989, he invested in the Canadian-based One-Stop Battery, Inc. That company's US operations went into Chapter 11 bankruptcy in December 1991. Phar-Mor itself also had financial problems. The company lost money in 1984 and 1985 and never cleared more than $1.4 million a year over the next three years. In June 1991, Corporate Partners, a Lazard Frères fund, paid $100 million for 17 percent of Phar-Mor. In October, the company pri-vately sold $112 million more of its stock. At about the same time, Phar-Mor raised its revolving credit to $600 million.

Shapira made his accusation in July 1992 only because he was tipped off to the fraud-embezzlement scheme. But why didn't outside investors, members of the board of directors, or the outside auditor, Coopers & Lybrand, exercise oversight? Coopers & Lybrand rejected any blame, maintaining that Phar-Mor executives had falsified financial statements. But there was much more going on than Coopers & Lybrand uncovered.

In September 1992, Phar-Mor filed for Chapter 11 and told its creditors it was closing stores and getting rid of unprofitable products. Antonio Alvarez, a New York turnaround specialist, was named as acting chief financial officer in September 1992. He argued for an immediate $50 million cash transfusion and made a commitment to stay with the company for three years in exchange for a $900,000 salary and an equity stake in Phar-Mor if it emerged from Chapter 11.

The Phar-Mor scandal promises to drag on for years as investors, suppliers, auditors, and principals trade charges and countercharges. In November 1992, a supplier, Corporate Partners, filed suit against Coopers & Lybrand, Shapira, and Giant Eagle Inc. Corporate Partners charged that Coopers & Lybrand had violated generally accepted accounting principles and sought $200 million as well as punitive damages. Corporate Partners further charged Shapira and Giant Eagle with providing false information about Phar-Mor's financial condition.[1]

Questions

1. What are the ethical, as well as the legal, responsibilities of outside directors?
2. Should someone have monitored Monus's sports activities? Should someone have asked from where Monus was getting his capital? Should any action have been taken if it became clear he was losing large sums of money? Who or what body was responsible for oversight?
3. What responsibility, if any, did Coopers & Lybrand have in uncovering the fraud?

The Ethics Debate

Beginning in the early 1960s, the historical ideologies of free market, supply and demand, and profit maximization discussed in Chapter 6 were no longer sufficient guidelines for managers. Business ethics became a major issue in the mid-1960s when Ralph Nader's book *Unsafe at any Speed* was published. Nader accused General Motors of knowingly developing and selling a poorly designed and dangerous car.

The 1970s brought a new scrutiny of US corporate activities. Dominant issues during that decade were foreign bribery, employment discrimination, false advertising, and pollution. When American companies were caught paying huge bribes to foreign political parties and officials, Congress passed the Foreign Corrupt Practices Act. Congress also responded to the Arab boycott of US firms doing business with Israel by passing the Antiboycott Bill.

In the 1970s, environmental issues came to the fore with the Love Canal problem. Hooker Chemical Company had dumped its toxic waste into the canal for a decade beginning in the mid-1940s. The City of Niagara Falls purchased the land from Hooker for $1 in 1953. Despite Hooker's warning

---

[1]"A Scandal Waiting to Happen," *Business Week,* August 24, 1992, pp. 32–33; G Stern, "Phar-Mor Inc. Is Considering Closing Stores," *The Wall Street Journal,* September 2, 1992, p. A3; G Stern, "Phar-Mor Cleared to Use $50 Million of Bankers' Collateral to Cover Costs," *The Wall Street Journal,* August 19, 1992, p. A5; K N Gilpin, "Specialist in Turnarounds Is Named to Run Phar-Mor," *The New York Times,* September 17, 1992; G Stern, "Fund Files Suit over Problems at Phar-Mor," *The Wall Street Journal,* November 2, 1992, p. B3.

about chemical contamination, the city subsequently built a school and subdivided the rest of the land into housing and shopping center plots. Throughout the 1970s, rains accelerated erosion and the chemicals oozed to the surface. By 1979, the community had suffered an unusually high percentage of health problems. On May 21, 1980, President Jimmy Carter signed an emergency order that forced families living on the Love Canal to abandon their homes.[2]

Who was responsible for telling residents the area was contaminated? Did Hooker Chemical Company do everything possible to warn residents and developers? Did the Niagara Falls board of education act ethically in building a school on the land despite warnings of contamination?

In the early 1980s, Ford came under attack for its handling of the Pinto issue. Pinto gas tanks were found to explode when the cars were hit from behind. Ford denied any wrongdoing, but there was compelling evidence that the company knew of the problem and did nothing to remedy it. In addition to product safety, occupational health and safety and corporate governance were added to the list of ethical issues during the 1980s.

In the 1990s, issues concerning business ethics centered around the environment, privacy, and financial governance. The public outcry against corporate crime, which increased dramatically in the 1980s, continues to be an important topic in the 1990s. Such acts have made citizens intensely skeptical about the ethical standards and behavior of corporations and their managers.

In 1991, at least 20 companies traded on national stock exchanges disclosed serious problems in their past financial statements. The research service, Securities Class Action Alert, reported it had seen a substantial rise in lawsuits charging "significant fraud and failures to disclose losses or poor earnings." Fraud cases seemed to increase when a strong stock market combined with a weak economy. Investors, especially institutional investors, bid up the stock of those companies that appeared financially sound and predicted strong performance. It was therefore very tempting for a financially shaky or poorly performing company to hide its weaknesses.

Richard C Breeden, chairperson of the Securities and Exchange Commission, suggested that moral standards were slipping. He said, "I think it's partly a function of the weakening of society's ethics . . . Less lying means less fraud."[3]

In the aftermath of the S&L debacle, the Drexel Burnham Lambert situation, the fraud by Phar-Mor executives, and other scandals, stakeholders questioned the ethical underpinnings of America's most powerful corpora-

[2]T S Mescon and G S Vozikis, "Hooker Chemical and the Love Canal," in W Michael and J M Moore, eds., *Business Ethics: Readings and Cases in Corporate Morality* (New York: McGraw-Hill, 1984), pp. 421–25.

[3]D B Henriques, "Falsifying Corporate Data Becomes the Fraud of the 90s," *The New York Times,* September 21, 1992, p. A1.

tions and industries and raised questions about corporate ethical performance. Multiple groups of stakeholders took different sides in each controversy.

For example, medical and pharmaceutical companies came under attack for exploiting the public by charging exorbitant prices for drugs. The companies defended their pricing structures, declaring they needed the profits to plow back into research. Patients blamed health care providers, drug companies, and the government for an inadequate safety net and high drug prices.

Environmental stakeholders argued that uncontrolled logging of Pacific Northwest forests was unethical. One group was concerned about the survival of the spotted owl. Another group protested the squandering of yew bark, the main ingredient in the cancer treatment drug Taxol. In election year 1992, Republican party pundits and forest industry stakeholders stressed the need to protect logging jobs at virtually any cost. The controversy became so explosive that President Bush told Northwest loggers that if Governor Clinton got elected, they would be up to their necks in owls but would have no jobs. Despite this prediction, Governor Clinton carried the states of Washington and Oregon in the November election.

When economic times are very bad, stakeholders begin to question whether society's basic institutions are working as they should. One question that goes to the heart of the business ethics issue is whether corporations themselves are *inherently* unethical. In the early 1990s, many believed moral and social standards in all societal institutions seemed drastically different than in earlier decades. Corporations were roundly criticized for inadequate ethical standards.

Craig P Dunn asks whether moral standards really have changed over time. Was once acceptable corporate behavior now unacceptable or even criminal? Do stakeholders believe corporate behavior today is fundamentally different than that in earlier times?[4]

Dunn concludes that the answers to these questions are to be found in analyzing the behavior of managers. He asserts that corporations themselves are morally neutral, but their structures may entice managers to set aside moral and ethical considerations. Dunn turns the ethics debate on the following observations:

> Because corporate [managers] have no clear burden for actions taken on behalf of the firm, corporate decision making seems to be devoid of any moral "flavor." . . . A radical rethinking of the basic charter of corporate governance is afoot . . . Corporations failing to institutionalize . . . changes, though hardly wicked in principle will nonetheless continue to promote wickedness in practice.[5]

---

[4]C P Dunn, "Are Corporations Inherently Wicked?," *Business Horizons* (July/August 1991), pp. 3–8.
[5]Ibid., p. 8.

Dunn notes that courts traditionally have been reluctant to punish corporations but in recent years have become more willing to press criminal charges against corporations and their top officers.

Clearly stakeholders do have higher expectations than in decades past. They receive more information about corporate activities and are more skeptical about corporate actions. All the major television networks produce investigative reporting shows for prime time viewing. For example, in December 1992, NBC's "Prime Time Live" reported that Wal-Mart's "Made in America" campaign was a sham. Most of its clothing, although advertised as American made, actually came from Asia. To make matters worse, child labor was used to sew many of the garments. Viewer response was so immediate and overwhemingly negative that Wal-Mart issued an immediate public apology and vowed to make its advertising more accurate.

In October 1992, *Time* ran a cover story on lying that revealed "a pervasive sense of moral moonscape where authority ought to reign."[6] Sissela Bok, author of *Lying: Moral Choice in Public and Private Life,* observes that "now there is something strange and peculiar; people take for granted that they can't trust the government."[7] The same cynicism applies to corporations and their management.

Fortune confirms these findings, noting that corporations are facing a new crisis in business ethics. Kenneth Labich attributes the "eruption" of questionable and even criminal corporate behavior to several factors. In his view, the causes of unethical behavior in the 1990s differ from those in the 1980s. Today's managers are not merely greedy; they are frightened of losing their jobs in an economic recession. They face a climate of increasing pressure to perform. For many managers, Labich says, inflating figures or fudging reports seems the only route to personal survival. Ethicist Michael Josephson reports his polls show that between 20 and 30 percent of middle managers have written deceptive internal reports.[8]

Ethics consultant Barbara Ley Toffler concludes the present corporate climate is extremely destructive. She says that because the effects are not immediately obvious, people rationalize their behavior. Eventually, however, "a kind of moral rot can set in."[9] People are frightened, and corporate innovation is stifled. But her view is not universally held—in fact, ethics is a hotly debated topic.

As the following section illustrates, the current business ethics debate rests on a variety of ideological arguments that has evolved over the past two decades.

---

[6]P Gray, "Lies, Lies, Lies," *Time,* October 5, 1992, p. 32.
[7]Ibid., p. 35.
[8]K Labich, "The New Crisis in Business Ethics," *Fortune,* April 20, 1992, p. 167.
[9]Ibid., p. 172.

Ideological Arguments

Stakeholders and managers have long debated what elements constitute corporate ethical behavior. All agree that business is an economic transaction, but they differ on the role values and ethics play in this transaction. This section explores some of the conflicting viewpoints.

Milton Friedman's perspective lies at one end of the spectrum. In his essay "The Social Responsibility of Business Is to Increase Its Profits," Friedman asserts that executives have the responsibility only to make a profit and to obey the law—that is their only ethical duty.[10]

Douglas S Sherwin acknowledges Friedman's perspective, but his view is more subtle and complex. He says owners, employees, and customers together form an interdependent system. Each of the three groups is essential to an enterprise's survival. Sherwin concludes that ensuring economic survival and profit in the short run is not management's only function, because long-run economic performance requires attention to the needs of all three groups.

Sherwin acknowledges that business is an economic transaction but points out that it cannot operate without values. Its values come from top managers, who must understand the concept of business as "a system of equal, necessary, and interdependent members." Profit, he says, is not the purpose of business. Rather, the purpose of business is equitable distribution of benefits and rewards to all stakeholders, because "if managers do not manage business as a system, some members of the system will reduce the values of their contributions, economic performance will suffer, and society's purpose for the business institution will be compromised."[11]

Ethics or moral principles help managers connect the purpose of business to the values business leaders should adopt. A top manager's individual cultural values and society's cultural values sometimes support and sometimes oppose each other. The underlying ethical duty of top management, according to Sherwin, is to join with other stakeholder leaders "to make public policy affecting business more reflective of the needs and desires of American society."[12]

In making a case for corporate social responsibility, Henry Mintzberg calls the Friedman argument "utterly false." In his view, one cannot make a tidy distinction between private economic goals and public social goals. When a large corporation makes an important decision to introduce a new

---

[10]W D Litzinger and T E Schaefer, "Business Ethics Bogeyman: The Perpetual Paradox," *Business Horizons* (March/April 1987), p. 18.

[11]D S Sherwin, "The Ethical Roots of the Business System," in *Contemporary Moral Controversies in Business,* ed. A P Iannone (New York: Oxford University Press, 1989), pp. 35–43.

[12]Ibid., pp. 35–43.

product line or close a division, it generates myriad social consequences. There is no such thing as a purely economic strategic decision in a large, divisionalized corporation.

But, Mintzberg warns, socially responsible behavior by business is not a solution to society's ills. Social responsibility has an important place alongside public policy to "tilt the efforts of a corporation toward what is useful to society, instead of what is useless or destructive."[13] Commitment and personal ethics are the bases for true corporate responsibility. Managerial ethics can raise the level of corporate responsibility and unlock the energy and ethics of the critical group of stakeholders—the employees.

John Dobson tries to reconcile the two apparently opposing points of view on the primary objective of business organization. He points out that corporate managers are taught that their first task is to maximize shareholder profit. At the same time, they are encouraged to adhere to statements on business ethics. These objectives are not *necessarily* in conflict. The two motivations can be reconciled by a company's desire to build and maintain its reputation. According to Dobson, a company's reputation is an implicit contractual enforcement mechanism built on four key characteristics:

1. A firm can have several reputations for different attributes.
2. A firm builds a reputation by demonstrating a consistent mode of behavior to its stakeholders (e.g., customers, creditors, shareholders, etc.).
3. The building or maintaining of a reputation can require net expenditures in the short-run, presumably in the expectation of net revenues in the long-run. Thus the decision whether to build or maintain a reputation at any time can essentially be viewed as a capital budgeting decision.
4. A firm's reputation can act as an implicit contractual enforcement mechanism: individuals may reject short-term opportunistic behavior in favor of actions which, albeit costly in the short-run, will be perceived as maximizing long run wealth through maintenance of their reputations.[15]

Other perspectives on ethics run the gamut from purely economic to purely social to purely individual concerns. For example, Peter Drucker observes that ethics is a private issue for each manager, who must make his or her own judgments.[16] Vernon R Loucks, Jr., CEO of Baxter Travenol, says ethics is a matter of trust related to the law and to moral codes of con-

---

[13]H Mintzberg, "The Case for Corporate Social Responsibility," in *Contemporary Moral Controversies in Business,* ed. A P Iannone (New York: Oxford University Press, 1989), p. 174.

[14]Ibid., p. 174.

[15]J Dobson, "Management Reputation: An Economic Solution to the Ethics Dilemma," *Business and Society* (Spring 1991), pp. 13–20.

[16]Ibid., p. 19.

duct. These moral codes affect *all* stakeholders of the firm, internal and external, direct and indirect.[17]

What guidelines, then, help managers make daily ethical decisions and create environments that are productive and understandable to employees and society? How does a corporation create and reinforce an ethical culture with clear standards? Who takes responsibility for creating the standards, culture, and environment? In the next section, we will explore these questions.

Ethics: Whose Responsibility?

We pointed out earlier that the macroculture creates the climate in which corporate microcultures operate. As the nation looked at the actions of some of its most influential political, corporate, and spiritual leaders during the late 1980s and early 1990s, there arose a collective uneasiness that direction and purpose had been lost.

Public opinion polls suggested the national character was "wallowing in a moral morass."[18] More than 100 members of the Reagan administration had ethical or legal charges filed against them under the 1978 Ethics in Government Act. Responsibility for ethical standards in business and government was shuffled among schools, government, and business. In a 1987 interview, President Reagan argued he was not to blame. "I am for morality," he declared. "In fact, I wish there was more of it taught in our schools."[19] But a *Time*/CNN poll conducted at the end of September 1992 found Americans had little faith in their leaders' morality and ethics. Seventy-five percent of those polled thought less honesty existed in government than a decade ago.[20] The central theme of the 1992 presidential election was which candidate told the fewest lies.

On December 24, 1992, President Bush pardoned six government officials who had been connected to secret missile shipments to Iran. His action led independent counsel Lawrence E Walsh to say, "it demonstrates that powerful people with powerful allies can commit serious crimes in high places—deliberately abusing the public trust without consequence."[21] President Bush's action led to intense media speculation that by pardoning all the actors in the affair, the president was ensuring that he would not be personally implicated.

[17]V R Loucks, Jr., "A CEO Looks at Ethics," *Business Horizons* (March/April 1987), pp. 3, 5.

[18]"Ethics: What's Wrong," *Time,* May 1987, p. 14.

[19]Ibid., p. 17.

[20]*Time,* October 5, 1992, p. 35.

[21]"Independent Counsel's Statement on the Pardons," *The New York Times,* December 22, 1992, p. A22.

Educating Managers in Business Ethics

Terence R Mitchell and William G Scott conclude that the most serious threat to American society is that corporate and political leaders abrogate their moral stewardship. They chronicle a litany of corporate debacles that illustrate the problem. The solution, they propose, lies in an intensive education program. They note that ethical and moral issues are usually treated as problems to be solved. Students are presented with ethical quandaries to be resolved through case analysis or role-playing exercises. In addition, faculty give lectures, guest speakers are invited to give their insights, and readings are assigned.

Mitchell and Scott conclude this approach is familiar to students and faculty, but it is ultimately unsatisfactory. The incorporation of ethics courses or modules is only a starting point, albeit an important one. Reform of business education must involve "a larger academic community." Major professional journals and professional associations should deal with moral philosophy. The function of ethics education should be "to instill an open, moral, loving, humane, and broadly informed mentality, so that students may come to see life's trials and business's ethical challenges as occasions to live through with integrity and courage."[22] Family, clergy, schools, and increasingly corporations are the institutions normally charged with imparting a national ethical code. As more parents work longer hours and fewer people attend organized religious services, schools and the workplace bear a heavier burden as the primary transmitters of the nation's ethical values.

Undergraduate and graduate business schools are taking on the initial responsibility of teaching business ethics to the country's prospective managers. However, educators and executives alike are realizing that to be effective, ethics education must be an ongoing process that does not stop when managers receive their academic degrees. Ethics education can become part of a corporate microculture that enhances a company's strategic advantage.

Although most corporate officers and business schools agree that ethics can and should be taught, they disagree about what the curriculum should be and who should teach it. John S R Shad, former ambassador to The Netherlands and former chairperson of the Securities and Exchange Commission, made some general observations about ethical attitudes and how business schools should respond. Shad noted it is not enough for professional schools to impart the fundamentals of law, business, medicine, and government: "The schools must hone their ability to certify that their graduates have the character and integrity to use the knowledge gained for the benefit—rather than the abuse—of society."[23]

---

[22]T R Mitchell and W G Scott, "America's Problems and Needed Reforms: Confronting the Ethic of Personal Advantage," *Academy of Management Executive 4*, no. 3 (1990), pp. 23–35.

[23]J S R Shad, "Business's Bottom Line: Ethics," *The Wall Street Journal,* July, 27, 1987, p. A19.

Shad made some specific suggestions for business schools. First, schools should use the admission process to keep out students who are "ethical misfits." Next, schools should develop cases with ethical components for use in every functional area, not for just a single course in ethics. The message Shad wanted to convey to students is:

· "Those who go for edges—like high rollers in Las Vegas—are eventually wiped out financially."

· As most successful individuals and companies demonstrate, the marketplace rewards quality, integrity, and ethical conduct. While quality, integrity, and ethical conduct are their own rewards, they also make good sense.

· In sum, ethics pays: It's smart to be ethical."[24] In a graphic example of "putting your money where your mouth is," Shad gave Harvard Business School $20 million to establish a program in ethics. The school responded to the challenge by designing and implementing a required ethics module for all incoming MBA students. Ethical issues are also raised and discussed in functional area courses.

An Academic Approach.   At the end of 1991, Harvard Business School tried to assess the value of its four-year-old ethics program. The program begins with a nine-session required module in the first semester of the MBA program. This module, called "Decision Making and Ethical Values" (DMEV), is designed to generate case discussion in all functional business areas.

Faculty from these areas team-teach in the three-week-long DMEV program. They examine the responsibility of management from three perspectives: (1) the purpose of corporations and the responsibility of managers and the ways these are shaped by political and social systems; (2) issues of leadership, concentrating on human relationships and the ethical climate managers create within corporations; and (3) basic questions about personal integrity and management.

Functional courses build on the DMEV and incorporate the discussion of ethical issues into case material for courses such as marketing, finance, accounting, manufacturing, organizational behavior, human resource management, and technology and operations management. Many faculty think the major achievement of the ethics initiative is encouraging classroom discussion of ethical issues. Harvard Business School reports "an increased awareness of the concepts of leadership, ethics, and corporate responsibility on the part of faculty and students . . . along with a new willingness to discuss them."[25]

Schools around the country are developing ethics modules and bringing the subject of ethics into course discussion. Over the past decade, case

---

[24]Ibid.
[25]"Ethics in the MBA Curriculum," *HBS Bulletin,* December 1991, pp. 42–52.

writers have had ample material on which to base ethical dilemmas. They are paying increasing attention to cultural diversity and national ethical standards. As universities have recruited increasing numbers of international students, the discussions have become more complex and richer for all participants. Ethical precepts that guide these students vary considerably. As all students struggle to find common intellectual ground, ethical issues provide a valuable focus for such discussion.

A Corporate Education Approach.   Susan J Harrington poses a number of questions about the impact of ethics education in the workplace.[26] She asks what corporations are trying to achieve with ethics training, who should receive it, what should courses include, and how executives can facilitate the effectiveness of the training.

Harrington notes that executives often link a strong ethical position with strategic advantage. Strategic issues such as human resource investment, modernization, product development, and executive salaries affect the firm's performance and bottom line. Harrington observes that companies face unforeseen threats and opportunities. By integrating an ethical perspective and ethical standards into long-term decision making, companies can avoid consequences that may adversely affect their bottom lines. She notes that 63 percent of Fortune 500 CEOs say strong ethics result in strategic advantage. Studies report that about 44 percent of companies offer some ethics training. Of that number, 53 percent use workshops and seminars as the educational vehicle. Managers receive most of the direct training, since they are the decision makers.

As with ethics training in academic institutions, the ultimate goal is to help participants—in this case, managers—avoid unethical behavior. Corporations try to develop employee awareness of ethics in business and to draw employees' attention to potentially pertinent ethical issues. An essential part of any ethics program is to emphasize commitment to ethical principles at all levels of the company and to develop procedures that reward ethical behavior and punish unethical behavior.[27]

Setting Standards for Ethical Behavior in Corporations

Business ethics are based on individual and collective moral decision making at every level at the corporation, from janitor to president. Standards for moral behavior are sometimes informal, but more often are explicit and embodied in a written document. Before a company can draw up a credo, design a code of ethics, or institute an ethics program, its managers must decide which ethical issues are important to them and how to identify and manage them.

---

[26]S J Harrington, "What Corporate America Is Teaching about Ethics," *Academy of Management Executive* 5, no. 1 (1991), pp. 21–30.
[27]Ibid.

In a widely read *Harvard Business Review* article, Laura L Nash suggests 12 questions top managers should pose in examining the ethics of a business decision.[28] She argues that these guidelines are a practical approach to considering the ethical dimensions of a decision.

Have You Defined the Problem Accurately?   Make sure you have a clear understanding of the problem. The more facts you collect and the more precise your use of those facts, the less emotional your approach will be.

How Would You Define the Problem if You Stood on the Other Side of the Fence?   This question demands that you look at the issue from the perspective of those who may question your ethics or those who are most likely to be adversely affected by your decision. Are you being objective?

How Did This Situation Occur?   Look into the history of the situation, and make certain you are dealing with the real problem rather than just a symptom. Doing so will help you gain perspective and contribute to your understanding of the views of others.

To Whom or What Do You Give Your Loyalties as a Person and as a Member of the Corporation?   Nash points out that "every executive faces conflicts of loyalty. The most familiar occasions pit private conscience and sense of duty against corporate policy. Equally frequent are situations in which one's close colleagues demand participation (tacit or implicit) in an operation or decision that runs counter to company policy."[29] Managers must ask themselves to whom or what they owe the greater loyalty.

One executive made his stand dramatically clear to subordinates. His predecessor, the head of a large division of a major corporation, had been jailed for price fixing. The new division head invited his four immediate subordinates to take a ride with him on his first day in the new job. He drove them to a vantage point from which they could see a nearby federal prison. He told them that if they ever felt any misguided sense of loyalty to the "good of the corporation" that might lead them to consider committing an illegal act, they should return to that spot in considering their decision.

What Is Your Intention in Making This Decision?   Ask yourself the simple question "Why am I really doing this?" If you are not comfortable with the answer, don't make the decision.

How Does This Intention Compare with the Likely Results?   Sometimes, despite the goodness of the intention, the results are likely to be harmful. Therefore, it is important to think through the probable outcome.

---

[28]L L Nash, "Ethics Without the Sermon," *Harvard Business Review 59* (November/December 1981), pp. 79–90.

[29]Ibid., p. 84.

Whom Could Your Decision or Action Injure?   Even if a product has a legitimate use, if it is likely to harm the consumer by falling into the wrong hands or being incorrectly used, managers should reconsider whether to produce and distribute the product. This issue is particularly difficult. Drain cleaner in the hands of a child can be lethal, but a "childproof cap" could prevent injury. An assault rifle, on the other hand, could theoretically be used for hunting, but it is more likely to be used by criminals. Thus, is it ethical to sell that rifle even if it is legal to do so?

Can You Discuss the Problem with Affected Stakeholders Before You Make a Decision?   If you are planning to close a plant, should you talk with affected workers and the community beforehand to help assess the consequences? If you are changing benefits packages, should you hold meetings to discuss the changes?

Are You Confident That Your Position Will Hold Up in the Long Run? Can you sustain the commitment you have made? Can you foresee conditions that are likely to make you change your mind? Will today's good decision be tomorrow's mistake?

Could You Disclose, without Qualm, Your Decision or Action to Your Boss, Your CEO, the Board of Directors, Your Family, or Society as a Whole? Arjay Miller, former president of Ford Motor Company and later dean of Stanford Business School, used to suggest the following public opinion test: "Ask yourself, would I feel comfortable in reporting my action on TV?" Decisions that seem very private and confidential often end up receiving full public disclosure.

What Is the Symbolic Potential of Your Action if Misunderstood?   The essence of this question is the issue of sincerity and others' perceptions of your action. Politicians campaigning for office engage in many symbolic acts to attract various voter groups. In the 1988, presidential campaign, for example, the Democratic candidate, Michael Dukakis, rode in a tank to appeal to the so-called "hawk" element of the electorate. George Bush, eager to attract conservationist groups, appeared in a variety of photos shot in park lands. In 1992, Bill Clinton and Al Gore took bus tours through Middle America. Their symbolic act seemed to attract voters.

However, such symbolic acts sometimes backfire, as they did in the 1988 campaign, and create more skepticism than goodwill. Corporate managers face the same problem. A CEO may hire a minority member to "sit near the door." But if she has not made a real commitment to providing opportunities for minorities, stakeholders are likely to greet the effort with cynicism.

Under What Conditions Would You Allow Exceptions to Your Stand?
Nash asks, What conflicting principles, circumstances, or time constraints
provide a morally acceptable basis for making an exception to one's normal
institutional ethos? For example, suppose you learn that a highly productive
and loyal office manager "borrowed" $250 and subsequently repaid that
amount to a petty cash fund. The company has a very strict policy against
personal use of company funds. The employee manual states clearly that
such actions will lead to immediate termination, without exception. What
would you do had the money been borrowed to pay emergency medical
bills? Would you act differently had the money been used to pay gambling
debts? What if the employee had been with the company only 18 months
instead of 12 years?

Benefits of Guidelines

The questions just raised help managers sort out their own perceptions of
ethical problems and provide various ways of thinking about them. The process of asking these questions facilitates group discussion about a subject
that has traditionally been reserved for the privacy of one's conscience. It
takes Drucker's position that ethics is a privately decided issue and moves it
into the public arena. The process:

· Builds understanding and consensus among managers. People from
different functional areas discover they share common problems. Raising
questions makes the company's values and goals explicit and an integral part
of determining corporate strategy.

· Encourages information sharing. Senior managers learn about other
parts of the company with which they may have little contact.

· Helps uncover ethical inconsistencies in the company's mission or
values statement or between those values and the company's strategy.

· Helps reveal sometimes dramatic disparities between the company's
values and their implementation. It helps the CEO understand how senior
managers think about and handle ethical problems. It helps the CEO assess
how willing and able senior managers are to deal with complexities. It also
reveals how individual managers' ethics and values interact with corporate
activity.

· Draws out individual managers' ethics and illuminates how they fit
into the corporate ethics system.

· Helps top management improve the nature and scope of alternative
strategies.

· Gives managers a chance to reduce stress and unload troublesome
problems.[30]

---

[30]Ibid., p. 88.

Ethics Credos, Programs, and Codes

In recent years, companies have developed credos, instituted corporate codes of conduct, and implemented ethics programs throughout the organization. Despite overwhelming evidence to the contrary, a 1992 *Industry Week* magazine poll reported that the ethical climate in American corporations is rising. Twenty-eight percent of respondents claimed business ethics were higher than they were in 1990. Over the past several years, more companies have written ethics codes, which may account for the belief that ethical standards are rising. Written codes may, in fact, lead to higher standards in practice.

Ethics Credos

A corporate *credo* is a short statement that delineates a company's values. Its objective is to provide a general set of principles and beliefs that give the company guidance. Gulf Oil's "Statement of Business Principles" (Exhibit 5–1) is one example of a credo or general approach to managing corporate ethics.

The Johnson & Johnson (J&J) credo (see Exhibit 2-3 on page 48) covers the essential issues for that company. When the Tylenol tragedy occurred, J&J managers based their response on the credo. The credo evolved from, and continues to influence, the J&J corporate culture. For 40 years the credo has been, as chairperson James Burke says, "the unifying force for our corporation . . . The Credo is our common denominator. It guides us in everything we do. It represents an attempt to codify what we can all agree upon since we have highly independent managers."[31]

In 1932 General Robert Wood Johnson, the son of J&J's founder, became the head of the company. He was convinced the company's highly centralized structure was counterproductive and broke up the company into several independent operating companies. The issue of independence is still very important at J&J. The company continues to be highly decentralized, and top management emphasizes individual autonomy and initiative. As this example shows, the concepts of decentralization and a strong set of commonly held values are compatible rather than contradictory.

General Johnson's personal belief in fair employee treatment, decentralization, and product quality were the essence of the document he formalized in 1945. The four central responsibilities of what was then called "An industrial Credo" were (1) customers, (2) employees, (3) communities in which they work and live, and (4) stockholders.

The J&J credo integrates profit and ethics. When reports of corporate misconduct proliferated in the 1970s, J&J's top managers discussed and

---

[31]Johnson & Johnson's Mission Statement, *Johnson & Johnson, 1982 Annual Report.*

EXHIBIT 5–1

*Gulf Oil's company
credo*

STATEMENT OF BUSINESS PRINCIPLES

Gulf will adhere rigorously to the highest ethical standards of business conduct. To this end the following specific principles are hereby confirmed as corporate policy, effective immediately, binding on all Gulf employees wherever located:

1. Gulf's business will be conducted in strict observance of both the letter and the spirit of the applicable law of the land wherever we operate.

2. Where a situation is not governed by statute—or where the law is unclear or conflicting—Gulf's business will be conducted in such a manner that we would be proud to have the full facts disclosed.

3. In case of doubt, employees should seek competent legal and other advice, which the Company is prepared to make available through regular channels.

4. Gulf reaffirms its conviction that in any democratic society proper and constructive participation in the political process is a continuing responsibility of individual citizens and groups of citizens, including Gulf employees and the Company itself. Such participation, however, must be in full accord with the regulations, laws, and generally accepted practice of the jurisdiction involved.

Strict adherence to the foregoing principles in hereby made a condition of continued employment.

rejected the idea of drawing up a more detailed code of ethics. Today most J&J managers report that the credo has a powerful influence on their decision making. It stands for day-to-day values.[32]

---

[32]J Keogh, ed., "Corporate Ethics: A Prime Business Asset," (New York: The Business Roundtable, 1988) pp. 1–138.

Ethics Programs

Ethics programs often provide more direction than credos do. More than 15 percent of US companies that employ 50,000 or more people have ethics offices that administer programs and maintain confidential hotlines. Most ethics offices and the programs they supervise were established because the companies faced public scandals or uncovered potentially explosive unethical behavior.

Nynex Corporation is one company with an active ethics program. Nynex was created with six other "Baby Bells" when American Telephone & Telegraph (AT&T) broke up in 1984. Within a few years, Nynex faced charges of graft, questionable financial transactions among its subsidiaries, and other troubling accusations. The company paid millions of dollars in penalties and generated very unfavorable publicity.

Finally, in 1990, Nynex's chairperson and CEO, William C Ferguson, set up an ethics office to help employees avoid mistakes and to channel complaints of misconduct. The office updated and standardized its ethics code, set up a hotline, and organized ethics seminars for managers. Senior officers took extensive training in ethics and then used videotapes and discussions to train their subordinates. Some subsidiary managers devoted part of their time to the promotion of ethical behavior in the firm. In the program's first year, the office handled 1,200 calls from employees and took 15 disciplinary actions.[33]

General Dynamics Corporation began its ethics program in 1985. Ethics officers had more than 30,000 contacts over the next six years. As a result, the company levied nearly 1,500 sanctions and fired 165 employees. A few cases were referred to public prosecutors for criminal action or to lawyers for civil lawsuits.

Pacific Bell (PacBell) was another AT&T spin-off. As at Nynex, the company's ethical climate turned stormy. Consumer groups filed suits charging PacBell with assigning phone numbers to companies that provided pornographic conversations to callers. They also charged PacBell used high-pressure tactics to load customers with expensive services and planned to sell lists of residential customers to direct marketers.

As part of PacBell's 1989 strategic business plan, the new president of the company made ethics his highest priority. His first initiative was to reevaluate the company's standards and practices. Next, PacBell established an ethics advisory council and ombudsperson's office. PacBell also decided to provide ethics training for more than 800 managers over the next year-and-a-half.

However, employees were confused about the purpose and function of the ombudsperson. An ombudsperson is "an official appointed to receive

---

[33]B J Feder, "Helping Corporate America Hew to the Line," *The New York Times,* November 3, 1991, p. E1.

and investigate complaints made by individuals against abuses or capricious acts of public officials."[34] An alternative definition is "one that investigates reported complaints (from students or consumers), reports findings, and helps to achieve equitable settlements."[35] Before the ombudsperson's appointment, disgruntled employees who wished to report fraud, waste, or abuse went to the Public Utilities Commission, the press, or elected officials rather than to company managers. The Bell culture did not support employees going over their bosses' heads. The new ombudsperson was a "safe" individual to whom employees could take grievances.

PacBell's ethics advisory council was composed of eight company officers and chaired by the executive vice president for external affairs. The council met six times a year but could be convened at other times as issues arose. It reported directly to the president on matters beyond the scope of the ombudsperson.

PacBell's top officers took part in a full-day off-site ethics seminar conducted by an ethics consultant. The officers used the J&J credo as a model for developing their own stakeholder principles. Eight hundred managers at the levels of district manager and above took two-day ethics seminars. The managers discussed "tools" for identifying and resolving ethical problems. After six weeks, the managers attended half-day follow-up sessions.[36]

The PacBell training program changed the way employees handled ethical issues. It also made top management far more responsible for dealing appropriately with employees' ethical dilemmas. Ethical issues that formerly had been tossed into the external indirect quadrant of the stakeholder influence map were now more likely to be resolved internally.

Ethics Codes

Ninety percent of Fortune 500 firms and nearly half of smaller firms have ethical codes or codes of conduct that provide specific guidance to employees in functional business areas. These documents clarify company expectations for employee conduct in a variety of situations. They also make it clear that the company expects its employees to recognize ethical issues in company policies and actions. Codes are generally considered the most effective way to encourage ethical conduct, but to work as their framers intend, they must be specifically tailored to the company's activities. The corporate culture and the specific nature of the company's business determine the exact statements to be included.

Norton Company, a diversified multinational industrial products manufacturer, began to draw up an explicit code of conduct in the mid-1970s.

---

[34] *Webster's New Collegiate Dictionary* (Springfield, MA: G & C Merriam Company, 1975), p. 800.

[35] Ibid.

[36] A Singer, "Pacific Bell: Dial E for Ethics," *Ethikos* (May/June 1990), pp. 4–7.

CEO Robert Cushman worked with the vice president of administration on what is now a 12-page document titled "The Norton Policy on Business Ethics." This code combines general guidelines with specific rules regarding legal compliance, responsibility to stakeholders, and the organizational process for ensuring that the standards are met.[37] Although it contains statements that are common to most codes, it specifically focuses on concerns unique to Norton.

Even before the code was written, the company had a highly developed, paternalistic set of policies toward employees. Framers found writing about employee issues fairly easy. Their most difficult task was to write and apply the code to indirect external stakeholders. It was particularly hard to delineate policies and programs dealing with operations abroad. They discussed and thrashed out positions on political contributions, gifts, favors, reporting procedures, grease payments, and antitrust.

General Code Contents   Ethics researchers examined 84 codes and clustered the categories of issues covered. Their results are shown in Table 5–1.[38] The majority of the issues fell into three major clusters. The first, "Be a dependable organization citizen," usually has very little to do with ethical conduct. Instead, statements from categories in this cluster exhort employees to be dependable and law abiding. An example from Bank of Boston's code tells employees, "Demonstrate courtesy, fairness, honesty, and decency in all relationships with customers, competitors, the general public, and with other employees." Codes of service organizations such as banks and utilities are represented heavily in this category.

Cluster 2 is titled "Don't do anything unlawful or improper that will harm the organization." Over 50 of the 84 companies' codes include statements in these categories. Statements in this cluster deal with obeying the law but go beyond it in categories dealing with bribery, confidentiality, and outside activities. Exxon Corporation's statement, for example, declares, "It is the policy of Exxon Corporation that all of its directors and employees shall, in carrying out their duties to the Corporation, rigidly comply with the antitrust laws of the United States and those of any other country or group of countries which are applicable to the Corporation's business." Hercules states categorically, "A payment is prohibited if: (A) It is illegal; (B) No record of its disbursement or receipt is entered into the accounting records of the Company; or (C) It is entered into the accounting records of the Company in a manner which is false or misleading."

The third cluster, "Be good to our customers," deals with ethical and legal behavior toward direct external stakeholders, namely customers. J C

---

[37]Ibid., pp. 115–30.

[38]D Robin, M Giallourakis, F R David, and T E Moritz, "A Different Look at Codes of Ethics," *Business Horizons* (January/February 1989), pp. 66–73.

TABLE 5-1 Clusters of Categories Found in Corporate Codes of Ethics

Cluster 1

"Be a dependable organization citizen."

1. Demonstrate courtesy, respect, honesty, and fairness in relationships with customers, suppliers, competitors, and other employees.
2. Comply with safety, health, and security regulations.
3. Do not use abusive language or actions.
4. Dress in businesslike attire.
5. Possession of firearms on company premises is prohibited.
6. Use of illegal drugs or alcohol on company premises is prohibited.
7. Follow directives from supervisors.
8. Be reliable in attendance and punctuality.
9. Manage personal finances in a manner consistent with employment by a fiduciary institution.

Cluster 2

"Don't do anything unlawful or improper that will harm the organization."

1. Maintain confidentiality of customer, employee, and corporate records and information.
2. Avoid outside activities that conflict with or impair the performance of duties.
3. Make decisions objectively without regard for friendship or personal gain.
4. The acceptance of any form of bribe is prohibited.
5. Payment to any person, business, political organization, or public official for unlawful or unauthorized purposes is prohibited.
6. Conduct personal and business dealings in compliance with all relevant laws, regulations, and policies.
7. Comply fully with antitrust laws and trade regulations.
8. Comply fully with accepted accounting rules and controls.
9. Do not provide false or misleading information to the corporation, its auditors, or a government agency.
10. Do not use company property or resources for personal benefit or any other improper purpose.
11. Each employee is personally accountable for company funds over which he or she has control.
12. Staff members should not have any interest in any competitor or supplier of the company unless such interest has been fully disclosed to the company.

Cluster 3

"Be good to our customers."

1. Strive to provide products and services of the highest quality.
2. Perform assigned duties to the best of your ability and in the best interest of the corporation, its shareholders, and its customers.
3. Convey true claims for products.

Unclustered Items

1. Exhibit standards of personal integrity and professional conduct.
2. Racial, ethnic, religious, or sexual harrassment is prohibited.
3. Report questionable, unethical, or illegal activities to your manager.
4. Seek opportunities to participate in community services and political activities.
5. Conserve resources and protect the quality of the environment in areas where the company operates.
6. Members of the corporation are not to recommend attorneys, accountants, insurance agents, stockbrokers, real estate agents, or similar individuals to customers.

Penney Company, for example, states that "advertising used by the Company is legally required to be true and not deceptive in any manner." Arizona Public Service Company goes beyond the letter of the law when it states that the company should "Manage our human, capital, and other resources to achieve excellence in service to our customers at the lowest attainable cost, consistent with reliability, quality, safety, and environmental standards."[39]

Employee Issues

Employees are expected to adhere to ethical standards and company ideals embodied in credos and codes and reinforced through programs. The degree to which employees do so depends largely on how the company treats them. Management creates a culture that represents an unwritten contract between the company and its employees. It also publishes written rules for behavior. That unwritten contract, along with the written rules, indicates the company's values, beliefs, behavior, and practices. In written documents and informal norms, it states management's expectations about the mutual obligations of employer and employee. When an employee is hired, he or she enters into a contract containing these mutual obligations.[40] For such contracts to be ethical, the company must meet four major requirements:

1. Both parties to the contract must have full knowledge of the nature of the agreement they are entering. Often gaps exist between what a company says in its policy and what it does on a daily basis. Despite good intentions, corporations may be unrealistic about their ability to deliver on their own expectations. In an economic downturn, they may be financially unable to carry out their stated policies. When companies change owners, as happened frequently throughout the 1980s, managers may have to deal with conflicting cultures that temporarily preclude full knowledge. Particularly in times of transition, managers may rely on their own imperfect interpretations of company values. Managers' assumptions about the new values may lead to situations in which actions are inconsistent with stated policies or are inequitable to employees.

2. Neither party to a contract may intentionally misrepresent the facts of the contractual situation to the other party.

3. Neither party to the contract can be forced to enter the contract under duress or coercion. This stipulation includes manipulation as well as threat. Some employees are skeptical about corporate values and the value of a contract and are unlikely to be susceptible to manipulation. Other employees have a strong need to belong and thus can be intimidated into behaving in a particular way. According to Manuel Velasquez, "Deception

---

[39]Ibid., pp. 67–73.

[40]B H Drake and E Drake, "Ethical and Legal Aspects of Managing Corporate Cultures," *Business and Society* (Winter 1988), pp. 109–10.

and manipulation are both attempts to get a person to do (or believe) something that the person would not do (or believe) if he or she knew what was going on."[41] Such agreements are not voluntary.

4. The contract must not bind the parties to an immoral act.[42] Any company that punishes an employee for whistle blowing or for voicing concerns over unethical practices acts unethically. In general, managers may not require employees to engage in immoral or unethical acts. On some occasions, however, employees go outside the company and expose issues that management has deliberately covered up.

Whistle Blowing. A *whistle blower* is an individual who discloses unlawful acts against the wishes of vested interests who seek to cover them up. The first legislation to protect whistle blowers was passed by the state of Michigan in 1981. The Whistle Blowers Protection Act covered any employee in private industry who was fired or disciplined for reporting alleged violations of federal, state, or local law to public authorities. If the employer could not show that treatment of the employee was based on proper personnel standards, the court had the power to award back pay, the costs of litigation, and attorneys' fees.[43]

This law came out of Michigan's PBB (polybrominated biphenyl) tragedy in the 1970s. Michigan Chemical Company accidently shipped poisonous fire retardant to a state feed grain cooperative. The PBBs were fed to livestock and contaminated their milk and meat. When farm animals began dying in large numbers, Michigan Chemical employees were warned not to tell investigators about the accident or they would be fired.

The number of instances of whistle blowing in both government and the private sector grew throughout the 1980s, and as it did, pressure for employee protection increased as well. Much of this pressure focused on new corporate grievance procedures and implementation of new internal policies. Historically courts were reluctant to meddle in what they saw as private contracts between employers and employees. With the precedence of the Michigan law, companies tried to ward off further legislation by voluntarily instituting due process for employees.

Lincoln Electric, Donnelley Mirrors, Pitney Bowes, Polaroid, and IBM pioneered this trend. By 1983, they had due process procedures in place. IBM, for example, created an "Open Door" program for employees who were unhappy about their bosses. An employee initiated the process by sending a message to the CEO. Within a week, a trained investigator interviewed

---

[41]M G Velasquez, *Business Ethics: Concepts and Cases* (Englewood Cliffs, NJ: Prentice-Hall, 1982), p. 332.

[42]E H Schein, *Organizational Cultures and Leadership* (San Francisco: Jossey-Bass, 1985), p. 9.

[43]A F Westin, "Michigan's Law to Protect Whistle Blowers," *The Wall Street Journal,* April 13, 1981.

those involved, operating on the assumption that the employee was right. Polaroid created an employee-elected committee to hear worker complaints. The committee members served for three years. Although their decisions were not binding, management usually adopted their recommendations.[44]

Some organizations still questioned employees right to publicly identify wrongdoers. In 1983, the National Association of Accountants drew up the first code of ethics for companies' internal accountants. The association urged employees to report improper behavior to superiors within the company. If the employee was legally required to report a practice to outside authorities, he or she should do so. However, the code suggested that if the law did not require whistle blowing and the wrongdoing was not corrected, the employee should resign. The president of the association, Charles T Smith, observed that "we cannot allow the minds of the public to be poisoned against business because a few businessmen are unethical."[45] In other words, the association believed its members' only obligation was that which the law required.

In 1986, Congress revised a Civil War era statute known as the False Claims Act. This law requires the Justice Department to investigate employee claims of fraud against the government. If the Justice Department finds substantial evidence of actions such as inflated billing or shifting cost overruns from one contract to another, an employee can earn as much as 30 percent of any damages awarded. Between 1986 and 1988, individuals filed more than 75 suits, mostly against defense contractors. In contrast, in the 1970s only 20 cases were filed.

Some companies questioned the legality of the act. Northrup, for example, asserted that Congress had violated the separation of powers provision of the Constitution by giving individuals the right to sue for fraud against the government. In 1987, two Northrup employees charged the company had falsified tests on its air-launched cruise missile. In July 1989, the government suspended its business with Northrup's Precision Products Division and agreed to help the plaintiffs litigate. In June 1991, Northrup finally agreed to pay about $9 million to the two former employees.

Despite Northrup's objections, use of the False Claims Act spread quickly to other industries. By 1991, suits alleging falsification of Medicare bills and environmental permits had been filed. Some likened the law to the Racketeer-Influenced and Corrupt Organizations Act (RICO) that acted as a "sword of Damocles" over Wall Street. *Business Week* speculated that

---

[44]D Warsh, "Employee Dissidents: Once a Rag-Tag Band, Now a Growing Army," *The Boston Globe,* January 4, 1983, pp. 45, 49.

[45]D B Hilder, "Accountants' Code Calls Whistle-Blowing Inappropriate Unless the Law Requires It," *The Wall Street Journal,* July 21, 1983, p. 6.

unless the Supreme Court ruled otherwise, the False Claims Act "would be to the 1990s what private securities cases were to the 1970s and RICO was to the 1980s."[46]

Regardless of the laws protecting whistle blowers, most employees will share the fate of A Ernest Fitzgerald, the Air Force cost analyst who blew the whistle on Lockheed's cost overruns. Fitzgerald spent 13 years in court before he won reinstatement in 1982. Whistle blowers usually lose their jobs and even their professions. Fitzgerald advises whistle blowers to think carefully before they pick up the whistle; he warns, "you just can't get away with throwing your body in the face of the juggernaut."[47] Companies' sanctions against whistle blowers do deter some employees from reporting wrongdoing. Others, however, are so outraged about a situation that their personal ethical codes demand action. In today's society, many whistle blowers become both victims and heros at the same time.

Some suggest the hero role should be emphasized. The Conference Board even proposes a model whistle blower policy that stresses a company's ethics system and makes employees believe that exposing internal wrongdoing is part of their job (see Table 5–2).

---

[46]T Smart with E Schine, "The 1893 Law That's Haunting Business," *Business Week,* January 21, 1991, p. 68.

[47]N R Kleinfield, "The Whistle Blowers' Morning After," *The New York Times,* November 9, 1986, pp. F1, F10.

TABLE 5–2 A Model Whistle Blower Policy

Shout It from the Rooftops.
Aggressively publicize a reporting policy that encourages employees to bring forward valid complaints of wrongdoing.

Face the Fear Factor.
Defuse fear by directing complaints to someone outside the whistle blower's chain of command.

Get Right on It.
An independent group, either in or out of the company, should investigate the complaint immediately.

Go Public.
Show employees that complaints are taken seriously by publicizing the outcome of investigations whenever possible.

SOURCE: L Driscoll, "A Better Way to Handle Whistle-Blowers: Let Them Speak," *Business Week,* July 27, 1992, p. 36.

Ethics in International Business

As noted earlier, countries and cultures have different standards of ethics and business practices. In fact, business ethics are becoming globalized very slowly. Unlike the United States, few countries impose their own cultures' ethical standards and practices on their corporations wherever their companies operate. The United States is an exception.

David Vogel notes, "the unusual visibility of issues of business ethics in the United States lies in the distinctive institutional, legal, social, and cultural context of the American business system. Moreover, the American approach to business ethics is also unique: it is more individualistic, legalistic, and universalistic than in other capitalist societies.[48]

In 1977, the US Congress passed the Foreign Corrupt Practices Act (FCPA). In effect, this act requires all publicly held US corporations to report to the Securities and Exchange Commission all payments of a substantial nature. This act specifically forbids American companies to make payments to foreign officials or political parties. It does allow small payments to individuals if such payments are a normal part of doing business. For example, a company may make an extra payment to a nighttime security guard above and beyond the person's salary if the salary structure for that position in that country is inadequate. This extra payment is a normal part of doing business in developing countries and is permissible under the FCPA.

US companies that violate the FCPA can be fined as much as $1 million. Executives may be sentenced to up to five years in jail and fined. Since the act was passed, US managers have complained bitterly that it places them at a competitive disadvantage in doing business abroad, where standards differ and bribery is commonplace. The reality is that the United States is the only country that forbids its companies from making payments to secure contracts outside its borders.

Bribery has a very different meaning and different consequences in Japan. The actions that constitute bribery in Japan are implicitly understood but poorly defined. The Japanese generally believe that whatever the group does is not only right but mandatory. The adage "a nail that sticks up gets pounded down" pervades every aspect of private life.

Although in 1982 Japan passed a bill making corporate payoffs illegal, the Japanese penchant for secrecy made it easy for corporations to circumvent the bill's restrictions. In the mid-1980s, there were reports that politicians, including Prime Minister Takeshita, had ties to organized crime families known as *yazuka.* Yazuka are involved in many illegal activities, from prostitution to gambling. *Sokaiya,* or gangsters who specialize in corporate crime, belong to or are associated with yazuka.

---

[48]D Vogel, "The Globalization of Business Ethics: Why America Remains Distinctive," *California Management Review* (Fall 1992), p. 30.

In Japan, sokaiya and their activities in politics and business are never discussed in public. However, they are so embedded as a part of Japanese corporate culture that a directory of several hundred sokaiya, listing names, addresses, and phone numbers, is readily available to companies. There is even a newsletter that provides details about sokaiya activities.

But in 1992, even the Japanese were stunned by revelations of corporate connections to organized crime. Officials of 22 of Japan's top companies were indicted for contributing to the sokaiya. Nomura Securities and Nikko Securities, for example, had loaned more than $200 million to a yazuka boss and then helped him manage a stock manipulation scheme. Nomura admitted a sokaiya had introduced the yazuka boss to a member of its board. Nevertheless, officials at the Tokyo Stock Exchange said the exchange had no policies on sokaiya and did not intend to conduct an investigation.

Sokaiya regularly manipulate stockholders' meetings. Secrecy and lack of managerial accountability tend to characterize Japanese corporate relations. In Japan, employees come first, then customers, then the government; shareholder interests come last or not at all. Unlike in corporation–stockholder relations in the United States, stockholders in Japan are not supposed to question management, because doing so will humiliate the company. An annual meeting that goes on for more than an hour is an embarrassment. In fact, the average annual meeting in Japan lasts less than 30 minutes.

Some sokaiya force publicity-averse executives to pay or be challenged at the stockholder meetings. In other cases, the company hires sokaiya to shout down questions from dissident shareholders. Some sokaiya are so adept at their business that they act as intermediaries between companies, much as lawyers do in the United States.

Because cultural expectations in the United States and Japan differ so sharply, the legal and ethical standards also differ greatly, as they do among all countries. However, some ethicists think there is a philosophical middle ground on which multinationals can and should stand, regardless of their countries of origin.

Multinational Corporations

Multinational corporations are a tremendously powerful force in today's global business environment. All of the largest 100 companies in the world are multinationals. Some of them have yearly earnings that surpass the GNPs of developing countries. Multinationals diversify their political and economic risk by expanding operations across the globe. They facilitate their search for lower-cost labor and natural resources by linking their subsidiaries with highly sophisticated technology and communications. Environmentalists and ethicists are paying increasing attention to the immense market power of these corporations. Stakeholders and others acknowledge that different countries have their own laws and customs that create unique national ethical environments for business. Nevertheless, they conclude that ethics transcend national boundaries and that managers in multinational corporations must try to develop and adhere to a global norm.

During the 1980s, US multinationals began to adopt the view that their ethics programs should cover corporate activities wherever those activities took place. The Bhopal incident, insider trading scandals, the controversy surrounding South African investment, toxic waste dumping in developing countries, and a host of other ethical issues all drew media attention. The impetus grew to develop global codes of ethics that addressed the rights of host country nationals. Thomas Donaldson looks at international ethics from this perspective and argues that multinational corporations must honor certain fundamental rights of citizens in whose countries they operate even if they are not required to do so (see Table 5–3).[49]

Who bears the responsibility for developing and implementing these basic rights? Is it the responsibility of corporate managers, shareholders, environmental activists, the US government, or multinational agreements such as the General Agreement on Tariffs and Trade (GATT)?

Karen Springen notes that codes are being developed to cover an increasing number of activities. Between 1989 and 1992, new codes were developed to cover everything from the environment to Mexican factories called *maquiladoras.* Springen suggests this proliferation reflects business's desire to police itself before the government gets involved. As we will see in

---

[49]J Sterngold, "Corporate Japan's Unholy Allies," *The New York Times,* December 6, 1992, pp. F1, F6.

TABLE 5-3   Citizens' International Rights

1. **The right to nondiscriminatory treatment.** Multinational corporations have a double obligation. It is not sufficient to refrain from discrimination in hiring or firing on the basis of sex, race, caste, or religion, or family affiliation. MNCs should go beyond that to establish procedures that protect the right to nondiscriminatory treatment and should make sure that lower-level managers adhere to reward or penalty systems based only on performance.
2. **The right to physical security.** Multinational corporations should provide safety equipment and safe procedures regardless of the stipulations of local law.
3. **The right to free speech and association.** Multinationals have an obligation to allow discussion about labor organization and association.
4. **The right of education.** Children are entitled to minimal education. In countries where MNCs use child labor, the company should not hinder a child's access to learning how to read and write.
5. **The right to subsistence.** A MNC should not become involved in activities that would result in people leaving land they need for growing food.

SOURCE: T Donaldson, *The Ethics of International Business* (New York: Oxford University Press, 1989), pp. 81–89.

the chapters on regulation, this view is consistent with corporate involvement in developing regulation.

These codes must take a "carrot-and-stick" approach. Since compliance is voluntary, companies must see that codes bring them benefits. There must also be a stiff public relations penalty for failure to observe a particular code. One of the best-known environmental codes is the Valdez Principles, discussed next.[50]

The Valdez Principles

In the aftermath of the Exxon *Valdez* disaster, stakeholders such as environmental groups, consumers, investment groups, individual shareholders, pension fund holders, and others pressured corporations to adopt principles of sound, ethical environmental management. Sanyal and Neves point out that these principles were modeled on the Sullivan Principles, which urged American firms to make workplace changes in their South African subsidiaries.[51] The underlying concept of the Sullivan Principles was to raise public awareness of the social and moral dimensions of apartheid.

The Valdez and Sullivan Principles had different targets. The Valdez Principles (see Table 5–4) applied to the environmental policies of firms worldwide; the Sullivan Principles applied only to US multinationals' treatment of South African host country employees. Unlike the Sullivan Principles, the 10 Valdez Principles did not establish specific standards or rewards and punishments.[52]

The framers of the Valdez Principles hoped to increase corporate awareness of the environment and raise ethical standards of environmental management. A group called the Coalition for Environmentally Responsible Economics (CERES) was formulated to administer the principles.

The impact these principles will have on corporate behavior is unclear. By the beginning of 1992, only 29 companies had signed the principles. Those companies included Aveda Corporation in Minneapolis; Domino's Pizza in Ann Arbor Michigan; and Stoneyfield Yoghurt in Londonderry, New Hampshire. Fortune 500 companies have been wary of signing a document that requires them to restore the environment and compensate people adversely affected.

However, companies that sign this or other codes of conduct may reap public relations dividends. As regional trade areas such as the newly signed North American Free Trade Agreement are implemented, companies may

---

[50]K Springen, "Codes to Live By," *Business Ethics* (January/February 1992), pp. 14–15.
[51]R N Sanyal and J S Neves, "The Valdez Principles: Implications for Corporate Social Responsibility," *Journal of Business Ethics* 10 (1991), pp. 883–90.
[52]Ibid.

TABLE 5-4   The Valdez Principles

---

1. **Protection of the iosphere.** Minimize the release of pollutants that may cause environmental damage.
2. **Sustainable use of natural resources.** Conserve nonrenewable natural resources through efficient use and careful planning.
3. **Reduction and disposal of waste.** Minimize the creation of waste, especially hazardous waste, and dispose of such materials in a safe, responsible manner.
4. **Wise use of energy.** Make every effort to use environmentally safe and sustainable energy sources to meet operating requirements.
5. **Risk reduction.** Diminish environmental, health, and safety risks to employees and surrounding communities.
6. **Marketing of safe products and services.** Sell products that minimize adverse environmental impact and that are safe for consumers.
7. **Damage compensation.** Accept responsibility for any harm the company causes to the environment; conduct bioremediation, and compensate affected parties.
8. **Disclosure of environmental incidents.** Public dissemination of incidents relating to operations that harm the environment or pose health or safety hazards.
9. **Environmental directors.** Appoint at least one board member who is qualified to represent environmental interests; create a position of vice president for environmental affairs.
10. **Assessment and annual audit.** Produce and publicize each year a self-evaluation of progress toward implementing the principles and meeting all applicable laws and regulations worldwide. Environmental audits will also be produced annually and distributed to the public.

SOURCE: K Sternberg, "New Pressure for Good Conduct," *Chemicalweek,* September 20, 1989, p. 23.

---

be encouraged to sign codes such as the Maquiladora Standards of Conduct. The act of signing communicates concern for the environment to every stakeholder group and encourages responsible environmental behavior by employees.

The AFL-CIO, Friends of the Earth, the YMCA, and more than 70 additional organizations forged a Coalition for Justice in the Maquiladoras. These principles ask American businesses in Mexico to comply with both US and Mexican environmental regulations. The coalition also wants corporations to maintain safe workplaces, pay fair wages, and develop communities in which their plants are located. Obviously each of these stakeholders has a somewhat different concern. The AFL-CIO wants to keep US workers competitive with lower-paid workers in Mexico, Friends of the Earth is concerned primarily with a clean environment, and the YMCA aims at fostering community activism.

As international ethics codes and principles become more numerous, companies may feel overly constrained by multiple, possibly conflicting demands. Multinationals are bound to think their degrees of freedom are reduced and the attractions of foreign markets, labor, and resources are diminished by the need to adhere to multiple, economically unrealistic codes. Yet stakeholder demands for ethical behavior are likely to keep increasing.

Summary

Business ethics are part of a country's social environment. Both macro- and microcultures determine the form ethical behavior will take. In the United States, there is an ongoing debate about what constitutes ethical behavior. Opinions range from solely economic to purely noneconomic concerns.

With the diminished role of the family and religious institutions, the transmittal of ethics and ethical behavior has been left largely to academic institutions. However, academics agree very little on how to carry out this effort or even on what guidelines they themselves should follow.

Managers should address several important questions before they try to design ethical credos, codes, or programs. These questions include defining a problem, determining how the problem occurred, examining internal company loyalties, finding out who will be affected by decisions, and assessing whether management can stick to a decision once it is made.

Each company selects its own approach to dealing with ethics. Most companies select some form of credo, code, or program to give structure to the firm's ethical climate. Each firm should rely on its own corporate history, leadership, and culture as it undertakes this task.

The employee is perhaps the most important stakeholder in the ethics implementation process. A company must treat its employees in an ethical manner on a daily basis, or its ethics programs will fail. In some cases, the implicit contract between firm and employee is broken and the employee becomes a whistle blower. Although whistle blowers are legally protected, they often lose their jobs and suffer other personal losses.

International business ethics are impossible to define. Each company operates on some internal ethical principle that it communicates to its foreign subsidiaries. Different national cultures and legal requirements are confusing and sometimes ethically contradictory. International managers have a particularly important role to play in transferring and rationalizing ethics throughout the corporation. Increasingly, international codes and principles are being developed and applied to the actions of multinational companies wherever they operate.

Projects

1. You are manager of a large computer manufacturing company that operates in the United States, Europe, and Japan. Research the efforts of the European Economic Community (EC) and Japan in dealing with ethics. Write an executive memo to your CEO that compares US, EC, and Japanese business ethics.
2. Your company is considering building a small assembly plant in Saudi Arabia. The king of Saudi Arabia is delighted; however, your board of directors is concerned that the company will be expected to comply with the Middle Eastern boycott of firms doing business with Israel. If

so, what do US law and your own conscience require? Prepare a report for your board on this topic.

3. Your mother has been president of a regional apple and pear growers' association and is now retiring. Members have chosen you to succeed her and have given you a major task. Your association has no statement on ethics. Stakeholders are pressuring you to commit the association to a stand on the use of pesticides and conditions for migrant workers. You decide you have to draw up a more comprehensive code that addresses issues important to your members. Write a complete ethics statement, including all the major issues that involve your association.

Questions

1. Review the 12 questions posed by Laura Nash (pp. 139–141). Which do you consider most helpful in assessing the ethics of a business decision? Why?
2. How large a role do you think business schools should play in teaching ethics?
3. What approach to teaching ethics do you think would be most helpful? Should faculty provide frameworks? Use cases to illustrate various decisions? Lecture on what ethical stand you should take? Why?
4. What do you think of whistle blowers? Would you ever blow the whistle on a company for which you worked? How would you deal with a situation in which you knew of a wrongdoing, reported it to your boss, and were subsequently ignored?
5. What is the future for international codes of conduct and principles of behavior for multinational corporations?

BETA CASE 5
ETHICS

One morning in June 1992, Ken Braddock picked up his morning *New York Times.* A front page article immediately seized his attention. It reported on an article in the *Annals of Internal Medicine,* written by researchers at the University of California at Los Angeles, that described a study of advertisements of prescription drugs carried in medical journals. The researchers had asked a group of 150 doctors and clinical pharmacists to study all of the 109 full-page advertisements in the first 1990 issues of 10 leading medical journals. The study concluded that advertisements often mislead doctors about the safety and effectiveness of the drugs being promoted.

Braddock was well aware that physicians got much of their information about new drugs from those advertisements. He also knew Beta spent a considerable amount of money promoting its own ethical drugs through those ads. In fact, Braddock had just looked at the industry data of advertising expenditures. In 1991, drug companies had spent $351 million on advertisements in medical journals.

Beta had safeguards in place to ensure the accuracy of its ads, Braddock reassured himself. Beta's medical director, Dr. Abigail Thompson, screened all of Beta's ads. In addition, Beta followed Food and Drug Administration (FDA) regulations and guidelines for advertising. It was company policy to adhere to FDA requirements that drug companies include only those data approved by the FDA and placed in the drug package insert.

However, Braddock still worried about the study's findings. *The New York Times* reported that the journals in which the ads were carried also published academic research papers. Although the papers were carefully reviewed and evaluated by medical experts, no one subjected the advertisements to the same standards of scientific rigor. The 150 expert reviewers concluded that many of the ads failed to highlight leading information, inadequately referenced or disleading information, inadequately referenced or distorted graphs, and generally inadequate scientific documentation.

Apparently not only those researchers found drug advertisements misleading. The director of the FDA's own drug marketing division had analyzed the same ads and found that half of them violated FDA guidelines. Her boss, Dr. David Kessler, FDA commissioner, wrote an editorial in the *Annals* claiming that "the problem of misleading drug advertisements is real" and the number "disturbingly high."

Braddock wondered whether Beta had unintentionally misled physicians with its ads and what, if anything, he should do. Perhaps, he mused, he should not do anything at all, since the company had followed FDA guidelines to the best of its knowledge. After all, the Pharmaceutical Manufacturers Association, the industry's Washington-based trade group, had disparaged the study, noting "Prescription drug advertising is the most regulated form of advertising in the United States."[53]

---

[53]L K Altman, "Study Says Drug Ads in Medical Journals Frequently Misleading," *The New York Times,* June 1, 1992, pp A1, B7.

6

THE ORIGINS OF BIG BUSINESS

*—Discussion Q on
origin of Big Business
+ rest of
chapter
—political emphases through
deals
182–187*

The first five chapters of this book emphasize how important it is for managers to develop and maintain a strategic perspective. Whether embarking on the strategic planning and implementation process or coping with crises, managers are always influenced by the historical background of their particular enterprise and the way the company evolved in its cultural environment.

Managers can derive great value from understanding and incorporating the positive attributes of their corporate histories. Corporate character, culture, and long-term success are not static but are a result of a historical process. Astute managers recognize that "the present is a monument in the past's trajectory into the future. Corporate history can be a way of thinking about the company, a way of comprehending why the present is what it is and what might be possible for the future."[1]

In this chapter, we survey the major components of the history of American business. We look at basic historical trends over time and the interrelationships between business and major stakeholders in society. We discuss the dramatic rise of big business as an American institution in the 19th century. We go on to consider the dynamic interaction that characterizes business and society in the twentieth century. The first half of the chapter focuses on the environmental conditions that support business growth. The second half reviews the later stages of capitalism and periods of business expansion that depended on that infrastructure.

In many respects, America was first and foremost a business venture. In the seventeenth century, mercantilist economic doctrine so heavily dominated European thought that it became the guiding ideology of the early colonists. Mercantilism called for the establishment of colonies to provide markets and sources of raw materials. British domestic manufacturers were to

---

[1]G D Smith and L E Steadman, "Present Value of Corporate History," *Harvard Business Review* 59 (November/December 1981), pp. 164–73.

turn the raw materials into finished goods and sell them back to the colonies and others, with value added. British mercantilists advocated extensive trade with other countries; a major objective was an excess of exports over imports so that Britain's treasury would swell with gold. To protect its markets, Britain imposed high duties on imports and strengthened its merchant fleet. According to historians Harry Carman and Harold Syrett,

> Four colonies subsequently part of the United States—not to mention others in Canada and the West Indies—were, in part at least, the work of trading corporations: Virginia, founded in 1607 by the Virginia Company of London; New Netherlands, planted by the Dutch at Fort Nassau in 1614; Massachusetts, established by the Massachusetts Bay Company in 1630; and Delaware, begun by a Swedish commercial company in 1638. Even the Pilgrims, who founded Plymouth in 1620, were financed by an English merchant, Thomas Weston, and his associates.[2]

Therefore, an "American business system" evolved over many years prior to the American Revolution.[3]

Although business and economic matters played a central role in the processes of colonization, the revolution, and the shaping of the new republic, the origins of *big* business were rooted in the period between the 1820s and the outbreak of the Civil War in 1861. As manufacturing and trade increased, financial institutions expanded to supply credit and banking services and transportation facilities to move goods from one place to another.

The impact of the dramatic growth in the business sector on the American way of life was profound. Historian Thomas C Cochran noted in 1900, "No culture can be satisfactorily characterized by a single phrase. Yet businesslike values and respect for them seemed the most pervasive common element in American culture, more so than religion, world mission, the democratic spirit, or similar formulations of American ideals."[4] Most observers agreed that business was the dominant American institution and that the culture of the United States was shaped in part by its business institutions.

Conditions Supporting Business Development in the United States

The United States began the nineteenth century as an agrarian society of 5 million people. By 1900, its 76 million people were producing twice the economic output of Britain.[5] Among the factors contributing to the develop-

[2]H J Carman and H C Syrett, *A History of the American People,* vol. 1 (New York: Alfred A Knopf, 1957), p. 24. © 1957 Alfred A Knopf, Inc.

[3]B Bailyn, *The New England Merchants in the Seventeenth Century* (Cambridge, MA: Harvard University Press, 1955).

[4]T C Cochran, *American Business in the Twentieth Century* (Cambridge, MA: Harvard University Press, 1972), p. 7.

[5]H E Krooss and C Gilbert, *American Business History* (Englewood Cliffs, NJ: Prentice-Hall, 1972), p. 145.

ment of a strong US business system were abundant natural resources, favorable social and political environments, rapid population growth and urban migration, the transportation revolution, and innovations in communication. Technological developments, especially the development of mass production techniques, also were critical to the growth of big business.

Companies using mass production techniques placed and operated their machinery to technologically integrate and synchronize stages of production. Their output at each stage of their operation was much faster and also much greater in volume. Managers using the new processes of production considered a high "throughput"—usually in terms of units processed per day—a critical criterion of performance.[6]

Plentiful Natural Resources

Abundant natural resources were a profoundly important contributor to economic growth in the preindustrial United States and even afterward. From the beginning, the United States possessed "a vast continent, irrigated by numberless rivers sweeping down the sides of the mountains fabulously rich in precious metals and inexhaustible supplies of fuel. America's soil was the richest in the world, her forests thick and varied. Deep harbors indented her coasts; her rivers and lakes beckoned trade."[7]

Agricultural output rose rapidly in the rich virgin soil. The many rivers facilitated power generation and transportation, and the timber and minerals provided the inputs to industrial processes. Other nations could claim a similar abundance of resources, but only the United States promised the opportunity for individuals to become owners of rich farmland. Land was given to early settlers in colonial New England.

According to Herman Krooss, "Most colonies . . . used the system of headrights to encourage settlement. Proprietors granted 50 acres of land to every settler who came over at his own expense and 50 more to every person who brought over another settler. Virginia supplied every family with 12 acres, a four-room house, and tools and provisions."[8] Later—and more dramatically—the Homestead Act of 1862 promised 160 acres of unoccupied public land to anyone who would cultivate it for five consecutive years.[9] Even though much of the land was of poor quality, by 1882 the government had distributed 50 million acres to farmers and would-be entrepreneurs.

Various legislative acts granted railroad companies ownership of approximately 200 million acres of prime land, which comprised nearly 10

[6]A D Chandler, Jr., *The Visible Hand* (Cambridge, MA: Belknap Press, 1977), p. 240–41.
[7]T C Cochran and W Miller, *The Age of Enterprise: A Social History of Industrial America* (New York: Macmillan, 1942), p. 1. © 1942 by Macmillan Publishing Co., Inc., renewed 1970 by Thomas C Cochran and William Miller.
[8]H E Krooss, *American Economic Development: The Process of a Business Civilization,* 3rd ed. (Englewood Cliffs, NJ: Prentice-Hall, 1974), p. 87.
[9]Cochran and Miller, *The Age of Enterprise,* p. 107.

percent of the continental land mass. Much of this land was sold to settlers at reasonable rates. Immigrants, attracted to the United States by the opportunity to share the plentiful natural resources, quickly found that entrepreneurship, whether in farming or in business, was a prevalent social value.

Favorable Social and Political Environments

Social Values.   In contrast to many Western European nations, the United States had no strong aristocratic class. Even the descendants of early settlers in Massachusetts and Virginia and of plantation owners in the southern states rejected a rigid aristocratic social structure and its values. Personal achievement was considered far more important than family name or birth order. Most Americans respected and emulated business leaders, particularly those who were self-made. William Letwin notes, "businessmen rose prior to the Civil War in the United States because they embodied the common aspirations and symbolized the working life of most Americans."[10] The unifying social ethic was individualism, hard work, and diligence—all prized virtues and all virtues of the successful businessperson.

Economist John E Sawyer comments on the unique social environment enjoyed by American entrepreneurs:

> In the classic era of the 19th and early 20th centuries American entrepreneurship grew and prospered in a society whose institutions and goals were as uniquely favorable to the individual entrepreneur as were its physical conditions. By inheritance and diffusion, America is, of course, part of a common Western civilization. But the historical timing of the American settlement and the extremely uneven weighting involved in the social and cultural transfer gave the United States a highly selective extraction of the European heritage.[11]

Sawyer referred to the transfer of values that supported individual growth and development. Perhaps the best examples of such values are those immortalized in the Horatio Alger success stories. Although they were not regarded as a high literary form, Alger's books were widely read in the post-Civil War era. Over 20 million copies were sold of such books as *Luck and Pluck, Tom the Bootblack,* and *Bound to Rise.*[12] Many people believed that by working hard and getting a few lucky breaks, they could achieve respectable middle-class membership. Although we now think of Alger's heroes as epitomizing the rise from rags to riches, in fact they usually became small-town businesspeople.

---

[10]W Letwin, "The Past and Future of the American Businessman," *Daedalus* Winter 1969, p. 8.

[11]J E Sawyer, "The Entrepreneur and the Social Order," *Men in Business: Essays on the Historical Role of the Entrepreneur,* ed. W Miller (New York: Harper & Row, 1962), p. 20.

[12]F L Allen, *The Big Change: America Transforms Itself, 1900–1950* (New York: Harper & Row), p. 63.

It was possible to get a start in business with extremely small amounts of capital. For instance, Andrew Carnegie's first major investment was $217.50 (borrowed without collateral) to buy a one-eighth interest in Woodruff's Palace Car Company, an investment that yielded an annual return of $5,000 in two years.[13] Many other entrepreneurs were able to start businesses with even smaller sums. In 1850, I M Singer borrowed $40 from a friend to build a model sewing machine. By the 1880s, Singer Manufacturing Company was the preeminent sewing machine company in the world. It had a huge sales network and giant factories abroad as well as in the United States.[14]

The Role of Government.   Throughout the nineteenth century, the government and the courts pursued policies and programs that supported business needs. As early as 1816, the government enacted tariffs to protect American textile interests from foreign competition. The government provided massive support for the railroad industry through grants, first-mortgage bonds, guaranteed loans, and remitted taxes. By and large, it left that industry free from regulation.[15] Although the Supreme Court had clearly established the right of the federal government to regulate interstate commerce by 1827, the government did not exercise that right until 50 years later.

As we shall see, the role of transportation was critical to business development. Business leaders quickly became acquainted with the dictum "There's no such thing as a free lunch." The advantages railroad magnates and other industrialists enjoyed had a price. According to Thomas Cochran and William Miller, "The politicians were eager to do business with Big Businessmen only because the latter offered the largest fees; in an age of fearful competition, such businessmen vied with one another in bribing legislatures, administrators, and judges to gain any advantage over their rivals."[16]

The same comment could have applied to other industries and their government relations. For instance, Henry Demarest Lloyd, then financial editor of the *Chicago Tribune,* said of John D Rockefeller that "the Standard [Oil Company] has done everything with the Pennsylvania legislature except to refine it."[17] Since US senators were appointed by state legislatures until the Seventeenth Amendment was passed in 1910, there was a strong incentive for big-business interests to attempt to control state senatorial votes. So many business leaders became US senators that the Senate was widely referred to as the "Millionaire's Club."

[13]J R T Hughes, *The Vital Few* (Boston: Houghton Mifflin, 1966), pp. 227–28.

[14]M Wilkins, *The Emergence of Multinational Enterprise: American Business Abroad from the Colonial Era to 1914* (Cambridge, MA: Harvard University Press, 1970), pp. 37–45.

[15]See S H Holbrook, *The Story of the American Railroads* (New York: Crown Publishers, 1947).

[16]Cochran and Miller, *The Age of Enterprise,* p. 158.

[17]H D Lloyd, *Wealth against Commonwealth* (New York: Harper & Row, 1894).

As might be expected, the Senate protected business interests during the last quarter of the nineteenth century. As a reaction to the excesses in the railroad industry between 1874 and 1885, the House of Representatives considered more than 30 bills to provide greater control over interstate commerce. The Senate, however, prevented the passage of any such bill until 1887, when the Interstate Commerce Act, which created the Interstate Commerce Commission, became law. (That law and subsequent legislation that tightened its provisions are discussed in Chapter 8.) The Sherman Antitrust Act, designed to prevent monopolies and restraint of trade, was passed in 1890. Like the Interstate Commerce Act, it was a weak act that subsequent legislation toughened. (The Sherman Act is also discussed in detail in Chapter 8.)

In 1900, the federal government operated on a budget of approximately $500 million, supported mainly by tax revenues from tariffs and excise taxes. There was no income tax at all. Also, the Federal Trade Commission, the Department of Commerce, the Food and Drug Administration, the Department of Labor, and the Federal Reserve System did not yet exist.

Thus, business was virtually unfettered, and it was widely believed that control of business was no affair of the federal government. In fact, as David Vogel notes, measures to ameliorate dangerous or unfair business practices "tended to be strongly opposed . . . and often were significantly weakened as a result of political pressure from industrialists."[18] However, as the country grew in population and became heavily urbanized, the role of the federal government expanded beyond merely increasing regulation.

Population Growth and Urbanism

Immigration fueled population growth. Such growth was heavy in prosperous periods and slow during economic declines, reaching an all-time peak of 1,285,000 in 1907.[19] Most immigrants, particularly toward the end of the nineteenth century, settled in industrial centers, such as New York, Boston, Philadelphia, and Chicago, where they were joined by migrants from rural America.[20] The number of Americans living in cities grew from 6 percent in the year 1800 to 33 percent in 1900. As eighteenth- and nineteenth-century migration to the West Coast continued and open areas were settled, the only remaining frontier was the city. Foreign-born Americans, who comprised 14 percent of the population, were twice as likely as native-born Americans to live in cities.[21]

---

[18]D Vogel, *National Styles of Regulation: Environmental Policy in Great Britain and the United States* (Ithaca, NY: Cornell University Press, 1986), p. 230.

[19]R Hofstadter, *The Age of Reform: From Bryan to F.D.R.* (New York: Vantage Books, 1955), p. 177.

[20]A M Schlesinger, "The Rise of the City: 1878–1898," in *A History of American Life,* vol. 10, eds. A M Schlesinger and D R Fox (New York: Macmillan, 1933), pp. 53–57.

[21]Krooss, *American Economic Development,* pp. 105–11.

The massive influx of workers to the cities created low-wage labor markets. It is important to note, however, that the scarcity of *skilled* labor, characteristic of the American work force since colonial times, persisted. Raymond Vernon observes that "labor in the United States has always been scarce, especially labor skilled in production techniques."[22] As a result, industrialists used the ample raw materials and capital available to generate large quantities of goods that used little skilled labor.

Although most of the workers were unskilled, they earned comparatively high incomes. Wages earned by both low-wage workers and the smaller pool of skilled workers led to the development of even larger markets for all types of consumer goods. Cochran and Miller note,

> It is impossible to exaggerate the role of business in developing great cities in America, and it is impossible to exaggerate the role of the cities in creating our business culture. The cities subjected hundreds of thousands of people to identical pressures, at the same time exporting to every rural river valley, plain and plateau uniform factory products. Creating a national market for standardized goods, they also created a national model of the successful man: the thrifty, shrewd, and practical clerk or mechanic who rose from the ranks to leadership.[23]

The Transportation Revolution

Shipping costs were high in the early nineteenth century. Toll roads and post roads were used to ship wagonloads of goods. The Erie Canal was only one of a network of canals and rivers, totaling over 4,200 miles in length. Surface and water routes led to a major reduction in shipping costs between 1825 and 1860. But it was the railroad that revolutionized shipping. On August 8, 1829, John B Jervis ran the first steam locomotive in the United States.[24] The massive, eight-ton "Stourbridge Lion" ran less than 200 yards before it crushed the wooden rails. Lighter engines, iron rails, and countless other innovations led to a rapid expansion of railroads after 1830. By 1865, 35,085 miles of track were in use.[25] Another 165,000 miles were lain by 1890.

The railroads were the nation's first big business. Unprecedented amounts of capital were required to build railways and maintain equipment. For instance, in the 1850s, a major textile mill might have cost $500,000 to build and as much as $300,000 per year to run with a work force of fewer than 800 workers. In contrast, railroad construction cost a minimum of $30,000 per mile. The New York Central cost over $30 million to build, cost $3 million per year to operate, and employed 4,000 workers.[26]

---

[22]R Vernon, *Sovereignty at Bay* (New York: Basic Books, 1971), p. 66.

[23]Cochran and Miller, *The Age of Enterprise*, p. 153.

[24]E E Morison, *From Know-How to Nowhere: The Development of American Technology* (New York: Basic Books, 1974), p. 52.

[25]D J Boorstin, *The Americans: The Democratic Experience* (New York: Random House, 1974), p. 120.

[26]Krooss and Gilbert, *American Business History*, p. 123.

The railroads generated massive requirements for steel rails and bridges, thus fostering the growth of a steel industry. Iron rails, which could be forged in small shops, were used only until the processes for producing steel were commercially perfected in the mid-1860s. Much more capital and equipment were required to produce the stronger and lighter steel rails, giving further impetus to the development of big business.

Many financiers made fortunes in the railroad industry, although they were rarely competent in railroad management. Alfred Chandler notes that "large sums of money were essential if the road was to be built at all, if it was to expand its physical equipment as the traffic grew, if it was to build feeders and branches necessitated by competition, or if it was to survive sudden contractions of the money market."[27] An executive who could command large sums of money was therefore a valuable asset to a railroad company.

Railroads were the first businesses in which a definite separation between ownership and management existed. However, there were exceptions, most notably the Pennsylvania Railroad, which was successfully managed and financed by a wealthy engineer, J Edgar Thomson. The need for sound operations management for the nation's railroads was apparent as early as 1850.

The most basic needs, however, were difficult to implement. For example, although standardization of time zones was essential, it took 11 years to reach a consensus to consolidate. Prior to 1883, a train crossing the continental United States might have gone through as many as 54 time zones instead of the present 4. Similarly, railroads adopted standardized rail widths, car couplings, and air brakes only after protracted delays.[28] One can imagine the delays and other difficulties passengers and shippers encountered as railroad workers switched trains from wide-gauge to narrow-gauge tracks and then back again.

Innovations in Communication

As businesses proliferated, they increasingly needed quick and easy communication. In 1844, Samuel F B Morse constructed a telegraph line from Baltimore to Washington that "hastened the pace of business . . . speeding news to the papers within a day after it happened."[29] By 1860, there were 50,000 miles of telegraph lines.

But the real boom came after Western Union achieved a monopoly in telegraphy. The company entered agreements with the railroads to use rights

---

[27]A D Chandler, Jr., "Henry Varnum Poor: Philosopher of Management, 1812–1905," in *Men In Business,* ed. W Miller (New York: Harper & Row, 1952), p. 283.

[28]E C Kirkland, "Industry Comes of Age: Business, Labor and Public Policy, 1860–1877" in *The Economic History of the United States,* vol. 6, ed. Henry Davis (New York: Holt, Rinehart & Winston, 1961), pp. 46–52.

[29]Boorstin, *The Americans,* p. 390.

of way and station houses in exchange for free telegraph service. By 1878, there were 200,000 miles of telegraph.[30] In that year, Theodore N Vail took over the management of the recently organized Bell Telephone Company. Over the next 34 years, under his skillful management, the telephone became an important part of American life.

Many other developments further improved the ability of Americans to communicate with one another. Table 6–1 briefly summarizes major innovations in communication. Each innovation provided opportunities for businesses to build and distribute needed equipment. Communication efficiency was extremely important to the growth of business. For instance, the development of carbon paper in the 1880s was one immeasurable improvement. Now businesspeople could create duplicates of memos and letters, a considerably useful achievement.[31]

Technological Developments

Technological advances in transportation and communications were, of course, not isolated events. Technological change played a central role in the development of many industries. But technology was not limited to

[30]Krooss, *American Economic Development,* p. 387.
[31]Chandler, *The Visible Hand,* part II.

TABLE 6–1   Selected Innovations in Mass Communications

1833	First penny paper, *The New York Sun.*
1839	Daguerre developed practical method of photography.
1844	Morse transmitted first telegraph message.
1853	Paper made from wood pulp.
1857	First trans-Atlantic cable.
1867	First practical typewriter.
1872	Process of photoengraving developed.
1873	First daily illustrated paper.
1876	Bell transmitted the first telephone message.
1877	Edison invented the phonograph.
1894	Motion picture projection perfected.
1895	Marconi sent and received a wireless message.
1904	Telephone wirephoto sent from Munich to Nuremberg.
1906	Human voice transmitted by radio.
1920	Beginning of regularly scheduled radio broadcasting.
1923	Picture televised from New York to Philadelphia.
1924	Tabloid newspaper.
1926	Beginning of book clubs.
1928	Beginning of regular, scheduled television broadcasting.

Source: W Schramm, ed., *Mass Communications,* 2nd ed. (Urbana, IL: University of Illinois Press, 1960), pp. 6–7.

mechanical objects. Management scientist Herbert H Simon observes that "technology is not things; it is knowledge—knowledge that is stored in hundreds of millions of books, in hundreds of millions or billions of human heads, and, to an important extent, in the artifacts themselves. Technology is knowledge of how to do things, how to accomplish human goals.[32] Future historians will doubtless add that computerization constituted nothing less than a transformation of and revolution in the storage and dissemination of technological knowledge.

It was difficult to develop or apply knowledge in the early nineteenth century. Engineers generally passed their knowledge on to apprentices. Prior to 1830, companies recorded very little in print about such subjects as canal building, steam engines, and textile machinery. The British deliberately withheld plans for textile machinery from American manufacturers. Indeed, the British had legislated against transporting machinery or even drawings of machines to the colonies. Thus, although steam engines and textile machines were introduced in Great Britain in the late eighteenth century, innovations appeared in the United States only after such engineers as Samuel Slater and Francis Cabot Lowell memorized and recreated British designs.

In the early 1800s, Britain imposed an embargo on British textile technology. British ships prowled the high seas, blockading American ports. For more than a decade, British sailors successfully confiscated plans American entrepreneurs tried to smuggle into the United States.

Francis Cabot Lowell, however, was not deterred. He and financier Nathan Appleton traveled through Scotland and Britain, memorizing the various configurations of textile machinery. During the return trip to Boston, British sailors boarded their ship several times to search for textile machinery plans. After coming up empty-handed, they finally let the ship proceed. Within several weeks of returning to Boston, Lowell and mechanic Paul Moody had built a prototype that became the foundation of the New England textile industry.[33]

The major innovations that sparked the business revolution included the Bessemer process for manufacturing steel, which was commercially implemented in the United States in 1872. The harnessing of electricity gave rise to the electrical equipment industry and the electric utilities. The refrigerated railroad car, introduced in 1875, led to the development of the meat-packing industry. The influence of technology was so great between 1850 and 1900 that historians deemed it "the precipitating factor in whatever transformation occurred in American society."[34]

---

[32]H A Simon, "Technology and Environment," *Management Science* 19 (June 1973), p. 1110.

[33]H Vernon-Wortzel, *Lowell: The Corporations and the City* (New York: Garland Publishing, 1992), pp. 4–5.

[34]Krooss and Gilbert, *American Business History,* p. 145.

Stages of Capitalism

One might adopt several frameworks from which to describe the stages of development in a business-oriented society. One approach is to consider the common stages of growth in a society that recognized private property. The late business historian N S B Gras delineates six stages of capitalism: prebusiness capitalism, petty capitalism, mercantile capitalism, industrial capitalism, finance capitalism, and national capitalism.[35] Although Gras's stages and labels are somewhat rigid and arbitrary, they are useful for dividing the capitalist orientation into chronological order.

Capitalism was and is today the ideological basis of US development. However, other countries have evolved under different systems that fall along a continuum from total central planning to totally free enterprise. Most countries combine some elements of government and business interaction.

The rigid central planning model is quickly disappearing. Only Cuba and a few other countries still cling to this model, and none of them have a thriving economy. The former Soviet Union, Eastern Europe, and many African and Latin American countries have largely abandoned central planning in favor of private enterprise. Even China has moved toward free enterprise and is rapidly loosening government control over most industrial sectors. Divestment programs have put state-owned industries around the world back into the private sector.

Many European countries combine aspects of capitalism and government control. Some countries retain control over airlines, telecommunications, and other "critical" industries. At the same time, they encourage free enterprise in consumer goods and other nonstrategic enterprises. Government responsibility for social programs and industrial relations also varies across cultures and countries. One should be wary of applying labels such as *communist, socialist, capitalist,* and so on to national policies. Most countries combine all of these aspects as they define and redefine the roles of government and the private sector.

While it is important to remember that real-life situations cannot be neatly classified and compartmentalized, categorizations such as the following provide a structure for discussion purposes.

Prebusiness and Petty Capitalism

Gras's stage, *prebusiness capitalism,* was rooted in the manorial estates and settled villages of Western Europe during the medieval period. Social mobility during this period was very low. A person born into a farming family was destined to be a farmer. Lords and ladies of the manors and peasants and

---

[35]N S B Gras, *Business and Capitalism: An Introduction to Business History* (New York: F S Crofts, 1939).

artisans in the villages worked and shared under a barter exchange system. They achieved a condition approximating self-sufficiency by trading goods and services. Society in rural colonial America had some of these elements, but even in those early days Americans were far more socially and geographically mobile.

The second stage, *petty capitalism*, prevailed in the North American British colonies in the seventeenth century and the first half of the eighteenth century. The petty capitalist was a shopkeeper or a traveling merchant. His enterprises were small, seldom extending beyond the town in which the store was located or the route the merchant followed. Businesses started and failed with great regularity. Because entrepreneurs required little capital to set up shop, the system encouraged "over competition, which would sooner or later be ruinous to all."[36] Of course, many petty capitalists survived and thrived. However, in terms of the dominant form of business, the petty capitalist yielded to the mercantile capitalist around 1750.

Mercantile Capitalism

In the American experience, the third stage, *mercantile capitalism*, consisted of two parts. The first period was that of the colonial merchant, who, as Chandler noted, was "an all-purpose, nonspecialized man of business. He was a wholesaler and a retailer, an importer and an exporter. In associations with other merchants he built and owned the ships that carried goods to and from his town. He financed and insured the transportation and distribution of these goods. At the same time, he provided the funds needed by planters and artisans to finance the production of crops and goods."[37]

By providing a market for agricultural and consumer goods, the merchant became the dominant business leader in the second half of the 1700s. By 1800, specialized intermediaries, such as importers, insurers, bankers, and wholesalers, had taken over.

Thus, in the second period of mercantile capitalism, intermediaries replaced merchants as the integrating force in the economy. Between 1800 and 1850, wholesalers directed the flow of goods from producers to consumers; financed the canals, turnpikes, and early railroads; and supplied the funds for the early steel and textile factories. According to Chandler, "They not only raised the funds for plants and machinery, but also supplied a large amount of the cash and credit that the new manufacturers needed as working capital to pay for supplies and labor."[38] But as manufacturing grew in importance, the role of the mercantile capitalist intermediaries became less and less critical.

---

[36]Ibid., p. 61.

[37]A D Chandler, Jr., "The Role of Business in the United States: A Historical Survey," *Daedalus,* Winter 1969, p. 24.

[38]Ibid., p. 26.

Industrial Capitalism

The era of *industrial capitalism* and the rise of factory-based manufacturing followed mercantile capitalism. The first fully integrated factory in the United States was owned by Boston Manufacturing Company, a group of Boston merchants who opened a textile plant in Waltham, Massachusetts, in 1814. This company, led by Nathan Appleton and Francis Cabot Lowell, was the first to process completely raw materials into finished goods and market the output. Until that time, home looms turned out goods that were sold in local markets. The expansion of the highly profitable textile factories into Lowell and Lawrence, Massachusetts, was followed by the development of the iron and agricultural implement industries. However, most manufacturers continued to rely on wholesalers for marketing and financial support. Once the railroads provided access to larger markets and technological progress provided economies to larger firms, many companies assumed their own marketing and financing functions.

Some saw the leaders of big business as "captains of industry"; others called them "robber barons." Both terms were appropriate for these complex individuals. Although the Industrial Revolution was in full swing before the Civil War, industrialists did not make their mark until after that conflict. In 1861, John D Rockefeller had a thriving wholesale business in Cleveland and Andrew Carnegie was the personal secretary to the powerful Thomas Scott, general superintendent of the Pennsylvania Railroad. Jay Gould operated a tannery in eastern Pennsylvania, J Pierpont Morgan had just opened an investment office in New York, James Hill (later president of Northern Pacific Railroad) was a merchant in what is now St. Paul, Missouri, and Edward Harriman (later president of Union Pacific Railroad) was a 14-year-old errand boy on Wall Street. In the West, members of the Pacific Associates—Collis Huntington, Leland Stanford, Mark Hopkins, and Charles Crocker—were merchants who would soon gain the rights to build the western part (Union Pacific) of the transcontinental railroad.

With the exception of members of the Pacific Associates, none of these industrialists was more than 26 years old, and only Morgan and Stanford had gone to college. In fact, most of them had left home by age 16 to make their way in the world. Historian Stewart H Holbrook describes the future "Robber barons" or "Captains of industry" as having had "a splendid audacity and a vital energy that erupted in astonishing ways . . . all were men of devout individualism . . . each had an overpowering sense of acquisitiveness . . . [each] held stoutly to the proposition that what is and shall be is determined by the forces at work."[39] With few exceptions, these self-made individuals came from poor families, were relatively uneducated, and entered the business world before age 16.

This generation of leaders was determined to dominate in all endeavors

---

[39]S H Holbrook, *The Age of the Moguls* (Garden City, NY: Doubleday, 1953), p. viii.

undertaken. The stories about Rockefeller's ascent to the position of monopolist in the oil industry are legion. "Reckafellow," as Carnegie called Rockefeller, was known for such tactics as offering to buy a competitor's business at about 40 percent of its asset value. If the competitor refused, Rockefeller would proceed to bankrupt the company through various ploys such as selling below cost or suggesting that railroads not handle shipments (or that they charge double or quadruple the normal rate). However, Rockefeller was unique only in his level of success, for his colleagues used similar strategies.

Additional factors were often involved in the emergence of big business. The diligence and attention to detail that characterized the business conduct of such business leaders as Rockefeller, Cornelius Vanderbilt, and J Pierpont Morgan helped them dominate others in business transactions. Rockefeller's most thorough biographer, Allen Nevins, offers an example that supports Rockefeller's quest for efficiency:

> He watched a machine for filling the tin cans. One dozen cans stood on a wooden platform beneath a dozen pipes. A man pulled a lever, and each pipe discharged exactly five gallons of kerosene into a can. Still on a wooden carrier, the dozen cans were pushed along to another machine where 12 tops were swiftly clamped fast on the cans. Thence they were pushed to the last machine in which just enough solder to fasten and seal the lid was dropped on each can.
>
> Mr. Rockefeller listened in silence while an expert told all about the various machines used to save labor and time and expense in the process. At last Mr. Rockefeller asked:
>
> "How many drops of solder do you use on each can?" "Forty."
>
> "Have you ever tried 38? No? Would you mind having some sealed with 38 and let me know?"
>
> Six or 7 percent of these cans leaked. Then 39 drops were used. None leaked. It was tried with 100, 500, 1,000 cans. None leaked. Thereafter every can was sealed with 39 drops.[40]

Nevins explains that "Rockefeller grasped early the great truth that inefficiency and waste are a form of dishonesty, a theft of wealth which might be used for the general good."[41] Nevins further notes that the savings from the use of less solder amounted to $2,500 in the first year, and as the business grew, "the savings accumulated into a fund of hundreds of thousands of dollars."[42]

Even the closest attention to detail could not help companies whose management was unable to ensure continuous sources of supply, transportation at competitive rates, and markets in which the output could be sold

---

[40]A Nevins, *Study in Power: John D. Rockefeller, Industrialist and Philanthropist,* vol. 1 (New York: Charles Scribner's Sons, 1953), pp. 280–81.
[41]Ibid., p. 281.
[42]Ibid., p. 428.

at equitable prices. The same free marketplace that allowed all firms to compete unhampered by restrictive taxes and government regulations also permitted financially strong and aggressive entrepreneurs to engage in predatory price cutting, gain rate concessions from railroads, and otherwise wreak havoc with highly competitive markets. The difficulty was compounded whenever a firm had a high investment in capital, as economist Alfred Eichner noted:

> The same force of technology which so greatly reduced the costs of production and made it possible to turn out goods of uniform quality in large numbers also required a substantial investment in fixed assets, thereby making the capital-output ratio significantly high. This meant that whenever the demand for a firm's produce fell, it was under considerable economic pressure to try to expand its sales by cutting its price and in this way spread its overhead costs over a larger volume.[43]

The typical response to price cutting in the 1870s and 1880s involved informal alliances, known as *pooling*, among competitors. Rival firms got together to agree on common prices for the various classes of products, establish output quotas, and divide market territories. Voting power in the pool was allocated on the basis of market power, with larger competitors having more votes. The pool also established fines for members that cut prices. The fines were often ineffective, however, because the excess capacity that existed in most industries encouraged companies to undercut the legally unenforceable prices and quotas.

A successful pooling arrangement in the oil industry, the South Improvement Company, was set up in 1872. But the Gunpowder Trade Association, established in the same year by Colonel Henry DuPont, served as a model for pooling arrangements.[44] Seven competitors met to agree on prices for black gunpowder and set a $1-per-keg fine for price cutting. There were 48 votes, with DuPont and two other large companies having 10 votes each. By 1877, Henry DuPont had bought interest in several other pool members, thus obtaining control of over 50 percent of the votes.[45] However, many members violated the pooling agreements. Between 1881 and 1883 alone, there were 230 separate, short-lived incidents of price cutting by members of the pool.[46] The Gunpowder Trade Association continued in operation until 1907, when the federal government successfully brought suit against DuPont for violation of the Sherman Antitrust Act. The suit, which was resolved in 1911, divided DuPont into three companies: DuPont, Hercules Powder, and Atlas Powder.

---

[43] A S Eichner, *The Emergence of Oligopoly: Sugar Refining as a Case Study* (Baltimore: Johns Hopkins University Press, 1969), p. 13.

[44] G C Zilg, *DuPont: Behind the Nylon Curtain* (Englewood Cliffs, NJ: Prentice-Hall, 1974), p. 66.

[45] Ibid., p. 67.

[46] Ibid., p. 89.

Industrialists quickly found a solution to the price cutting in pooling arrangements: Competitors joined into one organization. The *trust,* as this form of business organization was called, is discussed in Chapter 8. Cochran and Miller observe, "Trusts could appear only in a society in which the corporation had become the dominant type of business organization, in which property rights were represented not by land or other physical assets, but by negotiable paper easily convertible into other types of negotiable paper."[47]

Soon trusts were created in the whiskey, salt, leather, cottonseed oil, sugar, and many other industries. Several states challenged the charters of companies that had become trusts, questioning whether such an "agreement tends to stifle competition and enhance prices, and therefore to work an injury to trade and commerce."[48] By 1889, cases had been successfully prosecuted against the Sugar Trust in New York, the Gas Trust in Illinois, and the Cottonseed Oil Trust in Louisiana.[49] The passage of the Sherman Antitrust Act in 1890 did little to dissolve trusts, partly due to vague wording and partly because the government was rather lax in its enforcement. Indeed, business leaders, realizing that some antitrust legislation was inevitable, worked diligently to ensure that the wording of the act made the law as weak as possible. Only one case was successfully prosecuted against a trust in the first 14 years of the Sherman Act.[50]

Horizontal combinations continued under a state law enacted in New Jersey in 1889. The New Jersey Holding Company Act allowed companies to achieve the price control purpose of trusts by buying controlling interests in competing firms. By 1904, the seven largest industrial companies in the country were chartered in New Jersey.[51] The strategy for many of the combinations was defensive. The primary concern was preservation of capital. However, the financial resources and expertise required to create trusts and holding companies resided not with the owner-managers of industrial capitalism but with the investment bankers who came to dominate business during the period from the mid-1890s to the depth of the Great Depression in 1933.

Finance Capitalism

The period from 1893 to 1933 marked the fifth stage of capitalism, *finance capitalism.* Bankers and investment brokers became the prevailing force in American business during this period. A major reason for their dominance was their ability to effect industrial combinations and subsequently gain

---

[47]Cochran and Miller, *The Age of Enterprise,* p. 142.
[48]Eichner, *The Emergence of Oligopoly,* p. 137.
[49]Ibid., p. 141.
[50]*United States* v. *Addystone Pipe and Steel Co., et al.,* 175 U.S. 211 (1899).
[51]Cochran and Miller, *The Age of Enterprise,* p. 190.

important directorships. Alfred Chandler observes that the railroad system most closely exemplified financial capitalism in the United States. The bankers, who sometimes outnumbered shareholders, were not strategists or operating managers but nevertheless had tremendous influence over board decisions.[52]

By 1893, it was apparent in many industries that economies of scale were to be achieved through merger. The national railroad system was essentially complete, providing access to vital markets. High tariffs protected nearly all major industries. Also, the federal government had failed to aggressively prosecute trusts and holding companies under the Sherman Act. In addition, the financial capitalists often were able to produce enormous profits for stock owners who entered into trusts and holding companies. The device used was to "overcapitalize" assets by offering the shares of the new corporation to the public at a much higher price than the par, or stated value, of existing assets. The public—perhaps believing large trusts and holding companies could earn more profits than the individual components would have earned—seldom disappointed the financiers.

By 1904, at the height of the merger movement, there were 318 industrial trusts involving 5,288 separate plants, 75 percent of which had been incorporated since 1897.[53]

The most visible example of the financial capitalist's dominance in business during this period was the formation of US Steel in 1901. The first billion-dollar corporation, US Steel was capitalized at $1,402,846,000, although its constituent parts had assets of only $626 million.[54] The major components were Federal Steel (a trust organized in 1898), Carnegie Steel, and the Mesabi Range iron ore interests of John D Rockefeller. The combine brought together over 60 plants in total, including mines, railroads, shipping companies, and steel mills with 60 percent of the nation's steel-producing capacity.

The major stumbling block to creating US Steel was Andrew Carnegie. He had neither joined nor participated in any of the trusts and had not come under the dominance of financial interests, since he had financed the growth of his $400 million enterprise through retained earnings. When the various smaller steel and iron trusts had been formed (wire, tin plate, nails, tube, and others) and threatened to discontinue purchase of Carnegie Steel, his response was to begin manufacture of the products made by the trusts. He not only could make the products but, in his well-known quest for efficiency, would probably do so at lower cost than the trusts. Financier J Pierpont Morgan (whose syndicate would clear $57 million for assembling US Steel)

---

[52]Chandler, *The Visible Hand*, p. 187.

[53]M Josephson, *The Robber Barons* (New York: Harcourt Brace Jovanovich, 1962), p. 387.

[54]F L Allen, *The Great Pierpont Morgan* (New York: Harper & Row, 1949), p. 144.

approached Carnegie through one of Carnegie's closest associates, Charles Schwab.[55] Carnegie recounted the story in his autobiography:

> Mr. Schwab told me Mr. Morgan had said to him he should really like to know if I wished to retire from business; if so he thought he could arrange it . . . I considered what was fair and that is the option Morgan got. Schwab went down and arranged it. I never saw Morgan on the subject or any man connected with him. Never a word passed between him and me. I gave my memorandum and Morgan saw it was eminently fair. I have been told many times since by insiders that I should have asked $100 million more and could have got it easily.[56]

Morgan's power was unequaled. Journalist Lincoln Steffens said of him, "In all my time, J.P. Morgan sat on the American throne as the boss of bosses, as the ultimate American sovereign."[57] N S B Gras wrote of Morgan, "For nearly a generation, Morgan rivalled kings and presidents as an object of interest, respect, and hate."[58] Among Morgan's achievements were the rescue of the US monetary system in 1895 and the prevention of a banking collapse of 1907. On both occasions, US presidents sought his counsel and followed his directions explicitly. Morgan was also responsible for the creation of such industrial giants as General Electric, International Harvester, and American Telephone and Telegraph.

However, Morgan also nearly destroyed the financial structure of the country in an incident that led to the first antitrust dissolution decision of the US Supreme Court. The following account describes the methods of finance capitalism.

In 1900, there were two major railroads in the Pacific Northwest: the Great Northern, owned and operated by James J Hill, and the Northern Pacific, controlled by Hill with the backing of Morgan. Hill and Morgan wished to extend the line eastward to Chicago by purchasing the Chicago, Burlington, and Quincy line and operating as a subsidiary of the Northern Pacific. However, Edward H Harriman, then president of the Union Pacific, also coveted the Chicago, Burlington, and Quincy line. His approach, which was totally unexpected, was to buy the operating control of the parent, Northern Pacific. He did so quietly on the open market, supported by the Rockefeller-controlled investment house of Kuhn and Loeb. By the time Morgan (who was on an extended vacation in Europe) found out, Harriman had nearly 50 percent of the Northern Pacific stock, at a cost of over $78 million. When Morgan and Harriman each made a last effort to obtain over half of the stock, they drove the price from $120 to $1,000 per share in less

---

[55]Ibid., p. 147.

[56]A Carnegie, *Autobiography of Andrew Carnegie* (Boston: Houghton Mifflin, 1920), p. 246.

[57]L Steffens, *Autobiography of Lincoln Steffens* (New York: Harcourt Brace Jovanovich, 1931), p. 587.

[58]Gras, *Business and Capitalism,* p. 247.

than two days. Those who had sold the stock scrambled to buy the extremely scarce shares to be able to participate in the price rise.

The result was that the vast majority of stocks on the New York Stock Exchange declined precipitously, and many fortunes were lost. Morgan and Harriman quickly made peace and prevented a total market collapse by offering to buy Northern Pacific shares at $150 per share. The Morgan and Harriman forces then created Northern Securities Holding Company to merge the assets of the Great Northern, Northern Pacific, and Chicago, Burlington, and Quincy railroads.

Shortly thereafter, Theodore Roosevelt, who had become president after McKinley was assassinated, brought suit against the Northern Securities combine under the Sherman Act. President Roosevelt differentiated between the "good trusts," which had acquired assets through efficient operation, and "bad trusts," which represented financial manipulation. These latter combinations, which he called "malefactors of great wealth," were represented by Northern Securities Company.

When Morgan heard of the antitrust suit, he was amazed he had received no previous warning. According to Frederick Allen, "He went to Washington and saw the President. 'If we have done anything wrong,' said he, 'send your man to my man and they can fix it up.' "[59] The president refused to withdraw the suit, and in 1904, by a five-to-four vote, the US Supreme Court ordered the dissolution of Northern Securities Company. Other antitrust cases followed, and by 1911 Standard Oil, American Tobacco, and DuPont were all ordered to divide into smaller companies.

The American public was informed of the excesses of the "money trust" during the 1912 hearings conducted by Senator Pujo of Louisiana. The widely chronicled testimony of J Pierpont Morgan and other New York bankers and investment brokers produced some astounding revelations. Although the then 75-year-old Morgan denied he had any power at all, he gave an insight into his methods when he insisted that what ruled the financial world was not money but character:

> "Is not commercial credit based primarily upon money or property?" asked [committee counsel] Untermayer. "No, sir," said Morgan, "the first thing is character." "Before money or property?" "Before money or anything else. Money cannot buy it . . . Because a man I do not trust could not get money from me on all the bonds in Christendom."[60]

The Pujo committee revealed to a shocked nation that Morgan and two other New York bankers and their associates controlled 341 directorships in 112 corporations having a combined capitalization of $22 billion.[61]

---

[59]F L Allen, *The Lords of Creation* (New York: Harper & Row, 1935), p. 68.

[60]Allen, *The Great Pierpont Morgan*, p. 8.

[61]R Hofstadter, ed., *The Progressive Movement, 1900–1915* (Englewood Cliffs, NJ: Prentice-Hall, 1963), p. 160.

The criticisms of the finance capitalists revealed by the Pujo committee were subsequently incorporated into the New Freedom program of Woodrow Wilson through the passage of the Federal Reserve Act and the Clayton Antitrust Act, which were intended to limit the powers of the private bankers. However, these acts had little immediate impact as the nation prepared to enter World War I. The War Industries Board was established under the direction of financier Bernard Baruch to mobilize production capacity. During World War I, the performances of large industrial firms were generally well regarded by the populace.

During the 1920s, business–government relations hit a new high, particularly with Herbert Hoover as secretary of commerce. Hoover openly encouraged trade association activity and was so strongly probusiness that he once acted as intermediary for a company inquiry about possible antitrust consequences of a proposed acquisition. Also during this period, Judge Elbert H Gary, as chief executive officer of US Steel, could announce price rises honored throughout the industry at quasi-public dinners, with no government action.

Also during the 1920s, holding companies became so widespread that by 1928 only 86 out of 573 firms listed on the New York Stock Exchange were nonholding companies.[62] The holding company, particularly as it functioned in public utilities, became so "complicated that it was difficult to arrive at even the vaguest idea of the actual worth of their soaring stocks."[63] There was no strong movement to change the holding company, since its stock prices were steadily rising.

Calvin Coolidge became president following Warren Harding's sudden death in 1923. The years that followed have often been referred to as the period of "Coolidge prosperity," because the nation enjoyed unprecedented economic growth. There were many reasons for the tremendous growth. First, the automobile became a necessity for many Americans; 23,121,000 cars were in service by 1929, compared to 6,771,000 in 1919. Second, the nation fell in love with the "wireless phoney" as the radio, commercially introduced in 1921, was called. Third, sales of cigarettes doubled in the 1920s. Fourth, demand for such products as rayon, telephones, refrigerators, and cosmetics increased dramatically. Fifth, urbanites went to the movies at an average rate of more than once per week. Finally, chain drug, grocery, and five-and-dime stores doubled and then tripled sales in the 1920s.[64] All these factors added to the ever-increasing demand for the products of business.

Coolidge prosperity owed its success to several factors. First, the nation

---

[62]A Rochester, *Rulers of America: A Study of Financial Capital* (New York: Harper & Row, 1949), p. 87.

[63]Allen, *The Lords of Creation,* p. 244.

[64]F L Allen, *Only Yesterday: An Informal History of the 1920s* (New York: Harper & Row, 1931), pp. 109, 163, 165, 166–68.

emerged from World War I intact both economically and physically, while most of Europe was devastated. As a result, the United States became the world economic superpower. Second, mass production methods developed by engineers such as Frederick W Taylor and Frank B Gilbreth were applied widely and with considerable success. Third, demand for new products, such as the automobile, created many jobs. For instance, out of a work force numbering just over 30 million, nearly 4 million workers were either directly or indirectly involved in auto production. Fourth, on the demand side, installment buying became popular; over 15 percent of retail purchases had been made on credit by 1929. Fifth, there was a widespread rise in advertising and sales techniques. These marketing tools became very important ingredients in the success formula for consumer goods companies.

A sixth factor contributing to Coolidge prosperity came from profits made in stock market speculation. Everyone seemed to be putting money into the stock market, often on credit by buying stock and then using it as collateral to obtain a loan to buy more stock. Such methods created leverage that worked beautifully when stock prices were rising rapidly. The same methods produced very different results when stock prices tumbled precipitously and the bottom fell out of the stock market in the period following "Black Monday," October 29, 1929. Table 6–2 shows the dramatic fall in selected stock prices from 1929 to 1932.

Hearings held by the Senate Committee on Banking and Currency in 1933 did much to discredit the bankers who dominated the era of finance capitalism. The findings showed widespread manipulation of stock prices, misuse of the holding company approach to business organizations, and tax dodges such as sales of stock (at a loss) to family members to eliminate income tax liability. Allen noted about the hearings, "Again and again, it

TABLE 6–2   Selected Stock Prices, 1929 High versus 1932 Low

	1929 High	1932 Low
Consolidated Cigar	$115	$ 2½
Erie Railroad	93½	2
General Foods	82	20
General Motors	91	8
New York Central	256	9
Radio Corporation of America	115	2½
Southern Railway	165	2½
US Steel	261	21
Wright Aeronautical	150	4

SOURCE: G V Axon, *The Stock Market Crash of 1929* (New York: Mason and Lipscomb, 1974), pp. 93–94.

showed how men occupying fiduciary positions in the financial world had been false to their trust."[65] Such revelations, coupled with the inability of big business to lift the country out of the Great Depression, lowered public confidence in big business and thus set the stage for the reform programs of the New Deal.

National Capitalism

Gras's sixth and final stage of capitalism is *national capitalism,* which involved rejection of the strict application of the laissez-faire theory of government nonintervention in the economy.[66] However, proponents of national capitalism differ on the extent and content of the broadened government role.

Gras identifies four major movements advocating the expanded use of government fiscal, monetary, and regulatory capability: the Progressive movement of the early twentieth century, the New Deal of the Great Depression, the Fair Deal of the late 1940s and early 1950s, and the New Frontier-Great Society programs of the 1960s. These movements "were essentially pragmatic in their approach to the use of state power and were inclined to decide whether or not to invoke the aid of the state in coping with any particular problem on the merits of the case rather than in accordance with some preconceived plan or idea."[67] However, these social movements differed with respect to particular objectives and programs.

The Progressive Movement.   The Progressive movement owed much of its origins to the Populist and Grange movements of the 1880s, which advocated equal opportunity for farmers, workers, and small-business owners. However, the national Progressive movement leadership was mostly urban and middle class. The formal program of the Progressive party, formed in 1910 to sponsor Theodore Roosevelt as a third-party candidate for president of the United States, hinged on restoring competition and equal opportunity for all.

Progressives had several goals. The first was to provide the underprivileged with a larger share of the nation's benefits. Progressives also wanted to make governments more responsive to voters' wishes and to regulate the economy for the public good. Progressives promoted the concept of the "living wage," an income sufficient for basic family needs such as education, recreation, health, and retirement.

---

[65]F L Allen, *Since Yesterday: The Nineteen-Thirties in America* (New York: Harper & Row, 1940), p. 169.

[66]Gras, *Business and Capitalism,* p. 323.

[67]S Fine, *Laissez-Faire and the General-Welfare State: A Study of Conflict in American Thought, 1865–1901* (Ann Arbor, MI: University of Michigan Press, 1956), p. 380.

Progressives were also strongly concerned with the preservation and sound use of natural resources. They called for conservation of forests and other public lands and for the orderly development of the nation's river basins. Progressives pushed for reform in state and municipal governments in order to control utilities and business more efficiently and to better manage the functions of government. With respect to big business, the Progressives pressed for repeal of protective tariffs and establishment of the National Industrial Commission, which would "compel publicity for the acts of corporations that it supervised, ensure honest capitalization, and check unwarranted price boosts, restrictions on production, and any other unfair practices."[68]

The Progressive movement ended in 1916 with the return of Theodore Roosevelt to the Republican party. President Woodrow Wilson enacted the major proposals of the Progressives in 1913 and 1914 under his New Freedom program. Major social and business reform movements remained dormant until 1932. However, as Franklin D Roosevelt was sworn into office as president on March 4, 1933, he began what he had earlier called "bold, persistent experimentation."

The New Deal.   In his inaugural address, President Roosevelt blamed the bankers for the country's troubles, declaring that "the money changers have fled from their high seats in the temples of our civilization."[69] Roosevelt had closed the nation's banks for several days to prevent mass withdrawals. The banking system was not the only part of the economy in disrepair; 25 percent of the work force was unemployed, and low commodities prices had made farmers destitute. Two days later, the president went on radio and, in the first of many "fireside chats," explained calmly and reassuringly how the banks would be reopened. Aided by his "brain trust" of economic advisers, his legislative program rapidly took shape. Its major thrust was "to gain a greater social justice" for the working class.

The National Industrial Recovery Act (NIRA), enacted in 1933, was aimed at restoring the business sector to full productivity. The act suspended the antitrust laws to allow trade associations to draw up codes of conduct governing prices, hours, and output to encourage production at "fair" rates of profit.

The NIRA included a clause that gave employees the right to organize and bargain through representatives of their own choosing, free from employer interference, restraint, or coercion. This clause encouraged labor to accept the act. Manufacturers, however, opposed the legislated right of labor to bargain collectively. Indeed, when Henry Ford refused to join the

---

[68]Fine, *Laissez-Faire*, p. 390.

[69]A Schlesinger, Jr., *The Coming of the New Deal* (Boston: Houghton Mifflin, 1958), p. 303.

automobile industry's effort to develop a code of conduct, his company suffered lengthy strikes at two plants. Ford fired many of the strikers following the strikes.

After the NIRA was declared unconstitutional in 1935, Roosevelt reintroduced collective bargaining legislation under the Wagner Act, which created the National Labor Relations Board to supervise the rights of employees to select a bargaining agent. Congress also enacted the Fair Labor Standards Act, which specified rights for employees not covered by collective bargaining agreements.

Under the New Deal, the federal government introduced regulatory controls over banks, issues of securities, securities exchanges, public utility holding companies, and motor carriers. Also, the New Deal provided relief and jobs for the needy and the unemployed, constructed public housing, and provided electrical power to farmers and others. It extended low-interest loans to a wide variety of individuals and institutions, generally expanding the entire program of natural resource conservation and introducing the national Social Security program. But despite all the programs and successes of the Keynesian-oriented New Deal, President Roosevelt told the nation in his second inaugural address in 1937, "I see one third of the nation ill-housed, ill-clad, ill-nourished."

By the close of the decade, the New Deal had effectively run its course. According to Cochran, "In spite of loud protests and mutual mistrust, the New Deal and World War II forced government and business to work more closely together, a relationship which grew in importance in later years."[70] Emerging from the war, the nation under the presidency of Harry S Truman entered a new stage of national capitalism.

The Fair Deal.   President Truman supported the basic concepts of the New Deal. His Fair Deal institutionalized the role of government as the stabilizing force in the economy. The Employment Act of 1946 established the three-member Council of Economic Advisers, whose role included assisting the president in formulating economic policy and publishing an annual economic report.

The remainder of the Fair Deal, outlined in a State of the Union Address in 1949, pledged, "Every segment of our population and every individual has a right to expect from his government a fair deal."[71] More specifically, this program included measures to improve the collective bargaining process while prohibiting certain types of strikes, strengthen the antitrust laws, improve farm output and prices, and improve Social Security, medical insurance, and public housing. While some major features of this program were enacted (notably in public housing and Social Security), much of the

[70]Cochran, *American Business,* p. 176.
[71]Quoted in L W Koenig, ed., *The Truman Administration: Its Principles and Practice* (New York: New York University Press, 1956), p. 93.

Fair Deal wallowed in the "do-nothing" 80th Congress of 1947–1948[72] and the "ho-hum" 81st Congress of 1949–1950.[73]

Much of the legislation sought by President Truman was enacted during the presidential tenure of Dwight D Eisenhower from 1953 to 1960. The Eisenhower years featured a middle-of-the-road domestic policy, preserving the social gains of the earlier reform movements while stressing the need for a balanced federal budget. From 1955 to 1960, President Eisenhower worked with an active Democratic Congress. The combination yielded noteworthy achievements in civil rights, air and water pollution control, aid to education, Social Security, highway construction, and agricultural support.[74]

President Eisenhower's cabinet included several business leaders. Indeed, the cabinet was known as "eight millionaires and a plumber." The former term referred to the large number of business leaders who served in the cabinet. The "plumber" was Secretary of Labor Martin Durkin, president of the Journeyman Plumbers and Steamfitters Union.

The New Frontier.   John F Kennedy continued the social progress begun under presidents Truman and Eisenhower. He supported programs to deal with structural unemployment through retraining and area redevelopment.[75] Other social legislation included a housing bill, a minimum-wage increase and extension of the minimum wage to additional groups, and an increase in Social Security benefits.

President Kennedy spoke of a "New Frontier" in economics under which the nation would experience unprecedented economic growth.[76] A major element of the New Frontier concept was the idea of a personal income tax cut to stimulate investment, consumption, and employment at a time when the federal budget was balanced and inflation, production increases, and unemployment were all at tolerable levels.[77]

Under the New Frontier, business was asked to voluntarily maintain price and wage levels in accordance with demonstrated increases in productivity gains. In 1962, an incident occurred that tested President Kennedy's "power of persuasion" to hold down inflation. Roger Blough, chairperson of the board of US Steel, announced a $6-per-ton price increase for steel

---

[72]*Politics in America: The Politics and Issues of the Post-war Years,* 3rd ed. (Washington, DC: Congressional Quarterly Service, 1969), p. 9.

[73]E F Goldman, *The Crucial Decade—And After: America, 1945–1960* (New York: Vantage Books, 1960), p. 95.

[74]J L Sundquist, *Politics and Policy: The Eisenhower, Kennedy and Johnson Years* (Washington, DC: Brookings Institution, 1968), pp. 390–91.

[75]*Structural unemployment* refers to unemployment brought about by the displacement of workers due to changes in the means of production, most notably through automation of previously manual work.

[76]E R Canterbery, *Economics on a New Frontier* (Belmont, CA: Wadsworth, 1968), p. 6.

[77]*Politics in America,* pp. 49–50.

shortly after signing a noninflationary wage settlement with the Steelworkers Union. Other major steel producers also increased prices. Kennedy responded immediately, bringing the full fiscal power of the federal government to bear by threatening to transfer government steel purchases to companies that had not raised prices. Three days after the announcements of increased prices, the major companies returned to the earlier prices. Many businesspeople saw Kennedy's effort as a major example of an "antibusiness" administration. The incident may have contributed to the remarkable price stability experienced from 1961 to 1965, a period during which consumer prices advanced at approximately 1 percent per year.

At the time President Kennedy was assassinated, the Tax Reform Act, the Equal Opportunity Act, and the Civil Rights Act had not yet been passed. All were passed in the year following his death. However, President Kennedy clearly initiated the basic ideas in the three measures.

The Great Society.   The Great Society of President Lyndon B Johnson extended national capitalism. From 1964 to 1968, Congress enacted programs to support medical aid for older Americans, improve consumer information and product safety, improve housing, and create the Office of Economic Opportunity to administer the War on Poverty program. Johnson also created the cabinet-level Department of Housing and Urban Development in 1965 and the Department of Transportation in 1966.

The role of government continually expanded in the Great Society years. Fine concluded,

> Americans would appear to have rejected the admonition that the government is best which governs least and to have endorsed the view that in the interests of the general welfare the state should restrain the strong and protect the weak, should provide such services to the people as private enterprise is unable or unwilling to supply, should seek to stabilize the economy and to counteract the cycle of boom and bust, and should provide the citizen with some degree of economic stability.[78]

The 1970s.   On the domestic front, the administrations of presidents Nixon, Ford, and Carter called for less government involvement in the private sector and less regulation of business. Nevertheless, federal legislation continued to influence nearly every aspect of business management.

By the late 1970s, the distribution of wealth in the United States was changing. The very rich had made up the smallest segment of the American public since the 1830s, and the middle class was suffering an increasing tax burden.

The overhaul of the United States Bankruptcy Code in 1978 set the stage for the explosion of corporate debt that lasted throughout the 1980s. For the

---

[78]Fine, *Laissez-Faire,* pp. 399–400.

first time, companies were permitted to stay in business while they resolved their financial problems.

The 1970s marked the proliferation and growth of international business as technologically sophisticated multinationals produced large volumes of chemicals, machinery, automobiles, and electronics. As international trade in these products and in developing-country raw materials expanded rapidly during the 1970s, the United States grew increasingly dependent on foreign markets. The control of the Organization of Petroleum Exporting Countries (OPEC) over world oil prices brought home the consequences of such interdependence. We will discuss the emergence and operations of multinationals in Chapter 17.

The Reagan and Bush Administrations.   As restructuring through takeovers, diversification, and consolidation became rampant, corporations changed in size, scope, and shape. In April and May 1988 alone, the Campeau Company bought Federated Department Stores for $6.6 billion and sold $1.1 billion of Federated assets to R H Macy & Company; West Point-Pepperell, Inc., agreed to buy J P Stevens & Company for $1.2 billion and sell nearly half of it to the rival bidder, Odyssey Partners; and General Electric and Whirlpool made a deal over the acquisition of Roper Corporation. Tax law changes in the late 1980s made it more attractive to carve up newly acquired assets among takeover bidders.[79]

Employees of these companies faced an uncertain future in the 1980s. In the late 1980s, middle management and even top-level ranks were slashed along with unprofitable divisions. The crash of the stock market on October 19, 1987, threw thousands of investment bankers and financial institution managers into the ranks of the unemployed. Fewer and fewer companies offered lifetime career opportunities.

Public concern about ethics was aired more frequently during the second Reagan term. On the corporate side, Ivan Boesky's conviction and the indictment and conviction of others who took part in insider trading rocked Wall Street. Heroes turned into villains almost overnight. As a result of the crash and the scandals, business schools began to examine their curricula. The study of ethics, long considered irrelevant or "unteachable," became a mandatory part of undergraduate and graduate programs in business.

Ethics in government came under closer scrutiny as members of President Reagan's staff and cabinet became involved in scandals ranging from military procurement to illegal lobbying to trading of arms for hostages. The scandals that rocked the administration were often linked to corporations and to the process through which corporations received government contracts.

Women made major inroads into lower- and middle-management

---

[79]E D Lee, "Takeover Predators New Share the Prey," *The Wall Street Journal,* April 29, 1988, p. 6.

ranks of American companies throughout the 1980s. However, they continued to hit the "glass ceiling" of top management and to earn less than their male counterparts. Minorities and people with disabilities fared even more poorly. The three Reagan appointees to the Supreme Court changed the court's ideological balance and opened some of the civil rights legislation of the 1960s and 1970s to reconsideration.

Concerns about the environment proliferated in the 1980s. During the last year of the Reagan administration, the hazards of acid rain, increased levels of atmospheric ozone, and ocean pollution became all too apparent. During the summer of 1988, as scorching temperatures broke records across the United States, bathers on Atlantic Ocean beaches had to dodge illegally dumped vials of contaminated blood and used hypodermic needles. Elderly people and people with respiratory or allergy problems gasped in smoggy cities from coast to coast, and farmers wondered whether the drought that stunted their crops was due to the "greenhouse effect."

Consumers continued to lobby for safer products and to sue when products failed to fulfill expectations or caused injury. Administration-sponsored legislation to limit damages and preempt state laws that were inconsistent with federal laws slowly worked its way through Congress.

By the 1992 election campaign, the public demanded a change. In mid-August, a Gallup poll asked voters how President Bush was doing. Only 30 percent approved of his performance.[80]

In the early 1990s, the country was mired in a recession that put millions of Americans onto the unemployment rolls. Most Americans no longer believed in unfettered upward mobility or in the "American Dream" of the nineteenth century. Clinton's election in November 1992 can be attributed as much to disenchantment with "Reaganomics" and the recession of the Bush administration as to enthusiasm for the young president. Clinton's promise of change was a siren song voters could not ignore. It remains to be seen whether the ship of state will find clear sailing or pile up on the rocks of inflation, unemployment, poverty, and other economic woes.

Summary

This chapter examined the development of business as the dominant institution in American society. It traced the factors leading to the development of big business and the major stages of business growth. Plentiful natural resources and favorable social and political environments were contributory factors.

The workforce, although growing and capable, was characterized by a shortage of skilled labor. As workers migrated to cities, they received rela-

---

[80]"As Bush Runs Again, History Is Nipping at His Heels," *The New York Times,* August 16, 1992, p. 1.

tively high wages and spent their discretionary income on a wide variety of consumer goods.

Additional factors fostering the growth of big business included the development of affordable and widely available transportation and the expansion of knowledge and know-how. No one of these factors explains the growth of big business in the United States, but together they served as a catalyst for economic and social development.

N S B Gras's six stages of capitalism suggest a framework for analyzing major trends and developments of big business. The periods of industrial capitalism and finance capitalism were dominated by relatively small numbers of individuals who created major business enterprises. The stage of national capitalism involved a larger role for government in guiding and controlling the business sector of the economy. The Progressive movement, the New Deal, the Fair Deal, the New Frontier, the Great Society, and the Reagan and Bush administrations differed in their causes and programs. Since World War II, the relationships between business and the economic environment have generally increased in complexity.

Questions

1. Are the conditions that enabled big business to grow in the United States the same as those that fostered big-business growth in Europe? Explain.
2. What are the common factors of big-business growth, if any, in the United States and Japan?
3. How has American ideology changed in the century since the passage of the Interstate Commerce and Sherman Antitrust Acts?
4. Are there "robber barons" in the 1990s in the sense of a few business leaders who enjoy immense economic power? Do the trends of the 1990s differ from those of the 1980s?
5. What are some fundamental changes in the business–government interaction proposed by the Clinton administration?

BETA CASE 6
THE ORIGINS OF BIG BUSINESS

Robert Mobley, Beta's general counsel and a senior partner of Sullivan, Timberlake, and Frawley, regularly attended the firm's monthly operating committee meeting. At the October meeting, he suggested that the company institute a "document retention" program. It soon became apparent to the committee that Mobley was proposing a program that should have been called a "document disposal" program.

Mobley wanted to implement a policy that would discard most company documents after five years. He argued that if Beta were involved in litigation with the government or another company, documents could be subpoenaed. These documents, however innocent, could be twisted and used for a corporate "witch hunt." Mobley detailed several cases in which memos and telephone messages were used as evidence against a company involved in litigation regarding patent infringement, antitrust, and other violations. On several occasions, damages to the company totaled millions of dollars.

Everyone on the committee seemed persuaded that the "document retention" program was a good idea. The only dissenter was Bill Parker, head of the company's Hospital Products Division. Parker, a history buff who enjoyed reading company chronicles, asked how Beta could hope to have any sense of its present and future if it systematically destroyed the record of its past. As the committee debated the two points of view, Joan McCarthy remembered the process she had gone through as she set company objectives for social issues. She had rummaged through boxes and boxes of old records to find out what the company used to do before she made recommendations for what it *should* do. These boxes were still in an old storeroom next to the boiler in the basement. If Mobley's plan were adopted, they would be destroyed along with other documents.

II

POLITICAL AND COMMUNITY RESPONSIVENESS

The management of social responsiveness is tied to the political and regulatory processes. An intricate web links firms to all levels of government and to the communities in which they operate. Part II establishes the ideological underpinnings of issues that we explore in much greater depth in subsequent chapters.

   The four chapters that follow deal with the company's ability to conduct its affairs legally, to influence its political and regulatory environment in a forthright and positive fashion, and to act as a responsible citizen within its worldwide community.

CHAPTER

7

MANAGING THE LEGAL AND POLITICAL PROCESSES

Managers who formulate and implement social goals strategy must understand the legal structures and political processes that both provide opportunities for and impose constraints on their companies. The underpinnings of the US legal and regulatory systems evolved from a series of uniquely American events and historical antecedents. Today's corporate stakeholders shape and are shaped by legal and political processes that have evolved over two centuries.

In this chapter, we discuss the legal and regulatory frameworks within which corporations and their stakeholders operate. We examine the ideology that led to America's unique governmental system and the process through which legal and regulatory issues are developed and pursued.

The legal framework helps us understand the interaction between business and the political process. We examine the actions a company can take to train managers to operate within the legal and political systems. We also discuss the specific managerial activities that influence the content and passage of legislation. We begin with a look at the legal system.

CASE *Product Liability Law*

During the 1970s and 1980s, product liability was a major issue for American companies. Business pointed to mounting numbers of lawsuits and huge judgments as evidence that the legal system was unfair and unbalanced. There was no nationwide, uniform law covering product liability; cases involving product liability were heard on a state-by-state basis. Huge judgments were awarded to plaintiffs in some states, while in others, awards for similar cases were relatively small. In some states, product liability cases were heard by judges; in others, juries made the decisions and allocated awards.

193

Trade organizations pressured Congress to pass federal legislation that would eliminate aspects of product liability law their industries found particularly oppressive. In some states, for example, companies could be held liable even if their misconduct was unintentional. Business wanted the law changed to award punitive damages only if the company's wrongdoing was deliberate.

Business also wanted Congress to enact statutes of repose. A *statute of repose* assumes a product has a limited useful lifetime and provides an outer limit of liability for that product. After a specified time, the product's useful life is assumed to be over, and the owner or user can no longer sue the manufacturer. Industry claimed it was unreasonable to assume a product could be used forever.[1] The reform movement gathered support when litigation studies showed the number of product liability suits in federal courts increased 758 percent from 1975 to 1985.

Equally troublesome to companies were their soaring insurance premiums. The genesis of the insurance crisis was complicated. State regulations mandate how much insurance companies can write using a formula based on a company's capital and surplus. Insurance companies collect dollars from the premiums of the firms they insure and invest those dollars to earn income. Investment income, coupled with the premiums, offsets expected losses from claims.

In the early 1980s, interest rates rose dramatically, leading insurance companies to drop their premiums. They expected they could write more policies to generate more money, which they could then invest at the higher interest rates. But, in 1984, interest rates began to fall, losses rose, and the insurance industry lost nearly $4 billion.

Insurance companies hit the ceiling on the number of policies permitted by state laws. Since they were forced to reduce the amount of insurance they could write, they hiked their premiums to reduce their losses. Businesses went to state legislatures, arguing that reform of tort law (civil law that allows recovery of damages) was necessary because they could no longer afford to buy sufficient insurance.

During the 1980s, some states passed reform laws covering some of the above issues and others. However, Congress repeatedly rejected any attempt to pass federal legislation.[2] Lobbyists and other interest groups continued to work furiously on behalf of their constituents.

Some consumer advocate groups argued that big business would take advantage of uniform limited-liability laws by foisting unsafe products on an unsuspecting public. They were convinced many businesses would try to save money in manufacturing if their legal liability for accidents or problems were limited. Many manufacturers and their lobbyists argued that the huge settlements and perpetual liability reduced their competitiveness and required them to pass unreasonable costs on to consumers.

In September 1992, after a decade of wrangling, a bill called the Federal Product Liability Fairness Act reached the floor of the Senate. If passed, the law would supersede most state laws. It had some important provisions.

Under this proposed law, the statute of limitations would begin to run only when claimants recognized they had suffered an injury and identified its cause. For exam-

---

[1]F E Zollers and R G Cook, "Product Liability Reform: What Happened to the Crisis?," *Business Horizons,* (September–October 1990), pp. 47–52.
[2]Ibid.

ple, an asbestos worker would have two years in which to file a claim after he was diagnosed with cancer, provided the cancer could be traced to asbestos exposure.

The bill also encouraged pretrial settlement. If a claimant rejected settlement and, after a trial, received less than the settlement offer, the claimant would have to pay the other side's legal costs.[3]

An important provision of the bill eliminated joint liability for "pain and suffering." *Joint liability* is the so-called "deep pockets" liability in which one defendant may be forced to pay for the acts of others. For example, suppose a plaintiff wins a $2 million lawsuit against a total of four companies, three small and one large. The three small companies are each held 30 percent responsible, and the one large company is held 10 percent responsible. The plaintiff can now collect the entire $2 million from the one large company, which is supposed to act as a collection agency for the three smaller companies.[4] Despite strong bipartisan support, the bill was defeated.

Immediately after Bill Clinton's inauguration in January 1993, stakeholders from both sides geared up for a new fight. One major issue, left over from the defeated bill, was the passage of legislation limiting the ability of companies to conceal internal safety records in federal suits over allegedly defective products. Any new law would be particularly important to ongoing litigation involving cigarettes, breast implants, and automobiles.

Pro-plaintiff stakeholders, including Ralph Nader's Public Citizen organization, planned to introduce legislation to require public disclosure of internal company documents. These same groups prepared to pressure Congress to expand the law to allow injured victims to sue polluters for personal injuries related to toxic dumping. (Current federal law allows recovery for cleanup but not for personal injury.) Another legal issue of concern was whether injured workers would be allowed to sue employers for damages in addition to civil penalties.[5]

Pro-business groups, insurance industry lobbyists, consumer groups, and other stakeholders agreed that these unresolved, contentious issues would not be settled easily.

Questions

1. Should a federal law that covers product liability law nationwide be passed? Why or why not?
2. If new federal legislation is passed, are plaintiffs likely to prevail against big business?
3. What are the relevant arguments big business should use to justify limiting damages?
4. Is it reasonable and just to have product liability awards differ vastly from state to state? Why or why not?

---

[3]V E Schwartz, "Finally, a Chance to Reform Product Liability Law," *The Wall Street Journal,* September 9, 1992, p. A15.

[4]D Frum, "High Noon," *Forbes,* September 14, 1992, p. 478.

[5]M Geyelin, "Product-Liability Groups Take Up Arms," *The Wall Street Journal,* January 29, 1993, p. B1.

The Legal Framework

The ideology and value system of a society both shape and are shaped by that society's legal framework. The US common law system evolved from British colonial laws. However, Britain had no written constitution, had no written fundamental law, and gave final power to the Parliament. Britain's system basically differed from those of its European neighbors. Most European countries operated under the civil law system, in which bureaucracies administer but do not interpret the rules and laws legislatures pass.

The US Constitution

The founders of the new United States were determined to create a stable system that limited the power of the people, prescribed rules of decisions that were binding on a nationwide court system, and set up a framework within which all government acts must be "subject to law, as interpreted by its traditional custodians, the judges."[6]

The US Constitution is the written foundation on which the nation's legal framework rests and provides the guiding principles by which the United States is governed. At the end of the eighteenth century, a Supreme Court justice defined a *constitution* as "the form of government, delineated by the mighty hand of the people, in which certain fundamental laws are established."[7]

The framers of the Constitution were determined to remedy what they perceived as major weaknesses of the colonial period's Articles of Confederation. The Articles of Confederation placed all authority with the state legislatures, leaving the Union with no coercive power over individuals unless specifically granted by the state. The framers were particularly troubled by government's inability to regulate commerce. What would happen, they mused, if Pennsylvania levied tariffs against goods coming from New Jersey? It was imperative to put enough power in the hands of the federal government to prevent what some called a "drift toward anarchy."

The framers of the Constitution were acutely aware they could provide no more than a framework for government. They could not possibly cover every contingency that would occur over time. The result was a constitution that generally rested on the authority of the nation over the people. It established a tripartite central government consisting of separate legislative, executive, and judicial branches, each of which had checks and balances on the other two. Above all, the Constitution created a rule of law over every private or public individual, no matter how highly placed.

The great power of the US common law system is that laws change over time and are based on previous decisions (precedents). Common law tends

---

[6]B Schwartz, *A Commentary on the Constitution of the United States, Part I: The Powers of Government* (New York: Macmillan, 1963), p. 21.
[7]Ibid., p. 1.

to be closely connected to the prevailing value system. Over the lifetimes of most American adults, values and laws have changed regarding such fundamental societal issues as abortion, minority rights, capital punishment, religious observance in schools, and equal opportunity.

As Table 7–1 shows, all legal issues are categorized:

TABLE 7–1   Legal Classifications

Private and Public Law

Private law establishes rights among private companies and individuals, as distinct from those in which society is involved. This classification includes contract and property law.

Public law is usually established by administrative regulations and statutes. The interests of society as a whole or protected classes of people are directly involved. They are usually represented by a government agency or its officer. These rules cover environmental law, securities law, antitrust law, and labor law. The issues may be constitutional, administrative, or criminal in nature.

Procedural Law and Substantive Law

Procedural law pertains to the operation of the court system and the conduct of trials. In other words, it is the mechanism by which rights and duties are enforced.

Substantive law establishes rights and duties. It defines the legal relationships among people and between people and the state.

Criminal and Civil Law

Criminal law covers violations of the public rules of behavior. It is divided into felonies and misdemeanors. Corporations can and do commit felonies for which their officers may be held criminally accountable.

Civil law covers lawsuits brought by one party to assert a private right. In a civil suit, the plaintiff may be a person, a corporation, or a government entity. Civil law covers many areas:

1. *Breach of contract* covers the legal relationships that individuals create by their own agreement.
2. A *tort* is a civil wrong other than breach of contract. The law gives the plaintiff the right to recover damages. Malpractice suits are a major area in today's society. A plaintiff seeks dollar damages but not punishment of the defendant.
3. *Law of property* concerns ownership and possession of real estate and personal property. A fundamental concept of property ownership is the right to exclude others from possession and use.

SOURCE: R N Corley, R L Black, and O L Reed, *The Legal Environment of Business,* 5th ed. (New York: McGraw-Hill, 1981), pp. 1–8; T W Dunfee, J R Bellace, and A J Rosoff, *Business and Its Legal Environment* (Englewood Cliffs, NJ: Prentice-Hall, 1983), pp. 5–6.

Informal Societal Rules

Politicians routinely declare that the United States is a nation of laws, and almost all citizens agree that no society can exist without a set of strongly enforced rules. But we know from experience that the formal legal apparatus determines only part of our behavior. In our society as well as others, complex written and unwritten rules guide individuals and organizations.

All communities, whether primitive or highly industrialized, develop social environments that dictate behavior the group considers vital to its welfare. When an individual or an institution violates these customs, mores, or norms, society may levy penalties as severe or even more severe than those for violating formally passed laws. In simple societies without written law, customs are de facto laws and the community informally enforces them. As communities become increasingly complex, they generally formalize their bodies of norms into laws.

Many new laws affecting the conduct of American businesses have been passed in the last two decades. But altering the business environment does not *necessarily* require the passage of new laws. In the United States, for example, a conservative president may appoint an attorney general who is less aggressive than his or her predecessor in enforcing antitrust laws. Or the president may issue executive orders that intensify or diminish equal employment efforts. In such instances, although Congress has not passed new laws, the effect on business may be profound.

When the chief executive's political philosophy differs from that of his predecessor, the government's administrative apparatus reflects different levels of commitment to the enforcement of legislation. Although it is too soon at this writing to draw firm conclusions, it is likely that the priorities of the Clinton administration will contrast sharply with those of the two previous Republican administrations.

Before the 1960s, executives were rarely held criminally responsible for actions of their corporations, but by the 1990s, the legal climate had changed. Holcomb and Sethi have explored the topic of corporate and executive criminal liability.[8] They suggest standards, remedies, and managerial responses. Since the early 1980s, society has become more determined to further define and curb corporate crime. The major task is to protect social welfare and balance that protect against corporate rights and power.

Holcomb and Sethi caution that it is difficult to assess criminal liability as it is applied to corporations and executives. It is equally difficult to determine penalties and evaluate the deterrent effect of a punishment. For executives to be found guilty, three elements must be considered:

· Did the individual make a choice to commit a wrongful act?
· Was this choice freely made?
· Did the individual know, or could he or she have recognized, the wrongfulness of this act?[9]

---

[8]J M Holcomb and S P Sethi, "Corporate and Executive Criminal Liability: Appropriate Standards, Remedies and Managerial Responses," *Business and the Contemporary World,* (Summer 1992), p. 92.
[9]Ibid., p. 92.

Similar determinations must be made about corporate intent. For example,

- Did a corporate practice or policy violate the law?
- Was it reasonably foreseeable that a corporate practice or policy would result in a corporate agent's violation of the law?
- Did the corporation adopt a corporate agent's violation of the law?[10]

Holcomb and Sethi suggest that a "corporate ethos test" be applied requiring the government to prove that a corporate agent or executive committed criminal conduct and that a preexisting corporate ethos, or set of values, encouraged the conduct. In the absence of such an ethos, the corporation could not be found guilty.

Once guilt *has* been established in so-called "white-collar crimes," a number of laws dictating the severity of punishments can be applied. For example, in recent years the Racketeer Influenced and Corrupt Practices Act (RICO) has been used against businesses to combat fraud. Originally RICO was passed to fight organized crime, but the court now interprets it to cover a wide range of business activities that can be loosely construed as racketeering. The government used the threat of RICO to persuade Drexel Burnham Lambert's Michael Milken to plead guilty and pay a huge fine. RICO allows the government to impose compensatory and punitive damages, court costs, attorney's fees, and treble damages and to freeze corporate assets.

Other laws applying to corporate crime include the following:

- The Mail and Wire Fraud statutes cover situations in which individuals have used the postal or telephone systems for illegal activities. Mail-order companies and telemarketers have been prosecuted under these statutes.
- The Insider Trading Sanctions Act increased penalties for insider trading to $1 million for individuals and $2.5 million for corporations. The act also included bounty payments to informers.
- Penalties for violating the Foreign Corrupt Practices Act were raised in 1988 to $2 million for corporations and $100,000 for individuals. Individuals can be imprisoned for as long as five years.[11]

The societal question yet to be answered is whether stiffer penalties will deter corporate crime. The US Sentencing Commission is currently working to establish penalty guidelines for white-collar crime. It is also encouraging firms to institute steps to deter crime. The commission recommends that companies develop comprehensive ethics codes and implement policies to persuade employees that the codes can have economic rewards.

---

[10]Ibid., p. 93.

[11]M T Tucker, "Corporate Crime and Punishment," *Business and the Contemporary World,* Summer 1992, pp. 160–62.

The Political and Legal Frameworks

The political and legal frameworks of business are inseparable. The political framework has both legal and quasi-legal components. The legal framework includes acts lawmaking bodies pass at all levels of government. There are quasi-legal influences on decision making that often have the same force as laws. For example, when the executive branch of the government establishes price and wage "guidelines," the guidelines are not legally enforceable. However, an executive who makes a decision to raise prices beyond the guidelines must carefully consider the possible consequences.

It is clearly illegal to participate in an explicit agreement among companies to divide the nation into exclusive territories to restrain competition. However, trade practice statements and trade association agreements, combined with sanctions ("violators will be subject to reprisals from other members of the group"), may influence companies more than the law itself does. Therefore, quasi-legal devices, coupled with implied sanctions for violators, often restrain business executives from taking certain actions whether or not those actions are in violation of the law.

The underlying purpose of most legal and quasi-legal regulation of business is simply to encourage and maintain a desirable level of competition. But different groups, such as industry competitors and customers, may have significantly different views as to what constitutes a "desirable" level.

Corporate Political Stakeholders

As one of the most central institutions in US society, business is deeply involved in and affected by the political and legal processes. In the view of Jeffrey Pfeffer and Gerald Salancik, a business organization is one part of the larger social and political system. Firms survive and prosper to the extent that they effectively deal with the other organizations that make up that larger system.[12] Pfeffer and Salancik observe that "effectiveness derives from the management of demands, particularly the demands of interest groups upon which the organizations depend for resources and support."[13] Chrysler Corporation might well have gone bankrupt had it not built an effective coalition of stakeholders who influenced the White House and pressured Congress to secure a bailout.

Stakeholder groups disagree over the role business plays or should play in the political process. Consumer activists may object to power companies' advocacy of nuclear energy because they are concerned about safety. On the other hand, shareholders in power companies may support nuclear energy because they want a good return on their investment. Both sides apply political and legal pressure to achieve their own group's goals. To understand this conflict, we need to look more closely at the question of corporate political power.

---

[12]J Pfeffer and G R Salancik, *The External Control of Organizations* (New York: Harper & Row, 1978), p. 11.

[13]Ibid., p. 2.

A large number of books and articles have been written about various aspects of corporate political power. They range from sensationalistic journalism and anticapitalist tracts to full-blown, scholarly treatises. Ira Millstein and Salem M Katsh observe that many people are concerned that corporations have virtually unlimited ability to exercise power in a wide spectrum of economic, social, and political issues.[14] While corporations do have considerable influence in shaping their environment, stakeholders can bring countervailing pressure to bear on firms' autonomy. Increasingly, companies are choosing to avoid adverse notoriety by acknowledging the legitimacy of stakeholder concerns.

Major Stakeholders Groups

Exhibit 7–1 shows the stakeholder influence map for seven major groups of stakeholders.

News and Broadcast Media.   The media provide information that shapes public opinion. Public opinion "establishes the intellectual and moral environment within which corporate managers formulate their own views of corporate responsibility; it establishes . . . the likely expectations of shareholders . . . and it defines the public will to which government officials must be responsive . . ."[15] The media affect corporate power by the way they report corporate policy issues, either positively or negatively.

---

[14]I Millstein and S M Katsh, *The Limits of Corporate Power* (New York: McMillan, 1981), p. xvii.
[15]Ibid., p. 231.

EXHIBIT 7–1

Stakeholder influence map for major political stakeholders

	Direct	Indirect
External	Institutional investors: Banks and insurance companies Government	Broadcast media: Television and radio Press: Newspapers and magazines Industry associations Intellectual community Public-interest groups Government
Internal	Employees: Management level and lower level	Labor unions

Industry Associations.   Some associations set industry standards to allow corporations to regulate their own behavior. Other associations promote product quality and safety guidelines that industry participants can treat as minimally acceptable standards. Still other associations, such as the US Chamber of Commerce, the Business Roundtable, and the National Association of Manufacturers, serve as informational conduits between industry and government. They also develop responses to the demands of other stakeholders. For example, nearly 100 companies contributed information on corporate ethics to the Business Roundtable's report on policy and practice in company conduct.

Employees.   Management-level employees express convictions about the social and ethical role of their corporations. Lower-level employees exert influence on their companies through their own and union demands for better working conditions and social responsiveness. Every employee influences corporate behavior through the way she votes in local, state, and federal elections.

Shareholders and Institutional Investors.   Shareholders elect the board of directors, which makes basic decisions regarding corporation structure. They also constrain corporate decisions to merge, acquire, or be acquired. Labor unions, banks, insurance companies, churches, universities, and other institutions can and do use their stock holdings to influence corporate behavior.

The "Intellectual Community."   This group of stakeholders consists of academics, students, professionals, and others who influence what many members of society think and do. Intellectuals write articles and books to raise issues concerning the corporate, legal, and political environments. Conservatives and liberals alike continue to debate the degree of influence of the written medium.

Public-Interest Groups.   Various public-interest associations advocate special perspectives on certain issues. Some have become very adept at soliciting funds from foundations and grass-roots supporters. They also have learned how to use the political process, the media, and the courts to further their causes. As we pointed out earlier in the nuclear energy debate, different groups espouse conflicting goals. Corporate managers confronted by the demands of organized public-interest groups must determine how each group's demands fit the economic, social, or legal constraints their company faces.

Government.   Government officials can apply subtle or even overt pressure on corporations to make them behave in a particular way. Ronald Reagan tried (unsuccessfully) to prevent Dresser Industries from selling its French-made turbines to the Soviet Union. John F Kennedy was more successful in his attempt to make US Steel roll back a price hike. Legislators can affect corporate policy by threatening to take legislative action if such policy does not change.[16]

Corporate Political Power

Edwin Epstein makes the critical point that power—the capacity to control or determine the behavior of others—should not be confused with *potential* power.[17] Epstein points out that both a *base* of power and the means of power may exist without power ever being exercised. For example, some interest groups have expressed concern about corporations' tremendous wealth. These groups point out that if even a small percentage of this money were used to pursue a political cause, the effect on society could be profound.

E I DuPont de Nemours, the number one chemical company in the Fortune 500 in 1987, had sales income of over $30 billion. Only 2 percent of that total would put $15 million at the company's disposal.[18] However, Epstein notes, "because there are so many internal demands on company monies, only a very small—one might even say minuscule—percentage of corporate assets or revenues is used for political purposes."[19]

A few companies have used large amounts of money to curry favor, typically in operations outside the United States. Prior to the passage of the Foreign Corrupt Practices Act in 1977, American corporations were party to numerous cases of bribery. For example, McDonnell Douglas admitted making payments on aircraft sales to Pakistan, Zaire, South Korea, the Philippines, and Venezuela between 1972 and 1977. General Tire and Rubber made payments of $500,000 in Morocco in 1969 to get approval of plant expansion. Burroughs admitted that $1.5 million in corporate funds might have been used to pay bribes to foreign officials.[20] In a much less dramatic case, Kenny International Corporation, a small stamp distributor, pleaded guilty to paying a $337,000 bribe to the prime minister of the Cook Islands in the South Pacific to keep the company's exclusive rights to distribute the island's postage stamps.[21]

Epstein assesses corporate political resources such as organization, access, and patronage.[22] *Organizationally,* corporations can draw on their own public or government relations staff to pursue their political agendas. They can also use employees, shareholders, suppliers, and customers to help them create a favorable corporate political identity.

---

[16]Ibid., pp. 229–55.

[17]E Epstein, *The Corporation in American Politics* (Englewood Cliffs, NJ: Prentice-Hall, 1969), p. 197.

[18]*Fortune,* April 25, 1988, pp. D33–D39.

[19]Epstein, *The Corporation,* p. 197.

[20]*U.S. News & World Report,* June 27, 1988, p. 46.

[21]B Jackson, Overseas Bribery Gets a Lot Less Attention, *The Wall Street Journal,* February 23, 1983, p. B1.

[22]Epstein, *The Corporation,* pp. 192–208.

Access means corporations have the opportunity to get a hearing and to make their case at a crucial time. Top executives of large corporations can easily make social as well as formal contacts with government officials. Bill Gates of Microsoft, Jack Welch of General Electric, and CEOs of other top firms are likely to be invited to social and business functions that bring them into contact with members of the administration or of Congress. Finally, large companies use *patronage* to obtain leverage with their employees, suppliers, subcontractors, state and local governments, and present and even former government officials. Sometimes former government officials end up on the payroll of a major company or trade association.

A 1986 survey by the General Accounting Office found that private companies had hired many former Pentagon officials to work on the same weapons projects they supervised while still in Congress.[23] Even before President Clinton's inauguration, Warren Christopher, head of the transition team and now secretary of state, announced new, more stringent legal guidelines covering former government officials who wish to become lobbyists. The new administration clearly hoped to avoid situations like that created by Michael K Dever. Dever, former director of the White House Office of Management and Budget, left the government to form a lobbying firm that represented the governments of Canada, Singapore, South Korea, Mexico, and Saudi Arabia, as well as domestic and foreign companies.[24] Former senator Richard S Schweiker, who had served as secretary of health and human services, took a job as president of the American Council of Life Insurance.[25]

Notwithstanding the fact that corporations have considerable political resources, business firms do not constitute a threat to political democracy in the United States. Epstein argues that (1) political resources are not synonymous with political power; (2) corporations do not have a monopoly over political resources (he points to countervailing special-interest groups such as farm groups, organized labor, and others); (3) the public is too deeply committed to social pluralism to allow business to become politically dominant; and (4) major constraints within the business system are played out in intercorporate competition.[26]

Political and Legal Stakeholder Groups

Stakeholder groups spend a great deal of time and money attempting to influence the political and legal processes. Many of the groups that fall into the external indirect quadrant of the stakeholder influence map include business associations, political action committees (PACs), other lobbies,

---

[23]J H Cushman, Jr., "Pentagon-to-Contractor Job Shift Is Profiled," *The New York Times,* August 31, 1986.

[24]M Tolchin, "Democrats Press Meese for Inquiry on Dever Ethics," *The New York Times,* April 25, 1986, pp. A1, A11.

[25]J R Dickenson, "Dever Isn't the Only One Lobbying His Former Colleagues," *The Washington Post National Weekly Edition,* May 26, 1986, p. 12.

[26]Epstein, *The Corporation,* p. 227.

and industry groups. In addition to these external stakeholders, managers within the corporation can affect the drafting of laws and passage of legislation by forming their own PACs or other stakeholder groups. In this section, we first look at the structure and the role of business associations. Next, we examine PACs and the various kinds of PACs that affect the political and legal processes.

Business Associations

A variety of business associations have political agendas. The National Association of Manufacturers (NAM) is one of the oldest and best known. The NAM follows issues that manufacturers consider important and disseminates information to its membership. Lobbyists who work for the NAM represent many companies that cannot afford to have their own Washington-based staff. Some areas particularly important to the NAM are international economic affairs, government regulation, and taxation policy.[27]

The US Chamber of Commerce has a membership of over 150,000 corporations and is the parent organization of regional and municipal chambers of commerce. The agenda of the US Chamber of Commerce is very broad. Its tasks include helping members testify before Congress and spreading information about pending legislation. In addition, the chamber represents business in court, publishes reports in support of business, and helps executives use the media to communicate their goals more effectively.

The Business Roundtable is an association made up of nearly 200 CEOs of the top US corporations. It was created in 1972 during the Nixon administration. The underlying concept of the Business Roundtable is that business and government have mutual interests that can affect corporate profits. The Roundtable prefers to deal with relatively apolitical issues such as American competitiveness, the budget deficit, and global trade.[28] From time to time, the Roundtable publishes reports on various issues. In its 1988 report, *Corporate Ethics: A Prime Business Asset,* the Roundtable compiled material from 100 companies on philosophies, policies, and procedures dealing with corporate ethics.[29]

Political Action Committees

A decade ago Gerald D Keim, Carl P Zeithaml, and Barry D Baysinger observed, "one of the most visible changes in the U.S. political landscape over the past ten years has been the increased participation of corporations in electoral and legislative processes."[30] *Political action committees (PACs)*

---

[27]R A Bucholz, *Business Environment and Public Policy, 3rd ed.* (Englewood Cliffs, NJ: Prentice-Hall, 1989), p. 528.

[28]"Knights of the Roundtable," *Business Week,* October 21, 1988, pp. 39–44.

[29]The Business Roundtable, *Corporate Ethics: A Prime Business Asset,* February 1988.

[30]G D Keim, C P Zeithaml, and B D Baysinger, "SMR Forum: New Directions for Corporate Political Strategy," *Sloan Management Review* (Spring 1984), p. 53.

are fund-raising organizations that solicit money from employees and share-holders to use as political campaign contributions.

Federal law allows corporations to donate, per election cycle, up to $10,000 to a candidate through a PAC. Although an individual can give only $2,000 per election cycle directly to a candidate, he can use a technique called *bundling* to give far more. Bundling is the practice of making contributions to a PAC in addition to the direct contribution to the candidate. In the 1990 election, executives and families employed by Shearson Lehman Hutton, Inc., gave $71,800 to Senator Bill Bradley, a member of the Senate Finance Committee.[31]

Labor unions invented PACs in the 1940s as a means of supporting prounion political candidates. The business community was upset by what it saw as a unified effort to affect legislation, but it did not immediately retaliate by forming its own PACs on a large scale. Until the 1960s, the more usual pattern was for business leaders to give large personal contributions to political candidates. In fact, individuals still give substantial sums. In the 1992 election, individuals gave more than $9 million to party committees whose contributions are not limited by federal election law.

Corporate PACs proliferated in the 1970s for two major reasons. First, federal election laws restricted the amount of money individuals could contribute to a candidate. Second, the Federal Campaign Act of 1971 officially sanctioned corporate PACs. In 1974, the last barrier to PAC activity was removed when the 1971 act was amended to allow corporations with government contracts to form PACs.[32]

PACs of all kinds began to proliferate in the early 1980s, but corporate PACs were the fastest-growing single segment. These PACs, which were set up by individual companies, numbered 89 in 1974, 1,682 in 1986, and 4,172 in 1990.[33] During the 1990 congressional elections, PAC money accounted for one-quarter of the campaign funds of winning senators and one-half of the funds of house winners.

In the 1992 elections, some corporations and other organizations spent huge amounts to support their favorite presidential and congressional candidates. For example, the American Federation of State, County, and Municipal Employees (AFSCME), which lobbies for job protection for striking public employees and opposes privatization, gave the Democrats $133,360.

Chevron Corporation produces petroleum products and natural gas. Its subsidiaries produce chemicals, fertilizers, coal, and other minerals and are involved in real estate development. Chevron gave $130,000 to the Republicans and $44,750 to the Democrats. Philip Morris, which makes Marlboro

[31]"PAC Supplements Are Growing, Study Shows," *The New York Times,* July 19, 1992, p. 19.

[32]A L Fritschler and B H Ross, *How Washington Works: The Executive's Guide to Government* (Cambridge, MA: Ballinger Publishing, 1987), p. 87.

[33]"Buying Attention But Not Votes," *Washington Post Weekly,* April 14, 1986, p. 33; "Small Dog Bites PAC," *The Economist,* May 9, 1992, p. 27.

and Virginia Slims cigarettes, Miller beer, Kraft products, Post cereals, and Jell-O puddings, gave the GOP $279,830 and the Democrats $32,000. These are just a few of the many corporations, interest groups, unions, and trade organizations that have filled political party coffers.[34]

The ethical issues surrounding PAC contributions have made some members of Congress very uneasy. Beginning in 1988, bills were introduced to limit the influence of PACs in congressional campaigns. Although they have not passed, the political process has intensified the debate over whether politicians should accept money from all PACs, pick and choose the PACs they believe match their own views, or reject all PAC money, regardless of the cause.

While the ethical issues are debatable, it appears that PACs will continue to participate actively in the political process. Corporations and industry groups will keep making contributions to political campaigns, and corporate PAC activities will continue to be part of the social issues process. PACs will monitor regulatory and legislative issues, develop issue and advocacy advertising, and foster employee and investor relations. To conduct their activities effectively, managers of corporate PACs should follow the same strategic formulation and implementation processes that companies do for other issues. Exhibit 7–2 shows where PAC money originates.

---

[34]S McIntosh, "Political Tycoons of '92 Campaign," *USA Today/International Edition,* June 12, 1992, p. 5A.

EXHIBIT 7–2
Origins of PAC money.

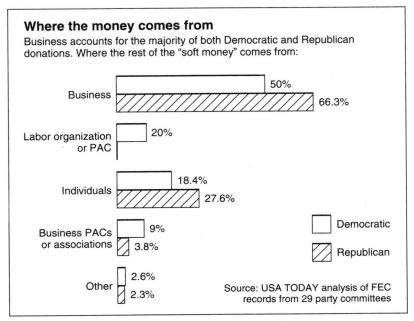

SOURCE: Marty Baumann, "Analysis of FEC Records from 29 Party Committees," *USA Today,* June 12, 1992.

The Corporate Political Program

Carl P Zeithaml and Gerald D Keim propose a five-phase framework for planning, evaluation, and integration of a corporate political program.[35] In *phase I,* the planning phase, it is critical that management at all levels understand and support the political program. Management should implement a program evaluation process that incorporates qualitative and quantitative measures of the political activity.

Phase II is the program assessment phase. The company should ask itself two questions. The first is "Why did the corporation develop a political action program?" Even the process of asking this question helps the company assess the personal commitment of the CEO and focus on operating problems that might be due to regulation. The second question is "What are the objectives and strategies of the corporation's political program?" As the manager identifies issues, he or she should apply the framework for strategy formulation discussed in Chapter 2. The corporation should take care to identify past, current, and potential issues. The product of this step should be a document that outlines each issue and its effect on the corporation.

During *phase III,* managers develop an issue database and a document that analyzes the effect each issue is likely to have on the corporation. Then senior managers from line and staff should prioritize the issues in terms of their impact on the corporation.

In *phase IV,* managers select a specific strategy and carry it out. They should appraise the probability of success realistically.

Phase V, program implementation and evaluation, should follow the guidelines in Chapter 3. During the implementation phase, managers should monitor costs and returns relative to the objectives they have set.

The Zeithaml and Keim recommendations just presented assume the manager understands the political process. However, most managers admit they know very little about the inner workings of the political process on the national level. Indeed, many do not even understand the steps in which a bill passes through Congress or the process of rule making in regulatory agencies. In the remainder of this chapter, we will discuss the skills a political manager must possess, the basic steps in the passage of bills through Congress, and the means by which laws and rules are administered.

Skills of the Political Manager

Formulation and implementation of social goals is a managerial skill that is becoming increasingly important in American companies. Michael Useem recommends the development of in-house programs for middle managers to help those managers understand the legislative process and the power of stakeholders to affect the firm.[36] As he notes, social goals must be imple-

---

[35]C P Zeithaml and G D Keim, "How to Implement a Corporate Political Action Program," *Sloan Management Review* (Winter 1985), pp. 23–31.

[36]M Useem, "The Rise of the Political Manager," *Sloan Management Review* (Fall 1985), pp. 15–26.

mented throughout the company; companies can no longer relegate them to a public affairs office. Useem observes that various levels of management require different political skills.

Entry-level managers often come into a large company with little or no interest in a political agenda. Their job is to gain control over functional area tasks and to learn the culture of the company. But they can be spokespeople for their firms.

Middle-level managers, the implementers of social issues, must participate if the company is to realize its goals. Some companies undertake a variety of activities to heighten political awareness and activity in the achievement of social goals. To foster participation, firms encourage employees to get involved in community activities and even give employees time off for this work. Company publications often feature articles about employees who accomplished fund-raising goals or serve on community boards of directors. Some companies conduct public affairs courses, both inside and outside the firm.

Senior managers must go beyond participation in public affairs courses. They should become directly involved in public affairs through service on the boards of directors of other companies. They should take part in the deliberations of business associations such as the Business Roundtable, serve on boards of trustees of nonprofit organizations, or meet with high-ranking government officials. They must also actively support programs and legislation on the national level.

In sum, the more involved managers at all levels become in the political process, the better able they will be to influence the issues that affect their firms. Participation in the political process will be more effective and more relevant to the firm if managers understand how laws and regulations are passed.

Some large, politically active firms establish offices in Washington. The Washington-based staff usually consists of lawyers or public affairs specialists who have experience in government. Often the office maintains close relations with trade organizations or lobbyists in the firm's industry. To be most effective, the Washington office staff works with all three branches of the federal government: the executive, the legislative, and the judicial. Its primary responsibility is to keep corporate headquarters informed about issues that have potential impact on the firm's strategy and to promote the interests of the firm to government officials. As in any policy-setting matter, the CEO's commitment and involvement are critical.[37]

Passage of Legislation

The politically effective manager deals with issues before they harden into laws and regulations. Throughout the history of the United States, managers

---

[37] R A Bucholz, *Essentials of Public Policy for Management* (Englewood Cliffs, NJ: Prentice-Hall, 1985), pp. 209–14.

and owners of corporations have been remarkably successful in influencing the design and content of legislation. The American legislative system provides for citizen participation at a number of points before a law is passed.

Prelegislative Phase

In the prelegislative phase, the politically astute manager realizes that public expectations of corporate behavior are changing. The manager notes that certain issues are beginning to attract the attention of community action groups or lobbies. Newspapers, television, and other media report on the particulars of the issues, and citizens may initiate petitions to get the issues on local or statewide ballots.

In the 1992 presidential election, we saw how important television and radio talk shows became in developing public awareness of a wide range of issues. The Ross Perot candidacy was fertilized by a new, grass-roots involvement of people who formerly were estranged from the political process. The Clinton campaign, and later the Clinton administration, continued to air and build consensus around issues through a televised "town meeting" forum. Sophisticated polling techniques gave political leaders on both sides of the aisle instant feedback about constituents' views. This information made it easier for politicians to anticipate the issues that might be politicized.

On the national level, firms find that nonprofit organizations, lobbies, and even individuals heighten public awareness of potentially harmful products or situations. In January 1993, two children died after eating hamburgers in Jack in the Box restaurants in the state of Washington. Consumer groups charged the company's food preparation standards were inadequate. Others put the blame on federal meat inspection policies. Secretary of Agriculture Mike Espy immediately recommended a series of steps to improve food safety. But it took 200 illnesses and several deaths of small children to generate new policies and procedures and ensure compliance with those already in place.

Legislative Phase

For an issue to become law or a regulation to be imposed, legislators have to take up the cause at some point. Very often people within a legislator's state or district have strong feelings about a cause. In 1977, amendments were added to the US Clean Air Act to require scrubbers in coal-fired generating plants. By 1988, public opinion had tilted so strongly in favor of increased legislation that many members of Congress supported drastic cuts in sulfur dioxide emissions. New laws will require that utility companies spend several billion dollars on the cleanup. Despite the high cleanup costs, legislators from New England, whose forests are suffering from the fallout known as "acid rain," are increasingly supporting strong laws to cut down emissions.

Their constituents are very concerned—and very vocal—about the death of fish in lakes and ponds, the defoliation of forests, and general harm to wilderness areas.

The National Legislative Process

To turn a concern into a law, legislators must follow the series of steps in Exhibit 7–3. The nuances and small procedural points need not concern us within the context of this book. We will deal only with bills initiated by senators and members of the House.

Step 1: Introduction of the Bill.   The *introduction of the bill* is the first step in the legislative process. Although the procedure Senate and House members use to introduce bills differs slightly, once the bill has been introduced in either house of Congress, it is given a number prefixed with *HR* for the House and *S* for the Senate. Then the bill is labeled with the sponsor's name and is sent to the US Government Printing Office to be copied.

Step 2: Committee Action.   The next step in both the House and the Senate is *committee action*—referring the bill to an appropriate committee. Then the bill is placed on the committeee's calendar. At this point, the committee makes its first major decision about whether to pursue the issue. If the designated committee does not act on the bill, the bill dies. If the committee decides to proceed, it refers the bill to a subcommittee and asks relevant federal agencies to comment.

The subcommittee holds hearings that may be public, private, or both. Once it completes its hearings, the subcommittee recommends actions and proposed amendments to the full committee. The full committee votes on recommendations, which are then sent to the House or the Senate. The committee sends the bill and its amendments to the chamber floor. The chamber must approve, alter, or reject the committee amendments before the bill can be put to a vote.

Step 3: Floor Action.   *Floor action* is the step that places the bill on the calendar, where it is debated and subsequently put to a vote. Senators and members of the House can use a variety of procedures to bring a bill to debate; the speed of the process lies in their hands. They vote on the amendments and the body of the bill separately. After all the votes are taken, the bill proceeds to the next step.

Step 4: Action in the Second House.   *Action in the second house* means that a bill initiated in the House goes to the Senate and a bill initiated in the Senate goes to the House. Members have three alternatives: They can either pass the bill as is, reject it, or alter it. If the bill is not substantially reworded and

EXHIBIT 7-3 *How a bill becomes law.*

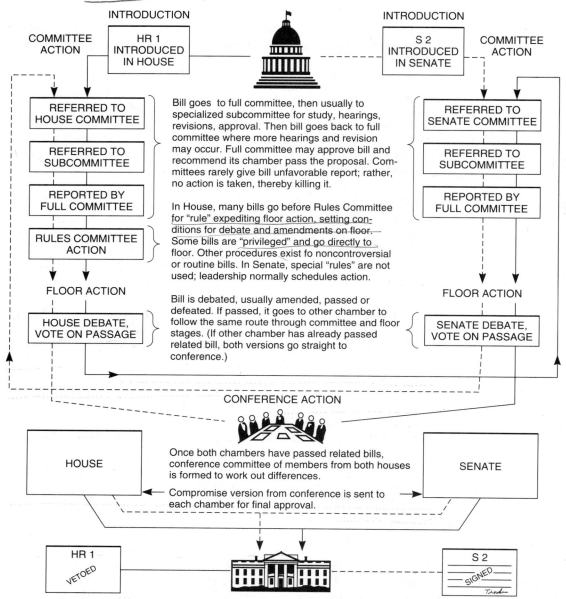

INTRODUCTION

COMMITTEE
ACTION

HR 1
INTRODUCED
IN HOUSE

INTRODUCTION

S 2
INTRODUCED
IN SENATE

COMMITTEE
ACTION

REFERRED TO
HOUSE COMMITTEE

REFERRED TO
SUBCOMMITTEE

REPORTED BY
FULL COMMITTEE

RULES COMMITTEE
ACTION

FLOOR ACTION

HOUSE DEBATE,
VOTE ON PASSAGE

REFERRED TO
SENATE COMMITTEE

REFERRED TO
SUBCOMMITTEE

REPORTED BY
FULL COMMITTEE

FLOOR ACTION

SENATE DEBATE,
VOTE ON PASSAGE

Bill goes to full committee, then usually to specialized subcommittee for study, hearings, revisions, approval. Then bill goes back to full committee where more hearings and revision may occur. Full committee may approve bill and recommend its chamber pass the proposal. Committees rarely give bill unfavorable report; rather, no action is taken, thereby killing it.

In House, many bills go before Rules Committee for "rule" expediting floor action, setting conditions for debate and amendments on floor. Some bills are "privileged" and go directly to floor. Other procedures exist fo noncontroversial or routine bills. In Senate, special "rules" are not used; leadership normally schedules action.

Bill is debated, usually amended, passed or defeated. If passed, it goes to other chamber to follow the same route through committee and floor stages. (If other chamber has already passed related bill, both versions go straight to conference.)

CONFERENCE ACTION

HOUSE

SENATE

Once both chambers have passed related bills, conference committee of members from both houses is formed to work out differences.

Compromise version from conference is sent to each chamber for final approval.

HR 1
VETOED

S 2
SIGNED

Compromise version approved by both houses is sent to President who can either sign it into law or veto it and return it to Congress. Congress may override veto by a two-thirds majority vote in both houses; bill then becomes law without President's signature.

This exhibit shows the most typical way proposed legislation is enacted into law. There are more complicated as well as simpler routes, and most bills fall by the wayside and never become law. The process is illustrated with two hypothetical bills, House bill 1 (HR 1) and Senate bill 2 (S 2). Each bill must be passed by both houses of Congress in identical form before it can become law. The path of HR 1 is traced by a solid line, that of S 2 by a broken line. However, in practice most legislation begins as similar proposals in both houses. SOURCE: A L Fritschler and B H Ross, *How Washington Works: The Executive Guide to Government* (Cambridge, MA: Ballinger Publishing, 1987), pp. 160–61.

is passed, it goes to the White House for signing. If, however, the second chamber makes basic changes, the bill is sent into a conference.

Step 5: Conference.   In *conference,* senior members of the House and Senate conference committee try to reconcile their conflicting versions. Working with their respective chambers, conferees try to forge language acceptable to their own colleagues. Once they reach an agreement, conferees prepare a report and, along with their recommendations, submit it to each house. If both the Senate and the House approve the compromise bill in identical form, the bill goes into the final legislative stages.

Step 6: Final Stages.   In the *final stages,* the clerk of the chamber prepares the bill on parchment paper, a process called *enrollment.* The clerk of the house in which the bill originated certifies that it is correct, and the speaker of the House and the president of the Senate sign it. Next, the bill is sent to the White House. Upon receiving the bill, the president has several options. The president can approve the bill and sign it, in which case it becomes law. If the president does not sign it within 10 days and Congress is in session, the bill becomes law. If Congress has adjourned and the president does not sign the bill, a *pocket veto* results and the bill does not become law. If the president refuses to sign the bill within the 10-day period and returns it to Congress along with reasons for the refusal, the bill is vetoed. The chamber in which the bill originated can let the bill die by refusing to take action. However, Congress can try to override the president's veto and pass the bill into law. For Congress to override the veto, there must be a quorum, the vote must be taken by roll call, and two-thirds of the members of both houses must vote in the bill's favor.[38]

Administrative Agencies   Obviously Congress cannot implement every law it passes and cannot write all the rules needed to run the programs it creates. As we noted earlier in the chapter, US laws are interpreted, refined, and rewritten as they are administered. Despite the attention to wording both houses of Congress give to bills, many bills that become law are ambiguous when applied to specific situations. All bills need to be fine-tuned as they are applied. Congress delegates much of its rule-making and writing authority to administrative agencies. Agencies receive and sift detailed information, set priorities on issues, solicit advice, and have wide discretion over actions they may take. Some agencies are part of departments in the executive branch of government, while others are independent of any government branch. In nearly every

[38] A L Fritschler and B H Ross, *How Washington Works: The Executive's Guide to Government* (Cambridge, MA: Ballinger Publishing, 1987), pp. 153–63.

case, the degree to which agencies enforce rules and laws depends on funding and support from both Congress and the White House. A full list of regulatory agencies appears in the appendix to Chapter 9.

All agencies have career staff who run them regardless of the politics of the administration in power. Political appointees who have the top jobs in federal agencies can set the tone for the agencies' activities. Sometimes an administration's political agenda comes into conflict with that of the permanent staff, but on those occasions the differences are usually resolved. Exceptions occur, of course, when career bureaucrats and others raise so much opposition to the agenda of the political appointee that a new appointment must be made. In 1983, EPA administrator Anne Burford Gorsuch, Rita M Lavalle, and other senior officials at that agency were removed when the staff accused them of deliberately mismanaging the agency's toxic waste superfund. Powerful members of the House demanded that Gorsuch turn over documents detailing her activities. She refused and was subsequently cited for contempt of Congress.[39]

Working with Agencies

Astute, politically aware managers understand they can have substantial input into agencies' processes for defining and writing the rules that affect their companies. Three major opportunities exist for managers, or people who represent their interests, to affect legislation. The first, as we already discussed, is during the passage of a bill. After the bill has been passed, agencies solicit public opinion twice, both before and after the rule has been made.

Any time an administrative agency passes a new rule or alters an existing one, it must publish that change in the *Federal Register.* This newspaper, in which the government publishes regulations, orders, and other documents, can be ordered from the Office of the Federal Register in Washington. However, it is also in the collections of most public, university, and even corporate libraries.

Many corporations monitor the *Federal Register* and notify their managers of proposed new rules or changes in existing rules. If a company wants input into the substance of a rule, it can comment by either writing to the agency or attending hearings held by the agency. A proactive, politically astute manager who influences legislation prior to passage will have fewer surprises than one who simply reacts to legislation after the fact.

Washington-based corporate offices know administrative agencies have wide discretion over their own actions. Agencies are also a source of information for legislators and government decision makers. Increasingly lobbyists, PAC members, and managers are spending more time trying to influ-

---

[39]P Shabecoff, "Former E.P.A. Aide Cited for Contempt," *The New York Times,* May 19, 1983, p. A1.

ence the agencies than individual members of Congress. Well-prepared managers and lobbying organizations can often alter the substance of rules and regulations through their participation with administrative agencies.[40]

Most experienced lobbyists are scrupulous about giving accurate and truthful information to regulators and agency staff. The manager or lobbyist who deliberately disseminates slanted or false information seriously damages his or her personal credibility and the credibility of the industry represented. However, managers should recognize that agency staffs also have political agendas. The political appointees who head the agencies often have goals very different from those of the career bureaucrats who carry out the work as apolitically as possible.

Summary

The US legal system is based on precedence and on interpretation of laws. Because laws change in response to the prevailing value system, managers have considerable opportunity to influence the political and legal processes. Laws are classified according to whether they are public or private, procedural or substantive, and criminal or civil. Instances of white-collar crime are rising, and the legal system is adjusting to cover those cases.

For legal and regulatory matters, managers should be aware of seven basic stakeholder groups: (1) news and broadcast media, (2) industry associations, (3) employees, (4) shareholders and institutional investors, (5) the "intellectual community," (6) public-interest groups, and (7) government.

Managers use a variety of methods to make their influence felt in the political and legal processes. Participation in political action committees (PACs) helps companies concentrate and focus specific industry concerns. Therefore, companies should consider designing a political action process and enhancing the political skills of managers at all levels.

It is critical for managers to understand the steps through which an issue goes to become legislation and the points at which it is possible to influence that legislation. It is also important that managers know what administrative agencies do and how their companies can work with those agencies.

Projects

1. From your own observation, what role does your local media play in defining social issues in your community?
2. Choose a specific industry association, write or telephone its headquarters, and assess its role in influencing legislation.

---

[40]J R Fox, *Managing Business-Government Relations: Cases and Notes on Business-Government Problems* (Homewood, IL: Richard D. Irwin, 1982), pp. 482–86.

3. Contact a public-interest group such as a state Public Interest Research Group (PIRG), Common Cause, Consumer's Union, Greenpeace, or any of the scores you are likely to find in your community. Ask a representative to address your class. Evaluate this spokesperson's message for objectivity, accuracy, and expertise.
4. In a memo to the CEO of your company, propose a detailed plan for using state or local legislators to promote your company's social goals.
5. Visit a municipal, state, or federal lawmaking body to observe a legislature or town government at work.
6. Choose a social issue and use the *Federal Register* to track its progress.

Questions

1. What are the seven major groups of stakeholders that exercise social and political influence?
2. What role do business associations and their PACs play in influencing legislation?
3. Describe the evolution of PACs, and discuss whether politicians should accept their donations.
4. Discuss the five-phase framework for planning, evaluation, and integration of a corporate political program.
5. Describe the six stages through which a bill passes before it becomes law.
6. Discuss the importance of administrative agencies in formulating public policy.
7. What are the different classifications of law?

BETA CASE 7
THE LEGAL AND POLITICAL ARENAS

Joan McCarthy had been struggling with the issue of PAC contributions since 1990. She had convened a committee to deal with the issue of PAC donations, but the committee's deliberations had been inconclusive and disappointing.

Part of the social issues formulation and implementation process in 1990 had been to develop explicit policy toward political stakeholders. In 1976, Beta formed its own political action committee and, until 1990, had regularly donated to all incumbent

members of the US House and Senate from Michigan. Although the company had not really asked itself why it followed this policy, the board of directors and top management hoped PAC money would foster good relations between Beta and the state legislators. Beta complied with the Federal Election Campaign Act by giving no more than the maximum allowable amount of $5,000 to each political candidate.

William G Flanders, the junior senator from

Michigan, had received his share of Beta PAC money six years earlier. In his bid for a second term, PACs, including Beta, gave generously. Flanders was easily reelected.

During the six years of his first term, Flanders repeatedly and vehemently criticized the pharmaceutical industry. From time to time, he gave speeches deriding pharmaceutical companies for selling unsafe products to developing countries. He accused the firms of inadequate testing procedures and making outrageous profits.

Flanders's opponent, Richard Devens, was far more conservative and was generally very supportive of the pharmaceutical industry. He spoke often about the prosperity the industry had brought to Michigan and from time to time singled out Beta as an example of a good corporate citizen. Devens's campaign received a great deal of PAC money from other pharmaceutical firms and trade organizations around the country.

This year, as McCarthy quickly discovered, Beta's PAC policy came under close scrutiny. During the campaign, committee member Bob Hodges argued for himself and several others that a contribution to Flanders constituted a "reward to the enemy." Hodges observed, "Flanders will cash the check, smile, and continue to attack us." Now that the election was over, Hodges told McCarthy and other committee members he was determined to change Beta's policy.

8   REGULATION

In 1976, the Congressional Budget Office defined *regulation* as "all governmental activities which somehow affect the operation of private industry or the lives of private citizens." This definition encompasses all federal, state, and local government activities.

Today we are accustomed to working and living with an "alphabet soup" of regulatory agencies and organizations that affect nearly every aspect of our working and private lives. In a broad sense, the government regulates major economic issues such as the size of the nation's money supply and the terms of borrowing and lending. It defines the nature and scope of competition in the United States and passes regulations to keep companies in conformance with its policies.

But the government also oversees a vast array of more personal activities. For example, regulations dictate how the products we use are marketed. They require advertising copy to comply with laws mandating that we receive truthful information. Federal, state, and local government agencies issue regulations that set standards for the food we eat and the cleanliness of the markets or restaurants in which we buy that food.

The government requires tests of the safety and effectiveness of our prescription and over-the-counter drugs, approving them only after it determines they have been properly tested. Government agencies tell us whether children's toys are safe and mandate the kind of information manufacturers must give us when we buy and use a wide variety of products.

As managers, we must deal with numerous regulations that affect our financial, production, marketing, and personnel decisions. Regulations tell us how and where to dispose of our waste by-products. We must comply with rules to make the workplace safe. We must provide facilities for the physically challenged. We are permitted to say some things to employees but must be careful not to refer to other topics. We must follow strict rules dealing with hiring and firing, administering tests, and providing health care. Yet only a century ago, very few managers were directly affected by government regulations, and even fewer were aware of their impact on managers' everyday activities.

Although the past decade-and-a-half has seen deregulation in some industries, managers still must formulate their strategies and operate in a regulated business environment that defines the nature of competition. The Clinton administration will have its own approach to regulation that may change the corporate playing field.

This chapter and the chapter that follows trace the evolution and implementation of regulation from the nineteenth century to the present. As we will see, the purpose of regulation and society's expectations of government's role in their personal and professional lives have changed over time. Economic and social conditions, coupled with technological developments, create pressure for increased regulatory action or for periods of government inaction.

In this chapter, we examine the development of early regulation and the balance between economic and consumer issues achieved through Franklin D Roosevelt's New Deal. The case at the end of the chapter explores the nature of competition and regulation in today's international arena.

CASE   *Regulation in Our Daily Lives*

Beverly Anderson's alarm clock jolted her out of a deep sleep. The clock, imported from Singapore, still had its Underwriters' Laboratory (UL) tag attached. Anderson knew UL approval meant she had a safe product. Sliding off her flameproof mattress, Beverly padded into the bathroom. After taking a shower, she stood in front of the mirror and plugged in her hair dryer. The dryer had tags attached to the cord warning her not to leave it plugged in near the sink or tub and assuring her that it was free of asbestos.

Before she put on her lipstick, Anderson used a lip balm. She noticed the tube weighed .15 ounces, or 4.2 grams. It contained petrolatums, lanolin, isopropyl myristate, and cetyl alcohol. The label told her the stick would help prevent dry and chapped lips and help heal her lips if they were sun- or windburned. It also warned her not to purchase the lip balm if the cap was not sealed. This little tube contained still more information, including the manufacturer's name, product division, and address, as well as the fact that the brand name was protected by trademark. A bar code running the length of the tube provided information useful to the retailer from whom Anderson had bought it. When Anderson brought the lip balm to the cash register, the scanner read the bar code and deleted the item from inventory. It also gave the drugstore comparative data about how that item was selling. Anderson's deodorant, soap, and cosmetics packages also had all this information, and more.

Anderson sprayed a little liquid cleanser on the sink to dissolve the soap lather. The plastic spray bottle contained twice as much information as the tube of lip balm, and even included a raised triangle on the bottom to tell her it could be recycled when empty.

Anderson settled for a quick breakfast of cold cereal. The cereal box packaging told her the ingredients of the cereal and how much fat, fiber, sodium, and cholesterol it contained. She could see how many calories a single serving contained with and without skimmed or regular milk.

The car in which Anderson drove to work had been built to comply with a variety of state and federal regulations. The previous week she had taken the car to her local garage, where a mechanic inspected it to make sure its emissions did not exceed state standards. A variety of safety features inside the car protected her in the event of collision.

By 8:15 AM, Anderson had encountered more than 20 different federal and state regulations covering every product she used. The rest of her day would bring her into contact with many more regulations.

As the controller for a large real estate corporation, Anderson was aware of the myriad regulations that covered her own industry. She knew she had to follow certain state and locally mandated procedures. Her industry had to adhere to state and federally defined rules on competition. The banks with which she did business were continuously under intense government scrutiny.

Yet Anderson, like most of us, was only dimly aware of the degree to which regulations affected nearly every action she took and every item she used. She took all the information for granted, not realizing that most of those rules had been implemented during her lifetime. In her great-grandparents' time, none of those regulations had existed.

Questions

1. Do consumers really need so much information about the products they use?
2. Does all the information about each product add unnecessarily to its cost?
3. Write down every regulation you encounter in the first hour after you awake in the morning. How many have you found?

Business Regulation from the Nineteenth Century to World War I

Before the late nineteenth century, people experienced little government intervention in their private lives. Even in business, regulations rarely constrained managerial decision making. Managers and other businesspeople were free to make nearly all major decisions for their companies as long as most Americans perceived that the free market was functioning smoothly and opportunity was made available to all individuals according to their abilities. Because most people believed competitive forces were working fairly and justly, there was no overwhelming public sentiment for regulatory control.

However, in the last two decades of the nineteenth century, large businesses began to squeeze their small competitors and dictate the terms of transactions. More and more people became convinced that huge corporations fettered competition. Large customers received more favorable rates and prices than small customers did. Suppliers became increasingly dependent on the companies they served, and in some cases became those firms' financial captives.

State legislatures and the federal government began to impose rules and regulations on specific industries that were deemed to be "clothed with the public interest."[1] These industries enjoyed large economies of scale and had the potential to exclude new entrants or force out competitors. Small businesses were prevented from entering industries in which only a handful of companies constituted a natural monopoly or oligopoly. Many small businesses also discovered they could not obtain the lower rates and rebates their large competitors enjoyed.

New regulations were particularly important to stakeholders in the upper left quadrant of the stakeholder influence map (see Exhibit 8–1). These were the external direct stakeholders, including suppliers, customers, competitors, potential entrants, and state and federal governments.

Interstate Commerce Act of 1887

In 1887, Congress passed the Interstate Commerce Act to regulate the railroads. Historically railroads were the pioneers of big business. Beginning in the 1830s, they developed new methods of management, new interactions

---

[1]A E Kahn, *The Economics of Regulation: Principles and Institutions,* vol. 1 (New York: John Wiley & Sons, 1970), p. 3.

EXHIBIT 8–1

Stakeholder influence map for the nineteenth century

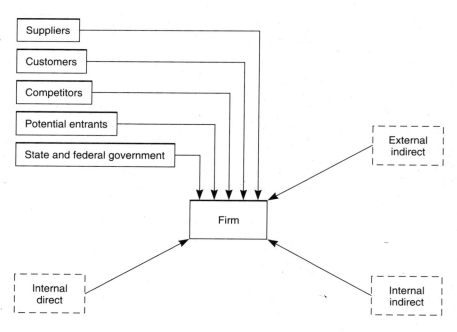

with organized labor, and new relationships with government. The capital for railroad expansion came from the federal government and a variety of investors, including private citizens and local and state governments. Money and investment markets that handled railroad stocks and bonds were centralized in new investment banking houses on Wall Street, close to the New York Stock Exchange building.

As railroad growth exploded, state legislatures tried to ensure that the companies lived up to their charters. They created independent regulatory commissions that Louis Galambos and Joseph Pratt call a "curious innovation."[2] These state commissions, which were initially established to regulate canal transportation, were a variation on a model that already existed in Great Britain. The British developed their regulation and enforcement process as a compromise to extend government control without requiring existing agencies to assume the burden. The independent commission "seemed to promise Americans a way to have more government without having more politics."[3]

In 1849, the state of Connecticut established the first independent special railroad commission to report to the legislature on safety inspections, land disputes, and rate discrimination. This was a fact-finding commission with very limited powers.

In 1869, Massachusetts set up a permanent advisory commission. It served as a model for other states, and by 1887, 15 states had working advisory commissions.[4]

As the railroads grew, they became fiercely competitive. Since fixed costs were very high, railroads tried to use as much of their carrying capacity as possible. At first they pursued the logical strategy of lowering rates, but competitive rate wars quickly followed. Railroad managers soon realized that if they did not cooperate, the combination of high fixed costs and destructive rounds of rate reductions would lead to the financial collapse of some lines. Monopolistic survivors would then be able to set rates at whatever levels they chose.

For a short time, railroad managers tried to bring order to their industry by creating cartels or "pools" to set rates and allocate traffic. However, these voluntary agreements broke down because they had no legal basis and because some railroads had offered "under-the-table" rebates to large customers.

Before long, external direct stakeholders, such as small-business owners, passengers, shippers, and farmers, pressured state governments to set maximum rates and prohibit the railroads' practice of charging higher rates for

---

[2]L Galambos and J Pratt, *The Rise of the Corporate Commonwealth* (New York: Basic Books, 1988), p. 45.

[3]Ibid., p. 47.

[4]R E Cushman, *The Independent Regulatory Commissions* (New York: Oxford University Press, 1941), pp. 20–25.

shorter hauls. Between 1874 and 1885, the US House of Representatives considered more than 30 bills to provide greater control over interstate commerce. Railroad and other big-business interests opposed the bills, and none were passed.

State legislators, who were more responsive to their grass-roots constituents, did pass the "Granger Laws" regulating railroads. However, all stakeholders, big and small, soon realized railroads and interstate commerce had to come under federal law rather than a hodgepodge of individual state regulations. In 1886, the Supreme Court ruled in the Wabash case, concluding that only Congress could regulate interstate commerce.

A year later, Congress passed the Interstate Commerce Act, which created the Interstate Commerce Commission (ICC).[5] The act mandated that all rates be "reasonable and just." Certain practices were expressly forbidden. Railroads could no longer discriminate in rates, fix prices, or furnish rebates.

Although the president of the United States nominated the five commissioners and the Senate confirmed them, ICC members were deliberately selected to balance conflicting perspectives on interstate commerce. The ICC was charged with carrying out the Interstate Commerce Act. When the act was drawn up, corporate leaders worked with sympathetic members of Congress to water down its provisions.

The Supreme Court heard 16 cases under the Interstate Commerce Act between 1887 and 1905. Of these cases, justices resolved 15 in favor of the railroads. Historian Edward C Kirkland concludes that "the court threw itself as an obstacle across the path willed by Congress and the public."[6] The sad truth was that a farmer or small supplier who appealed high railroad rates to the ICC was likely to die of old age before receiving relief.

Hepburn Act of 1906.   To strengthen the provisions of the Interstate Commerce Act, Congress passed the Hepburn Act in 1906. The new legislation expanded the scope and jurisdiction of the ICC and added two more commissioners, bringing the number to seven. One important provision of the Hepburn Act gave the ICC the power to require corporations to use a unified system of accounting. Prior to 1906, companies used a wide variety of accounting systems, which made it difficult for the ICC to obtain reliable information. Yet another provision made ICC rulings binding until the courts could review them.

---

[5]G Porter, *The Rise of Big Business, 1860–1910* (Arlington Heights, IL: AHM Publishing, 1973), pp. 27–39.

[6]E C Kirkland, "Industry Comes of Age: Business, Labor and Public Policy, 1860–1897," in *The Economic History of the United States,* vol. 6, ed. Henry Davis (New York: Holt, Rinehart & Winston, 1961), p. 134.

Sherman Antitrust Act of 1890

The Sherman Antitrust Act was the second major piece of congressional regulatory legislation. It was titled "an act to protect trade and commerce against unlawful restraints and monopolies." Like the Interstate Commerce Act, the Sherman Antitrust Act at first primarily affected external direct stakeholders.

Throughout the 1870s and 1880s, other industries followed the railroads' example of horizontal growth and increasing complexity through mergers. Manufacturers integrated vertically, either to control access to raw materials or to move closer to consumers. For example, lumber companies integrated forward into furniture making and backward into forest acquisition. Oil refineries integrated vertically into footwear, chemicals, and explosives.

Although few companies actually gained total control over an entire industry, some firms' activities were so comprehensive that they constituted what many considered to be a monopoly position. In effect, these large firms attempted to control suppliers, customers, and competitors in a single industry by dictating terms of trade. As Exhibit 8–2 shows, they formed trade associations and lobbies that worked to set prices and establish production quotas among participants.

Like the railroad cartels, these industry agreements fell apart when the terms no longer suited one of the participants. Rather than lobbying Congress for legalization of cartels, owners of leading firms in a single industry

EXHIBIT 8–2

Stakeholder influence map

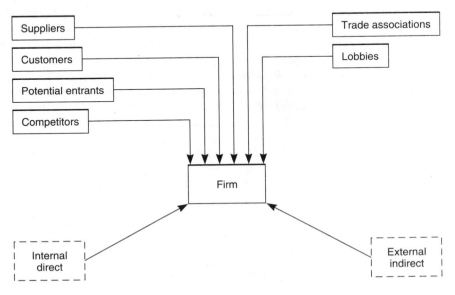

purchased stock in one another's firms and in their smaller competitors. When this strategy also failed to provide the control manufacturers desired, they devised an organizational structure called a trust.

A *trust* was an arrangement in which companies turned over their stock certificates and voting rights to a group or board of trustees, who then became directors. Directors were invested with the power to make operating decisions and determined investment strategies for the companies that comprised the trust. Directors were the new group of stakeholders in the internal direct quadrant of the stakeholder influence map.

As with legislation to control railroads, a diverse group of competitors and potential market entrants gathered together and attacked trusts in state and federal courts and in state legislatures.[7] With Populist support, the state of Kansas passed the first antitrust act in 1889. The following year, Congress passed the Sherman Antitrust Act.

One of the most important stipulations of the Sherman Act appears in section 1. It declares, "Every contract, combination in the form of trust or otherwise, or conspiracy, in restraint of trade or commerce among the several States, or with foreign nations, is hereby declared to be illegal."[8] It was left to the courts to decide what constituted combination in restraint of trade.

In section 7, the Sherman Antitrust Act actively encouraged competitors to sue for damages. Section 7 stipulates, "Any person who shall be injured in his business or property by any other person or corporation by reason of anything forbidden or declared to be unlawful by this law, may sue . . . without respect for the amount in controversy, and shall recover three fold the damages by him sustained." Even though much of the law was vague, the prospect of realizing triple damages encouraged litigation.

Clayton Act of 1914.   The Sherman Antitrust Act was so broad that it left companies uncertain as to what actions constituted violations and what did not. In 1914, Congress passed the Clayton Act to tighten and clarify the Sherman Act and address specific business practices that might lessen competition. The Clayton Act barred price discrimination if it lessened competition or created a monopoly. It prohibited *tying agreements,* in which a seller required a buyer to purchase unwanted goods to get goods the buyer *did* want. It also prohibited *exclusive dealing arrangements* in which buyers could not deal with seller rivals. In addition, the Clayton Act prohibited interlocking directorates among competing firms if those directorates would tend to create a monopoly.

---

[7]A D Chandler, Jr., *The Visible Hand: The Managerial Revolution in American Business* (Cambridge, MA: Belknap Press, 1977), pp. 317–19.

[8]R H Bork, *The Antitrust Paradox* (New York: Basic Books, 1978), p. 19.

Federal Trade Commission Act of 1914

Lawmakers recognized that laws prohibiting monopoly and restraint of trade needed to be enforced in a systematic way. The Federal Trade Commission Act (FTCA) created the Federal Trade Commission (FTC), which was charged with investigating unfair methods of competition among businesses. Congress directed the FTC to prohibit unfair and deceptive acts or practices. The FTC had broad discretion to define business practices that constituted "unfair methods of competition."

Like the Interstate Commerce Commission, the FTC was created as an independent commission with commissioners appointed by the president and confirmed by the Senate. The commission's charge was to protect consumers against "unfair methods of competition in or affecting commerce." Congress, the US Chamber of Commerce, and nearly all trade associations supported the mission of the FTC. However, the commission had little real clout. Since the law did not stipulate what elements constituted unfair competition, the FTC made its own determination. Although it had the power to investigate business practices, it could not compel companies to comply with its regulations.

Wheeler-Lea Amendment (1938).   A portion of the Wheeler-Lea Amendment, passed in 1938, stated that the FTC could intervene when trade practices were deemed "unfair or deceptive acts or practices in commerce." The change in wording from the original act meant the FTC did not have to prove competition was affected. The FTC generally relied on companies' voluntary compliance until the 1940s, when the courts showed more interest in pursuing violators.[9]

regardless of whether it affected competition

amended sections which outlawed unfair comp. + unfair acts or practices

These early acts and commissions responded to society's widespread conviction that corporations required government oversight. The public demanded that Congress preserve a competitive business environment in which small participants were treated equitably and were not excluded from participation.

Among business leaders, antitrust legislation created great uncertainty. They fiercely resisted new legislation until they realized it was inevitable. Then they worked with Congress and other government entities to make the laws and regulatory agencies as "business-friendly" as possible. However, the vagueness of the resulting acts led to inconsistent court rulings that constrained executives in developing their strategic initiatives.

The legislative process reflected business's ambivalence about whether government regulation was helpful or harmful. As a result, initial legislation was usually weaker than it would have been had business not eventually

---

[9]*Federal Regulatory Directory,* 6th ed. (Washington, DC: Congressional Quarterly, 1990), p. 262.

cooperated in its development. These early acts and the regulatory bodies they created focused stakeholders' attention on competition, price fixing, and deceptive business practices. Government refused to address the public policy issue of how economies of scale should be treated in a growing and more technology-based economy. According to Galambos and Pratt, "Technologically and organizationally the business system was changing in fundamental ways, but public officials had yet to work out how society could best capture the long-range economic benefits offered by modern large-scale enterprise while maintaining a satisfactory level of competition."[10]

Consumer Regulation from the Nineteenth Century to World War I

Although the term *consumerism* was not coined until the 1960s, public concern about accurate information, product content, and product use dates from the end of the nineteenth century. As urban populations grew and new products and processes proliferated, industries operating without regulation often manufactured unsafe products. Reformers organized to deal with the problems created by unregulated industries and hazardous products. In 1891, activists formed the first Consumers' League in New York City. Within a few years, a number of local groups formed a national federation, the National Consumers' League. By 1903, the league had 64 branches in 20 states. The National Consumers' League joined a variety of other organizations in alerting the public to the dangers of impure, mislabeled, and misrepresented food and drugs then on the market.

Pure Food and Drug Act of 1906

Drugs.   Growing markets and technological advances motivated forces for change in the delivery of medication to the public. After the Civil War, concentration of capital, labor, and control was evident in the growth of large-scale prescription pharmaceutical manufacturers and the explosion of the patent medicine industry.

Traditionally pharmacy schools trained pharmacists to compound drugs, and some physicians filled their own prescriptions. They routinely used substances such as morphine, quinine, iodine, chloroform, and carbolic acid in their potions. These substances had tremendous potential to do harm as well as good. As the market for mass-produced pharmaceuticals grew, the public demanded that an oversight body ensure quality control.

The patent medicine industry garnered much of the stakeholder concern. Its misuse of toxic, narcotic, and addictive substances was nothing short of scandalous. Patent medicine makers routinely turned out substances such as Hostetter's Bitters, Radam's Microbe Killer, and Swain's Panacea. Fretful babies were given opium-laced Winslow's Soothing Syrup

---

[10]Galambos and Pratt, *The Rise of the Corporate Commonwealth*, p. 62.

to stop their crying. Elixir Terpin Hydrate with heroin was a popular over-the-counter cough syrup.

Working together, pharmaceutical and medical associations pressed for passage of pure food and drug legislation. They were motivated, in large part, to eliminate the quackery of the patent medicine industry and remove harmful products from the marketplace.

Food.   Food-processing companies also came under attack. By the turn of the century, refrigerated railroad cars carried processed food from coast to coast. Packers and canners had only rudimentary knowledge of food preservation and bacteriology. They added preservatives such as formaldehyde to canned meats and copper sulfate to vegetables to make them look and smell fresher.

Lobbying groups were particularly vocal in pressuring Congress for pure food and drug legislation. External indirect stakeholders such as the General Federation of Women's Clubs, the National Consumers' League and chemists' organizations joined together after bills failed to pass Congress in 1892 and 1902. When Theodore Roosevelt was elected in 1904, these groups tried to enlist presidential support. In his annual message to Congress in 1905, Roosevelt urged the enactment of a pure food and drug law.

The law passed the Senate at the same time Upton Sinclair's *The Jungle* was published. Sinclair drew the public's attention to the meat-packing industry, writing, "Men, who worked in the tank rooms full of steam . . . fell into the vats; and when they were fished out, there was never enough of them to be worth exhibiting—sometimes they would be overlooked for days, till all but the bones of them had gone out to the world as Durham's Pure Leaf Lard."[11]

When federal inspectors bore out Sinclair's charges, Roosevelt threw his full support behind a meat inspection bill. Packers, worried about foreign competition and consumer concern about their products, realized a federal law would help them save their reputations.

Finally, in 1906, Theodore Roosevelt signed the Pure Food and Drug Act. The act required manufacturers to give truthful information about the contents of their products. Although dangerous substances had to be listed on labels, other ingredients did not. Interpreted generously, the act meant manufacturers could not deliberately mislead the public.

The Sherley Amendment (1912).   The Sherley Amendment, enacted in 1912, tightened restrictions against deceptive labeling. As with the railroads and other industries, the courts did very little to interfere with the patent medicine business. Not until 1938 did the Food and Drug Administration receive congressional authority to require proof that any new product, whether prescription or over-the-counter, was safe.

---

[11]U Sinclair, *The Jungle* (New York: Doubleday, 1906), p. 117.

Business Regulation Summary

In the late nineteenth and early twentieth centuries, legislators and the public were very concerned about the nature of competition. American ideology supported the notion of unfettered competition as long as that competition was "fair." Fairness demanded access to the industrial environment and at least the possibility of an equitable chance. Very few legislators on the national level considered widespread consumer protection, workplace, or environmental legislation. During this early period, newly formed groups of external indirect stakeholders such as trade associations and lobbies began to exercise their power, a trend that would continue to build. As cataclysmic events often do, World War I precipitated fundamental changes in business and government relations.

World War I to the New Deal

Before World War I, most regulatory legislation concentrated on the railroad, oil, steel, and coal industries. As we noted in the previous chapter, Secretary of Commerce Herbert Hoover pursued policies to make production more efficient and competition less destructive. Trade associations flourished. The government, supported by the US Chamber of Commerce and the National Association of Manufacturers, grew more supportive of price and production agreements. But agencies like the Department of Commerce had a difficult time drawing the line between legitimate standards for improved trade practices and criminal price fixing. Courts ruled gingerly and narrowly on competition and trade practice cases.

Consumer-focused regulation drew new attention in the postwar era. Companies eagerly responded to pent-up demand for consumer products. Issues such as market entry and competitive practices began to take a back seat to more pressing problems dealing with marketing a vast variety of goods to mass markets.[12] The FTC began to focus on deceptive trade practices such as misleading advertising. Its rulings were still once removed from direct intervention to protect consumers. Instead, it tried to prevent fraud that indirectly injured consumers.

The Great Depression led legislators and legal scholars to question the US economic order. However, the courts waffled on many issues, and neither they nor government policy produced a reasoned approach to regulation. A few Supreme Court decisions supported government price and production controls. On the other hand, when small retailers demanded protection from chain stores, several states passed "fair trade laws" that restrained price cutting. Morton Keller notes that ". . . as so often before,

---

[12]M Keller, "The Pluralist State: American Economic Regulation in Comparative Perspective, 1900–1930," in T K McCraw, ed., *Regulation in Perspective* (Cambridge, MA: Harvard University Press, 1981), p. 74.

administrative implementation and court interpretation of the law came to be thoroughly muddled by the gulf between the public policy goal and economic realities, by the sheer complexity and multiplicity of the interests involved."[13]

Regulation in the New Deal

The administration of Franklin D Roosevelt heralded a new era in regulation. The New Deal's major goal was to pry the economy out of the depression. A cooperative Congress created regulatory agencies of three basic types: functional, economic, and social.

Functional Agencies

Functional agencies regulated a particular function within an industry. They dealt with labor relations or financial transactions.

The Federal Home Loan Bank Board (FHLBB) was an independent agency organized under the executive branch. It regulated federally chartered savings and loan associations. The S&Ls were the major source of private funding for building and buying housing.

The National Labor Relations Board (NLRB) was established by the Wagner Act in 1935. This independent commission protected the rights of employees to bargain collectively and was intended to prevent "unfair labor practices."

The Securities and Exchange Act of 1934 created the Securities and Exchange Commission (SEC). The SEC, also an independent agency, began operations in 1934. Its job was to protect the public against fraud and deception in the securities and financial markets. For the first time, the government had a powerful presence in the securities industry and could require companies to disclose financial information.

The Banking Act of 1933 (or the Glass-Steagall Act) created the Federal Deposit Insurance Corporation (FDIC). Operating under the executive branch, this independent agency regulated state-chartered, insured banks that were not members of the Federal Reserve System. In addition to separating commercial and investment banking functions, the FDIC protected small depositors by insuring their bank deposits.

Economic Agencies   Industry Specific

Economic agencies regulated an entire industry. The Motor Carrier Act of 1935 created an agency to regulate the trucking industry. The act also brought the entire industry under the ICC, which regulated entry, rates, and

---

[13]Ibid. p. 94.

IRS
NLRB
BATFA
SEC

mergers. The Federal Communications Commission (FCC), formed in 1934, was charged with consolidating federal regulation of radio, telephone, and telegraph.

The Civil Aeronautics Authority (CAA), formed in 1938, lasted for two years before it was replaced by the Civil Aeronautics Board (CAB). The CAB handled the coordination of airline routes and regulations covering airlines.

Social Agencies

Like the economic regulators, social agencies applied across industries. The Social Security system was the only major social body created during the New Deal. Social agencies did not proliferate until the 1960s.[14]

CASE   *Antitrust Legislation and Foreign Competition in the 1980s*

In the century between 1890 and 1990, various presidential administrations developed their own ideology about how the Sherman and Clayton Acts were to be interpreted. As membership on the Supreme Court changed, justices interpreted the acts in a variety of ways. The framers of the original legislation could not have anticipated the development of modern business enterprises. The nature of competition changed, and the competitive environment took on global dimensions.

By the 1980s, the uniquely American practice of settling antitrust action in the courts was becoming extremely costly. No industrialized country other than the United States used the traditional court system for trade matters. Great Britain, for example, had a Restrictive Trade Practices Commission that settled private antitrust suits. These suits comprised up to 90 percent of all antitrust cases. The European Community (EC) drew up rules regarding competition that expressly prohibited price-fixing agreements and discriminatory pricing. However, the EC pragmatically avoided litigation by developing a system of block exemptions from the rules governing competition.

When the Reagan administration took office in 1981, one of its greatest concerns was the effectiveness with which American companies were competing in the global arena. Japanese and European competition presented a serious challenge to American companies. Japanese and West German competitors had captured large shares of US domestic markets in autos, steel, electronics, and chemicals. Many legal scholars, economists, and politicians concluded that national boundaries were increasingly irrelevant in defining the competitive market in a number of industries.

The Reagan administration, which was committed ideologically to a laissez-faire regulatory environment, began to look for ways to enhance American corporations' international competitiveness. The administration settled on a policy that punished price fixers but approved mergers. Its view was that size was unimportant and efficiency should be encouraged. In 1984, the Justice Department gave the "go-ahead" to vertical integration between suppliers and customers. It also made horizontal mergers between competitors much easier. For the first time in the history of

---

[14]C M Kerwin, "Introduction," *Federal Regulatory Directory,* 6th ed. (Washington, DC: Congressional Quarterly, 1990), pp. 1–5.

antitrust legislation, the government defined markets *internationally* instead of domestically.

In 1985, Secretary of Commerce Malcolm Baldrige called for a repeal of section 7 of the Clayton Act that prohibits mergers that "may . . . substantially lessen competition . . . or may tend to create a monopoly." Baldrige insisted that foreign competition was behind his proposal and that the Clayton Act stopped "the kinds of efficiency-creating mergers we need to become internationally competitive."[15]

The administration's new attitude toward antitrust created the climate within which the biggest nonoil company merger in history took place: General Electric Company purchased RCA Corporation for $6.3 billion. This event created the nation's seventh largest industrial company. GE chairperson John F Welch, Jr., declared this colossus would be a new breed of US corporation and would be powerful enough to beat its Japanese rivals. While not everyone agreed with Welch that sheer size was a critical competitive variable, the international arena became the new venue for any discussion of competition.

In December 1988, Attorney General Richard Thornburgh and Secretary of Commerce C William Verity debated the issue of antitrust and foreign competition on the editorial page of *The Wall Street Journal.* Thornburgh asserted that US firms faced unprecedented international competition in the global marketplace. He pointed to foreign inroads in superconductors, high-definition television, robotics, and computer-aided design and manufacturing. Although US firms were bringing products to market, so were its major trading partners. The costs of R&D and demand for customization were extremely high, often exceeding the resources of any single firm.

Thornburgh noted that foreign firms had entered cooperative production ventures but American companies had failed to do so because they feared an antitrust challenge. He pointed to the Sherman Act's triple damages in private suits and to huge attorney's fees. He recommended two approaches. First, a company that wanted to enter a joint production venture would apply to the government through the Commerce and Justice Departments. The departments would make sure the venture did not threaten competition. They would jointly issue a certificate saying the conduct covered by the certificate could not be challenged under state or federal antitrust laws in either a government or a private suit. The second approach used the stipulations of the National Cooperative Research Act (1984), which prohibited a court from stopping a joint-research venture without considering its competitive benefits.

Verity observed that US firms were losing the race in the global marketplace. He suggested protecting US firms engaged in cooperative research from antitrust legislation. Two possible high-tech sectors worthy of this protection were high-definition television and flexible computer-integrated manufacturing. In his view, "permitting qualified firms jointly to finance, construct, or operate such [facilities] would aid technology development and product diversity. The net result is increased competition and its benefits."[16]

The Bush administration took a much more activist role in global antitrust enforcement. It used US antitrust law to punish foreign competitors if they stifled American firms in the global market. The Justice Department's antitrust division

---

[15]A Reilly, "Reagan Turns a Cold Eye on Antitrust," *Fortune,* October 14, 1985, p. 31.

[16]"U.S. Firms Get Tripped in Race to the Marketplace," *The Wall Street Journal,* December 27, 1988, p. A10.

looked for ways to reach beyond US borders to strike at bid rigging, price fixing, and cartellike behavior that hurt US exports.

The administration pointed to several examples of this behavior. One hundred forty Japanese construction firms were suspected of rigging bids at the Yokosuka US naval base near Tokyo. Allied Signal alleged it had been shut out of Japan's $100-million-a-year market for electrical transformers, because the Japanese utilities claimed Allied's transformers were too noisy, expensive, and unsafe. In yet another example, Japanese carmarkers favored Japanese part suppliers in their US operations.[17]

The Bush administration took yet another step in the spring of 1992. The Justice Department issued a statement extending US antitrust enforcement policy to non–US markets. The department announced that it would, in "appropriate" cases, take antitrust enforcement action against "conduct occurring overseas that restrains U.S. exports whether or not there is direct harm to U.S. consumers if it is clear that:

1. the conduct has a direct, substantial and reasonable effect on exports of goods or services from the U.S.;
2. the conduct involves anticompetitive activities which violate the U.S. antitrust laws—in most cases, group boycotts, collusive pricing and other exclusionary activities; and
3. U.S. courts have jurisdiction over the foreign persons or corporations involved in such conduct."

London's *Financial Times* pointed out the complications for foreign companies whose countries' legal systems differ from that of the United States. It noted that few other countries endorsed US triple-damage private lawsuits. Unlike laws in most other countries, US law did not distinguish between protecting a domestic market from foreign-source abuse and protecting the domestic rights of citizens abroad from abuse in the foreign market.[18]

Many antitrust issues remain unresolved. The competitive international environment, coupled with the ideological predisposition of political parties and presidential appointees, challenges the courts and legislators to wrestle with evolving policy. Application of one of the most fundamental and basic pieces of legislation, the Sherman Antitrust Act, is difficult and subject to change in a global competitive environment.

Questions

1. Should the Sherman Act be altered to do away with private suits and triple damages?
2. Should antitrust be negotiated and resolved by committees or by arbitration as it is in many other countries?
3. What activities should exempt US firms from antitrust legislation?

[17]"Return of the Big Stick," *US News & World Report,* June 4, 1990, pp. 54–55.
[18]C Hampton, "Long Arm of US Antitrust Law," *The Financial Times,* April 30, 1992, p. 12.

4. Are the issues that led to the passage of the Sherman Act irrelevant in today's world?
5. If you could construct the ideal policy on competition for US corporations, what would it be? Why?
6. Should the United States (or any other country) be able to bring charges against foreign firms for activities outside its own borders if the foreign firm's actions do not affect US firms, or the foreign firm's actions do affect US firms?

Summary

During the decade-and-a-half of the 1940s and 1950s, business, government, and other stakeholders developed expectations that fundamentally changed the nature of regulation from economically focused to socially activist. The period between the end of the New Deal and the 1960s was relatively uneventful in terms of developing regulation. Stakeholders gathered their strength and resources to face the turbulent social and environmental events of the 1960s and 1970s.

This chapter laid the foundation for the regulatory process. It discussed the major regulatory agencies created between 1887 and the New Deal. The debates that led to the passage of legislation and the role business played in developing the new regulatory agencies were peculiarly American. No other industrialized country took exactly the same approach to the interaction among business, government, and special-interest groups. Debate continues over the nature of competition, the degree of government oversight, and the development of public policy. Issues shift with changing economic conditions and partisan politics. Groups of stakeholders coalesce around their "pet" issues. The activities of external indirect stakeholders continue to gain strength. Lobbyists, special-interest groups, and advocacy organizations on all sides of issues use many of the same organizational skills that made corporate interests so powerful.

Projects

1. Examine the role the courts play in the US regulatory process. Does our legal framework contribute to or detract from the competitive environment?
2. Interview a top manager of or legal counsel to a newly merged firm to find out the impact the Sherman Act had on the merger.
3. Interview a member of the legal division of a multinational company. What does he or she consider the most pressing regulatory issues for the company? Would those issues be different if the company were purely domestic?

Questions

1. What were society's main concerns that led to the passage of the Interstate Commerce Act and the Sherman Antitrust Act?
2. What role do lobbying or special-interest groups play in the passage of legislation in the United States?

9

REGULATION AND DEREGULATION FROM THE 1960S TO THE 1990S

The previous chapter traces the development of regulation from the end of the nineteenth century through the New Deal. This chapter introduces the development of social legislation from the 1960s to the 1990s. Subsequent chapters examine social legislation in great detail. Deregulation in general and the consequences of economic deregulation in particular are this chapter's primary topics.

CASE   *Air Florida: Aftermath of the 1970s*

Between 1980 and 1982, recession plagued the airline industry. A bitter and highly publicized air traffic controllers' strike in 1981 slowed air traffic at the same time small, regional, low-cost airlines proliferated. As fare wars reduced prices and more people flew, overburdened hub-and spoke-airports became unable to handle the huge traffic snarls in the sky. Passengers suffered chronic flight delays, missed connections, lost luggage, and dealt with surly airline personnel.

Air Florida was widely touted as proof that deregulation had worked. Founded in 1972 by a Florida entrepreneur, the airline confined its market to inter-Florida flights. In 1977, the year before deregulation, Air Florida earned $7.8 million in profits.

That same year C Edward Acker, a former Braniff official, became chairperson of Air Florida. Acker began using the new deregulated environment to expand. The airline established routes north to New York and south into the Caribbean and Central America. In 1980, when some other airlines were in the red, Air Florida made a profit of $5.1 million.

But 1981 and 1982 were bad years for Air Florida. Acker left to become chairperson of Pan American and was replaced by Eli Timoner. In January 1982, Air Florida was devastated by a tragic crash that killed 78 people. In full view of a riveted national television audience, rescuers plucked survivors from the icy Potomac River.

For months thereafter, management was preoccupied with the aftermath of the crash. In June, Timoner recruited Donald Lloyd-Jones from American Airlines. A month later, Timoner suffered a severe stroke and Lloyd-Jones took over as chief executive.

Air Florida soon began to suffer the effects of intense competition spurred by deregulation. Low-fare carriers, such as People Express, Northeastern, and American International, flooded the Florida market. Hoping to cut costs, Lloyd-Jones cut Air Florida's routes, sold off airplanes, and fired employees. He tried to attract new investors, but had very little success.

On January 4, 1984, Interfirst Bank, Air Florida's largest lender, declared the carrier in default of its $48.1 million debt. General Electric Credit Corporation stepped in with a $6 million loan and an option to buy up to 55 percent of Air Florida stock. However, this lender's move merely served as a bandage to stem a hemorrhage.

In May 1984, Lloyd-Jones abruptly resigned, and on July 3, 1984, Air Florida joined its predecessors, Braniff and Continental, in filing for protection under Chapter 11. By this time, Air Florida had a negative net worth of $81 million, and its troubles were mounting.

Air Florida no longer owned any of its planes. Creditors had already repossessed two that were leased and were planning to repossess more. The airline's remaining chief assets were its international routes from Miami to London and Central America. After Air Florida went into Chapter 11, even casual observers predicted the airline would never fly again.[1]

Questions

1. Should government regulate the airline industry to ensure that all airlines have a good chance of economic survival?
2. To what extent should government be involved in the airline industry, and what role should it play?

Regulation in the 1960s

In the decade after World War II, people had both the leisure and the affluence to think about what an ideal society *should* be. Women entered the workforce in greater numbers, the civil rights movement shifted into high gear, and a young President Kennedy asked the American people what they could do for their country. Stakeholder demands galvanized Congress into creating social programs and regulatory controls at a frenzied pace. The spate of regulation that gushed forth in the 1960s and 1970s touched nearly every aspect of American corporate and personal life.

---

[1]M S Beelman. "Air Florida Files under Chapter 11 and Lays Off 1200," *The Boston Globe,* July 3, 1984, p. 1; A Salpukas, "Air Florida Seeks Bankruptcy; Planes Grounded," *The New York Times,* July 3, 1984, pp. A1, D3; "Behind the Rise, and Fall of Air Florida," *Business Week,* July 23, 1984, pp. 122–23, 125.

Consumer advocate Michael Pertschuck notes that until the 1960s and early 1970s, consumer advocates could point to only a few successes against the "determined opposition of business." He observes that "for consumer entrepreneurial politics to succeed in the 1960s, consumer goals had to harmonize with public attitudes and the political environment."[2] He attributes stakeholders' new interest in social regulation to the liberal political agenda of the Kennedy and Johnson administrations. It is equally plausible that stakeholder interest promoted the agenda rather than the other way around.

Richard Harris and Sidney Milkis assert that social regulation was a direct result of "new conceptions about the relations among business, government, and society."[3] They point to two competing theories. First, Theodore Lowi, in *The End of Liberalism,* suggests that the social regulation of the 1970s represented a more mature phase of New Deal ideology. Second, Irving Kristol, a neoconservative spokesperson, promotes a contradictory idea. Kristol sees the push for social legislation as a betrayal of the New Deal by the New Left. The New Left, Kristol says, was hostile to and suspicious of market forces that were inherent in the New Deal.

Harris and Milkis contend that neither perspective is entirely accurate. The ideas of the New Deal and the New Left came together in a tense and uneasy union: "The difficulty in devising adequate responses derives from the idea of participatory democracy as being rooted in the ideals and suspicions of the New Left and as being practiced in an institutional environment established in the New Deal."[4]

Regardless of ideology and the roots of the new forces, nothing less than a social revolution swept the country. People took sides in the antiwar movement, the women's movement, civil rights activities, environmental activism, and product safety initiatives. Public demonstrations supporting all sides of nearly every issue were commonplace. External indirect stakeholders' activities helped legislation proliferate. Nearly every cause, from toxic-waste dumping to abortion rights, had multiple, highly vocal proponents and detractors. People joined shifting and sometimes conflicting coalitions.

Companies found themselves in the middle of these controversies, taken to task by some for what they did do and by others for what they neglected to do. Newly implemented rules and regulations constrained their decision making and strategic options.

Susan and Martin Tolchin point out that many companies supported regulatory efforts at the same time they complained bitterly about them. Companies looked to Congress to protect them "from the vagaries of the

---

[2]M Pertschuck, *Revolt Against Regulation: The Rise and Pause of the Consumer Movement* (Berkeley, CA: University of California Press, 1982), pp. 12–13.

[3]R A Harris and S M Milkis, *The Politics of Regulatory Change* (New York: Oxford University Press, 1989), pp. 53–96.

[4]Ibid., pp. 53–96.

marketplace."[5] Not surprisingly, both firms and individuals were inconsistent in their demands. Products and services had proliferated dramatically in the post-World War II period. Stakeholders in every quadrant of the stakeholder influence map wanted protection from discriminatory practices and unsafe products as well as the freedom to grow and innovate (see Exhibit 9–1). These needs sometimes conflicted.

Congress passed regulations that covered consumer products, employment discrimination, product safety, consumer finance, workplace safety, and the environment.[6] The passage of one regulation led to the need for others. Douglas Needham points out that stakeholders often make multiple, interdependent demands for corporate regulation. When regulation changes one aspect of a firm's behavior, all parts of the firm are affected. Stakeholders call for additional regulation to cover the new behavior and unregulated activities.[7]

From Regulation to Deregulation, 1960–1978	The surge of regulation during the Kennedy, Johnson, Nixon, and Ford administrations created vast networks of regulatory agencies and large government bureaucracies through which companies had to maneuver. By the late 1970s, all businesses faced new demands and constraints in a growing regulatory environment. On local, state, and federal levels, legislators responded to constituents' pressure to make working conditions hazard free, the environment cleaner, and products safer. Murray Weidenbaum asserts there was also a widespread belief that unless the government regulated corporate activities, businesses would not voluntarily respond to public demands.[8] Americans evinced a growing skepticism about business's willingness to implement the policies needed to achieve their vision of a "proper" society.

The costs of burgeoning regulations and agencies to enforce them were substantial. According to Weidenbaum, the operating expenses of the major regulatory agencies totaled $1.9 billion in 1974 and rose 48 percent over the next two years. Regulatory agencies hired inspectors, reviewers, and rule-makers to monitor and enforce rules. (See Appendix 9–1 for a list of regulatory agencies.)

The public paid directly or indirectly every time a new rule went into effect. For example, if the EEOC reviewed and assessed a company's affir-

---

[5]S J Tolchin and M Tolchin, *Dismantling America: The Rush to Deregulate* (Boston: Houghton Mifflin, 1983), pp. 11–12.

[6]M L Weidenbaum, *Business, Government, and the Public* (Englewood Cliffs, NJ: Prentice-Hall, 1977), p. 5.

[7]D Needham, *The Economics of Regulation: A Behavioral Approach* (Boston: Little Brown 1983), pp. 258–63.

[8]Weidenbaum, *Business, Government, and the Public*, p. 16.

EXHIBIT 9–1

*Stakeholder influence
map, 1960s and
1970s*

		Direct	Indirect
External		Customers Government Suppliers	Social activists Lobbies Religious institutions Environmentalists Community groups Regulators Local politicians
Internal		Employees Management	Unions Shareholders

mative action plan, the salaries of compliance officers were added to the government's payroll and the taxpayer eventually picked up the bill. When an electric appliance company added safety features to a toaster oven, the consumer paid for them directly in the purchase price. For the time being, stakeholders found the costs acceptable.

Public enthusiasm for ever-increasing regulation was tied to the health of the economy. The liberal agenda of the Kennedy and Johnson administrations coincided with substantial economic growth. As a result, says Pertschuck, "the prevailing public mood in the mid-1960s remained buoyant, confident, generous."[9]

But by the mid-1970s, the public mood, corporate interests, and the national political perspective had changed. People began to see some of the rules and constraints under which companies operated as frivolous and arbitrary. The national mood switched just as agencies were about to implement the far-reaching industrywide regulations they had developed and written over the previous decade. Businesses and professions, both large and small, faced additional government interference with their strategic decision-making powers and were forced to bear much of the cost.

Important and powerful special-interest groups gathered to oppose more social and economic legislation. Trade associations and other lobbyists called for a new assessment of the regulatory process. The so-called liberal lobbies that had pushed social legislation found their popular support waning.

---

[9]Pertschuck, *Revolt Against Regulation,* p. 13.

As opposition to more regulation grew, so did business and government interest in deregulation. However, there was little agreement on what *deregulation* actually meant. Cornish Hitchcock, legal director for the Aviation Consumer Action Project in the late 1980s, writes,

> [T]he word "deregulation" has been used in so many contexts to mean so many different things that the currency of the term has been devalued. I think the result has been confusing to the public, and "deregulating" the airlines is certainly different from deregulating the FTC or "deregulating" financial institutions, yet the debate on these and many other topics has come down to a question of whether you are for or against deregulation generically. That oversimplification has tended to cloud discussion of specific topics because there may be valid reasons for some types of deregulation, but not others.[10]

The Carter Administration

The Carter administration, eager to cut costs and bureaucracy, began the economic deregulatory process in 1978. Leaving social legislation virtually untouched at first, President Carter emphasized the need for greater market competition. Carter issued executive orders that systematically reduced the quantity of paperwork businesses were required to submit to the government. Next, he instituted a group called the Regulatory Council to oversee and monitor executive agencies' structure and activities. Carter also organized the Regulatory Analysis Review Group (RARG). Charles L Schultze, chairperson of the president's Council of Economic Advisers, headed this top-level committee. RARG reviewed and conducted cost-benefit analyses on regulations that cost more than $100 million a year.

Carter made some haphazard attempts to intervene in environmental issues such as cotton dust and strip-mining standards. However, stakeholders raised such a storm of protest that he immediately backed off and focused his attention on economic deregulation of the transportation and communications industries.

The Airline Industry

Prior to deregulation, most air carriers charged passengers similar fares. Airlines differentiated themselves by promising friendly service and a variety of menu offerings. Determined to open the industry to competition, President Carter actively supported the passage of the Airline Deregulation Act of 1978. The act mandated the gradual dismantling of the Civil Aeronautics Board (CAB). The Federal Aviation Administration (FAA), whose major responsibility was airline safety, remained intact.

Carter appointed economist Alfred E Kahn to preside over the CAB's

---

[10]Harris and Milkis, *The Politics of Regulatory Change,* p. 280.

demise. Kahn concluded the government should remove itself from making technical decisions about air routes, pricing, and services. Those duties should be left to industry managers. As Kahn put it, "I have more faith in greed than in regulation."[11]

Deregulation led to the swift proliferation—and equally rapid bankruptcy—of commuter lines. In addition to financial instability, these lines also suffered major safety problems. Between 1975 and 1980, commuter lines had eight times as many accidents per 100,000 flights as the major carriers did. Poor plane maintenance, fewer experienced pilots, and less safety equipment all contributed to the problem.

By December 1981, the CAB had given up much of its authority over domestic routes. Two years later, it relinquished control over domestic fares, domestic mergers, and interlocking relationships among airlines. Finally, on January 1, 1985, the CAB ceased operations.

Airline deregulation will be discussed in greater detail later in this chapter.

The Trucking Industry

The Carter administration also supported the passage of the Motor Carrier Act of 1980. Before the act went into effect, truckers had to apply to the Interstate Commerce Commission (ICC) for operating rights. An *operating right* gave a trucker exclusive permission to follow a certain route carrying certain commodities. Beginning in the 1960s, the ICC began to limit operating rights. Truckers immediately created a market in operating rights, buying and selling them to one another. Like any limited commodity, rights soared in price. The rights were carried as intangible assets on truckers' balance sheets and had actual monetary value. On average, they totaled 15 percent of trucker equities.[12]

After July 1980, the ICC began granting operating rights to nearly anyone who asked. In the first year after deregulation, the ICC processed 28,700 applications for new or expanded operations. Companies that had held operating rights before deregulation suffered major financial losses.

What was the consequence of having such valuable assets become virtually worthless overnight? Major truckers simply wrote the amounts off on their balance sheets. Roadway Express, one of the nation's largest truckers, wrote off all of its $26.8 million in operating rights in its third quarter of 1980. This action, which represented a significant loss for Roadway, was catastrophic for smaller competitors. Some truckers' entire equity was literally wiped out overnight.

---

[11]E Holsendolph, "The U.S. Drive for Deregulation," *The New York Times,* October 7, 1980, pp. D1, D19.

[12]"Reality Takes the Wheel," *Forbes,* October 27, 1980, pp. 133–35.

The Communications Industry

Television.   In 1978, the Federal Communications Commission (FCC) created a special staff to investigate television networks. The staff's report strongly supported deregulation. It concluded that beginning in 1952, the FCC had protected NBC, CBS, and ABC from potential competitors. The advent of cable television in the 1960s brought consumers new and original programming, but the three established major networks persuaded the FCC that cable threatened "free" networks. The FCC promptly imposed severe limits on the cable industry, an action that inhibited its growth for a decade.

In 1972, the FCC began to remove some of cable's programming restrictions, and the industry flourished. In 1978, the FCC's deregulatory efforts increased competition. The commission eliminated restrictions on the programs that pay television was permitted to carry. It allowed cable television systems to use a wider variety of stations on channels and removed the barriers to direct satellite broadcasting. Finally, the FCC licensed hundreds of new, low-power broadcast television stations. Charles Ferris, chairperson of the FCC in 1980, declared, "The FCC is allowing new technologies and new entrepreneurs to achieve the potential that burdensome regulation denied them in a previous era."[13]

Radio.   Before long, the FCC deregulated radio's nearly 9,000 stations. Stations were no longer required to poll listeners to ask what they wanted to hear, offer news or other forms of "nonentertainment," or place time limits on advertising.

Telex.   The telex business was plunged into turmoil when the FCC decided to open the domestic telex market to international carriers. Before 1979, Western Union had a monopoly on the domestic message market. It relayed international telexes to their domestic destinations. This business accounted for 10 percent of its revenues.[14] Deregulation brought both domestic and foreign competition.

The First Reagan Administration, 1980–1984

President Reagan's election in 1979 demonstrated that a new conservative mood was sweeping the nation. The initiatives of the Carter years were a mere trickle presaging a flood of economic and social deregulatory activity. The Tolchins assert the Reagan administration was dedicated ideologically to nothing less than the dismantling of America. They note that he vowed to get the government off people's backs during his campaign. In their view,

---

[13]T Schwartz, "F.C.C. Battleground: Deregulation of TV," *The New York Times,* October 22, 1980, p. D1.

[14]"Deregulation Roils the Telex Market," *Business Week,* December 22, 1980, pp. 62, 66.

"the new President initiated a crusade against government regulation and quickly laid the groundwork for the direction of regulation in the 1980s."[15]

Social and economic regulation were clearly on the wane. Barbara S Thomas, a commissioner of the Securities and Exchange Commission, articulated the new ideology very clearly:

> We need to reform the regulatory system and lessen our reliance on regulations as a means of controlling business. In the past we thought a vastly better society could be achieved if only we could specify . . . the procedures that business had to follow . . . In recent years, however, we have become acutely aware of the limitation of such regulatory techniques. We now understand that they have negative consequences, subtle in their operation, but devastating in their overall impact. They can stifle creativity, erode an individual's sense of responsibility, and impose societal costs that may far exceed the benefits provided.[16]

Presidents Carter and Reagan had fundamentally different ideological goals for the deregulatory process. Both presidents wanted to encourage investment, reduce inflation, and foster productivity. However, Carter's approach was far narrower in scope. He limited economic deregulation to a few industries such as airlines, trucking, communications, and financial institutions.

Using an economic rationale, the Reagan initiatives cut into nonmarket social areas such as health, safety, and the environment. Reagan chose new appointees with similar ideologies and philosophies to carry out his programs. He and his appointees avoided the outcry that stymied Carter's tentative forays into social regulation reform. James C Miller, head of the Office of Management and Budget under Reagan, crowed about the differences between the two presidencies. Reagan was tough, he said, but "Carter folded on his first big issue, cotton dust."

But toughness was not as important as planning. Miller noted the new administration did all its homework during the transition period. As soon as Reagan took office, he put the full force of his administration behind deregulation, which, with political astuteness, he called "regulatory relief."[17] Table 9–1 lists the major principles behind the administration's deregulation approach.

Gary Bryner points out that ideological compatibility was President Reagan's major criterion for appointing senior administrative officials.[18] Reagan insisted his appointees demonstrate absolute loyalty in their pursuit of his objectives. Many business leaders applauded Reagan's initiatives and the single voice with which his administration now spoke. These leaders

---

[15]Tolchin and Tolchin, *Dismantling America,* pp. 20–22.

[16]B S Thomas, "Overregulating the Regulators," *The New York Times,* May 1, 1981, p. B10.

[17]Tolchin and Tolchin, *Dismantling America,* pp. 56–58.

[18]G C Bryner, *Bureaucratic Discretion: Law and Policy in Federal Regulatory Agencies* (New York: Pergamon Press, 1987), p. 66.

TABLE 9–1   Reagan Administration Principles

* Impose regulations only if benefits exceed costs.
* Choose least expensive methods to achieve regulatory goals.
* Rely on economic incentives and penalties to encourage companies to meet standards. Eliminate rigid compliance.
* Tailor regulatory burdens to size and nature of affected companies.
* Reduce unnecessary paperwork and regulatory delays.
* Shift regulatory control from the federal government to the states.
* Support legislation requiring Congress periodically to assess the current relevance of regulation.

SOURCE: "Deregulation: A Fast Start for the Reagan Strategy," *Business Week,* March 9, 1981, p. 63.

asserted they could safely put resources into productivity instead of facing endless paperwork.

The administration sent regulatory agencies new guidelines requiring them to conduct cost-benefit analyses of all their objectives. In June 1981, the president's Task Force on Regulation Relief praised the government's rapid movement toward deregulation. The task force predicted businesses would save more than $18 billion by not having to comply with regulations from which the administration had withdrawn support. In fact, the administration wrote very little new deregulatory legislation. Instead, it took action to cut the budgets of existing regulatory agencies, reorganized agency leadership, and issued directives to limit enforcement.

Inaction and budget cutting had major and minor consequences. In some cases, the consequences were fairly trivial. The Department of Education eliminated regulations that caused schools to lose federal funding if their dress codes distinguished between boys and girls. The Postal Service had to show the benefits of the nine-digit ZIP code outweighed the costs before it could implement the code. The Department of Energy eliminated paperwork demands on the private sector by 820,000 hours.[19]

Other consequences were more profound. During the first nine months of the Reagan administration, the National Highway Traffic Safety Administration opened only four investigations into automobile defects; the Carter administration had begun 15 investigations each year. The number of monthly investigations conducted by the Occupational Safety and Health Administration plummeted 17 percent between February and August 1981. Average monthly follow-up inspections dropped 68 percent.

Some of the most dramatic effects occurred at the Environmental Protection Agency (EPA). The agency abolished its Office of Enforcement and

---

[19]C H Farnsworth, "Reagan Group Predicts Curbs on Regulatory Agencies Will Save Billions," *The New York Times,* June 14, 1981, p. 20.

split its functions into several offices. It cut the number of enforcement lawyers dramatically, from 400 to 40. On the regional level, lawyers were instructed to check with Washington before beginning any new initiatives. Under President Carter, the EPA had referred an average of 200 cases per year to the Justice Department. In 1981 it referred only 30, and EPA administrator Anne Gorsuch asked the Justice Department to return more than 40 pending cases to the EPA, declaring they lacked sufficient evidence to go forward.[20]

The FTC's consumer protection policy was "reduced to ashes." Barry Boyer proposes that the White House's insistence on cost effectiveness and data collection undermined any meaningful, rational analysis of its policies. He notes that FTC staff members quickly assumed the process of regulatory analysis was really a political filter. Commissioners "seemed primarily concerned with the practicalities of enforcing any rules they might adopt and finding ways to replace detailed . . . regulations with self-enforcing, market incentives."[21]

The Reagan administration was eager to develop a new perspective on the nature of competition. The ideological underpinnings of its philosophy were consistent with Robert Bork's carefully reasoned thesis in *The Antitrust Paradox*. Bork, a conservative jurist, laid out his recommendations for reform of antitrust doctrines. He concluded that

(1) The only goal that should guide interpretation of the antitrust laws is the welfare of consumers. Departures from that standard destroy the consistency and predictability of the law . . .

(2) In judging consumer welfare, productivity efficiency, the single most important factor contributing to that welfare must be given due weight along with allocative efficiency. Failure to consider productive efficiency . . . is probably the major reason for the deformation of antitrust's doctrines.

(3) The law should be reformed so it strikes at three classes of behavior:

   (a) The suppression of competition by horizontal agreement . . .

   (b) Horizontal mergers creating very large market shares (those that have fewer than three significant rivals in any market).

   (c) Deliberate predation engaged in to drive rivals from a market, prevent or delay the entry of rivals, or discipline existing rivals . . .

(4) The law should permit agreements on prices, territories, refusals to deal, and other suppressions that are ancillary . . .[22]

[20]C Mayer, "Reagan Gets Tough with Regulation," *The Boston Globe,* November 29, 1981, p. 67.

[21]B Boyer, "The Federal Trade Commission and Consumer Protection Policy: A Postmortem Examination," in K Hawkins and J M Thomas, eds., *Making Regulatory Policy* (Pittsburgh: University of Pittsburgh Press, 1989), pp. 93–132.

[22]R H Bork. *The Antitrust Paradox: A Policy at War with Itself* (New York: Basic Books, 1978), pp. 405–07.

The Justice Department and the court system crafted a deregulatory framework that turned academic discourse into action.

Antitrust Legislation

Antitrust enforcement and an evolving definition of competition were core concerns of Reagan's deregulatory process. In 1984, J Paul McGrath, the assistant attorney general in charge of the Antitrust Division, looked back over the first four years of the Reagan presidency. He spoke for the administration when he asserted, "bad mergers ought to be prevented but mergers which are not bad shouldn't be blocked out of ignorance of our law enforcement policy."[23]

McGrath's predecessor, William F Baxter, established the ideology that McGrath followed. Baxter had taken a strict constructionist view of antitrust legislation. In rewriting the Justice Department's merger guidelines in 1982, Baxter gave a green light to both vertical and horizontal combinations. His policy, which allowed mergers between suppliers and customers, also fostered the formation of conglomerates by companies that had been competitors. For the first time, the government determined what constituted a "bad" merger by looking at its potential effects on international competition.

The administration established new measures of product markets. The relevant product market was now international rather than local or national. This new definition gave merger-minded companies much more leeway. For example, Baxter adopted a "5 percent rule," under which antitrust officials would try to determine what would happen in a product market if manufacturers raised prices 5 percent. The questions they asked themselves were (1) how many new competitors would enter the market in six months and (2) how many customers would switch to other products within a year.[24] The answers to these questions as based on the 5 percent rule helped officials decide whether or not a merger was acceptable.

The Justice Department also adopted a "fix-it-first" approach. Antitrust officials told prospective merging companies what their objections were and gave them time to eliminate the causes of their objections. For example, when DuPont and Conoco were planning a merger, Baxter informed the companies he would block the deal unless Conoco ended its joint venture with Monsanto, DuPont's largest competitor. When DuPont agreed to buy out Monsanto's share in its joint venture plant, Baxter agreed to the merger.

Baxter adopted yet another test based on the Herfindahl index, which measures the degree of concentration in an industry. Baxter modified the

---

[23]"Now the Antitrust Guidelines Are Clearer—and Looser," *Business Week,* June 25, 1984, p. 38.

[24]A Reilly, "Antitrust Policy after the Steel Veto," *Fortune,* March 19, 1984, pp. 85–86, 90–91.

index to take into account the market shares of all competitors, both domestic and foreign, instead of basing the index on the market shares of only the four largest domestic competitors.[25] The index rating helped the Justice Department decide whether or not to approve a merger.

Reagan's first term established a clear trend toward increased numbers and scope of mergers and acquisitions. Whether that trend would be healthy for business and for the economy remained to be seen. Deregulation and a laissez-faire antitrust policy affected all major industries. The technicalities of specific antitrust measures remained a mystery to most ordinary citizens. However, the effects of the policy were widely felt.

The Second Reagan Administration, 1984–1988

By the mid-1980s, many questioned whether deregulation was working as it should. There was no doubt prices had fallen for a variety of goods and services, but some wondered whether the rash of mergers and acquisitions had fostered such a high degree of concentration that new entrants would be unable to compete with established giants. Instead of enhanced competition and productivity, new oligopolies resulted. Even Alfred E Kahn, former chair of the now defunct CAB, expressed reservations about the anticompetitive side effects of deregulation. Small companies often became clients and even captives of the large players in their industries.

Although the promoters of deregulation recognized their policies might have anticompetitive side effects, they maintained the benefits outweighed the liabilities. Critics charged that regulatory agencies had mishandled the transition and that if no remedial steps were taken, the pendulum could swing too far toward deregulation.

Benefits were spread unevenly across the nation. Sparsely populated and rural areas found services disappearing and prices skyrocketing. Deregulation wiped out the "hidden subsidies" on which rural areas had depended. For example, before the telecommunications industry was deregulated, the FCC required phone companies to charge urban and rural customers the same prices for service. This new policy meant relatively fewer customers covered the phone companies' fixed costs in rural areas. After deregulation, phone companies could pass on more of the actual cost to rural customers. One customer in Nebraska saw her phone bill go up 300 percent between 1984 and 1987, from $7 to $27 per month. Although the dollar amount was fairly trivial in this case, the trend was chilling.

Transportation deregulation hit rural areas particularly hard. Many small towns that had already lost bus routes found that they were paying higher fares for airline service or that the airlines too had simply abandoned the routes.

[25]Ibid.

Residents of South Dakota's panhandle had to pay twice as much to fly to Denver as they had paid before deregulation. Four local airlines came and went between 1984 and 1987. Only the federal government's Essential Air Service program, which subsidized commuter lines serving otherwise unprofitable rural areas, guaranteed any service at all, and even that safety net was snatched away in 1988.[26]

By the end of 1986, five major industries had felt the full force of deregulation: the airlines, the trucking industry, the railroads, the telephone industry, and the bus industry.

Airlines

By 1986, six air carriers controlled 84 percent of the market, compared to 78 percent in 1978. Hub-and-spoke configurations replaced direct flights. This system allowed the airlines to dominate traffic patterns and, indirectly, to control prices in those concentrated markets.

Trucking

Large LTL (less-than-truckload) companies also adopted the hub-and-spoke systems for satellite terminals. Since profits were tied to optimal loads, these companies used state-of-the-art dispatch systems to create economics of flow. The LTL segment was extremely well developed and dominated by a few large companies that earned 90 percent of the profits. Most full-truckload (TL) companies did not fare well under deregulation: Between 1978 and 1986, nearly 30 percent of all new entrants in the TL trucking industry failed. A spokesperson for Consolidated Freightways Inc. observed, "There's no question the big guys are getting bigger and the bottom end is getting squeezed.[27] This was true for both LTL and TL companies.

Railroads

In 1978, there were 13 large rail freight carriers. By 1986, there were only six, three in the East and three in the West. Together they carried 86 percent of the rail freight and earned 93 percent of the profits. In the early 1980s, these railroads acquired trucking and ocean shipping companies that had been run by smaller railroads.

In March 1984, the ICC opened new opportunities for railroads to become supertransportation companies. The ICC approved CSX's acquisition of a large barge operation, American Commercial Line. CSX, a major railroad holding company, started operations in 1981. During the next three

---

[26]B Richards, "Deregulation Raises Prices, Cuts Services in Many Rural Areas," *The Wall Street Journal,* October 5, 1987, p. 1.

[27]"Is Deregulation Working?," *Business Week,* December 22, 1986, p. 52.

years it convinced the ICC it could achieve greater efficiencies with a combination of rail, water, pipeline, and air operations. Over that period, CSX acquired Beckett Aviation to service corporate jets, Texas Gas Resources, a barge company operating on the Mississippi River, and a Kentucky-based pipeline. By mid-1984, CSX had become an "intermodal monster."[28] Although CSX's bid to become a supercompany seemed headed for success, few observers were willing to conclude deregulation had brought about a transportation revolution.

Telephone Industry

In January 1982, the Justice Department ordered the breakup of AT&T and imposed a 1984 deadline. At the time of the initial judgment, AT&T controlled $137 billion in assets, more than those of Exxon, General Motors, and US Steel combined and more than the GNP of all but 20 nations. AT&T owned 24,000 buildings, 177,000 motor vehicles, 142 million telephones, and 1.7 billion miles of cable, microwave, radio, and satellite circuits.

Under the terms of the breakup, AT&T agreed to divest itself of its 22 local telephone companies. In exchange, the company would be allowed to enter deregulated computer and information-processing businesses. The surviving company would continue to provide most of the country's long-distance service to other nations, continue to sell and lease communications equipment manufactured by its giant Western Electric subsidiary, and retain Bell Labs, one of the world's best R&D facilities. In addition, AT&T could use its newly streamlined but still integrated structure to offer computer products and services and new methods of voice data storage and transmission.

In 1985 and 1986, American households received ballots allowing them to choose their long-distance carrier. AT&T, MCI Communications, and GTE Sprint were the major contenders. However, AT&T's dismantling did not mean competitors flourished. By 1987, MCI and Sprint had incurred huge losses. The Justice Department added to their woes by urging the courts to allow so-called Baby Bells (former local Bell companies) to get into the game. Although the courts refused to go along with the Justice Department, the industry remained intensely competitive and increasingly complex.

The real import of the breakup was that companies and individuals could now purchase their own equipment. By 1986, large numbers of competitors were fighting for the corporate market. Even Japanese companies such as Toshiba vied for market share. In long-distance service alone, 300 companies offered lower rates than AT&T. On the local level, three dozen vendors sold hundreds of complex systems. New companies sprang up to

---

[28]P Brimelow, "Where Those Hybrid Haulers Are Headed," *Fortune,* March 24, 1984, pp. 114–20.

offer confused businesspeople telephone consulting services. One consultant assured potential clients that "there are no bargains in parachutes, brain surgery, or telephones."[29]

Buses

The Bus Regulatory Reform Act of 1982 deregulated the intercity bus industry, 60 percent of which was served by Greyhound Lines. The act left safety regulations intact, but state regulators could no longer compel bus lines to serve rural areas.

In 1983, Greyhound suffered a 47-day strike. After the strike, Greyhound cut 2,500 employees from the payroll and lowered the wages of those who remained. The strike exacerbated the effects of deregulation. The company sold most of its terminals, restructured its route system, and dropped hundreds of stops.[30] In Illinois alone, Greyhound cut service to 61 communities.

Greyhound officials announced they expected to eliminate service to one-third of their scheduled stops. Those in favor of deregulation assured customers that smaller bus lines would fill the vacuum.[31] But by 1987, more than 3,000 US towns and cities had lost their bus service permanently. Once again, rural areas had been hit hardest.

The Reagan-Bush Transition: The Banking Industry

The Reagan administration allowed eight years of unfettered competition to rule in the banking industry. Ralph Nader's Public Citizen issued a scathing report on the effects of bank deregulation. Soon charges of criminal mismanagement rocked the industry. For many people, the S&L failures epitomized the problems deregulation had brought to banking.

In 1988, Congress's General Accounting Office (GAO) recommended that the newly elected George Bush improve enforcement of the banking industry. The GAO observed that bank deregulation had resulted in "a risky hodgepodge of banking and other functions that could imperil the safety and soundness of the banking system."[32] In fact, the GAO concluded, nearly one-third of US savings and loan institutions had become insolvent due to poorly implemented deregulation. (For the details of deregulation, see the S&L case on pages 255–256.)

---

[29]R L Simison, "Wrestling with Choice," *The Wall Street Journal,* February 24, 1986, pp. 1D, 4D.
[30]R W Stevenson, "Greyhound Restructuring Is Planned," *The New York Times,* August 16, 1985, p. D1.
[31]R Lindsey, "Bus Line Deregulation to Cut Off Many Stops," *The New York Times,* February 21, 1983, p. B7.
[32]R L Berke, "Deregulation Has Gone Too Far, Many Telling New Administration," *The New York Times,* December 11, 1988, p. 1A.

The banking industry was in a state of flux between 1988 and 1991. *The Economist* attributed "today's [January 1991] shaky financial structure" to 60 years of haphazard legislation. Diversification was a major issue with which the banking industry had struggled for decades. Nearly everyone involved in banking agreed many banks had gotten into trouble through their own mismanagement. However, banks were constrained by regulations that prohibited diversification into new businesses such as insurance and underwriting. Also, they could not enter markets outside their home states. To remain competitive, commercial banks had loaned too much money to borrowers who could not repay. The credit crunch pushed the economy deeper into the recession.[33] Bankers, lawyers, Congress, and the Bush administration all agreed bold new reforms were overdue. However, there was little agreement on the exact details of that reform.

New Banking Regulation

It took three years for the Bush administration to propose its banking plan. In February 1991, the administration recommended a sweeping overhaul of the banking system. Treasury Secretary Nicholas F Brady declared the legislation had two main goals: to strengthen the banking system and to make banks more competitive internationally. The bill contained five major provisions:

1. *Bank ownership.* Industrial companies would be allowed to own banks, but insured deposits would be held in a separate affiliate to reduce opportunities for speculation. These banks would be able to have affiliates that sold mutual funds and insurance and underwrote corporate securities. The administration held that banks would be able to attract more capital and diversify risk. Opponents said this provision might create another S&L debacle and would make banks more vulnerable to recession.

2. *Nationwide banking.* The bill would authorize full nationwide banking by 1994. National banks would be able to open branches in additional states more easily. The administration declared this move would result in huge financial savings, but critics maintained community-based banks would be at an unfair competitive disadvantage.

3. *Banks and insurance.* States would decide whether to allow banks to sell insurance in the states in which they were chartered or operated. The administration said this provision would allow positive diversification. Critics noted the insurance industry was already weak and the states had been ineffective insurance regulators.

4. *Regulatory restrictions and consolidation.* S&L and bank regulation would be consolidated from four agencies into two. This consolidation would eliminate layers of regulators and conflicting directives. The Federal Reserve Board would regulate all state banking organizations. A new federal

---

[33]"A Brave New World for America's Banks," *The Economist,* January 12, 1991, p, 69.

banking agency under the Treasury Department would regulate all national banking and thrift organizations. The FDIC's sole function would be as an insurer. While everyone agreed consolidation was a correct move, some critics wanted a single regulatory body instead of two.

5. *Federal deposit insurance.* The coverage of this insurance would be scaled back by limiting the number of insured accounts an individual could hold in one bank. Bank failure standards would be changed to limit coverage in any one bank to two deposits of $100,000, one being a retirement account. Coverage would end for brokered deposits (certificates of deposit sold through brokerage houses to raise funds for banks). Institutional investors such as pension funds and securities firms that break down deposits into $100,000 increments to obtain insurance would no longer be covered. Critics pointed out most families would be able to circumvent the $100,000 limit simply by opening an account at another bank.[34]

The Bush administration plan provided the basis for media and interest group discussion about the American banking industry. In a special report on the future of banking, *Business Week* concluded the banking industry was dying and the administration's bill was far too limited in scope. Although the Brady legislation would make banking more competitive, even greater deregulation was needed. *Business Week* saw a future in which "most of today's banks will be just another set of participants in a financial services free-for-all where everyone will be able to invade rival turf."[35]

Few observers thought Congress would take the bank reform bill seriously. However, by July 1991, the House Banking Committee had passed much of the proposal. The major difference between the administration's bill and the Senate Banking Committee's draft was that in the Senate version, commercial companies would not be allowed to own banks.

The Economist applauded the Senate version, concurring in the decision not to let industrial companies own banks. It assessed America's record at regulating and supervising banks as "lousy." In the case of thrifts, it declared, "the record is one not just of incompetence but also of political interference and outright corruption."[36]

The optimism of summer 1991 turned to gloom in autumn. Unhappy with the House and Senate banking committees's revisions, the administration and big banking stakeholders successfully pressured the House to reject the entire bill. Treasury Secretary Brady, representatives from American Express, J P Morgan, Citicorp, and the American Bankers Association com-

---

[34]S Labaton, "Administration Presents Its Plan for Broad Overhaul of Banking," *The New York Times,* February 6, 1991, p. A1; K H Bacon, "Financial Overhaul: Big Banks Would Get Vastly Broader Powers under Treasury's Plan," *The Wall Street Journal,* February 6, 1991, p. A1.

[35]"The Future of Banking," *Business Week,* April 22, 1991, pp. 72–81.

[36]"A Needless Risk," *The Economist,* July 6, 1991, p. 16.

bined forces to lobby for defeat of the altered bill. In November, the House overwhelmingly turned it down.[37]

By the end of that month, lawmakers passed a leaner and more limited banking law. Congress rejected most of the administration's proposals to expand bank functions. In fact, the new legislation approved a much tougher regulatory system. Under the new law, regulators would have to move more quickly to close banks before those banks became insolvent. After 1994, the FDIC would lose its authority to reimburse foreign deposits and uninsured deposits over $100,000 when large banks failed. However, the bill added $70 billion in borrowing authority to support deposit insurance.

Banking experts differed in their assessment of the bill. The president of a Washington-based financial consulting firm concluded, "this legislation creates a system of arbitrary, Draconian and inflexible regulatory criteria designed to ensure that no bank will ever again fail." Robert Litan of the Brookings Institution thought the bill was "modest good news for taxpayers." Consultant Edward Furash concluded, "the bottom line is the bill doesn't help the outlook for banking one bit . . . Congress walked away from the worst financial crisis the country has faced since the 1930s."[38]

Unwilling to make a commitment before the upcoming presidential election, Congress continued to debate the bill into the summer of 1992. National banking was the one aspect of the bill everyone agreed would come to fruition. President Clinton's appointment of Lloyd Bentsen as secretary of the treasury opened up new possibilities and the opportunity for innovative initiatives. However, no new bill would mitigate the devastating costs of the S&L fiasco.

CASE   *The Savings and Loan Debacle*

In March 1980, outgoing president Jimmy Carter signed legislation that ended the cap on interest paid to S&L depositors. S&Ls had to pay interest as high as 18 percent to attract investors, but they were not allowed to diversify their investments. To help the struggling thrifts, Congress raised the level of insured deposits from $40,000 to $100,000 and permitted riskier investments.

In 1981, the Federal Home Loan Bank Board (FHLBB), the industry's supervisory body, permitted single individuals to own S&Ls instead of the previously mandated minimum of 400 owners. Deregulating even further, the board allowed real estate developers to use property cash as collateral for investment. By 1982, S&L

[37]S Labaton, "House Turns Down Banking Overhaul by 324-to-89 Vote," *The New York Times,* November 5, 1991, p. A1.
[38]K H Bacon, "The New Banking Law Toughens Regulation, Some Say Too Much," *The Wall Street Journal,* November 29, 1991, p. A1.

owners could use $1 of capital in cash or real estate to raise $33 in federally insured deposits.

Savings and loan directors, however well-intentioned, often did not understand the new, sophisticated financial transactions that allowed S&Ls to sell off mortgages to Wall Street firms that in turn sold the mortgages as securities to investors. Directors relied for advice on managers, many of whom were tied to real estate developers or securities firms.

Independent accounting firms that were required to approve S&L financial reports often filed inaccurate audits. For example, the GAO found that 29 of 31 insolvent California S&Ls had had clean audits shortly before the government was forced to take them over. Some accounting firms refused to get involved in S&L auditing, but others actively pursued S&L clients, and many of those firms approved inaccurate and even fraudulent real estate appraisals.

Experts concluded federal accounting rules rather than auditors were often at fault. They claimed the FHLBB and Congress had put into place a set of accounting "gimmicks" rather than rules. Those poorly conceived rules masked the problems that beset the S&Ls and contributed to the industry's eventual collapse.

In the mid-1980s, the number of FHLBB examiners was reduced at the same time S&Ls were making even riskier investments. As investigators subsequently discovered, hundreds of S&Ls were not examined at all. Frederick D Wolf, the GAO assistant comptroller, observed the White House's attitude was that S&Ls should do what the marketplace allowed and supervision should be lax.[39]

Early in 1986, a GAO report said 1,300 of the 3,180 federally insured S&Ls were in financial trouble. This number represented 42 percent of the industry's total assets. There was ample blame to spread around. Members of Congress from both parties denied the seriousness of the situation. The White House refused to own up to the problem, trying to delay publicity until after Bush was elected.

The silence continued as the 1988 election approached. Both political parties avoided any discussion of bailout legislation. Soon after taking office, President Bush proposed that taxpayers fund the S&L bailout and a federal agency be created to manage the process. By this time, the best estimates were that the bailout would cost $71 billion.[40]

Questions

1. What has happened recently in the S&L situation?

2. What policies should the government adopt to ensure those problems do not recur?

3. Interview a top officer in an S&L institution. What are the major issues she faces in the industry? To what extent is regulation a help or a hindrance?

---

[39]J Gerth, "A Blend of Tragedy and Farce," *The New York Times,* July 3, 1990, p. D1.
[40]S V Roberts with G Cohen, "Villains of the S&L Crisis," *U.S. News & World Report,* October 1, 1990, p. 22.

Reregulation in the 1990s

Much to the surprise and consternation of the Bush administration's conservative supporters, Reagan's deregulatory policies did not endure. Although the administration's rhetoric continued to echo earlier themes of limited government control, the S&L crisis and intense foreign competition precipitated a new discussion of government's relationship to business.

A June 1991 editorial in *The Wall Street Journal* called President Bush the "Reregulation President." The article noted that agencies had issued 17 percent more rules than in the 1980s. It attributed a new wave of regulation to the inactivity of the White House Office of Information and Regulatory Affairs (OIRA). Begun under President Carter, OIRA reviewed regulations and was supposed to stop those it considered wasteful. The office had been without a director since the beginning of 1990 because, the *Journal* averred, certain Democratic senators were delaying confirmation hearings.[41]

Although the president seemed to support and even initiate much of the new regulatory legislation, he also created Vice President Dan Quayle's Council on Competitiveness to examine prospective rules and oppose any that were "antibusiness." The council was composed of six high-ranking members: the treasury secretary, commerce secretary, attorney general, director of the White House budget office, chairperson of the president's Council of Economic Advisers, and White House chief of staff. They, along with six full-time aides, were swamped by the tremendous numbers of proposed regulations. By the end of 1991, nearly 5,000 federal regulations were in the process of being written, 25 percent more than at the end of the Reagan years. Few of these regulations were examined by the Council, even though the costs attendant to their passage were high. The Quayle council concentrated on examining proposed health, safety, and environmental rules.

The council proposed a number of changes in these critical social issues. Among its suggestions were changes in the definition of wetlands to permit commercial development of animal and plant habitats. It also proposed more than 100 changes in rules covering air pollution emissions permits.

The council joined with the Food and Drug Administration (FDA) to urge a new system of approving new drugs more quickly. It concurred with the administration's Office of Management and Budget's decision to eliminate an EPA proposal that 25 percent of municipal waste be recycled before the rest was burned.[42]

Quayle and his council received new support early in 1992. In his state of the union address, President Bush declared a 90-day freeze and review of

---

[41]"The Reregulation President," *The Wall Street Journal*, June 17, 1991, p. A10.

[42]J H Cushman, Jr., "Federal Regulation Growing as a Quayle Panel Fights It," *The New York Times*, December 24, 1991, p. A1.

all federal regulations. Quayle gleefully announced, "We are the ones who are going to run this operation—and it's not going to be Congress." He also declared the rule review would save the United States $10 billion to $20 billion per year.[43]

The moratorium had immediate effects. Within 90 days, the Department of Labor delayed rules it was drafting to protect worker health and safety. President Bush rejected EPA administrator William K Reilly's view that the Clean Air Act specifically required the public to be notified of increased auto emissions. He agreed with the council's conclusion that public review would take too long and would hold up changes in manufacturing.

Several federal agencies proposed relaxing safety rules for testing and producing live, genetically altered organisms. The SEC made it easier for small companies to sell stock and for mutual funds to invest in new, small companies. The FDA speeded up testing of new drugs for safety and delayed deadlines for food processors that had been ordered to put more detailed nutritional labeling on products.[44]

As the 1992 presidential election drew closer, the administration and the Democrat-controlled Congress evaluated regulations in terms of their political utility. President Bush, who was vulnerable in the polls, tried to appeal to the conservative wing of the Republican party. Bill Clinton, weighed down by attacks on his character, tried to develop a regulatory policy. Many members of both the House and the Senate decided not to stand for reelection in 1992. Congress reeled under White House charges of mismanagement and obstructionism. The House banking scandal, the Postal Service scandal, and the ongoing recession contributed to the public's mistrust of and disgust with the entire government process. It would be up to the Clinton administration to establish the regulatory strategy for the mid-1990s and possibly beyond. Indeed, in October 1993, President Clinton issued an executive order that effectively abolished the council.

Summary

Stakeholder interaction regarding regulation became very complex after the 1960s. Economic and social regulation waxed and waned. Many new products and processes were developed during this period. As stakeholders began to use those products and as the environment was affected by them, pressure for regulatory control increased. Presidents Carter, Reagan, and Bush each had different political and social agendas as they developed regulatory policy. Coalitions of stakeholders in the external direct and indirect quadrants of the stakeholder influence map shifted.

---

[43]R D Hershey, Jr., "Quayle Says Rule Review Is Saving U.S. $10 Billion," *The New York Times,* April 3, 1992, p. A10.

[44]D E Rosenbaum, "Bush Is Extending Regulation Freeze with a Fanfare," *The New York Times,* April 29, 1992, p. A1.

At the end of the 1970s, the government took major initiatives to deregulate specific industries. President Carter's view of deregulation was quite narrow, concentrating on competition in a few industries. President Reagan did very little to overturn existing regulations but substantially diminished the ability of regulatory agencies to carry out their mandates. President Bush waffled back and forth on regulation. His rhetoric supported social regulation, while his Supreme Court nominations demonstrated a more conservative view of society and the interpretation of law. Some of his cabinet appointments appeared to mollify more liberal elements of his party, whereas others toed the strict conservative line. No clear strategy emerged.

Regulation, deregulation, and reregulation overlapped and conflicted, leaving most stakeholders confused and concerned. The election of Bill Clinton signaled a sharp break with past policies. Exactly what new policies will be implemented is still unclear.

Questions

1. What are the ideological problems a nation faces as it tries to balance regulation and free market forces?
2. What are the societal drawbacks to unregulated transportation industries? What are the benefits?
3. Are partisan politics helpful or harmful to regulatory policy? Explain.

Projects

1. Interview your local member of Congress about his stand on banking legislation.
2. Compile a list of new technologies that are coming under the regulatory process. What kinds of regulations should be put in place to address the concerns of stakeholders?

BETA CASE 9
REGULATION AND DEREGULATION

Brian Madison drummed his fingers on his desk and rocked back and forth in his large leather swivel chair. He no longer had to worry about what President Bush's regulation moratorium would mean to Beta. He knew the FDA was speeding up the testing of new drugs. But would Beta be held responsible if its drugs, tested under the relaxed guidelines, developed problems later? What policy would the Clinton administration and the director of the FDA adopt?

Drug-testing requirements were of utmost importance to Beta. All of its operating divisions spent huge amounts on testing and meeting FDA requirements. Any substantive change in those requirements had profound strategic and monetary implications.

Back in 1990, Beta began to make generic drugs.[45] The company hired David Shapiro, the vice president of a small, successful generic company in New Jersey, to run the new division. Shapiro had spent endless hours with regulators trying to move his previous company's application process through the FDA's maze of paperwork. He had explained the problems to Madison at the time he was interviewed: "Those folks at the FDA are totally inept, especially when it comes to evaluating generic drugs. I personally know three generic drug manufacturers that have submitted phony data. I know Beta does everything by the book, but there's a risk of losing out to the company that gets quick approval. I really have a lot of admiration for the folks at Mylan."

Madison was impressed with Shapiro's candor and expertise. Everyone in the industry knew about Mylan Laboratories and the generic-drug scandal. Mylan blew the whistle on FDA procedures in 1989. The company realized it was losing millions of dollars because the FDA sat on its applications but passed competitors' applications quickly. After complaining to the FDA about favoritism and payoffs for two years, Mylan executives hired private detectives. The detectives uncovered evidence of payoffs, which they quickly delivered to the House oversight committee. After the committee investigated, the FDA withdrew its approval of several drugs that competed with Mylan products.[46] Eventually, the FDA recalled or suspended more than 150 drugs and inspected more than 20 major companies.

The FDA regulatory process continued to be a concern. Drug testing was a major topic of conversation every time pharmaceutical industry executives got together. No one really knew what the Bush administration or FDA commissioner Dr. David Kessler would do about drug testing. Early in 1991, Kessler announced he would get a lot tougher on the violators, take a fresh look at regulations, and revamp the structure of the FDA. In fact, in April 1991, four FDA employees went to jail for accepting bribes from generic drugmakers.

But presidential politics stirred the murky waters. When President Bush extended his regulatory moratorium in the spring of 1992, Madison, Shapiro, and every other generic or brand-name drugmaker had to operate without clear direction or standards. They had to develop policies that would protect them if existing regulations were enforced or new regulations were imposed. What new directives would come from the Clinton administration, and how did the company anticipate the changing regulatory environment?

---

[45]Generic drugs are less expensive versions of brand-name medicines. Generics account for more than one-third of all prescription drugs sold. When drug patents expire, generic companies use the formulas to make generic versions. By 1995, patents will have expired on brand-name prescription drugs with estimated annual sales of $10 million. Increasingly, large pharmaceutical companies are producing both generic and brand-name drugs. Squibb, Warner-Lambert, American Cyanamid, and Ciba-Geigy all have generic businesses. Beta's generic business is very small compared to these four giants, whose production accounts for more than 25 percent of all prescriptions for generic versions of drugs.

---

[46]"Mylan Is Glad It Opened This Can of Worms," *Business Week,* September 18, 1989, p. 30.

APPENDIX 9–1
US REGULATORY AGENCIES

Major Regulatory Agencies

Consumer Product Safety Commission
Environmental Protection Agency
Equal Employment Opportunity Commission
Federal Communications Commission
Federal Deposit Insurance Corporation
Federal Energy Regulatory Commission
Federal Reserve System
Federal Trade Commission
Food and Drug Administration
Interstate Commerce Commission
National Labor Relations Board
Occupational Safety and Health Administration
Securities and Exchange Commission

Other Regulatory Agencies

Architectural and Transportation Barriers Compliance Board
Commodity Futures Trading Commission
Farm Credit Administration
Federal Election Commission
Federal Housing Finance Board
Federal Maritime Commission
National Credit Union Administration
National Mediation Board
National Transportation Safety Board
Nuclear Regulatory Commission
Pension Benefit Guaranty Corporation
Postal Rate Commission
Resolution Trust Corporation
Small Business Administration
United States International Trade Commission
United States Postal Service

Departmental Agencies

Department of Agriculture
Agricultural Marketing Service
Agricultural Stabilization and Conservation Service
Animal and Plant Health Inspection Service
Commodity Credit Corporation

Farmers Home Administration
Federal Grain Inspection Service
Food and Nutrition Service
Food Safety and Inspection Service
Foreign Agricultural Service
Forest Service
Federal Crop Insurance Corporation
Packers and Stockyards Administration
Rural Electrification Administration
Soil Conservation Service

Department of Commerce
Board of Export Administration
Economic Development Administration
International Trade Administration
National Institute of Standards and Technology
National Oceanic and Atmospheric Administration
Patent and Trademark Office

Department of Defense
Army Corps of Engineers

Department of Energy
Conservations and Renewable Energy
Economic Regulatory Administration
Environment, Safety and Health
Environmental Restoration and Waste Management
Fossil Energy
International Affairs and Energy Emergencies

Department of Health and Human Services
Office for Civil Rights
Social Security Administration
Family Support Administration
Health Care Financing Administration
Office of Human Development Services
Office of the Inspector General
Public Health Service
Regional Offices

Department of Housing and Urban Development
Office of Fair Housing and Equal Opportunity
Office of Housing
Office of Community Planning and Development
Government National Mortgage Association

Department of the Interior
Bureau of Indian Affairs
Bureau of Land Management

Minerals Management Service
United States Fish and Wildlife Service
United States Geological Survey
National Park Service
Bureau of Reclamation
Office of Surface Mining Reclamation and Enforcement

Department of Justice
Antitrust Division
Civil Rights Division
Drug Enforcement Administration
Immigration and Naturalization Service
Office of Justice Programs
Bureau of Prisons
Criminal Division
United States Parole Division

Department of Labor
Employment Standards Administration
Employment and Training Administration
Mine Safety and Health Administration
Office of Labor-Management Standards
Pension and Welfare Benefits Administration
Veterans' Employment and Training Service

Department of Transportation
Federal Aviation Administration
Federal Highway Administration
Federal Railroad Administration
Maritime Administration
National Highway Safety Administration
Research and Special Programs Administration
Saint Lawrence Seaway Development Corporation
United States Coast Guard
Urban Mass Transportation Administration
Office of Aviation Analysis
Office of Aviation Enforcement and Proceedings
Office of Commercial Space Transportation
Office of Hearings
Office of Intergovernmental and Consumer Affairs
Office of International Aviation

Department of the Treasury
Bureau of Alcohol, Tobacco and Firearms
Comptroller of the Currency
Internal Revenue Service
Office of Thrift Supervision
United States Customs Service

Department of Veterans Affairs

Regulatory Oversight and Coordination
Administrative Conference of the United States
General Accounting Office
Office of Management and Budget
Regulatory Information Service Center

Executive Office of the President

10 PHILANTHROPY AND CORPORATE GIVING

This chapter focuses on philanthropy and cause-related marketing. Philanthropic giving is a major business in the United States. Individuals, foundations, and corporations all contribute to a vast panoply of causes from the extreme political right to the fringes on the left. Philanthropy helps support constituencies and organizations that are not funded by federal, state, or local governments. It also supports causes that are government funded but have inadequate resources.

In recent years, many corporations have tied their marketing programs and products to social causes. Increasingly they are using their marketing function to promote political and social agendas important to top managers or to potential customers.

All countries have some form of philanthropic activity, and many also embrace cause-related marketing. This chapter examines the programs and strategies used by two of the United States's largest trading partners: Great Britain and Japan.

CASE *United Way*

United Way of America is a network of more than 2,000 local chapters that collect contributions through the workplace. Employees make workplace donations and often authorize payroll deductions for local charities. About one cent of every dollar donated to local chapters goes to the United Way of America's national association in Alexandria, Virginia. The national organization helps the affiliates with activities such as advertising and training charity workers. In 1992, affiliates donated $29 million to United Way of America. But the purposes to which some of that money was put engendered a tremendous amount of negative publicity.

In February 1992, William Aramony was forced out of his job as president of United Way of America. Newspapers and other media across the United States uncovered a number of Aramony's activities that eventually led United Way's board to ask for his resignation. Why did the media single out Aramony for criticism, and what was so noteworthy about his situation?

The *Washington Post* and *Regardie's Magazine* of Washington, DC, reported that Aramony had been using contributions to finance an extravagant personal lifestyle. The stories focused on Aramony's salary and benefits package of $463,000, his travel habits, and entertainment paid for by the charity.

Aramony was not the only highly paid head of a tax-exempt institution. According to the *Chronicle of Philanthropy*, 37 of the biggest 100 charitable foundations paid their chief executives more than $200,000 in salary and benefits. The median salary in 1991 was $155,000. Three foundations—the W M Keck Foundation, the J Paul Getty Trust, and the Ford Foundation—paid their top executives even more than United Way paid Aramony.[1] But these foundations were not publicly supported.

The newspapers pointed to Aramony's lavish lifestyle. They noted he used chauffeured cars costing United Way of America more than $90,000 a year. On two occasions, Aramony flew to Europe on the supersonic Concorde, running up an airline bill of $41,000. Whenever Aramony traveled, he purchased first-class tickets.

While president, Aramony unilaterally authorized the formation of two spin-off organizations incorporated as profit-making enterprises. One of these companies, Partnership Umbrella, Inc., bought Aramony an apartment on New York City's Upper East Side and a Florida apartment, together valued at $1.3 million. Partnership Umbrella refused to disclose its finances despite the full disclosure policies of the standard-setting agency, the National Charities Information Bureau. The other affiliate, Sales Service/America, hired Aramony's son Robert as its top executive even though professional fund raisers agreed he was not qualified.[2]

The public outcry was loud and furious against what many perceived as Aramony's excesses. Economic and social concerns at that time made Aramony's actions seem particularly flagrant. First, there was the public perception of what the motivation for the head of a nonprofit organization *should* be. According to an editor of the *Nonprofit Times,* a monthly trade publication, "The average Joe or the average Jane who makes maybe $25,000, when they see someone working for a charity, that's supposed to be mission-driven, they think these people should be doing it for the love of the mission and not to make money."[3] Clearly a disparity existed between the average donor's perception of United Way's mission and the reality of its operations.

This happened at a time when the US economy was in a seemingly endless recession. Many of the communities in which United Way campaigned were suffering job losses and threats of more layoffs. People who were themselves barely surviving economically were exhorted to give to those less fortunate.

Another concern was that donors could not designate the specific charities to which their money would go. Various stakeholder groups had very different visions of what United Way should support and were not reluctant to make their voices

---

[1]"Philanthropic Pay," *The Wall Street Journal,* September 8, 1992, p. A1.

[2]F Barringer, "United Way Board Discusses Leaders," *The New York Times,* February 27, 1992, p. A2.

[3]F Barringer, "Pay for Charity Leaders Raises Uneasy Question," *The New York Times,* March 16, 1992, p. A12.

heard. They wanted to target their donations to causes they liked and away from those they disliked.

In Rochester, New York, for example, the local offices of Planned Parenthood had been part of the campaign for 20 years. In 1991, Planned Parenthood announced the opening of an abortion clinic at the same time the campaign got under way. Anti-abortion groups promptly mounted a movement to deny donations to the local United Way.

Historically United Way supported very few environmentally oriented philanthropies even though by 1991 such organizations were the fastest-growing category of charities soliciting workplace donations. At the same time United Way chapters in Los Angeles, San Diego, and San Francisco were having a hard time raising funds, Earth Share of California enjoyed a 42 percent increase in gifts. Critics accused United Way of being old-fashioned, out of touch, and unresponsive to donors' concerns.[4]

By the beginning of 1993, United Way had lost its position as the "blue chip" of charities. For the first time since 1946, contributions were down. Local chapters cut budgets and extended campaigns. In some cities, such as San Diego and Denver, donations were behind 1991 levels by as much as 30 percent.

United Way made some major changes after William Aramony's departure. Former Peace Corps director Elaine L Chao took over as president of United Way of America. Chao instituted new policies covering financial controls, governance, travel expenses, and donors' choice. Managers became accountable for their budgets, which senior vice-presidents monitored on a monthly basis. In turn, outside auditors reviewed the senior vice-presidents' expenses.

Fifteen new seats on the board were created for officials from local chapters. Local officials were appointed to six new steering committees, including budget, ethics, and compensation committees. At the same time, the administrative staff was reduced from 275 to 186 employees. Travel expenses were severely curtailed. All business trips, including the president's, were at coach fares, and meal allowances were imposed on everyone.

For the first time, local chapters initiated programs that allowed donors to target their contributions to the charity of their choice, whether or not it was an official United Way agency. Many corporations matched their employees' donations with corporate gifts.[5]

Questions

1. What are appropriate benchmarks for the salary and benefits structure for top managers of charities? How can charities attract outstanding managers while responding to the concerns of donors?

2. Should the standards of compensation for employees of nonprofit institutions, such as universities and hospitals, differ from those for employees of charitable

---

[4]F Barringer, "United Way Says Slump and Scandal May Bring Sharp Drop in Donations," *The New York Times,* November 20, 1992, p. A14.

[5]T Segal and C Del Valle, "They Didn't Even Give at the Office," *Business Week,* January 25, 1993, pp. 68–69.

organizations such as the National Wildlife Foundation, Greenpeace, or United Way? If so, why and how? If not, why?

3. As a class project, volunteer for a fund-raising campaign. Find out what methods the charity uses to solicit funds. Are you as a fund raiser, informed as to how funds are allocated? What proportion of the funds is used for administration, and what portion goes directly to the designated recipients? What promises does the charity make with respect to how your donation is used?

Individual Giving

Corporate giving is a twentieth century phenomenon. Before that time, individual philanthropy was considered a more appropriate means of giving than corporate donations. Most of the so-called "captains of industry" such as Rockefeller, Carnegie, Frick, Morgan, and Vanderbilt gave very large sums from their personal fortunes.

These donations were not always appreciated, as the following anecdote shows. In 1905, a public outcry occurred over the refusal by a missionary group to accept a $100,000 gift from John D Rockefeller (even though, as it turned out, the group had sought the aid). The group rejected the "tainted money" as a disparagement of Rockefeller's business methods. In a subsequent incident following the 1906 San Francisco earthquake and fire,

> Mr. Rockefeller sent large sums of money to subordinates in San Francisco to be used as they saw fit. One of the Standard Oil managers, who specialized in clergymen, gave a number of them "bank orders" of $150 each but told them he wanted it distinctly understood that this was "tainted money." One of the clergymen replied, "The taint wears off the moment it passes from your hands into ours." Another stated, "It's the motive that makes money tainted or not." The third one commented, "All money is tainted." The fourth said, "Tain't enough!"[6]

Andrew Carnegie had such strong negative feelings about corporate giving and such a great commitment to individual giving that he wrote a book called *The Gospel of Wealth and Other Timely Essays.* His essays, written between 1886 and 1899, were compiled into this book that was published in 1900. Carnegie mused about the administration of wealth and concluded that the duty of a rich person was "to set an example of modest, unpretentious living . . . to provide modestly for the legitimate wants of those dependent upon him; and . . . to consider all surplus revenues which come to him . . . to administer in the manner which, in his judgment, is best calculated to produce the most beneficial results for the community."[7]

[6]K G Patrick and R Eells, *Education and the Business Dollar: A Study of Corporate Contributions Policy and American Education* (New York: Macmillan, 1969), p. 4.
[7]A Carnegie, *The Gospel of Wealth and Other Timely Essays,* ed. E C Kirkland (Cambridge, MA: The Belknap Press, 1962), p. 25.

Carnegie went on to disparage indiscriminate charity. He suggested the rich should give to institutions that would build healthy habits among the less fortunate. These institutions included universities, public libraries, hospitals, parks, meeting and concert halls, swimming pools, and churches.[8] Carnegie apparently never considered it appropriate to use corporate money for other social causes. Like many other philanthropists, he was convinced people should be helped only by providing facilities that would allow them to help themselves. He and other philanthropists were not entirely selfless givers. They used their personal fortunes to achieve high social and civic prestige as well as to support worthy institutions.

Individual Giving in the 1990s

Individual and household giving still generate the highest percentage of total philanthropic activity in the United States. In 1990, 75 percent of US households donated a total of $122.6 billion to charities. Adjusting for inflation, Americans gave more than three times as much as they did in 1955. Over 96 percent of this money stayed in the local communities.

According to Independent Sector, a Washington-based group representing the nation's nonprofit institutions, of those households that gave, each donated an average of $978 to a variety of causes, including religious institutions, the environment, health care, education, homelessness, the arts, and nuclear disarmament. Fifty-three percent of charitable gifts went to religious organizations, 10 percent to education, 9.6 percent to human services, and 8 percent to health care.[9]

Table 10–1 shows the leading recipients of charitable gifts in 1990. These charities are a very diverse group and reflect a wide variety of interests and commitments. They include universities, health organizations, young people's groups, religious organizations, and food banks. This mix of organizations changes according to the nation's economic condition, the prevalence of particular diseases, the growth or wane of religious fervor, and international catastrophes. The list of leading charitable contributions will probably look quite different in the year 2000.

In 1991 charities that relied on small gifts lost ground, but groups with major capital campaigns did better. Overall, private donors increased their contributions to America's 400 most popular charities by 5.8 percent. The underlying impetus for some of the increase in these gifts is interesting.

Organizations facing emergency situations generated a spate of donations. For example, the United Jewish Appeal (UJA) forged ahead of the Salvation Army in percentage gain in 1990. During 1990–1991, the UJA

[8]Ibid., pp. 32–47.

[9]F Barringer, "In the Worst of Times, America Keeps Giving," *The New York Times,* March 15, 1992, p. E6.

TABLE 10-1   Who Gets the Most

Leading recipients of charitable contributions in the United States. Figures are for 1990, except as noted.

Recipient	Private Support	Total Income*
All local United Way groups	$3,110,000,000	Not Applicable
United Jewish Appeal (includes all local fundraising)	1,100,000,000	Not Applicable
Salvation Army	658,755,399	$1,215,463,189
American Red Cross	520,169,000	1,465,557,000
Second Harvest[1]	394,830,019	395,989,532
American Cancer Society	281,785,285	356,404,566
American Heart Association	215,860,000	264,391,000
Catholic Charities	210,887,523	1,538,590,851
Y.M.C.A.	207,372,958	1,438,455,518
Harvard University	195,521,227	1,107,920,674[β]
Boy Scouts of America	194,491,000	430,001,000
Y.W.C.A.	185,600,000	323,570,000§
Stanford University	180,922,245	1,000,000,000[β]
Cornell University	177,100,000	1,164,209,000[β]
Shriners Hospital for Crippled Children	173,308,245	372,970,694
Boys and Girls Clubs of America	157,319,431	239,560,786§
University of Pennsylvania	143,384,184	1,100,000,000[β]
Catholic Relief Services[2]	141,856,000	220,027,000
World Vision[2]	138,653,464	215,515,930
Yale University	130,100,000	700,000,000

*Includes such sources of funds as government and private fees and research grants, tuition and income from investments. Local United Way and United Jewish Appeal groups are conduits of funds to charitable organizations.

[1]Most contributions are in the form of food.

[2]Includes in-kind gifts.

[β]Figures are from 1991.

§Figures are from 1989.

SOURCE: The Chronicle of Philanthropy

Who Gives How Much

A glimpse at donations in the United States. The figures for donors to the arts, environmental and youth organizations reflect total giving to all kinds of charities by those households. Figures are from 1989, the latest year available.

	All Donors	Art Donors	Environmental Donors	Youth Donors
Average household contribution	$978	$2,115	$1,091	$1,128
Average percentage of household income donated	2.5%	4.0%	2.2%	2.6%
Percentage of U.S. Population	75.1%	9.6%	13.4%	21.7%

SOURCE: Independent Sector.

helped fund the settlement of Soviet Jews in Israel through its Operation Exodus and supported Israel during the Gulf War. Because of these activities and an aggressive fund-raising campaign, donations to the charity reached unprecedented levels.

In 1991, contributions to the Salvation Army, which generally receives large numbers of small gifts, fell 1.5 percent from 1990. The Red Cross, which also receives small gifts and gifts-in-kind such as food, clothing, and medical supplies, also lagged; donations fell 26 percent in 1991. Experts speculated that the steep drop was partly due to the previous year's outpouring of disaster relief following Hurricane Hugo and the San Francisco earthquake.[10]

The 1990s promise to be a decade in which traditional patterns of individual giving change. As mentioned in the opening case, United Way used to dominate in the payroll deduction form of individual giving. This has changed as new interest in the environment and other causes grows and organizations such as Earth Share become increasingly important.

Earth Share, founded in 1988 as the Environmental Federation of America, is a network of 40 national environmental agencies. Its affiliates include the Environmental Defense Fund, the Izaak Walton League of America, the National Audubon Association, and the World Wildlife Fund. More than 50 major companies, including J P Morgan and Company, Apple Computer, Polaroid, and Safeway, participate in Earth Share's program of payroll deductions. Companies wishing to participate in Earth Share simply add it as an addition to United Way. Some companies add information on Earth Share to United Way literature, while others hand out an additional pamphlet. Earth Share provides its own materials to participating companies at a cost of less than $1,000 a year.

Earth Share has generated local- and state-level spin-offs. California, Oregon, and Washington have state groups affiliated with national Earth Share. California's affiliate, the Environmental Federation, collected $1.4 million in 1991, a 50 percent increase over 1990.

Earth Share and its affiliates do not appear to divert contributions from other charities. According to Jim Abernathy, executive director of the Environmental Support Center, "The phenomenon isn't that employees turn away from other organizations. When given a choice, they give more money."[11]

In 1990, Independent Sector conducted a survey called "Giving and Volunteering in the United States." It found that more than 98 million Americans volunteered their time to help charitable institutions, a three-year rise of 23 percent. Baby boomers became more involved with specific

---

[10]P Sebastian, "Small-Gift Charities Had a Weak Year in Fiscal '91 But Bigger Ones Did Better," *The Wall Street Journal,* November 2, 1991, p. B6.

[11]C Warner and D Bihler, "Giving at the Office," *Business Ethics* (December 1992), p. 34.

societal problems, volunteering their time as well as money. They worked
with youth programs and with health and human services, the areas that
had suffered the deepest cuts under the Reagan and Bush administrations.
Virginia A Hodgkinson, vice president of Independent Sector's survey,
reported,

> The behavioral patterns we are seeing now reflect a number of influences on this
> population group: Young adults in their child-bearing years tend to become
> more altruistic. This group is more highly educated than preceding generations.
> They are at the peak of their earning careers. They are more concerned about
> values. They were in the vanguard of the peace movement in the 60s. These
> influences add up to more charitable giving and more volunteering for com-
> munity service.[12]

Women's Giving

As women's incomes grew in the 1990s, more women gave money to charities. But philanthropy meant active involvement in addition to writing a
check. Women worked in organizations and communities for the causes
they supported. Some formed networks to increase the impact of their
efforts. Often the beneficiaries were groups that were too young, too radical,
or too inexperienced to attract money from established philanthropies.

Women's donations rarely exceeded $50,000 annually, although a few
very rich women like Sawnee Hunt gave much more. Hunt donated about
$1 million a year to help battered wives and teenage mothers. Like less afflu-
ent women, she formed foundations to pool funds for greater impact.

Although women have worked for and organized charities since before
the Civil War in the mid-1800s, the first modern women's charitable foundation was organized in 1973, when *Ms. Magazine* used profits to set up the
Ms. Foundation for Women. In the mid-1980s, women began to address the
problems created by the feminization of poverty (the growing numbers of
women living below the poverty line). By 1990, the foundation had an
endowment fund of $4 million.

Studies show divorce and single motherhood were often accompanied
by low incomes, poor support services, and a diminished standard of living.
Few of the established charities, such as United Way, focused on women's
issues. In 1987, only 18 percent of United Way's nearly $2 billion in dona-
tions went specifically to women's causes.[13]

A number of organizations channel contributions through women's
networks. The North Star Fund, for example, was started in 1978. Based in
lower Manhattan, it gives away more than a half-million dollars per year to

---

[12]K Teltsch, "'Baby Boomers' Donate More, a Survey Says," *The New York Times,*
October 17, 1990, p. A17.

[13]"Now It's 'Sister, Can You Spare a Dime?'," *Business Week,* January 29, 1990, p. 58.

groups that organize new immigrants, teenagers from lower-income families, and South Asian women suffering from domestic abuse. The typical donor is a professional woman in her 30s or 40s who received an inheritance or income from a family business.

Haymarket People's fund in Boston runs workshops for potential donors. Between 1989 and 1992, participation by women increased from 582 to 709.[14] Haymarket's director of development noted that "women are taking a leadership role today and altering the face of traditional philanthropy."

Despite the growth of women's charitable organizations and the pooling of funds, the amount of money these organizations give away is still a very small proportion of the operations of more traditional philanthropic organizations.

Charitable Organizations

Organized charitable institutions began to proliferate at the end of the nineteenth century. Four ministers calling themselves the Associated Charities organized the first Community Chest in 1887.[15] By 1892, 15 similar organizations had formed. The movement continued to grow; by 1919 there were 40 Community Chests, and by 1929 nearly 350 existed.[16]

However, business firms resisted giving. According to business historian Morrell T Heald, "some challenged the validity and efficiency of welfare work . . . Others . . . doubted the propriety, the necessity, or the legality of company—as opposed to individual—contributions."[17] A major concern of corporate officers was that charitable giving might be considered an activity outside the corporate charter. It is difficult to assess whether this concern was valid or whether it was a rationalization for not giving.

Company Towns

The establishment of company towns proved to be notable exceptions to the generally limited involvement of companies in community welfare. In the 1880s, George M Pullman, who made a fortune building railroad passenger cars, invested $8 million to build the company town of Pullman outside Chicago. The town provided housing, recreational, and church facilities for

---

[14]K Teltsch, "Shaking Up the Old Ways of Benevolence," *The New York Times*, September 15, 1992, p. B1.

[15]J R Seely et al., *Community Chest: A Case Study in Philanthropy* (Toronto: University of Toronto Press, 1957), p. 17.

[16]M T Heald, *The Social Responsibilities of Business: Company and Community, 1900–1960* (Cleveland: Press of Case Western Reserve University, 1970), p. 122.

[17]Ibid.

employees, all built at company expense. Heald noted that the company benefited greatly from his investment:

> Pullman's motives were practical, too. Outstanding among them was the desire to attract skilled labor beyond the immediate vicinity of Chicago's trade unions and union organizers. His philanthropy was further tempered by a determination to realize a profit in good times or bad. Pullman saw no inconsistency or impropriety in permitting the company-built church on the town square to stand vacant when no group could raise the money to rent it at a rate which would assure a 6 percent return on investment.[18]

While Pullman's primary concern was to avoid union interference, other founders of company towns were more interested in improving living conditions for employees. For instance, in 1909 Metropolitan Life Insurance Company donated money to build a hospital to serve its employees. When a disgruntled stockholder filed a suit against Metropolitan Life, the courts found in favor of the company on the grounds that by benefiting the workers, the gift benefited the company.[19]

Mutual self-interest led the Young Men's Christian Association (YMCA) and the American railroads to work closely together in the period between 1872 and 1903. The YMCA movement needed physical facilities, and the railroads needed a moral, healthful environment for traveling employees. The railroads contributed over half of the $1.8 million needed to build the 113 YMCA buildings constructed by 1903.[20]

Other industries also came to support the YMCA, and in the years before World War I, the growth in company giving for community-related welfare and social programs was closely associated with the work of the YMCAs. The YMCA thus was a key institution in gaining legitimacy for corporate giving.

Two other events ensured legitimacy for corporate giving. First, the Revenue Act of 1935 allowed a deduction of up to 5 percent of pretax income for charitable contributions (this allowance was raised to 10 percent during the Reagan administration). The second major event was a 1953 court decision. The case, *Smith* v. *Barlow,* involved a small New Jersey manufacturing company that had given $1,500 to Princeton University to test the legal definition of acceptable tax-deductible corporate contributions.[21] A stockholder filed suit, but the court found the contribution acceptable. The continuous availability of college-trained people for managerial positions and preservation of the free enterprise system were found to be sufficient benefits to the small company to justify the gift.

---

[18]Ibid., p. 8.

[19]R L Thomas, *Policies Underlying Corporate Giving* (Englewood Cliffs, NJ: Prentice-Hall, 1966), p. 53.

[20]P Williams and F E Croxton, *Corporate Contributions to Organized Community Welfare Sources* (New York: National Bureau of Economic Research, 1930), p. 52.

[21]Thomas, *Policies Underlying Corporates Giving,* p. 53.

Foundation Giving

Private Foundations

Private foundations are usually funded by a single individual or family. Many of the foundations that are public today were started as private foundations by people with a net worth of less than $1 million. These foundations are nonoperating. That means they do not do their own research or provide services directly; rather, they give money to other charities of the founder's choice.

Some people endow foundations for self-serving taxation purposes. Legally, a taxable estate is cut by the endowment of the foundation. An individual who endows a foundation also receives a current income tax deduction of up to 30 percent of adjusted gross income. The law stipulates that one must disburse at least 5 percent of the foundation's total assets each year. The only tax burden on the foundation itself is a 1 to 2 percent excise tax.

Anyone who wants to undertake such an endeavor should hire a good lawyer and an experienced accountant. The founder will need their help in drafting the articles and filing with the Internal Revenue Service (IRS). The IRS applies multiple tests to ensure that the foundation does not qualify as a public foundation. The lawyer and the accountant will also help establish the required trust agreements.[22]

About 30,000 private foundations exist in the United States, and they support many different causes and activities. Sharon L Monsky, for example, decided to establish a foundation to find a cure for her own illness, scleroderma, which primarily affects women of childbearing age. The cause is largely unknown, and the genetic link, while present, is not fully understood. At the time Monsky began the foundation, there was no cure, no treatment, and very little research under way.

Monsky formed the Scleroderma Research Foundation in the mid-1980s. By 1990, the foundation had raised $750,000 from companies such as Apple Computer, American Airlines, and Gap, Inc. From her experience, Monsky developed some helpful rules:

· Keep your goals short range and attainable.
· Create a board that includes people with business contacts.
· Enlist celebrities whenever possible.
· Hire a good, competent office staff.
· Ask for help—don't try to do everything by yourself.

Monsky applied these rules so successfully that she was able to attract volunteers and create a lobbying strategy to increase federal research. By all reports, she achieved far more than anyone could have expected in creating

---

[22]J Warner, "Foundations: They're Not Just for Rockefellers," *Business Week,* April 13, 1992, p. 103.

awareness of the affliction and developing research for its treatment and cure.[23]

Corporate Foundations

The creation of corporate foundations has been one of the most dramatic developments in corporate giving. Of the estimated 1,500 corporate foundations in existence in 1980, 1,095 were created between 1950 and 1961.[24] Some of the Fortune 500's largest industrial firms now have foundations.

There were two reasons for the rapid growth of corporate foundations. First, excess-profits taxes instituted during World War II and the Korean War led companies to seek means of reducing taxes. By contributing to a corporate foundation, a firm could reduce its taxes even if the foundation gave little of the money away. Because too many foundations were simply accumulating dollars, the law was changed, and foundations are now required to pay out annually the equivalent of 5 percent or more of their assets.[25] Second, according to legal scholar Marion R Fremont-Smith, the advantages of a foundation were "stability of giving despite instability in company earnings; better planning, particularly with regard to long-term commitments; and greater efficiency through centralized administration and more independent review of solicitations, including isolation of company officers from customer pressure."[26]

In 1985, as stock prices rose, the nation's 2,400 foundations gave record amounts. By 1987, foundation giving had reached an all-time high with contributions of $6.38 billion, an 8.1 percent increase over the previous year.[27] Despite this increase, however, foundations accounted for only 6.9 percent of total giving in 1988.

Historically most foundations have chosen to support noncontroversial causes. They subsidize medical research, higher education, and secular good works of religious groups. A few (usually the biggest) have made some important new contributions to the philanthropic movement. The Ford Foundation donated the seed money for the Public Broadcasting System. Both the Rockefeller and Ford Foundations were important contributors to environmental causes.

---

[23]Michael Lev, "Success Comes to a Start-Up Charity," *The New York Times,* November 6, 1990, p. D5.

[24]F E Andrews, "Introduction," *The Foundation Directory,* 3rd ed. (New York: Russell Sage Foundation, 1967), p. 29.

[25]K Teltsch, "Charity Donations Set a Record in '85," *The New York Times,* May 7, 1986, p. C13.

[26]M R Fremont-Smith, *Philanthropy and the Business Corporation* (New York: Russell Sage Foundation, 1972), p. 69.

[27]K Teltsch, "Increase in Charitable Donations in '87 Was Lowest in 12 Years," *The New York Times,* May 26, 1988, p. 18.

Foundations traditionally shy away from politically charged issues. The Dayton-Hudson Foundation's experience with Planned Parenthood illustrates the problems foundations may encounter in their giving programs.

In 1990, abortion became a major problem for the Dayton-Hudson Foundation. The foundation was blindsided by the vigorous opposition of some pro-life local groups to its funding of Planned Parenthood. For more than 20 years, the Dayton-Hudson Foundation had supported Planned Parenthood and family-planning educational programs sponsored by several well-established local associations.

Much to the foundation's surprise, the Christian Action Council threatened to boycott the company. The foundation's president wrote a letter to the executive director of Minnesota Planned Parenthood stating the grant would not be renewed because "the foundation and the corporation don't want to be part of the national abortion-rights debate." When questioned by the media, the foundation's managers vehemently denied the threatened boycott had made it withdraw its contribution.

Pro-choice activists quickly responded with a threatened boycott of their own. Stakeholders on both sides of the issue demanded Dayton's compliance with their own position. Pro-choice customers vowed to stay away from Dayton-Hudson stores until the foundation reversed its decision. Some sent back their mutilated charge cards and returned merchandise. Sales associates, anticipating the Christmas season, worried more about lost commissions than about ideology.

Individual shareholders, some pro-life, some pro-choice, inundated the company with letters. New York City Comptroller Elizabeth Holtzman, a trustee for the New York City Employees Retirement System, vigorously expressed concern about potential losses to the system's investment if Dayton-Hudson stock fell. The Dayton-Hudson Foundation, caught in the middle, announced it might reconsider its decision.[28]

Three weeks later, the Dayton-Hudson Foundation reversed its decision and announced the continuation of its policy of giving to educational programs. The threatened boycott by pro-life forces did not materialize, and the furor quickly died. But other foundations, having observed the uproar and the difficult position in which the Dayton-Hudson Foundation and the department store chain found themselves, might have screened prospective recipients for potential objections.

Part of the prevailing conservative foundation ideology seems to lie in the tradition of foundation leadership. A 1990 study of 75 foundations conducted by the Women and Foundations/Corporate Philanthropy found that most foundations were run by older, wealthy white men. In fact, 80 percent

---

[28]K Kelly, "Dayton Hudson Finds There's No Graceful Way to Flip-Flop," *Business Week,* September 24, 1990, p. 50.

of the governing boards of the 25 largest private, corporate, and community foundations were composed of high-income, white males.

Women held 39 percent of the seats on foundation boards, but 23 foundations had no women at all on their boards. At least 30 foundations had no men or women of color on their boards. Of 641 major foundation trustees, African-Americans comprised 10 percent. Three percent of trustees were African-American women, and overall 12 percent were minorities. As might be expected, corporate foundations had the fewest women and minorities as board members and trustees, while community foundations had the highest. However, even in community foundations, only 18 percent of the trustees were minorities.[29]

By and large, major foundations are not interested in—or capable of— compensating for federal and state budget cuts in social services, training, community development, and local advocacy. All these causes, which have been adversely affected for more than a decade, have encountered major difficulties in attracting private money. Foundations cannot and will not fill the gap.

Unless leadership changes along with the ideology of the majority of trustees, many foundations will continue to pursue strategies of highly visible but noncontroversial giving. Kenneth A Macke, chairperson and CEO of Dayton-Hudson Corporation, commented on the problems his company and the foundation faced, remarking, that "one very real possibility is that companies will contribute only to 'safe' causes, avoiding anything that has the slightest hint of controversy."[30] He advised activists to heed the warning of *The St. Paul Pioneer Press* that "targeting charitable givers is not only inappropriate but also potentially counterproductive to the needs of a society that values and encourages philanthropy."[31] The admonition is particularly relevant to foundation giving. Individual philanthropy is anonymous, but foundations make their contributions publicly and therefore are prey to special-interest group pressure.

How is Your Money Spent?

As noted in the United Way case, William Aramony used donations to support his lavish lifestyle. Many charities use most of the money they receive to raise even more money. Few Americans know what proportion of their charitable donations is allocated to the cause, how much is used for administration, and how much is used to raise still more money. In fact, charities vary considerably in what they spend on each activity. Until recently, most

---

[29]M Cogen, "Too Few Women, Minorities Run Big Charities, Study Says," *The Boston Globe,* March 31, 1990, p. 7.

[30]K A Macke, ". . . With Some Attendant Risks," *The New York Times,* December 30, 1990, p. F11.

[31]Ibid.

Americans have been rather indifferent toward the way their charitable contributions have been spent. But in 1990, the media began to focus their attention on nonprofit institutional spending.

The Wall Street Journal featured a front-page headline titled "Organized Charities Pass Off Mailing Costs as 'Public Education.'" In 1987, movie star Doris Day founded the Doris Day Animal League as a tax-exempt, nonprofit lobbying group. The organization's purpose was to develop petition drives to prevent animal cruelty and product testing on animals. The petitions were sent to members of Congress and state officials, asking them to support animal rights legislation.

Day's organization mailed millions of direct-mail pieces to prospective donors. By 1990, it had raised $7 million, but 75 cents of every dollar it spent went into sending out more mail to raise more money. Accounting rules allowed the organization to pay 96 percent of the public advocacy expenditure to a profit-making, direct-mail company, National Direct Marketing. The direct mailer acknowledged that its fees for marketing the foundation were substantial but maintained they were reasonable.[32]

All observers agreed that Doris Day's goals were altruistic and that she did not benefit personally. However, the unregulated allocation of donations points out the absence of control over foundation expenditures that leads to the potential for abuse.

Under current rules, charities can designate a substantial portion of their direct-mail costs as "public education." *Public education* is defined as material that raises public awareness of a problem. The critical question is how much *should* be spent on fund raising, how much on administration, and what proportion should go directly to those for whom the charity was formed.

Forbes was so interested in how charitable contributions were used that it conducted a study in 1991 to provide prospective donors with statistics about the commitment and efficiency of the US's 127 leading charities[33] (see Table 10–2). It based its study on the Form 990 financial statements tax-exempt organizations file with the IRS. Because *Forbes* had to rely on organizations' self-reporting, the statistics were not completely accurate.

Forbes used two indexes to assess the organizations's operations. The Program Commitment Index showed how much of the total funds from all sources an organization spent on the cause for which it was created. The Fundraising Efficiency Index showed the percentage of the funds raised from the general public that was available for the organization's general purposes. It is important to note that some regional charities may have had a low program commitment ratio because they were funneling funds to a national

---

[32]C Crossen, "Organized Charities Pass Off Mailing Costs as 'Public Education,'" *The Wall Street Journal,* October 29, 1990, p. A1.
[33]J Cook, "Charity Checklist," *Forbes,* October 28, 1991, pp. 180–84.

TABLE 10–2   **Charity Checklist**

Direct Public Support

$ Million	As % of Total Revenue	Organization	Program Commitment Index[1] (%)	Fund Raising Efficiency Index[2] (%)
$288	20%	American National Red Cross[7]	89%	92%
282	79	American Cancer Society (Group)[7]	42	82
214	79	United Jewish Appeal of New York	85	91
176	98	United Way of Tri-State	96	98
153	70	Nature Conservancy	73	88
152	40	Shriners Hospital (National)[7]	95	100
138	98	World Vision Inc.[7]	70	79
137	98	Institute of International Education	97	100
136	51	American Heart Association (Group)[7]	79	76
124	88	Campus Crusade for Christ (Intl. HQ)[5]	85	92
108	91	Muscular Dystrophy Association	67	79
93	99	United Way Crusade of Mercy (Chicago)	93	95
88	86	Christian Children's Fund	82	88
87	88	March of Dimes Foundation (Group)[7]	53	88
79	40	Metropolitan Museum of Art (NY)	92	98
78	86	American Lebanese-Syrian Associated Charities[7]	79	78
75	89	Jewish Federation Council Greater LA	84	89
73	89	Billy Graham Evangelistic Association	86	95
70	112[4]	Covenant House (National)[7]	23	78
64	67	Rotary Foundation of Rotary International	87	90
63	39	Christian Broadcasting Network	77	76
61	97	United Way National Capital Area	91	93
58	96	United Way Southeastern Michigan	90	93
55	53	Educational Broadcasting Corp.	75	74
55	84	Disabled American Veterans[7]	70	65
53	98	United Way Southeastern Pennsylvania	2	93
52	57	Lincoln Center for the Performing Arts	89	98
50	44	Metropolitan Opera Association	88	84
46	94	Mothers Against Drunk Driving	70	75
42	86	United Negro College Fund	75	78
41	46	Save the Children Federation	84	83
41	62	Jewish Communal Fund of New York	99	100
38	17	Catholic Relief Services	92	87
35	76	Project Hope (People-to-People Health Fndn.)	90	93
35	80	Greenpeace USA[3,7]	55	74
33	20	New York Public Library	89	86
32	79	Compassion International	84	89
32	93	Jewish Welfare Federation	88	91
31	11	CARE	92	59
30	75	National Merit Scholarship Corp.	97	98
30	77	Combined Jewish Philanthropies (Boston)	83	94
29	68	Jewish Community Federation of Cleveland	87	94
28	11	Smithsonian Institution	96	87
28	91	Foster Parents (Plan International USA)[7]	76	84
25	24	WGBH Educational Foundation	79	71
24	37	March of Dimes Foundation (National)[7]	65	64

TABLE 10–2 Charity Checklist *(continued)*

Direct Public Support

$ Million	As % of Total Revenue	Organization	Program Commitment Index[1] (%)	Fund Raising Efficiency Index[2] (%)
$23	21%	Art Institute of Chicago	67%	86%
23	57	Father Flanagan's Boys Home[7]	82	72
23	51	Planned Parenthood Federation of America[7]	64	72
22	78	American Friends Service Committee	75	88
22	47	United States Olympic Committee	80	75
22	82	Music Center of LA County[7]	87	91
22	84	North Shore Animal League	64	67
22	78	The Associated Jewish (Baltimore)[7]	92	93
21	37	City of Hope	75	75
21	73	United States Committee for UNICEF[7]	13	75
20	91	Statue of Liberty–Ellis Island Foundation	85	85
20	32	John F Kennedy Center	70	86
20	99	Amnesty International of the USA	66	71
18	36	Cystic Fibrosis Foundation (Group)[3,7]	30	89
17	84	Trust For Public Land	83	96
17	29	Museum of Modern Art (NY)	85	94
17	15	The New York Community Trust	87	98
16	51	Leukemia Society of America (Group)[7]	43	81
16	83	St. Labre Indian School[4,5]	73	84
16	21	Museum of Fine Arts (Boston)	44	95
16	20	National Wildlife Federation[7]	86	70
15	19	National Gallery of Art	59	96
13	35	National Audubon Society[7]	72	78
13	42	Arthritis Foundation (National)[7]	69	75
13	87	Environmental Defense Fund	78	80
12	16	National Benevolent Association (Disciples)	89	74
12	42	Special Olympics International[7]	70	69
12	97	Oxfam-America	76	83
11	20	New York Zoological Society	90	78
11	16	Colonial Williamsburg Foundation[3]	71	79
11	29	Sierra Club[7]	66	54
10	16	American Museum of Natural History	83	91
10	97	American Civil Liberties Union Inc.[3,7]	22	84
9	78	American Civil Liberties Union Foundation[3,7]	71	93
9	61	Boys & Girls Clubs of America (National)[7]	76	83
9	30	National Multiple Sclerosis Society[7]	69	59
9	29	Lighthouse (NY Association for the Blind)	86	86
9	83	Epilepsy Foundation of America	66	70
9	47	ASPCA	60	60
9	23	International Rescue Committee	93	90
9	33	Shriners' Hospital (Mass.)[7]	100	100
8	61	Whitney Museum	78	90
8	32	Orange County Center (Performing Arts)[3]	65	83
8	27	Philharmonic-Symphony Society of NY	79	85
8	22	Population Council	88	98
8	48	Toledo Museum of Art (Ohio)	74	90

TABLE 10–2 **Charity Checklist** *(concluded)*

Direct Public Support

$ Million	As % of Total Revenue	Organization	Program Commitment Index[1] (%)	Fund Raising Efficiency Index[2] (%)
$ 7	10%	Zoological Society of San Diego[3]	72%	89%
7	28	Museum Associates (LA)	74	96
7	85	American Foundation for AIDS Research	86	88
7	10	Children's Television Workshop	86	94
6	71	Sierra Club Legal Defense[7]	70	77
6	8	American Heart Association (National)[7]	86	45
6	37	United Service Organizations (World HQ)[3,7]	78	74
6	25	National Urban League	78	88
6	89	NAACP (Special Contributions Fund)	78	83
6	5	Legal Aid Society of New York	95	93
6	93	Sierra Club Foundation[7]	76	88
5	20	Museum of Science and Industry[3]	50	88
5	32	National 4-H Council[4]	82	88
5	48	YWCA of the USA National Board[7]	79	92
5	26	Walker Art Center	56	90
5	20	Field Museum of Natural History	67	53
5	24	New York Shakespeare Festival	82	87
4	16	American Diabetes Association (National)[7]	64	38
4	6	Guideposts Associates	92	50
4	28	MSPCA (Mass.)	81	78
4	13	Children's Aid Society	89	85
4	5	Boy Scouts of America[7]	80	97
4	37	National Easter Seal Society[7]	84	76
4	11	United Way of America[7]	90	94
4	100	American Heart Disease Prevention Foundation	5	10
3	3	Devereux Foundation	92	85
2	35	Huntington Library & Art Gallery	79	89
3	21	United Charities (Chicago)	81	88
3	40	Helen Keller International	77	84
3	97	Friends of the Earth (Environmental Policy Inst.)	84	91
3	56	Runyon-Winchell Research Fund	84	84
3	39	National Kidney Foundation[7]	88	87
2	4	Jewish Board Family and Children's Services	88	73
2	31	NAACP (National)[7]	81	90
2	6	Cystic Fibrosis Foundation (HQ)[3,7]	77	−39
4,497	—	Average[7]	76	82

[1]Program services as a percent of total expenses.
[2]Percent of direct public support remaining after fund-raising.
[3]Fiscal 1989.
[4]Fiscal 1991.
[5]Data from financial report.
[6]Exceeds 100 because of accounting for extraordinary loss.
[7]Unconsolidated data of national and affiliated groups may skew results.
[8]Does not include organizations with no fund-raising costs.
SOURCE: J. Cook, "Charity Checklist," *Forbes,* October 28, 1991, pp. 180, 182, 184.

organization. On the other hand, a national organization such as the American Diabetes Association might have been fund-raising for its affiliated groups.

According to the study, some charities spent a tremendous proportion of their donations on more fund-raising. Yet few donors seemed to realize their donations were often used to employ professional, profit-making, fund-raising organizations, buy mailing lists, and accrue substantial mailing costs. In the case of the American Heart Disease Prevention Foundation, these fees amounted to 90 percent of the total amount the group took in. In 1990, that foundation spent only 5 percent of the income on its program.

Prospective donors can find out where their money goes by contacting the National Charities Information Bureau in New York City. This organization collects a variety of data about nonprofits. It also scrutinizes their tax returns, financial statements, and solicitation letters.

Founded in 1918, the bureau initially helped the public assess the effectiveness of World War I relief organizations. Over the years, it evolved into a rating and standard-setting agency for the nonprofit sector (see Exhibit 10–1). The bureau generates about 300 reports on 400 agencies each year. Many of the individuals, corporations, and foundations that use the bureau's research reports also contribute to its annual operating budget of nearly $900,000. A vice president for the American Cancer Society, commenting on the work of the National Charities Information Bureau, observed, "They're sort of a self-appointed watchdog organization that charities allow themselves to be regulated by."[34]

Corporate Philanthropy	The Reagan administration held the view that the private sector should give more and government should give less to alleviate social problems. The Bush administration said very little on the subject of corporate philanthropy, but President Bush himself encouraged private philanthropy, which he characterized as "a thousand points of light." Despite the analogy, the administration never articulated a real plan or philosophy. As a practical matter, while corporate donations rose steadily during the 1980s, they did not nearly make up for federal and state cuts in social spending.

Despite the recession of the early 1990s, companies continued to give. The Internal Revenue Service reported that corporate giving more than doubled during the 1980s from $2.4 billion in 1980 to more than $5.2 billion in 1990. The levels dipped a little in 1991, but experienced observers expected the 1990 levels to rise steadily through the decade. There are several reasons this rise is likely to continue.

---

[34]A L Cowan, "The Gadfly Who Audits Philanthropy," *The New York Times,* October 7, 1990, p. F9.

Standards in Philanthropy

NATIONAL CHARITIES INFORMATION BUREAU

The National Charities Information Bureau was founded in 1918 by a group of national leaders who were concerned that Americans were giving millions of dollars to charitable organizations, particularly war relief organizations, that they knew little or nothing about.

Through the years, NCIB has evolved into an organization that promotes informed giving. NCIB believes that donors are entitled to accurate information about the charitable organizations that seek their support. NCIB also believes that well-informed givers should ask questions and make judgments that will lead to an improved level of performance by charitable organizations.

To help givers and charitable organizations, NCIB collects and analyzes information about charities and evaluates them according to the following standards.

EXHIBIT 10–1

(continued)

Preamble

The support of philanthropic organizations soliciting funds from the general public is based on public trust. The most reliable evaluation of an organization is a detailed review. Yet the organization's compliance with a basic set of standards can indicate whether it is fulfilling its obligations to contributors, to those who benefit from its programs, and to the general public.

Responsibility for ensuring sound policy guidance and governance and for meeting these basic standards rests with the governing board, which is answerable to the public.

The National Charities Information Bureau recommends and applies the following nine standards as common measures of governance and management.

NCIB Standards

Governance, Policy and Program Fundamentals

NCIB Interpretations and Applications

1. Board Governance: The board is responsible for policy setting, fiscal guidance, and ongoing governance, and should regularly review the organization's policies, programs, and operations. The board should have

Fiscal guidance includes responsibility for investment management decisions, for internal accounting controls, and for short and long-term budgeting decisions.

    a. an independent, volunteer membership;

The ability of individual board members to make independent decisions on behalf of the organization is critical. Existence of relationships that could interfere with this independence compromises the board.

    b. a minimum of 5 voting members;

Many organizations need more than five members on the board. Five, however, is seen as the minimum required for adequate governance.

    c. an individual attendance policy;

Board membership should be more than honorary, and should involve active participation in board meetings.

    d. specific terms of office for its officers and members;

    e. in-person, face-to-face meetings, at least twice a year, evenly spaced, with a majority of voting members in attendance at each meeting;

Many board responsibilities may be carried out through committee actions, and such additional active board involvement should be encouraged. No level of committee involvement, however, can substitute for the face-to-face interaction of the full board in reviewing the organization's policy-making and program operations. As a rule, the full board should meet to discuss and ratify the organization's decisions and actions at least twice a year. If, however, the organization has an executive committee of at least five voting members, then three meetings of the executive committee, evenly spaced, with a majority in attendance, can substitute for one of the two full board meetings.

    f. no fees to members for board service, but payments may be made for costs incurred as a result of board participation;

Organizations should recruit board members most qualified, regardless of their financial status, to join in making policy decisions. Costs related to a board member's participation could include such items as travel and daycare arrangements. Situations where board members derive financial benefits from board service should be avoided.

    g. no more than one paid staff person member, usually the chief staff officer, who shall not chair the board or serve as treasurer;

    h. policy guidelines to avoid material conflicts of interest involving board or staff;

In all instances where an organization's business or policy decisions can result in direct or indirect financial or personal benefit to a member of the board or staff, the decisions in question must be explicitly reviewed by the board with the members concerned absent.

    i. no material conflicts of interest involving board or staff;

    j. a policy promoting pluralism and diversity within the organization's board, staff, and constituencies.

Organizations vary widely in their ability to demonstrate pluralism and diversity. Every organization should establish a policy, consistent with its mission statement, that fosters such inclusiveness. An affirmative action program is an example of fulfilling this requirement.

EXHIBIT 10–1

(continued)

2. **Purpose:** The organization's purpose, approved by the board, should be formally and specifically stated.

The formal or abridged statement of purpose should appear with some frequency in organization publications and presentations.

3. **Programs:** The organization's activities should be consistent with its statement of purpose.

4. **Information:** Promotion, fund raising, and public information should describe accurately the organization's identity, purpose, programs, and financial needs.

Not every communication from an organization need contain all this descriptive information, but each one should include all accurate information relevant to its primary message.

There should be no material omissions, exaggerations of fact, misleading photographs, or any other practice which would tend to create a false impression or misunderstanding.

5. **Financial Support and Related Activities:** The board is accountable for all authorized activities generating financial support on the organization's behalf:

   a. fund-raising practices should encourage voluntary giving and should not apply unwarranted pressure;

   b. descriptive and financial information for all substantial income and for all revenue-generating activities conducted by the organization should be disclosed on request;

   Such activities include, but are not limited to, fees for service, related and unrelated business ventures, and for-profit subsidiaries.

   c. basic descriptive and financial information for income derived from authorized commercial activities, involving the organization's name, which are conducted by for-profit organizations, should be available. All public promotion of such commercial activity should either include this information or indicate that it is available from the organization.

   Basic descriptive and financial information may vary depending on the promotional activity involved. Common elements would include, for example, the campaign time frame, the total amount or the percentage to be received by the organization, whether the organization's contributor list is made available to the for-profit company, and the campaign expenses directly incurred by the organization.

6. **Use of Funds:** The organization's use of funds should reflect consideration of current and future needs and resources in planning for program continuity. The organization should:

   a. spend at least 60% of annual expenses for program activities;

   b. insure that fund-raising expenses, in relation to fund-raising results, are reasonable over time;

   Fund-raising methods available to organizations vary widely and often have very different costs. Overall, an organization's fund-raising expense should be reasonable in relation to the contributions received, which could include indirect contributions (such as federated campaign support), bequests (generally averaged over five years), and government grants.

   c. have net assets available for the following fiscal year not usually more than twice the current year's expenses or the next year's budget, whichever is higher;

   Reserve Funds
   Unless specifically told otherwise, most contributors believe that their contributions are being applied to the current program needs identified by the organization.

   Organizations may accumulate reserve funds in the interest of prudent management. Reserve funds in excess of the standard may be justified in special circumstances.

   In all cases the needs of the constituency served should be the most important factor in determining and evaluating the appropriate level of available net assets.

   d. not have a persistent and/or increasing deficit in the unrestricted fund balance.

   Deficits
   An organization which incurs a deficit in its unrestricted fund balance should make every attempt to restore the fund balance as soon as possible. Any organization sustaining a substantial and persistent, or an increasing, deficit is at least in demonstrable financial danger, and may even be fiscally irresponsible. In its evaluations, NCIB will take into account evidence of remedial efforts.

EXHIBIT 10–1

(continued)

Reporting and Fiscal Fundamentals

7. **Annual Reporting:** An annual report should be available on request, and should include

   Where an equivalent package of documentation, identified as such, is available and routinely supplied upon request, it may substitute for an annual report.

   a. an explicit narrative description of the organization's major activities, presented in the same major categories and covering the same fiscal period as the audited financial statements;

   b. a list of board members;

   The listing of board members should include some identifying information on each member.

   c. audited financial statements or, at a minimum, a comprehensive financial summary that 1) identifies all revenues in significant categories, 2) reports expenses in the same program, management/ general, and fund-raising categories as in the audited financial statements, and 3) reports all ending balances. (When the annual report does not include the full audited financial statements, it should indicate that they are available on request.)

   In particular, financial summaries or extracts presented separately from the audited financial statements should be clearly related to the information in these statements and consistent with them.

8. **Accountability:** An organization should supply on request complete financial statements which

   a. are prepared in conformity with generally accepted accounting principles (GAAP), accompanied by a report of an independent certified public accountant, and reviewed by the board;

   To be able to make its financial analysis, NCIB may require more detailed information regarding the interpretation, applications and validation of GAAP guidelines used in the audit. Accountants can vary widely in their interpretations of GAAP guidelines, especially regarding such relatively new practices as multi-purpose allocations. NCIB may question some interpretations and applications.

   and

   b. fully disclose economic resources and obligations, including transactions with related parties and affiliated organizations, significant events affecting finances, and significant categories of income and expense;

   and should also supply

   c. a statement of functional allocation of expenses, in addition to such statements required by generally accepted accounting principles to be included among the financial statements;

   d. combined financial statements for a national organization operating with affiliates prepared in the foregoing manner.

9. **Budget:** The organization should prepare a detailed annual budget consistent with the major classifications in the audited financial statements, and approved by the board.

   Program categories can change from year to year; the budget should still allow meaningful comparison with the previous year's financial statements, recast if necessary.

NCIB believes the spirit of these standards to be universally useful for all nonprofit organizations. However, for organizations less than three years old or with annual budgets of less than $100,000, greater flexibility in applying some of the standards may be appropriate.

National Charities Information Bureau, Inc.
19 Union Square West • New York, NY 10003-3395 • (212) 929-6300
This publication was made possible by a grant from the Exxon Corporation.

1/91

SOURCE: National Charities Information Bureau, *Standards in Philanthropy* (New York: NCIB, 1993).

First, corporations no longer tie their donations to pretax earnings. Even though pretax earnings have fallen since 1989, companies have continued to make donations. Experienced observers think corporations have a philosophical commitment to philanthropy that leads them to give even as profits decline.

Second, more corporations are funneling their money into their own foundations. The number of corporate foundations grew markedly through the 1980s, and in many cases they have been managed better than the parent companies. While corporate profits have declined, foundations have enjoyed very healthy annual earnings. Much of the corporate foundation giving stays in the local communities; thus, it directly enhances the business-community relationship.

Third, corporations are keenly aware of the problems they will face if the workforce is inadequately prepared for the future. Studies have concluded that the US public education system is failing to prepare children to enter the workforce as productive prospective employees. In response to that concern, 41 percent of all corporate giving went to education in 1991. Although 80 percent went to colleges and universities, corporations are becoming increasingly apprehensive about the quality of kindergarten-through-12th-grade education. Giving to education has become the socially responsible corporation's mandate for the 1990s.

If the economy slides into a new recession in the 1990s, corporations will likely give less money but will donate more in terms of volunteers' time, energy, and expertise. They will also donate more in equipment and even low-interest loans. Most experts believe that today corporate giving is part of the fabric of American society and that companies will not back away because of hard economic times.[35]

The Strategic Marketing Approach to Corporate Giving: Doing Well by Doing Good

Cause-Related Marketing

P Rajan Varadarajan and Anil Menon generalize the strategic marketing approach to marketing social issues.[36] *Cause-related marketing (CRM)* is a marketing program that links charitable contributions to the firm's products and/or services. These authors note that for many years companies have tried to enhance their corporate images by publicly supporting worthy causes. Firms use CRM to achieve a variety of objectives, including

- Gain national visibility.
- Promote corporate image.

---

[35]"They Still Give Away Money," *Business Ethics* (March/April 1992), p. 16.

[36]P R Varadarajan and A Menon, "Cause-Related Marketing: A Coalignment of Marketing Strategy and Corporate Philanthropy," *Journal of Marketing* 52 (July 1988), pp. 58–74.

- Thwart negative publicity.
- Pacify consumer groups (indirect external stakeholders).
- Generate incremental sales.
- Promote repeat purchases.
- Promote multiple-unit purchases.
- Promote more varied usage.
- Increase brand awareness.
- Increase brand recognition.
- Enhance brand image.
- Broaden customer base.
- Reach new market segments.
- Increase retail activity.

CRM is a strategic management tool because top managers are involved in key decisions about the program, have a long-term commitment to it, and invest substantial resources. To be effective, CRM must evaluate performance based on objective criteria such as profitability, market share, dollar sales volume, and so on. However, Varadarajan and Menon acknowledge there are many less quantifiable goals that are much harder to measure. CRM, it must be remembered, is a strategy to sell more of the product, not to make philanthropic contributions.[37]

Nevertheless, CRM is a tool managers can use to incorporate philanthropy into the routine workings of the firm and do well by doing good. Beginning in the early 1980s, corporate officers began to look more closely at the strategic implications of their giving programs. Some tried to direct their giving programs into areas that would directly generate business and tie their products to the causes in which they were interested. The strategic focus was particularly important in the marketing function.

Company Examples

One of the first explicit connections between marketing and philanthropy began in 1981, when American Express's marketing department established its own contributions program. For two months, American Express made a small donation to the Atlanta Arts Alliance each time an American Express customer charged an item on the card or used a travel service in the 15 counties surrounding Atlanta. The alliance received 5 cents each time the American Express card was used, $2 for each new American Express card issued, and $5 each time travel arrangements in excess of $500 (excluding air fare) were made through one of its travel offices. When it instituted the program,

---

[37]Ibid.

American Express estimated it would donate more than half a million dollars to alliance members in addition to spending more than $300,000 on local media advertising. This promotion was added to American Express's regular program of philanthropy.[38]

During the 1980s, marketing departments and corporate-level strategists worked to heighten consumer awareness of socially responsible marketing. Understandably, marketing managers were worried about consumer backlash if their companies' opinions differed from consumers'. Traditional marketers equated controversy with corporate disaster. But by the early 1990s, the very nature of marketing practices, particularly in mass markets, was changing. Companies were besieged by social-cause agencies that themselves were full-service marketers. The agencies developed sophisticated promotional activities and awareness programs to attract new sources of funds that would make up for the shortfall in government funding.

Corporations, solicited by charities, examined their giving programs as part of a total marketing mix rather than as an ad hoc activity. Many instituted marketing programs that directly supported causes. Roger Lipker, vice president of a marketing services agency, noted, "as a marketer, you have to be careful . . . and make sure your product or service has a 'direct relation to a topic' or cause with which you tie in."[39]

Some companies, after assessing the product-cause relationship, simply do not care whether or not their giving programs are controversial. They rely on the patronage of people who are sympathetic to their programs. Working Assets Funding Service is a good example. Working Assets solicits customers for a long-distance telephone service. The company donates 1 percent of the charges to a variety of causes, including the American Civil Liberties Union, Greenpeace, and Amnesty International. The company also lets consumers donate a nickel from each credit card purchase to "hard-hitting advocacy groups."

Although the company has been boycotted by the Christian Action Council and other religious fundamentalist groups, Peter Barnes, president of Working Assets, is not worried. As he points out, the nature of marketing is changing in the 1990s. Instead of a mass market being all things to all people, the market is being segmented into smaller pieces. Barnes notes he is serving a niche market of people who believe in "controversial" causes: "Sure, we're not trying to please everybody, like AT&T, MCI and Sprint do. It's fine with us that people who oppose a woman's right to choose not become customers."[40]

---

[38]"AmEx Shows the Way to Benefit from Giving," *Business Week,* October 18, 1982, p. 44.

[39]H Schlossberg, "Surviving in a Cause-Related World," *Marketing News,* December 18, 1989, p. 1

[40]S Elliot, "When Products Are Tied to Causes," *The New York Times,* April 18, 1992, p. 33.

Body Shop International is another company whose social activism embodies a 1990s "in your face" assertiveness. Body Shop promotes its causes at the point of sale. Point-of-sale advertising places the company's message on packaging, on aisle displays, on signs on the cash registers, and at other points in the store at which people make decisions about whether to buy the product.

Anita Roddick, Body Shop's founder, opened her first cosmetic and personal care products store in Brighton, England, in the mid-1970s. By 1993, she had more than 900 stores and franchises in 42 countries. The shops emphasize her strong political concerns about saving the rain forests and the whales. She also works against animal testing and human rights abuses. Posters and flyers in her stores advocate recycling and environmental responsibility.

Roddick argues she is not rushing around the world "as some kind of loony do-gooder."[41] She asserts her primary concern is trade. She has seen profits rise by as much as 50 percent each year and now has a business worth more than $300 million. She says, "we're simply making a product good enough for people to want it and to give us a profit for it. What is interesting, what is even brave, is all the other things we're trying to do to keep ourselves from being bored out of our brains."[42]

Roddick links socially responsible products to causes that are important to her. She is totally unconcerned about negative political fallout, and her dedicated customer following confirms that the marketing program drives her company. Although several companies have been very successful using strong political statements, most still shrink from controversy and develop more conventional, risk-averse social marketing strategies.

The Marketing Approach to Responsive Management

Keith B Murray and John R Montanari observe that managers find it very difficult to justify social responsibility in the usual context of profit and loss if it is not tied to specific consumer behavior. But, they note, the company can promote a good or a service (in this case, corporate giving) as a long-range social benefit based on "the needs, wants, interests, and moral expectations of target publics and [can] adapt the organization to deliver the desired satisfactions more effectively and efficiently than its competitors."[43]

Murray and Montanari propose a *marketing approach to responsive management (MARM),* shown in Exhibit 10–2. They recommend the marketing department be accountable for social responsibility, since corporate

---

[41]"Anita Roddick Interview," *Business Ethics* (September/October 1992), p. 27.
[42]Ibid.
[43]K B Murray and J R Montanari, "Strategic Management of the Socially Responsible Firm: Integrating Management and Marketing Theory," *Academy of Management Review* 11 (October 1986), pp. 815–827.

EXHIBIT 10–2

Continuous management model of social responsibility activities

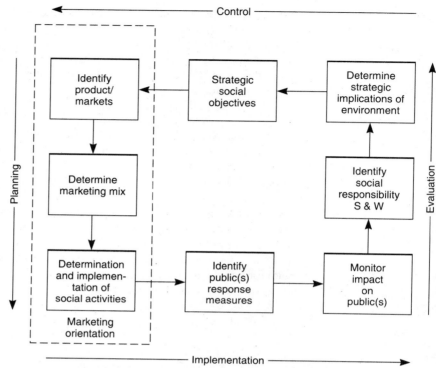

SOURCE: K B Murray and J R Montanari, "Strategic Management of the Socially Responsible Firm: Integrating Management and Marketing Theory," *Academy of Management Review* 11, no. 4 (October 1986), p. 822.

social policies and behaviors are "products" offered to stakeholders. They argue that a firm's range of products could be extended to include all social goods.

Step 1 in the marketing orientation portion of the model identifies both direct and indirect stakeholders using marketing research techniques, historical data, and managers' personal judgments.

Step 2 specifies the marketing mix variables (product, place, price, and promotion) associated with each stakeholder group. In the case of product, "offerings of the firm should focus on important social morality issues that can be addressed by the firm and may include actions such as energy conservation, supporting local charities, engaging in fair hiring practices . . ."

Step 3, determining and implementing social responsibility activities, consists of deciding on a set of activities based on "technological feasibility, management capacity, cost-effectiveness, and strategic relevance."[44] Keith and Montanari argue that the MARM model focuses on the notion that corporations and society are interdependent and have mutual goals. It effi-

---

[44]Ibid, pp. 815–827.

ciently allocates the company's resources and increases the firm's strategic options. The model also focuses on quantifying and measuring results, a major weakness in most companies' strategy.

Ethics and Corporate Giving

In the 1990s, stakeholders are keenly aware of ethical considerations attached to corporate giving. The media have pointed out an occasional ethical gap between the products a company sells and the effects of that product on the consumer. Major cigarette and liquor manufacturers are examples of companies that give large sums to philanthopy yet make harmful products with no health or societal benefit. To help lessen public criticism, some cigarette makers give generously to hospitals specializing in lung diseases and cancer, the very ailments their products cause.

Philip Morris has a very sophisticated giving program designed to foster the sale of its cigarettes. In 1991, Philip Morris donated more than $17 million to schools, hospitals, and cultural and charity groups. As the public became increasingly aware of the dangers of tobacco in the 1980s, questions were raised about the ethics of the company's corporate giving program. In 1992, the controversy was exacerbated by the leak of internal documents to the media. The documents, written between the early 1980s and 1991, tied Philip Morris's charitable donations to a prosmoking political and social agenda. They showed Philip Morris gave charitable donations, sponsored events, and provided honoraria to influence politicians to withdraw their objections to antismoking programs. The company also made donations to minority groups, including teenagers, Hispanics, African-Americans, and women, hoping to cultivate new populations of smokers.

Corporate ethics was not an issue to most citizens a decade ago. The Philip Morris program generated very little controversy because the public was not fully aware of the dangers of smoking or of the company's agenda. In fact, many considered Philip Morris's interest in and support of the arts an outstanding example of corporate philanthropy.

CEO and chair of the board George Weissman talked about why the company had become so interested in giving to the arts. Like many other top corporate officers, he subscribed to the notion of enlightened self-interest: "Our fundamental interest in the arts is self-interest. There are immediate and pragmatic benefits to be derived as business entities, and long range benefits as responsible corporate citizens . . . They go together. This self-interest, endowed now with a more comprehensive definition, accounts for business's strong support and continuing commitment to the arts."[45]

---

[45]"Philip Morris and the Arts: Remarks by George Weissman," The First Annual Symposium, Mayor's Commission on the Arts and Business Committee for the Arts, Inc., Denver, Colorado, September 5, 1980, p. 2.

In 1987, the surgeon general's report and other data underlined the dangers of smoking. Health-conscious and antismoking groups accused Philip Morris of using gift giving to cultural activities to build respectability. A spokesperson for the American Cancer Society observed, "the company is engaged in manufacturing a product that has killed thousands, if not millions. The recipients should start to raise very, very serious questions about that association." The acting director of the American Lung Association also questioned the motivations of Philip Morris and of R J Reynolds Industries, another tobacco company and large contributor to the arts. He said, "I think the people who accept the money without soul-searching . . . are contributing to the illusion that these are ordinary corporations."[46]

Tobacco companies rebutted the charges. Top executives equated cigarette company donations with donations made by banks doing business in South Africa. Weissman asked critics why they did not try to stop the Bolshoi from coming to the United States because the ballet company was Russian. A Philip Morris vice president referred to the company's generosity in donating a $3 million-plus exhibition of Vatican art treasures to the Museum of Modern Art in New York in 1983. At the opening banquet, Cardinal Cooke of New York led a prayer for Philip Morris executives. The vice president noted, "We are probably the only cigarette company on this earth to be blessed by a cardinal."[47]

The recipients of the companies' largesse also defended accepting the money. The director of the Joffrey Ballet asked who would help them if Philip Morris did not. New York's Lincoln Center, a major recipient of Philip Morris money, hosted a soirée at which it passed out bags of favors including Philip Morris cigarettes. A Lincoln Center official equated tobacco with chocolate as a promotional device. One director for the Whitney Museum observed that if one looked at donations too closely, one would find they are all "tainted." Even Michael Pertschuk of the Advocacy Institute admitted benefits accrue when tobacco companies or other firms make donations that feed the homeless, display artwork, and do other good works.

During the 1990s, charitable organizations will face major ethical dilemmas. If they refuse contributions from tobacco companies or other firms whose products are deemed harmful, they will jeopardize their programs and lose favor with the constituents they serve. How will they determine whether the greater good is served by accepting or refusing contributions? This concern will become even more difficult to resolve as federal and state support continues to diminish.

---

[46]N Ravo, "Tobacco Companies' Gifts to the Arts: a Proper Way to Subsidize Culture?" *New York Times,* March 8, 1987, p. 32.
[47]Ibid.

An International Perspective on Charitable Giving

So far, we have been concerned with charitable giving in the United States. But the United States is unique in its approach to philanthropy. No other country in the world relies so heavily on individual and corporate philanthropy to solve social problems. Each culture approaches the concept of philanthropy very differently.

Like the United States, some other countries have well-developed structures through which individuals and corporations donate money or in-kind services and goods. Most European countries, however, relegate primary responsibility for social issues to government. Countries in Asia, the Middle East, and Africa depend on an extended family structure to provide a variety of support services.

Many developing countries rely on international charities to provide basic social services. Sometimes even a consortium of such organizations is inadequate. The famine in Somalia, for example, was so profound that no single government structure, charitable organization, or even international group could cope with the devastation without massive intervention.

In this section, we examine the British and Japanese approaches to philanthropy. Great Britain and Japan are two of our major trading partners. Their philanthropic activities at home and in the countries in which they invest are very different in scope and ideology. Like the United States, both countries have developed programs consistent with their own histories, government structures, and competitive needs.

The British Example

Great Britain, like many other European countries, has relied heavily on local and national government funds to support social causes. As social spending diminished in the 1980s, philanthropy was forced to take up the slack. Today philanthropy has become a big business in its own right. In the late 1980s and early 1990s, philanthropic organizations burgeoned to support health issues, care of the elderly, child advocacy, the environment, and other causes.

The Charities Aid Foundation, an oversight group, reported that in 1990 the top 10 fund-raising charities were the National Trust, the Royal National Lifeboat Institution, Oxfam, the Imperial Cancer Research Fund, the Cancer Research Campaign, the Salvation Army, the Save the Children Fund, Barnados, Help the Aged, and the Guide Dogs for the Blind Association.[48]

The mix of top charities is uniquely British. Britain's mainland is an island nation with a deep historical tradition, few natural resources, and a

---

[48]"No Free Lunch," *The Economist,* August 29, 1992, pp. 52, 54.

comprehensive government social welfare program. Reflecting these characteristics, philanthropic giving supports the natural environment and architectural preservation, the coastline and shipping, and relief of hunger worldwide.

Britain's charities, unlike those in the United States, are monitored by a national oversight body, the Charity Commission. Created by the Charities Act, the commission is charged with policing against fraud and ensuring that trustees carry out their responsibilities properly. Until the new Charities Act was passed in March 1992, the commission's powers were relatively weak. The new legislation charged the government with drawing up precise rules to increase transparency, reducing the number of fraudulent fund-raisers, and monitoring corporate giving more closely.

In Great Britain, a fund-raiser is defined as anyone, including a company, who is rewarded for soliciting on behalf of a charity. Rewards can take the form of up-front payments for services, income from licensed product sales, or endorsements. Under the new rules, fund-raisers must draw up legal contracts with the charities they represent. They must also reveal to prospective donors and to the public how much of the money collected will go to the charity itself.

The 1992 Charities Act also greatly strengthened trustees's responsibilities. As in the United States, typical trustees of philanthropic organizations are middle-aged, white, Anglo-Saxon Protestant men from professional backgrounds. Organizational agendas reflected the interests of these trustees, but until 1992 they provided few guidelines for their oversight function.

A report published by the National Association for Voluntary Organisations and the Charity Commission found that many of Great Britain's 1 million trustees had no idea what their duties were. Although trustees had major legal, financial, and managerial responsibilities under the new act, only 20 percent received a formal introduction to the work of the organization and fewer than 15 percent received training directly related to their work. This absence of formal procedures was due to the rapid growth of philanthropy and the shift of social services from government to the private sector in the late 1980s and early 1990s. Britain's regulatory and legal structure failed to keep pace with this transition. Full-time professional managers who took over much of the management of charities left voluntary workers and trustees unsure of their roles and responsibilities.

The Charities Act called for radical changes in trustee recruitment and training. It charged the Charity Commission with ensuring that trustees received training in committee work, decision making, negotiating, and related skills. One trustee described it, "Start as an energetic ignoramus; make every possible mistake for five years; leave as an exhausted expert."[49]

---

[49]A Pike, "Good Intentions Are Not Enough," *Financial Times,* September 28, 1992, p. 9.

In Great Britain and the rest of Europe, the private sector continues to take on many of the social support activities previously funded and administered by governments. As the recession continues and government resources diminish, administration and strategic decision making will necessarily become part of the philanthropic apparatus. Skilled managers will be as important to these organizations as they are to corporations. Managers will have to assume many of the same duties they perform in the profit-making sector, but apply them to nonprofits. As more nonprofits compete for fewer pounds, francs, and marks, the techniques they use to attract contributions will become more professional.

The Japanese Example

Japanese philanthropic activities are beginning to receive a great deal of attention at home and abroad. Japanese society is facing many structural changes. As in all industrialized countries, the population is aging rapidly and values are changing. Lifetime employment, which at its peak applied to less than 40 percent of the population, is rapidly disappearing.

In 1990, people ages 65 and over made up 25 percent of the population. According to Japan's Ministry of Health and Welfare, by the year 2020 half the Japanese population will be over age 65. The percentage of national income spent on supporting the elderly will be enormous. The Japanese government, while pledging to help those who need it, is urging Japanese corporations and individuals to develop and expand their philanthropic activities.

The Japanese culture supports group rather than individual activity so it is not surprising that corporations are being asked to shoulder much of the philanthropic burden. The Keidanren is the overarching organization of Japanese businesses. Established under the Occupation forces in 1946, the Keidanren quickly became the consensus-building unit among large corporations. Its members meet regularly and transmit industry's views to the government. It has immense influence over public policy and the corporate community.

In 1990, the Keidanren announced that corporate philanthropy is the "fourth pillar" of corporate strategy along with contributions to consumers, shareholders, and employees. A resolution adopted at the Keidanren's General Assembly called for establishing a new public image for private corporations joining society under the slogan "New economic democracy."

The implementation of this call is uniquely Japanese. It focuses heavily on philanthropy *outside* Japan. The Keidanren itself has raised money for a variety of activities. In Japan, it helped establish the Foundation for Cultural Heritage, the National Assembly for Youth Development, and the Sports Fund Foundation. Abroad, it contributed to the construction of the Japanese galleries of the British Museum and the Metropolitan Museum of Art in New York. It also contributed to the Japan Festival '91 in Britain.

The Keidanren's Council for Better Corporate Citizenship (CBCC) devotes its activities to overseas corporate philanthropy. The CBCC's goal is to help the efforts of Japanese companies abroad to integrate more closely with the societies in which they operate. An unstated goal is to improve the image of Japanese firms operating abroad. The CBCC holds seminars on community relations and minority problems in overseas communities.[50]

Japanese corporations and managers are beginning to take this new charge very seriously. Charitable contributions by Japanese companies tripled between 1976 and 1989. According to a survey by Asahi Mutual-Life Insurance Company, Japanese companies donated $3.13 billion to charities in 1989. However, only 10 percent of Japanese companies participated. Some Japanese observers believe companies are making corporate contributions because they want to avoid overseas criticism that they do not share the concerns of the communities in which they operate abroad. They note that charity is not part of the Japanese culture and predict it will be a temporary phenomenon.[51]

Japanese corporations in the United States are very involved in philanthropic giving. The *Corporate Philanthropy Report,* a Washington-based newsletter, reported that in 1986 Japanese subsidiaries in the United States gave $30 million to American nonprofits and in 1990 they gave $300 million. By comparison, France, West Germany, and Great Britain collectively gave only $60 million in 1990.

In 1990, three trade groups representing Japan's automobile, electronic, and computer industries formed a company called International Business Communications (IBC). This group, which includes Nissan, Sony, and Toshiba, is trying to boost the reputation of Japanese companies in the United States through charitable giving.

IBC launched its campaign in October 1991 with a $350,000 gift to the Children's Health Fund. Unlike other Japanese groups that give to highly visible causes like the Metropolitan Museum and major universities, the IBC is concentrating on smaller, grass-roots causes.[52] These causes are likely to have considerable local visibility.

Some Japanese companies in the United States have created foundations through which to funnel their philanthropic giving. The Hitachi Foundation, which appointed an American president to oversee its activities, set aside $2.5 million for nonprofit giving. The American Honda Foundation,

---

[50]"Keidanren Promotes Corporate Philanthropy," *Keidanren Review,* no. 126 (December 1990), pp. 8–9.

[51]S Alexander, "Japanese Firms Embark on a Program of Lavish Giving to American Charities," *The Wall Street Journal,* May 23, 1991, p. B1.

[52]N M Better, "Japanese Benevolence Low Profile Indeed," *The New York Times,* November 24, 1991, p. F21.

based in California, is managed by an American woman. In 1991, this foundation gave $1.2 million to youth and science education programs.[53]

Hitachi, Toyota, and Mitsui make grants to minority funds. These companies, however, have been roundly criticized for discriminatory hiring and promotion practices. Some critics charge the Japanese government is behind the foundation's giving program and that its goal is to influence American recipient institutions. These assertions may have some validity.

In 1990, the Japanese government allowed Japanese companies to deduct 2.5 percent of pretax earnings for overseas contributions—double the rate for donations made in Japan. Supporters of Japanese philanthropy counter the critics by asserting that the United States has so many social problems that it should encourage Japanese contributions. Moreover, they argue, American companies give for essentially the same reasons Japanese firms do: to foster goodwill, increase profits, and improve the communities in which they operate.

Summary

Over the past 100 years, Americans have changed their approach to philanthropy. In the nineteenth century, wealthy people gave to causes that helped individuals develop the skills they needed to help themselves. Individuals continue to give to philanthropic causes, but as society has become more complex, the number of charities and nonprofit institutions has proliferated.

Today individuals give even though most are not wealthy and many are only marginally more affluent than those to whom they give. People support a vast variety of causes, many of which are linked to religious and educational institutions. Increasingly, however, the environment and social welfare organizations are receiving a greater proportion of funds than they did a decade earlier. As women's wages have increased, women have given more in money and in time to causes associated with gender and family issues.

Charitable organizations such as foundations have grown in size and scope throughout the twentieth century. In the early days, some foundations supported company towns. In recent years, tax law revisions and court decisions have supported the establishment of private or public foundations through which corporate funds and individual fortunes have been funneled.

The US legal and regulatory systems have not closely monitored how philanthropic donations are used. Nonprofits can legally give as little as 5 percent of donations to the causes for which the money was raised. Watchdog agencies are now tracking many of these charities and disseminating information on their allocation of funds.

---

[53]Alexander, "Japanese Firms Embark on a Program," p. B1.

Corporations continue to give even when profits fall. They are increasingly recognizing the benefits of tailoring their giving to their marketing programs and fostering public awareness of their good citizen role. Cause-related marketing has become big business.

It is not always clear what ethical considerations are attached to corporate giving or whether a company's motives or products should be considered before its money is accepted. Does the good done by the money outweigh the harm caused by the product?

Each country's culture is unique and influences the structure and goals of its philanthropic programs. As countries invest across borders, they are expected to become participants in one another's social structures. The extent to which they participate in cross-border giving will depend largely on how important philanthropy is to their images in the host country.

Questions and Projects

1. Choose three charitable organizations whose causes interest you. Find out what proportion of their income goes to the cause being promoted. Learn how each charity does its marketing to you and to others. Discover how each targets potential donors.

2. Volunteer your services for a fund-raiser. You might take part in a phone campaign, a school fund-raiser, or a mail solicitation. Analyze the material you are asked to convey to potential donors. Does it accurately reflect the aims of the cause? Are all parts literally and figuratively truthful? Is the potential donor misled in any way? If so, how? If there are any discrepancies, what is your ethical responsibility to call attention to them?

3. What role are corporate foundations likely to play during the 1990s? Why do you think so?

4. Choose a product associated with a particular cause. Examine the marketing campaign to see how effectively the target audience is identified and persuaded to buy the product. Ben & Jerry's ice cream and Aveda personal care products are two companies whose products and causes are intertwined. (Don't forget to taste test Ben & Jerry's ice cream as well as examine its program!)

5. Choose a country outside the United States and examine its approach to philanthropy.

6. To what causes do you think businesses should give?

7. As head of corporate giving, you are worried about having sufficient profits at the end of the year. Make an argument to the CEO for cutting your company's contributions to a minority corporate day care program.

8. Devise a cause-related marketing program using the MARM structure.
9. Contact a Fortune 500 firm and interview a corporate giving officer. Find out what the individual does, to whom she reports, and how she is evaluated.
10. Contact a local merchant who gives to charity. Find out how that person selects the charity and determines the amount to give.

BETA CASE 10
COMMUNITY SUPPORT AND
PHILANTHROPY

Brian Madison was delighted. He had been asked to join the board of directors of the National Arts Stabilization Fund (NASF). The founding donors of the fund were the Ford Foundation, the Andrew W Mellon Foundation, and the Rockefeller Foundation. Madison would join a distinguished group of business leaders that included William M Ellingham, former president of AT&T; Howard W Johnson, honorary chairperson of the corporation at MIT; and Juanita M Kreps, former US secretary of commerce. Madison was especially pleased that he would be working with Kenneth N Dayton, a member of the fund's Affiliates Council.

The NASF, which began in 1983, was dedicated to the following goals:

- To strengthen the long-term financial health of selected national and regional organizations of artistic merit
- To encourage arts organizations to adopt a balance sheet strategy as a means of identifying financial priorities and quantifying long-term fund-raising goals
- To assist arts organizations in developing effective management systems by providing technical assistance
- To improve the ability of arts organizations to withstand financial stress
- To promote a better understanding of the range of basic capital resources required to

stabilize arts organizations in the United States
- To change the public's perception of the ability of arts organizations to manage their financial affairs in a prudent and businesslike fashion
- To demonstrate that fiscal responsibility and artistic integrity are compatible and mutually supportive.[54]

Madison was pleased with his appointment to the board for several reasons. First, he was a patron of the arts in Detroit and looked forward to supporting a cause that was personally meaningful to him. More important, Madison believed he would be able to bring to the NASF his expertise in strategic planning and fiscal accountability. He was impressed by the performances of arts organizations in the four localities in which NASF currently operated.

Boston was the first NASF stabilization project. A local consortium of business interests had joined with NASF and solicited 33 corporations for funds. Of those approached, 31 contributed. By 1987, NASF had awarded grants aggregating more than $3.5 million to five Boston arts organizations. Part of this grant money was used to liquidate the organizations'

---

[54]"National Arts Stabilization Fund, The First Phase," (New York, 1987), p. 5.

debts; the rest was used to establish restricted working capital reserves.

In Kansas City, Missouri, NASF signed an agreement with a consortium of foundations and corporations to create a $4.4 million project for the arts. Kansas City was selected because of its aggressive leadership in the local philanthropic community.

Arizona was the first state and the third project. The Flinn Foundation, Arizona's largest grantmaking organization, began a three-year pilot program in the arts. In January 1987, NASF earmarked $1.5 million to strengthen the financial position and managerial skills of Arizona's cultural organizations.

Seattle was the fourth locality to receive NASF help. The Seattle Arts Fund Committee set about raising $5 million to be contributed to NASF for a local stabilization project.[55]

_____

[55]Ibid., pp. 11–15.

By 1993, however, companies were scaling back on cash donations and switching their support to marketing sponsorships funded mainly by their advertising and promotion budgets. Brian Madison was intrigued by the possibilities of developing corporate sponsorship programs for the NASF.

As he contemplated the task ahead, Madison decided he would make every effort to ensure that Detroit was the next NASF city. In addition, he determined he would dedicate Beta to a contributions program that would enhance its reputation as a market-driven company with a bottom-line approach to philanthropy. At the next board meeting, scheduled in two weeks, he wanted to propose a program that would emphasize Beta's commitment to the community and, he hoped, enhance the company's market position as well. He wondered what that program should be.

PART

III

HUMAN INVESTMENT

Expertise in managing people and allocating resources to support them is an important determinant of a firm's success. The three chapters in Part III deal with the many issues that directly affect employees in the internal direct segment of the stakeholder influence map. Employees, and society as a whole, expect companies to provide physical, psychological, and economic support. Stakeholders also expect companies to create an environment in which people perceive they are treated fairly and given opportunities to grow, meet challenges, and find satisfaction.

11

WORKPLACE ISSUES FOR THE LATE 1990s

know what some issues are [handwritten annotation]

CASE   *Jennifer Stills Workday*

Note: Jennifer Stills case covers issues in Chapters 11, 12, and 13.

Jennifer Stills is the young human resources manager for Prime Office Equipment, a company that manufactures, sells, and services a wide variety of high-quality office equipment. As she unlocked her office at 6:30 AM Monday morning, she mused that nothing in her educational experience had prepared her for the complexity of this job.

Stills had majored in international relations in college, but she knew she had very little chance of using her academic experience in the workplace. When she graduated, she took a job with a head-hunting firm that placed administrative and secretarial personnel in a wide variety of local companies and industries. She quickly developed a strong client base, mastered interviewing techniques, and discovered she had an uncanny ability to choose the right candidate for the job. After three years, she had learned as much as she could from this job and decided to switch to corporate human resources. She had developed excellent contacts in the business community and had several offers from which to choose.

Prime was Stills's first choice, because she would be the company's first full-time human resources manager. Until she was hired, the company kept very few records, had sketchy employee policies, and did a dismal job of recruiting and dealing with the human resources function. Stills recognized the tremendous learning opportunities Prime offered. She would be able to set up systems, develop policy, and work with top management. She was also a bit frightened, because she was inexperienced in so many aspects of the job.

But Stills was pleased with the company's willingness to let her set flexible hours. As a "morning person," she liked to get to work early and leave by 4 PM. She also liked being able to work at home on weekends and in the evenings, which gave her more autonomy in her personal life. Her benefits were good and her salary well above those of her college peer group.

Stills knew this was going to be a frantically busy day. She had spent the weekend going through résumés of 200 applicants for customer service representative jobs.

She had selected 60 applicants to interview by Monday and had to call each one to set up an interview. She had to make 15 offers by Thursday.

At 7 AM Don, her "morning person" boss, poked his head into her office and told her the security officer had caught an employee trying to steal hundreds of dollars' worth of computer software late Friday afternoon. Could Don summarily fire the alleged thief? What was company policy? What did the law require? He asked Stills to get back to him within the hour.

A few minutes later Marc, her assistant, arrived. After plugging in the coffee-maker he and Stills began reviewing some of the voice mail messages left over the weekend. Taken in order, the messages were:

- A welder in the factory reported to her supervisor that she had just tested positive for AIDS. The welder was distraught and didn't know what to do. The supervisor asked if he could arrange a meeting with the welder and Stills to discuss the company's AIDS policy, its short-term and long-term disabilities policy, and medical benefits. The supervisor wanted this meeting held first thing Monday morning.

- A customer service representative left a message reminding Stills that she was in her ninth month of pregnancy and wanted to know when she could start her maternity leave.

- A phone representative wanted to know whether her husband, who had lost his job and had a nervous breakdown, was covered under her medical plan.

- Dorothy, the receptionist, wanted to talk immediately about Chuck, the inventory manager. He had called her "honey" again and told her she ought to shorten her skirts because she had such nice legs. Her message to Jennifer stressed that she had asked him repeatedly not to call her familiar names or comment on her anatomy. Dorothy was so outraged that Stills could hear her hyperventilating on the voice mail tape.

- Bob Trask, Prime's president and CEO, had left a message at 10 PM on Friday. He wanted to talk about layoffs in the furniture department. Should Prime offer more comprehensive outplacement services? Were the company's present policies sufficient? "Before I forget," he added, "my son thinks we ought to consider subsidizing day care for employees. What's our current policy? Would you look at what the competition does, how much it would cost Prime, and send me a memo by Tuesday at 4:00 PM?"

- Diane Forbes, the company lawyer, with whom Stills had an excellent relationship and on whom she relied for advice, had left a message saying she had accepted a job with another firm. Forbes said she was sorry to leave Stills at this time. She knew Stills needed legal advice on Jean Tyrone's claim that Prime practiced racial discrimination. Tyrone's formal complaint to the State Commission Against Discrimination had just been filed.

- Leroy Aspin had left his message on Sunday. He had been cleaning the employee kitchen floor when he slipped in a pool of leftover oil and broke his left ankle. He angrily informed Stills that he was going to sue Prime for every penny it had.

- The last message came from Tim Strunk's sister. Strunk, who worked on the showroom floor, was riding his motorcycle home from work on Friday evening and was hit from behind by a truck. He was killed instantly. The wake was being held that afternoon, and his sister hoped Stills would handle all the details for her and the Strunks' two young children. Would she please notify Strunk's co-workers, find out about benefits, and let the family know as soon as possible?

Stills momentarily wondered why she had ever gone into human resources. The issues she faced affected many lives and were profoundly important. She had to be an expert in just about everything. Her on-the-spot judgments had to be correct, she had to know when she needed outside advice, and she had to know how to handle the emotional needs of multiple stakeholders. She was fortunate that her personal life was in such good order and her husband was so understanding and sympathetic.

Questions

1. If you were Jennifer Stills, which issues would you handle first? Make a decision on each issue with which she has to deal.
2. How should a company develop a strategy for handling workplace issues? Looking back to Chapters 2 and 3, which elements of strategy formulation and implementation can be applied?
3. What priorities should a company set regarding human resources issues? What makes some issues more important than others?

Introduction

This chapter and the two that follow discuss the important workplace issues with which Jennifer Stills deals every day. Stills would readily agree that the problems she must solve today are very different from those she would have faced five years ago and will face in the future.

The composition of the US labor force already differs substantially from that of past decades. As demographics change, white males are making up a smaller and smaller percentage of the workforce. They are being replaced by a much more diverse group, including Asians, African-Americans, Hispanics, women, teenagers, and older people. These new workers will experience some of the same workplace issues their white male predecessors did and also present their companies with new challenges.

The changing family structure is placing new demands on management. As the baby boom generation aged, the proportion of households with children under age 18 dropped from 48.4 percent in 1960 to 34.6 percent in 1990. In 1940, nine in ten American households were married-couple families. In 1992, slightly more than 50 percent fit that description. Single parents now head one in ten households.[1] Single women, homosexual couples, unrelated adults, and parents with grown children identify themselves as

---

[1]J Gaines, "In Pursuit of the Unmarried Life," *The Boston Globe,* June 24, 1993, p. 1.

family units and are now demanding the benefits and services hitherto reserved for traditional male-headed households.

Working parents, whether single or married, are pressing for quality child and family care, better health benefits, and more flexible working conditions. Firms are exhibiting increased concern for workers by generating new corporate programs to meet employees' needs. Companies that correctly assess employee concerns, plan strategically to address them, and implement policies carefully will make better use of their human resources and enhance workers' productivity. Those that react only to the most pressing demands as they occur will use their human resources far less effectively.

In June 1993, *Business Week* carried a cover story on work and the family. Continental Corporation's CEO, John "Jake" Mascotte, noted, "It's time for business to get in step with this country's evolving social patterns. Corporate America can't afford to ignore or pay lip service to the work-family agenda anymore."[2]

Employee Privacy

Employee privacy has always been a workplace issue. In the nineteenth century, managers involved themselves in every aspect of employees' lives. The Lowell, Massachusetts, mill girls were required to go to church on Sunday and were chaperoned by the owners of the boarding houses in which they were required to live.

As we noted in Chapter 6, George Pullman, the railroad sleeping car magnate, built a company town south of Chicago. In his town, company spies delved into every aspect of employees' lives, even reporting on domestic spats and visitors' political leanings. In the early twentieth century, Ford Motor Company sent social workers to employees' homes to assess whether workers' lifestyles made them worthy of the yearly bonus. Companies continued to intrude in employees' private lives, but until computer technology became commonplace, they were constrained by the time and effort required to collect meaningful data.

In the mid-1970s, the *Harvard Business Review* interviewed the then chairperson of the board and CEO of IBM, Frank T Cary. IBM had instituted a privacy code that went far beyond legal requirements in protecting employees from the collection and improper use of personal data. The company gathered only the information it needed to make initial employment decisions and conduct periodic performance evaluations. IBM did not concern itself with employees' off-the-job behavior unless it interfered with their regular job assignments. From the time managers were hired, IBM made

[2]M Galen, A T Palmer, A Cuneo, and M Maremount, "Work and the Family," *Business Week,* June 28, 1993, pp. 81–82.

clear the principles the company followed. All IBM employees were expected to bring code infringements to management's attention.[3]

IBM's policy was unusual in the 1970s. Most corporate upper-level managers agreed that an employee could object to a company policy on workplace privacy but maintained the company had the right to fire the employee for objecting. Although many companies now ascribe to policies like IBM's, changes in management ideology and technological advances have raised new concerns about employee privacy.

Today computers can gather so much information that virtually nothing about an individual is truly private. Computers can also store information about employees easily and inexpensively. As personnel files proliferate and companies accumulate more and more data, employees are becoming increasingly concerned about how the information is collected and used.

In November 1991, *Time* published a Yankelovich Clancy and Shulman poll of 500 adults. The pollsters asked whether people were concerned about the amount of computerized information about them that business and the government collected and stored. The pollsters asked a variety of questions about whether employers should or should not be allowed to

- *Listen in on employee phone conversations.* Ninety-five percent of respondents said the practice should not be allowed; 4 percent said it should be permitted.

- *Check job applicants' credit history.* Sixty-seven percent said it should not be allowed, while 31 percent said it should.

- *Scan work areas with video cameras.* Fifty-six percent objected, and 38 percent said it should be allowed.

- *Require job applicants to take psychological tests.* Respondents were nearly evenly split on this item. Forty-five percent said tests should be allowed, and 46 percent said they should be prohibited.

- *Require employees to take drug tests.* On this issue, 76 percent of respondents said employers should be allowed to conduct drug testing; 19 percent said such testing should not be allowed.[4]

An ongoing Louis Harris poll shows how the public's attitude toward privacy has changed. In 1970, when the poll was first taken, respondents were asked whether they were concerned about invasion of their privacy. Thirty-four percent reported they were somewhat or very concerned. In 1977, 64 percent were concerned; in 1990, 79 percent answered yes; and in 1993, 83 percent of the 2,506 respondents reported they believed their privacy was being invaded. In this latest poll, 67 percent were concerned about

---

[3]Interview conducted by D E Ewing, "IBM's Guidelines to Employee Privacy," *Harvard Business Review* (September–October 1976), pp. 82–90.

[4]R Lacayo, "Nowhere to Hide," *Time,* November 11, 1991, p. 36.

companies using public lists to sell their products, and 80 percent objected to individuals' ability to obtain public records on others.[5]

The Privacy Act of 1974 was the first major piece of legislation designed to protect employee privacy. This act aimed to "make sure that records maintained by federal agencies on individuals were accurate, complete and relevant."[6] The legislation also created the Privacy Protection Study Commission to examine the rights of state government, local government, and corporate employees. In its 650-page report, the commission determined that corporations had far more power than government to affect employee privacy.[7]

Companies collect information ranging from employees' cholesterol levels to the kinds of cars they own. Although the law and individual company policies restrict the use of this information, the potential for invasion of privacy still exists. Very few companies share with employees their reasons for intrusiveness and surveillance. As data collection techniques have become more sophisticated and uncertainty about how the data can be used grows, many employees are becoming increasingly apprehensive.

In 1993, the Clinton administration took steps to show its concern about electronic eavesdropping on telephone calls and electronic mail. The administration is developing measures to ensure privacy that are consistent with the government's right to eavesdrop only for law enforcement and national security reasons. Although this plan is limited to government workers, it may herald a new era in the corporate workplace.

To prevent unauthorized eavesdropping, the government will introduce a new system to encode voice and computer transmissions. The coding device, called Clipper Chips, will be deployed first to law enforcement and intelligence agencies and to civilian services like the Internal Revenue Service. Observers expect the devices will be extended to the country's commercial and computer networks and will become the *de facto* industry standard. Communications or computer companies that do business with the government, such as IBM and AT&T, will probably have to incorporate the technology into their products.[8]

Polygraph Testing

Until 1989, many companies used lie detectors in preemployment screening and investigations of workplace theft. Legislators, civil liberties groups, medical personnel, and corporate organizations all had very different

---

[5]"U.S. Public Is Worried about Privacy," *The Boston Globe,* September 6, 1993, p. 13.
[6]"New Push for Employee Privacy," *Dun's Review,* March 1979, p. 112.
[7]Ibid.
[8]J Markoff, "New Communication System Stirs Talk of Privacy vs. Eavesdropping," *The New York Times,* April 16, 1993, p. A1.

perspectives on whether polygraph tests worked and whether they should be used.

Many scientific and medical groups asserted that polygraph responses were often unconnected to the question being asked and resulted in false conclusions. Increasing numbers of legislators and civil liberty groups objected to the tests for a variety of ideological and practical reasons. Polygraph operators, however, insisted their results were accurate. Even though many managers had confidence in the tests, others questioned whether the results were accurate enough to justify their use given possible adverse legal action.

In November 1987, the US House of Representatives approved a bill that severely restricted the use of polygraphs to screen job applicants or test employees in private industry. In March 1988, the Senate approved a similar bill. Congress rejected the Reagan administration's assertion that polygraphs were valuable tools in combating business theft.

Finally, in December 1988, Congress enacted a law making illegal approximately 80 percent of polygraph applications in the workplace. The law banned all random polygraph examinations and most uses for pre-employment screening. With only a few exceptions, the law prohibited an employee from being dismissed, disciplined, or discriminated against solely for refusing to submit to a polygraph examination.

Today an employer can ask a worker to take a polygraph test only if the worker had access to missing or damaged company property and the employer notifies the worker in writing that there is a reasonable suspicion that he was involved in the loss or damage. The test cannot include any questions about personal beliefs or sexual behavior.[9]

As soon as polygraphs were banned, a new external indirect stakeholder emerged. Security companies marketed written tests for assessing employee honesty and began pushing their wares more aggressively. Although these tests had been around since the 1940s, when they were initially developed for the military, corporations had not used them widely. Stakeholders who objected to lie detectors used the same arguments to draft legislation to prohibit written tests.[10]

States began banning the tests in the early 1990s, charging they were overly intrusive and some discriminated disproportionately against minorities. In late 1990, the congressional Office of Technology Assessment issued a report that cast doubt on whether these so-called integrity tests worked as advertised.[11]

---

[9]"Use of Polygraph in Hiring is Curbed by U.S.," *The New York Times,* December 28, 1988, p. A13.

[10]C Harlan, "Written 'Honesty' Tests Attract Interest as Polygraph Ban Begins," *The Wall Street Journal,* January 3, 1989, p. B4.

[11]G Fuchsberg, "Integrity-Test Firms Fear Report Card by Congress," *The Wall Street Journal,* September 20, 1990, p. B1.

Security companies were not deterred, however. Wackenhut Corporation, for example, acquired marketing rights to a written honesty test called Phase II Profile and advertised the test in trade publications for security personnel.[12] Pinkerton Investigation Services advertised in the human resources publication *Personnel Journal,* offering preemployment checks and introducing IntelliView, a "computerized interview system that helps add structure to the process—provides important documentation." Pinkerton also offered a hiring guide it called "an invaluable source of information about hiring practices, promoting honest behavior in the workplace and various types of employee investigations."[13]

Electronic Surveillance

The Fourth Amendment to the US Constitution bars the government from unreasonable search and seizure of an individual's written material kept at home. Currently, however, companies are free to listen in on employees' telephone conversations, access their personal computer data, go through their E-mail messages, and videotape their activities.

As workplace technology has become more sophisticated, employers have developed new techniques to intrude in employees' work. A 1987 congressional report concluded organizations were monitoring nearly 7 million employees, many without employees' knowledge. Nearly 90 percent of the 110 firms surveyed for the report collected electronic performance data on employees. Some insisted the data were used only for planning and cost control, but other firms acknowledged they were used for employee evaluations.[14]

The computer magazine *Macworld* surveyed 301 companies from various industries. Investigators found supervisors in 22 percent of the companies surveyed had examined employees' computer files, E-mail, or voice mail. In companies with 1,000 or more employees, the number rose to 30 percent.[15] Supervisors insisted they were only trying to prevent theft or were simply measuring performance.[16]

Less skilled people involved in telephone sales or data processing are those most likely to be electronically monitored. Such jobs include airline reservations, telephone service, data processing, and insurance prospecting.

---

[12]Harlan, "Written 'Honesty' Tests," p. B4.

[13]"Smart Tools of the Trade" is an advertisement of Pinkerton Investigations Services. This ad was placed in *Personnel Journal* (May 1993), p. 54.

[14]R Gelbspan, "The Boss May Be Listening," *The Boston Globe,* November 30, 1987, p. 41.

[15]L Tye and M Van Schuyver, "Technology Tests Privacy in the Workplace," *The Boston Globe,* September 6, 1993, p. 13.

[16]L Smith, "What the Boss Knows about You," *Fortune,* August 9, 1993, p. 93.

Technology is so highly developed that it is possible for a firm to automatically count a computer operator's keystrokes as a measure of productivity.[17]

Some companies do not listen in on conversations but do keep track of the number of telephone calls each employee makes. Personal calls made while at work can cost a large company millions of dollars a year. Phone monitoring systems print out a record of every call, the telephone number of the recipient, and the contact time of the call.[18]

Many employees report that constant monitoring creates tremendous job stress. Some think a company that monitors mistrusts its employees. Employers insist quite the contrary. They argue that monitoring is a tool to help employees do their jobs better. Employers claim monitoring even reduces worker stress if supervisors use the data to provide regular, positive feedback. Companies that monitor are within their legal rights. Under federal privacy laws, companies can listen in as long as eavesdropping is part of an established, ongoing performance evaluation program.[19]

The "smart badge" is one of the newest technological advances in monitoring. Olivetti patented this electronic identification card, which is designed to be clipped onto an employee's clothing each morning. The badge emits infrared signals read by sensors placed around the building in which the employee works. The sensors are wired to a computer, which collects and distributes information on the employee's whereabouts.

The badge technology has tremendous potential application in the US workplace, some positive and some negative. It can instantly route telephone calls to the phone closest to a badge wearer. Badges can allow access to secure laboratories. For example, the Media Laboratory at Massachusetts Institute of Technology has electronic doors that open automatically for badge wearers. Smart-badge systems can locate doctors in hospitals immediately without paging or beeping.[20]

While badges may facilitate efficiency and control, they can also invade employees' privacy. Managers who wear them often find them convenient and time saving. Lower-level employees may resent the constant monitoring of their whereabouts and the widespread access to their activities.

Stress

Stress is a pervasive workplace issue that over the past several years has often escalated into employee violence. A number of factors cause stress, some inherent in today's general work environment and some job specific. In general, the stress level is rising in nearly all businesses and in most jobs.

---

[17]Ibid.
[18]Ibid.
[19]"Memo to Workers: Don't Phone Home," *Business Week,* January 25, 1988, p. 89.
[20]P Coy, "Big Brother, Pinned to Your Chest," *Business Week,* August 17, 1992, p. 38; L Smith, "What the Boss Knows about You."

Employees have to make decisions so quickly that they have no time to recharge. One stress therapist noted, "Twenty-five years ago, we had more intermittent stress. We had a chance to bounce back before we encountered another crisis. Today, we have chronic, unremitting stress."[21]

Employees at every level appear to be stress victims. Managers as well as hourly workers blame stress for health and personal problems. Some observers trace the current concern about workplace stress to the wave of corporate restructuring and cost cutting that began in the early 1980s.

Between 1977 and 1988, Fortune 500 companies cut 2.8 million employees from their payrolls and encouraged many more to take early retirement or pay cuts. A manager at US Steel noted, "Around here, we refer to a guy who brings his lunch on Friday as an optimist."[22]

As the economy lagged in the early 1990s, Americans worked harder to maintain their standard of living. In a 1991 Northwestern National Life Insurance survey of 600 US workers, 46 percent of respondents rated their jobs as highly stressful. Thirty-four percent said their jobs were so stressful that they were thinking of quitting.[23]

Workers blamed stress for a variety of physical ailments. In states that allowed workers to sue in cases of job-connected stress, stress-related compensation claims skyrocketed. California compensated workers for "mental-mental injuries." According to California state law, courts could award compensation if intangible (mental) injury resulted from an intangible (mental) cause such as stress. In 1990, the state paid $380 million to both employed and unemployed workers claiming stress-caused insomnia, headaches, and other physical problems.[24]

Stress is particularly prevalent in jobs that require a great deal of customer contact or long hours in front of a computer. These jobs are often boring and repetitive and require high, easily measurable output. Other high-stress jobs require instant decision making or involve life-threatening situations. Some examples of high-stress occupations are inner-city high school teacher, data processor, police officer, air traffic controller, miner, medical intern, stockbroker, customer service/complaint representative, and secretary.[25]

The consequences of stress-related problems are often very costly for employers. According to the National Council on Compensation Insurance, employees who brought legal action against companies in 1987 accounted for about 14 percent of occupational disease claims in 1988, up from only 5

---

[21]"Stress on the Job," *Newsweek,* April 25, 1988, p. 40.

[22]T F O'Boyle, "Loyalty Ebbs at Many Companies as Employees Grow Disillusioned," *The Wall Street Journal,* July 11, 1985, p. 27.

[23]A Farnham, "Who Beats Stress Best—and How," *Fortune,* October 7, 1991, p. 71.

[24]R Grover, "Say, Does Workers' Comp Cover Wretched Excess?," *Business Week,* July 22, 1991, p. 23.

[25]A Miller, "Stress on the Job," *Newsweek,* April 25, 1988, p. 43.

percent in 1980.[26] Experts estimate stress costs the economy as much as $150 billion a year.[27]

People interpret stress subjectively, especially at the managerial level. What may cause one manager to have a nervous breakdown is challenging and exciting for another. Most people, however, react positively to a supportive environment and to top management that seeks to reduce rather than magnify stress-producing factors. Jobs that give employees control, autonomy, and time to enjoy home and family life are less stressful than those that demand total devotion and military-style discipline.

Some companies, albeit a minority, actively try to raise stress levels because they believe stress leads to higher productivity. PepsiCo deliberately created a high-pressure environment designed to weed out people early in their careers. PepsiCo moved its managers from job to job and place to place whenever it chose. It expected managers to put in a seven-day workweek to achieve measurable results quickly. Those who complied enjoyed a variety of rewards, including first-class air travel, huge bonuses, and a magnificently appointed health club. When told he was not PepsiCo material, a terminated manager asked his reviewer why he had failed. The reviewer looked him straight in the eye and said, "You're not enough of a bastard."[28]

Most human resources experts recommend that managers become more flexible and help employees balance work and family. A 1993 study of Johnson & Johnson showed employee morale and productivity increased when the company offered help in resolving work and family conflicts. Fifty-eight percent of employees surveyed said stress-reducing policies such as flextime and family leave policies were "very important" in their decision to stay at the company.[29]

Workplace Violence

Companies are finding that employees may turn to violence when they cannot relieve their stress. The Centers for Disease Control report that murder is now reaching epidemic proportions as a workplace health problem. Between 1980 and 1988, homicide accounted for 12 percent of workplace injury deaths.[30] Murder is, however, only the most dramatic manifestation of the much larger problem of workplace violence. Companies routinely deal with on-site beatings, stabbings, rapes, suicides, and assorted psychological trauma.

Experts on workplace violence attribute the increase to downsizing in the late 1980s and recession in the early 1990s. They also point to domestic

---

[26]Ibid., p. 41.
[27]O'Boyle, "Loyalty Ebbs at Many Companies."
[28]B Dumaine, "Those Highflying PepsiCo Managers," *Fortune,* April 10, 1989, p. 80.
[29]M Galen, "Work and Family," *Business Week,* June 28, 1993, p. 82.
[30]"Labor Letter," *The Wall Street Journal,* June 15, 1993, p. A1.

upheavals and even to workers' exposure to toxic chemical substances. An article in *Security Management* noted more than 9 million workers are routinely exposed to solvents. Solvent exposure causes a variety of side effects, including inexplicable rages, severe mood swings, reduced inhibitions, and unfounded feelings of physical strength. The author urged security officers to be alert to this problem and document all instances of solvent exposure.[31]

In 1990, *The Wall Street Journal* reported on revenge in the office. Management consultants, managers, and psychologists reported the workplace was on the way to becoming "a breeding ground for vengeful acts."[32] In one case, an employee who had been demoted after years with a high-tech company was found with a loaded gun in his company's parking lot. He was lying in wait for the supervisor he held responsible for the demotion.

In July 1993, mortgage broker Gian Luigi Ferri walked into a San Francisco law office, took out a semiautomatic pistol, killed eight people he had never met, then shot himself to death. In a rambling letter found in his bag, Ferri blamed the law firm for giving him bad investment advice a decade earlier.[33]

Although present or former employees commit most office homicides and other acts of violence, workplaces are vulnerable to anyone who holds a real or imagined grudge. Experts note pressures and deadlines have always been part of office life. However, in the past it was easier for employees to cope. Employment was more stable, families were supportive, and the economy was healthier. Today society is less supportive and life in and out of the workplace has become more unpredictable and hence more stressful.

Studies show men and women respond differently to stress. Women employees tend to become depressed and seek counseling, while men become aggressive and even violent.[34]

The US Postal Service Example.   The US Postal Service is particularly prone to employee violence. Between 1983 and 1993, 10 postal workers went on rampages, killing 34 co-workers and supervisors. Countless additional acts of violence stopped short of murder.

A 1992 Postal Inspection Service study examined 350 of the 2,000 cases of postal workers' assaults that took place between 1989 and 1992. The study defined assaults as hostile acts ranging from verbal threats to armed

---

[31]J J Prince, "Fuming over Workplace Violence," *Security Management,* March 1993, p. 64.

[32]L A Winokur, "Sweet Revenge Is Souring the Office," *The Wall Street Journal,* September 19, 1990, p. B1.

[33]"Victims of Chance in Deadly Rampage," *The New York Times,* July 7, 1993, p. A10.

[34]D L Johnson, "The Best Defense Against Workplace Violence," *The Wall Street Journal,* July 19, 1993, p. A10.

attacks. Postal officials hoped to develop a psychological profile of 8 to 10 characteristics that would help them identify potential killers among the service's 700,000 civilian workers. The Postal Service intends to use this profile to screen job applicants.

However, some experts in workplace violence say the Postal Service is addressing the wrong issue. Instead of trying to predict violent behavior among new hires, the Postal Service should improve working conditions at post offices. Critics charge that a high-pressure, hostile, and authoritarian work environment at the Postal Service fosters emotional instability among otherwise "normal" workers.[35]

The Postal Service operates under a quasi-military system in which many supervisors communicate only by issuing orders. Frontline supervisors frequently lie in wait for an employee to make a mistake and even time workers' trips to the restroom.

Although top management appears to be more concerned about workers than in the past, all 20 employees interviewed in the Oklahoma City post office reported they had recently had a clash with an overbearing supervisor. They claimed they were treated like boot camp recruits. Oklahoma City's post office management is well aware of the problem and is working actively to ameliorate it. However, systems constantly remind workers of the military. For example, workers punch in by sliding a plastic time card through a slot calibrated in military time. At 11 PM, the clock reads 2300 hours. Workers punch special buttons when they go to lunch, when they return, when they change workstations, and when they end their shifts.

Workers report supervisors use these precise records against them. If employees are even a few seconds late, they are called AWOL (Away Without Leave) and are penalized by LWOP (Leave Without Pay). Workers say supervisors suspend them for minor infractions, although the union-management grievance resolution procedure usually reinstates them. Reinstated employees return to the same job, where many are often suspended again and again for minor infractions. Workers who threaten to commit violent acts are suspended with pay until the case is resolved, but are rarely counseled or monitored.

Typically supervisors are former line workers. Although they earn about the same pay as regular line workers do, they have their own lounges and preferred parking. They do not receive special supervisory training when they are promoted. Unlike line workers, supervisors are rarely suspended. If they create problems, they are reprimanded in private or transferred.[36]

[35]"Postal Study Aims to Spot Violence-Prone Workers," *The New York Times,* July 2, 1993, p. A9.
[36]P T Kilborn, "Inside Post Offices, the Mail Is Only Part of the Pressure," *The New York Times,* May 17, 1993, p. A1.

What steps can the Postal Service and other organizations take to discourage violent behavior? What kind of training programs and other intervention should they institute to help supervisors and managers recognize potentially aggressive behavior? What measures can they take to reduce employee trauma after a violent act has taken place?

"People who cannot find time for recreation are obliged sooner or later to find time for illness."

John Wanamaker

Medical Issues in the Workplace

Federal law, state law, and company policies all affect individuals' services, treatment, and work environment. In this section, we address three of the most prevalent issues in which managerial decision making and medical concerns overlap: substance abuse, AIDS, and policy toward physically challenged or handicapped workers. The law designates a number of physical conditions as "handicaps" and offers limited job protection, medical care, and access to special working conditions.

Substance Abuse

Substance abuse is a pervasive corporate problem. In 1988, the National Institute on Drug Abuse and other groups estimated that at least 10 percent of the workforce suffered from some form of substance abuse. American industry was losing nearly $100 billion a year to drugs and alcohol in the form of absenteeism, workforce turnover, and rehabilitation services.[37]

The Rehabilitation Act of 1973 classified substance abuse as a "handicap." Under that law, an employer cannot discriminate against an employee addicted to drugs or alcohol solely on that basis. The act extends to any company with federal contracts that provides goods or services exceeding $2,500.

Before hiring a job candidate, an employer can condition employment on the results of a medical exam for drug or alcohol addiction if all prospective employees undergo the same exam. The employer can use the results only to verify the employee's ability to perform the job. Once a person is hired, an employer is limited in taking actions against an employee with a substance abuse problem. Unless an employer can demonstrate that an employee's current drug or alcohol abuse (1) prevents the employee from performing the duties of the job or (2) causes the employee to constitute a direct threat to property or the safety of others, the employer cannot fire or otherwise discriminate against that person.[38]

---

[37] J Hoerr, "Privacy," *Business Week,* March 28, 1988, p. 61.
[38] CCH editorial staff, "Drugs and Alcohol in the Workplace" (Chicago: Commerce Clearing House, 1989), p. 48.

EXHIBIT 11–1

Stakeholder influence map: substance abuse

	Direct	Indirect
External	Insurers	Federal government Local governments State government Chamber of Commerce American Medical Association Credit bureaus Civil liberties group Testing companies
Internal	Managers Employees	Unions

Drug use is clearly illegal and can be detected in routine screening tests. Alcohol consumption, however, is legal and socially sanctioned. Unlike drugs, alcohol is quickly metabolized and hard to detect several hours after consumption. It is difficult to define the point at which alcohol consumption becomes alcohol abuse. However, it is an equally pernicious workplace problem.

The stakeholder influence map in Exhibit 11–1 shows some multiple stakeholders in the substance abuse issue.

Alcohol Abuse.   Drug abuse is rare among top-level managers of large companies, but experts estimate alcohol abuse affects at least 10 percent of senior executives. The Alcohol, Drug Abuse, and Mental Health Administration estimated that in 1990, alcohol abuse cost the nation $41.7 billion in lower productivity and treatment.[39]

In the 1980s, most large companies developed employee assistance programs (EAPs) to treat alcoholism and other personal problems affecting work performance. These programs have been very cost effective. In companies with comprehensive, long-term EAPs, the success rate for alcohol abuse is between 65 and 70 percent, 15 to 20 percent higher than the national average. In the cost-containing 1990s, companies are shortening EAPs and introducing "managed care" that ostensibly tailors the treatment

---

[39]W C Symonds and P Coy, "Is Business Bungling Its Battle with Booze?," *Business Week,* March 25, 1991, p. 77.

program to the employee. In practice, managed care means employees who would have entered an inpatient facility will have to fail in an outpatient program before obtaining access to hospitalization.[40]

Drug Abuse.   By the mid-1990s, drug testing was widespread in larger companies. In January 1993, 84 percent of the corporate members of the American Management Association (AMA) had drug-testing programs. AMA members—mostly large corporations—account for 25 percent of all American workers.[41]

Drug-testing laboratories are doing a booming business. In 1989, drug testers earned $230 million; in 1990, revenues from drug testing rose to $340 million. As testing has become more widespread, experts are noting that the percentage of workers testing positive seems to be declining. SmithKline Beecham Clinical Laboratories, one of the nation's five largest testing labs, confirmed that between 1988 and 1992, fewer and fewer Americans tested positive for drugs. Conducting tests in its 18 laboratories around the nation, SmithKline Beecham reported that in 1988, 13.6 percent tested positive; in 1989, 12.7 percent; in 1990, 11 percent; and in 1992, only 9 percent.[42]

A SmithKline Beecham spokesperson said the decline might be due to more sophisticated tests as well as to the public's awareness that prescription and over-the-counter drugs can affect test results.[43] Other experts attributed the decline to employer leverage over jobs. Another possible reason is that as drug testing has broadened, it is reaching populations with lower rates of drug use.

Ira Lipman, chairperson and president of the private security company Guardsmark, Inc., observed, "Aren't employers in the rare position of possessing both this desire [to stop employee addiction] and this power? They have both the means—control over jobs—and the motive—slashing the economic cost of drug abuse—to stop addiction."[44] An employee assistance manager, observing the tendency of young American workers to use illicit drugs and alcohol, commented, "it is hardly surprising that many companies have opted for hardball methods, heeding the law and conventional notions of human rights only when faced with unequivocal prohibitions."[45]

Stakeholders, concerned about employee privacy, note drug tests are not foolproof. Although critics claim urine tests are more reliable than blood

[40]Ibid., pp. 76–78.

[41]I A Lipman, "Fight Drugs with Workplace Tests," *The New York Times,* July 18, 1993, p. F15.

[42]Ibid.

[43]"Tester Finds Less Drug Use in Workplace," *The New York Times,* February 12, 1992, p. A16.

[44]Lipman, "Fight Drugs."

[45]J T Wrich, "Beyond Testing: Coping with Drugs at Work," *Harvard Business Review* (January–February 1988), p. 120.

tests, employees can still switch or alter urine samples. Testing cannot distinguish between the one-time user and the hardened addict. Even when an employee is drug free, many legal substances may cause the sample to be suspect. A flu patient who took a dose of Tylenol Plus 3 with codeine could still test positive for drugs three weeks after recovery.[46] In some cases, an employee who drank a cup of herbal tea or ate a piece of poppy seed cake for breakfast tested positive for drugs.

Even when drug tests are correctly conducted and interpreted, their cost to the company is very high. Small companies or companies that hire large numbers of young workers for low-wage, unskilled jobs such as security guards may well find that level of cost unacceptable.[47]

Corporations find they must make a series of decisions about testing. First, a company must decide whether to test applicants, employees, or both. If the firm decides to test, it must also decide how often to test. Procedures must ensure fair administration and proper interpretation. In some companies, unions may object to any procedures no matter how sophisticated or accurate they are. Employees who test positive may sue the company, which can be very costly even if the company wins the suit. If an employee tests positive, the firm must deal with the issue of rehabilitation.

James T Wrich, president of Employee Assistance Services for Parkside Medical Services Corporation, suggests that if an organization wants to set up a drug-testing program it should

1. Have an effective employee assistance program already in place.
2. Familiarize itself with the technical and legal limitations of a DTI [drug-testing initiative] and consider the possible negative effect on employee relations.
3. Place control and direction of the DTI in the hands of its human resource department, with input from its legal department—not the other way around.
4. Convince supervisors and employees of the need for drug testing and give them reasons to trust and support the program.
5. Require drug testing of everyone in the organization from the CEO on down.
6. Establish criteria in advance for maintaining confidentiality and evaluating effectiveness.[48]

The Motorola Example.   Motorola developed a simple drug policy: "No use of illegal drugs; no use of legal drugs illegally." Motorola's drug-free policy focused on providing total customer satisfaction. The company found the average drug user was late three times more often than the nonuser and

---

[46]A Kupfer, "Is Drug Testing Good or Bad?," *Fortune,* December 19, 1988, p. 134.
[47]Ibid.
[48]Wrich, "Beyond Testing," p. 122.

was absent three and one-half times more often. The drug user filed three and one-half times more medical claims and five and one-half more workers' compensation claims. The drug user was 30 percent less productive than the nonuser and therefore was not working in concert with Motorola's stated objectives.

Motorola developed a drug-testing program that cost between $750,000 and $1 million a year to operate. It extended its testing program from pre-employment testing to random on-the-job testing. The human resources department compiled a computer database on all of Motorola's 55,000 US employees, from the president to contractors on site more than 30 days. Each day, a computer program selected a certain number of employee names for testing. Every employee in the company was tested at least once in three years, but it was possible for some employees to be selected more often. If an employee was sick or away from the job site when the computer chose his or her name, the name was randomly selected again within three months.

A human resources clerk informed employees' supervisors of the names selected that day and at what time the employee should report for testing. If a test was positive, Motorola's medical review officer was notified and discussed the situation with the employee. The officer tried to find out whether the employee was taking a prescription drug that might have accounted for the positive result.

If the employee had a true drug problem, she could opt to enter a company-paid rehabilitation program. All employees, except those in safety or security-sensitive positions, continued working at their jobs during rehabilitation. Those in safety or security jobs were transferred to less sensitive posts. After employees completed rehabilitation, they were put into a special computer pool and randomly tested every four months for a year thereafter. If they tested positive during that year, they were fired. If all tests were negative, they went back into the three-year pool.[49]

Disabled Workers[50]

In 1989, Congress passed the Americans With Disabilities Act (ADA), a sweeping antidiscrimination bill. Prior to the passage of this act, workers with disabilities were minimally protected by three pieces of legislation: the Civil Rights Act of 1964, which bars discrimination on the basis of race, sex, or national origin; a 1973 law prohibiting the federal government, federal contractors, or entities that receive federal funds from discriminating

---

[49]D Gunsch, "How Motorola Enforces its Drug-Free Policy," *Personnel Journal* (May 1993), p. 54.

[50]We use the term *disabled* in this section because it is the word used by the US government in its legislation. Readers may find other terms, such as *physically or mentally challenged,* more acceptable.

against people with disabilities; and a 1988 housing law forbidding discrimination in the sale or rental of housing. The Equal Employment Opportunity Commission (EEOC) administers the ADA. It writes the guidelines for enforcing the act and negotiates with other federal and state agencies regarding specific coverage and implementation.

A 1985 Louis Harris & Associates poll showed 74 percent of people with disabilities shared "a common identity" and 45 percent believed they were "A minority in the same sense as are blacks and Hispanics." In 1980, a worker with a disability made only 77 percent of a nonchallenged colleague's earnings; in 1984, she made only 64 percent as much. The 1985 Harris poll found 70 percent of working-age people with disabilities were unemployed and two-thirds of that number were prevented from working because they faced discrimination in hiring or lacked transportation.[51]

Even though one-fifth of the nation's population has some form of disability, ranging from mental retardation to total physical immobility, people with disabilities had never demonstrated in the streets for civil rights as women, Hispanics, and African-Americans have. In the mid-1980s, however, a new, more enlightened attitude toward disabilities supported change and the development of new legislation. People with disabilities were more independent and better educated than in the past. Newly created independent-living centers became advocacy sites. The onslaught of the AIDS epidemic added thousands of involuntary recruits to the ranks of physically challenged people.

During the 1988 presidential campaign, candidate George Bush endorsed a bill extending civil rights legislation to people with disabilities. At the end of that year, Senator Lowell Weicker, then senator from Connecticut and father of a Down syndrome child, introduced the first version of the bill. Senator Kennedy of Massachusetts, whose son had lost a leg to cancer and whose sister was mentally retarded, proclaimed, "This legislation will go down as one of the most important accomplishments in the history of the Congress."[52]

The final version of the Americans with Disabilities Act went into effect on July 26, 1990. It defined *disability* as "(a) a physical or mental impairment that substantially limits one or more of the major life activities of such individuals; (b) a record of such impairment; or (c) being regarded as having such an impairment."[53]

As Exhibit 11–2 shows, the ADA set up a timetable for adaptations for people with disabilities. Beginning in July 1992, more than one-half million

---

[51]J P Shapiro, "Liberation Day for the Disabled," *US News & World Report,* September 18, 1989, pp. 20–23.

[52]S F Rasky, "How the Disabled Sold Congress on a New Bill of Rights," *The New York Times,* September 17, 1989, p. E5.

[53]J P Kohl and P S Greenlaw, "The Americans with Disabilities Act of 1990: Implications for Managers," *Sloan Management Review* (Spring 1992), p. 88.

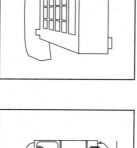

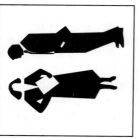

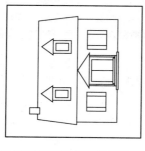

EXHIBIT 11–2

Major requirements of the Americans with Disabilities Act

ACCOMMODATIONS

Public facilities must be made accessible to the disabled.

Jan. 26, 1992: Buildings and businesses employing over 25 people must actively strive to eliminate barriers to disabled individuals.

July 26, 1992: Businesses employing 25 or fewer people, but having annual revenue over $1 million must conform.

Jan. 26, 1993: Buildings constructed for occupancy after this date must be accessible to the disabled.

EMPLOYMENT

Employers may not discriminate against qualified, disabled individuals in hiring, promoting, compensating, or training. Employers must make necessary adaptations to the workplace. Companies having fewer than 15 employees are exempt.

July 26, 1992: Companies employing over 25 people must comply.

July 26, 1994: Companies employing 15 to 24 people must comply.

TRANSPORTATION

New buses, trains, and subway systems must be wheelchair accessible.

Jan. 26, 1992: New vehicles built for public bus and train systems must be wheelchair accessible.

July 26, 1993: Rail stations must be made wheelchair accessible.

July 26, 1995: One car per train must be wheelchair accessible.

July 26, 1996: Private transportation providers must purchase accessible vehicles. Small operators are exempt.

July 26, 1997: Small operators must comply.

TELEPHONES

Telephone companies must provide, to the extent possible, relay services allowing hearing- or voice-impaired individuals to use ordinary telephones.

July 26, 1993: Companies should have telecommunications services available 24 hours a day to hearing- and voice-impaired individuals.

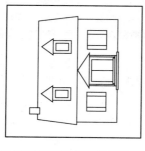

324

businesses with 25 or more employees had to comply with a new set of regulations mandating accessibility to public property, job sites, public transportation, and telephone communication.

Many companies reported their actual investments were very small compared to the benefits of compliance. For example, a blind United Parcel Service (UPS) worker became a computer programmer and trainer. He used a voice synthesizer and headset attached to his computer to convert the words on his screen to speech. UPS paid about $11,000 for special equipment, but it gained a very productive worker. A UPS spokesperson said the company looked on the ADA as an opportunity.[54]

EEOC and employment specialists advised businesses to take steps to avoid lawsuits and improve job prospects for workers with disabilities. They advised managers to take a new look at all hiring, firing, and promotion practices and follow these rules:

· *Don't ask job candidates or their references about applicants' disabilities.* The law does not allow a prospective employer to even mention physical limitations.

· *Don't ask about the following before you offer a job: medical history; prescription drug use; prior workers' compensation or health insurance claims; work absenteeism claims; worker absenteeism due to illness; and past treatment for alcoholism, drug use, or mental illness.* The law does allow companies to ask health-related questions *after* a candidate has accepted the offer as long as management asks the same questions of all applicants in the job category.

· *Don't require a job candidate to take a medical exam before you offer the job or require current employees to take medical exams unless the business has a specific reason for the request.* A company cannot withdraw a job offer based on a medical exam unless there is a job-related reason, such as the need to have an employee available every day for a specific time period.

· *Don't refuse to hire people because you are concerned that they or their dependents with disabilities will cost you more in health insurance.* Keep in mind that you can refuse to cover preexisting conditions as long as they do not completely exclude employees with disabilities or their disabled dependents from your health insurance plans.[55]

The Supreme Court ruled that self-insured employers can reduce their coverage for treatment of AIDS, since they are not subject to state insurance law requirements that would bar this action. This decision was based on the federal Employee Retirement Income Security Act (ERISA) rather than on the ADA. However, the EEOC is developing health coverage rules for AIDS

---

[54]P T Kilborn, "Big Change Likely as Law Bans Bias Toward Disabled," *The New York Times,* July 19, 1992, p. 1.

[55]J S Lublin, "Disabilities Act Will Compel Businesses to Change Many Employment Practices," *The Wall Street Journal,* February 7, 1992, p. B1.

under the ADA and has specifically been charged with deciding whether the ADA allows employers to discriminate in insurance coverage among AIDS and other physical illnesses such as cancer and heart disease.[56]

· *Revise all union contracts to reduce conflicts between the ADA and seniority rules.* The law is unclear about whether it is mandatory to fill a vacancy with a worker with a disability if a more experienced worker is senior under union rules. The National Labor Relations Board and the Equal Employment Opportunity Commission are working out rules on this and other union-related issues.

· *Take a tough stand with employment agencies by demanding that at the least they obey the law.* A firm can be liable for its employment agencies' actions. Agencies' employment ads must comply with the ADA and offer services such as a special telephone number for hearing-impaired people.[57]

The ADA and Litigation.   Between July 1992 and June 1993, 11,760 complaints of employment discrimination were brought under the act. Successful plaintiffs won $11 million.[58] As the ADA evolves, claims are being filed over issues the framers never intended the law to cover. Phrases used in the act are sometimes ambiguous. It is difficult to tell what constitutes "reasonable accommodation" and "undue hardship." A lawyer said, "It's like a recipe for bread where they don't tell you how much flour or yeast to use. But the penalty if you don't make a good loaf is a violation of the law."[59]

Some employees tried to use the lack of preciseness in the ADA to win damages for injuries suffered on the job. In most states, workers' compensation claims are the only remedy for job-related injury. Now workers are trying to use the ADA to collect damages if their bosses will not transfer them to jobs that accommodate their injuries.

In a unique case, a professor at a Midwestern university collected his mother's Social Security checks for five years after she died. When the school fired him, he filed a suit under the ADA claiming his criminal behavior on the job was due to the disability of clinical depression.[60]

A Connecticut lawyer used the law's language to challenge smoking in public places. He contacted three mothers whose children had asthma and filed claims on their behalf. He charged a local McDonald's restaurant

---

[56]F Swoboda, "New US Disability Law Taking Shape," *The Boston Globe,* January 5, 1993, p. 43.

[57]Lublin, "Disabilities Act."

[58]B Wade, "Slow Going for Disabled on Private Buses," *The New York Times,* August 29, 1993, p. XX3.

[59]C Yang, "The Disabilities Act Is a Godsend—for Lawyers," *Business Week,* August 17, 1992, p. 29.

[60]E Felsenthal, "Disabilities Act Is Being Invoked in Diverse Cases," *The Wall Street Journal,* March 31, 1993, p. B1.

excluded people with lung problems because customers were allowed to smoke in the building.[61]

As the EEOC continues to clarify the ADA's language and more closely define policies, the workplace will change for mentally and physically challenged people. Advocates, many of whom have disabilities themselves, are becoming more vocal in their demands for access to quality jobs and fair remuneration. They are demanding that workplaces be equipped with better wheelchair ramps, raised-letter signs, accessible light switches, and a wide range of other modifications. It will be months or even years before the act is fully implemented. It remains to be seen whether the ADA will eliminate more subtle discriminatory workplace behavior.

AIDS in the Workplace

AIDS is one of the most pervasive and difficult workplace issues. As we noted in Chapter 2, companies deal with economic, social, technological, and legal and political environments. Exhibit 11–3 shows the environmental impact of AIDS in all four sectors.

The increasing presence of AIDS in the workplace has crystallized a number of concerns for both employers and employees. By late 1988, more than 1.5 million people had tested positive for the HIV virus that causes AIDS. Of 2,000 companies with more than 50 employees surveyed in 1988, 10 percent had at least one worker with AIDS. Among firms with more than 10,000 employees, 59 percent had one or more workers with AIDS.[62] AIDS is the second most frequent cause of death among men ages 25 to 44 and the sixth leading cause of death among women in the same age group. This age group comprises more than 50 percent of the US workforce.[63]

All observers agree the number of AIDS cases is increasing and companies must address the cost of medical treatment. In 1992, 365 life and health insurance companies responded to a poll asking how much they had paid out in AIDS claims. The poll, conducted by the American Council of Life Insurance and the Health Insurance Association of America, reported respondents paid $1.4 billion in claims. This was a 7 percent increase over 1991 and four times as much as in 1986, the year first surveyed. Group health claims showed the largest increase, up 15 percent to $525 million. The figures do not include payments made directly to self-insured employees or claims paid by Blue Cross–Blue Shield.[64]

Title I of the Americans with Disabilities Act covers employees infected with the HIV virus. The act prohibits employers, employment agencies,

---

[61]Ibid.

[62]"AIDS in Workplace a Reality in 10% of Surveyed Firms," *Journal of Commerce* (February 2, 1988), p. 9A.

[63]B Harrison, "AIDS Enters the Office," *Financial Times,* January 20, 1993, p. 8.

[64]"Insurers Pay $1.4b for AIDS Claims," *The Boston Globe,* August 10, 1993, p. 35.

Exhibit 11-3

Environmental forces affecting social issues strategy for companies in high-AIDS environments

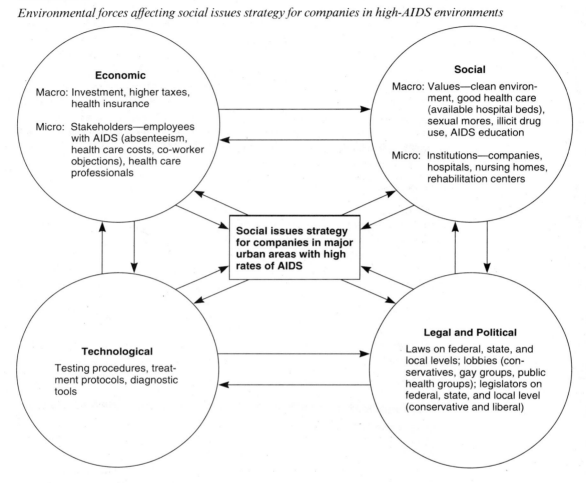

labor organizations, and joint labor-management committees from discriminating against individuals with AIDS or ARC (AIDS-related complex). The act does not require that the infected person manifest symptoms of the disease. Title I applies to job application procedures, hiring, promotion, discharge, training, employee compensation, and other terms and conditions of employment.[65]

States have different fair employment laws that apply to people infected with AIDS. In many states, including Florida, Massachusetts, and Ken-

---

[65]*AIDS in the Workplace* (Chicago: Commerce Clearing House, 1990), p. 5.

tucky, employers cannot require an AIDS test as a condition of employment. In Minnesota, public employers are prohibited from discriminating against any employee or job applicant because of the person's sexual orientation or AIDs infection. In Rhode Island, an AIDS test can be required as a condition of employment only if a prospective employer can demonstrate a "clear and present danger of the AIDS virus to others."[66]

In practice, an employer can exclude someone from a job only if the person cannot perform the essential tasks associated with that job. For example, an AIDS-afflicted employee who normally stands while checking books out of a library cannot be disqualified if he or she can do the job sitting down. The employer is required to make a "reasonable accommodation" to the individual's needs and requirements.

On the other hand, an employer need not accommodate the individual if it can show accommodation would impose "undue hardship" on the business's operation. For example, a hospital need not keep an AIDS-afflicted nurse in an operating room setting in which other patients may be at risk. The hospital may be required to place the nurse elsewhere in the hospital in a job in which she could not infect others accidentally.

Corporate Policy for AIDS.   Some companies argue they do not need to develop a separate policy for AIDS because it is an illness like any other and is covered by the same policies and procedures. Many people are still uninformed about how the HIV virus is passed, how the disease affects people over time, and how it affects an individual's ability to perform his job. Employers without explicit policies are more vulnerable to charges of discrimination. Clear written policies minimize employee uncertainty, fear, and mistrust. Even if a company does not have a written policy, an articulated philosophy can be very helpful.

Levi Strauss & Company has made a moral commitment to employees throughout the firm. Although it does not have a point-by-point written philosophy, Levi Strauss distributes an "AIDS Information Sheet" stating, "The company has an overall commitment to health education. AIDS is a national health problem and the company feels a responsibility to educate its employees so that prejudice and unwarranted fear about the disease in the workplace can be eliminated."[67]

The information sheet reassures workers they will be treated with dignity and respect and can continue to work as long as they are physically able. The company also assures employees complete confidentiality when seeking counseling or medical referral assistance.[68]

---

[66]Ibid., pp. 73–74.
[67]Ibid., p. 55.
[68]Ibid.

The Citizens Commission on AIDS of New York City and Northern New Jersey developed a set of principles that several companies have adopted as a sample policy. The principles state,

- People with AIDS or the HIV infection are entitled to the same rights and opportunities as people with other serious or life-threatening illnesses.
- At the very least, policies should comply with all relevant laws and regulations.
- Policies should be based on the scientific fact that HIV cannot be transmitted through ordinary workplace contact.
- Upper-level management should support policies and programs and communicate their support to employees.
- Employers should provide up-to-date information on risk-reduction in employees' lives.
- Employers should protect the confidentiality of employee medical information.
- Employers should institute education programs for all employees before any problems in the workplace arise.
- HIV screening should not be required as part of preemployment or routine workplace medical examinations.
- In settings where there is potential risk of HIV exposure—in hospitals, for example—employers should provide training and appropriate equipment to ensure that infection-control procedures are followed.[69]

Family and Child Care Benefits

Family and child care are two of this decade's most pressing workplace issues. Changing demographics are responsible for this profound attitudinal change. As we note throughout this book, women, single parents, and dual-career couples dominate the workforce. They are searching for child care at the same time they are trying to cope with the problems of aging parents. The adult workforce today is a "sandwich generation," caught between the needs of young and elderly dependents. In 1990, only 10 percent of over 1 million firms with more than 10 employees offered help with child care needs.[70] Help for dependent elderly family members was even harder to find. A coalition of interest groups began to push for a federal family leave bill.

---

[69]B P Noble, "AIDS Awareness Goes to the Office," *The New York Times,* December 6, 1992, p. F25.

[70]L T Thomas and J E Thomas, "The ABCs of Child Care: Building Blocks of Competitive Advantage," *Sloan Management Review* (Winter 1990), p. 31.

The Family Leave Bill

Although the Reagan and Bush administrations loudly touted their commitment to family values, they adamantly opposed implementation of a national family leave bill. In 1990, when President Bush vetoed a family leave bill, the bill's supporters in Congress lacked the votes needed to override the veto.

In September 1992, the House of Representatives gave final approval to a watered-down version of the 1990 bill and once again sent it to the White House. This law applied only to employers with 50 or more employees. Democrats accused President Bush of hypocrisy for opposing the measure. The Women's Legal Defense Fund, a major backer of the bill, estimated that 300,000 workers had lost their jobs since 1990 due to a lack of a federal family leave bill. Some conservative Republicans warned the president a veto would hurt his chances of reelection. Bush retorted that he supported the family leave bill in principle but would veto it because it would impose new employee benefits on business groups. He maintained employees and employers could voluntarily work out an agreeable policy without legislation from Washington.[71]

On the eve of the president's second veto, 11 of the nation's leading corporations announced they would join with more than 100 smaller businesses to collaborate on a $25.4 million project to help provide their employees with care for children and aging family members. The companies were IBM, American Express, Exxon, Eastman Kodak, Xerox, Travelers Corporation, Johnson & Johnson, Amoco, Allstate Insurance, Motorola, and AT&T. The money would be used to finance 300 local programs in 44 cities. The programs included new child care centers, in-home care for elderly family members, vacation programs for school-age children, and vocational training for at-home mothers.

A joint statement issued by the 11 corporations said, "The basic principle guiding our collaboration is the belief that we can accomplish more by working together than by working alone."[72] A spokesperson for IBM, which initiated the collaboration in the spring of 1991, declared, "These are family issues, not women's issues . . . We're doing this because we have to. We have to attract and retain the best people we can find, more and more of whom have issues regarding their family lives."[73]

True to his word, President Bush vetoed the measure. Campaigning vigorously for another term, Bush presented his own plan to grant small businesses tax breaks if they gave workers family medical leave. His opponent,

---

[71]M Kranish, "Family Leave Bill Is Sent to President," *The Boston Globe,* September 11, 1992, p. 1.

[72]T Lewin. "Top Businesses Join in Plan to Provide Dependent Care," *The New York Times,* September 11, 1992, p. A26.

[73]Ibid.

Bill Clinton, strongly supported the federal bill and made a campaign promise to sign it.

Senate leaders immediately scheduled an override vote, which passed easily. Republican House members delayed the House vote as long as possible. They hoped President Bush would be elected and they could sustain his perfect veto record.

In February 1993, President Clinton won an early victory when the House approved the family leave bill. The bill had to go back to the Senate, because Senate Republicans had tacked on an innocuous statement about homosexuals serving in the military.

On February 5, 71 senators voted for and 27 opposed the family leave bill, and President Clinton signed it into law.[74] The bill went into effect on August 5, 1993. It is still much too soon to predict what the impact will be. Table 11–1 details the basic points of the Family Leave and Medical Act of 1992.

Child Care

The rapid increase in the number of women in the paid labor force and the prevalence of single mothers are among the most significant social changes of the past two decades. In August 1993, the US Bureau of the Census reported that single motherhood was on the rise. In 1982, 15 percent of unwed women between ages 18 and 44 bore a child. In 1992, 24 percent of women in that age group were mothers.

Substantial differences occurred across racial lines. In 1982, out-of-wedlock births as a percentage of all births among women between ages 18 and 44 were 10 percent among white women and 49 percent among African-American women. A decade later, 17 percent were white and 67 percent were African-American.

There were also differences across educational lines. More educated women are having children out of wedlock. In 1992, 11 percent of unmarried mothers had some college education and 8.3 percent had a managerial or professional occupation. In 1982, only 5 percent were professional employees. Lesbians are a growing segment of this educated, more affluent group of single mothers. Although the Census Bureau's definition does not consider their households to be traditional, many are part of two-parent families.[75]

There seem to be several reasons single-parent households are increasing so rapidly in the United States and throughout the entire industrial world, except Japan. As the gap between men's and women's wages continues to narrow, women have fewer financial reasons to get married. The

---

[74]A Clymer, "Family-Leave Bill Passes the Senate and Nears Signing," *The New York Times,* February 5, 1993, p. A1.

[75]T Mashberg, "More Mothers Unwed, Unwistful," *The Boston Globe,* July 15, 1993, p.1.

TABLE 11-1   The Family Leave and Medical Act of 1992

Employees' Rights and Obligations

1. Employees are allowed to take up to 12 weeks of unpaid leave in any 12-month period for the birth or adoption of a child; to care for a child, spouse, or parent with a serious health condition—or for the worker's own health condition that makes it impossible to perform the job.

    Employees must have worked at least 25 hours a week for the company for at least one year prior to applying for the leave. They are also required to give their employers 30 days' notice for foreseeable leaves.

2. Employees must be returned to their old jobs or equivalent positions upon returning to work. An equivalent position must have the same pay, benefits, and working conditions and must involve the same or substantially similar duties and responsibilities.

3. Employees can keep their health benefits during the leave, as though they were still employed, but the employer is not required to pay workers' salaries. An employee may choose not to retain health coverage during the leave but must be reinstated on the same terms when he returns to work.

4. The employee cannot collect unemployment or other government compensation while on leave.

Employer's Rights and Obligations

1. Any employer with fewer than 50 workers is exempt.

2. An employer can deny leave to a salaried employee within the highest-paid 10 percent of its workforce if letting the employee take the leave would create "substantial and grievous injury" to the business operations.

3. An employer may require the employee to provide medical certification or opinions needed for the leave.

4. The employer may ask the employee to repay the health care premiums paid by the employer during the leave if the employee does not return to work.

SOURCES: A Clymer, "Family-Leave Bill Passes the Senate and Nears Signing," *The New York Times,* February 5, 1993, p. A1.; "Nutter, McLennen & Fish Client Advisory," February 9, 1993.

women's movement that began in the 1970s made women feel more capable and independent. Social taboos against out-of-wedlock births have diminished. For example, many movie stars, who often serve as role models for young women, celebrate unwed motherhood openly and loudly.

Single parents often have less flexibility, fewer alternatives, and fewer financial resources than traditional two-parent families. But all working parents are finding the costs of child care rising and the pressures of balancing work and family escalating. The Family Leave and Medical Act helps families deal with the immediate period after childbirth or adoption, but it does not solve the long-term problem of choosing and paying for children's day care.

Weekly child care costs began to exceed rises in the consumer price index in the late 1980s. In 1990, child care costs rose 8 percent a year, while the consumer price index rose 6.1 percent. Child care often exceeds 75 percent of the second income of a two-income household. Child care costs vary by region and nature of the facility. Some child care choices are much more expensive than others.[76]

The cost of nannies' and in-home baby sitters has risen precipitously. In some parts of the country, nannies' salaries have jumped by more than 10 percent a year. In major East and West Coast cities, nannies receive up to $500 a week, health care benefits of $150 or more per month, room and board, two weeks' paid vacation, and the use of a car. Top agencies report demand exceeds supply.

About 80,000 child care centers operate in the United States, three times the number 20 years ago. Nationally, 20 percent of all children under age five are in child care centers. Commercial child care centers' costs have risen more slowly than nannies' salaries. Most child care centers charge between $50 and $250 per week.[77] However, the increase in cost has not been accompanied by an increase in providers' salaries. Since the mid-1970s, staff salaries have decreased by 25 percent. Full-time child care workers make an average of only $11,000 a year.[78]

Child care providers who care for other children in their homes usually charge between $25 and $125 per week depending on the facilities and location. There are more than 265,300 licensed family child care providers nationwide and more than 1 million unlicensed caregivers. Thirty-eight states require training before issuing a license to family child care homes.[79]

Despite the rise in nannies' wages, most child care workers are not well educated and are paid very poorly. Their average pay ranks in the bottom 10 percent of all wage-earning categories. Many receive no health, employment, or disability benefits. Low morale contributes to an extremely high turnover rate.

The Child Care Employee Project in Oakland, California, reported that 70 percent of child care teachers left their jobs between 1988 and 1992.[80] The Child Care Action Campaign, a child care advocacy group, estimated the breakdowns in child care cost US businesses $3 billion a year.[81]

As we noted earlier in the chapter, some companies are becoming more "family friendly" and acknowledge the difficulties of managing the pressures of work and family. When the 11 major corporations mentioned earlier joined together just prior to President Bush's 1991 veto of the family leave bill, child care was very much on their minds. Several of the companies entered partnerships with others in the consortium.

---

[76]S Shellenbarger, "Work and Family," *The Wall Street Journal,* July 22, 1991, p. B1.
[77]Ibid.
[78]N Carroll, "Day Care Centers," *USA Today,* February 9, 1993, p. 4D.
[79]T Henry, "Family Day Care," *USA Today,* February 9, 1993, p. 4D.
[80]S Shellenbarger, "Work and Family," *The Wall Street Journal,* April 12, 1993, p. B1.
[81]S Shellenbarger, "Companies Team Up to Improve Quality of Their Employees' Child-Care Choices," *The Wall Street Journal,* October 17, 1991, p. B1.

IBM teamed up with American Express, Allstate Insurance, Duke Power, and a research park developer to build a $2 million child care center in Charlotte, North Carolina. The center accommodates nearly 200 children and is open to the public as well as to sponsors' employees. The teacher-child ratio is half that required by the state, and employee wages and benefits are above average. IBM's affirmative action officer acknowledged costs were high but said the high quality of child care justified the expense.[82]

Training and professionalization of child care providers are likely to result in better-quality care. IBM joined with Travelers Insurance to fund and set up a training program for child care providers in Dallas–Fort Worth. This $375,000 program recruits and trains family child care providers. At the end of the program, each provider is qualified to care for four to six children in her own home. The program teaches health and safety as well as parent interaction and documentation of the children's daily activities.[83]

In the Rochester, New York, area, Eastman Kodak, Xerox, Bausch & Lomb, and other companies arranged for low-cost health care benefits for child care workers. Morale improved, child care workers stopped looking for new jobs, and the pool of applicants with good experience grew. Other child care centers in the area improved their working conditions to increase their competitiveness, thereby raising the quality of child care across the region.[84]

Despite corporate initiatives, training programs for child care workers, and government family leave policies, the problems of balancing work and family continue to pose a national problem and a corporate challenge.

Child Care Abroad. Sweden has the highest female employment in Western Europe. Nearly 85 percent of women with children under school age work. In 1991, about 13 percent of the nation's annual budget went to support families and children. The government provides a supplementary allowance for each child in the family, as well as additional money for 15 months after the birth or adoption of a child. For the first year, the family member taking leave receives payments of up to 90 percent of previous income and can use this benefit package at any time up to the child's eighth birthday. In practice, parents can extend their leave for two years or much longer if they have additional children. Federal and local governments split the costs with parents, paying about 10 percent. Child care is widely available and affordable in Sweden. About 60 percent of preschool children are in some kind of state-supported child care center.[85]

---

[82]Ibid.

[83]Ibid.

[84]Ibid.

[85]R Taylor, "Sweden's Working Women Enjoy a Baby Boom," *Financial Times,* July 30, 1991, p. 2.

Great Britain's child care provisions are the poorest in the European Community (EC). According to the chairperson of Britain's Equal Opportunity Commission (EOC), "Lack of childcare remains one of the major barriers to equality of opportunity for women, inhibiting their access to training and good employment prospects."[86]

Great Britain's paid maternity leave is the lowest in the EC, and regulated child care is available to fewer than 8 percent of children under age five. Nannies and private day nurseries cost about the same as in the United States. Childminders (baby-sitters) provide the most available child care next to relatives, but only one minder in five is registered with local-authority social services.

Although Britain has play groups, parent-toddler groups, and infant crèches, these options require parental involvement and do not cover regular work hours. As children reach school age, the problem gets even worse. Schools finish in mid-afternoon and are closed for 175 days a year. About 30 percent of British school-age children are completely unsupervised when school is not in session. British corporations are showing more interest in getting involved in child care, but, as the EOC observes, "Everyone is waiting for a lead from government."[87]

Health Care

Health care is one of the country's most pressing social issues. The United States spends more on health care than any country in the world. In 1992, health care spending rose to 14 percent of the nation's gross national product (GNP). The Department of Commerce estimated it would continue to rise by 12 to 15 percent each year unless the system is reformed.[88] In 1992, Japan spent 6.8 percent of its GNP on health care and Great Britain spent 9 percent.[89] Technically, US health care can be superb for the affluent or well insured. But the United States is the only industrialized country that does not insure all of its citizens and leaves many families open to financial disaster.

During his 1992 campaign, presidential candidate Bill Clinton promised to develop a new national health care plan to serve all stakeholders. After the election, he charged Hillary Rodham Clinton with developing the plan. The first deadline passed in mid-May 1993. Most observers agreed the plan will not reach Congress before mid-1994 and the political machinations through which it will go will delay implementation even further.

---

[86]D Summers, "The Little Things That Mean a Lot," *Financial Times,* January 13, 1992, p. 10.

[87]Ibid.

[88]"Too Sick to Wait," *The Economist,* January 16, 1993, p. 30.

[89]J Sterngold, "Japan's Health Care," *The New York Times,* December 28, 1992, p. A1.

Perhaps more than any other issue, health care policy and delivery has propelled both groups and individuals into a national debate. The debate was raging even before the 1992 election. In April 1991, *The New York Times* published a five-part series entitled "The Price of Health." Researchers found most Americans had health insurance coverage through their jobs. Federal, state, and local governments accounted for 40 percent of all health care spending.[90]

Medicare covered all elderly people, including those who could afford other forms of insurance. The very poorest people were covered by Medicaid, but half the population with incomes below the poverty line were still too affluent to qualify. About 33 million Americans, or 13 percent of the population, had no coverage. Of this number, most were low-income workers and their families. Tens of millions more had such limited policies that a major illness could wipe out all of their financial assets.[91]

In 1991, Congress took up the issue of health care reform with an energy not seen since the 1960s, when it created the Medicare and Medicaid programs. All stakeholders agreed a new policy had two major goals: health care for everyone regardless of income and cost cutting while preserving quality care.

However, there was no consensus on how to reach the goals. The cost of implementing new policies was a major stumbling block. Even the mention of new taxes was politically unacceptable.[92] Both Republicans and Democrats came up with plans, but none was acceptable to the majority of legislators.

Stakeholders floated different strategies for controlling costs:

- *Managed care:* Government and large corporations would contract with health maintenance organizations (HMOs) for all care. A new bureaucracy would scrutinize doctors' decisions and encourage people to enter HMOs.
- *Malpractice limitations:* The law would be changed to hold down awards in malpractice suits. Legal changes would also cut down the number of procedures used to rule out even slight risks.
- *Single payer:* A national health plan would be created to allow all medical bills to be paid by a single public entity. This entity would have bargaining power over fee levels and medical practices. Some private insurers could channel their payments through this entity.
- *Annual cap on expenditures:* The government would develop annual health budgets for the nation, the states, local communities, and even individual hospitals. If budgets were reasonable, care could be

[90]E Eckholm, "Rescuing Health Care," *The New York Times,* May 2, 1991, p. A1.

[91]T Lewin, "High Medical Costs Affect Broad Areas of Daily Life," *The New York Times,* April 28, 1993, p. 1.

[92]Eckholm, "Rescuing Health Care," p. B. 12.

high in quality with strong incentives, on every level, to offer only cost-effective treatment.

· *Explicit rationing:* Insurers could refuse to pay for treatments they considered low priority. Ethicists would resolve divisive issues.[93]

Harvard Business School professor Regina Herzlinger proposed a scheme in which each employed adult American would have to shop for his own insurance. The policies would reimburse the individual for any medical expenses greater than 5 percent of his salary. Under this plan, doctors and hospitals would not have to bear the cost of treating catastrophic injuries or illnesses. Premiums would be tax deductible up to a set amount roughly comparable to what companies currently spend on insurance. All taxpayers would have to show on their tax returns that they had purchased insurance. Insurers would be required to take a certain number of high-risk clients with preexisting medical problems.[94] Poor and unemployed people were not included in Herzlinger's plan, but other scholars suggested the government could give them tax credits that would eventually replace Medicare and Medicaid.[95]

Corporate chief executives put health care costs at the top of their worry list. In a 1991 poll of CEOs of Fortune 500 and Fortune 500 service companies, 63 percent of executives surveyed said runaway medical bills were one of their greatest worries (see Exhibit 11–4). The respondents were overwhelmingly opposed to national health care but acknowledged such a plan might be the only solution if cost escalations continued. The executives preferred cost sharing, having employees pay higher premiums and settle for higher deductibles.

Increasingly companies are urging employees to join HMOs or other managed care networks. In a managed care system, employees agree to use a certain group of designated physicians, specialists, and hospitals. They may go outside the system but must bear the costs themselves. An insurance company manages this network by obtaining volume discounts from the physicians and ensuring that they do not order unnecessary tests or treatments.[96]

Business Week promoted its own plan based on the "managed competition" concept. All employers, regardless of size, would be required to provide health care benefits to employees. Small businesses would buy into a regional health care purchasing corporation that had government sponsorship and operated as a "superinsurer." Corporations would develop a variety of health care options by negotiating among competing companies. Employees would select among the options. In the plan, the government

---

[93]Ibid.

[94]L Smith, "A Cure for What Ails Medical Care," *Fortune,* July 1, 1991, p. 49.

[95]Ibid.

[96]W E Sheeline, "Taking on Public Enemy No. 1," *Fortune,* July 1, 1991, pp. 58–59.

EXHIBIT 11–4

Fortune *CEO Poll*

Q Some employers believe the rising expense of health insurance will be their greatest cost problem in the 1990s. Do you agree or disagree?

A
Agree, one of the greatest problems 63%
Agree, the greatest problem 35%
Disagree 1%
Not sure 1%

Q Given problems such as the rising cost of health care and the more than 30 million Americans who remain uninsured, should the US adopt a nationalized health care system, financed by taxpayers?

A
Yes 24%
No 69%
Not sure 7%

Q At what rate do you expect health care costs per employee to climb at your company over the next five years? An annual rate of . . .

A
Less than 5% 2%
5% to 10% 29%
11% to 15% 46%
16% to 20% 19%
More than 20% 3%
Not sure 1%

Q Costs aside, are you generally satisfied with the quality of health care your employees receive?

A
Yes 95%
No 4%
Not sure 1%

Q Of the following factors, which two or three do you consider the most important when it comes to driving up the cost of health insurance for US companies?

A
Liability awards and malpractice insurance 79%
Expensive new technology 59%
Unnecessary surgery and other procedures 52%
Inefficient hospitals 28%
Excessive paperwork 27%
Overuse of other benefits by employees 23%
Overpaid doctors 22%
Overuse of mental health benefits 17%
Other 12%
Adds to more than 100% because of multiple responses.

SOURCE: W E Sheeline, "Taking on Public Enemy No. 1," *Fortune,* July 1, 1991, pp. 58–59.

would determine minimum coverage, price, and quality standards. The market would work by giving power to individuals and small companies to choose among competing options.[97]

The Bush administration floated a long-promised plan during the 1992 presidential campaign. The plan's core was a combination of middle-class tax deductions and low-income tax credits to offset the cost of private health insurance. Money saved from restraining Medicare and Medicaid costs would fund the plan. Few health experts took this plan seriously, and many characterized it as a Band-Aid approach that would do little or nothing to curb spiraling costs.

President Clinton's campaign plan focused on extending medical coverage to 35 million people who had no insurance. He also pledged to contain the growth in health care expenditures and cap annual increases in the nation's overall health budget.

Clinton's election mobilized a broad spectrum of health care lobbyists and other stakeholders, both supporters and detractors. However, there was no doubt in anyone's mind that a major overhaul was on the way. The proposed Clinton plan took on special urgency.

At the end of January 1993, Hillary Rodham Clinton began developing the legislation for overhauling the health care system. Her team included several domestic advisers, the secretaries of Health and Human Services, the Treasury, Commerce, Defense, Veterans Affairs, and the director of the Office of Management and Budget.[98] As deliberations began, additional people, including state governors, joined the group.

The team deliberated through the spring and summer, far longer than the first 100 days promised in the campaign. Congressional leaders, appearing on weekly news shows, doubted anything would be signed before 1994. Finally, in mid-September, details of the health care plan began to emerge. Every day national newspapers and magazines "floated" new elements of the plan. The White House wanted to make sure the public understood and supported the administration's initiatives before formally announcing the plan at the end of September.

The Clinton Health Care Reform Plan

Under the plan, each American citizen will receive a health security card certifying her right to medical care regardless of income, health status, job, or state of residence. Everyone will receive a basic care package that includes benefits such as hospitalization. In addition, the package will include some long-term care, with a focus on in-home and community-based care, mental health assistance, treatment for drug and alcohol addiction, and preventive

---

[97]S B Garland "A Prescription for Reform," *Business Week,* October 7, 1991, pp. 58–66.

[98]T L Friedman, "Hillary Clinton to Head Panel on Health Care," *The New York Times,* January 26, 1993, p. A1.

health services such as childhood immunization and dental care. The administration will probably seek to have abortions included in this package.

The federal government will establish a national health board to set the rate of growth in health care costs for each state, establish guidelines for quality care, and update the benefits package in the national plan. Although the federal government will establish the guidelines, each state will implement and administer its own plan and establish doctors' fee schedules.

Most people will obtain their coverage through large purchasing cooperatives called health *alliances.* Each state will decide how many competing alliances it will allow. Large corporations, called *corporate alliances,* can form their own alliances and offer their own plans. They will have to meet federal standards regulating the scope of benefits, financial reserves, and prudent use of money held in trust for employees. They will also have to comply with the national health board's "cost containment goals."

All alliances will offer a choice of health plans, each with a minimum package of benefits. There will be three basic plans. In the traditional *fee-for-services plan,* the patient will choose all of her doctors and the patient or insurer will be billed directly by the provider. This will be the most expensive option. The *managed care plan* will provide all services under one roof. Patients will pay a small fee (about $10) for each service and a maximum yearly fee of about $3,000. A *preferred provider organization (PPO) plan* will provide a network of doctors and hospitals that will be paid a set fee to provide care to a group of patients. Patients will be able to see doctors outside the PPO, but will be reimbursed at a lower rate.

All employers and employees will pay for health care. Unemployed people will be asked to contribute what they can. Medicaid recipients will be integrated into the new system. Elderly people currently under Medicare will continue to receive benefits unless they want to join the new system. Eventually both Medicare and Medicaid will be eliminated.[99]

Summary

Workplace issues of the 1990s have their roots in earlier decades. As the United States shifted from a manufacturing- to a service-oriented society, the composition of the workforce changed and new stakeholders emerged. Innovative technologies gave employers new tools with which to assess

---

[99]R Toner, "Clinton Facing Reality of Health-Care Reform," *The New York Times,* May 21, 1993, p. A14; Dentzer, "Clinton's Master Plan," *US News & World Report,* May 24, 1993, pp. 22–28; E Neuffer, "Health Overhaul: A Policy Primer," *The Boston Globe,* August 26, 1993, p. 1; R Pear, "Health Planners at White House Consider Lid on Medicare Costs," *The New York Times,* August 30, 1993, p. A1.

employee performance. Computerization of employee files and electronic devices allowed employers to compile huge masses of data about each employee without his explicit consent.

The polygraph, or lie detector, is used much less frequently today, but written tests are being used to identify potential problem employees. Electronic surveillance is used very widely, particularly to monitor employees in low-skilled jobs. Innovations like the "smart badge" promise new opportunities to track workers' activities.

Stress on the job is a major workplace problem. It costs companies in terms of absenteeism, lower productivity, and hostility. Unfavorable economic conditions, family problems, and productivity pressures exacerbate stress. In the most extreme cases, stress can lead to worker aggression and even homicide.

Companies face a variety of medical issues, many of them difficult to resolve. Substance abuse has grown over the past decade. Companies cannot discriminate against workers with substance abuse problems. Rehabilitation programs have proven effective in returning workers to productivity.

Individuals with disabilities have become more activist in the 1990s. Their efforts were given impetus by the passage of the Americans with Disabilities Act in 1990 and its subsequent implementation. Generally, companies have discovered it costs comparatively little to meet national guidelines, and they have expanded their pool of productive employees. The courts are still trying to interpret the act's exact meaning, but new EEOC guidelines should clarify Congress's intent.

HIV infection and AIDS will present employers with major challenges for the foreseeable future. Companies of all sizes will have to deal with the social and financial burdens created by AIDS. The Americans with Disabilities Act is explicit regarding how employers must accommodate AIDS patients. Legal issues such as insurance coverage are still being worked out through the courts.

Family and child care are two of the most pressing workplace issues of the 1990s. Many baby boomers are caring for small children and elderly parents at the same time. Although the Family Leave and Medical Act of 1990 provides short-term help, companies are just beginning to tackle this concern. They have not come up with universally acceptable answers. It remains to be seen whether the federal government will develop its own plan or the government and corporate America will work together to provide these essential services.

The government is developing health care policy to bring basic coverage to every American regardless of income or job status. This issue is tremendously complex and has engendered strong stakeholder controversy. A new model will present huge opportunities for some industries and will probably diminish opportunities for others. Overall, a profound national reorientation is under way, but it will take considerable time to evolve.

Projects

1. You are the CEO of a highly regarded security firm. You have taken on a new client who requires 30 additional security personnel to guard his premises. Develop a recruitment and training plan that satisfies your own standards for high-quality, well-trained personnel and still meets your customer's six-week deadline. Pay particular attention to standards of employee reliability, honesty, and expertise. Discuss how you will meet those standards without violating the new recruits' privacy.

2. As human resources manager in a medium-size computer firm, you collect data on employee absences. You notice that during the past year, many of the firm's engineers have been reporting sick for one or two days at a time. Absenteeism is clearly up, but you don't really know why. Office gossip leads you to think the engineers are feeling stressed and anxious about changes in the firm's environment. Analyze the economic, social, legal and political, and technological environmental factors for the high-tech industry. Devise a plan to reduce stress and restore a more productive working environment.

3. In your community, find three companies that will let you interview their benefits manager. Before the interview, draw up a questionnaire that will give you information about each company's choice of health care program. Find out what decision process was used and whether the company has changed health care plans in the past two years. If the company has changed plans, ascertain what led to that change. Based on your interview, draw some conclusions about the companies' decision rules in selecting a health care plan. If you have an opportunity, interview employees to find out what they want from their health care plan and whether they are satisfied. Ask the companies to what extent the new Clinton plan will alter their offerings.

Questions

1. Discuss the benefits and drawbacks of a drug-testing program for a company's truck drivers.
2. Discuss the factors that create the greatest stress in (*a*) a word processing job and (*b*) a marketing management job.
3. *a.* What would be the ideal form of child care in this country? Discuss alternatives.
   b. Discuss the appropriate role of the local, state, and federal governments in providing that ideal form of child care.

Beta Case 11
Workplace Issues for the 1990s

John West, Beta's vice president of human resources, usually looked forward to his routine of a quiet early morning cup of coffee and a sweet roll at the kitchen table before he left for work. This morning, West was distracted by the papers he had brought home the previous night in preparation for today's meeting with Sam Powell, vice president of the Biotechnology Division. Powell had requested the meeting to report he had discovered some very serious breaches in his division's security system.

Powell's division was developing the new drugs everyone hoped would generate Beta's future profits. Secrecy was imperative in developing new products. Earlier in the week, a concerned employee had told Powell he suspected two co-workers were leaking Beta's secrets to the competition. "These turkeys are both druggies," he told Powell. "The money they get for the secrets goes right up their noses."

Powell was stunned by this graphic description of security violations. Beta did not have a random drug-testing program, and Powell had no idea what to do next. He questioned the suspects, but both denied any wrongdoing.

This is a potentially disastrous situation, thought West. We are not talking about petty theft; we are talking about the future of the company and a drug problem of unknown proportions. I've got to get my legal facts straight and then make some important policy decisions.

12 EQUAL EMPLOYMENT AND AFFIRMATIVE ACTION

HIGH PRIORITY CHAPTER

— Know Legal cases

— Know Civil Rights acts

— EEOC - does doesn't do

Title 7

diversity v. affer mact

CASE *Diversity Training*

Prime Office Furniture wanted to find out why so few women and minorities were being promoted. At the urging of Don, her boss, Jennifer Stills organized a workshop to increase sensitivity among the company's department heads. She consulted with several diversity training companies and collected a number of frequently used exercises. One exercise asked supervisors to mention stereotypes they had heard or used about women and minority group members. Although Stills had some concerns about using this exercise and bringing unpleasant stereotypes to the surface, experts assured her the results were usually very positive. The idea was to expose potential prejudice and deal with it.

Stills sent a memo to each of the 10 department heads asking them to reserve a full morning the following Wednesday. Nine of the department heads were men; none was African-American, Asian, or Hispanic. Sue Fielding, head of the accounting department, was the only female in the group. She was 50 years old and had worked for Prime since her college graduation.

Stills arranged for a breakfast of juice, bagels, doughnuts, and coffee. After everyone had eaten, they got down to work. She explained the exercise to the participants and stressed its purpose was to help stereotypes surface but not to attack or criticize any person or group.

"Women cry when they're criticized," one manager said.

"Blacks are lazy," said another.

"Hispanics just want to take life easy," declared a third.

Sue Fielding kept silent. She thought, "Why should I open my mouth? I've worked really hard to get where I am, and nothing I say is going to make these guys behave differently. If I say that white males are self-centered, insensitive to gender issues, or exclude people who don't look like them, they'll gang up on me. Even worse, they'll remember it for years after this session is over."

John Martin, head of the paint department, stood up. "You know," he said, "I really hate being here. I feel as if we are dumping on all the groups that aren't represented in this room. What good does it do to talk about people who aren't here to defend themselves?"

"No way!" said Tom Johnson. "Minorities get all the benefits. We are catering to them instead of giving the jobs to the people who can do them best."

Jennifer Stills realized the exercise was definitely not going the way she had anticipated. She glanced at Fielding's stony face and knew she would get no help there. She did not want to create an in-group and an out-group. Instead of bringing people together, this exercise was polarizing the participants.

Questions

1. What should Stills do? Should she stop the exercise where it was?
2. Should Stills try to focus the conversation differently? If so, how?
3. Should Stills ask Fielding directly for her input?
4. In retrospect, should Stills have refused to do the training herself? Should she have told Don she felt more comfortable bringing in a professional trainer?

Introduction

Managers use the term "level playing field" to describe the environment in which they would like their firms to compete. It means all players' chances of winning are based solely on their talents and abilities. Within the firm, the concept of a level playing field is fairly recent. Applicants of equal ability and qualifications have not always had the same legal access to employment and, in some cases, still do not. Promotions and pay were not—and still are not—color- or -gender blind. In the past, employers could terminate workers on a whim for reasons that had nothing to do with job performance. Since the passage of the Civil Rights Act of 1964, Congress and the courts have strengthened employees' rights.

This chapter discusses the historical background of landmark employment legislation and the issues companies and employees face more than 30 years after the passage of that landmark legislation. These issues include race and gender discrimination, sexual harassment, and age discrimination.

Civil Rights Act of 1964

Background

The movement for equal opportunity in employment dates from World War II, when President Franklin D Roosevelt issued Executive Order 8802. This order prohibited racial discrimination in employment by companies with federal contracts. It established the first Fair Employment Practices

Committee (FEPC). The effects of the order were widespread, since most manufacturing companies were operating under wartime federal contracts.[1]

When large numbers of young white men left the factories to go off to war, blacks and women were hired into jobs they previously were not allowed to hold. Once peace was declared, many of the blacks and women were fired so that returning white servicemen could reclaim their jobs. Although the FEPC was disbanded at the end of the war, some legislators and other stakeholders continued to agitate for a permanent federal FEPC law through the late 1940s and the 1950s. States and cities did pass FEPC laws, but nothing was done on the federal level.[2]

A number of companies also took steps to end discrimination in hiring during the postwar period. They were motivated by two convictions. First, they believed business, rather than government, could best solve social problems. Second, they were convinced that if they failed to address the issues voluntarily, restrictive and possibly oppressive legislation would result.

The disparity in opportunity and treatment between blacks and whites became glaring in the 1950s. Equal opportunity was a privilege enjoyed primarily by white males, a point brought home by Rosa Parks, an African-American, in December 1955. Parks, a department store employee, refused to give her seat on the bus to a white man. Blacks, led by Martin Luther King and others, conducted a bus boycott and followed it with years of demonstrations and marches. The media were critical stakeholders in this movement. Television in particular brought the struggle for racial equality into living rooms around the country.

The public grew increasingly aware that basic workplace rights were the prerogative of only one segment of the population: white men. This awareness renewed the call for federal equal rights legislation. Race was the primary focus of the civil rights struggle. As in the pre-Civil War antislavery movement, gender discrimination was a secondary focus. Women active in the civil rights movement were told to put their gender demands aside until the primary issues of racial discrimination were settled.

Employee Qualifications

Throughout the early 1960s, most proponents of equal job opportunities emphasized the hiring of *qualified* employees without regard for race or ethnicity. This "color-blind" perspective on equal opportunity prohibited overt discrimination against racial and ethnic groups. However, some claimed it fostered a more subtle form of discrimination because it failed to right past

---

[1]S M Gelber, *Black Men and Businessmen* (Port Washington, NY: Kennikat Press, 1974), p. 24.
[2]P S Foner, *Organized Labor and the Black Worker, 1619–1973* (New York: Praeger Publishers, 1974), pp. 269–70.

wrongs. No special attention was paid to those people who were unqualified for employment due to past discriminatory practices.[3]

By the early 1960s, it was clear that voluntary policies had failed to make a substantial dent in black unemployment. Blacks and other stakeholders called for "affirmative action" to make up for past inequities.

In 1961, President John F Kennedy issued Executive Order 10925 establishing the President's Commission on Equal Employment Opportunity (PCEEO). The commission had the power to investigate complaints and enforce a ban on discrimination by federal contractors. In addition, the order required government contractors to "take affirmative action to ensure that applicants are employed and that employees are treated during employment, without regard to their race, creed, color, or national origin."[4] The PCEEO could terminate contracts of noncompliant employers, prevent them from obtaining further government contracts, and recommend that the Department of Justice bring criminal or injunctive action against them.

Title VII of the Civil Rights Act of 1964

Title VII extended many provisions of Executive Order 10925. The act covered all employers of 25 or more people, employment agencies, and labor unions with 25 or more members. It also added a prohibition against gender discrimination.[5]

Title VII, which took effect in 1965, was amended in 1972 and again in 1979. As amended, Title VII covered nearly all employers with more than 15 employees except private clubs, religious organizations, and Native American reservations. Section 703(a) of Title VII was the most important provision. It stated, in part, "It shall be an unlawful employment practice for an employer—(1) to fail or refuse to hire or discharge any individual, or otherwise to discriminate against any individual with respect to his [sic] compensation, terms, conditions, or privileges of employment, because of such individual's race, color, sex or national origin."[6] The amendments did not change the intent of the law; they merely broadened its scope and made it more inclusive.

Title VII provided that employers did not have to hire employees if it was unreasonable to do so. It declared, "Nothing contained in this title shall be interpreted to require any employer . . . to grant preferential treatment to any individual or to any group because of the race, color, religion, sex, or

---

[3]Gelber, *Black Men and Businessmen,* p. 165.

[4]Ibid., p. 140.

[5]Bureau of National Affairs, The Equal Employment Opportunity Act of 1972 (Washington, DC, 1973), p. 1.

[6]Subcommittee on Labor, Committee on Labor and Public Welfare, US Senate, *Compilation of Selected Labor Laws Pertaining to Labor Relations, Part II* (Washington, DC: US Government Printing Office, 1974), p. 591.

national origin of such individual or group on account of an imbalance which may exist with respect to the total number or percentage of persons of any race, color, religion, sex, or national origin employed by any employer."[7] The law also stated, "Notwithstanding any other provision of this title, it shall not be an unlawful employment practice for an employer to apply different standards of compensation, or different terms, conditions, or privileges of employment pursuant to a bona fide seniority or merit system . . . provided that such differences are not the result of an intention to discriminate . . ."[8]

The 1964 Civil Rights Act emphasized equal opportunity for the individual. Employers were not required to give preferential treatment, and indeed were expressly forbidden to do so. It viewed discrimination as an intentional, calculated act to exclude some people from work.

Equal Employment Opportunity Commission (EEOC)

In 1965, Congress created the Equal Employment Opportunity Commission (EEOC) as an independent agency to implement antidiscrimination legislation. The EEOC was composed of five commissioners, not more than three of whom could belong to the same political party. The president appointed the commissioners, and the Senate confirmed them for five-year terms. The EEOC also had a presidentially appointed general counsel who served for four years. As with other federal agencies, Congress specified the basic criteria the EEOC was to use in implementing congressional directives.[9] Table 12–1 lists the major responsibilities of the EEOC.

In 1990, President Bush appointed Evan Kemp, Jr., to the job of commissioner. Kemp, who was confined to a wheelchair with a polio-type disease, vowed to be the chairperson for all Americans.[10] His appointment was concomitant with the passage of the ADA. When Kemp resigned, long-time commissioner Tony Gallegos became acting commissioner and still holds that post.

When an individual complains to the EEOC, the agency processes the complaint in three phases:

1. *Investigation.* The EEOC may examine the complaint itself or refer it to a state EEOC agency if that state has EEOC laws that meet federal standards. Usually the state or federal agency interviews the people involved and examines relevant records. Both state and

---

[7]Ibid., p. 610.

[8]Ibid., p. 612

[9]J R Fox, *Managing Business-Government Relations* (Homewood, IL: Richard D Irwin, 1982), p. 143.

[10]"Equal Employment Opportunity Commission," *Federal Regulatory Directory,* 6th ed. (Washington, DC: Congressional Quarterly, 1990), p. 115.

TABLE 12–1 Major EEOC Responsibilities

- Prohibit employment discrimination on the basis of race, color, national origin, religion, or sex.
- Prohibit employment discrimination based on pregnancy, childbirth, or related medical condition.
- Protect men and women against pay discrimination based on sex.
- Protect workers age 40 or older from arbitrary age discrimination in hiring, discharge, pay, promotions, and other aspects of employment.
- Prohibit discrimination against individuals with disabilities within the federal government.

Also, the EEOC

- Coordinates all federal equal employment efforts.
- Oversees all affirmative action plans to eliminate discriminatory practices.
- Has jurisdiction over federal employees' complaints concerning equal employment.

SOURCE: "Equal Employment Opportunity Commission," *Federal Regulatory Directory,* 6th ed. (Washington, DC: Congressional Quarterly, 1990), p. 109.

federal EEOCs can compel companies to produce information they want. Once the EEOC collects the information, the agency decides whether there is "probable cause" to believe the employer has violated Title VII.

2. *Conciliation.* If the EEOC does not find probable cause, it ends the process and tells the complainant she can file a private suit in federal district court. If the EEOC finds probable cause, it undertakes the process of conciliation or negotiation. The complainant, the employer, and the EEOC try to work out a compromise acceptable to all parties and consistent with Title VII's requirement that the employer compensate the victim for the discrimination suffered.

3. *Litigation.* If the two sides cannot reach an agreement, the EEOC may litigate by filing suit against the employer in federal district court. Usually, however, the EEOC drops the case unless it has an excellent chance of winning. The complainant still retains the right to sue in federal district court.[11]

Affirmative Action

President Kennedy's Executive Order 10925 was the first order to use the term *affirmative action.* This order declared employers should make sure qualified minority group members were informed of job openings and had

---

[11]J Ledvinka, *Federal Regulation of Personnel and Human Resource Management* (Boston: Kent Publishing, 1982), pp. 30–31.

an equal chance to be hired. President Johnson's Executive Orders 11246 (issued in 1965) and 11375 (1967) required companies with federal contracts to have affirmative action programs that recruited workers on a nondiscriminatory basis. Companies with federal contracts of over $50,000 and 50 or more employees had to develop and put into effect written affirmative action programs.[12]

Department of Labor guidelines issued in February 1970 emphasized affirmative action programs should be "result oriented." Further guidelines, under Revised Order No. 4, were issued 11 months later. They stated, "An acceptable affirmative action program must include an analysis of areas within which the contractor is deficient in the utilization of minority groups and women, and further, goals and timetables to which the contractor's good faith efforts must be directed to correct the deficiencies and, thus, to increase materially the utilization of minorities and women, at all levels and in all segments of his workforce where deficiencies exist."[13] The order said further, "Affirmative action programs must contain the following information: . . . An analysis of all major job classifications at the facility, with explanation if minorities are currently being underutilized in any one or more job classifications (job 'classification' herein meaning one or a group of jobs having similar content, wage rates, and opportunities). 'Underutilization' is defined as having fewer minorities or women in a particular job classification than would reasonably be expected by their availability."[14]

Although these guidelines applied only to federal contractors, the EEOC and the courts interpreted the Civil Rights Act as having similar provisions so that most large employers were affected. What began as equal opportunity came to mean "statistical parity."[15]

The benchmark for minority employment became the proportion of the minority group in question living in the area or of the overall workforce in the Standard Metropolitan Statistical Area (SMSA) surrounding a business. The emphasis of affirmative action shifted from discrimination against individuals to discrimination against an entire *class* of people. For example, if the area in which a plant is located had 20 percent African-American residents or workers, a company should aim for a workforce that is 20 percent African-American—and at all levels, not only the lowest ones. Evidence of discrimination was either a conspicuous underrepresentation of women or minority group members among a company's employees or concentration of these groups at the lower levels of employment.

---

[12]US Equal Employment Opportunity Commission, *Affirmative Action and Equal Employment: A Guidebook for Employers,* vol. 1 (Washington, DC: US Government Printing Office, 1974), p. 13.
[13]Ibid., vol. 2, p. D-28.
[14]Ibid.
[15]N Glazer, *Affirmative Discrimination: Ethnic Inequality and Public Policy* (New York: Basic Books, 1975), pp. 33–49.

TABLE 12–2 Steps in an Affirmative Action Plan

An employer must:

- Conduct a utilization analysis that shows (1) the percentage of the employer's work force that belongs to the group in question and (2) the percentage of the available labor supply in that group.
- Determine which employment policies are contributing to the underutilization of the target group.
- Establish goals, timetables, and plans for action increasing the utilization of the target group in deficient areas.
- Apply good-faith efforts to meet the goals. The term *good faith* is nonspecific and usually means the company must make a real effort to remedy underutilization.
- Take steps to meet goals in the next planning cycle if they are not met in the current one.
- Report progress to the OFCCP.

SOURCE: N Glazer, *Affirmative Discrimination: Ethnic Inequality and Public Policy* (New York: Basic Books, 1975), pp. 33–49.

The law does not require companies to hire unqualified workers. It does require them to go beyond the Civil Rights Act of 1964 and undertake an active search for qualified minorities, women, and people with disabilities to fill positions. Employers are also expected to upgrade the skills and utilization of these same groups. Affirmative action requires the employer to make as wide a search as possible for qualified applicants and to upgrade present target group employees. The Office of Federal Contract Compliance Programs (OFCCP) monitors the effort. Table 12–2 shows the steps in an affirmative action program.

Landmark Supreme Court Decisions

Despite the profusion of legislation, guidelines, and court decisions, ambiguities and other problems with the implementation of affirmative action programs persist. To some white males, the preferential treatment being given to women and minority group members amounts to "reverse discrimination." Affirmative action quotas usually dictate that if a white man, a woman, and a minority group member are equally qualified for a job, an individual in one of the latter two groups should be hired since he or she is likely to be underrepresented in the firm.

After the passage of the Civil Rights Act of 1964, a number of lawsuits were filed claiming companies were discriminating in favor of women and minorities and this "reverse discrimination" violated the act. However, in April 1975, the New York State Supreme Court declared remedial legislation to be legal.

The severe recession of the early 1970s hindered company efforts to hire women and minority group members. Since seniority was the basis for lay-offs and firings, at least in unionized companies, the recently hired women and minority group members were the first to lose their jobs.

During this period, the proportion of recently hired women and minorities declined sharply. Some of these fired employees filed suits, claiming the seniority system discriminated against them because it enabled white male workers to keep their jobs while members of other groups were fired.

Minority group employees contended their low seniority stemmed from prior discrimination. Companies considered several remedial alternatives, including laying off women and minority workers in the same proportion as the company's overall layoff and paying minority workers' salaries until those employees could be called back to work.[16]

Layoffs by percentage, however, violated seniority rules, which were an important part of most union contracts. Since management implemented workforce reductions to save money, remedial payments to laid-off workers could defeat the reduction's purpose. Lower court decisions were mixed until 1984, when the Supreme Court upheld seniority as a legal basis for layoffs.

There are several landmark cases on reverse discrimination. The four most important are (1) *Regents of the University of California* v. *Bakke;* (2) *U.S. Steelworkers, etc.* v. *Weber;* (3) *Memphis Fire Department* v. *Shotts;* and (4) *City of Richmond* v. *J. A. Croson.*

Allan Bakke *v.* The Regents of the University of California

Allan Bakke, who contended he was refused admission to medical school because of reverse discrimination, brought his case before the California Supreme Court. The school to which he had applied, the University of California at Davis, had a special admissions program for minorities. Of the 100 openings for entering classes in 1973 and 1974, 84 were filled by the usual admissions process. For the remaining 16 places, nonwhite applicants received preference.

The university admitted the 16 minority applicants had college grades and standardized examination scores well below those of the white applicants. Bakke asserted this program violated the US Constitution's Fourteenth Amendment rights of equal protection to everyone regardless of color. The California Supreme Court, in a six-to-one decision, banned minority quotas in the graduate schools of California's state system.[17]

The University of California appealed the decision to the US Supreme Court. The Court split five to four on the decision, supporting the California court's order admitting Bakke to the medical school. The Supreme Court

---

[16]*Business Week,* March 9, 1976, p. 166.
[17]*Allen Bakke* v. *The Regents of the University of California,* 553 P.2d 1152 (1976).

held the admissions program of the University of California at Davis violated Title VI of the Civil Rights Act of 1964, which forbade racial discrimination in programs or activities receiving federal financial assistance.

The Court also ruled, however, that a university could take race into account in admissions in the same way it considered geography, athletic ability, or other special talents. As a result of the inconclusive *Bakke* decision, the EEOC issued new guidelines. It would not support charges that companies were violating the civil rights of white men in cases where "reasonable" affirmative action programs favored women or minorities.

The *Bakke* case had a postscript. The 1980 medical school class at the University of California at Davis had no African-Americans; in 1981, only two enrolled. Although the school made numerous offers, African-Americans rejected them. Apparently the Supreme Court's decision to admit Bakke was the single most important factor in the candidates' decision.[18]

United Steelworkers, etc. *v.* Weber[19]

In 1974 Brian Weber, a white man, was a lab analyst at a Kaiser Aluminum and Chemical plant in Gramercy, Louisiana. Kaiser and the United Steelworkers agreed to establish a program to train workers for high-paying, skilled craft jobs. At least 50 percent of the trainees were to be minority group members. Kaiser had not been ordered to establish such a program, but both the company and the union wanted to improve minority participation to head off government interference. The federal government had already observed that at Kaiser Aluminum, "prior to 1974, there were fewer than 2 percent blacks among craft workers . . . compared with a 39 percent black labor force in the area."[20]

When Brian Weber applied to the new training program, he was turned down in favor of minority group members with less seniority than he. Weber sued on grounds that the 1964 Civil Rights Act clearly prohibited discrimination against anyone on the basis of race. The Fifth Circuit Court of Appeals agreed with Weber, but the case was appealed to the Supreme Court.

By a five-to-two majority, the Court ruled that employers could *voluntarily* give preferences to minorities and women in hiring and promoting for traditionally segregated job categories. In a concurring opinion, Justice William Brennan noted the Kaiser plan did not require the discharge of any

---

[18]W King, "School Still Feels Bakke Effect," *The New York Times,* December 6, 1981, p. A2.

[19]For a review of lower court decisions in this case, see B Lindemann Schlei and P Grossman, *Employment Discrimination Law, 1979 Supplement* (Washington, DC: Bureau of National Affairs, 1979), pp. 194–96. The Supreme Court decision may be found in the *Supreme Court Reporter* 99, no. 18 (July 15, 1979), pp. 2721–31.

[20]*The Wall Street Journal,* June 28, 1979, p. 30.

white workers and did not pose an absolute barrier to their promotion. He described the plan as a "temporary measure" designed "simply to eliminate a manifest racial imbalance."[21]

Memphis Fire Department *v.* Shotts

In 1980, the city of Memphis agreed to integrate its fire department by filling half of its vacancies with African-Americans. In 1981, the city suffered a major budget crisis and had to lay off some city employees under the "last hired, first fired" rule that was part of its seniority plan. About 40 firefighters lost their jobs. The local district court ordered the city to modify its seniority plan to protect the African-American firefighters hired under the 1980 affirmative action plan. Since 15 of the 40 were African-American, the plan would have reversed the movement toward an increased percentage of African-Americans on the force.

In 1984, the Supreme Court had to decide whether the lower court had exceeded its authority by requiring the city to protect the African-American firefighters. The Reagan administration lobbied furiously against the affirmative action protection and for the seniority plan. The Supreme Court sided with Reagan administration policy. Six Supreme Court justices ruled the district court had exceeded its powers and the existing seniority plan, with its "last hired, first fired" provision, should stay intact.[22] Justice White wrote for the majority, "Title VII protects bona fide seniority systems and it is inappropriate to deny an innocent employee the benefits of his seniority in order to provide a remedy in a pattern or practice suit such as this."[23]

City of Richmond *v.* J. A. Croson

In 1983, the Richmond City Council, five of whose nine members were African-American, passed a plan designed to increase the participation of minority firms in public works projects. The council heard testimony that although half of the city's residents were African-American, only 0.67 percent of its prime construction contracts had been awarded to minority businesses. The plan (called a "set-aside") required that prime contractors subcontract at least 30 percent of the dollar value of each contract to one or more minority business enterprises. *Minority* was defined as at least 51 percent owned and controlled by African-American, Hispanic, Asian, Native American, Eskimo, or Aleut citizens.

---

[21]Ibid.

[22]"A Ruling That Could Roll Back Affirmative Action," *Business Week,* July 2, 1984, p. 31; L Greenhouse, "Bias Remedy Vs. Seniority," *The New York Times,* June 14, 1984, p. A12.

[23]"Supreme Court Decides Seniority, Not Race, Should Govern Layoffs," *The New York Times,* pp. 1, B12.

In 1983, J A Croson Company, a white-owned mechanical plumbing and heating contractor, challenged the plan. Croson had lost a bid to supply toilets for the city jail because he could not certify he would use a minority-owned subcontractor. The city denied Croson's request for a waiver of the 30 percent set-aside.

The US Court of Appeals for the Fourth Circuit, in Richmond, ruled the Richmond ordinance violated white contractors' constitutional rights to equal protection of the law. In January 1989, the Supreme Court ruled six to three to uphold the lower court ruling. In effect, the Supreme Court said laws favoring African-Americans over whites had to be judged by the same constitutional test that applied to laws favoring whites over African-Americans. Justice O'Connor, who wrote the majority opinion, noted that no racial discrimination, even that undertaken for a laudable purpose, is "benign." She added, "Racial classifications are suspect, and that means that simple legislative assurances of good intention cannot suffice."[24]

Equal Opportunity and Affirmative Action in the 1980s

Decisions in the Memphis and Richmond cases were consistent with the Reagan and Bush administrations' philosophies. As soon as the Reagan administration took office, it abruptly reversed EEO and affirmative action enforcement. Raymond Donovan, Reagan's labor secretary, said he and the president believed in affirmative action but "not the push-pull, slap-punch, police approach."[25]

In 1982, William Bradford Reynolds, head of the Justice Department's Civil Rights Division, announced he hoped to get the Supreme Court to reverse its decision in the *Weber* case.[26] He expanded on his statement, spelling out the administration's philosophy: "By elevating the rights of groups over the rights of individuals, racial and sex preferences are at war with the American ideal of equal opportunity for each person to achieve whatever his or her industry and talents warrant. This kind of 'affirmative action' needlessly creates a caste system in which an individual must be unfairly disadvantaged for each person who is preferred."[27]

The Reagan administration's rhetoric continued despite the findings of a 1983 study by the Department of Labor. This study concluded the affirmative action plan so roundly criticized by President Reagan had indeed

---

[24]L Greenhouse, "Court Bars a Plan Set Up to Provide Jobs to Minorities," *The New York Times,* January 24, 1989, pp. A1, 16, 19; E Bronner, "A Plan to Help Minority Firms Is Struck Down," *The Boston Globe,* January 24, 1989, pp. 1, 7.

[25]"The New Bias on Hiring Rules," *Business Week,* May 25, 1981, p. 123.

[26]B R Bergmann, "An Affirmative Look at Hiring Quotas," *The New York Times,* January 10, 1982, p. A1.

[27]L Denniston, "Changes in Affirmative Action Policy," *The Boston Globe,* January 5, 1982, p. 9.

been highly effective in promoting the employment of African-Americans, women, and Hispanics.[28]

Two years after the *Memphis* decision, Attorney General Edwin Meese III declared, "the idea that you can use discrimination in the form of racially preferential quotas, goals and set-asides to remedy the lingering social effects of past discrimination [is] nothing short of a legal, moral and constitutional tragedy."[29] Despite the administration's unequivocal opposition, the Supreme Court still supported affirmative action programs in some cases.

Corporate restructuring in the mid-1980s eliminated large numbers of management-level jobs. Particularly hard hit were staff support positions heavily populated by African-Americans and women. Public affairs, community relations, and human resource jobs were the first to go. In 1987, the Black Executives Agency (BEA), an association of African-American directors of social service agencies in New York, tried to organize a meeting with African-American executives of major corporations. They dropped their plans for the meeting because so many African-American managers had lost their jobs. John N Odom, director of the BEA, observed, "The ranks of blacks in corporations have been so decimated there just wouldn't be enough people to come."[30]

In a 1988 survey of African-American managers, 43 percent said they believed they had less opportunity to move up through corporate ranks than they had in 1983. Only 15 percent reported their chances of promotion had improved. Most blamed the Reagan administration for the retreat from affirmative action.[31]

The Supreme Court's 1989 ruling on the Richmond set-aside program cast doubt on set-aside programs in 190 cities and 36 states. In March 1989, for example, the Supreme Court used the precedent of the *Richmond* decision to reject two additional affirmative action plans, one in Michigan and the other in Florida. Many observers concluded this and subsequent decisions sounded the death knell of affirmative action.

Gelvin L Stevenson, chairman of CommonWealth Capital Group, Inc., observed the "ruling will be a major setback for minority firms and for minority employment . . . Affirmative action cracked open a door, and now it's shutting . . . Affirmative action has finally allowed qualified blacks . . . to start doing business. It did not level the playing field, it let them onto the playing field."[32]

---

[28]R Pear, "Study Says Affirmative Rule Expands Hiring of Minorities," *The New York Times,* June 19, 1983, p. 16.

[29]S Taylor, Jr., "Breaking New Ground on Affirmative Action," *The New York Times,* May 21, 1986, p. A28.

[30]C H Deutsch, "The Ax Falls on Equal Opportunity," *The New York Times,* January 4, 1987, p. F1.

[31]"*The Wall Street Journal,* February 9, 1988, p. 1.

[32]"Prospects," *The New York Times,* January 29, 1989, p. 1F.

The Civil Rights Act of 1991

[handwritten marginalia: Know key issues × Disparate impact]

In October 1990, the Democratic Congress, dismayed and angered by Reagan Supreme Court appointments and decisions, submitted a new civil rights bill to the White House. If passed, the legislation would make it easier for victims of job discrimination to sue and collect damages. President Bush promptly vetoed the bill, asserting it encouraged unacceptable hiring and promotion quotas.

In May 1991, Democratic leaders outlined a compromise worked out by members of the House Judiciary Committee. They changed the legislative language of the bill to make it conform to language negotiated by the Business Roundtable and the Leadership Conference on Civil Rights. The new language allowed employers to defend employment practices as necessary if they bore "substantial and manifest" relationship to the jobs at issue. The bill prohibited the use of discriminatory employment testing and the adjustment of test scores on the basis of race, color, sex, national origin, or religion.

Eleanor Holmes Norton, who headed the EEOC under President Carter, wrote a thoughtful editorial on the issue of quotas in *The Wall Street Journal.* She pointed out that quotas were explicitly barred in the language of the bill and damage awards were rare and small. Yet the Bush administration persisted in raising quotas as a scare tactic. Norton wrote, "[The quota scare] poisons the racial atmosphere already polluted by racial incidents and by the mutual suspicion between blacks and whites that is the legacy of retrenchment, resistance, and resentment on racial issues that began in the 1980s."[33]

President Bush promptly denounced the bill. He charged the Democratic leadership with proposing a quota system that would allow employers to establish personnel systems based on numbers rather than merit. The White House promptly moved to ease even further federal regulations intended to prevent discrimination in employment tests. Civil rights leaders, lobbyists, and Democratic members of Congress were furious. The Leadership Conference on Civil Rights, an umbrella lobbying organization, called President Bush's remarks "almost Orwellian" in the way they turned the truth about quotas upside down.[34]

On June 6, 1991, the Civil Rights Act passed the House of Representatives with a vote of 273 to 158, exactly the same number of votes its predecessor had received. As with the previous bill, the vote was 17 short of the 290 votes needed to override the president's veto.[35]

---

[33]E H Norton, "Quota Scare Must Not Destroy Civil Rights Bill," *The Wall Street Journal,* May 16, 1991, p. A17.

[34]A Clymer, "Bush Denounces Civil Rights Bill Advocated by House Democrats," *The New York Times,* May 31, 1991, p. A1; S A Holmes, "White House Change in Job Discrimination Rules," *The New York Times,* May 31, 1991, p. B6.

[35]A Clymer, "Rights Bill Passes in House But Vote Is Not Veto-Proof," *The New York Times,* June 6, 1991, p. A1.

TABLE 12-3 Civil Rights Act of 1991

Disparate impact: Disparate impact deals with suits involving hiring or promotion practices. Tests that seem fair on the surface but have a disparate impact may result in a company hiring, for example, proportionately more whites than African-Americans or more men than women. These tests and other practices sometimes result in "unintentional discrimination" cases.

In a 1989 case, *Wards Cove Packing* v. *Antonio,* the Supreme Court held that once complainants had shown a disparate impact had resulted from an employment practice, they still had to prove there was no business necessity for the practice.

Under the new act, once disparate impact was proven, the burden of proof shifted from the complainant to the employer. The concept of disparate impact was written into law for the first time. It said employers must show employment practices were "job related for the position in question and consistent with business necessity." The act eliminated the standard set by *Wards Cove* and ordered the courts to interpret the law as it existed before that decision.

Discrimination and harassment: In the 1989 case *Patterson* v. *McLean Credit Union,* the Supreme Court held that the right to sue for damages for racial job discrimination under an 1866 law did not apply to on-the-job harassment or other forms of discrimination after someone was hired. Under the new act, the *Patterson* decision was rejected and the 1866 reconstruction law was clearly defined as applying only to hiring, firing, promotions, and all other terms of employment.

Victims of intentional discrimination or harassment based on sex, religion, national origin, or disability were protected under the 1964 Civil Rights Act. The 1964 law was amended to allow complainants to sue for back pay, compensatory damages, and punitive damages.

Reopening old discrimination cases: In the 1989 case *Martin* v. *Wilkes,* the Supreme Court ruled that since some white firefighters in Birmingham had not been parties to two earlier suits challenging discrimination in the city's fire department, they had a right to go into court later to attack hiring and promotion practices. People could not sue to reopen employment cases if they had actual notice of the decree at the time it was entered and a reasonable opportunity to object if their cases were adequately represented in the original case.

SOURCES: T Noah and A R Karr, "What New Civil Rights Law Will Mean," *The Wall Street Journal,* November 4, 1991, p. B1; "The Compromise on Civil Rights," *The New York Times,* October 26, 1991, p. 7.

Rather than precipitate another presidential veto and increase congressional animosity, Republican Senator John Danforth tried to develop a proposal acceptable to all sides. After the White House objected repeatedly to elements of his compromise, Danforth announced he had enough Republican votes to override any veto.[36]

The White House capitulated almost immediately and declared the quota issue dead. President Bush now supported a measure he had adamantly opposed. He dropped his assertion that the measure would lead employers to hire racial minorities on the basis of strict percentages to avoid lawsuits charging indirect discrimination.

The proposed new law extended for the first time punitive damages to victims of employment discrimination based on sex or disability as well as on race. It also countered seven Supreme Court decisions, most of them from 1989, that made it more difficult for job bias plaintiffs to win lawsuits.

[36]A Clymer, "President Rejects G.O.P. Compromise on Rights Measure," *The New York Times,* August 2, 1991, p. A1.

With no objections from the administration, Congress passed the act and it was signed into law.

Legal experts quickly pointed out that the most important aspect of the new law was not racial discrimination but sexual discrimination. They declared that as a practical matter, people claiming racial discrimination were already able to sue under a separate law. The 1991 bill's biggest impact was the increased likelihood that women complaining of sexual discrimination would come forward with claims.[37]

Sexual Harassment

In recent years, women have fared better than minorities in the courts in terms of access to jobs and promotions. But they face a special problem: sexual harassment in the workplace. In 1980, the EEOC wrote its guidelines defining sexual harassment as "[unwelcome] sexual advances, requests for sexual favors, and other verbal or physical conduct of a sexual nature . . . when (1) submission to such conduct is made either explicitly or implicitly a term or condition of an individual's employment, (2) submission to or rejection of such conduct by an individual is used as the basis for employment decisions affecting such individual, or (3) such conduct has the purpose or effect of unreasonably interfering with an individual's work performance or creating an intimidating, hostile, or offensive working environment."[38] This definition prohibited two specific types of sexual harassment: (1) situations in which sexual harassment created a hostile work environment and (2) cases in which a supervisor demanded sexual favors in exchange for job benefits.[39]

Men and women generally agree on the actions that constitute sexual harassment, but they have very different views concerning its impact. In a 1988 study of business school graduate students, 46 percent of the men surveyed thought women would be flattered by actions that constitute sexual harassment; only 5 percent of the women agreed.[40] A consultant specializing in sexual harassment observed, "men have been brought up to behave toward women in a social-sexual manner and have a hard time adjusting in an office."[41]

Some companies have taken steps to ensure that the workplace remains free of discrimination and specifically sexual harassment. As Exhibit 12-1 shows, AT&T has a corporate policy that clearly defines sexual harassment and sets up a process to deal with sexual harassment charges. The exercise

---

[37]S Faison, Jr., "Rash of Sex-Bias Suits Seen After Rights Act," *The New York Times,* November 30, 1993, p. 1.

[38]29 C.F.R. 1604. 11 (a) (1987).

[39]*Shrout* v. *Black Clawson,* 689 F. Supp. 774, 780 (1988).

[40]A Bennett, "Managing," *The Wall Street Journal,* August 5, 1988, p. 19.

[41]"Hands Off at the Office," *US News & World Report,* August 1, 1988, p. 58.

Exhibit 12–1

AT&T's antiharassment policy

It is company policy that all employees have a right to work in an environment free of discrimination, which encompasses freedom from sexual harassment. A.T.&T. prohibits sexual harassment of its employees in any form.

Such conduct may result in disciplinary action up to and including dismissal. Specifically, no supervisor shall threaten or insinuate either explicitly or implicitly that any employee's submission to or rejection of sexual advances will in any way influence any personnel decision regarding that employee's employment, evaluation, wages, advancement, assigned duties, shifts or any other condition of employment or career development.

Other sexually harassing conduct in the workplace, whether physical or verbal, committed by supervisors or non-supervisory personnel is also prohibited. This includes repeated offensive sexual flirtation, advances, propositions, continual or repeated abuse of a sexual nature, graphic verbal commentary about an individual's body, sexually degrading words to describe an individual and the display in the workplace of sexually suggestive objects or pictures.

Employees who have complaints of sexual harassment should in appropriate circumstances report such conduct to their supervisors. If this is not appropriate, they should seek the assistance of their equal opportunity complaint investigator. Where investigations confirm the allegations, appropriate corrective action will be taken.

of defining the problem and drawing up a policy helps sensitize and protect all employees—men as well as women.

The number of firms that developed sexual harassment policies grew steadily from 1980 on. Grievances rose from 4,272 in 1981 to more than 6,300 in 1984. The 1991 Anita Hill–Clarence Thomas controversy generated a new awareness of the problem. In the first half of the 1992 fiscal year, sexual harassment charges increased more than 50 percent, to 4,754, over the same reporting period a year earlier.[42]

The Anita Hill–Clarence Thomas Controversy

In July 1991, President Bush nominated Judge Clarence Thomas to the Supreme Court. Judge Thomas, a 1974 Yale Law School graduate, had served in government agencies before he was appointed to the federal court. In 1981, he went to the Department of Education as an assistant secretary in the Office of Civil Rights. In 1982, he was nominated and confirmed as chairperson of the EEOC.

---

[42]J Gross, "Suffering in Silence No More: Fighting Sexual Harassment," *The New York Times,* July 13, 1992, p. A1.

Anita Hill, a professor of law at the University of Oklahoma, graduated from Yale Law School in 1980. While she was working for a Washington law firm, a friend introduced her to Clarence Thomas. He told her he was anticipating a political appointment and asked if she would like to work with him. After he received the Department of Education post, Hill became his assistant. When he accepted the EEOC post, she moved with him. In the spring of 1983, she accepted a job teaching law at Oral Roberts University, and in July she left Washington, DC.[43]

Events Leading to the Senate Hearings.   The Senate Judiciary Committee scheduled its hearings on Judge Thomas's nomination to begin on September 10, 1991. In August, one of Anita Hill's male law school classmates called Nan Aron, head of the Alliance for Justice, which opposed Thomas's nomination. The classmate told Aron Thomas had sexually harassed Hill when she worked for him at the Department of Education and the EEOC. It was unclear whether Hill knew the classmate was making the call.

Aron contacted Democratic Senator Howard Metzenbaum, the only member of the Senate Judiciary Committee to vote against Thomas's nomination to the federal appeals court in 1990.[44] On September 3, Senator Metzenbaum's office asked Professor Hill about the rumors, but Hill did not mention that she herself had been harassed. Later she called back and told her story to a staff member.

On September 5, staff members of Senator Edward Kennedy, another member of the Judiciary Committee, contacted Professor Hill and asked about the rumors. Hill replied she needed time to think about whether she would discuss being sexually harassed.

On September 9, Hill agreed to talk to a Metzenbaum lawyer. On September 10, the day the hearings began, Hill outlined her allegations to the lawyer, who forwarded them to a Judiciary Committee nominations counsel.[45]

On September 12, Anita Hill repeated her allegations to the counsel. She asked Senator Joseph Biden, the Senate Judiciary chairperson, to keep the allegations confidential and not notify Thomas or the FBI. At this point three members of the 14-member Judiciary Committee—Metzenbaum, Kennedy, and Biden—knew about the charges. Biden decided to keep the charges from the other committee members, and the Thomas confirmation hearings proceeded.

On September 19, Hill again called the Judiciary Committee nominations counsel and said she wanted all the members of the committee to know

---

[43]R W Apple, Jr., "Thomas Accuser Tells Hearing of Obscene Talk and Advances," *The New York Times,* October 12, 1991, p. 1.

[44]D A Kaplan, "Anatomy of a Debacle," *Newsweek,* October 21, 1991, pp. 25–32.

[45]J Abramson and D Shribman, "Sex Harassment Furor Jeopardizes Thomas, Embarrasses Politicians," *The Wall Street Journal,* October 9, 1991, p. A1.

her story, but did not want the FBI involved. Biden insisted the FBI had to be notified before he went further. Finally, on September 23, Hill agreed. She then faxed a four-page statement to the committee, and Biden passed it on to the White House and the FBI.[46]

The FBI completed its investigation on September 25. Biden, under White House pressure to get the nomination through the Senate, scheduled the committee vote for Friday, September 27. He knew he could not brief the seven Democrats on the committee until the next day. Some committee members on both sides of the aisle later reported they were incompletely briefed just moments before the vote. The vote, along party lines, was a seven-to-seven deadlock.

Most observers agreed Thomas would win a revote, but a week later, on October 6, National Public Radio broke the story of Hill's allegations. The next day Hill went on television with her charges, and on October 8 the Senate decided to hold public hearings on them.[47]

The Sexual Harassment Hearings. The hearings riveted the American public and began a nationwide discussion on sexual harassment. The central issue was Anita Hill's allegation that Judge Thomas had repeatedly harassed her sexually between 1981 and 1983. The six questioners on the 14-member Judiciary Committee were committee chair Joseph Biden (D-Delaware), Patrick J Leahy (D-Vermont), Howell Heflin (D-Alabama), Strom Thurmond (R-South Carolina), Arlen Spector (R-Pennsylvania), and Orrin Hatch (R-Utah).

The details of the hearings, allegations, and responses are far too complex to recount in detail. They were extremely acrimonious and sexually explicit. Between October 11 and October 15, the 14 white male members of the Senate Judiciary Committee questioned Hill and Thomas, both articulate, professional, highly educated African-American lawyers. They also heard the testimonies of a stream of witnesses, some supporting Hill and others supporting Thomas. The proceedings were carried live on the major television and radio networks, as well as on CNN, PBS, and cable outlets.

There was more at stake than Thomas's confirmation. Hill quickly became a surrogate for every woman who believed she had experienced unwanted and unsolicited attention from male colleagues in the workplace. A *New York Times* telephone poll taken on October 9 asked 294 women whether they had ever been "the object of sexual advances, propositions, or unwanted sexual discussion from men who supervise you or can affect your position at work." Four out of 10 women said they had encountered sexual harassment, but very few had reported the incidents to their companies.[48]

---

[46]Kaplan, "Anatomy of a Debacle," p. 28.

[47]Ibid.

[48]E Kolbert, "Sexual Harassment at Work Is Pervasive, Survey Suggests," *The New York Times,* October 11, 1991, p. A1.

Thomas became a surrogate for the Bush administration's policies and male hegemony in the workplace. President Bush was already less popular among women than among men, and political pundits suggested Bush would pay an electoral penalty even if Thomas won the nomination.

After the nation heard Hill's charges and Thomas's spirited defense, additional witnesses appeared corroborating both sides. Hill and Thomas stated their cases with such conviction that it was difficult for viewers to believe either one was deliberately lying. The issue came down to whether the senators believed Thomas or Hill.

One critical question that arose during the hearings was why Anita Hill remained in Thomas's employ in the Department of Education and why she moved with him to the EEOC. Lynn Hecht Schafran, an attorney with the National Organization for Women, said the answer was economic necessity. She recounted a recent conversation with a judge on New York Governor Cuomo's Task Force on Rape and Sexuality. The judge told her victims of sexual harassment, like victims of sexual assault, rarely make an immediate outcry because they are so afraid of how their disclosures will be received.[49] Virtually all such incidents take place in private; no witnesses are available to corroborate the victim's charges.

On October 16, the Senate confirmed Clarence Thomas as a Supreme Court justice by a 52-to-48 vote. Phone calls from President Bush and lobbying from interest groups and colleagues continued up to the last moment. Most senators gave Thomas the benefit of the doubt. Even most of those who voted against him would not state flatly that they believed Anita Hill's allegations.

Sexual Harassment since the Hearings

Within weeks after the confirmation, sexual harassment awareness training became the new managerial fad. Faced with the publicity on sexual harassment and the penalties sanctioned by the Civil Rights Act, employers rushed to educate employees. A woman lawyer at a prestigious Chicago law firm observed, "The hearings made them [employers] concerned about the issue. The act raised the concern of the bottom line."[50]

A year after the hearings, studies found sexual harassment was still widespread. In a 1992 survey by the National Association for Female Executives, 60 percent of the 607 women polled said they had been sexually harassed. More than half the women said their companies still had not addressed the problem. Most of the companies that made serious efforts to deal with sexual harassment were concerned about the problem before the hearings. The

---

[49]L H Schfran, "The Harsh Lessons of Professor Hill," *The New York Times,* October 13, 1991, p. F13.

[50]T Segal, "Getting Serious about Sexual Harassment," *Business Week,* November 9, 1992, p. 78.

companies that were galvanized into action by the hearings usually contracted for abbreviated, unrealistically short programs.[51]

Surveys found sexual harassment even pervaded educational institutions from secondary school through universities. The Acadia Institute in Maine reported its survey findings on sexual harassment in academia at the American Association of Advancement of Science meetings. The institute surveyed 2,000 graduate students and 2,000 faculty members at 98 universities. One-quarter of all students and faculty questioned said they had observed or had direct knowledge of faculty engaging in sexual harassment. Forty percent of female faculty reported incidents, compared to 20 percent of male faculty.[52]

Reports of sexual harassment continued to proliferate, but it was not clear whether progress was being made in ameliorating its effects. Competition for jobs brought about by the 1991–1992 recession and continued corporate downsizing may have contributed to male hostility toward women.

What became of the woman whose charges against Clarence Thomas drew the nation's attention to the problem? Anita Hill went back to the University of Oklahoma to teach. The state and the law school are still gripped in an argument over whether she was a courageous spokesperson or a perjurer. Minnesota State Representative Gloria Segal and former Lieutenant Governor Marlene Johnson raised $120,000 to endow the Anita Faye Hill Professorship Chair at the University of Oklahoma.

Professor Hill's opponents argued that outsiders had no business raising money for a chair. A computer consultant who still leads the fight against her said, "if Fidel Castro sent the University of Oklahoma $500,000 saying he'd like to endow the Lee Harvey Oswald chair, we don't think the regents ought to give it to him." State Representative Leonard Sullivan said he wanted to see Anita Hill in prison.[53]

Hill's supporters include the dean of the law school, who resigned on June 30, 1993. Supporters say she has been targeted by the extreme right and opposition to the chair is motivated by "blatant racism and sexism."[54]

Sexual harassment remains a pervasive workplace issue. As people question who bears the burden of sexual harassment charges, they need only look at Anita Hill and Clarence Thomas now. Thomas pursues his private life and holds one of the most respected jobs in the country. Hill is still embroiled in controversy and is likened by her detractors to the murderer of President Kennedy.

---

[51] Ibid.

[52] A Bass, "Survey Finds Wide Sexual Harassment in Academic Science," *The Boston Globe,* February 11, 1993, p. 4.

[53] "Hill Professorship Stirs Passions in Oklahoma," *The Boston Globe,* September 7, 1993, p. 4.

[54] S Labaton, "For Oklahoma, Anita Hill's Story Is Open Wound," *The New York Times,* April 19, 1993, p. A1.

Age Discrimination

Major Legislation

The EEOC also administers the Age Discrimination in Employment Act (ADEA). The act protects workers between ages 40 and 70 from arbitrary age discrimination in employment. When Congress passed the ADEA in 1967, the law covered people up to age 65; in 1978, the age limit was raised to 70. The ADEA encompasses issues of hiring, firing, pay, promotion, and fringe benefits. It does not cover cases in which age is a bona fide occupational qualification.

In 1990, the Older Workers Benefit Protection Act (OWBPA) was signed into law. It prohibited discrimination based on age in connection with all employee benefit programs. It reestablished the requirement that benefits for older workers be the same as for younger workers, except to the extent the employer can show a greater cost is attached to providing for older workers.[55]

Under the OWBPA, companies can ask outgoing workers to sign a promise, or waiver, not to sue for age discrimination. To be legal, a waiver must meet the following requirements:

- The company must give workers some kind of compensation in addition to the benefits and severance pay they would ordinarily get.
- The waiver must be in plain English, not legal jargon.
- The waiver cannot cover issues arising after the date of the waiver.
- The company must suggest the employee talk to a lawyer.
- The company must give the employee at least 21 days to sign the waiver and 45 days if the employee is leaving because of mass layoffs or buyout incentives. Employees have seven days after signing to change their minds.
- Employers must give employees a list of job titles and ages of everyone potentially affected by the cutback, including people who were not fired.
- Employers must specifically refer to the Age Discrimination in Employment Act in their discussions with employees.[56]

In the spring of 1993, the Supreme Court ruled that employers are not necessarily barred from firing older workers to avoid paying them pensions. Such firings would violate the age bias law only if age rather than years of service were the actual reason for the firing. Writing for the majority, Justice Sandra Day O'Connor observed, "It is the very essence of age discrimination

---

[55]*Labor Law Legislative Update* (Boston: Nutter, McClennan & Fish 1991), p. 1.

[56]J Woo, "Ex-Workers Hit Back with Age-Bias Suits," *The Wall Street Journal,* December 8, 1992, p. B1.

for an older employee to be fired because the employer believes that productivity and competence decline with old age. When the employer's decision is wholly motivated by factors other than age, the problem of inaccurate
and stigmatizing stereotypes disappears."[57]

The 1980s retrenchment hit older workers particularly hard. Massive
layoffs brought a huge wave of age bias suits. These suits could be brought
by workers as young as 40. Between 1990 and 1991, a 156 percent surge
occurred in inquiries to the American Association of Retired Persons
(AARP) about age discrimination. In the first half of fiscal 1992, 22,800 age
discrimination suits were filed with the EEOC and state agencies. The suits
were filed against a variety of companies in many industries. The defense
industry, which suffered mass layoffs, was particularly hard hit.

The McDonnell Douglas Corporation Example

In 1990 and 1991, McDonnell Douglas reduced its St. Louis-area work force
by 25 percent. Ten thousand employees were cut or forced to retire. Of this
number, about 900 were at least 55 years old and nonunion employees.
More than 100 McDonnell Douglas employees filed with the EEOC
between 1990 and 1992.[58]

In 1993, McDonnell Douglas and the EEOC agreed the company would
pay $20.1 million to resolve charges that it had discriminated against the
older workers. This was the second largest age discrimination suit ever
brought before the EEOC. In the settlement, the 900 workers divided $10
million and had an additional $10.1 million added to their pensions on a
scale tied to age and experience. In addition, McDonnell Douglas agreed to
rehire 200 St. Louis-area workers for four years. Forty-five former employees who had filed private lawsuits against the company were each offered
$20,000 to withdraw their suits.[59]

Age discrimination suits can be very costly to companies. Most settlements run from $50,000 to $400,000 per employee. IDS Financial Services,
a unit of American Express, paid $35 million to settle an age discrimination
suit brought by 32 division managers. A lawyer who specializes in age discrimination suits warns companies that if it can be inferred that age is the
basis for layoff decisions, a flashing light goes off at EEOC agencies for potential age discrimination suits.[60]

---

[57]L Asseo, "Court Limits Age-Discrimination Law," *The Boston Globe,* April 21, 1993,
p. 47.
[58]K G Salwen, "EEOC Gets Settlement from McDonnell in Crackdown on Age-Based
Layoffs," *The Wall Street Journal,* March 2, 1993, p. A4.
[59]Salwen, p. A4.
[60]Ibid.

Managing an Aging Workforce

In an *Academy of Management Executive* article, Robert J Paul and James B Townsend point out that by the year 2000, nearly half of all Americans will be older than 45 and more than 36 million will be over 65 years of age. They say American business tends to undervalue the importance and experience of older workers. Forty million Americans age 60 and older have more than 1 billion years of cumulative work experience that should not be wasted. They suggest managers follow these guidelines for employing older workers:

· *Talk with your legal department.* You should discuss the ADEA and its amendments, the Senior Community Service Employment Program of 1973, the Employee Retirement Income Security Act (ERISA), the Job Training Partnership Act of 1982, the Social Security Act and its amendments, and the Tax Reform and Budget Conciliation Acts of 1986.

· *Review your strategic plan.* The HRM manager should forecast personnel needs to determine whether the company has adequate policies on recruitment, orientation, retention, and retirement.

· *Reconsider your human resource policies.* Older workers should be accommodated by using flexible benefits and work schedules, part-time work, and incentives for continued employment. The company should also consider arrangements with older workers such as consulting, seasonal work, reduced hours with reduced pay, job sharing, compressed work weeks, expanded or reduced shifts, voluntary demotions, and job rotation.

· *Think about job redesign.* The company should consider individual job preferences of older workers. Older workers are proficient at teaching, counseling, research, long-range planning, security, arbitration, and other tasks. Jobs that require accuracy, judgment, and reason are more appropriate than those that require speed, innovation, and creativity.

· *Provide for career-long training.* Training for older workers should take place in a non-threatening environment that builds confidence for learning new skills. Verbal assurances, adequate learning time, and privacy are important.

· *Examine your benefit plans.* Make sure older workers have a choice of insurance plans, pension credits, extended leaves, and vacation days to meet their needs.

· *Reconsider incentives.* Older workers may have different incentives than younger workers. Stress recognition of accomplishments, financial rewards, and peer recognition instead of promotions and more responsibility.

· *Ensure that performance appraisal programs are current.* These data form the basis for many personnel decisions.[61]

---

[61]R J Paul and J B Townsend, "Managing the Older Worker—Don't Just Rinse Away the Gray," *Academy of Management Executive* 7, no. 3 (1993), pp. 67–74.

Summary

The passage of the Civil Rights Act of 1964 fundamentally changed companies' criteria for hiring, firing, and rewarding employees. The act established the Equal Employment Opportunity Commission to write and administer rules and regulations. The EEOC's job is to investigate employees' discrimination charges and litigate on their behalf if the charges are sufficiently grave.

Affirmative action, a policy embodied in a series of executive orders, goes beyond equal treatment. It is directed primarily at minorities and women and requires companies to redress past discrimination. The Office of Federal Contract Compliance Programs monitors corporations' affirmative action efforts and suggests models for formulating and implementing programs.

Since the mid-1970s, the Supreme Court has ruled on several precedent-setting affirmative action cases. Over the past 15 years, the ideological composition of the court has changed, and so has the direction of its decisions. The Supreme Court of the early 1990s has been far more conservative and less likely to support affirmative action cases than the pre-Reagan era Court. Some recent decisions have upheld affirmative action for women, but minority programs have fared poorly. It remains to be seen how much the Clinton appointees will change the Supreme Court's positions.

Although more women have entered the workforce and are moving upward through the management hierarchy, they are still encountering difficulties, including sexual harassment. The law prohibits sexual harassment, but it is very difficult to prove and the EEOC is reluctant to take cases to court. Some companies have instituted procedures and policies aimed at diminishing sexual harassment. As with all other issues of social responsibility, top management's commitment is critical. Programs that foster fair and equitable treatment benefit all employees.

The passage of the Age Discrimination in Employment Act protects workers between ages 40 and 70 from discrimination in hiring, firing, pay, and promotion. In recent years, more and more employees have been filing grievances under this act. Faced with expensive pensions and health costs, companies are trying to find ways to minimize their burden. But firms face an indefinite future of court-mandated payments and damages if they are found guilty of violating age discrimination regulations.

Questions

1. Even if top management is committed to an affirmative action program, middle managers and supervisors often resist implementation. Suppose you are the head of personnel for a large

manufacturing company. Send the CEO a memo suggesting how to secure middle management support.

2. Discuss the problems women face in the workplace, and determine what issues, if any, are unique to women. How do women's issues differ from those of minorities and elderly workers? How do they differ, if at all, from the issues men face?

3. How should a company assess its social performance in the area of affirmative action?

4. Since the passage of the Civil Rights Act, how has government policy affected the law's implementation? Discuss the role of the Supreme Court in determining civil rights issues.

Projects

1. Contact the EEOC in your state to find out what it does to monitor the status of minorities in the workplace.

2. Find out from your state or the federal EEOC how it decides which cases to litigate and which cases to drop.

3. Conduct a diversity awareness workshop in class. As a semester-long project, each student should pick a diversity issue with which he or she is not familiar. Some examples might be problems of gay and lesbian employees, people with disabilities, elderly people, women, African-Americans, Hispanics, or other minorities. Students should interview members of their lobbying or support groups and write a comprehensive paper. The paper should include the problems as they are described by the chosen group, relevant legislation, and a personal statement about what students have learned. Students should examine their own stereotypes and assess whether they have changed as a result of the project. Students may do this project individually or in small groups.

BETA CASE 12
EQUAL EMPLOYMENT AND
AFFIRMATIVE ACTION

Joan McCarthy, vice president of public affairs at Beta, decided she had put off the "woman" issue long enough. Shortly after she joined Beta, McCarthy and her task force found women were substantially underrepresented in the ranks of top management, craftspeople, and service workers. In fact, she remembered, the only category in which women were fully represented was office, clerical, and staff. In 1980, only 3.66 percent of Beta's managers and professionals were women; in 1993, that number had grown to only 4.12 percent.

McCarthy reflected that not one woman had made it through the managerial ranks to the vice president level in more than a decade. Even she had been hired from outside the company to fill the public affairs position. Of all the vice presidential slots in companies, public affairs was the one most likely to be held by a woman or minority group member.

The glass ceiling against which Beta's women managers banged their heads as they tried to rise was clearly intact. Certainly women had been at Beta long enough to have made it farther up the ladder. McCarthy decided to do a little research before she discussed the matter with John West, vice president of human resources. She wondered why upward mobility at Beta was so low. Was it because the women were undervalued? Was it because they did not do their jobs as well as the men? Were they stalled because of factors that had little or nothing to do with Beta?

McCarthy studied data on women in a variety of managerial and professional jobs. A 1993 Department of Labor study of the 1,000 largest US companies showed women represented only 16 percent of more than 31,000 managers. In the largest accounting firms, only 5 percent of partners were women, up from 1 percent a decade ago.[62]

Korn/Ferry International and the UCLA Anderson Graduate School of Management surveyed 400 top women executives. The survey found that since the last study in 1982, the percentage of women surveyed who held the title of executive vice president had doubled from 4 to 8.7 percent. During the same period, those at the senior vice presidential level rose from 13 to 23 percent. Average compensation for women doubled over the decade to $187,000 compared to the male average of $289,000 reported in a 1989 survey of male executives.[63]

Women in ad agencies said they thought they were narrowing the gender gap in some areas but declared they had been denied top positions and salaries. A study conducted by Advertising Women of New York reported that 35 percent of women employed at ad agencies believed they had suffered sex discrimination. The median individual income for women was $38,500 compared with $73,400 for men.

The men surveyed denied the existence of a glass ceiling. Seventy percent of those surveyed said women had equal opportunity to attain more responsibility, promotions, and salary increases. Thirty-seven percent of women respondents said they had equal access to compensation and top jobs.[64]

McCarthy's research on the status of women in the nation's large pharmaceutical firms found Beta was consistent with the norm in number of women in top positions. Over the next several weeks, McCarthy discussed the "women issue" with several of the top male managers at Beta. Generally they prefaced their responses with "Of course, we don't mean you, Joan, but . . ." Some observed women were not interested in sports or other topics men liked to talk about informally. Many were afraid women would get "emotional" if they had a professional disagreement. A few mentioned their wives would object if they had to travel with a woman.

Overwhelmingly, the men said they did not want to hire or promote women because if the women had children, they would want special privileges. All the training and time invested in them would be lost if the women did not come back to work or had extended maternity leaves.

There was no question that the men's concerns were reflected in *The New York Times* article McCarthy had just read. In 1978 Congress passed the Pregnancy Discrimination Act, which made it illegal for employers to treat pregnancy differently from any other disability. In 1992, for the first time in several years, the number of pregnancy discrimination complaints to the EEOC rose. The EEOC complaints were only the tip of the iceberg, experts said. Women who returned to work after childbirth frequently

---

[62]L Berton, "Deloitte Wants More Women for Top Posts in Accounting," *The Wall Street Journal,* April 28, 1993, p. B1.

[63]N J Perry, "More Women Are Executive VPs," *Fortune,* July 12, 1993, p. 16.

[64]C Miller, "Women at Ad Agencies Say Top Pay, Positions Denied to Them," *Marketing News,* June 21, 1993, p. 1.

found their performance evaluations were far lower than before. Staff cuts and management overhauls gave companies the opportunity to save money by firing employees whose personal circumstances might require special attention.[65]

As McCarthy pulled into her driveway after an exhausting day, she reflected on her conversations with male colleagues and on her other findings. The month she had spent on this issue had been intensely unsettling for McCarthy. She was very concerned about women's access to top management jobs and dismayed at her male colleagues' attitude toward women with families.

After working 14-hour days for the last 10 years, McCarthy and her husband were contemplating starting a family. Although she had every intention of continuing to work after her child was born, she wondered whether she would find herself relegated to another job. She also wondered whether her colleagues' treatment of her would change when her pregnancy became obvious.

[65]B P Noble, "An Increase in Bias Is Seen Against Pregnant Workers," *The New York Times,* January 2, 1993, p. 1.

13

UNIONS, OCCUPATIONAL SAFETY, AND HEALTH

FILM—development North Ms. South

CASE   *Jennifer Stills and Workplace Safety*

Jennifer Stills hated mornings like this. Betsy Stanford, an employee in the customer service department, was still causing a problem. Six months ago, Stanford fell in the parking lot and claimed her back was broken. Physicians' diagnoses were inconclusive. One corroborated the claim, while two others said she had simply suffered a very bad sprain. Both agreed she was sufficiently recovered to return to work. However, Betsy refused, insisting she was in terrible pain and could not sit for long periods as her job required.

When the accident occurred, Stills notified the state workers' compensation board and Prime's insurance company. Stanford was still receiving 66 percent of her pay from the insurance company. Since she refused to return to work, Prime filed for arbitration with the state board of industrial accidents. Now Bill Kelley at the board told Stills the arbitration could drag on for as long as two years, during which time Prime's insurance company would have to continue to pay. Stanford was willing to compromise, however. She agreed to settle for $15,000 and leave the company.

Stills was furious that over the past six months her time had been taken up by someone who she believed just wanted to make money at Prime's expense. She was sure Stanford never intended to come back to her job. Stills was thoroughly disgusted with a system that rewarded a malingering employee at the expense of the company.

Questions

1. What responsibility should a company have toward a worker who appears to be taking advantage of an inefficient legal system?
2. Should Jennifer Stills recommend fighting the issue to its conclusion regardless of how long it takes?

3. If Prime gave Betsy Stanford the $15,000, what message would it send to other employees?

4. The Clinton administration is considering abolishing separate workers' compensation. Under the new plan, workers' compensation would be incorporated into the general health care system. What do you think will be the consequences of bypassing the insurer?

Introduction

Before 1970, American workers relied on a combination of labor union intervention, voluntary corporate responsibility, state law, and luck to make the work environment even moderately safe. Across industries, union organizers pressed business to raise wages, improve benefits, and implement workplace safety standards. Unions were workers' only consistent major advocates for workplace safety.

After Congress passed the Occupational Safety and Health Act in 1970, the federal and state governments assumed major responsibility for rule setting and enforcement of workplace safety. The Occupational Safety and Health Administration (OSHA), created by the act, has gone through periods of underfunding and minimal activity and times of rigorous enforcement. Although unions still have serious concerns about workplace safety, their strength has greatly diminished in recent years. It is unclear what the mid- and late 1990s will bring in terms of workplace safety and what role unions will play as workers' advocates.

Labor Unions

US workers were slow to organize labor unions, for some very good reasons. Unlike European countries, the United States never had a politically or religiously active working class. The tightly knit, highly structured European guild system was incompatible with an America of boundless land, abundant natural resources, and an unshakable belief in individualism.

In colonial America, workers had little need to form labor unions to preserve or improve working conditions. In the few formal associations of employees, workers were limited to a single craft such as shoemaking or carpentry because

· The market for the employer's product was local and usually not competitive.

· Workers had close contact with their employers and often shared the same living quarters. Therefore, they tended to resolve their differences amicably.

· Skilled labor was in short supply. A formal apprentice system included the stipulation that workers could not be fired without good reason.

- Land was cheap, and dissatisfied workers could always move west and become farmers or practice their crafts in new surroundings.
- The ratio of labor to resources was low, enabling many people to afford luxuries.

The Development of Nationwide Unions

Workers began to unionize in the early nineteenth century, when the influx of unskilled immigrant labor forced them to compete for wages. Unions' membership and vitality fluctuated with the nation's economic peaks and depressions. When the economy prospered, so did the unions. Recessions and depressions, which created intense job competition, sapped unions' strength and solidarity.

In 1827, Workingmen's Associations of several crafts joined together under one umbrella organization to push for political and industrial goals. Their first objective was to shorten the workday from 12 to 10 hours. Some participants in the union movement diluted economic and workplace safety concerns with social goals, such as free education, women's suffrage, and abolition of imprisonment for debt. These early efforts at organization were short-lived, however, because workers could not agree on a common set of economic and social goals or their relative importance.

The depression of 1837 nearly wiped out union activity. An influx of Irish immigrants during the 1840s fostered a new element of wage competition. With the return of economic prosperity in 1850, the unions regained strength, concentrating on issues of higher wages and a shorter workday. Labor leaders also began to see the need to press for standardized wages and common bargaining demands.

The Civil War (1861–1865) brought a new spurt of union activity. By the end of the war, 2 percent of the northern population was unionized, up from less than 1 percent four years earlier. Workers became more interested in joining unions because (1) more immigrant competitors were working for low wages, (2) changing technology was replacing workers with machines, and (3) prices were rising faster than wages, preventing workers from buying as much as before.

William Sylvis of the Iron Moulder's Union formed the National Labor Union in 1866 while the economy was still healthy. He made the first attempt to unite all unions into a single federation of American labor. A collection of farmers' groups, women suffragists, and blacks promoted the eight-hour day, female suffrage, and free libraries. Because many of the goals were social and the participants had very little in common ideologically, the union quickly folded.

In 1873, business collapsed into a five-year-long depression. Once again unions disbanded, but the embers of the union movement continued to glow. Employers, sensing a chance to smother unionism entirely, engaged in lockouts, hired spies to identify union organizers, and employed strikebreakers.

A secret organization called the Noble and Holy Order of the Knights of Labor emerged from the chaos. Organized in 1869, the Knights of Labor was a huge general union of skilled and unskilled workers. When good times returned in the 1880s, its charismatic leader, Terence Powderly, embarked on an organizing campaign. By 1886, the Knights of Labor had 700,000 members. However, this union, like its predecessors, fell apart. Skilled and unskilled workers had very few common interests in the various political, economic, and social issues of the time. By 1900, the union had virtually disappeared.

Unlike earlier unions, the American Federation of Labor (AFL), founded in 1886 and led by Samuel Gompers, was a well-organized federation of craft unions that concentrated on economic goals rather than political or social issues. Membership in trade unions grew rapidly in the early 1900s, reaching 5 million in 1920.[1]

During World War I, economic growth and labor shortages facilitated union growth. As unions grew stronger, business owners applied countervailing pressure through trade associations. Business leaders, fearing that organized labor would usurp their prerogatives, actively campaigned against the unions. The National Association of Manufacturers (NAM), founded in 1895, became the most notable antiunion trade association. Management used blacklists, yellow-dog contracts (agreements by employees that if hired they would not join a union), strikebreakers, and accusations of communist infiltration to fight the burgeoning unions.

Some employers took a more subtle approach to undermining unions: They began offering worker benefits such as provided profit-sharing plans, pension plans, unemployment benefits, guaranteed wages, and employee stock ownership. But employers made it quite clear to workers that they were granting privileges and were not conceding rights to the labor unions.

The stock market crash of 1929, followed by the Depression of the 1930s, ended public support for antiunion activity. As the epidemic of unemployment spread across the country, in a remarkable and fundamental change of attitude, public opinion turned in favor of organized labor. The Depression was so profound that people looked to labor unions as their only hope.

Franklin D Roosevelt's election and the establishment of the New Deal signaled a new stage in organized labor. The Norris-LaGuardia Act, passed in 1932, ended the use of injunctions and made yellow-dog contracts unenforceable. Prior to this act, when a company was struck or workers formed picket lines, government could get a court order called an *injunction* to force strikers to return to work.

---

[1] S Cohen, *Labor in the United States,* 4th ed. (Columbus, Ohio: Charles E. Merrill, 1975), p. 51.

Employers still were not obliged to recognize unions as bargaining agents for employees. Unions lobbied Congress to pass a law that would require employers to deal with them. In 1935, the National Labor Relations Act (better known as the Wagner Act) set up the National Labor Relations Board (NLRB) to hear union appeals and peacefully resolve disputes between labor and management.

In 1935, John L Lewis, unhappy about the craft orientation of the AFL, combined his United Mine Workers of America with several other unions to form the Congress of Industrial Organizations (CIO). The CIO promoted the idea of industrywide unions instead of the AFL federation. After a massive membership drive and successful strikes against the automobile and steel industries, most large businesses began to recognize industrial as well as craft unions. Over the next 15 years, the AFL and CIO spent huge sums of money competing for new members. Finally, in 1955, they decided to call a truce and merged into one labor movement, the AFL-CIO. George Meany was elected president and represented the interests of over 16 million workers.

Not all post-World War II legislation was prolabor. In the chill of the Cold War, employers again charged that communists were involved in union leadership and American productivity was jeopardized by unions' monopolistic control. In 1947, they persuaded Congress to pass the Taft-Hartley Act over President Truman's veto. The act broadened employers' range of options in dealing with unions and further defined and limited the rights of employees. It also gave the president the right to declare a national emergency if, in his judgment, a strike created major health or safety problems. A court order could force strikers to go back to work for a "cooling-off period" of 80 days while both sides tried to resolve their differences. This provision was used 35 times between 1947 and the early 1980s.

During the 1970s, the percentage of unionized members in the total workforce declined from 29.3 percent in 1968 to 24.9 percent in 1979. The growth of nonunion operations in construction, trucking, and mining accounted for some of the decline. Other reasons for membership decline included growth in high-technology, science-based, and service industries. Workers in these industries did not have a tradition of union activity as they did in steel and automobiles. In addition, employers in the new industries vehemently resisted union efforts to organize.[2]

Union Activity in the 1980s

Union membership dropped sharply between 1980 and 1985. As noted above, deregulation and recession in the early 1980s, coupled with a shift from manufacturing to service industries, were major factors in the decline.

---

[2] E M Kassalow, "The Future of American Unionism: A Comparative Perspective," *Annals of the American Academy of Political and Social Science* 473 (May 1984), pp. 52–63.

The Bureau of Labor Statistics reported 23 percent of wage and salary earners belonged to unions in 1980. Four years later, only 18.8 percent of that population held union membership.[3]

Realizing its power was rapidly eroding, the AFL-CIO executive council met to develop a new strategy. The council acknowledged new issues had emerged that required innovative approaches. Unions began to stress concerns for pay equity, day care, advancement for women, office automation, job security, and health and safety in the workplace.[4] A prominent labor leader commented that labor would have to confront corporations "not as street-fighters but as professional opponents."[5]

In the 1980s, unions and management leaders began working together over workplace issues and compensation. Some corporate boards, like their counterparts in Europe, appointed worker-directors. Former United Auto Workers (UAW) President Douglas A Fraser became the first union director at a major corporation when he joined the Chrysler Corporation board in 1980. The trend toward union participation on boards began to change the historically adversarial relationship between labor and management. Although antipathy continued, a more cooperative relationship between labor and management began to emerge for the first time in American labor relations.

In 1988, unions faced major problems in negotiating for increased pay. Wages took a back seat to job security. The Conference Board (a business research organization) anticipated union pay hikes would average 2.5 percent, half the rate of inflation. In a period of weak unions, fierce foreign competition, and widespread restructuring, unions had very little clout. Lower pay in a secure job was clearly preferable to no job at all. Unions still expressed concern about workers' health and safety, but they more frequently left enforcement to government regulators and inspectors.

Many union leaders believed President Reagan set the tone for the decade when he broke the Professional Air Traffic Controllers' strike and its union in 1981. Steel union members declined by half during the 1980s. Greyhound Bus Lines strikers lost their battle when the company went into bankruptcy. At Continental Airlines, Frank Lorenzo broke the pilots' union and tried to repeat the process at Eastern Airlines.[6] Douglas Fraser observed, "unions will have to offer innovative and different services. We can expand the employee assistance programs . . . and social services. They have to be available near where people work to do much good."[7]

---

[3]W Serrin, "U.S. Cites Continued Drop in Union Membership," *The New York Times,* February 8, 1985, p. B5.

[4]L M Apcar and C Trost, "Realizing Their Power Has Eroded, Unions Try Hard to Change," *The Wall Street Journal,* February 21, 1985, p. 1.

[5]Ibid.

[6]J Holusa, "Unions Are Expanding Their Role to Survive in the 90's," *The New York Times,* August 19, 1990, p. F12.

[7]Ibid

By 1990, unions no longer dominated major industries like automobiles, steel, and rubber. Audrey Freeman, a labor economist at the Conference Board, said 39 percent of all people represented by unions were in the public sector, and it [the union movement] will probably be over by the end of the decade [in the year 2000].[8]

The recession of the early 1990s did little further damage to the union movement. Most unions had already dealt with the restructuring of the 1980s and with sharp cuts in jobs and pay. Productivity had even risen in many industries. At USX (formerly the US Steel Corporation), management had already made massive cuts in employee compensation and slashed its unionized workforce by more than one-half. Although the United Steelworkers union was not happy with the company's 1991 offer of an 8 percent pay raise over four years, at least unionized workers' wages were likely to match inflation.[9]

The United Auto Workers and the Big Three

When Americans think of unions, they often consider them in the context of the automobile industry. Historically, the United Auto Workers (UAW) has been a very powerful American union. Since 1990, however, that power has been waning and new, more conciliatory auto industry–union relationships have begun to emerge.

When contract negotiations between the UAW and the Big Three automakers began in July 1990, the union admitted its power to force widespread work stoppages had diminished. On the other side, the automakers were less willing than previously to extract painful economic concessions from the unions. Nonunion Japanese plants in the United States were particularly strong competitors. The Big Three automakers had a higher wage base than workers in the US-based Japanese companies. A strike would only help the Japanese, hurt the American companies, and ultimately undermine unionized workers.

The following table shows US hourly wage rates in 1989:

General Motors	$ 15.94	Mazda Motor Corp.	$15.16
Chrysler	15.73	Toyota Motor Co.	14.95
Ford	15.48	Honda Motor Co.	14.55
		Nissan Motor Co.	14.23

SOURCE: D P Levin, "Detroit Set for Talks with U.A.W.," *The New York Times,* July 16, 1990, p. D3.

Due to differences in manufacturing strategy, automobile workers in the Big Three plants were also less productive than their nonunionized Japanese competitors. GM averaged 4.99 workers per car per day, while Nissan averaged 2.94.

---

[8]Ibid.
[9]A Bernstein, "Been Down So Long," *Business Week,* January 14, 1991, p. 31.

During the 1980s, General Motors had lost market share to Japanese and other foreign car companies. Between 1986 and 1989, GM's share of the US car market slid from 41 to 35 percent. By 1990, GM's factories were working at 70 percent of capacity. Every time the company's share declined a percentage point, GM needed 10,000 fewer workers. By September 1990, GM had placed 30,200 workers on layoff and idled four plants.[10]

In October 1990, UAW president Owen F Bieber offered union members a contract. The UAW's two major issues were job security and health benefits. Next to wages, health benefits were the single biggest expense in building cars and trucks. The agreement recognized the reality that more plants would be closed and more workers laid off for an indefinite period.

But GM paid a very high price for union peace. The company agreed that laid-off workers with 10 years' seniority would get 95 percent of their pay for three years, up from two years. Other laid-off workers would get 95 percent of their pay for 18 months, up from 12 months. GM would also give layoff benefits to the 8,000 workers at the four plants closed since 1987. GM agreed to give training or other work and full pay to workers laid off more than 36 weeks. Base wages would rise to $17.88 per hour by 1993.[11]

A new round of negotiations began in June 1993. Like most other unions, the UAW believed it had a more sympathetic ear with President Clinton in the White House. General Motors, more than Ford or Chrysler, suffered a huge productivity gap in domestic car and truck operations. The economy was still stalled, and foreign competition was even fiercer than it had been in 1990.

The North American Free Trade Agreement (NAFTA) with Mexico added to growing uncertainty about the future. Autoworkers rejected the theory that NAFTA would bring new jobs. A 35-year-old autoworker spoke for most of his co-workers when he called the agreement a bad deal: "I'm of the belief," he said, "that most of our jobs are going to follow it [to Mexico]."[12]

GM President John F Smith, Jr., was determined to make domestic operations profitable by switching to "lean production" (also called **synchronous production** or **reengineering**). Basing its production on Toyota's techniques, GM hoped to make more car parts with fewer errors in less time with a reduced workforce.[13] The UAW faced tough car company demands for lower wages, a demand it had resisted since its organization in the 1930s.

---

[10]D Woodruff, "The UAW May Be Chasing an Impossible Dream," *Business Week,* September 10, 1990, p. 40.

[11]D Woodruff, "The UAW Ceers Closer to Reality," *Business Week,* October 1, 1990, p. 33.

[12]R Toner, "In Auto-Making Country, Trade Accord Is the Enemy, *The New York Times,* September 14, 1993, p. A18.

[13]N Templin and J B White, "GM Drive to Step Up Efficiency Is Colliding with UAW Job Fears," *The Wall Street Journal,* June 23, 1993, p. A1.

GM insisted that workers in its US parts operations take wage cuts. The UAW had already capitulated to that demand in its 1992 contract with Champion Spark Plug. The UAW had accepted a two-tier wage contract. Current employees would receive a base wage of $15.74 per hour; new workers would start at $9.12 an hour. Future retirees would lose their health care insurance upon retirement, and active workers would pay a bigger portion of their health care costs. The UAW accepted Champion's terms after the company threatened to move its factory out of town.[14]

As part of its lean production strategy, GM planned to cut workers. Smith and his top managers ordered GM plants to shrink the number of hourly workers by 272,000 people, one-third of its total workforce. GM slated 23 factories for closure. Union members knew they faced layoffs. If they did not help to reduce costs and increase productivity, their workplaces would be closed permanently rather than downsized.

As negotiations over the 1993 contract between the UAW and the Big Three automakers reached its September 14 deadline, GM, Chrysler, and Ford found themselves in different bargaining positions. However, the Big Three and the UAW still faced the threat that any strike by the UAW would likely give Japanese carmakers an even greater share of the US market.

By mutual agreement, the first contract negotiated between one of the Big Three and the UAW would be the model for the other two. The target company would have the greatest freedom to select which concessions to grant the union. If, for example, a healthy Ford Motor Company were chosen as the model and agreed to increasing benefits for laid-off workers, a bloated, unhealthy GM would be badly hurt.

Ford relied on overtime to increase production. The UAW made reducing overtime a priority, hoping the auto companies would hire more workers. GM had no overtime problem and thus would not be hurt by this particular UAW demand. At the end of August, the union picked Ford, the healthiest of the Big Three, to be the lead company in negotiating its 1993 basic labor contract.[15]

All three automakers faced tremendous health care costs, averaging $5,700 a year per worker. In 1993, General Motors was the largest private purchaser of health care in the United States. The company had spent $3.7 billion in 1992. For union members alone, GM's health care costs amounted to $711 for every car and truck it built in North America. Virtually all Big Three employees paid nothing for health care.

As part of the 1993 negotiations, the Big Three insisted that autoworkers assume some of the health care cost burden. The UAW called that demand

---

[14]N Templin, "GM Kicks Off Contract Talks with UAW by Seeking Lower Wages at Parts Plants," *The Wall Street Journal,* June 24, 1993, p. A7.

[15]J Bennet, "Auto Union Set to Aim at One of Big Three," *The New York Times,* August 30, 1993, p. D1.

unfair, maintaining workers had accepted health care benefits instead of wage increases. The union predicted that if a strike occurred, it would be to preserve health care benefits. Both sides agreed the Clinton health care plan would not affect the terms of the 1993 contract.[16]

The 1993 contract between the autoworkers and their employers was negotiated in a spirit of compromise rather than antagonism. Each side recognized and appreciated the other's problems and needs. Both sides wanted to avoid giving comfort to foreign competitors operating on US soil. A UAW assembly line worker looking back over the previous six years could appreciate the difficulties and the intense competition in the auto industry worldwide. Her problems were similar to those every unionized worker in the country faced.

Negotiated at Ford's world headquarters in Dearborn, Michigan, the contract served as a model for bargaining at GM and Chrysler, where current contracts were extended indefinitely. Once the UAW contract was ratified by the membership at each Big Three company, it would cover about 400,000 workers and 390,000 retirees and their spouses.[17] Negotiators bargained through the night of September 14, with both sides expecting to arrive at an agreement. When discussions hit a last-minute snag, negotiators agreed to continue talks without a strike.

September 14, 1993, was also the deadline for auto industry–labor talks with the Big Three in Canada. The Canadian Auto Workers (CAW) union was engaged in discussions with Chrysler, which served as its model. The CAW's primary demands were wage increases and more vacation time. As the deadline approached, both sides seemed optimistic that they would reach an agreement.[18]

On September 15, the UAW and Ford reached a three-year agreement that pundits declared would be good for Ford and bad for General Motors. The Ford model included a 3 percent wage hike, followed by 3 percent bonuses, and an additional cost-of-living adjustment to wages (equal to about 90 percent of the inflation rate). In addition, Ford would keep a small portion of each worker's hourly wage to defray health care expenses. This money would otherwise have been paid as part of the quarterly cost-of-living increase. Ford also pledged $1.2 billion to compensate laid-off workers. Finally, Ford agreed to a reduction of 85 percent to 70 percent of starting pay for new hires.[19]

---

[16]J Bennet, "Health Care Looms as Major Issue for Big 3 Auto Makers and Union," *The Wall Street Journal,* September 6, 1993, p. A1.

[17]"Both Sides Optimistic on Talks at Ford," *The New York Times,* September 13, 1993, p. D1.

[18]N Templin and M Heinzel, "Auto Accords, Near Deadline Appear Likely," *The Wall Street Journal,* September 14, 1993, p. A6.

[19]J B White and N Templin, "Auto Pact Leaves GM Hard Choice," *The Wall Street Journal,* October 4, 1993, p. A1; J Bennet, "Health Cost Payment in Ford Pact," *The New York Times,* September 18, 1993, p. 33; D Woodruff, "The Ford Deal Won't Throw GM into a Skid," *Business Week,* October 4, 1993, p. 36.

It remained to be seen whether GM President John F Smith, Jr., would be able to persuade UAW President Owen Bieber that GM's cost of labor structure needed fundamental changes. Bieber vowed GM would not be allowed to break the new pattern that guaranteed strong job and income security protection. GM Executive Vice President Harry J Pearce stressed that GM had to have relief in a number of areas and had to establish a new relationship with the UAW.[20]

The Future of US Unions

protection of Unionist mgt rights

As Bill Clinton took office in January 1993, one-sixth of all workers and only one-ninth of workers in the private sector were unionized. Union strike activity in the United States was at a post-World War II low. In the year beginning May 1992, only 1/10,000 of all worker hours were lost due to strikes. Several decades earlier, 10 times that number of work hours would have been lost due to strikes. The number of unfair labor practice charges filed annually with the National Labor Relations Board totaled about 35,000, well below the number filed in the 1960s and 1970s. Ninety percent of the cases were amicably settled.[21]

The Cesar Chavez Workplace Fairness Act, which would bar employers from hiring permanent replacements for striking workers, was organized labor's major issue. The underlying question in this bill was whether union workers should earn only the lower pay and benefits nonunionized workers would accept to replace the strikers. If the bill were enacted, unions would get a big boost in collective bargaining power.

The 1938 Supreme Court decision *NLRB* v. *Mackay Radio* gave employers the right to replace striking workers, but until the 1980s employers rarely exercised this right. Some labor experts thought the pattern would change when Ronald Reagan fired and replaced the PATCO air traffic controllers in 1981, but in reality very little changed.

Congress's General Accounting Office reported that only 4 percent of all strikers were replaced in 1985 and 3 percent in 1989. However, more than 30 percent of all companies involved in strikes in the late 1980s reported they would hire permanent replacements. Companies such as International Paper, Greyhound, Eastern Airlines, and Trans World Airlines all replaced workers. The mere threat of replacement made many union workers willing to accept concessions without striking.[22] Although the actual percentages of replaced workers appear small, each percentage point represented thousands of people.

Unlike the Reagan and Bush administrations, Clinton and his labor secretary, Robert Reich, supported the Chavez bill. Reich asserted, "the

[20]Ibid., p. A6.

[21]"Unions and Strikers: A Huge Nonproblem," *Fortune,* May 31, 1993, p. 175.

[22]L Uchitelle, "Labor Has a Big Job for Its New Friend Clinton," *The New York Times,* June 27, 1993, p. E5.

availability of [a strike] is a crucial counterweight to the economic powers that business owners and managers bring to the bargaining table."[23]

Although the House of Representatives passed the Chavez bill in mid-June 1993, the Senate showed very little interest in supporting it. Business groups like the US Chamber of Commerce and the National Association of Manufacturers argued the bill would "unwisely" tilt the balance of power in the unions' favor. Republican House member Cass Ballenger said the bill "would grant big union bosses powers to paralyze small business and the American economy unseen since Jimmy Hoffa began pushing up daisies under the 5-yard line."[24] As enthusiasm waned in the Senate, the Clinton administration backed away from a Senate showdown, and the bill simply faded away.

In fact, unions faced a rough bargaining year. On the health care front, many unions agreed to limit workers' ability to choose their own doctors. Unions accepted pay increases that often were lower than the 3.2 percent inflation rate. For the first time since 1988, new contracts provided smaller wage increases than the contracts they were replacing. The Bureau of Labor Statistics reported wage boosts in the first quarter of 1993 averaged 2.8 percent.[25]

The federal government offered a new model of management–union cooperation. In August 1993, President Clinton signed into law his bill to "reinvent" the government. An estimated 252,000 federal jobs would be eliminated. Unions acknowledged that while attrition and early retirement would comprise much of the decrease, some workers would be fired.

However, the administration saw new opportunities for workplace cooperation. The administration envisaged the creation of a national partnership council composed of the heads of federal agencies and AFL-CIO federal union representatives. Unions and agencies would work together to decide which facilities to close, how to increase productivity, and how to manage workloads. Unions were highly satisfied with the trade-off between the lost jobs and pay boosts for the most productive workers.[26]

Occupational Safety and Health

Development of Worker Health and Safety Concerns

Throughout most of the nineteenth century, employers rarely concerned themselves about occupational safety and health. During the early days of the Industrial Revolution, accidents were common in many occupations.

---

[23]K G Salwen, "Ban on Replacing Strikers Seen Facing Bleak Future as House Prepares to Vote," *The Wall Street Journal,* June 15, 1993, p. A2.

[24]C Krauss, "House Passes Bill to Ban Replacement of Strikers," *The New York Times,* June 16, 1993, p. A23.

[25]K G Salwen and D Milbank, "Recent Labor Contract Results Portend a Rough Bargaining Year for Unions," *The Wall Street Journal,* June 25, 1993, p. A2.

[26]K G Salwen, "Reinventing the Government," *The Wall Street Journal,* September 8, 1993, p. A2.

Machines had few, if any, protective devices. Local newspapers in mill cities such as Lowell, Massachusetts, reported horrendous accidents on a nearly daily basis. It was quite common for mill workers to be seriously injured when their hair or clothing got caught in machinery. With depressing regularity, Lowell workers fell into the water-driven turbine pits and were swept to their deaths in the Merrimack River.

Miners and construction workers were maimed or died by the thousands in the nineteenth century. Railway brakers had to clamber to the tops of trains to use the hand brakes; rarely did a braker retire with all 10 fingers. Open vats of chemicals were left on factory floors, where employees inhaled the fumes or even fell into the vats. In the days before antibiotics and tetanus shots, a cut finger could be a death warrant. In 1925, the *Monthly Labor Review* reported that one-third to one-half of all electric line workers were killed on the job.[27]

Although accidents were more dramatic than complaints from long-term exposure to chemicals, the effects were no less frequent or incapacitating. Workers called their debilitating ailments "brass chills," "painter's colic" (from lead poisoning), and "grinder's consumption" (lung diseases acquired from inhaling dust).[28] Hatmakers were poisoned by the mercury they used to cure beaver pelts. Even fictional characters like the Mad Hatter in Lewis Carroll's *Alice in Wonderland* exhibited symptoms of real-life hatters' occupational ailment.

Before 1900, companies and unions did very little to make the workplace safer. There were several reasons for their apathy. Calvinist ethics promoted a general sense of fatalism and the expectation that life would be full of tribulation and adversity. Although skilled workers were in chronically short supply in the United States from the colonial era on, large numbers of unskilled immigrant workers were available to take the places of incapacitated employees. Training requirements were minimal, and experience was unnecessary. Companies made the economic decision to replace workers rather than install safety mechanisms to protect them.

Employees and employers ascribed to three doctrines that US courts generally accepted. These doctrines made it difficult for workers to recover damages when they sued their employers. Legal fees were so high that even in the rare cases in which workers won, they actually kept little, if any, of the awards. The doctrines were as follows:

- *Assumption-of-risk doctrine.* This doctrine held that when workers took jobs, they were aware of and accepted the risks involved.
- *Fellow-servant doctrine.* According to this doctrine, the employer was not responsible for an employee's injury if the injury was caused by a co-worker's negligence. For example, if a worker did not sufficiently tighten a

---

[27]*Monthly Labor Review*, May, 1925, p. 172.

[28]W B Catlin, *The Labor Problem in the United States and Great Britain* (New York: Harper & Row, 1935), p. 193.

steam valve and a co-worker was scalded, the employer could not be held responsible.

· *Contributory negligence doctrine.* This doctrine held that if an accident occurred, the employee was at least partially responsible. The courts generally assumed injured workers had demonstrated some degree of negligence.

The concept of workers' compensation was established in Germany in the 1880s, but it was not until 30 years later that Congress passed the United States' first workers' compensation law. Early laws required employers to carry insurance to pay for injuries. If they did not have insurance, they would have to pay damages out of their own pockets. Although employers were obliged to assume responsibility for job-related injuries, they could handle safety issues as they saw best.[29]

Some states passed laws against unsafe working conditions, often after a tragedy such as the Triangle Shirtwaist Company fire in New York City on March 25, 1911. One hundred fifty employees, mostly young women, were killed either directly in the fire or when they jumped from the top floors of the building to the sidewalk below. Bodies were found heaped against emergency doors that were bolted "to safeguard employers from the loss of goods by the departure of workers through fire exits instead of doors."[30]

In the aftermath of the fire, the New York state legislature set up a factory-investigating commission whose findings led New York and other states to enact comprehensive safety legislation. In the absence of federal legislation, safety regulations remained the province of the states. But in many states, laws did not allow inspectors to enter workplaces against the wishes of management. Inspectors were few and poorly trained, and employees were denied access to inspection reports.

Occupational health was more difficult to define and legislate than accidents were. Although it was common knowledge that miners and textile workers suffered respiratory problems, the connection was hard to prove in court. Employers tended to blame alcoholism for symptoms that are now known to have been brought on by industrial diseases.[31]

It was difficult to establish that illness was work related because the effects of exposure to toxic substances often do not appear until years later. Even after symptoms appeared, it was easy to blame other, non-work-related causes for the illness. For example, in 1978 20 workers at an Occidental Chemical Company plant in Lathrop, California, were made sterile by exposure to dibromochloropropane, a pesticide. Although researchers

---

[29]R A Buchholz, *Business Environment and Public Policy: Implications for Management and Strategy Formulation* (Englewood Cliffs, NJ: Prentice-Hall, 1986), pp. 342–43.

[30]M B Schnapper, *American Labor: A Pictorial Social History* (Washington, DC: Public Affairs Press, 1972), p. 358.

[31]A Hamilton, *Exploring the Dangerous Trades* (New York: Harper & Row, 1948), pp. 5–6.

knew the chemical caused sterility in animals, 16 years passed before Dow Chemical Company and Shell Oil, which made the chemical, acknowledged it caused sterility in people.[32]

In the 1950s and 1960s, many American corporations established the position of safety director and stressed educating employees in safe workplace habits. During this period, manufacturing processes introduced new chemical compounds, and the number of illnesses and accidents began to rise. After Ralph Nader and others pointed out serious flaws in industrial safety practices, public concern about the hazardous substances to which workers were exposed mounted.

The Occupational Safety and Health Act

In 1964, Congress held public hearings that criticized the weak enforcement of workplace safety and health. In 1968, President Lyndon Johnson asked Congress to enact comprehensive federal safety and health legislation. Business strongly opposed the measures, charging the federal government was infringing on states' rights.

President Nixon introduced the Occupational Safety and Health Act (OSHA), which Congress passed in 1970. The act gave states the option to administer standards set by the federal government. In 1971, the federal government created the Occupational Safety and Health Administration (OSHA) to administer federal government standards. Twenty-three states immediately created their own OSHA programs, which were "at least as effective" as the federal health and safety regulations.[33] Specifically, OSHA had responsibility to

- Encourage employers and employees to reduce workplace hazards and implement new or improved existing safety and health programs
- Provide for research in occupational safety and health and develop innovative ways to deal with occupational safety and health problems
- Maintain a reporting and recordkeeping system to monitor job-related injuries and illnesses
- Develop mandatory job safety and health standards and enforce them effectively
- Provide for the development, analysis, evaluation, and approval of state occupational safety and health programs[34]

---

[32]V Cahan, "The Overhaul That Could Give OSHA Life under Reagan," *Business Week,* January 19, 1981, p. 88.

[33]"Occupational Safety and Health Administration, *Federal Regulatory Directory,* 6th ed. (Washington, DC: Congressional Quarterly, 1990), p. 380.

[34]*All about OSHA,* US Department of Labor, OSHA 2056, 1982 (revised), p. 2.

OSHA began to develop health and safety standards from existing federal regulations and from standards established by groups such as the American National Standards Institute and the National Fire Protection Association. In its first month of operation, OSHA adopted more than 4,000 health and safety rules, some of which were outdated and irrelevant. Businesses complained bitterly that the penalties for violation were unfair and the cost of compliance was unnecessarily burdensome. Paperwork and documentation requirements were enormous and time consuming.[35]

Between 1974 and 1976, OSHA set stringent health standards for substances linked to cancer and lung disease. OSHA required employers to reduce worker exposure to the lowest possible levels even if there was no evidence that those levels were necessary to prevent significant risk. The operating principle was that no level of a carcinogen was safe.[36]

In 1977, the Carter administration adopted a cost-cutting strategy. Carter eliminated standards advisory committees made up of research, business, labor, and government representatives. These committees had defined and recommended health standards. Nearly 1,000 safety standards were revoked during the first month of fiscal year 1977, and the number of inspections decreased dramatically.

In 1978, the Supreme Court ruled on an OSHA-related case, *Marshall v. Barlow.* The court found that an employer had the right, based on the Fourth Amendment, to refuse to allow an OSHA inspector to enter the premises unless the inspector had a search warrant. In practice, very few businesses demanded warrants, and inspections went on without them.[37]

Fines for OSHA violations were very low. The Interagency Task Force on Workplace Safety and Health reported in 1978 that "an inspection system alone cannot rely on indirect costs, embarrassment, or inconvenience to convince recalcitrant employers to invest in safety and health." The report suggested that fines for violators should run into the thousands of dollars.[38] Yet in 1981, the average fine for a serious violation was still only $800.

Presidential candidate Ronald Reagan promised to abolish OSHA, but settled for appointing Thorne G Auchter as a commissioner dedicated to reducing government involvement in workplace health and safety.

The Reagan and Bush Years

In April 1981, the White House issued new policies. OSHA would have to measure potential worker health risks against the costs to business of meeting required health standards. In effect, OSHA was required to conduct a cost-benefit analysis of workplace safety measures. OSHA was also directed

---

[35]Ibid.
[36]Cahan, "The Overhaul," p. 88.
[37]Ibid.
[38]Ibid., p. 89.

to give business more options for meeting standards. In pragmatic terms, businesses could issue earplugs to workers in a noisy environment instead of having to reduce noise levels.[39]

In 1982, penalties assessed by OSHA fell by 65 percent. OSHA Administrator Thorne Auchter ordered federal investigators not to investigate workplaces in states that had their own OSHA programs. He declared, "This Administration is committed to using federal intervention as the last, not the first, resort in solving problems."[40] Business executives were delighted, noting they could now focus on the big picture instead of "nit-picking."

Workplace fatalities continued to rise throughout the mid-1980s. In 1984, workplace deaths rose to 3,740 from 3,100 a year earlier. Occupational injuries and illnesses climbed to 5.4 million from 4.85 million. Between 1980 and 1985, workplace inspections declined by 40 percent in US factories. Between 1980 and 1986, OSHA issued only three new standards covering toxic materials.[41]

Union officials placed the blame squarely on the administration. Eric Frumin, health director of the Amalgamated Clothing and Textile Workers Union, observed, "OSHA under Reagan is a disaster. They have virtually abandoned the responsibility Congress gave them to set standards and then vigorously enforce them."[42]

In 1986, OSHA changed its laissez-faire attitude. In April, it fined Union Carbide $1.4 million for alleged bookkeeping, safety, and health violations. Several months later, it levied a $2.6 million fine on Occidental Petroleum's meat-packing subsidiary, charging the company had doctored its accident and illness records. Next, it went after General Dynamics for recordkeeping violations and hit Uretek with a $480,000 fine for health and safety infractions. Fines skyrocketed from a total of $14,166 in 1981 to $9 million in 1986. Industry became increasingly nervous about OSHA's activities, wondering if the agency was simply trying to score political points.[43]

As the Reagan administration drew to a close in 1988, none of the stakeholders in the workplace safety issue was satisfied. Companies charged the agency with petty rule making. Labor unions and employee lobbying groups accused OSHA of internal disarray and lax enforcement. They noted the agency had only 1,000 inspectors to cover nearly 5 million employers. Margaret Seminario, the AFL-CIO's health and safety director, charged that

---

[39]S E Teeley, "Reagan Plan Would Slash OSHA Role," *The Boston Globe,* April 12, 1981, p. 12.

[40]"As Regulation Relaxes, Critics Flex Their Muscles," *Business Week,* April 12, 1982, p. 44B.

[41]T Lewin, "Archives of Business," *The New York Times,* March 23, 1986, p. F8.

[42]P Perl, "Corporate Experience Can Be Hazardous to Your Health," *The Washington Post National Weekly Edition,* September 8, 1986, p. 33.

[43]H Bradford, "OSHA Awakens from Its Six-Year Slumber," *Business Week,* August 10, 1987, p. 27.

"when you get behind the headlines and banners, you see thousands of workers being killed every year from occupational injuries and scores of thousands suffering from occupational disease, and OSHA doesn't have a coherent plan on how to deal with those problems."[44] The president's Council of Economic Advisers expressed the administration's philosophy: "Government . . . has no clear advantage over workers, labor unions and employers in using this information to determine appropriate levels of workplace safety or the best way to reduce hazards."[45]

In 1989, the National Safety Council reported on a disturbing trend. Along with rising productivity, the workplace was becoming more dangerous. Permanent work-related disabilities jumped 16 percent between 1986 and 1987, from 60,000 to 70,000. In manufacturing industries, injuries and illnesses climbed nearly 12 percent in that year. Safety experts suspected the increase was much greater, citing industry's propensity to underreport industrial accidents.[46]

In 1989, Secretary of Labor Elizabeth Dole appointed Gerard Scannell as OSHA commissioner. Scannell, the former safety chief at Johnson & Johnson, proposed new rules and guidelines. At J&J, he reduced the number of workdays lost to injuries by 92 percent between 1979 and 1989. Both business and organized labor had praised his efforts.[47]

Scannell's efforts successfully reduced workplace fatalities. Scannell also increased the maximum penalty for willful violation from $10,000 to $70,000. But critics continued to point to OSHA's poor inspection record. In July 1991, there were only 1,290 US OSHA inspectors for 6 million work sites.[48]

Hoping to harness OSHA's new-found energy, Senator Howard Metzenbaum (D-Ohio) introduced a bill to revamp OSHA. He sought criminal penalties of up to five years in prison for employers who willfully caused bodily harm to employees. OSHA's existing rules allowed criminal prosecution only in cases where negligence led to death. The Bush administration vigorously opposed the bill and was able to prevent it from coming to a vote.[49]

On September 3, 1991, the nation's attention once more focused on workplace safety. A catastrophic fire broke out at Imperial Food Products, a Hamlet, North Carolina, poultry-processing plant. A hydraulic hose burst,

---

[44]K B Noble, "The Long Tug-of-War Over What Is Hazardous," *The New York Times,* January 10, 1988, p. E5.

[45]Ibid.

[46]C Ansberry, "Workplace Injuries Proliferate as Concerns Push People to Produce," *The Wall Street Journal,* June 16, 1989, p. A1.

[47]S B Garland, "A New Chief Has OSHA Growling Again," *Business Week,* August 20, 1990, p. 57.

[48]D E Lewis, "Is It Time to Revamp OSHA?," *The Boston Globe,* July 5, 1991, p. 1.

[49]Ibid.

spraying a mist of oil near the plant's chicken fryers. The burners, which heated the cooking oil to 400 degrees, ignited the mist from the hose. Twenty-five workers were killed and 54 injured in the inferno.

Not one door in the plant met fire exit criteria. Several doors were locked or blocked by vehicles parked alongside the plant. The plant was not equipped with automatic sprinklers and had never developed an evacuation plan. Workers charged management routinely locked the doors to prevent workers from stealing chickens. Local officials said the doors were locked to prevent outsiders from selling illicit drugs to employees inside the plant.

Deborah Berkowitz, health chief at the United Food and Commercial Workers Union, accused the state of North Carolina of attracting food processors by advertising the state's loose safety standards. She charged that was the reason Imperial moved to Hamlet from Pennsylvania in 1980. Berkowitz said the fire should "finally show the American public that . . . ten years of deregulation, of turning the Occupational Safety and Health Administration from a policy force into a nice guy agency, ends up in these tragic consequences."[50]

As details of the fire emerged, it was found that federal and state investigators had never visited the factory. In fact, state records showed state inspectors had checked only about half the poultry-processing plants in North Carolina. The injury rate in North Carolina's poultry industry was three times that for all private businesses.[51]

Federal law permitted North Carolina and other states to set up their own regulatory monitoring and inspection programs. Although OSHA monitored the programs, it did nothing to enforce the rules. All 23 states with OSHA agencies ran their own shows. The penalties imposed by state-run OSHAs were considerably smaller than the fines levied by the federal agency. For example, in 1989 North Carolina fined Perdue Farms Inc. $39,000 for exposing workers to repetitive-motion injuries in two plants. OSHA fined Cargill, Inc., in Georgia and Missouri nearly $1 million for similar violations.[52]

When Gerard Scannell left OSHA in January 1992 to return to Johnson & Johnson, a variety of stakeholders applauded his efforts. Harold Coxson, a management-oriented labor lawyer, said Scannell had been "practical, not ideological." Joseph Kinney, head of the National Safe Workplace Institute, initially had been one of Scannell's detractors. Now Kinney commented he would not mind if Scannell stayed on the job for an additional 100 years. Even Deborah Berkowitz, who had been so critical of OSHA's role in the

---

[50]L Tye, "Poultry Plant Blaze Lights Era of Neglect," *The Boston Globe,* September 8, 1991, p. 1.

[51]"North Carolina Faults Poultry Plant Checks," *The Boston Globe,* November 12, 1991, p. 3.

[52]S B Garland, "What a Way to Watch Out for Workers," *Business Week,* September 23, 1991, p. 42.

North Carolina poultry fire, said Scannell injected "a great deal of professionalism" into the agency.[53]

Despite these plaudits, there was still room for much improvement. Safety experts in industry and academia suggested ways to make OSHA more effective. In a thoughtful article in *Technology Review,* Charles Noble, a professor at California State University, pointed out that OSHA had two major functions: standard setting and enforcement. In his view, OSHA did a poor job in both areas.[54]

Standard-setting efforts were very expensive and met strong corporate resistance. Presidents Reagan and Bush gave the White House's Office of Management and Budget (OMB) unprecedented authority to delay or kill proposed OSHA standards. The White House sent lawyers to the Supreme Court to support industry challenges to the economic feasibility of standards on lead and cotton dust levels.

Although standard setting improved under Scannell, he did very little to speed up the standard-setting process. Many safety hazards, such as repetitive-motion injuries and work in confined spaces like sewers and furnaces, were partially regulated at best.[55]

Enforcement also was limited. Between 1982 and 1992, OSHA's funding dropped 10 percent in real dollars while the number of workers covered by the Occupational Safety and Health Act rose by one-third. In 1992, only about 11 percent of employees benefited from regular safety inspections. State agencies were underfunded and were likely to remain so.

Almost all investigations focused on the most dangerous industries, including construction, oil and gas extraction, maritime industries, and some dangerous manufacturing operations. Even with this narrow focus, OSHA inspectors saw fewer than 1 in 10 high-hazard job sites in a given year.

In 1989, OSHA took an important and aggressive step in enforcement when it fined USX $7.3 million for recordkeeping and safety violations. In 1990, Congress boosted most maximum fines, but OSHA officials argued it was more productive to foster corporate safety programs than to levy heavy fines. Officials further argued that OSHA should concentrate on helping employers with research, training, and coordination of safety and health initiatives.[56]

Charles Noble suggests the following reforms:

- OSHA should accelerate standard-setting processes.
- OSHA should develop timetables for rule making and set priorities for that process.

---

[53]A R Karr, "Outgoing Chief Leaves Tranquil OSHA Legacy," *The Wall Street Journal,* January 17, 1992, p. A5.

[54]C Noble, "Keeping OSHA's Feet to The Fire," *Technology Review* (February/March 1992), pp. 43–51.

[55]Ibid.

[56]Ibid., p. 47.

- Where feasible, OSHA should adopt "generic" regulations—across-the-board rules covering related problems. Generic standards could be applied to chemical substances with similar properties or to toxic chemical monitoring and worker education programs.
- The National Institutes for Occupational Safety and Health (NIOSH) should have its responsibilities, status, and funding strengthened. Congress created NIOSH to play a lead role in researching workplace hazards and developing exposure criteria for OSHA, but its recommendations were often ignored.
- Congress should ensure that the OMB could not use political influence to manipulate cost-benefit tests or assumptions about potential dangers.
- Congress should strengthen the Occupational Health and Safety Act's criminal penalties and give government the authority to seek felony charges against employers who willfully exposed workers to bodily injury.[57]

OSHA and the Clinton Administration

In April 1993, President Clinton appointed Joseph Dear, director of Washington State's Labor and Industries Department, to head OSHA. Dear had run Washington's OSHA agency since 1987.[58] He inherited a federal agency badly in need of reform. The agency's compliance staff numbered 1,120, 25 percent below the number of inspectors when Reagan took office. OSHA's computer system was antiquated and unable to target the work sites with the greatest safety risks.

Dear's greatest challenge was political: How would he manage a sweeping overhaul of safety laws proposed by liberal Democrats? The Democrats, under Senator Edward Kennedy's leadership, proposed that employers with 11 or more workers be required to form joint labor-management safety and health committees with elected representatives. The proposal's supporters said the proposal would promote the kind of cooperation between labor and management that the administration wanted. Executives opposed this measure, calling it a "sham for union organizing."[59]

The Clinton-Gore government streamlining plan, released in September 1993, drew fire from both sides of the workplace safety issue. Vice President Gore's task force on workplace safety proposed the Labor Department "let employers self-certify health and safety standards." Margaret Seminario, AFL-CIO safety and health director, was no happier with Clinton's proposal than she had been with the Reagan policies years earlier. She said,

---

[57]Ibid.

[58]"Joseph Dear Selected by President Clinton to Be Head of OSHA," *The Wall Street Journal,* April 2, 1993, p. A4.

[59]D Frost, "Stepping into the Middle of OSHA's Muddle," *Business Week,* August 2, 1993, p. 53.

"This idea was tried under the Reagan administration. It failed because companies lied on their safety reports. Finally the policy was abandoned. It shouldn't be tried again."[60]

Edward Kennedy (D-Mass.), chairperson of the Senate's Labor and Human Resources Committee, was stunned by the self-certification proposal. As author of the proposed labor-management safety councils, he did not support the notion that companies police themselves. Vice President Gore's task force suggested giving employers two options for "certified self-inspection." OSHA would set reporting standards and conduct random audits and inspections to ensure compliance. The first option would be to let companies hire outside parties to conduct safety inspections. Alternatively, companies could train and certify employees to conduct inspections.[61]

None of the proposals were likely to take effect quickly. It would be months before a consensus emerged and a meaningful OSHA overhaul took place.

Video Display Terminals (VDTs): A Workplace Safety Issue

Beginning in 1984, the media began focusing on potential safety hazards associated with video display terminal operation. Most of the 10 million VDT operators were women. Women operators became increasingly worried that their jobs could cause miscarriage, birth defects, or sterility. The concern was precipitated by reports of "clusters" of pregnancy problems among US and Canadian VDT operators.

Tests had established that VDTs sent out tiny amounts of X-ray and microwave radio frequency radiation. However, the emissions were 1/1,000 of the federal safety standard level. Researchers *had* established that VDT operation was accompanied by eye strain and backaches, but these problems could be remedied with proper lighting and office equipment.

Researchers at NIOSH began a major study to discover whether VDTs were to blame for reproductive problems. Preliminary investigations at problem sites had been inconclusive, so a full-scale project got under way.[62]

However, VDT users were unwilling to wait until the study was completed. Pregnant workers demanded and often won transfers to jobs that did not require VDT use. By mid-1984, eight US and Canadian unions won transfer rights, extra unpaid leave, or the right of pregnant VDT workers to wear lead aprons.

---

[60]M Vaillancourt, "OSHA Reform Plan Draws Fire," *The Boston Globe,* September 9, 1993, p. 43.
[61]Ibid.
[62]"Pregnancy and VDT Workers: Pressure Leads to a Quest for Hard Facts," *Business Week,* April 23, 1984, pp. 80–81.

Computer makers lobbied hard against any legislation requiring employers to provide alternative work. An official of the Computer Business and Equipment Manufacturers Association, a trade group, said it was "like protecting them from light bulbs."[63] In reality, neither side had conclusive evidence about reproductive hazards.

A 1988 California study found women who worked extensively on VDTs early in their pregnancies were more likely than other women to miscarry. The Kaiser-Permanente Medical Care Program in Oakland studied 1,583 pregnant women. Study results showed women who used VDTs more than 20 hours a week in early pregnancy had nearly twice the number of miscarriages other office workers did. The authors did not study other factors that might have accounted for the miscarriage rate, such as job-related stress, poor working conditions, or even the possibility that women who had miscarriages were more likely to report having spent long hours at a VDT. One of the researchers acknowledged the study's design would not have identified differences between people who worked 20 hours on a VDT and those who worked 40 hours. Nor would the study have made any distinction between workers in an office with one VDT and those in computer rooms with hundreds of terminals.[64]

In fact, scientists and safety experts knew relatively little about the potential dangers of electromagnetic emissions and VDT radiation. By 1988, more than 15 million VDTs were in use nationwide. Despite widespread concern, very few independent studies were under way. IBM was the only manufacturer helping to pay for independent research on VDT radiation.

A *Fortune* magazine article recommended that in light of all the uncertainty, responsible companies should use terminals designed to reduce emissions. The article pointed out these terminals were not being marketed in the United States. In Sweden, where IBM sold reduced-emission terminals, the cost of each terminal was 10 to 15 percent more than that of a comparable European model.[65]

A NIOSH study released in 1991 found pregnant women who worked all day at VDTs ran no greater risk of miscarriage than did women in similar jobs without terminals. Between 1983 and 1986, government researchers studied 730 telephone operators who had at least one pregnancy in that period. One group of women worked at computer terminals, while the other group worked on machines that had small neon tubes. The terminals emitted a considerably higher level of electromagnetic radiation than the neon

[63]J S Lublin, "Fearing Radiation, Pregnant Women Win Transfers from Work on Video Terminals," *The Wall Street Journal,* April 6, 1984, p. B1.

[64]T Lewin, "Pregnant Women Increasingly Fearful of VDT's," *The New York Times,* July 10, 1988, p. 19.

[65]D Kirkpatrick, "How Safe Are Video Terminals?," *Fortune,* August 29, 1988, pp. 66–69.

tubes did. The study found the proportions of live births, stillbirths, and miscarriages were similar for both groups. The rate of miscarriages for terminal users was 14.8 percent and for nonusers 15.9 percent.[66]

A subsequent NIOSH study of 2,430 women found no difference in risk between women who sat in front of a VDT for more than 25 hours a week and those in similar jobs who did not use VDTs. A senior epidemiologist for NIOSH concluded this and previous studies answered some major questions related to VDT use and incidence of miscarriage.[67]

Although the question of reproductive hazards associated with VDT use seemed to have been resolved by the early 1990s, other problems associated with their use proliferated. Faulty keyboard design was responsible for a spate of repetitive-stress injuries (RSIs). More and more workers began to flood the courts with damage claims.

RSIs plagued a number of industries in which people repeated the same small motions. In the meat-packing industry, for example, 800 out of 10,000 full-time employees reported RSIs. The Newspaper Guild found 4.5 percent of its membership—over 1,500 people—cited repetitive-stress injuries. About 63 percent of operators polled by Communications Workers of America suffered wrist and hand pain. Twenty percent had been diagnosed with tendinitis or carpal tunnel syndrome (a hand and wrist nerve disorder).[68]

Cases of RSIs in factories and offices doubled between 1985 and 1992. In 1990, there were 185,000 cases of these injuries. By 1993, such injuries accounted for nearly 60 percent of all workplace illnesses.

Most lawsuits were filed by reporters, data processors, and telephone operators against manufacturers such as AT&T and Unisys. Under workers' compensation laws, workers were barred from suing their own companies. Aetna Life & Casualty estimated workers' compensation claims and other expenses from these injuries could cost employers $20 billion a year.[69]

Management Strategy for Workplace Safety Issues

Managers rarely learn in school how to implement health and safety programs, and many have no experience in assessing the costs and benefits of workplace safety. As with any social issue plan, introducing occupational safety and health measures is likely to meet organizational resistance. Health and safety are emotional issues because accidents and illness bring intense

[66]W K Stevens, "Major U.S. Study Finds No Miscarriage Risk from Video Terminals," *The New York Times,* March 14, 1991, p. A22.

[67]P H Lewis, "Trying to Assess the Potential Hazards of Video Terminals," *The New York Times,* April 21, 1991, p. F9.

[68]B Goldoftas, "Hands That Hurt," *Technology Review* (January 1991), pp. 43–50.

[69]M Galen, "Repetitive Stress: The Pain Has Just Begun," *Business Week,* July 13, 1992, pp. 142–44.

personal suffering and financial loss to victims and their families. They also add to worker compensation costs, disrupt productivity, increase downtime, and add to hiring and training costs. Further, unfavorable press can follow accidents and seriously impair a firm's image in a community or throughout the country.[70]

The US government, the Minerva Education Institute, and US corporations jointly sponsor a variety of educational activities to encourage business schools to educate prospective managers about occupational health and safety. The institute makes specific recommendations about how companies can use their control systems to monitor progress and assess costs of worker safety programs. It recommends corporate-level managers ask themselves the following series of questions as they plan, organize, and control for workplace safety.

Planning. How do other companies develop a corporate philosophy regarding safety and health matters? How do these philosophies incorporate public affairs, media interaction, regulations, and litigation?

How do managers in high-hazard industries comply with occupational and environmental safety and health standards? What actions do they take to ensure they have relatively few adjustments to make when these standards and other requirements become effective?

How do managers in high-hazard industries set occupational health and safety goals, and to what extent is their staff involved in the goals' exercise? How does the company measure goals?

What constitutes a reasonable budget for activities within an organization of a specified size, mission, hazard category, and geographic spread of operations?

Organizing. Within the organization, where is the most effective place to locate the safety and health function? Should it be located under operations, personnel, employee relations, or some other department?

To what extent do joint labor-management safety and health committees within an industry influence management decisions about occupational safety and health matters? Can such committees be structured for greater effectiveness? If so, how?

Controlling. Managers should examine the effects of variations in economic conditions on issues relevant to workers' health and safety. For example, why and how does a recession affect the injury and illness experiences of workers within specific industries? How can such effects be minimized?

---

[70]*Research in Occupational Safety and Health for Business Schools: A Resource Guide* (Cincinnati: Minerva Education Institute, 1988), pp. 1–20.

Managers should examine the costs of compliance with provisions of the Occupational Safety and Health Act in (1) a low-risk industry, (2) a moderate-risk industry, and (3) a high-risk industry. They should also assess the impact of the Americans with Disabilities Act.

Managers should investigate both budgetary and nonbudgetary methods of control as they relate to the safety and health function within an organization. They should ask: What are the strengths and limitations of each method? Should both methods be used? If so, in what balance?

Managers should try to calculate dollar losses due to safety and health incidents. They should assess the benefit mechanisms of setting up special accounts for this purpose and ask how the accounts would be handled in internal financial and managerial accounting reports. Top managers must devise their plan to effectively communicate the benefits to middle managers and employees and assess costs to the company.

Summary

The unionization movement in the United States was disorganized and weak until the 1930s. In a country of high social and physical mobility and abundant land, workers had very little incentive to organize. The early unions emphasized social goals rather than economic aims. This approach divided rather than united America's diverse ethnic, social, and religious groups. Finally, in the 1930s, New Deal legislation provided protection for the AFL and CIO and fostered the aims of organized labor. As the US economy has concentrated on service and high-technology industries, labor unions have lost much of their clout and effectiveness. Increasingly, union leaders are pressing for job security rather than economic gains.

Workplace safety and health has never been a corporate priority in the United States. Although some companies have voluntarily incorporated occupational safety and health programs, most companies have responded to legislation and the regulations of the Occupational Safety and Health Administration. OSHA activities have been both praised and criticized.

Stakeholders hotly debate the agency's effectiveness in reducing accidents and illness in the workplace. Most observers agree reporting procedures and recordkeeping have improved workers' compensation, but much more progress is needed. John Mendeloff, who served on the National Academy of Sciences panel on occupational safety and health statistics, concluded, "OSHA policies have at best a small effect—up to 10%—on the rate of injuries and fatalities."[71]

---

[71]J Mendeloff, "The Hazards of Rating Workplace Safety," *The Wall Street Journal,* February 11, 1988, p. 30.

Questions

1. Why did the union movement have less impact in the United States than in Europe?
2. How do US unions compare in structure and goals with Japanese unions? (To answer this question, you should research the unique relationship between Japanese unions and companies.)
3. What predictions can you make about how unions will do in the remainder of the 1990s? What data led you to these conclusions?

Projects

1. In 1988 OSHA, the meat-packing industry, and its unions disagreed vehemently about safety and working conditions in plants. Research this issue, and write a three-page paper about it. Make recommendations to management in a one-page executive memo.
2. OSHA has been a highly controversial agency. Interview the safety director of a local company to determine advances in the measurement of occupational health and worker safety and the extent to which OSHA has contributed to them.

BETA CASE 13
UNIONS AND WORKPLACE SAFETY

Donald Drees, Beta's president and COO, could not believe it: The clerical and office workers were threatening to unionize. The Service Employees Union of America was passing out literature describing the hazards of video display terminals (VDTs). Beta had succeeded in keeping labor union activity to a minimum by providing competitive wages, safe working conditions, and generous benefits. All the company's hard work could be ruined if unionization occurred.

Daphne Malone, Drees's assistant, came back from lunch with a manila envelope full of union material. "May I see that propaganda?" Drees asked. Malone silently handed him the packet. Drees began to read:

Danger from Your VDT

Did you know that nearly 40 million workers, 15 million of whom are women, receive and process information on video display terminals? VDTs cause miscarriages. The Northern California Kaiser-Permanente Medical Care program found twice as many miscarriages among those women who remembered spending long hours in front of screens while pregnant than among those who did not. Many occupational health and technology experts warn that babies of women who work in front of VDTs may be harmed by very-low-frequency, pulsed, nonionizing electromagnetic radiation.

Even if you are not planning to have a baby, do you know that you risk severe hand and wrist damage from the repetitive motions you must use in your work?

Drees read a little further, then threw the paper on his desk. "Daphne," he snapped, "get me Bob Mobley!" Drees fidgeted with a paper clip until Mobley, the corporate counsel, answered. "Hello, Bob, we've got trouble," Drees began. "The union's trying to organize the women who work on the VDTs. The union is saying pregnant women are going to have miscarriages unless they wear lead aprons or are transferred to some other noncomputer work. They're also predicting all sorts of vision and hand problems for VDT workers. Do we know whether the union is telling the truth? Are we liable if an employee has a miscarriage and sues? What do you think the chances are that the union will be successful? We've got to tell Brian about this issue so we can plan our strategy."

PART

IV | CONSUMER WELFARE

Part IV covers consumer information and product safety. Chapter 14 discusses the evolution of the consumer movement, issues of information dissemination, and product promotion. Chapter 15 explores product safety, total quality management, and the role of the Consumer Product Safety Commission (CPSC).

To survive, businesses must build trusting relationships with consumers. Customer retention, in fact, is a major concern in the 1990s. A concern for consumer welfare is both a societal obligation and a necessity for business success. Customer retention begins before the sale is made through providing appropriate information about the firm's products or services.

Consumers need good information to make sound buying decisions. The better the quality of information, the better able the consumer is to choose among buying options and the more likely the consumer is to be happy with his or her choice.

If a product is unsafe or its advertising misleading, all the stakeholders involved with that product suffer. We define *consumer welfare* as the provision of products and services of appropriate quality that are presented to prospective buyers in an honest and comprehensive manner to ensure to a reasonable degree the safety, well-being, and satisfaction of those customers. Consumer welfare and the welfare of the firm are inextricably linked.

CHAPTER

14

CONSUMERS AND INFORMATION

- Consumer movement
- class discussion

CASE   *The High Cost of Prescription Drugs*

One ongoing news story in 1993 was the high prices charged for prescription drugs. Although the media first raised the issue during the Bush administration, President Clinton's health care policy development generated new stakeholder concerns.

Consumers who complained most loudly about high prices were, for the most part, people whose purchases were not covered by insurance. Consumers who were insured largely ignored the price of drugs, because they paid only a small flat fee out of pocket.

A 1990 Tufts University study reported that drug companies claimed it cost an average of $231 million to bring a drug to market. One-half of the money consisted of development costs; the other half was the opportunity cost, or the return the company could have expected had it invested the money instead of developing the drug.[1]

A 1992 US General Accounting Office study of 29 widely used prescription drugs found most prices doubled or even quadrupled between 1985 and 1991. For example, Parke-Davis, a division of Warner Lambert Company, made huge profits on its antiseizure drug Dilantin. In the six-year period covered by the study, the price for 1,000 100-milligram Dilantin capsules rose by 349 percent. Nitrostat, a heart drug, rose by 247 percent. Prices for almost all 29 drugs exceeded the consumer price index increase of 26 percent.[2]

Stakeholders quickly responded to this study. Ron Pollack, director of the advocacy group Families USA Foundation, said, "Companies making the top 20 prescription drugs are experiencing skyrocketing profits and they are making those profits the new-fashioned way—by price gouging."[3]

---

[1]E Rosenthal, "Drug Companies' Profits Finance More Promotion Than Research," *The New York Times,* February 21, 1993, p. A1.

[2]E Tanouye, "GAO Study of Prescription Drugs Finds 1985–91 Prices Doubled, or Quadrupled," *The Wall Street Journal,* August 26, 1992, p. B2.

[3]R A Knox, "Drug Firms Gouge Public, Report Says," *The Boston Globe,* September 11, 1992, p. 1.

Some members of Congress hopped on the legislative bandwagon. Senator David Pryor, the Democrat who headed the Senate special committee on aging, and Senator William Cohen, the ranking Republican, called for legislation to remove pharmaceutical companies' tax breaks if their profits outpaced the general inflation rate.

The Pharmaceutical Manufacturers Association defended the price rises, noting price increases were moderating. Senator Pryor retorted that drug prices were still rising at four times the rate of inflation.

Spokespersons for the pharmaceutical companies were quick to justify the price increases, claiming that R&D spending warranted the hikes. Wyeth-Ayerst's representative reported that its estrogen replacement product, Premarin, cost the consumer 35 cents per day, or $127 a year. "For what it does," she said, "that's not really expensive."[4]

Drug companies, concerned about growing consumer anger and activism, promised to hold price increases below the 1992 inflation rate. They assured the Clinton administration that government price controls were unnecessary because the industry was policing itself. However, Senators Pryor and Cohen released a report in February 1993 showing the major drug companies had broken their promise. In 1992, wholesale price increases for all prescription medicines rose more than 6 percent—twice the inflation rate.

Responding quickly, the major drug companies faulted the data because they did not include rebates to Medicaid, discounts, and other price reductions. The companies were particularly frustrated by their inability to present a formal and unified pricing structure to the government. Their lawyers warned them any discussion about pricing would violate federal antitrust laws.[5]

Later in February 1993, the Office of Technology Assessment, a bipartisan congressional agency, issued its own report, concluding, "the market for prescription drugs is broken."[6] The report estimated the aftertax cost of bringing a drug to market at $194 million, well below the industry's figure of between $231 million and $259 million. The researchers also found drug companies spent an average of 22.5 percent of total sales on advertising and promotion, which was considerably more than they spent on research.[7] Other critics argued that much of drug research was aimed not at developing new cures and treatments for diseases but at developing drugs to compete with preparations already on the market.

President Clinton jumped into the fray. He blasted the prices of prescription drugs as "shocking" and especially blamed vaccine makers for pursuing profits at the expense of children's health. His attack came one day after Hillary Rodham Clinton chided drug companies for making 1,000 percent profits on childhood vaccines over the past decade.

Drug companies retorted that the 17-year patents on their drugs forced them to recoup their investments quickly. They asserted that since most drugs take 12 years to develop and get FDA approval, they had only five years in which to make a profit.

---

[4]Ibid.

[5]E Tanouye, "Senate Study of Drug Prices Could Prove a Bitter Pill for Pharmaceutical Makers," *The Wall Street Journal,* February 3, 1993, p. B1.

[6]P J Hilts, "U.S. Study of Drug Makers Criticizes 'Excess Profits,' " *The New York Times,* February 26, 1993, p. D1.

[7]Ibid.

Often, after a patent expires, generic-drug makers enter the market with their own versions, which sell at considerably lower prices.

The drug companies also argued that they plowed back profits into new drugs. Wyeth-Ayerst insisted that the profit it made on Premarin and Inderal (a heart medication) helped finance research for the implantable contraceptive Norplant.[8]

On March 2 1993, the Pharmaceutical Manufacturers Association addressed a full-page ad in *The Wall Street Journal* to "The American People From the People Who Work In Pharmaceutical Companies." The advertisement said there were facts every American should have:

- Increases in the price of prescription drugs are not a major cause of America's spiraling health care expenditures. Prescription drugs represent less than 7 percent of the nation's total health care bill each year [and] while health care costs have grown to 14 percent of GNP, pharmaceuticals have remained consistently below one percent of GNP for decades.
- Contrary to recent reports from a Senate Committee, pharmaceutical companies who voluntarily pledged to limit price increases to the consumer price index have been true to their pledge.
- Although Americans pay more for some drugs than the citizens of other countries, in fact Americans work significantly fewer hours to pay their average annual bill for pharmaceuticals than do citizens of many other industrial nations. Americans work 14.4 hours to pay for their average annual supply compared to 22.5 hours for Germans, 22.1 hours for Japanese, and 16 hours for Canadians.
- While prescription drugs are often blamed for rising health care costs, in fact they are one of the most dramatic ways to reduce costs. They eliminate the need for surgery, shorten hospital stays, reduce nursing home admissions, and keep people productive.[9]

This barrage of claims and counterclaims hardly mentioned a most important group of stakeholders. Physicians were the prime targets of drug companies' promotional efforts. The nation's half-million physicians, not users of prescription drugs, determine which drugs enjoy good sales.

Because most prescription drugs have competition, their makers must spend heavily on advertising and promotion. Drug companies send armies of "detailers" with their sample bags to visit individual physicians. Nationwide, drug companies employ 30,000 detailers, one for every 18 physicians. They inundate doctors with information about drug efficacy, but rarely mention price. Their goal is to get physicians to prescribe their particular brands of drugs.

In the past, drug companies offered doctors lavish gifts and other incentives to use their products. Although the FDA and medical associations imposed a variety of restrictions on these practices, they have not closed all the loopholes.

The industry has found ways to promote its products despite new restrictions. Some drug companies hire prominent doctors as "consultants" who tout the drugs at medical conventions and in hospitals. Drug companies also sponsor newsletters or supplements in peer-reviewed journals.

---

[8]"Ouch," *Time,* March 8, 1993, pp. 53–55.
[9]*The Wall Street Journal,* March 2, 1993, p. B5.

In some cases, the companies teach doctors how to administer the medications. When Wyeth-Ayerst began marketing Norplant, it trained doctors in the technique of inserting the device. A few drug companies have become major charitable donors to hospitals. Marion Merrell Dow, for example, gave an undisclosed amount of money to cardiovascular research at a Cincinnati hospital and called its gesture "strategic philanthropy."

In an effort to hold prices up and keep consumers from switching to cheaper generic drugs, some companies even began advertising to the general public. Marion Merrell Dow marketed a hypertension and angina medication called Cardizem. With the patent due to expire on one form of the drug in 1994, Marion Merrell Dow ran television advertisements in which a pharmacist urges a patient to ask his doctor about switching to Cardizem CD. The ad implied the patient would save money by making the switch. However, the real savings went to Marion Merrell Dow, because Cardizem CD's patent still had some time before it expired—and the patient would continue using Marion Merrell Dow's product instead of a cheaper generic equivalent.

The controversy over drug costs is far from over. It will continue to rage until legislation is passed or health care policy dictates profit levels. Regulation of drug pricing will bring its own problems and opportunities, many of which cannot be anticipated. Stakeholders in an unregulated market will continue to argue over appropriate profit levels and policy for bringing new drugs to market at affordable prices.

Questions and Exercises

1. What public policy issues surround drug pricing? Should Congress or some other body regulate prices, or should drug companies be left alone to set prices as they wish?

2. As a class, debate the issue of drug pricing. One team takes the part of the drug manufacturers. A second team takes the part of an AIDS patient whose insurance has expired and who needs AZT and other expensive drugs. A third team becomes a member of Mrs. Clinton's health care policymaking group. A fourth team assumes the role of a congressional legislative committee on health care issues.

3. Was Marion Merrell Dow's advertising of Cardizem to consumers a clever marketing ploy or an effort to deceive consumers? Is such an advertising campaign likely to affect the relationship between the physician and the drug company? Why or why not?

Consumerism

As we discussed in Chapter 8, the term *consumerism* was not widely used until the 1960s, although consumers' organizations flourished from the nineteenth century onward. The early period of the consumer movement is covered in the discussion of the development of American regulatory legislation on pages 219–224.

Regulation of marketing and its role in the government process increased in the 1920s. The 1920s ushered in the era of modern marketing. Consumers were inundated with billboard, magazine, and newspaper advertising. Radio, the new medium, also promoted new and exciting products. Automobiles, refrigerators, vacuum cleaners, and phonographs sold briskly, but consumers had to purchase them with very little real information. Whatever information was available came from manufacturers and retailers, both marketer-dominated sources.

Concerned about the objectivity of these sources, some consumers began organizing groups to press for scientific product testing and uniform product standards. In 1927, Stuart Chase and F J Schlink wrote a book titled *Your Money's Worth* in which they strongly criticized companies' high-pressure sales tactics and suggested that consumers sponsor organizations to conduct scientific product testing. In 1929, Consumers' Research, Inc., began scientific testing of new products in the laboratory. Around the same time, a few major department stores and trade associations also formed testing laboratories.

The Great Depression heightened consumer awareness of price and value. People became more determined to get the best and safest buys for their money. The New Deal under Franklin D Roosevelt responded to consumer pressure. Legislators reinforced the Pure Food and Drug Act and extended the powers of the Food and Drug Administration to ensure that the food and drug industries met consumer demands.

By the late 1930s, the business community had become very wary of the growing power of consumer groups. The Advertising Research Foundation, a trade association, commissioned George Gallup to conduct a survey assessing the impact of the consumer movement. In 1940, Gallup reported the movement had generated substantial support, particularly among more educated and upper-income consumers. Gallup concluded the consumer movement would be likely to grow because of its strength among influential groups.[10]

During the 1940s, the consumer movement was quiet as people focused on the war effort. The movement again flourished in the 1950s and blossomed fully in the 1960s. President John F Kennedy's Consumer Message to Congress in March 1962 outlined needed reforms in existing programs

---

[10]R O Herrman, "The Consumer Movement in Historical Perspective," in D A Aaker and G S Day, eds., *Consumerism: Search for the Consumer Interest,* 2nd ed. (New York: The Free Press, 1974), pp. 10–18.

and suggested new initiatives in product safety, particularly in food and drugs. His Consumer Bill of Rights had four major components:

1. *The right to safety.* The consumer has the right to be protected from dangerous products and from the thoughtless actions of other consumers.
2. *The right to be informed.* The consumer has the right to easily available, accurate information to use in making buying decisions.
3. *The right to choose.* The consumer has the right to select among products from competing firms.
4. *The right to be heard.* The consumer has the right of access to some person or some body that will respond to legitimate complaints about abuses in the marketplace and about products that do not meet expectations.

In the late spring and summer of 1965, the government held hearings on tire and auto safety. Manufacturers argued that drivers, not they, were responsible for auto safety. A few months later, Ralph Nader came out with his book *Unsafe at Any Speed,* which presented evidence that faulty engineering, construction, and design were to blame for many auto accidents. General Motors (GM) tried to undermine Nader's credibility, even hiring private detectives to stage a seduction scene to bring Nader's integrity into question. When GM's tactics became public, the backlash was so great that Congress had enough consumer support to pass safety legislation easily.

Between the 1960s and 1980s, numerous incidents heightened public awareness about product safety. As television became a fixture in nearly every home, people heard about product problems on TV news programs as soon as they occurred. While there was enormous publicity about unsafe or harmful products, the agencies set up to protect consumers paid relatively little attention to the quality of information marketers provided to consumers.

The Reagan administration was a low point for consumerism. Business organizations such as the Business Roundtable and the US Chamber of Commerce aggressively pursued the business agenda. Consumer groups seemed to have run out of steam.

But as the Bush administration took office in January 1989, consumerism was infused with new life. Suddenly Ralph Nader and consumer groups were back in the headlines with new initiatives and new programs. Exhibit 14–1 shows the broad range of public-interest and consumer groups under Nader's umbrella organization. The US Public Interest Research Group (PIRG) is perhaps one of the most interesting. It is the national organization for state PIRGs organized on college campuses. The state PIRGs are lobbying groups that provide a training ground for young people interested in environmental and consumer rights issues. In some states, they have had a considerable impact on legislation and obtained the respect of local

EXHIBIT 14–1

Consumer groups

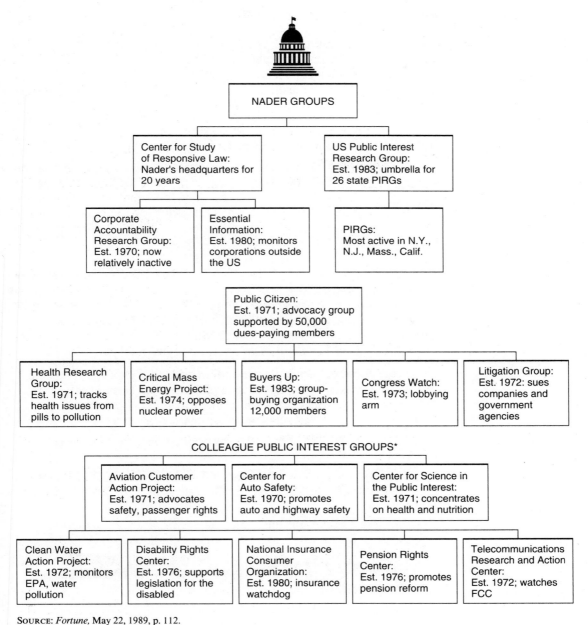

NADER GROUPS

Center for Study of Responsive Law: Nader's headquarters for 20 years

US Public Interest Research Group: Est. 1983; umbrella for 26 state PIRGs

Corporate Accountability Research Group: Est. 1970; now relatively inactive

Essential Information: Est. 1980; monitors corporations outside the US

PIRGs: Most active in N.Y., N.J., Mass., Calif.

Public Citizen: Est. 1971; advocacy group supported by 50,000 dues-paying members

Health Research Group: Est. 1971; tracks health issues from pills to pollution

Critical Mass Energy Project: Est. 1974; opposes nuclear power

Buyers Up: Est. 1983; group-buying organization 12,000 members

Congress Watch: Est. 1973; lobbying arm

Litigation Group: Est. 1972: sues companies and government agencies

COLLEAGUE PUBLIC INTEREST GROUPS*

Aviation Customer Action Project: Est. 1971; advocates safety, passenger rights

Center for Auto Safety: Est. 1970; promotes auto and highway safety

Center for Science in the Public Interest: Est. 1971; concentrates on health and nutrition

Clean Water Action Project: Est. 1972; monitors EPA, water pollution

Disability Rights Center: Est. 1976; supports legislation for the disabled

National Insurance Consumer Organization: Est. 1980; insurance watchdog

Pension Rights Center: Est. 1976; promotes pension reform

Telecommunications Research and Action Center: Est. 1972; watches FCC

SOURCE: *Fortune,* May 22, 1989, p. 112.

politicians. Consumer safety and consumer rights continue to be critical issues in the 1990s.

Regulation and Consumer Protection	In this section, we discuss the two major regulatory agencies that deal with consumer information and safety: the Federal Trade Commission (FTC) and the Food and Drug Administration (FDA). Chapter 15 covers the responsibilities of the Consumer Product Safety Commission, the independent consumer watchdog agency established in 1972.

The Federal Trade Commission (FTC)

The FTC is an independent agency headed by five commissioners nominated by the president of the United States and confirmed by the Senate. The commissioners serve seven-year terms. The president also chooses the FTC's chairperson. To avoid partisan politics, no more than three commissioners can be from the same political party. Exhibit 14–2 shows the organization of the FTC in January 1993.

Responsibilities of the FTC.   The FTC is responsible for issues relating to competition, consumer information, and consumer protection not covered by the Consumer Product Safety Commission. It deals especially with advertising that makes false or deceptive claims to consumers. Following is a list of consumer-related duties of the FTC. Much of it comes from the 6th edition of the *Federal Regulatory Directory,* published in 1990.[11] The FTC

- Protects the public from false and deceptive advertising. In the late 1980s, cases involved advertising of food, drugs, cosmetics, therapeutic devices, art, jewelry, and travel.
- Requires accurate labels on fur and textile products.
- Regulates the packaging and labeling of consumer products to prevent deception.
- Informs consumers and industry about major FTC decisions, programs, statutes, and rules defining the legality of certain business practices.
- Prohibits credit discrimination on the basis of sex, race, marital status, national origin, age, or receipt of public assistance.
- Requires sellers to give consumers notice of their three-day cancellation rights for sales made away from the seller's place of business, such as door-to-door sales.

---

[11]"Federal Trade Commission," *Federal Regulatory Directory,* 6th ed. (Washington, DC: Congressional Quarterly, 1990), pp. 262–85.

EXHIBIT 14–2

Organization of the FTC, January 1993

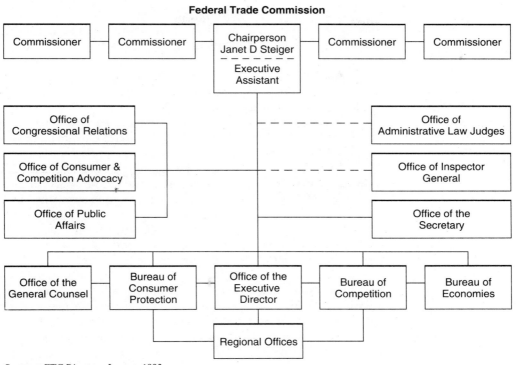

Federal Trade Commission

SOURCE: *FTC Directory*, January 1993

· Requires nondepository creditors, including retailers and finance companies, to give borrowers accurate and complete information about the true cost of credit.

· Prohibits the sending of unordered merchandise to consumers and then charging for it.

· Requires that consumers ordering merchandise through the mail be informed if shipment cannot be made by the promised date (or within 30 days). Customers must then be given the opportunity to agree to a new shipping date or to cancel the order and receive a full refund.

As noted above, the pre-World War II antimonopoly activities of the FTC are covered in Chapter 8. In this chapter, we focus on the agency's consumer-related functions.

The FTC was inactive during the World War II years, but in the late 1940s it began to investigate consumer complaints of deceptive advertising.

The courts supported the FTC's activities in this area, and deceptive advertising quickly became one of the agency's main targets.

The FTC's responsibilities grew after Congress passed the Wool Products Labeling Act, the Fur Products Labeling Act, the Textile Fiber Products Identification Act, and the Flammable Fabrics Act in the 1940s. In the 1970s, responsibility for the Flammable Fabrics Act was shifted to the Consumer Product Safety Commission.

In the 1950s and 1960s, the FTC's major task was warning the public about the hazards of smoking. In 1964, the FTC tried to enforce a rule that would have required cigarette packages and advertising to carry a health hazard warning. Successful lobbying by the tobacco industry resulted in weakened legislation called the Federal Cigarette Labeling and Advertising Act (1965). However, industry pressure did not prevail for long.

In 1969, the Public Health Cigarette Smoking Act prohibited cigarette advertising on radio and television and mandated stronger health warnings on cigarette packages. Successive laws continued to strengthen and expand antitobacco legislation. In 1986, the Smokeless Tobacco Act added chewing tobacco and snuff to the list of products banned from television and radio advertising. Antitobacco lobbying groups continue to succeed in fostering regulation and restriction of tobacco use.

FTC Leadership.   Richard Nixon's administration rejuvenated the FTC's activities with the 1969 appointment of Caspar Weinberger as chairperson. Under Weinberger and his successor, Miles Kirkpatrick, the FTC hired activist lawyers, updated rules, and placed greater emphasis on consumer affairs. During this period, the FTC's activities antagonized many of the industries it scrutinized. Some businesspeople charged the FTC was pandering to consumers at business's expense.

President Jimmy Carter's appointee, consumer advocate Michael Pertschuck, continued to press for consumer protection. An angry House of Representatives tried to stall industrywide rulemaking in 1977. The House attached a requirement to the FTC's authorization bill directing the FTC to submit proposed trade regulation rules to Congress for approval before they took effect.

The Senate and President Carter objected, calling a legislative veto unconstitutional because it encroached on the executive branch's authority. A stalemate between the executive branch, the Senate, and the House held up funding for the FTC. Finally, in 1980, a compromise agreement authorized FTC funds, but also allowed a two-house veto of the commission's rules. The 1980 bill also restricted FTC rulemaking authority over commercial advertising to cover deceptive (but not unfair) practices. The bill forbade the FTC to go forward with studies of the insurance industry and children's advertising.

The House and Senate skirmishes were not over. They continued until 1989, when the Senate passed a bill to reauthorize the FTC. This bill also imposed curbs requiring the FTC to notify Congress before it gave testimony or made comments before any other federal or state body.

Throughout the 1980s, the FTC's budget was whittled down and personnel was cut from 1,800 under Pertschuck to fewer than 900 under his successors James Miller III and Daniel Oliver.

President Bush appointed Janet Steiger, who at the time seemed inclined to make the commission more active, particularly in the area of merger and antitrust. Steiger vowed to look hard at the advertising and marketing of tobacco products, the alcohol industry, and food advertising and labeling. Her term continues until September 1995.

The Concept of Materiality in FTC Rulings on Advertising.   The issue of *materiality* is key to FTC involvement in a claim. The FTC is empowered to rule on advertisements only if they are both deceptive and material. If a company's claim is not important to the buyer (that is, material), the FTC has no power to take action regardless of how far the ad stretches the truth.

Section 5(b) of the Federal Trade Commission Act of 1914 incorporated the concept of materiality into the FTC's standard of deceptive advertising. Under the US system, regulatory agency rulings are tested and refined by the judicial system. Some rulings eventually make their way to the Supreme Court, which decides their constitutionality.

In FTC rulings tested in the 1930s, the courts ruled that purchasers were entitled to receive what they intended to buy. The FTC's materiality test rested solely on whether the deceptive claim was likely to induce purchase. The FTC was charged with protecting the public interest by stopping unfair trade practices before the public was injured.

In 1938, Congress amended the FTC Act to include a definition of false advertisement that made a direct reference to materiality:

> The term "false advertisement" means an advertisement, other than labeling, which is misleading in a material respect; and in determining whether any advertisement is misleading, there shall be taken into account (among other things) not only representations made or suggested by word, design, device, sound, or any combination thereof, but also the extent to which the advertisement fails to reveal facts material in light of such representations or material with respect to consequences which may result from the use of the commodity to which the advertisement relates . . .[12]

This clause clarified any potential conflicts between the duties of the FTC and those of the Food, Drug, and Cosmetic Act, now the FDA. It focuses the FTC on what advertisers say about the product or service rather than on the attributes of the product or service itself. It also recognizes that omitting facts, like making false statements, is deceptive.

---

[12]Wheeler-Lea Act, 1938, Pub. L. No. 447, 52 Stat. 111.

In 1964, the FTC expanded the range of conditions under which omissions of information were considered material and that justified the FTC's action ordering a company to make an affirmative disclosure:

- Where the seller has created in consumers' minds a false impression of the quality or merits of a product.
- Where undisclosed facts are made material by virtue of affirmative claims by the seller.
- Where the seller has made no affirmative claims about country of origin, but consumers believe and prefer that the product be from a country other than its actual origin.
- Where the seller has made no affirmative claim about safety, but the product is hazardous and the hazards are not disclosed.

The Supreme Court heard a number of cases testing these conditions. Through its decisions, the court granted greater regulatory latitude to the FTC in determining materiality, allowing the commission to presume materiality under any reasonable circumstances.

The judicial finding concerning an Anacin ad illustrates this precedent. The ad falsely implied (but did not explicitly state) that Anacin contained a "secret" ingredient other than aspirin. In 1981, an administrative law judge decided that a significant difference in price between Anacin and plain aspirin constituted materiality. If consumers were willing to pay more, the judge reasoned, they must have believed there was a difference in the product's effect, and this difference was important enough to induce them to pay the higher price.

By the early 1980s, the FTC's power to infer materiality was so broad that most advertisers could not effectively defend an argument claiming immateriality. When James Miller III became the FTC chairperson, he asked Congress to amend the FTC Act to more closely define "deceptive acts or practices." In his testimony, he said, "I believe that we should allocate our resources only to cases in which consumers have been hurt . . ." In effect, if that standard prevailed, it would return FTC powers to their 1938 parameters.

Miller won a new definition of deception and a modified definition of materiality. The new definition of materiality states, "A 'material' misrepresentation or practice is one which is likely to affect a consumer's choice or conduct regarding a product [and] material information may affect conduct other than the decision to purchase a product."

The Case of Kraft Singles (1991).   The Kraft case represented the first time an advertiser challenged the FTC by presenting its own data collected specifically to test the materiality of its claims. In February 1991, the FTC determined that a Kraft General Foods Group campaign exaggerated the amount of calcium contained in a slice of Kraft Singles cheese. The FTC said the ads *implied* the slice had more calcium than five ounces of milk.[13] The words used in the text of the advertisement were "Imitation slices use hardly any milk. But Kraft has five ounces per slice. Five ounces. So her little bones get the calcium they need to grow." Kraft's own analysis showed that each slice contained 70 percent as much calcium as five ounces of milk.

When the FTC charged the ad was deceptive, Kraft hired a New York University professor to test whether calcium was important in consumers' decisions to buy Kraft Singles. The issue was whether the difference between 70 percent and 100 percent of the calcium in five ounces of milk was material to consumers and thus would affect either their decision to purchase the cheese and/or the way they used it.

The professor administered a telephone survey to people who had purchased Kraft Singles. One hundred ninety-three questionnaires were completed. An analysis of the results supported Kraft's position that the calcium claim was unlikely to affect consumers' choice or conduct. When told that a Kraft Single had only 70 percent of the calcium in five ounces of milk, 172 respondents said they would buy the cheese anyway.

But the results did not deter the FTC from pursuing its complaint. The administrative law judge (ALJ) contended that the survey did not ask (1) whether consumers reduced their milk consumption as a result of Kraft's claim or (2) whether they would have have decreased their Kraft Singles purchases had they known the product contained only 70 percent of the calcium in five ounces of milk. The ALJ also suggested that because the survey was conducted on the telephone, respondents did not get a chance to see the ad. Nor were respondents told the ads represented Singles as having 100 percent of the calcium in five ounces of whole milk.

The FTC supported its materiality finding by concluding the claim would be difficult for consumers to evaluate or verify; therefore, consumers would be likely to rely on the ad. The FTC also said that since Kraft spent $15 million a year to promote the product, the company must have found the claim valuable and likely to sway consumer decisions.

Although Kraft lost in this complaint, the case marked the first time a company used the defensive technique of producing its own research to buttress its argument. It seems likely that in the future, companies under FTC attack will take note of the FTC arguments in the Kraft case and frame their own defense to meet them.[14]

The Food and Drug Administration (FDA)

The Food and Drug Administration is an agency within the Department of Health and Human Services (HHS). The Secretary of HHS appoints the

---

[13]"Suddenly, Green Marketers Are Seeing Red Flags," *Business Week,* February 25, 1991, p. 74.

[14]J I Richards and I L Preston, "Proving and Disproving Materiality of Deceptive Advertising Claims," *Journal of Public Policy and Marketing* 2 (Fall 1992), pp. 45–56.

FDA commissioner, who does not have to be confirmed by the Senate. Seven associate commissioners, who are responsible for legislation and public information, planning and evaluation, management and operations, and regulatory, health, and consumer affairs, assist the commissioner.

Responsibilities of the FDA.   As we discussed in Chapter 8, the Food and Drug Act of 1906 was the first piece of legislation to protect the public from potential health hazards created by adulterated and mislabeled foods and drugs. The Department of Agriculture's Bureau of Chemistry administered the act from 1907 until 1927, when the department's newly created Food, Drug, and Insecticide Department took over this responsibility. In 1931, the new agency's name was changed to the Food and Drug Administration.

The FDA

- Regulates the composition, quality, safety, and labeling of food, food additives, colors, and cosmetics and conducts some research in those areas
- Monitors and enforces regulations through inspection of food and cosmetic producers' facilities; also oversees advertising and media reports by investigating consumer complaints
- Regulates the composition, quality, safety, effectiveness, and labeling of all drugs for human use and establishes scientific standards to carry out this task
- Requires premarket testing of new drugs and evaluates new-drug applications and requests to approve drugs for experimental use
- Develops standards for safety and effectiveness of over-the-counter (OTC) drugs
- Develops guidelines for proper drug-manufacturing practices and makes periodic inspections of drug-manufacturing facilities in the United States and abroad
- Monitors the quality of marketed drugs
- Recalls or seizes products that violate federal laws and pose human health hazards
- Conducts research and establishes standards for the manufacturing and use of biological products; inspects and licenses biological products
- Regulates the safety, effectiveness, labeling, and pretesting of medical devices
- Conducts research on the effects of radiation exposure and determines standards for radiation-emitting products.[15]

---

[15]"Food and Drug Administration," *Federal Regulatory Directory,* 6th ed. (Washington, DC: Congressional Directory, 1990), pp. 290–303.

In 1938, the passage of the Food, Drug, and Cosmetic Act greatly increased the FDA's powers. A year earlier, 100 people had died from taking a "miracle drug" called elixir of sulfanilamide. There was nothing wrong with the sulfanilamide itself, but its manufacturer, S E Massengill Company, had dissolved the drug in ethylene glycol, which is poisonous. To prevent a similar tragedy, the new act required that a manufacturer prove the safety of a new drug and the ingredients used in making a dosage from it before the FDA would allow the drug to be placed on the market.

In 1940, the FDA moved from the Department of Agriculture into the Federal Security Agency, a new agency formed to protect the public health. This agency was incorporated into the Department of Health, Education, and Welfare (HEW) in 1953. In 1979, HEW was split into a new Department of Education and Department of Health and Human Services.

When the Bush administration took office, the FDA was widely regarded as one of the most professionally run regulatory agencies in the federal government. President Bush reappointed Reagan's commissioner, Frank Young, in 1989. But within a year, scandal in the FDA's Generic Drugs Division drove Young out of office. The Mylan scandal, discussed in the Beta case in Chapter 9, rocked the FDA. The Generic Drugs Division was downgraded and folded into the agency's Center for Drug Evaluation.

In February 1991, HHS secretary Louis W Sullivan appointed Dr. David Kessler as FDA Commissioner. Most observers agreed this was a crucial period for the FDA. The effects of the Mylan scandal still lingered, and the agency's staff was smaller than it had been a decade earlier while demands on it had grown. By 1991, the FDA had responsibility for the safety and effectiveness of one-quarter of the nation's GNP. However, its budget was only $690 million a year, about the same as that of Albert Einstein Hospital in New York City.

Kessler immediately announced that over the next two years, he would create a team of 100 criminal investigators to pursue cases of fraud. He also announced his top priorities would be to beef up enforcement and eliminate the multilayered approval process for new drugs and medical devices.[16]

Within a few months, Kessler began a sweeping review of 400 food and drug safety measures that had been proposed but never acted on between 1960 and 1990. He also embarked on a reorganization plan to divide the FDA into five management centers. In addition, he created a new policy center to ensure that proposed regulations were written and issued promptly.

Some consumer groups and federal officials questioned whether the FDA had adequate powers to protect the public from dangerous drugs and medical devices. They pointed out that the FDA did not do any of its own

---

[16]P J Hilts, "New Chief Vows New Vitality at F.D.A.," *The New York Times,* February 27, 1991, p. A12.

TABLE 14-1   FDA Issues, 1992–1993

November 17, 1992: The FDA recommends that Taxol, an anticancer drug made from the yew tree, be approved for treatment of ovarian cancer.

November 25, 1992: The FDA proposes guidelines aimed at preventing drug companies from illegally promoting their drugs under the guise of continuing medical education for healthcare professionals.

May 17, 1993: The FDA proposes rules to stop almost all health claims for dietary supplements.

May 18, 1993: The FDA orders the smoked-herring industry to gut freshly caught fish before salting them.

June 10, 1993: The FDA orders restaurants to back up nutrition claims made on their menus.

---

testing but relied entirely on the results submitted by manufacturers. The FDA was also the only federal agency without subpoena power. Without that power, the FDA could not force drug companies to turn over documents when its suspicions were aroused. As the Dow Corning case in Chapter 4 shows, trial lawyers knew there had been complaints about breast implants for eight years, but without subpoena power the FDA lacked access to sealed court records.[17]

Over the past several years, the FDA has become much more active and assertive in a variety of issues. Table 14–1 lists some of the issues the FDA took up in late 1992 and 1993.

The Case of Medical Devices.   The controversy over the FDA's approval and oversight process for medical devices heated up in the early 1990s. A 1989 congressional audit found that out of 53,000 reports on adverse incidents filed with the FDA by device manufacturers, 55 percent involved serious injuries to patients and others and 3 percent resulted in deaths. Malfunctioning devices from heart valves to infant-monitoring devices were to blame for 42 percent.

Critics charged that the Center for Devices, one of the FDA's major centers, had disregarded entire sections of the 1976 medical device law it was supposed to enforce. The Center for Devices was created in 1982 but was chronically short of funding and personnel from the beginning. The center's charge was to set mandatory safety standards for 830 categories of medium-risk devices such as surgical saws and resuscitators. It was also supposed to review 140 categories of high-risk devices on the market before 1976. By March 1992, none of the standards for medium-risk devices had been written. In the high-risk category, only artificial heart valves and implanted nerve stimulators had been declared safe.

---

[17]G Kolata, "Questions Raised on Ability of F.D.A. to Protect Public," *The New York Times,* January 26, 1992, p. 1.

To assess device safety, FDA inspectors are supposed to inspect the manufacturing plants in which the devices are made. However, the FDA did not know exactly how many medium- and high-risk-device manufacturers came under its oversight. FDA officials inspected US manufacturing practices once every four years, although the law called for inspection every two years. The agency inspected overseas manufacturers exporting to the United States once every eight or nine years.

In the late 1980s and early 1990s, the FDA cited more than half of the US companies it inspected for manufacturing problems. From 1983 through 1988, the General Accounting Office reported that 74 percent of all recalls involved devices for which the FDA had failed to set mandatory standards.

In the absence of performance standards, the FDA relied on the principle of "substantial equivalence." FDA policy allowed manufacturers to introduce a new device if they assured the FDA it had the same intended use and substantially the same technical attributes as a pre-1976 medium-risk device. In practice, more than 98 percent of the devices received FDA approval. Legal loopholes allowed companies to introduce into the market, without FDA review, products based on brand-new technologies.

In 1990, congressional overseers gave up trying to make the FDA write new standards. They passed a new law requiring hospitals, nursing homes, and outpatient clinics to report deaths and serious injuries involving medical devices. The new requirements were expected to generate many more reports than the FDA, with its limited staff, could evaluate. The shift from premarket review to postmarket surveillance gave the FDA new enforcement powers. In 1991, the FDA seized 67 defective products, up 109 percent from the previous year.

The industry was unhappy with the new scrutiny. It argued technology was being stifled and entrepreneurs were being impeded. They noted that foreign manufacturers, which were not subject to the same restrictions, would gain a market edge and threaten US competitiveness.[18]

In March 1992, the FDA fired the director of medical devices, Robert Sheridan. At the same time it proposed tracking systems for 35 classes of medical devices, including heart valves, breast implants, and life support systems. Manufacturers would have to report a malfunction with the patient's name and device location to the FDA within three working days. Manufacturers would also be required to maintain records on each device in use and audit its performance every six months.

In March 1993, FDA internal investigators found safety studies for some medical devices were "not up to the level of fifth-grade science."[19] An

---

[18]B Ingersoll, "Amid Lax Regulation, Medical Devices Flood a Vulnerable Market," *The Wall Street Journal,* March 24, 1992, p. A1.

[19]P J Hilts, "F.D.A. to Toughen Testing of Devices," *The New York Times,* March 5, 1993, p. A18.

FDA spokesperson noted that although safety tests were inadequate, untested devices were not necessarily unsafe.

The director of the Health Industry Manufacturer's Association, the trade group that represents the device makers, blamed the FDA for past problems. He said that if the new rules were fair and clear, manufacturers could comply. He expressed relief that under the new rules, manufacturers would not have to get involved in a "giant guessing game" but could instead meet reasonable and consistent FDA requirements.

Consumers' Sources of Information

Despite the myriad regulations covering nearly every product and process, most consumers assume they must take some responsibility for protecting themselves and learning about products they buy. What do consumers need to know, and how do they go about acquiring and using the necessary information? Consumers use a variety of sources of information. They also vary considerably in the amount of detail they want to know about the products they buy.

There is compelling evidence that many consumers are in a hurry to buy and are unwilling to use a great deal of energy to seek the "perfect purchase." Often they "satisfice," that is, gather just enough information to make them believe they have made an acceptable decision. In some circumstances, the information needed to make a "perfect purchase" is simply not available. For example, the "perfect purchase" of a refrigerator might require the assurance that it will operate for 20 years. However, there is no reliable method for predicting whether a particular refrigerator purchased today will actually last 20 years. Faced with such a situation, consumers believe uncovering every bit of product information is a waste of time and energy.

A variety of resources is available to consumers willing to make the effort to become better informed. Very often, however, people rely on their accumulated experience, general knowledge, and informal recommendations as their major sources of product information.

Although marketer-dominated sources of information are usually the most prevalent, consumers do not always see those sources as the most reliable, trustworthy, or objective. A number of objective or "unbiased" publications specialize in providing detailed and comparative information about products. Some consumers rely on information from private testing laboratories, such as Consumers' Union and Consumers' Research.

Other popular information sources include the consumer magazine *Changing Times* and certain newspaper columns. A growing number of books aim to help consumers buy insurance, food, automobile repairs, prescription drugs, and many other products and services. The US Government Printing Office publishes specialized reports from federal consumer agencies and also furnishes comparative test data on consumer products bought with public funds.

Consumers Index is a guide to product evaluations and information sources. Published each quarter by Pierian Press in Ann Arbor, Michigan, it aims at individual consumers and the education/library community. The publishers emphasize articles that reflect the financial or physical health and well-being of consumers, libraries, and educational institutions. *Consumers Index* divides its subjects into 17 main groupings. It provides general information about the products and addresses a variety of relevant information categories designed to help consumers make better decisions.

Local Better Business Bureaus (BBBs) are also good sources of information, especially about local businesses. In 1911, John I Romer, publisher of *Printer's Ink,* suggested that local advertising clubs form "Vigilance Committees." The committees worked to eliminate abuses in advertising codes and to create and set advertising standards.

In 1912 George Coleman, a Boston advertising executive, formed the National Vigilance Committee to extend the effort to regional and national advertising. This group became an independent corporation in 1926 and changed its name to the National Better Business Bureau. An overarching Council of Better Business Bureaus was formed in 1970, when the National Better Business Bureau and the Association of Better Business Bureaus International merged.

BBBs are private, nonprofit, self-regulatory agencies. The BBB's Virginia headquarters disseminates information about charitable solicitations and performs consumer education and public information functions. Table 14–2 lists the 24-hour consumer counseling information available by phone to consumers in eastern Massachusetts, Maine, and Vermont.[20]

What Is Good Information?

Consumers have become more sophisticated over time. Raymond Bauer pointed out over 30 years ago, "As the persuaders become more sophisticated, so do the people to be persuaded. One way of reading the history of the development of techniques of persuasion is that the persuaders have been in a race to keep abreast of the developing resistance of the people to be persuaded."[21] Bauer's words have turned out to be prophetic as well as historical.

Business generates a huge volume of material to influence consumers to buy particular products and services. Consumer advocates assert that full disclosure of every aspect of the product is necessary for the consumer to make a wise choice.

---

[20]"History & Traditions," *Consumer Counseling Information,* Better Business Bureau, Inc., 1991.
[21]R A Bauer, "The Limits of Persuasion," *Harvard Business Review* 36 (September–October 1958), p. 105.

TABLE 14–2 Better Business Bureau Counseling Topics

The following information is available 24 hours a day, 7 days a week.
Please call 617–426–9000. From area code 802, please call 800–4–BBB-811.
A Touch Tone phone is necessary for this free service.

Automotive
Automobile Shipments
Automobile Take Over Payments
Buying a New Car
Car Buying and Selling Services
Car Care on the Road
Car Rental Insurance
Cosigning a Loan
Leasing a Car

Charitable Giving
Charitable Telephone Solicitations
Child Sponsorship Programs
Coin Collection Devices
Donating to Charity
Homeless Assistance Programs

Education & Employment
Career Counseling
Door-to-Door Sales
Employment Services
Job Listings
Mideast Employment Opportunities
Overseas Employment
Trade and Vocational Schools
Traveling Sales Crews

Financial
Bill Paying Services
Biweekly Mortgages
Business Opportunities
Consumer Liability on Lost or Stolen
    Credit and ATM Cards
Cosigning a Loan
Credit Card Offers
Credit Card Offers from Third Parties
Credit Card Billing Disputes
Credit Doctors
Credit Records

Credit Repair
Debt Collection
Federal Housing Administration
    (FHA) Loan Locators
Financial Planning
Foreign Lotteries
Get Rich Quick Schemes
Government Land Sales
Home Equity Loans
Home Mortgage Scams
Investment Fraud
Investments
IRAs
Mutual Funds
Penny Stocks
Real Estate Brokers and Agents
Reverse Mortgages
Tax Preparers
Title Insurance
Using Credit Cards When Purchasing
    by Telephone or Mail
Wills and Probate

Food & Food Supplements
Vitamin Sales by Direct Marketers

Health & Personal Improvement
AIDS Treatment
Baldness and Wrinkles
Diet Programs
Health Spas
Home Exercise Equipment
Tanning Salons and Tanning Pills
Vitamin Sales by Direct Marketers
Weight Loss

Home Improvements & Construction
Air Conditioners
Furnace Repair and Maintenance

Home Landscaping
Home Repair Scams
Home Remodeling Contractors
Lawn Care
Pest Control
Selecting Carpet
Swimming Pools
Water Purifiers

Real Estate
Buying a Home
Home Inspectors
Real Estate Appraisals
Real Estate Brokers and Agents
Timeshare Resales

Retail
Mail Order
Going Out of Business Sales
Membership Warehouse Clubs
Record and Book Clubs
Refunds and Exchanges
Service Contracts
Unordered Merchandise

Services
Bill Paying Services
Buying Clubs
Coupon Book Promotions
Dating Services
Invention Promoters
Modeling and Talent Agencies
Moving
Obtaining a Patent
Planning a Funeral
Publishing
US Government Surplus Sales

SOURCE: "24-Hour Consumer Counselling Information," (Boston: Better Business Bureau, Inc., 1991), p. 3.

The term *full disclosure* means different things to different people. To most it means disclosure of the hazardous characteristics of a product, such as its poisonous or inflammable nature. A second meaning is the disclosure of terms-of-sale information, component ingredients, and net contents. The statement of a product's performance characteristics is a third kind of disclosure. Full disclosure may also require a statement about the ratings of product-testing agencies and whether the products subscribe to industry codes or practices. There is no widespread consensus on the definition of full disclosure, and costs as well as benefits are associated with additional disclosures. Perhaps the materiality concept is the best guideline for what a marketer should disclose.

Advertising

Advertising Goals

Advertising is "any form of nonpersonal presentation of ideas, goods, and services by an identified sponsor."[22] The goal of advertising is to make potential customers *aware* of the product's existence and then to *inform* those customers of product characteristics leading to a favorable *purchase* decision. The firm's goal is to have consumers *insist* on purchasing its brand.

Advertising is big business. In the United States, thousands of advertising agencies do billions of dollars' worth of business each year. In 1940, advertising expenditures in all media in the United States were $2 billion. In 1978, they totaled around $43 billion and reached $55 billion in 1986. The advertising industry estimates the average American family is exposed to more than 1,500 ads per day on television, in newspapers and magazines, and on radio.

But do all these ads directly result in sales? The answer is, obviously not. Sometimes sales are not the primary object of advertising. A company may simply be trying to increase awareness of its brands in a particular market or to build a positive company image and then rely on personal selling to close the deal. Whether or not the company uses ads to generate sales, only a small percentage of those ads' content has any meaningful effect on consumers' buying decisions.

A 1968 study by Raymond A Bauer and Stephen A Greyser concluded that "the average American adult is aware of 76 advertisements a day in the major media."[23] Of that total, 84 percent of the ads were not notable enough for people to categorize their reactions or the strength of their feelings. It is unlikely that in the 25 years since that study was conducted, people's ability

---

[22]R P Bagozzi, *Principles of Marketing Management* (Chicago: Science Research Associates, 1986), p. 372.

[23]R A Bauer and S A Greyser, *Advertising in America: The Consumer View* (Boston: Harvard University Press, 1968), pp. 385–86.

EXHIBIT 14–3

Statement by the chairperson of Exxon

AN OPEN LETTER TO THE PUBLIC

On March 24, in the early morning hours, a disastrous accident happened in the waters of Prince William Sound, Alaska. By now you all know that our tanker, the Exxon Valdez, hit a submerged reef and lost 240,000 barrels of oil into the waters of the Sound.

We believe that Exxon has moved swiftly and competently to minimize the effects this oil will have on the environment, fish and other wildlife. Further, I hope that you know we have already committed several hundred people to work on the cleanup. We also will meet our obligations to all those who have suffered damage from the spill.

Finally, and most importantly, I want to tell you how sorry I am that this accident took place. We at Exxon are especially sympathetic to the residents of Valdez and the people of the State of Alaska. We cannot, of course, undo what has been done. But I can assure you that since March 24, the accident has been receiving our full attention and will continue to do so.

L. G. Rawl

L.G. Rawl
Chairman

to assimilate information has changed; rather; their willingness to assimilate information from advertising has likely decreased.

Nevertheless, advertising is ubiquitous and uses the most advanced audiovisual and psychological techniques to reach consumers. Thirty-five years ago, historian David M Potter argued, "advertising now compares with such long-standing institutions as the school and the church in magnitude of its social influence. It dominates the media, it has vast power in the shaping of popular standards and is really one of the very limited group of institutions which exercises social control."[24] The power and sophistication of advertising companies and the media have grown enormously since Potter made his observation.

Yet it is clear that people do not believe every advertisement they read or hear. In fact, some advertisements do a company much more harm than good. The statement by the chairperson of Exxon, shown in Exhibit 14–3,

---

[24]D M Potter, *People of Plenty* (Chicago: University of Chicago Press, 1954), p. 167.

hurt the company's credibility when it became clear that Exxon was *not* cleaning up the oil spill from the Exxon *Valdez*. The ad brought into question all of Exxon's efforts and generated public cynicism rather than support.

Deceptive Advertising

Advertising claims and techniques of personal selling can be deceptive. No universally accepted definition of deceptive advertising exists. A working definition states that *deceptive advertising* occurs when the advertisement in some people's minds differs from the reality of the situation and adversely affects those consumers' buying behavior. In some cases the advertisement contains explicit falsehoods, but more frequently the advertisement is not explicitly false. Even then, however, consumers may misinterpret the message or perceive that it is deceptive.[25] Exhibit 14–4 outlines some generally accepted principles that help clarify what constitutes deceptive practices.

Deceptive sales practices have come under increasingly heavy criticism. Such practices as bait-and-switch, lowballing (advertising a price lower than the price that will actually be charged for the product), fear selling, chain referral selling, and free gimmicks are increasingly being brought under control by strengthened state laws and city ordinances. Most of these practices are not subject to federal control, because the perpetrators do not engage in interstate commerce. Even when they do, they generally affect an insufficient number of consumers to meet the public-interest requirements for federal action.

Counterfeit Products.   Some producers engage in outright fraud by selling counterfeit products under famous brand names such as Gucci, Cartier, and Apple Computer. One of the most tragic results of counterfeit products was the crash of a Bell Helicopter when a counterfeit replacement part was accidentally used.

In most cases, however, the losses from counterfeit products are primarily financial. They are borne by both the company that developed a trademark or other intellectual property and the consumer who has purchased an inferior product. Most often the culprits are developing-country producers hoping to cash in on American, European, or Japanese design and technology. In some cases, these products are sold only in the counterfeiters' home countries; in other cases, they enter world trade.

In 1988, a US government study found American companies lost between $8 billion and $20 billion in worldwide sales. The most frequent offenders were firms from Taiwan, followed by Mexican, South Korean, and Brazilian companies. Counterfeiting and foreign violation of intellectual

---

[25]D A Aaker, "Deceptive Advertising," in D A Aaker and G S Day, eds., *Consumerism: Search for the Consumer Interest,* 2nd ed. (New York: The Free Press, 1974), p. 137.

EXHIBIT 14–4

Generic standards for advertisers

- Who is your audience? The nature of the audience will be a factor in determining whether an advertisement is deceptive. Advertisements directed at vulnerable groups such as children receive closer scrutiny than others. However, in reviewing misleading advertising, the FTC does not always adopt law schools' traditional "reasonable person" standard. Rather, they can be concerned with the public, "that vast multitude which includes the ignorant, the unthinking and the credulous, who, in making purchases, do not stop to analyze, but are governed by appearances and general impressions." In summary, the appearances and general impressions you convey to the lowest common denominator—the audience segment that is more likely to be influenced by an impression gleaned from a first glance and not tempered by mature reflection or judgment—may be controlling.

- The FTC will view an advertisement in its entirety; total net impression governs. A headline will outweigh any subsequent disclaimers or clarifying material.

- Literal truth will not save your advertisement if it is misleading when read in the context of the entire advertisement. Here you must avoid deception by half-truth or the failure to disclose material facts. The advertisement usually does not have to state all the facts, but must contain a reasonably complete statement.

- An advertisement may be found false and deceptive if either of two possible meanings is false.

- Expressions of subjective opinion (puffery) are not actionable unless they convey the impression of factual representations or relate to material terms. Opinion of the superiority or the merits of a product seems to be generally acceptable until the phrase becomes a fact. "We believe (an opinion) that our razor blades will never cut your face (fact)." The claim of fact may cross the line from puffery to deception. Likewise, exaggerating the qualities of a product is usually permissible, but assigning qualities that do not exist reaches too far. Stating that you're the "number one" seller requires substantiation with supporting evidence and documentation.

- If you are employing a mock-up that is not an accurate representation of a consumer experience, it must not pertain to the product you are specifically selling.

- All research quoted must be significant and must have been professionally obtained through state-of-the-art research techniques.

- You have a *continuing* obligation to make sure all your material claims are substantiated, including test results, price claims, and endorsements.

   Throughout its history, the FTC has tried to follow the ideal that its regulation would serve two objectives—to provide useful and truthful data and to maintain effective competition. One way to accomplish this is to enforce minimal standards of marketplace compliance such as the examples above. Another way is to affirmatively encourage broader consumer information.

SOURCE: R J Posch, Jr., *The Complete Guide to Marketing and the Law* (Englewood Cliffs, NJ: Prentice-Hall, 1988), pp. 391–92.

property rights remains a very serious problem for companies in the industrialized countries.[26]

In 1991, Levi Strauss & Company encountered an unprecedented flood of counterfeit jeans. The previous year the company had seized 1.3 million pairs of jeans, more than five times the normal yearly amount. Levi Strauss was very worried because the new copies, made mostly in China, were indistinguishable from the real thing. The fakes duplicated the originals even down to the trademarked colored tab and stitched pocket design. Levi Strauss insisted the fakes were likely to fall apart after a few washings and the company's image would be hurt by their poor quality. The company spent $2 million to hire a network of informants in Asia and Europe to try to build legal cases against the counterfeiters.

Political changes in China have made that country a world center for counterfeit manufacturing. As the central government loosened its control over Chinese factories in the late 1980s, intermediaries claiming to be Levi Strauss representatives approached the factories to sign contracts for the goods. These intermediaries shipped the fake Levis through Panama, then overland through Mexico into the United States. Levis going to Western Europe took a different route through Eastern Europe into European Community markets; once there, they were sold in small, local stores. It was very difficult for law enforcers to trace and seize those goods.

In one case that eventually came to court, Levi Strauss used Hong Kong investigators to tip off Chinese officials about a factory in Tianjin that was making fake Levis. The Chinese authorities raided the factory and seized about 100,000 pairs of jeans. The confiscated jeans were "de-Levied" by Chinese workers, who had to pick out the pocket stitching and remove all the tabs and labels.[27]

The Levi Strauss situation points out the problem companies and consumers have in determining the attributes of a product. As more and more manufacturing becomes globalized, industrialized countries are applying pressure on developing countries to protect intellectual property. However, even when all the labeling laws are followed and no intent to defraud exists, it may be difficult for consumers to judge a product by its advertising or labeling.

Food Labels. The Food and Drug Administration, the Department of Agriculture, and the Federal Trade Commission all monitor and regulate food advertising. Even with oversight by three federal agencies, however, consumers often get conflicting information or information they cannot

---

[26]M Harney, "A New Way to Combat Product Counterfeiting," *Business Horizons* (July–August 1988), p. 19.

[27]C Dolan, "Levi Tries to Round Up Counterfeiters," *The Wall Street Journal*, February 19, 1991, p. B1.

understand. Some labels are so full of confusing detail that the average consumer *cannot* exercise the right to know guaranteed in the Consumer Bill of Rights.

Although information is readily available on an item's label, it is often neither relevant nor accurate. One example of confusing labeling is the use of the word *light* or *lite*. The average consumer does not know whether the product is light in color, light in calories, or light in texture. Light beer can be a 12-ounce can of Michelob Light, which has 134 calories, or Miller Lite, which has 95. Schaefer regular beer has only 139 calories, just 5 calories more than Michelob Light.[28] Happily for consumers, new FDA regulations will soon remedy this situation.

The Bush administration announced the first major changes in food labels in many years. Health and Human Services Secretary Louis W Sullivan said, "The grocery store has become the Tower of Babel, and consumers need to be linguists, scientists, and mind readers to understand the many labels they see."[29] Bush's plan called for mandatory nutrition labeling on nearly every food product. After a year of public discussion, companies would be required to provide information about amounts of saturated fat, fiber, and cholesterol and the percentage of calories coming from fat. Booklets at stores would give consumers the same information about fresh fruits and other produce. The plan would also give formal definitions for "low-fat" and "high-fiber," thereby taking the responsibility for those designations away from manufacturers or processors.

In May 1990, the food label bill passed the House Energy and Commerce Committee and the Senate Labor and Human Resources Committee and went to the floor of the House and the Senate. Finally, in October, the Senate passed the bill, which had been approved by the House three months earlier. It remained for the president to sign the bill and the FDA to write the detailed regulations for more than 14,000 food products. The bill was scheduled to go into effect in May 1994. The FDA estimated the cost of relabeling at about $40 million.

In April 1991, the Department of Agriculture announced it would coordinate its efforts with the FDA by requiring meat and poultry processors to list nutritional data. The proposal covered processed meat and poultry products from chicken soup to lunchmeat. Labels would contain calories, total fat, saturated fat, cholesterol, protein, sodium content, and serving size. Supermarkets and retail stores would be requested to supply similar information for fresh meats and poultry.[30]

---

[28]C Schaeffer, "Food Labels: The Hype Behind the Type," *Changing Times,* July 1989, p. 38.

[29]P J Hilts, "U.S. Plans to Make Sweeping Changes in Labels on Food," *The New York Times,* March 8, 1990, p. A1.

[30]B Ingersoll, "USDA Proposes Nutritional-Data Rules for Labels on Processed Meat, Poultry," *The Wall Street Journal,* April 2, 1991, p. B5.

Shortly after becoming the FDA commissioner, Dr. David Kessler announced he would go after products that implied they might prevent heart disease and that used heart symbols or heart logos on their labels. He noted that even no-cholesterol products might contain other fats suspected of leading to heart disease.

The involvement of the Department of Health and Human Services, the Department of Agriculture, the FDA, and Congress pointed out the complexity of interactions among various jurisdictions. Congress was not asked to pass labeling legislation on fresh meats and poultry that went into processed foods. Therefore, a sausage pizza could be under the jurisdiction of the Department of Agriculture, which regulates pork, while a cheese pizza might come under the FDA, which covers dairy products. The Federal Trade Commission, which regulates advertising, might allow food companies to use terms in television commercials that the FDA and the Department of Agriculture would not permit on labels.

In June 1991, the FDA targeted labeling practices of the juice industry. It decided to require companies to list percentages of each juice in blends as well as the total percentage of juice in juice cocktails and punches. The proposal, which covered about 3,000 products, included fruit sparklers, sparkling cider, carbonated fruit drinks, soft drinks, and carbonated waters.

Consumer groups were delighted with the FDA proposal. Bruce A Silverglade of the consumer advocacy group the Center for Science and the Public Interest noted that juice processors would have to make major labeling changes. Under the old rules, juice blend drinks could be identified as tropical guava or passion fruit drinks even though most of their liquid was plain apple juice.

Manufacturers were given one month to comment on the rules and were required to have new labels by November 1991. A New Jersey manufacturer noted her company would have to change 2,500 labels to comply with the new rules. She doubted the nation's printing presses could handle her company's requirement and those of all the other juice manufacturers in time to make the deadline.[31]

For the most part, consumers were pleased they would have access to so much new information. About half of all consumers said they depended on labels to decide which foods to buy. A casual stroll through the supermarket, however, showed how easily consumers could be deceived. Budget Gourmet Light and Healthy Salisbury Steak was labeled "low fat," but derived 45 percent of its total calories from fat. Diet Coke and Diet Pepsi each contained more than the one calorie per can listed on the label. Post Fruity Pebbles contained no fruit at all, and Mrs. Smith's Natural Juice Apple Pie contained artificial preservatives.

Nearly half of all consumers reported they were "highly skeptical" about the information they read on grocery packages. Medical experts said they

---

[31]Tim Golden, "Juice Label Asked by F.D.A," *The New York Times,* July 2, 1991, p. D1.

were right to be concerned and pointed to the inherent dangers in mislabeled food. For someone with heart disease, high blood pressure, or diabetes, inaccurately labeled quantities of salt or sugar in a product could have fatal consequences. A spokesperson for the American Dietetic Association noted some Stouffer diet products contained almost half the total amount of salt allowed daily on a salt-restricted diet. Stouffer labeled the salt content in grams rather than milligrams (one thousandth of a gram).[32]

Although a dispute between Bush administration officials briefly delayed label implementation, in December 1992 the administration gave the plan the green light. Dr David Kessler, kept on by the Clinton administration, has continued the FDA's aggressive consumer education plan. It seems clear that the food-labeling law will greatly enhance consumers' ability to choose products based on their actual contents and attributes.

"Green Products." Earth Day 1990 marked the beginning of a flood of environmentally sound products. Since then, many companies have asserted their products or services are environmentally sound or environmentally friendly. However, it is often very difficult for consumers to make reasoned judgments about whether such claims are valid.

In 1990, for example, John Hancock Life Insurance Company boasted that its $53 million Freedom Environmental Fund was a good way to "participate in the coming environmental mobilization." A consumer advocate group in California sent letters to the SEC charging the Hancock fund deliberately misled the public because Waste Management Inc., a company with multiple Environmental Protection Agency violations, was one of the fund's biggest investments. The fund manager insisted there were no perfectly environmentally pristine companies and Waste Management ran the cleanest landfills in the business.

Environmental fund managers rode the tide of public interest in the wake of the Exxon *Valdez* debacle. The Merrill Lynch Environmental Technology Trust opened two portfolios of pollution cleanup stocks. Within a few days after the first one opened, the trust reached its $50 million goal.

Organizations as well as individuals questioned their portfolio managers about companies' environmental records. The director of the Prudential-Bache Capital Funding Group's social research service reported the environment was the single most important social issue among institutional investors.

However, assessing a company's "green" credentials becomes very complicated when that company both pollutes *and* cleans up the pollution. DuPont Company, for example, makes chlorofluorocarbons (CFCs) that contribute to global warming. On the other hand, DuPont has promised to phase out CFCs by the year 2000 and is developing new substitute technol-

---

[32]C Gorman, "The Fight over Food Labels," *Time,* July 15, 1991, pp. 50, 52–59.

ogies. How does a consumer decide whether to buy DuPont stock or invest in a fund that holds this stock?

Some investors use an independent screening service to ensure that their investments are environmentally clean. The screening service researches and eliminates funds that own any of the 150 major toxic waste dumps identified by the World Wildlife Foundation or own stock of firms identified as environmental culprits.

Many experienced investors were skeptical about the green craze. Some warned consumers not to be taken in but instead to contribute some of their traditional investment profits to organizations that clean up their local areas. Most experts agree environmental investing requires consumers to make trade-offs between profitable investments and environmental commitment.[33]

In the early 1990s, the green craze spread to other countries. Governments established panels to judge the truthfulness of companies' claims. In Great Britain, the Independent Television Association, a trade group representing Britain's independent television companies, devised guidelines for green television commercials. The Advertising Standards Authority, the trade group for press advertisements, advised companies not to make absolute claims.

This group suggested advertisers call a product "environmentally *friendlier*" rather than simply "environmentally friendly." It also suggested advertisers tell the consumer what attributes make the product green. For example, an ad should state that a product has no CFCs or is biodegradable rather than simply environmentally sound.[34]

Japanese advertisers also latched on to the environmental theme. The Japanese Advertising Council reported respondents chose "nature preservation" as the most important ad campaign theme of 1990. The quasi-governmental Japanese Environmental Association (JEA) developed a seal of approval called an "Ecomark." More than 500 Japanese companies received the seal for eco-activities such as using cans with stay-on tabs rather than the pull-off variety. Even department stores took up the environmental theme, creating "earth-friendly" corners where consumers could buy environmentally sound products.[35]

In the United States, private companies hustled to provide green ratings for industry. Scientific Certification of California, a private, profit-making organization, announced it would award the "Green Cross" to products it certified. It planned to charge companies fees ranging from several hundred dollars to $10,000 to verify the environmental soundness of their products.

---

[33]E C Gottschalk, "Investments Promoted as Ecologically Clean Pop Up Like Weeds," *The Wall Street Journal,* April 10, 1990, p. A1.

[34]"Friendly to Whom?," *The Economist,* April 7, 1990, p. 83.

[35]R Neff, "Now, Japan's Advertisers Are Nuts about Nature," *Business Week,* July 16, 1990, p. 44.

Four retail and supermarket chains in western states with more than 400 stores in total announced they would adopt strict standards for products making environmental claims and promptly hired Scientific Certification. To qualify for the Green Cross seal, products would have to contain at least 50 percent materials recycled from consumer waste. Product and packaging manufacturers would have to meet all local, state, and federal requirements. In addition, manufacturers would have to nearly eliminate plant emissions of any substance known to cause cancer or reproductive system damage.[36]

McDonald's.   Eco-stakeholders pressured companies to adopt environmentally sound practices. McDonald's, which generated mountains of trash, became a prime target. Polystyrene hamburger boxes became the symbol of a throw-away society. Environmentalists agreed it took hundreds of years for those boxes to rot.

McDonald's had tested a pilot program to collect and recycle the polystyrene boxes. The program failed because most customers carried the boxes out of the restaurant and discarded them elsewhere. Customers eating in the restaurants were confused when confronted with multiple bins for trash. Even when the hamburger boxes were cleaned and recycled, they had very limited use.

Young people, McDonald's largest consumer group, became its severest critics. During 1989 and 1990, schoolchildren demonstrated outside the restaurants and wrote thousands of letters to corporate headquarters. McDonald's management had to respond.

McDonald's enlisted the environmentalists' help. In August 1990, the company signed an agreement with the Environmental Defense Fund (EDF), an environmental research and lobbying group. The EDF and McDonald's agreed to work together to reduce the company's trash output. Initially McDonald's wanted to continue trying to recycle the hamburger boxes, but the EDF wanted the company to concentrate on reducing the amount of packaging material. McDonald's took EDF's advice and announced it would replace the polystyrene box with a quilted wrap made from a layer of tissue between a layer of polyethylene and a sheet of paper. Although the wrap could not be recycled, it was only 10 percent as bulky as the box and used far fewer natural resources.

Initially the EDF wanted McDonald's to use washable plates instead of disposable containers. McDonald's managers resisted, pointing out that outlets served two to three times as many people per square foot than a conventional restaurant did. They also argued that dishwashers use water, detergents, and energy.

---

[36]R B Smith, "Four Store Chains to Set Strict Standards for Environmental Claims of Products," *The Wall Street Journal,* April 3, 1990, p. A2.

The alliance between McDonald's and the EDF has flourished. McDonald's adopted a policy of "reduce, reuse, and recycle." Some experiments to reduce waste worked, while others did not. Consumers found that when the company narrowed its straws to save paper, their milkshakes were too thick to suck through the new straw. However, when McDonald's reduced the size of its napkins, consumers did not use more napkins.

Recycling efforts continue with McDonald's experiments in composting. Almost half the waste from a typical restaurant consists of food scraps and paper, which eventually can be used for fertilizer. In time, McDonald's should be able to dispose of nearly 80 percent of its trash without adding to landfills.[37]

McDonald's responsiveness to consumers and to green corporate strategy has paid off for the company and greatly enhanced its image. However, there is evidence that the green industry is maturing. Consumers are making hard calculations between price and environmental attributes. In recessionary times, price often wins even when environmental products last longer or can be used more sparingly.

The Future of the Green-Product Movement. Manufacturers say it is too soon to tell whether the current consumer apathy toward green products is temporary or more lasting. The Roper Organization found green products have not gained mass acceptance. Some people do not like the appearance, texture, or performance of recycled products and paper in particular. Disposable diapers are a major contributor to landfills, but most parents are unwilling to switch to cloth diapers.

Price seems to be the biggest obstacle to the widespread use of green products. Green products are usually more expensive. Consumers report they would buy environmentally sound products if they were the same price as or cheaper than conventional products, but are reluctant to pay a premium for them.

Some companies have found innovative ways to address both environmental concerns and price issues. Procter & Gamble, for example, has reduced the amount of plastic it uses and at the same time saves consumers money. P&G's refillable laundry detergent and fabric softener bottles have gained market share because they are cheaper for the manufacturer, retailer, and consumer and incidentally are also environmentally sound.[38] Virtually all detergent manufacturers are offering more concentrated products, which saves packaging material.

---

[37]"Food for Thought," *The Economist,* August 29, 1992, pp. 64, 66.

[38]V Reitman, " 'Green' Product Sales Seem to Be Wilting," *The Wall Street Journal,* May 18, 1992, p. B1.

Summary

For a century, consumers have been concerned about access to product information. The number of available products has increased rapidly, and potential sources of information have proliferated. Organized consumers' groups help make public information about unsafe or harmful products. After World War II, consumers movements grew in both size and influence.

The Federal Trade Commission and the Food and Drug Administration are the two key government agencies dealing with consumer protection. In some instances their duties appear to overlap, but together they dictate industry rules and regulations for consumer protection. They oversee advertising, labeling, and content requirements, allowing consumers to make more confident choices based on more accurate information.

Consumers use a variety of sources to get the information they want and need. Often they do not have complete information about their product choices and have to question what constitutes good information or complete disclosure about a product.

Advertisers try to attract new customers and keep old ones. Nearly all consumers are bombarded with far more product information than they can or are willing to absorb. Many consumers are sophisticated enough to reject messages in advertisements that are obviously misleading.

Food labeling is one of the FDA's major responsibilities. Although food products in the United States have more comprehensive labels than do those in most other countries, they still provide too little information for consumers to make really informed choices. New standards, due to take effect in 1994, will improve labels even further and eliminate much of the confusion over contents and dietary requirements.

Consumers' desire for environmentally sound products has created new offerings of goods and services in the United States and abroad. Nevertheless, consumers are ambivalent about green products; price seems to be the major impediment to mass acceptance of these products. However, manufacturers and advertisers are finding innovative ways to make standard products greener at little or no extra cost.

Questions

1. Define *consumer welfare.* What are the various issues involved in consumer welfare?
2. What are the major sources consumers might use to obtain product information? What are the costs associated with using each source?
4. What are the Federal Trade Commission's responsibilities with respect to advertising?
5. What are the Food and Drug Administration's responsibilities to consumers?

6. Evaluate the Federal Trade Commission's concept of *material.* What are the pros and cons of a position that *all* information is material?

Projects

1. Buy several magazines available at the supermarket check-out counter. Carefully read the advertising copy for over-the-counter drug ads. List the ads and any copy you consider deceptive or potentially deceptive. Use these ads as a basis for class discussion.
2. Find out whether your state has passed legislation against deceptive advertising. Contact your state office for consumer affairs to find out what the state government has done to protect consumers. Ask how your state and the federal government work together on this issue.
3. Find out the procedure by which one registers a complaint with the Federal Trade Commission or the Food and Drug Administration.

BETA CASE 14
CONSUMERS AND INFORMATION

As Detroit baked in the July heat, Beta's board members steamed in their walnut-paneled meeting room. A memo from the marketing department had led to shouting matches among directors. The memo recommended that Beta acquire a license to RU486, the so-called "abortion pill." RU486 was developed and patented by Groupe Roussel Uclaf in France. The German chemical company, Hoechst AG, owned 54½ percent of Roussel; the French government owned the rest.

All tests confirmed that RU486 was safer than surgical abortion and was 95 percent effective when used within the first five weeks after conception. The pill had to be administered by a physician and the patient closely supervised. To avoid having babies born with birth defects, women using the pill were required to sign a paper agreeing to a surgical procedure if the pills didn't work.

In October 1988, an international furor erupted when Roussel decided to suspend distribution of the drug. The company had been pressured by anti-abortion groups to stop production. The suspension coincided with the meeting of the World Congress of

Gynecology and Obstetrics. Representatives of the World Health Organization, the World Bank, and the Rockefeller Foundation, as well as physicians from many countries, deplored Roussel's action. The doctors pointed out that worldwide 500,000 women died each year from pregnancy-related causes, and more than 200,000 of those deaths were due to botched abortions. A panel of scientists who worked with the drug reported the compound had other uses, such as ending an ectopic (tubal) pregnancy, treating breast cancer in women, and treating prostate cancer in men.[39] Two days after the suspension, the French government ordered Roussel to resume production.

In the spring of 1989, the US Food and Drug Administration approved an "investigational new drug" application by the Population Council, a non-profit biomedical research organization. One staff member of the FDA observed, "If the drug is safe, the data is good and abortion is legal, I don't see what

---

[39]M Simons, "A Medical Outcry Greets Suspension of Abortion Pill," *The New York Times,* October 28, 1988, pp. A1, A8.

choice we would have [other than to give full approval]."[40]

Beta's marketing department pointed out the FDA had approved another drug that caused abortions: Cyotec, produced by G D Searle & Company, which was used to prevent ulcers in arthritis patients. Searle argued the drug should have been approved because it was developed for ulcer treatment rather than abortion.[41]

Beta's marketing department reasoned that because RU486 had other uses, Beta could reasonably take advantage of an extremely attractive entrepreneurial opportunity as well as serve a useful and legitimate purpose. It would only be a matter of time before some company obtained the license and the profits. The department also pointed out that even if some groups of consumers objected to Beta's decision to make the drug, consumer boycotts of companies making abortion or contraceptive drugs had been ineffective.

Beta's directors were deeply split. Some wanted nothing to do with a drug that caused abortion even

if it had other beneficial uses. Others favored manufacturing a drug that was safer, cheaper, and more effective in producing abortions. The drug would, after all, require a physician's prescription, and all Beta would be doing was giving the physician another choice for performing a legal procedure. The directors pointed out that *Roe* v. *Wade* was still the law of the land.

Other directors had no moral objection to the drug, but were very concerned about how it could be marketed. They pointed to the possibility of lawsuits similar to those that had sent A H Robins into bankruptcy. These directors insisted management explore the risk to Beta's other product lines and its manufacturing operations.

One director was adamant that, as a matter of principle, pharmaceutical companies should always avoid controversy and keep a low profile. Another countered that in a time of consumer hostility toward the industry, Beta's willingness to introduce RU486 could result in positive public relations.

All members agreed the marketing department should explore the size of the potential US market. They were acutely aware that President Clinton had signaled a willingness to reconsider the Bush administration policy barring RU486 from the United States and that their time to make a decision was running out.

---

[40]"Abortion in the Form of a Pill," *Newsweek,* April 17, 1989, p. 61.

[41]G Kolata, "U.S. May Allow Anti-Ulcer Drug Tied to Abortion," *The New York Times,* October 29, 1988, pp. 1, 5.

15 PRODUCT USE ISSUES

Chapter 14 explored what a company should do to ensure that consumers have the right information about the quality and other attributes of products they buy. This chapter discusses issues of product quality. It covers the major trends in quality management and examines the role of the Malcolm Baldrige Award and ISO 9000 in fostering quality among US companies.

The chapter also describes the components of product quality, the evolution of product safety, company liability, and the changing legal environment for managers and consumers injured by defective products. As we shall see, companies are liable when their products do not perform as expected. A thorough understanding of quality management is essential, not only as a competitive weapon but as a critical means for avoiding product liability lawsuits.

CASE   *General Motors and Its Pickup Trucks*

Between 1973 and 1987, General Motors Corporation (GM) made its GMC and Chevrolet pickups with side-mounted dual gas tanks placed outside the frame rails. In 1988, GM altered the trucks' design and put a single tank *inside* the frame.

In November 1992, the media began to draw attention to the fact that when these original-design trucks were hit from the side, they were more likely than other pickups to burst into flames. By the time the problem was widely known, GM was involved in more than 100 lawsuits. The company had made payments of over $1 million to some of the families of the more than 300 people who had been killed due to the safety defect. At the end of 1992, however, 4.7 million of those trucks were still on the road.

GM documents suggest that prior to 1983, the company tried to better protect the fuel tanks. Federal rules mandate that fuel tank systems must be able to withstand a collision from the side with another vehicle moving at 20 miles per hour. According to GM's director of engineering analysis, after the company installed a plastic shield around the tank, the truck passed a 50-mile-an-hour crash test.

But critics demanded a recall, claiming the plastic shield was only a "Band-Aid fix." They asserted the test results did not take into account the buildup of corrosion and rust around the fuel tank, which made the trucks much more likely to catch fire as they aged.[1] General Motors told the media it would resist any decision to recall the trucks. Company spokespersons said a recall would be illegal and would represent ad hoc regulation.

On December 9, 1992, the National Highway Traffic Safety Administration (NHTSA) sent a letter to GM asking whether the company had conducted its tests on cars that differed from those sold to the public. The NHTSA also asked GM for missing and incorrect data concerning failed tests. In addition, it restored the 20 mph standard. These moves meant the agency believed there was "reasonable possibility" that GM would issue a recall.

On November 17, the television program "Dateline NBC" showed crash tests in which a 1977 Chevrolet CK pickup ignited when hit from the side by a car going 30 miles per hour. A 1980 GM truck, subjected to the same test, did not catch on fire.

GM called the tests rigged and unfair. NBC later admitted the network had used "sparking devices" but maintained the results would have been the same had the devices not been used. In January, NBC told GM the vehicles used in the demonstration had been destroyed and thus could not be examined.[2]

Early in February 1993, GM suffered another public relations disaster. A Georgia state jury found GM responsible for the death of teenager Shannon Moseley. Moseley was burned to death when his 1985 GMC Sierra pickup burst into flames when it was hit in the side. The jury awarded his parents, Thomas and Elaine Moseley, $105 million in damages.[3]

A spokesperson for the NHTSA immediately declared the verdict would have no impact on the possible recall. But GM took very little solace in that statement. The company had lost more than $10 billion in the previous seven quarters, and GM chairperson Robert C Stempel had been forced to resign. A former GM safety engineer had been the chief witness against the company in the Moseley case, telling the jury the company had intentionally hidden knowledge of the safety defect. Regardless of whether or not NBC had staged the crash test, public opinion against GM was mounting.

Within a few days, GM adopted a tough, stonewall strategy in dealing with the Moseley verdict and the NBC segment. Regarding the jury verdict, GM accused "plaintiff attorneys and others of creating a poisoned public and litigation climate in which an objective engineering evaluation and fair assessment are very hard." Commenting on the NBC program, Harry J Pierce, GM's executive vice president and

---

[1]B Meier, "Data Show G.M. Knew for Years of Risk in Pickup Trucks' Design," *The New York Times,* November 17, 1992, p. A1.

[2]M Maynard, "GM Suit Attacks NBC Report, *USA Today,* February 9, 1993, p. 1A.

[3]P Applebome, "G.M. Is Held Liable over Fuel Tanks in Pickup Trucks," *The New York Times,* February 5, 1993, p. A1.

general counsel, asserted that the company was cooperating with the NHTSA and that the crash test was a "blatant deception."[4]

NBC capitulated and made an on-the-air apology to GM on February 9. Nevertheless, GM announced it was suspending advertising on all NBC news programs, although it did agree to drop a suit it had filed a few days earlier.

GM executives were delighted with NBC's apology, stating they and the company had been vindicated. GM continued to resist any pressure to recall the 4.7 million older trucks. Although it maintained the pickup trucks were safe, the company issued a recall for a different problem in March. Nearly 2 million 1988–1993 full-size pickup trucks and large sports-utility vehicles were called in to replace defective hoses that could spark and cause a fire under the body. GM admitted it had received reports of 400 incidents, including some minor fires that started when transmission fluid ignited near the catalytic converter.

GM, safety critics, and the federal government faced an impasse. On April 7, 1993, safety advocates called a news conference in Washington. They suggested a practical and relatively inexpensive solution to the safety problems in the trucks. Clarence Ditlow, director of the Center for Auto Safety, noted that GM could solve the problem without bankrupting itself. For little more than $200 million, GM could install a protective cage around the side-mounted gas tanks. Ditlow released an internal GM document that described the side-mounted tanks as "potential leakers." The same document, released to GM salespeople in the late 1980s, touted the new inside frame design, claiming it reduced the chance of fuel spillage. GM called the document "a fluke."[5]

On April 9, the NHTSA formally asked GM to recall the 4.7 million pickup trucks and correct the fuel tank design. This recall request was the fourth largest in the agency's history and was the first formal step toward a mandatory recall. William A Boehly, NHTSA's top enforcement officer, said the side-mounted placement of the tanks created a risk of a crash fire 2.4 times greater than the risk in a comparable full-size Ford or Dodge pickup. The NHTSA gave GM until the end of April to explain why the trucks should not be recalled. In response, GM issued a statement claiming the trucks met "all applicable safety standards and General Motors does not agree with any suggestion that they should be recalled because of their side-mounted tanks."[6]

On April 30, GM rejected the recall request. GM officials said that if they honored the NHTSA request, all of the company's past and future products could be exposed to government action. GM's position drew support from those who had charged the government with inconsistent and lax policies. After all, they noted, NHTSA acknowledged that the trucks were safe overall and that GM's internal testing was even more stringent than the government's.

[4]D P Levin, "In Suit, G.M. Accuses NBC of Rigging Crash Tests," *The New York Times,* February 9, 1993, p. B6.

[5]D Lavin and B Ingersoll, "GM Is Offered Plan to Resolve Truck Dispute," *The Wall Street Journal,* April 7, 1993, p. B1.

[6]F Swoboda and W Brown, "GM Refuses Request to Recall Pickups," *The Boston Globe,* April 10, 1993, p. 1.

GM and its supporters charged that government policy changed after President Clinton entered the White House. Under Presidents Reagan and Bush, safety inspectors had worried more about the expectations of political employees who ran the agency than about product safety. The new secretary of transportation, Frederico Peña, vowed to make public safety his top priority and to use recalls to implement his policy. With neither side willing to budge, the NHTSA and GM seemed to be hunkering down for a protracted fight.

The issue was economic as well as moral and ethical. The NHTSA estimated that if all 4.7 million trucks remained on the road until the year 2003, 50 to 60 more people would die in them. If a recall actually cost the estimated $1 billion, GM might spend $16 million to $20 million to save one life. Today government agencies value a life at $3 million to $7 million, depending on the victim's age, gender, and profession. One fundamental question is whether GM should spend $1 billion to save comparatively few lives.[7]

Questions

1. Did GM adopt a wise strategy in dealing with the safety problem?
2. If you were GM's chief counsel, what legal issues would you need to take into account?
3. How should a company handle situations in which political perspectives determine the regulatory process?
4. Is there a single most ethical position open for GM to take?
5. Should the government force GM to spend $1 billion in view of the economics involved?

Product Quality

When producers and consumers talk about product quality, they often have very different concepts of what the term means. How do managers know when they have made a product of acceptable quality? How can they set product quality goals for their companies and determine when those goals have been met?

Industry discussions about product quality have taken on almost mystical significance in the 1990s. During the 1970s and 1980s, American consumers lost confidence in the ability of the nation's manufacturers to make high-quality products. Japan's success—which came at the expense of US producers—drove home the importance of quality production. Manufacturers and service companies looked back to the postwar period, when product quality advocates were ignored by American manufacturers but eagerly listened to by Japanese companies.

---

[7]A E Serwer, "GM Gets Tough with Its Critics," *Fortune,* May 31, 1993, pp. 90–92, 94, 96–97.

History of Quality Control

W Edwards Deming.   In 1950, W Edwards Deming became a leader of the Japanese quality control revolution. Deming exhorted managers on both sides of the Pacific to concentrate on continuous improvement of products and services, to innovate, and to commit resources to ongoing quality improvement. Quality, he stressed, had to be built into all goods and services.

Deming's key to quality management was statistical process control (SPC). Deming acknowledged that some variation from product to product was inevitable, but managers could use statistical probability to distinguish an acceptable variation from a problem situation.[8]

Joseph M Juran.   More than 30 years ago, Joseph M Juran wrote the *Quality Control Handbook*. He too had a significant impact on Japanese quality control. Juran proposed that *quality* was another term for "fitness for use." This means that people who use a product or service should be able to count on it to perform up to expectations. If a person ships a package from New York to California, it should arrive within the time period specified by the shipper and in the same condition in which it was sent. Juran identified five major dimensions of fitness for use: quality of design, quality of conformance, availability, safety, and condition after it reached customers' hands. Juran developed an analytical method to identify areas needing improvement. He advocated a cost-of-quality (COQ) accounting system that defined avoidable and unavoidable costs. Avoidable costs resulted from product defects and manufacturing process failures. In other words, with proper quality control, the manufacturer could avoid having to refinish a piece of furniture or a car body. Unavoidable costs were those associated with sampling, sorting, and inspection procedures. Juran assumed that as the number of defects continued to decrease, failure costs approached zero.[9]

Armand Feigenbaum.   In the mid-1950s, Armand Feigenbaum introduced the idea of *total quality control (TQC)*. This approach called for the establishment of "interfunctional teams" from functional business areas such as finance, marketing, engineering, and manufacturing. In Feigenbaum's view, every functional area and activity of the firm should be focused on producing the best-quality product at the best price to the consumer.[10]

---

[8]A March, "A Note on Quality: The Views of Deming, Juran, and Crosby," Harvard Business School #9-687-011, pp. 1–4.

[9]D A Garvin, "Competing on the Eight Dimensions of Quality," *Harvard Business Review* (November/December 1987), pp. 101–109.

[10]R B Chase and N J Aquilano, *Production and Operations Management: A life Cycle Approach* (Homewood, IL: Richard D. Irwin, 1989), p. 166.

David A Garvin. In the 1960s and 1970s, US companies adopted various quality control procedures but failed to keep pace with foreign competitors in Germany and particularly in Japan. In 1987, David A Garvin noted the United States was falling behind and suggested that companies ask themselves tough questions about how much quality is enough and what quality looks like from the customer's perspective. He proposed eight critical dimensions of quality that could serve as a framework for strategic analysis. Garvin suggested that companies use this framework to explore opportunities to distinguish their products from those of other companies.[11] The following discussion elaborates on this framework.

Eight Dimensions of Quality

1. Performance. *Performance* refers to a product's primary operating characteristics. In a bank, for example, it includes how quickly a service representative handles a customer's needs and how efficiently problems are resolved. For instance, consumers judge the performance of a microwave oven by how evenly and quickly it cooks food.

To a "typical" consumer who buys a self-defrosting refrigerator, the fact that the refrigerator keeps food cold and does not build up a wall of ice in the freezer is not sufficient evidence of product quality. Other operating characteristics are whether the compressor is quiet, the motor is energy saving, the refrigerator is easy to clean, and shelves are sturdy and easy to adjust. Consumers do not always agree on what constitutes high quality in refrigerators, since their needs differ. Some people are more concerned about an appliance that operates quietly than about energy-saving features. Generally good performance includes objective technical attributes of the product as well as subjective personal judgment.

Safety is a critical attribute of performance that Garvin does not explicitly include in his formulation. However, if making a refrigerator more energy efficient also makes it more likely to catch fire, the energy-saving quality is negated. As is pointed out later in this chapter, a company ignores the product's or process's safety aspect at its peril.

2. Features. *Features* are a product or service's "bells and whistles." Sometimes it is difficult to draw the line between a product's primary performance and its secondary features. For example, some consumers have no need for a browning element in a microwave oven because they use the oven only to warm up conventionally cooked food or leftovers. A home computer that has enough power only for word processing may be sufficient for one consumer, but another may need much more power to run graphics software or complex spreadsheets.

---

[11]D Garvin, "Competing on the Eight Dimensions of Quality," pp. 104–108.

A customer may use the teller at the bank to process transactions but not use the advice of the bank's service representative on buying certificates of deposit or investing in mutual funds. To many consumers, the more features built into the product or service, the more favorable their perception of it is. To others, the greater the number of features, the greater the likelihood that something will go wrong.

Let us return to our earlier example of the refrigerator and add ice and chilled-water dispensers on the outside door, an ice maker inside the freezer, separate butter, egg, meat, and vegetable bins, and an electronic voice that tells the owner when the door has been left ajar. Some consumers would consider the quality of this refrigerator better than that of its basic, no-frills counterpart; others would not. Individual preference thus plays a major role in assessing quality in performance and features.

3. Reliability. *Reliability* is the probability that the product will function properly for a reasonable period of time. Some brands are more reliable than others. Some will not need a major repair over their lifetime, while others will be a constant source of trouble. Brands that need very frequent repairs are called "lemons." The more features built in and the greater the number of interrelated parts that depend on one another to function, the more likely it is that the product will malfunction.

Unreliable products can result from a variety of factors. The product may be badly designed, materials may be shoddy, workmanship may be poor, or some unexpected variable may crop up in its use. To most consumers, the longer the time the product is out of service and the more expensive it is to fix, the more important the issue of reliability becomes.

If the copier in a busy office breaks down, a restaurant's ovens malfunction, or an airplane's engine stalls in flight, reliability becomes the product's most important attribute. On the other hand, if a lightbulb burns out or an electric toothbrush stops working, the consumer's concern about reliability is much less pressing.

4. Conformance. *Conformance* is the degree to which the product's design and operation meet established standards. All products have established specifications that constitute a "central point." Consumers will tolerate a certain amount of deviation from that point as long as it stays within an acceptable range. In some cases, consumers tolerate a fairly wide deviance. For example, one can of minestrone soup may have 15 chunks of onion and seven pieces of potato, while another has 12 chunks of onion and nine of potato, yet both are still acceptable to most consumers. However, a person with heart trouble can tolerate only a very small margin of deviation in medication. Also, consumers in different countries have different expectations of conformance. Japanese consumers expect every seam of a garment to be stitched perfectly; American consumers are less exacting.

5. Durability. *Durability* is the amount of use a consumer gets from a product before it reaches the point at which replacement is preferable to repair. Many consumers make the decision to purchase a particular item or brand on the basis of its estimated life. Retailers and consumer magazines are frequently used sources of information about products' expected longevity.

A product's life can be significantly affected by the frequency and intensity of operation and the attention given to its maintenance. A car whose oil is rarely changed will break down and wear out more quickly than one that is maintained according to the manufacturer's recommendations. Likewise, a humidifier is less likely to clog up with dust when its filters are changed regularly.

Increasingly consumers are throwing away products they used to repair. Calculators, portable radios, hair dryers, videocassette recorders, and even television sets can cost more to repair than their initial purchase price. In addition, the inconvenience of doing without the product for a long period while it is in the repair shop may be sufficient reason for the consumer to make the choice to discard it. Even when a consumer throws the product away, its initial purchase price may have been low enough that the consumer believes the product was of sufficient quality given its features and price.

In other instances, a consumer or a company discards a product because it has become obsolete. An obvious example is major airlines' substitution of jet planes for propeller-driven aircraft. In this case, obsolescence was selective. Airlines still use propeller-driven planes for short trips and where runways are too short to accommodate jets.

However, faster travel did not make conventional jets obsolete when the supersonic Concorde was introduced. Although the Concorde cut trans-Atlantic flying time in half, other considerations were more important. The Concorde's tendency to make sonic booms, its cramped quarters, and its expensive operation diminished its attractiveness for mass transportation.

Automobile manufacturers used to be extremely successful in persuading the consumer that his current car was obsolete. Some consumers traded in their cars every two years to get the newest style. In 1972, Ralph Nader wrote,

> The stylists' . . . function has been designated by automobile company top management as *the* prerequisite for maintaining the annual high volume of automobile sales—no small assignment in an industry that has a volume of at least $20 billion every year. It is the stylists who are responsible for most of the annual model change which promises the consumer "new" automobiles. It is not surprising, therefore, to find this "newness" is almost entirely stylistic in content and that engineering innovation is restricted to a decidedly secondary role in product development.[12]

---

[12]R Nader, *Unsafe at Any Speed: The Designed-In Dangers of the Automobile* (New York: Grossman Publishers, 1972), p. 211.

When styling was the paramount purchase determinant, durability mattered little. Consumers traded in their cars before the autos needed major repairs. Consumers changed their car-buying habits, however, as automobiles became more expensive. Many consumers recalculated the elements of product quality. Serviceability, reliability, and performance became more important than style. As this change occurred, Japanese cars became more attractive to a sizable segment of consumers.

Even in the ever-changing fashion industry, consumers are paying more attention to durability in their clothes. In 1987, designers and manufacturers tried to revive flagging sales by switching their new lines from the long skirts of the earlier 1980s to miniskirts. In 1993, they switched back to long skirts. To the fashion industry's dismay, women did not replace their wardrobes. They simply added the new long fashions to their existing wardrobes. Some even took their old long skirts out of closets where they had been stored for five years or longer.

6. Serviceability.   *Serviceability* is the speed, courtesy, competence, and ease of repair. How much time will it take to fix a broken product? Consumers often find the repair process frustrating and sometimes infuriating. Many consumers feel like the physician who called her plumber on a Saturday to report that the only toilet in the house was stopped up. The plumber advised the physician to drop two aspirins down the toilet and call him on Monday. When repairpeople are courteous, quick, and efficient, consumers attribute higher quality to the company's product.

7. Aesthetics.   *Aesthetics* refers to how the product looks, feels, tastes, and smells. Chocolate candy manufacturers always refer to "mouth feel" in judging quality. High-quality leather goods always have a distinctively appealing scent. Because people have individual aesthetic preferences, companies have to develop their own niches.

8. Perceived Quality.   Consumers often get their information about quality from advertising copy, acquaintances, television, and other indirect sources. Many make buying decisions with imperfect information and sketchy data. A product's reputation is often based on *perceived quality* that may in fact belong to an older model or an established company image rather than on the intrinsic quality of the product.

Total Quality Management

In the 1960s and 1970s, US industry focused on the cost of making a particular product or service rather than on its quality. Companies believed they had to choose between quality and cost reduction or cost maintenance. If costs went down, profit would increase. Very little effort was made to involve employees in production decisions. The assumption was that management knew best.

Japanese companies had a different mindset when they approached cost, quality, and employee involvement issues. Japanese consumers demanded higher-quality products than American consumers expected. Japanese manufacturers had to ask themselves how they could provide high quality and still keep costs low. In many cases, they found that with clever engineering, higher quality could lead to *lower* costs. Japanese firms looked to their customers' needs to drive quality improvements and were far more customer directed than their US counterparts.

As Japanese productivity continued to improve in the 1970s and 1980s, US performance declined. There were three major reasons for Japanese companies' excellent performance:

1. They achieved a major competitive advantage by reducing the time needed to complete processes.
2. They adopted a habit of continuous improvement.
3. They focused first and above all on the customer.[13]

Finally, in the early 1980s, US companies realized that if they were to keep their global market share, they would have to develop new leadership skills. They would have to take a multifaceted approach to the technical, physical, and behavioral aspects of their businesses. By the mid-1980s, *total quality management (TQM)* was touted as the new, best approach to remedy US industries' problems. Typically the major elements of TQM were as follows:

· *Technical expertise,* including just-in-time manufacturing. Companies experimented with reducing lead times, work-in-process inventories, and finished-goods inventories. They demanded that suppliers deliver defect-free parts as they were needed and that suppliers assume the task of inspection before delivery. Predictability and conformance were the watchwords.

· *Organizational development* techniques that fostered better team management and greater team interdependence. Management focused on building the interpersonal relationships that would lead to more effective strategic decision making.

· *Strategic approaches* to markets and customers that defined and clarified the important organizational imperatives.

· *Concern for the customer* is the element that makes the organization look outward rather than inward. Companies recognized the negative results from offering poor-quality products. They shared

---

[13]D Ciampa, *Total Quality* (Reading, MA: Addison-Wesley, 1992), pp. 9–14.

customer feedback with employees so that all organization members could be involved in product improvement.

In short, TQM is a form of organizational change. Organizational change drives the process of quality improvement. Often a change agent triggers the process. The change agent may be a person (usually the CEO), competition, customer demand, a new start-up venture, or a restart. Competitors and demanding customers influence CEOs to change their perceptions and actions.[14]

The Malcolm Baldrige National Quality Award

In 1987, President Reagan's secretary of commerce, Malcolm Baldrige, died in a rodeo accident. An award was established in his memory to encourage American businesses and other organizations "to practice effective quality control in the provision of their goods and services."

Award criteria have two result-oriented goals: to project key requirements for delivering ever improving value to customers and, at the same time, maximizing the overall productivity and effectiveness of the delivering organization. To achieve these goals, the organization must have in place a set of values that addresses and integrates the overall customer and company performance requirements.

The National Institute of Standards and Technology (NIST), a branch of the Department of Commerce, manages the Baldrige Award. Any for-profit company in the United States or its territories is eligible to apply. Governments—federal, state, or local—are not eligible, nor are not-for-profit companies, trade associations, and professional societies. There are three categories of award, with two awards per category. The categories are Manufacturing, Service, and Small Business (fewer than 500 full-time employees). However, there is no obligation to give all six awards unless companies meet the criteria.

Each fall, NIST chooses a board of examiners from a pool of applicants. The board tries to provide a balance among a number of constituencies such as universities, trade associations, government agencies, health care organizations, and industry. The board of examiners assesses companies' performances in the following areas: Leadership, Information and Analysis, Strategic Quality Planning, Human Resource Development and Management, Management of Process Quality, Quality and Operations Results, and Customer Focus and Satisfaction.

In the first stage of the award process, the company must pass a review. In the second stage, at least four members of the board of examiners and a

---

[14]D M Lascelles and B G Dale, "Quality Improvement: The Motivation and Means of Starting the Process," in M Hand and B Plowman, eds., *Quality Management Handbook* (London: Butterworth-Heinemann Ltd., 1992), pp. 22–23.

senior examiner review each applicant. A panel of judges decides who will
go on to the third stage, the site visit review. In this stage, five board members
and a senior examiner visit the site over three to four days to verify information and clarify issues. In the final stage, the panel of judges recommends
award recipients to NIST. Then NIST presents the judges' recommendations to the secretary of commerce, who presents the award.[15]

Cadillac: A Controversial Winner.   In 1990, Cadillac Motor Car Company,
a division of General Motors, won a Baldrige award. In making the award,
the judges noted that in 1985, Cadillac had seriously misjudged customers'
expectations and the market. Predicting a gasoline shortage that never mate-
rialized, the company downsized its cars and lost its customers.

Cadillac management asked W Edwards Deming to consult with
employees and top management about remedies. Deming stressed that
management itself was the problem and advised Cadillac to look to its own
management systems for the solution.

Cadillac instituted an approach it called *simultaneous engineering,*
or "the process in which appropriate disciplines are committed to work
interactively to conceive, approve, develop, and implement product programs . . ."[16] The company used teamwork and group decision making to
improve its manufacturing process. Cadillac asked customers what specifications it should use for its cars. The company collected data from a variety
of sources. Marketing firms conducted surveys, customers and noncusto-
mers evaluated models of proposed car designs, dealers gave feedback on
customer suggestions, and Cadillac employees spoke directly with customers at clinics, auto shows, and auto dealerships.

By 1989, Cadillac had turned its situation around. It applied for a Baldrige Award and was one of the finalists. Using the feedback from the Baldrige
judges, Cadillac applied again in 1990, and this time it won.[17]

As noted above, the process of applying for the Baldrige Award requires
a major organizational effort. Winners are rewarded by the prestige the
award confers and the right to use it to promote their products and services.
In Cadillac's case, however, such promotion caused problems. Parent company General Motors and Cadillac came under fire for the way they touted
the Baldrige Award. In 1991, General Motors ran a two-page ad that said,
"of the 167,000 different companies that applied for consideration this year
alone, fewer than 240 were judged qualified just to go on to the next level."
The Department of Commerce quickly corrected General Motors, noting
that only 97 companies had applied. The larger number was also inaccurate;
180,000 companies had asked for applications but had not filed.

[15]Bureau of Business Practice, *Profiles of Malcolm Baldrige Award Winners* (Boston:
Allyn and Bacon, 1992), pp. 7–18.
[16]Ibid, p. 10.
[17]Bureau of Business Practice, *Profiles of Malcolm Baldrige Award Winners,* pp. 61–64.

General Motors ran a second version of the ad in *Fortune* in January 1992. This version was also inaccurate. It said, "of the thousands of different companies that applied for consideration this year alone, fewer than 100 were judged sufficiently qualified to go on to the final round." The director of public affairs for NIST noted that the numbers and the award process description were still incorrect.

A Cadillac spokesperson agreed that both ads had mistakes. McCann-Erickson USA, the company that prepared the ad, took the blame, declaring it did not understand the Baldrige process well enough to make the ads accurate.

The Department of Commerce was not through with Cadillac, however. In yet another ad, Cadillac asserted that "the government cited the 4.9 liter V-8 as a prime example of Cadillac's ongoing product refinement." The NIST director protested the suggestion that the Department of Commerce was endorsing a particular engine. He charged Cadillac with extrapolating the ad from a Department of Commerce news release citing improvements in "performance attributes of several models such as acceleration and horse-power . . ."[18]

In a letter to the editor of *The Wall Street Journal,* Murray Hillman, president of Strategy Workshop Inc., pointed out ironies in the Department of Commerce's selection process. Cadillac, he declared, let its quality drop to very low levels compared to Japanese competitors. When Cadillac finally decided to improve its quality, "its *rate of improvement, not its level of quality,* was significantly higher than most of its competitors. Today [February 1991], Cadillac still turns out a larger number of new-car defects per thousand than its sister division at Buick."[19] Hillman pointed to the inability of the new Cadillac Allante to win market share. If customer satisfaction is one of the Baldrige Award's seven criteria, he asked, how did Cadillac win it with a marketing failure?

Department of Commerce officials met with Baldrige Award winners to develop clearer standards regarding what companies could say about their awards and how they said it. Since the department did not have the authority to censor ads, it hoped to work toward a community standard of permissibility.

ISO 9000 — *know*

ISO 9000 is a series of quality standards developed in 1986 under the International Organization for Standardization (ISO), headquartered in Geneva, Switzerland. The purpose of ISO 9000 is to set common specifications for a wide range of products and services and to accredit the products and services

---

[18]G Fuchberg, "Let Restraint Guide Your Advertising, Baldrige Prize Winners to Be Warned," *The Wall Street Journal,* January 11, 1992, p. B5.

[19]"They're the Top and the Bottom," *The Wall Street Journal,* February 21, 1991.

that meet the standards. The organization consists of the national standards bodies of 90 member countries. Countries participating in ISO 9000 include all of the European Community (since 1989), the European Free Trade Association (EFTA), Japan, and the United States. The organization is non-governmental and is not a part of the United Nations; it does, however, have technical liaisons with some UN agencies. Member countries voluntarily participate in nearly 1,000 technical committees and subcommittees that develop and revise international standards covering service industries as well as manufacturing.

Companies begin the accreditation process by consulting a 100-page ISO 9000 guidebook. The guide directs companies to document how workers perform every function affecting quality. Then companies institute mechanisms to ensure that workers follow through on stated routines. They develop internal teams to check that procedures are followed in each of 20 functions, including design, process control, service, purchasing, inspection and testing, and training.

When a company decides it has these processes in place and operating, the International Standards Organization sends independent auditors to the company to inspect it and, if it passes, to award it a certificate of compliance. The auditors are certified by agencies in their own countries; for example, the Registrar Accrediting Board licenses US auditors. The accreditation process can take as long as 18 months to complete and can cost a company more than $200,000.

ISO 9000's underlying concept is that companies can standardize certain generic management practices consistently to produce products at a given level of quality. While ISO 9000 does not mandate that a company raise its quality, it forces the firm to follow a uniform standard in its production.

In the United States, Underwriters' Laboratories has incorporated ISO 9000 standards as its first-phase requirement to use the UL approval in specific product certification plans. However, the United States is well behind Europe in adopting ISO 9000 standards. A 1992 survey of US manufacturing executives found that 15 percent of the respondents planned to certify their plants by 1994, but nearly 50 percent had never even heard of ISO 9000.[20]

US domestic companies are losing contracts to ISO-certified European competitors. However, companies with European subsidiaries are well aware of the benefits of certification. For example, the 3M subsidiary in France has been responding to its customers' requirement for ISO 9000–registered products since 1989.

Other companies conforming to the standards include Volkswagen, DuPont, Eastman Kodak, Renault, Corning, Exxon Chemicals, Sandoz,

---

[20]J B Levine, "Want EC Business? You Have Two Choices," *Business Week,* October 19, 1992, pp. 58–59.

and many others. Government ministries and departments also have made ISO 9000 a requirement for their large contract suppliers. The US Department of Defense and the Food and Drug Administration, for example, mandate that their suppliers be registrants.

Pall Corporation of New York recognized the importance of ISO 9000 several years ago. Hyman Katz, corporate vice president of quality assurance and regulatory affairs at Pall Corporation, noted that his company began its efforts to comply with ISO 9000 in its UK manufacturing plants in 1987. The company, which makes filters and other fluid clarification devices that remove contaminants, has manufacturing facilities worldwide. If its operations did not comply with ISO 9000, prospective purchasers would not be assured of a fixed standard of quality and might look to Pall's competitors for that assurance.[21]

ISO 9000 requirements contribute to a TQM process. ISO 9000 requires documentation and product assessment, two important aspects of TQM. But total quality management goes beyond ISO 9000 by dealing with issues such as leadership, strategic planning, and employee empowerment.

US Corporations That Use Japanese Quality Models

Japanese manufacturing success was the driving force behind many of the manufacturing changes US corporations made in the 1980s. Companies invested billions of dollars in quality circles and just-in-time parts delivery. After a decade of experimentation and adaptation to these techniques, some US companies have concluded that Japanese systems do not work very well in American companies.

A leading management consultant observed that what American companies learned from Japanese systems had not really made them competitive. He noted that "companies have been obsessed with one fad idea or another at the cost of their overall focus." In 1992, Arthur D Little Inc. surveyed 500 manufacturers to find out how well they were doing with Japanese methods. Those companies had spent $800 billion in capital investment and $150 billion in worker training over the preceding decade. Most were disappointed with the results.[22]

Auto parts manufacturer Federal-Mogul of Lancaster, Pennsylvania, is one such example. The company had assumed Japanese firms realized a major cost advantage from computers, robots, and other automated equipment. In 1987, seeking to reduce its labor costs, the plant installed state-of-the-art automation based on Japanese systems. Although the plant turned parts out more quickly than before, it could not switch easily from making

---

[21]Bureau of Business Practice, *ISO 9000: Handbook of Quality Standards and Compliance* (Needham Heights, MA: Allyn and Bacon, 1992), pp. 7–111.

[22]A K Naj, "Some Manufacturers Drop Efforts to Adopt Japanese Techniques," *The Wall Street Journal,* May 7, 1993, p. A1.

one part or one size of part to another. The sophisticated machinery required extensive maintenance and realignment.

Federal-Mogul failed to lower costs, but—more important—it lost flexibility in switching among models to meet customer needs. In 1992, the company removed the robots and many of the computers. Workers who switched the assembly apparatus by hand were able to produce three times as many varieties as before in the same amount of time.

Quality circles, which were in great vogue in the mid-1980s, are also disappearing. Companies such as Whirlpool and General Electric found workers did not know why they were in the groups, their discussions were unfocused, and they talked about issues unrelated to their jobs. Although both Whirlpool and General Electric continued to solicit ideas from workers, they focused on those that saved money. GE rewarded individual workers for their ideas, giving them gift certificates and stock options.

Just-in-time inventory works well in Japan, where manufacturers and suppliers are located close together. In the United States, suppliers are more likely to be greater distances away. Some companies, such as GE Appliances, found they were able to respond more quickly to customer needs by keeping higher levels of inventory. John Cassidy, director of research at United Technologies Corporation, observed, "we misplaced the goal. In order to eliminate inventory, we focused our efforts on materials-handling. We forced our supplier to take extraordinary measures to solve our [own] inventory problem, rather than looking at our manufacturing process."[23]

Many Japanese firms, in fact, are rethinking their commitment to just-in-time manufacturing. The very frequent deliveries (sometimes several a day) required by just-in-time are clogging the roads with delivery trucks and contributing to air pollution.

Regulation of Product Safety

Consumers have become increasingly concerned about the safety of the products they buy and use. As we discussed in the previous chapter, the concept that a product should be safe under reasonable use is fairly new, but it has become generally accepted. Manufacturers cannot ignore safety-in-use considerations in their quest to offer products that satisfy other quality dimensions.

In 1972 Congress passed the Consumer Product Safety Act, which created the Consumer Product Safety Commission (CPSC). The CPSC is an independent regulatory body charged with protecting the public against unreasonable risk of injury by unsafe products. The commission is composed of five members appointed by the president and is located in Washington, DC. The CPSC also supervises regional offices and testing laboratories around the country. Jacqueline Jones-Smith has headed the CPSC

---

[23]Ibid.

since 1989. Her recent initiatives emphasize public education, making better use of CPSC resources, and redefining the agency's direction.

The CPSC's duties are to

- Develop and enforce uniform safety standards for consumer products, including design, construction, content, performance, and labeling
- Initiate and monitor recalls of products deemed to be hazardous
- Help industry develop uniform safety standards
- Help consumers evaluate comparative safety standards of consumer products
- Promote and conduct research and investigation into the causes and prevention of injury, illness, and death caused by consumer products
- Help minimize the conflicts among local, state, and federal product safety laws

In the first six years after the CPSC's creation, the commission issued more than 1,200 recalls affecting over 7 million specific products.[24] Recalled products included toys, electrical appliances, and flammable clothing. The commission banned such products as flammable contact adhesives, products containing asbestos, and unstable refuse bins. Most of these actions resulted from negotiations between the CPSC and the companies producing the products. Of the 600 actions taken by the commission, fewer than 10 required court action.[25]

In 1981, the first year of the Reagan administration, Congress passed the Consumer Product Safety Amendments, which gave industries the right to develop their own safety standards. The Reagan administration's real goal was to abolish the CPSC, but it settled for slashing the commission's budget and appointing inexperienced commissioners.

Between 1981 and 1989, the CPSC's budget fell from $42.1 million to $34.5 million. In mid-1989, its budget was approximately the same size it had been 15 years earlier.[26] Its staff shrank from 978 members in 1981 to 519 in 1989.[27] When George Bush took office in 1989, the commission had only two members, one of whom was the acting chairperson, Anne Graham. Graham observed that the reliance on voluntary standards became "a signal for everything to go in slow motion."[28]

Over the past several years, consumer groups have criticized the Consumer Product Safety Commission for the length of time it takes to complete

---

[24] *The New York Times,* February 9, 1979, sec. 3, p. 1.

[25] W Guzzardi, Jr., "The Mindless Pursuit of Safety," *Fortune,* April 9, 1979, p. 60.

[26] J Bodnar, "Whatever Happened to the Consumer Movement?," *Changing Times,* August 1989, p. 50.

[27] M D Hinds, "Troubles of a Safety Agency: A Battle to Keep Functioning," *The New York Times,* March 18, 1989, p. 52.

[28] Ibid.

EXHIBIT 15–1

CPSC accomplishments, 1990–1992

U.S. CONSUMER PRODUCT SAFETY COMMISSION
WASHINGTON, D.C. 20207
ACCOMPLISHMENTS IN 1990–1992

1. Mandatory Standards

Action taken

• Glue removers containing acetonitrite and hair-wave neutralizers containing bromates	– Mandated child-resistant packaging to help prevent poisonings
• Test protocol for child-resistant packaging	– Proposed change in test protocol to make child-resistant packaging easier for older people to open.
• Infant "bean-bag" cushions	– Banned because of suffocation hazard.
• Reloadable shell fireworks	– Banned because of severe injuries.
• Crib toys	– Advance notice of proposed rulemaking to address strangulation deaths.
• Art materials and household chemicals	– Proposed chronic hazard labeling guidelines.
• Cigarette lighters	– Issued advance notice to proposed rulemaking to require child-resistant lighters.
• Automatic garage door operators	– Codified UL standard as federal mandatory standard to prevent crushing injuries to children.
• Over-the-counter ibuprofen	– Mandated child-resistant packaging to help prevent poisonings.
• Lidocaine and dibucaine	– Proposed child-resistant packaging to help prevent poisonings.
• Lead	– Published notice of regulatory investigation soliciting information on lead-in-paint.
• Clacker balls	– Granted petition to review the current regulation.

2. Voluntary Standards

Voluntary standards are developed and implemented by industry, with technical support by CPSC. CPSC also reviews industry conformance with selected voluntary standards. Examples of voluntary standards for which CPSC provided technical support include:

- All-terrain vehicles
- Chain saws
- High chairs
- Carriages and strollers
- Chimney liners
- Fireplace stoves
- Room heaters
- Hair dryers
- Immersion-detection circuit-interrupters
- Pacifiers
- Play yards
- Carbon monoxide detectors
- Crib cornerposts
- Art materials labeling
- Child resistant closures
- Riding lawnmowers
- Balloon package labeling
- Safety signs and labels
- Covers for swimming pools, spas and hot tubs
- Barriers for residential swimming pools, spas and hot tubs (to prevent child drownings) developed by CPSC staff and adopted by code organizations and by state and local jurisdictions.
- Electrical outlets
- Home playground equipment
- Indoor air quality
- Playground surfacing
- Toy safety
- Formaldehyde/pressed wood products

3. Recalls and Corrective Actions

In 1990–92, CPSC obtained recalls affecting more than 98 million products that failed to comply with a regulation or presented product hazards to consumers. Some models of the following products have been involved in corrective actions:

- Water coolers containing lead (lead poisoning)
- Infant "bean-bag" cushions (suffocation)
- Five-gallon buckets (drownings) (warning issued, not a recall)
- Swinging cradle (suffocation)
- Baby walkers (children choking on plastic decals)
- Playground equipment (finger entrapment)
- Storage containers (child entrapment)
- Exercise devices (spring breakage)
- Toys (choking hazard)
- Coffeemakers (thermal cut-off fuse failure)
- Strollers (pinch points and accidental collapse)
- Electrical converters (overheating)
- Ceiling fans (falling)
- Toddler bed (entrapment/strangulation)
- Pacifiers (choking hazard)
- Rattles (choking hazard)
- Children's products with excess lead (lead poisoning)
- Oil-filled electric heaters (fire hazard)
- Miniature Christmas light string sets (fire hazard)
- Cribs (slat width and entrapment hazard)

investigations. The commission's rules require that it must give manufacturers a chance to review and dispute data; The CPSC cannot release preliminary data to the public.

Exhibit 15–1 lists the 1990–1992 accomplishments of the Consumer Product Safety Commission.

The Legal Environment

Prior to 1916, US product liability law was based on the concept of privity. *Privity* meant that if a manufacturer was negligent in making an unsafe product, the consumer's only legal recourse was to sue the firm. But if the consumer bought the product from an intermediary such as a wholesaler or retailer, the manufacturer was immune from liability for negligence.[29] While the privity concept might have been appropriate when a consumer bought a product directly from the craftsperson who made it, it did not serve the public interest in a time of mass production and mass distribution.

The courts ended privity with the case of *MacPherson* v. *Buick Motor Company.* In that case the defendant, Buick Motor Company, sold a car to a retailer, which in turn sold it to Mr. MacPherson. As MacPherson was driving the car, one of its wooden wheels crumbled. Buick had bought the wheels from another manufacturer that had not inspected them prior to the sale. The charge was negligence rather than fraud, because there was no intent to deceive. The court found that Buick, which sold the car to the retailer, was guilty because it was responsible for the finished product and should have tested the component parts.[30] Once privity was no longer applicable, the issue of product safety was thrown wide open to judicial interpretation.

Theories of Product Liability

Negligence

Negligence is the failure to exercise reasonable care in manufacturing or selling a product, resulting in injury to a person or property. The concept of reasonable care extends to all parts of the production and distribution process, including the salesperson who presents the product to the consumer. For example, if a salesperson overpromotes a product, thereby causing the consumer to overlook warning labels, the salesperson can be found guilty of negligence.

When products are sold to vulnerable consumers such as children or the elderly, companies have to be particularly careful. A company can be guilty

---

[29]R J Posch, Jr., *The Complete Guide to Marketing and the Law* (Englewood Cliffs, NJ: Prentice-Hall, 1988), p. 3.

[30]Ibid., p. 5.

of negligence if it fails to warn the user about potential hazards. Suppose a company makes a toy for a five-year-old. That toy may be perfectly safe for a five-year-old but not for her two-year-old sibling. Unless the toy carries a warning about dangers to toddlers, the manufacturer or retailer may be guilty of negligence.

But warnings may not be enough if the product is still dangerous in normal use. The Consumer Affairs Committee of the Americans for Democratic Action published a report in 1988 criticizing the CPSC for "pitiful ineptitude" in overseeing toy standards. The report asserted that with ordinary use, toys caused 131,000 injuries in 1987, including 105,000 to children under 15 years old. The ubiquitous baby walker alone caused nearly 21,000 injuries.[31]

In 1992, the Institute for Injury Reduction, a nonprofit group founded by trial attorneys, said the CPSC tested fewer than 1 percent of all toys for sale. Its report claimed that in 1991, 67 children were killed by toys and 163,000 were injured. The institute's president urged the Clinton administration to reverse Reagan and Bush cutbacks and give the CPSC more money and staff to expand its testing and recall programs.[32]

The Marble Case.   In mid-1992, the Consumer Product Safety Commission decided not to ban balloons, marbles, small balls, crayons, and other toys that failed to carry labels warning that toddlers could choke on the objects. According to statistics, less than one death results from the sale of 1.5 billion marbles each year, and an average of six deaths occur from yearly sales of 1.2 billion balloons.

The CPSC decided the effectiveness of warning labels could not be demonstrated for these products. It also noted that studies of labeling indicate it has no effect on the use of common products that have obvious hazards. The CPSC staff concluded multiple warning labels would be necessary for any product that contains both marbles and balloons or balloons and small balls.[33]

Design Defect

Manufacturers are legally bound to design products with reasonable care. Even if a product is carefully made, it may be defective because it is unreasonably dangerous to use. It is up to the manufacturer to anticipate the way

---

[31]T Ahern, "Consumer Group Warns Shoppers of Hazardous Toys," *The Boston Globe,* November 22, 1988, p. 3.

[32]R Green, "1 in 6 Toys Tested by US Is Unsafe for Children, Group Says," *The Boston Globe,* November 19, 1992, p. 6.

[33]C Lochhead, "Child Safety Bill Is Hard to Swallow," *The Wall Street Journal,* July 7, 1992, p. A14.

a product will be used and design it so it can be put to use safely. Manufacturers are not expected to use designs that are impractical or prohibitively expensive; therefore, a balance exists between the likelihood that injury will occur and the cost of taking precautions to ensure that it does not.

The Case of Automobile Seat Belts.   There is overwhelming evidence that seat belts in America are obsolete and prone to improper use. Lap belts installed in rear seats can actually kill. The belts themselves may crush vertebrae, internal organs, and the spinal cord when the passenger is thrown forward in a crash. Rear shoulder belts ameliorate some of the risk.

However, recent studies show many American and Japanese cars have insufficiently anchored back seats. When these cars are hit from the rear, back-seat passengers may be crushed by the collapsing rear end of the car regardless of the kind of seat belt they are wearing. Spokespeople for the National Highway Safety Commission (NHSC), which regulates automobile safety, assert automobile manufacturers are more interested in getting people to buckle up than scaring them about seat belt safety.

Jeffrey Miller, a NHSC deputy administrator, said, "Sure there are people injured by lap belts and lap-shoulder belts, but on balance, the belts have proven repeatedly . . . to be very effective in reducing death and injury. Why haven't we told people about the risks? Our top prority is to save lives, and you save lives by encouraging seat-belt usage. You don't encourage usage by scaring people out of using the equipment."[34]

Warranty) + Lecture

A *warranty* indicates the seller's willingness to stand behind its product. A seller who issues a written warranty assumes responsibility for the quality and suitability of the goods sold for a specified period of time. If a written warranty is issued, it must be given at the time of sale and must be part of the sale. The consumer must not have to pay any additional fees for the warranty.

Sellers are not required to offer warranties regardless of the price or type of product. However, once the seller issues a written warranty on a product that costs more than $10, that warranty must be designated as a full or a limited warranty. A *full warranty* promises the consumer that a defective product will be replaced or fixed in a reasonable period of time. A *limited warranty* promises less than the stipulations of a full warranty. For example, a seller may decide to issue a limited warranty that covers parts but not service.

---

[34]M D Hinds, "Some Seat Belts Found Inferior (or Lethal)," *The New York Times,* October 22, 1988, p. 50.

Strict Liability

Under *strict liability* standards, the company is held to much tighter standards than it is under negligence or design defect standards. The quality of the product is the key issue.[35] A manufacturer of a defective product may be held responsible for an injury caused by a product "regardless of privity, foreseeability, or due care."[36] The injured party must show only that the manufacturer or seller was connected with a defective product, the product was dangerous when it was sold, and it caused injury. Under strict liability, everyone in the distribution chain is responsible for the safety of the product.

The United States has the most litigious legal climate in the world. Courts have been willing to compensate injured parties with huge settlements. Although Vice President Dan Quayle railed against the legal profession and large monetary awards, he was unsuccessful in effecting change. It remains to be seen whether Congress and the Clinton administration will press for new legal procedures and compensation standards.

CASE   *Cellular Phones and Electromagnetic Fields: Are They Safe?*

Cellular phones were sold commercially for the first time in 1984. By November 1992, more than 10 million people had subscribed to the service. In January 1993, David Reynard of St. Petersburg, Florida, appeared on CNN's "Larry King Live" show. He announced he was suing a phone maker, NEC America, and a GTE subsidiary, GTE Mobilnet. He asserted his wife had developed brain cancer and died because she used a cellular phone.

A few days later, Reginald Lewis, chairperson of TLC Beatrice Company, died of brain cancer and Michael Walsh, a top executive at Tenneco, Inc., was diagnosed with the disease. People also remembered Lee Atwater's death from brain cancer; as George Bush's campaign manager, Atwater had used a cellular phone incessantly.

Cellular phone transmitters operate at very high frequencies at one-half to three watts of power. Unlike car phones and low-powered cordless home phones, cellular phones place the radio transmitter beside the user's head. Scientists know radio waves enter the brain as they seek out the nearest transmitter site, but they do not know whether those waves are harmful.

Most research has centered on the effects of low-frequency electromagnetic radiation from power lines and video display terminals rather than on cellular phones. Scientists do agree that cellular phones create only a negligible risk due to heat or thermal damage to tissues. But there are no hard data on the effects of radio waves from cellular phones.

Within hours after Reynard's charges were made public, cellular phone manufacturers vehemently denied the product posed health risks. Edward F Staiano, pres-

---

[35]F W Morgan, "Marketing and Product Liability: A Review and Update," in A P Iannone, ed., *Contemporary Moral Controversies in Business* (New York: Oxford University Press, 1989), pp. 353–64.

[36]Posch, *The Complete Guide,* p. 14.

ident of the cellular phone division of Motorola, said independent studies showed "no existence of health risks from the use of cellular phones." His judgment was echoed by the president of a communications market research firm, who called the charges a "tempest in a teapot."[37]

Scientists pointed out that consumers are exposed to the dangers of electricity in many other ways and recommended means to avoid exposure. M Granger Morgan, head of the Department of Engineering and Public Policy at Carnegie Mellon University, offered some tips for avoiding electric and magnetic fields:

- Don't use electric blankets, electric mattress pads, or waterbed heaters. Older designs of these products create strong magnetic fields. If you are determined to warm your bed, preheat it, then unplug the devices. Remember that newer devises have low-field electricity.
- Don't sleep next to bedside clocks or fans. They also produce strong magnetic fields. Switch to wind-up clocks, or place motorized clocks across the room.
- Ask your local utility company to measure electric fields around your bedroom, and place your bed in the area of the lowest field.
- If you use a computer, put at least 24 inches between you and it. Get strong reading glasses if you need them to see the screen.
- Don't stand near your dishwasher, refrigerator, clothes dryer, or oven.
- Don't use a hair dryer.

Morgan acknowledged at the bottom of his list, "once you have done whatever seems reasonable to you, then it is probably wise to forget about it."[38]

Shifting the public's attention to the dangers of other products did not stop the cellular phone controversy. Cellular phone companies hastened to assure consumers that health risks were minimal. However, the companies acknowledged they were caught in a dilemma. They had no way of knowing whether the health risk was real or imagined. They had to decide quickly whether to address negative news stories or ignore the issue. In fact, there was very little information, either positive or negative, to report. Could the firms be held legally responsible if sued for selling an unsafe product? Had they protected themselves against problems that might surface years later?

On February 26, 1993, the EPA called for a major, comprehensive study of the potential dangers from electromagnetic fields. The agency said consumers had virtually no information on which they could rely to assess the danger of exposure from sources ranging from hair dryers to power lines.

Results of a reassuring study in California were released in March. The study, funded by Southern California Edison, was published in the journal *Epidemiology*. The researchers noted the study did not address the possible relationship between childhood leukemia and exposure to electromagnetic fields identified in a Swedish study. However, it did cover workplace exposure.

Researchers evaluated health data from 36,221 workers who were employed by Southern California Edison for at least a year between 1960 and 1988. They found

---

[37]"Motorola Denies Cellular Phone Risk," *The New York Times,* January 26, 1993, p. D7.

[38]"Some Tips to Reduce Exposure to Electricity," *USA Today,* February 4, 1993, p. 13A.

no evidence of unusual levels of leukemia, brain cancer, or lymphoma in the group, even among those whose occupations exposed them to very high levels of electromagnetic contact.[39]

As quickly as it had occurred, the public's concern about cellular phones seemed to disappear. There may be several reasons why the cellular phone scare did not have staying power. Apparently people find it difficult to believe danger exists if they cannot see, feel, hear, or smell it or if the consequences are deferred. Articles about electromagnetic fields pointed out the dangers associated with every electric household and office appliance. To avoid all sources of electromagnetic exposure, a person must stop using or alter the use of the conveniences that make life pleasant and easy—with no assurance that the effort is worthwhile.

Questions

1. Should cellular phone companies lease or sell their products if they cannot guarantee their use will not harm consumers?
2. Is a warning label on the headset sufficient to absolve the companies from responsibility?
3. Based on the information in the case, would you stop using a cellular phone if you had one? If not, what data would convince you to stop?

Summary

The term *product quality* has many meanings. However, some basic elements and criteria define product quality. Until the 1990s, the issue of product quality was taken more seriously in Japan and Europe than in the United States. The dimensions of quality are performance, features, reliability, conformance, durability, serviceability, aesthetics, and perceived quality.

Total quality management (TQM) became a national obsession in the late 1980s as American companies lost market share. The major elements of TQM are technical expertise, organizational development, strategic approaches, and concern for the external customer. Many companies have applied for the Malcolm Baldrige Award for Quality. The award process is difficult and time consuming, but it provides important organizational feedback.

Companies are beginning to use ISO 9000 standards as a benchmark for quality worldwide. ISO 9000 is the standards the European Community uses across countries to ensure standardization of quality. US companies and government agencies are also adopting the standards to enhance their competitiveness abroad.

---

[39]Bill Richards, "Southern California Edison Study Finds No Workplace Tie Between Cancer, EMF," *The Wall Street Journal,* March 15, 1993, p. B5.

Product quality and TQM are liability and safety concerns as well as competitive issues. A good quality management program considers how and by whom the product will be used and whether such use will be safe. Such a program will not sacrifice safety for other elements of performance. Unsafe products, as well as poor-quality products, negatively affect a firm's profits.

The Consumer Product Safety Act created the Consumer Product Safety Commission (CPSC). The commission was supposed to enforce uniform safety standards, monitor product recalls, help develop safety standards, evaluate safety standards, promote safety research, and minimize legal conflicts. The CPSC was very active initially, but its budget and staff were cut severely in the late 1980s.

The original legal basis for product liability law was privity. When privity was eliminated as a legal concept, product liability law was developed on a state-by-state basis. The theories of product liability include negligence, design defects, warranty, and strict liability.

Liability laws are in a state of transition. Although the Reagan administration tried repeatedly to pass a uniform federal law, stakeholders successfully thwarted its efforts. There seems to be a new trend toward a more conservative and pro-business legal climate. The courts may be able to achieve the goals of the Reagan era without federal legislation.

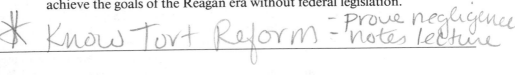
Know Tort Reform - Prove negligence - notes lecture

Questions

1. What are the basic elements of product quality?
2. What is the significance of the Malcolm Baldrige Award? What benefits accrue to the winners?
3. How are ISO 9000 standards important to US competitiveness?
4. What are the duties of the Consumer Product Safety Commission as delegated by Congress? How effective has the commission been?
5. What is the legal concept of privity?
6. What are the theories of product liability?
7. Are manufacturers of marbles or balloons exercising reasonable care when they make those products? Should a toy store be charged with negligence if it sells the product to a parent whose child puts it in his mouth and chokes? What constitutes reasonable care in making and selling these products?

Projects

1. Suppose you are a toy manufacturer. Write an executive memo to your staff defining what product safety should mean in your industry.

2. Talk to a lawyer in your city or town who deals in product safety issues. Ask her what legal trends seem to be emerging.
3. Call your state legislator's office and find out your state's laws regarding product safety.

BETA CASE 13
PRODUCT USE ISSUES

Robert Mobley, general counsel for Beta, was having a terrible day. Not only was the March downpour flooding his new basement family room, but problems were mounting at the office. In January, Mobley was notified that one of Beta's products—E-Targa, a form of vitamin E—may have been responsible for the deaths of four premature babies in a Boise, Idaho, hospital. Beta, which had distributed the solution to hospitals the previous July, at first attributed the deaths to routine nursery problems. In August and September, when other hospitals began to report deaths, Beta took the solution off the market. But now, Mobley discovered, parents of the infants had filed a class action suit against Beta.

Vitamin E is an important nutrient for premature babies, but it is not very effective when taken orally. Babies' immature stomachs cannot handle oral doses, and their limited muscle area makes intramuscular injections impractical. E-Targa, however, was in a solution that could be injected directly into the veins.

Beta had not sought FDA approval for E-Targa because, in its counsel's opinion, the drug was not new. Although the means of dispensing it to infants was an innovation, the substance was simply a variation of others that had been on the market for years. When Beta found out about the deaths in January,

Mobley recommended the company not inform the FDA. According to the law, any company that markets a product that needs federal approval must report severe reactions within 15 working days of its discovery. But since Beta had not asked for or received approval for the drug, the reporting requirement was not clear.

Also, doctors at the Boise hospital did not report the deaths. They did call the regional FDA office to find out whether E-Targa had been approved, but they did not mention any problems. They also notified a prominent pediatrician whose close ties to the FDA, they thought, would lead him to inform the agency.

The Food and Drug Administration had been told repeatedly that the solution was being marketed without approval, but it took no action until it learned about the mounting death toll. FDA officials explained that vitamin E had been used safely for decades and that its intravenous form was similar to that of other vitamin E products. Moreover, the entire class of vitamins was under review, and it would be premature to act on an individual vitamin.

Now, Mobley mused, he, Beta's board of directors, and Brian Madison would have to decide how best to handle the impending lawsuits.

V THE ENVIRONMENT AND MULTINATIONAL CORPORATIONS

The three chapters in this part cover the critical topics of the domestic and international environments and social issues management in multinational corporations. At no time in the world's history has industry brought people and resources closer together through mass communications, transportation, and access to information. At the same time, people and communities have had to endure the breakdown of political systems and the resulting ethnic, religious, and civil strife.

Governments and corporations are concerned about the shrinking ozone layer, toxic waste, and the disappearing rain forests even as they create and perpetuate those problems. These two major stakeholders have tremendous potential to either ameliorate or add to social and environmental problems and solutions.

Managing the environment is a global problem that becomes increasingly difficult as economic development progresses. Without a doubt, economic development has improved the standard of living of people around the world. But, as Table V shows, it has come at a high cost to the environment. Today the world faces significant environmental problems that adversely affect health and productivity.

TABLE V Principal Health and Productivity Consequences of Environmental Mismanagement

Environmental Problem	Effect on Health	Effect on Productivity
Water pollution and water scarcity	More than 2 million deaths and billions of illnesses a year attributable to pollution; poor household hygiene and added health risks caused by water scarcity.	Declining fisheries; rural household time and municipal costs of providing safe water; aquifer depletion leading to irreversible compaction; constraint on economic activity because of water shortages.
Air pollution	Many acute and chronic health impacts: excessive urban particulate matter levels are responsible for 300,000–700,000 premature deaths annually and for half of childhood chronic coughing; 400 million–700 million people, mainly women and children in poor rural areas, affected by smoky indoor air.	Restrictions on vehicle and industrial activity during critical episodes; effect of acid rain on forests and water bodies.
Solid and hazardous wastes	Diseases spread by rotting garbage and blocked drains; risks from hazardous wastes typically local but often acute.	Pollution of groundwater resources.
Soil degradation	Reduced nutrition for poor farmers on depleted soils; greater susceptibility to drought.	Field productivity losses in range of 0.5–1.5 percent of gross national product (GNP) common on tropical soils; offsite siltation of reservoirs, river-transport channels, and other hydrologic investments.
Deforestation	Localized flooding, leading to death and disease.	Loss of sustainable logging potential and of erosion prevention, watershed stability, and carbon sequestration provided by forests.
Loss of biodiversity	Potential loss of new drugs.	Reduction of ecosystem adaptability and loss of genetic resources.
Atmospheric changes	Possible shifts in vector-borne diseases; risks from climatic natural disasters; diseases attributable to ozone depletion (perhaps 300,000 additional cases of skin cancer a year worldwide; 1.7 million cases of cataracts).	Sea-rise damage to coastal investments; regional changes in agricultural productivity; disruption of marine food chain.

SOURCE: *World Development Report: Development and The Environment* (New York: Oxford University Press, 1992), p. 4.

464

CHAPTER

16

ENVIRONMENTAL ISSUES

poll. credits
CEQ

CASE *Buying and Selling the Right to Pollute*

In the summer of 1991, the Chicago Board of Trade voted to create a private market for buying and selling rights to emit sulfur dioxide. The Clean Air Act of 1990 required the Environmental Protection Agency to allot pollution allowances to individual plants. A unique feature of this act was the provision that a plant that exceeded clean air requirements could sell pollution rights, while a plant that did not meet those requirements could buy those rights rather than having to invest in additional pollution control equipment. Exhibit 16–1 shows how the trading system will work.

The act left to power station operators the task of deciding how to meet clean air requirements. The clean air allowance program was divided into two phases:

Phase I: takes effect in 1995 and requires the 110 most heavily polluting power plants in 21 states to reduce their total sulfur dioxide emissions to about 60 percent of their aggregate 1980 levels of 8.9 million tons a year.

Phase II: takes effect in the year 2000 and affects about 800 additional, less heavily polluting plants. Phase II cuts annual sulfur dioxide emissions to less than half of their 1980 level.[1]

The Chicago Board of Trade devised a plan that would permit it to begin trading "cash forward" contracts in 1993. These contracts were promises to deliver allowances after the EPA issued them in 1995. The Chicago Board of Trade also decided to ask the Commodity Futures Trading Commission for permission to establish an ongoing futures market that would allow anyone to gamble on emissions rights in 25-ton allotments up to three years in advance.

In theory, a utility might buy 100 contracts due in 1997. The utility would then have the right to emit an extra 2,500 tons of sulfur dioxide that year. A potential seller

---

[1]B Durr, "Creating a Future for Pollution," *Financial Times,* July 24, 1991, p. 8.

EXHIBIT 16–1

The pollution rights trading system

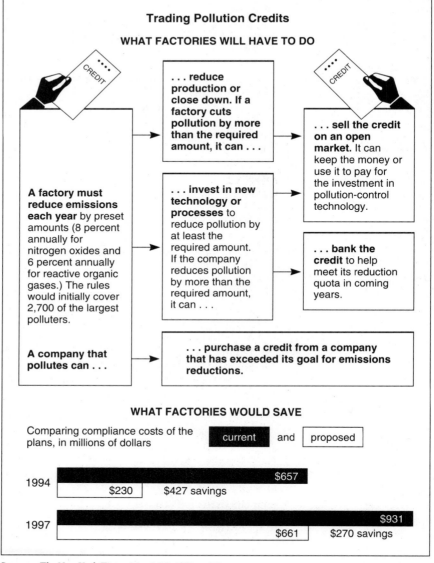

Trading Pollution Credits

WHAT FACTORIES WILL HAVE TO DO

A factory must reduce emissions each year by preset amounts (8 percent annually for nitrogen oxides and 6 percent annually for reactive organic gases.) The rules would initially cover 2,700 of the largest polluters.

A company that pollutes can . . .

. . . **reduce production or close down. If a factory cuts pollution by more than the required amount, it can . . .**

. . . **invest in new technology or processes** to reduce pollution by at least the required amount. If the company reduces pollution by more than the required amount, it can . . .

. . . **purchase a credit from a company that has exceeded its goal for emissions reductions.**

. . . **sell the credit on an open market.** It can keep the money or use it to pay for the investment in pollution-control technology.

. . . **bank the credit** to help meet its reduction quota in coming years.

WHAT FACTORIES WOULD SAVE

Comparing compliance costs of the plans, in millions of dollars   current   and   proposed

1994 $657
$230 $427 savings

1997 $931
$661 $270 savings

SOURCE: *The New York Times,* March 25, 1992, p. D6.

might be an old coal plant that is due to be closed in 1997. Another participant in the market might be the mutual funds manager of a brokerage house who expects the price of allowances to fall and is prepared to gamble the assets of the fund.

Experts estimated that contracts initially would trade at about $400 per ton, although their value might fluctuate with the changing demand for electricity or with new developments in scrubber technology. The price per ton would not exceed

$2,000, since that was the amount of the fine for each ton emitted over a company's legal limit.[2]

In March 1992, the state of California also decided to adopt a market approach to pollution. The South Coast Air Quality Management District began to work out the details. Exhibit 16–1 shows what factories would have to do and what they would save by adopting the plan. The underlying principle was to reduce *total* emissions in the most cost-effective way.[3] The district also planned to allow trading in emissions of hydrocarbons, nitrogen oxide, and sulfur oxide by 1994.[4]

In another case, Wisconsin Power and Light Company entered into a deal to sell pollution rights to the Tennessee Valley Authority (TVA) and Duquesne Light Company in Pittsburgh. In May 1992, the TVA bought from Wisconsin Power and Light the right to emit 10,000 tons of sulfur dioxide. Wisconsin Power and Light, which had shifted to a lower-sulfur fuel, agreed to reduce its emissions 10,000 tons below the requirements of the 1990 Clean Air Act. The TVA would get additional time to install scrubbers or replace the sulfur dioxide with cleaner fuel. Duquesne Light Company bought the right to emit up to 25,000 tons of sulfur dioxide.

The state of Massachusetts also hopped on the emissions trading bandwagon. It announced it was setting up a stock market-like system to buy and sell emission rights. The Massachusetts plan was similar to the Chicago Board of Trade model but did not include a formal auction; instead, trading would be left to private brokers. The Massachusetts system allowed trade in all kinds of pollution in addition to sulfur dioxide.[5]

The first auction at the Chicago Board of Trade took place on March 29, 1993. By this time, the EPA had distributed 5.7 million permits among the 110 worst polluters. Each permit allowed a discharge of one ton of sulfur dioxide per year to be used between 1995 and 2000. The auction was based on sealed bids from power companies, coal producers, environmentalists, and smokestack industries. When the auction was over, traders discovered that successful bids ranged between $122 and $439 per ton of sulfur dioxide. Experts agreed the prices were substantially lower than the cost of developing technology for reducing emissions under the 1990 Clean Air Act.

Questions

1. If the pollution rights trading concept is broadly applied, what result will the market produce?
2. What are the implications of this plan for labor? Will companies sell their pollution rights, close plants, and move to Mexico or other developing countries where pollution is poorly controlled?

---

[2]P Passell, "A New Commodity to Be Traded: Government Permits for Pollution," *The New York Times,* July 17, 1991, p. A1.

[3]R W Stevenson, "Trying a Market Approach to Smog," *The New York Times,* March 25, 1992, p. D1.

[4]"Now, One Company's Poison Is Another's Cash," *Business Week,* July 13, 1992, p. 134F.

[5]S Allen, "State Touts Give-and-Take on Clean Air," *The Boston Globe,* January 8, 1993, p. 1.

3. Can you apply this permits model to automobile emissions? What elements would such a plan entail?

History of Air and Water Pollution

Pollution and cities developed together. In the first century BC, the Romans built one of the first sewer systems in history to protect Rome's municipal water supply. In the thirteenth century, London had such a severe smoke control problem that city officials passed a law forbidding the burning of coal when Parliament was in session. By the eighteenth century, most large European cities were still drawing drinking water from rivers. Sewers did little to remove the effluvia from city streets.[6]

Industrial pollution began in England and Scotland in the 1830s as the Industrial Revolution gathered steam. Factory jobs brought many people into cities ill prepared to house them. These jobs also brought sickness and pestilence. To employers, workers' health problems were important only because they interfered with worker productivity.

In the early nineteenth century, town leaders passed strict environmental controls. Gradually, as controls became more expensive to implement, industrialists pressured officials to allow increasing amounts of solid waste particles to be released into the air and water.

In the United States, pollution and industrialization also went hand in hand. Factories and cities dumped untreated sewage directly into lakes and rivers. Regular epidemics of typhoid, yellow fever, and dysentery ravaged nineteenth-century American cities. As industrialization progressed through the twentieth century, smoke and chemical by-products poured out of pipes and chimneys, automobile exhausts filled city streets with haze, and hazardous waste dumps proliferated.

In the mid-1960s, environmentalists and other concerned stakeholders, realizing environmental pollution could irrevocably damage the nation's natural resources and the health of its people, began to pressure Congress for remedial legislation. The environmental movement and subsequent regulation came out of the same ideology that led to the establishment of regulatory bodies, such as OSHA, EEOC, CPSC, and others, discussed in earlier chapters.

At first, environmental regulatory groups were scattered among government agencies and executive departments. They did not work closely with one another, nor did they coordinate activities. Finally, in 1969 and 1970, Congress reorganized environmental affairs oversight into two bodies, the Council on Environmental Quality (CEQ) and the Environmental Protection Agency (EPA).

---

[6]F Braudel, *Capitalism and Material Life, 1400–1800* (New York: Harper & Row, 1973), pp. 159–62.

Regulatory Agencies

Council on Environmental Quality (CEQ)

In 1969, Congress established the three-member Council on Environmental Quality (CEQ). As part of the executive office, the council's task is to recommend to the president policies for improving environmental quality. It also administers the environmental impact process when federal agencies prepare their statements. The council's role is limited to the executive branch, and the council is not involved with industry or with other stakeholders.

Environmental Protection Agency (EPA)

Prior to 1970, separate programs for control of air pollution, water pollution, pesticides, radiation, and waste management were located in independent agencies and executive departments. President Nixon sent to Congress a reorganization plan that combined them into a new, single agency, the Environmental Protection Agency (EPA). The EPA is now an independent agency in the executive branch. Exhibit 16–2 shows the organization of the EPA and its reporting relationships.

The EPA's mission is to control and lessen pollution in the areas of (1) air, (2) water, (3) solid waste, (4) pesticides, (5) radiation, and (6) toxic substances. Congress charged the EPA with integrating efforts in research, monitoring, standard setting, and enforcement. In short, the EPA was "designed to serve as the public's advocate for a livable environment."[7]

The EPA encourages voluntary compliance by government agencies, private industry, and communities. It also urges state and local governments to meet local standards. If state and local agencies fail to develop or implement effective plans to reduce pollution, the EPA is authorized to intervene. The EPA's Office of Enforcement and Compliance Monitoring oversees enforcement activities. It gathers and prepares evidence and conducts enforcement proceedings for water quality, air pollution, radiation, pesticides, solid waste, toxic substances, hazardous waste, and noise pollution.[8]

The EPA starts enforcement proceedings by notifying an alleged polluter of a violation. If the violation is not corrected, the EPA begins informal negotiations with the polluter. If the situation cannot be resolved, the hearings become public. Finally, the EPA can initiate civil proceedings in a US district court to force compliance. It can file criminal charges if a polluter engages in certain activities, including willfully discharging waste into waterways, dumping toxic waste, and deliberately falsifying environmental reports.

---

[7]*U.S. Government Manual* (revised June, 1988), p. 527.

[8]"Environmental Protection Agency," *Federal Regulatory Directory,* 6th ed. (Washington, DC: Congressional Quarterly, 1990), pp. 71–105.

EXHIBIT 16–2
Organization of the EPA

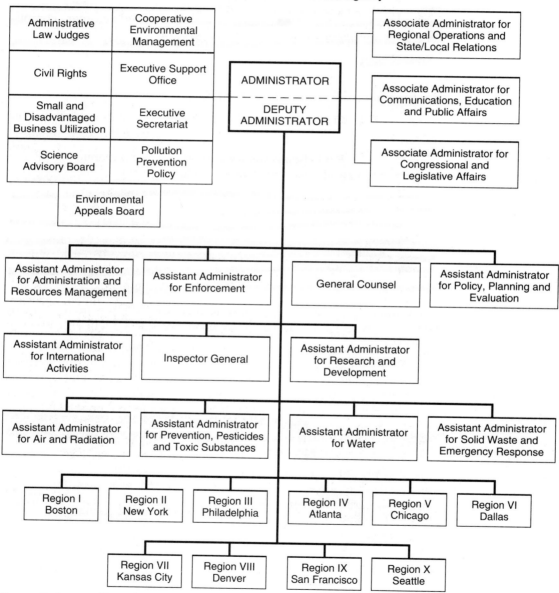

U.S. Environmental Protection Agency

Administrative Law Judges | Cooperative Environmental Management

Civil Rights | Executive Support Office

Small and Disadvantaged Business Utilization | Executive Secretariat

Science Advisory Board | Pollution Prevention Policy

Environmental Appeals Board

ADMINISTRATOR
DEPUTY ADMINISTRATOR

Associate Administrator for Regional Operations and State/Local Relations

Associate Administrator for Communications, Education and Public Affairs

Associate Administrator for Congressional and Legislative Affairs

Assistant Administrator for Administration and Resources Management | Assistant Administrator for Enforcement | General Counsel | Assistant Administrator for Policy, Planning and Evaluation

Assistant Administrator for International Activities | Inspector General | Assistant Administrator for Research and Development

Assistant Administrator for Air and Radiation | Assistant Administrator for Prevention, Pesticides and Toxic Substances | Assistant Administrator for Water | Assistant Administrator for Solid Waste and Emergency Response

Region I Boston | Region II New York | Region III Philadelphia | Region IV Atlanta | Region V Chicago | Region VI Dallas

Region VII Kansas City | Region VIII Denver | Region IX San Francisco | Region X Seattle

SOURCE: Environmental Protection Agency, May 1993.

470

EPA History. During the 1970s, the EPA actively designed and implemented environmental policy but in the early 1980s, the agency became highly politicized and fractious.

EPA administrator Anne McGill Burford was very critical of environmental laws. Claiming she was simply applying cost-cutting measures to reduce the agency's budget, Burford sharply reduced the number of enforcement cases slated to be heard by the courts. She insisted voluntary compliance with regulations was preferable to coercion. In December 1982, the House of Representatives cited Burford for contempt for refusing to turn over documents on Superfund management. Although the action was subsequently dropped, the EPA suffered tremendous political damage. Finally, in March 1983, Burford resigned.

William Ruckelshaus, who had been the first administrator of the EPA in 1970, replaced Burford. He led the agency into a quieter, scandal-free period, although the Reagan administration largely ignored many of his recommendations. Ruckelshaus was very frustrated by his inability to get the administration to address certain issues, such as acid rain. At the heart of the problem was the cost of cutting sulfur dioxide emissions and allocating the costs of doing so. The Reagan administration took the side of the coal and utility industries, maintaining insufficient data about acid rain existed to warrant intervention.

In November 1984, Ruckleshaus resigned and was succeeded by Lee M Thomas. Thomas stepped up the agency's activities. During 1987, the EPA brought the largest number of legal actions in its history, referring 372 civil cases and 59 criminal cases to the Justice Department.[9] Nevertheless, environmentalists continued to charge that the EPA was tilted in favor of business, while industrialists complained incessantly about unreasonable controls.

George Bush, who stressed environmental affairs during his presidential campaign, chose William Reilly to head the agency. The former president of the Conservation Foundation and the World Wildlife Fund, Reilly was the first person from the conservation community appointed to the EPA in its 19-year history. The new administration began to formulate policy to deal with the main problems of the environment: clean air, clean water, and toxic and nuclear waste. During the four years of the Bush administration, Reilly's views often clashed with those of industry and even more heavily with Vice President Quayle's Council on Competitiveness.

Following his election in 1992, Bill Clinton appointed Carol M Browner, who was Florida's secretary of environmental regulation. In May 1993, the US Senate approved a bill to elevate the EPA to full cabinet status.

---

[9]P Shabecoff, "E.P.A. Record Set in Pollution Cases," *The New York Times,* December 9, 1988, p. A24.

If the bill is signed into law, the EPA will become the Department of Environmental Protection. The measure will disband the Council on Environmental Quality.[10]

The EPA's current priorities are

- To quicken the pace of EPA decision making across a wide range of issues from water pollution to pesticide use
- To improve management of the Superfund (discussed later in this chapter) to clean up toxic waste and end monetary waste
- To restore credibility to the EPA and its programs[11]

Within a few weeks, Browner concluded the EPA had "a total lack of management." She found agency contracts suffered from cost overruns and highly paid professionals were assigned duties such as caring for lab animals. Millions of dollars had been misallocated and improperly spent in laboratories across the United States.

Experts on the environment shared Browner's view. They noted that environmental laws developed since 1980 had created a tangle of regulations that cost industry more than $100 million per year and cost the government $40 billion annually. Many of the laws were not backed by sound research or cost-benefit analysis.

Industry leaders, government officials, and environmentalists all argued for a new environmental policy that was more reflective of real risk rather than of public perception of risk. All observers agreed the toxic waste program and the Superfund were the most wasteful programs of all.

Clean Air

The first major federal legislation for controlling air pollution was enacted in 1955. It left most of the responsibility for clean air to individual states. States were required to file State Implementation Plans (SIPs) to show how they would meet acceptable concentrations of particular pollutants. In 1970, Congress passed the Clean Air Act. The act mandated federal regulation and enforcement of federal air quality standards and emission thresholds through the EPA. States were still required to develop their own SIPs and work with the EPA to achieve them.

Congress passed a subsequent Clean Air Act in 1977, but implementation stalled. Interagency conflict, which had lessened after Burford's departure, continued. Industry dragged its heels, and state plans were consistently delayed. An EPA official observed, "We were beset with interagency politics, and we just stopped requiring states to provide attainment demonstration.

[10]R Beamish, "Senate Approves EPA for Cabinet," *The Boston Globe,* May 5, 1993, p. 3.
[11]K Schneider, "New Type of Watchdog for the E.P.A.," *The New York Times,* December 17, 1992, p. B20.

Since we have not pressured the states, the states have not pressured industry."[12]

In the 1980s, the EPA devised two mechanisms to foster industry compliance. First, some plants were allowed to pretend they operated under a bubble. They could measure the total quantity of pollution gathered under the bubble rather than the quantity emitted by each smokestack. They could then use their own discretion in working toward reducing total pollution. The second mechanism allowed companies to buy and sell pollution "credits." If a company shut down a smokestack that emitted particulate matter, it could sell that amount of pollution credit to another company, which could use the credit instead of reducing its own pollution.

In 1987, Congress began to push for more and stricter clean air laws. States cracked down on the dirtiest polluters, the steel and utility companies. This flurry of activity was due in part to the development of new technology that could pinpoint polluters more precisely and clean up emissions more efficiently. Although the 1977 act badly needed revising, Congress was unable to muster enough support to do so.

In 1989, after more than a decade of legislative stalemate, the Bush administration declared, "we will make the 1990s the era for clean air," and proposed a greatly revised Clean Air Act. The proposal addressed three critical clean air issues:

1. *Acid rain.* The plan suggested a 10-million-ton (nearly 50 percent) reduction in emissions of sulfur dioxide from coal-burning electric power plants by the year 2000. It also proposed a 2-million-ton-per-year (1 percent) reduction in nitrogen oxides. When midwestern smokestacks emit sulfur and nitrogen oxides, the emissions travel long distances and change chemically. Eventually particles fall on Canadian and Northeast lakes and forests as acid rain, snow, or smog. Under the proposed law, companies would be free to decide how to meet EPA goals. They could use scrubbers that chemically remove sulfur residue from smokestacks; they could burn coal with lower sulfur content; they could encourage consumers to conserve electricity; or they could adopt new technologies.

2. *Selling the right to pollute.* As we discussed earlier in the chapter, polluters who exceeded the reduction requirements could sell or transfer their pollution rights to other companies within the same state. The pollution rights would be bought and sold like securities, with brokers managing the parties. An EPA official estimated the initial price of pollution rights would be the marginal cost of pollution reduction, or between $1,000 and $2,000 per ton at 1989 prices.[13]

---

[12]C H Deutsch, "The Pollution Hounds Get Ready to Pounce," *The New York Times,* September 6, 1987, p. F6.

[13]R W Stevenson, "Concern Over Bush Clean-Air Plan," *The New York Times,* June 14, 1989, pp. D1, D6.

3. *Ozone reduction.* Ozone in the stratosphere protects the Earth from harmful ultraviolet radiation. On Earth, ozone is a main component of smog and causes serious respiratory problems. Sunshine acts on nitrogen oxides and volatile organic compounds to produce what an environmental physician called "pound for pound . . . by far the most toxic of the usual outdoor pollutants."[14] Motor vehicle exhausts, bakeries, dry cleaners, petroleum refineries, and paint shops all contribute to ozone pollution. New measures would place stricter controls on motor vehicle tailpipe emissions and encourage the use of clean-burning motor fuels like methanol. The 20 cities with the worst ozone problems would have to reduce pollution by 3 percent per year.

As soon as the Bush proposal became public, stakeholders such as members of Congress, environmentalists, and state officials pointed out its shortcomings. Most contended it did not go far enough in limiting automobile emissions. Some criticized possible loopholes in smog reduction. The congressional Office of Technology Assessment reported the EPA was overly optimistic and unrealistic about how rapidly cities could reduce urban ozone pollution.[15] On the other hand, some industry spokespeople, especially automobile manufacturers, asserted the measures were too burdensome. As Congress began its debate on the new bill, the only issue on which all stakeholders agreed was that strict and prompt measures to restore clean air were critical.

The Clean Air Act of 1990

On November 16, 1990, George Bush signed the first new clean air act in 13 years. The proposed acid rain provision went into effect along with the "rights to pollute." The early estimate of the initial price to pollute of between $1,000 and $2,000 per ton was grossly optimistic, as the case at the beginning of the chapter demonstrates.

The ozone depletion provision mandated the complete phaseout of chemicals that deplete the ozone layer by the year 2000. Motor vehicles had to conform to new standards. The Clean Air Act lowered the limit on smog producing hydrocarbon emissions by 40 percent and nitrogen oxide emissions by 60 percent. A new program phased in alternative-fuel cars for fleets. The act mandated on-board canisters to trap vapors during refueling and doubled extended warranties on emissions control equipment to 100,000 miles. The act also required factories to install technology to reduce the release of nearly 200 toxic chemicals by the year 2000. Finally, chemical safety boards would be formed to investigate chemical release accidents.[16]

---

[14]E Faltermayer, "Air: How Clean Is Clean Enough?," *Fortune,* July 17, 1989, p. 58.

[15]"Bush's Clean-Air Plan Is Seen Falling Short," *The Boston Globe,* July 18, 1989, p. 58.

[16]M Kranish, "Bush Signs Historic Clean Air Act," *The Boston Globe,* November 16, 1990, p. 3.

The Decade of the "Clean Car"

In 1991, California passed a clean air act that was far more stringent than the federal act passed a year earlier. By 2003, all new cars sold in California could produce no more than one-fifth of the pollution emitted by 1991 automobiles.

California quickly became the laboratory in which carmakers experimented in making the automobile of the future. None of the major manufacturers was willing to give up a market of 1.7 million car and truck sales per year. The manufacturers realized the California law represented the wave of the future and its standards were likely to be adopted in much of the United States and eventually overseas. Any company that achieved a technological breakthrough in reducing pollution would have a competitive advantage. (See Exhibit 16–3.)

Automakers tried electric power, methanol power, natural gas, and other systems using fuel cells. To use any of these new power sources, nearly all the parts that powered the car, from fuel injection systems to hoses, had to be redesigned. The major carmakers settled on these three alternatives as the most promising.

Electric Cars.   Electric cars, which run on batteries, produce no emissions at all; in fact, some prototypes have no exhaust pipe. Electrically powered cars require different motors, drivetrains, and battery systems than conventional automobiles. In 1991, the average operating cost of an electric car was estimated at 25 to 36 cents per mile. The cars had a driving range of 50 to 120 miles before they had to be recharged for six hours. Fiat's Electra was the only electric car on the market made by a major manufacturer. It retailed for $22,000, had a top speed of 45 miles per hour, and ran out of power after 100 miles. Still, this made it considerably more reliable than Fiat's existing gas-powered car.

Batteries were the major environmental problem posed by electric cars. Existing electric car batteries were filled with toxic lead acid, cost about $1,500 each, and had a lifetime use of 2,000 miles. Early in 1992, ABB Asea Brown Boveri, a Swiss-Swedish company, and Britain's Chloride Silent Power, Ltd., began pilot production of a more ecologically sound, lightweight, sodium-sulfur battery. Test results were promising, and it appeared a commercial product could be ready by 1994.

In April 1993, the Big Three automakers announced they were discussing collaboration to build an electric car. All three companies already had expensive prototypes with limited driving range and high price tags compared to conventionally powered autos. The last time these companies had worked together was in the early 1960s, when the first pollution control rules were proposed. At that time, the Justice Department raised antitrust questions that led the companies to drop their joint effort. In 1984, the rules were changed, and today manufacturers are exempt from antitrust complaints as

Exhibit 16–3

*Automobile
Alternatives*

Choosing a new type of car

Each of the gasoline alternatives offers a mixed bag of benefits and problems.

METHANOL (WOOD ALCOHOL)

Advantages: Flexible-fuel cars use methanol or gasoline; can be fueled in 4 locations in New York. Provide slightly better horsepower than gasoline-powered cars.

Disadvantages: Cars have limited range; start hard in cold weather; cannot now be fueled in New England. Fuel is highly flammable and very corrosive, requiring special tanks and fuel lines and posing environmental hazard; costs as much as gasoline.

ETHANOL (GRAIN ALCOHOL)

Advantages: Flexible-fuel cars use ethanol or gasoline; provide slightly better horsepower than gasoline-powered cars. Fuel is nontoxic and a renewable resource.

Disadvantages: Cars hard to start in cold weather; cannot now be fueled in Northeast. Fuel is expensive, costly to produce, highly flammable and very corrosive.

COMPRESSED NATURAL GAS

Advantages: Cars eligible for federal tax deduction and can be run cheaply because fuel is only two-thirds the cost of gasoline; car engine lasts longer than with gasoline models. Fuel is plentiful, clean, nontoxic and disperses quickly if it leaks.

Disadvantages: Cars require large fuel tanks that may eliminate some trunk space; can be fueled at only one public station in Massachusetts (Springfield). Cars prohibited from travel in Mass. tunnels.

PROPANE

Advantages: Car engine lasts longer than with gasoline models; car qualifies for tax deduction. Fuel is widely available (41 locations in Mass.) and slightly cheaper than gasoline.

Disadvantages: Cars prohibited from travel in Mass. tunnels; require tanks that limit trunk space. Fuel is costly, in limited supply and poses a safety hazard in event of leak.

ELECTRICITY

Advantages: Cars are the cleanest available, are quiet and have few moving parts, so they require little maintenance and should last long. Can be recharged at home at low cost. Eligible for tax credit. Fuel poses no fire or explosion hazard in case of an accident.

Disadvantages: Cars are costly, accelerate slowly and perform poorly in very cold weather; cannot easily be refueled away from home because few public stations available.

SOURCE: *Boston Globe*, May 23, 1993, p.1.

long as they notify the Justice Department and the Federal Trade Commission of their activities in advance. As managers of the carmakers point out, there is no possibility of antitrust violation in any case because no market to monopolize exists. If a market develops, the consortium members may need to proceed independently.[17]

Compressed Natural Gas. Some carmakers decided to develop compressed natural gas technology. The United States has a large surplus of natural gas, and experts agreed pipeline capacity could be added at a relatively low cost. Existing cars could be retrofitted with pressure regulators, fuel-metering systems, and aluminum tanks. This technology is particularly attractive to companies with fleets of cars. Federal Express and United Parcel Service, for example, can refuel their cars at central pumps during the night. Because the demand is still small and the technology fairly new, compressor pumps are costly. In 1991, high-pressure compressors for commercial fleets cost $2,500 apiece. Home fill-up pumps cost $2,500, but experts agree the price would go down quickly if sales increased.[18]

Clean Air and Jobs. The Bush administration dragged its heels in implementing the Clean Air Act, citing potential job losses as the reason. President Bush and Vice President Quayle's Council on Competitiveness responded to complaints from manufacturers and utilities by limiting the Clean Air Act's effectiveness. For example, in March 1992, Bush told a group of Detroit businesspeople he was waiving the Clean Air Act rule requiring automakers to install fume-capturing canisters. In June, the Bush administration issued a rule allowing each of 35,000 chemical, pharmaceutical, and other plants to increase hazardous emissions by up to 245 tons a year. Citizens' groups, environmentalists, and Democratic members of Congress charged that industry lobbying was hindering implementation of the act.[19]

In a *Wall Street Journal* article, Philip K Verleger, Jr., a researcher at the Institute for International Economics, tied clean air regulations to the cause of the riots in South Central Los Angeles after the Rodney King verdict.[20] Verleger asserted the primary reason for the riots was not the jury verdict but closed factories and lost jobs. He pointed to the furniture and metal fabrication industries, which, he noted, might provide appropriate employment enterprise zones in the South Central LA area. Unfortunately, he declared, these industries went elsewhere because they used toxic substances

---

[17]M L Wald, "Clean-Air Laws Push Big 3 to Cooperate on Electric Car," *The New York Times,* April 14, 1993, p. A1.

[18]"The Greening of Detroit," *Business Week,* April 8, 1991, pp. 54–60.

[19]K Schneider, "Bush on the Environment: A Record of Contradictions," *The New York Times,* July 4, 1992, p. A1.

[20]P K Verleger, Jr., "Clean Air and the L.A. Riots," *The Wall Street Journal,* May 19, 1992, p. A14.

limited by California's air quality rules. He implied that had people had jobs in these and similar industries, they would not have rioted. Verleger did not mention the unhealthy workplace conditions that often prevail in those industries.

Verleger proposed a solution. He noted that about half the air pollution in the Los Angeles area came from automobile emissions and the rest from stationary sources. He suggested cracking down on pollution from existing automobiles while allowing more pollution from stationary sources. He declared, "the cycle of poverty . . . is unlikely to be broken unless a second cycle—that of increasingly stringent environmental regulation—is broken as well."[21]

In Verleger's view, private investment would not return to California unless the state relaxed its environmental regulations. Verleger pointed to a study conducted by Southern California Edison. Sixty-three percent of the companies that moved to Las Vegas from Los Angeles told researchers their move was influenced in part by "government and/or environmental regulations." In a second study, done on behalf of California utility companies, respondents stated environmental laws and regulations were a significant factor in their decisions to relocate or build new factories.

Several questions emerge from Verleger's article. How should one assess the reliability of information given by the big utilities, one of the industries most heavily affected by the new laws? What assumptions does the author make about the mix of industries needed for revitalization in South Central Los Angeles? Are industries such as metal working and furniture most appropriate? Should the disadvantaged be the group most at risk? If so, why? If not, why not? What are the societal trade-offs between mobile and stationary sources of pollution? Would strict, uniform national (or global) laws lead to less job flight?

Clean Water

The Rivers and Harbors Act of 1899 was the earliest act prohibiting pollution of navigable waters or adjoining banks without a permit. Throughout the first half of the twentieth century, Congress passed other antipollution water acts, but none was as far reaching or comprehensive as the Federal Water Pollution Control Act of 1972. This act, administered by the EPA, set national standards for reducing water pollution. The EPA defined pollutants as solid waste, incinerator residue, sewage, garbage, sewage sludge, munitions, chemical wastes, radioactive materials, and a variety of other substances.

---

[21]Ibid.

The states and the EPA had to work together to draw up comprehensive plans for river basin and regional water quality planning.[22] The act, which came to be known as the Clean Water Act, called for national action to create "fishable, drinkable, swimmable" waters. It required industries and cities to clean up their sewage and led to the establishment of a national, multibillion-dollar water treatment program.

In 1977, Congress passed amendments to the 1972 legislation that tightened rules dealing with the discharge of toxic chemicals into water supplies. Environmentalists thought the amendments were too lax, while industry representatives contended that costs for compliance were prohibitive.[23]

When the bill came up for renewal in 1982, the Reagan administration proposed what it called "minor revisions." Environmentalists immediately pointed out that the Reagan proposal threw out the rule mandating national standards for treatment of industrial wastes discharged into municipal water systems. It also extended the time limit for cleanups for four years and doubled the time limit for industry pollution permits.[24]

Contention among the EPA, the Reagan administration, Congress, and other stakeholders continued throughout the 1980s. When President Reagan vetoed a $20 billion 1987 bill aimed at cleaning up the nation's water, Congress promptly overrode his veto. The bill enjoyed enormous popularity with politicians, because it provided $18 billion in aid to state and local governments for construction of sewage treatment plants through 1994.[25]

At the end of the Reagan years, the United States Geological Survey reported that while most of the nation's underground water was of good quality, contamination was on the rise. Industrial waste, garbage dumps, septic tanks, underground storage of gasoline, and agricultural pesticides had all contributed to increasing contamination.

Coastlines near major cities came under major assault from contamination. In New York City, for example, household waste mixed with rainwater was eventually conveyed through 6,200 miles of pipeline to treatment plants. During storms, the capacity of the treatment plants was overwhelmed, and millions of gallons of raw sewage flowed into the city's harbors and along nearby shorelines. The city estimates that if more than three-quarters of an inch of rain fell, 500 million gallons of mixed, untreated sewage was discharged.

---

[22] *Toward Cleaner Water* (Washington, DC: Environmental Protection Agency, 1974), p. 5.

[23] P Shabecoff, "New Rules for Clean Water: Attacks on 2 Fronts," *The New York Times,* June 29, 1982, p. A20.

[24] "15 Changes Asked in U.S. Water Act," *The New York Times,* May 28, 1982, p. A12.

[25] B Weintraub, "Clean Water Bill Passed by House Over Reagan Veto," *The New York Times,* February 4, 1987, p. A1.

New York City was no different than Boston or any other old city with antiquated sewage treatment systems. However, pollution affects waterways and the fishing industry in every part of the United States. Experts say 14 of the most valuable food fish are threatened with commercial extinction. This means commercial fishers would catch so few fish that the effort would not be worth the cost. Between 1986 and 1991, the finfish and shellfish catch off the lower 48 states declined by 500 million pounds.

Nearly half of the US population lives within 50 miles of a coastline. Due to population pressure, coastal wetlands in which fish breed are disappearing. Bays and estuaries are polluted with sewage, runoff from fertilizers and pesticides, and factory wastewater. More than one-third of the nation's shellfish beds are closed at any time because of pollution.

The Clean Water Act and its amendments have somewhat ameliorated but not eliminated pollution of the nation's water supply. Pure drinking water, the survival of the commercial fishing business, the cost of harbor cleanup, and the elimination of pollutants were all agenda items for the Clinton administration.

A major piece of bad news came in April 1993. A General Accounting Office (GAO) report found state programs to insure safety of drinking water were in shambles. Forty-five states had not complied with EPA directives to evaluate all components of their public water systems. Blame for this situation was placed squarely on the EPA, which for many years had failed to request enough money from Congress to allow the states to meet the requirements.

Environmental officials agreed the situation was as dismal as the study depicted. Nationally, states failed to check half of the large water systems and 20 percent of the smaller ones to ensure they were not contaminated by pesticides or sewage runoff. States did not check their systems as often as the EPA required, a situation that was graphically brought to public attention when, in 1993, the city of Milwaukee's water supply became contaminated by a parasite. Thousands of people became ill, and some with other medical conditions died.[26]

The Boston Harbor Cleanup.   In Massachusetts, the EPA charged the Massachusetts Water Resources Authority (MWRA) with cleaning up Boston Harbor. Experts conservatively estimated the cost at $4.3 billion. The MWRA developed a 10-year schedule raising water and sewage rates assessments in the cities and towns surrounding Boston Harbor. In the procedure for collecting the assessments, cities and towns send quarterly bills to homes and businesses; when the municipalities have collected the revenues, they turn them over to the MWRA.

---

[26]M D Hinds, "Survey Finds Flaws in States' Water Inspection," *The New York Times,* April 15, 1993, p. A14.

As assessments rose in 1992 and 1993, stakeholders in the MWRA area became increasingly enraged over having to bear the cost of cleaning up a mess created more than 100 years ago. Shortly after the May assessments were due to the cities and towns, homeowners and businesspeople protested by dumping their bills into nearby Quincy Harbor. They sent the same message their colonial Boston Tea Party forebears had sent to the British.

The symbolism was not lost on local and state politicians. The town of Weymouth voted to withhold $508,144, the amount equal to what it was unable to collect from residential and commercial users. A few days later, Woburn city council members voted to withhold their $1.6 million payment. As stakeholder protest mounted, Massachusetts governor Weld and state officials searched for other ways to pay for the cleanup.

The governor promised about $30 million in state aid to lighten the 1993 burden on MWRA customers. He also lobbied to insert a $100 million item for the harbor cleanup into President Clinton's budget. State treasurer Joseph Malone and others pushed for a fleet of floating casinos to sail around the harbor while gamblers played the roulette wheels and one-armed bandits. The revenues from the casinos would help defray the cleanup costs. The Massachusetts House Natural Resources Committee endorsed a study of a proposed lottery ticket called "Splash Cash," whose proceeds would go to the MWRA.

MWRA officials worried about the link between gambling and revenues. However, they realized they could not afford to dismiss any potential income scheme, since MWRA bills were expected to top $1,200 per year for a family by the year 2000.[27]

Hazardous Waste

In 1980, the EPA estimated that at least 57 million metric tons of the nation's total waste could be classified as hazardous. Hazardous waste emissions, which contaminate air and water, come under EPA jurisdiction. In a 1973 report to Congress, the EPA recommended passage of a federal law to regulate disposal of this waste on land. This law was called the Resource Conservation and Recovery Act (RCRA). Subtitle C of RCRA imposed strict controls over the management of hazardous waste over its entire life cycle from "cradle to grave." Some estimated the costs of complying with RCRA would exceed the combined costs of the Clean Air and Clean Water Acts. The RCRA program included

1. Identification of hazardous waste.
2. Standards for generators and transporters of hazardous waste.

[27]J Rakowsky, "Woburn Votes to Withhold $1.6m to Protest Increase in MWRA Rates," *The Boston Globe,* May 19, 1993, p. 27.

3. Performance, design, and operating requirements for facilities that treat, store, or dispose of hazardous waste.

4. A system that issues permits to such facilities.

5. Guidelines describing conditions under which state governments can carry out their own hazardous waste management programs.[28]

In 1980, Congress created the Superfund of $1.6 billion to clean up oil and chemical spills, as well as abandoned toxic waste dumps such as Love Canal. The money for the fund would come from taxes on petroleum and chemical companies, from fees on polluting substances, and from the US Treasury. Over the years, the Superfund has had problems maintaining and increasing its funding levels. Oil and petroleum manufacturers wanted to shift the burden to manufacturers as a whole, EPA administrators tried to limit its use of funds, and Congress attended to other issues. But public support for the Superfund prevailed, and by 1989 the EPA had $8.5 billion in the cleanup program.

NIMBY (Not in My Backyard)

Hazardous waste and routine garbage are shipped across state lines each day. In 1991, 15 million tons of municipal garbage was shipped among states, much of it going to Pennsylvania and Ohio. New Jersey was a net importer until the late 1980s, when it closed landfills and shipped its own garbage elsewhere.

Importers began levying high dumping fees, and some banned garbage imports altogether. When exporters complained, federal courts held that shipments across state borders were protected by the constitutional right to conduct commerce across state borders.

But opposition to hazardous waste and garbage dumps grew in the late 1980s and 1990s. Opposition to the shipment of hazardous waste was particularly contentious. In 1991, only 15 states had commercial hazardous waste dumps (see Table 16–1).

The states that housed these dumps found themselves taking hazardous waste from all over the country. Increasingly residents near these sites adopted a defiant "Not in My Backyard" (NIMBY) stand against further dumping. Until the Supreme Court ruled, none of the stakeholders could prevail. Residents, state governments, waste disposal companies, and disposal site managers were in legal and regulatory limbo.

Legal Challenges to Waste Disposal.   In March 1992, the Supreme Court agreed to rule on two separate constitutional challenges in which the states of Alabama and Michigan had passed laws to keep out waste from other

---

[28]*Everybody's Problem: Hazardous Waste* (Washington, DC: Environmental Protection Agency, 1980), p. 10.

TABLE 16–1   **States with Hazardous Waste Dumps, 1991**

	Number of Dumps		Number of Dumps
California	3	Nevada	1
Illinois	2	New York	1
Louisiana	2	Ohio	1
Texas	2	Oklahoma	1
Alabama	1	Oregon	1
Idaho	1	South	
Indiana	1	Carolina	1
Michigan	1	Utah	1

SOURCE: *The Wall Street Journal*, August 16, 1991, p. B1.

states. Alabama was very persistent in its attempt to ban waste from outside the state. In 1991, the state won an Alabama Supreme Court decision that upheld its imposition of a $72-per-ton fee for the disposal of out-of-state hazardous waste.

Waste treatment firms appealed the decision. Trade organizations representing heavy-manufacturing industries argued that if the state supreme court decision was allowed to stand, other states would enact similar laws. They painted a picture of train- and truckloads of hazardous waste wandering from state to state looking for a place to dump their cargo. The Bush administration Justice Department sided with the waste management companies and industry representatives, declaring that Alabama should not be allowed to place a financial burden on out-of-state waste that it would not impose on its own citizens.[29]

A third case involved the state of Illinois. The court agreed to consider how far state governments could go in regulating hazardous waste dumps that were also covered by federal worker safety rules.[30] That case has not yet been decided.

Nevertheless, hazardous waste had to be stored somewhere. Some groups succeeded in ensuring that their "backyards" would not get sullied. But others, primarily low-income groups and minorities, were not so fortunate or were more willing to take the risk for a price.

In June 1992, the EPA issued a report citing evidence that racial and ethnic minorities suffered disproportionate exposure to dust, soot, carbon monoxide, ozone, sulfur dioxide, and lead. Some of this exposure occurred because the disadvantaged tended to live in poorly maintained inner-city

[29]P M Barrett, "High Court to Enter Waste-Disposal War," *The Wall Street Journal*, March 23, 1992, p. B1.

[30]Ibid.

conditions. But other sources of contamination were directly traceable to dump sites, sewage treatment plants, and storage and disposal problems near minority and poverty-stricken communities. The EPA found a large minority population was the most significant factor contaminated communities had in common.[31]

Native Americans became a targeted minority group. Some tribes were pressured to open their reservations to all sorts of hazardous waste from nuclear residue to ordinary garbage. Beginning in 1990, commercial waste management companies approached Native American tribes across the country, offering millions of dollars for sites. Even the federal government made offers.

The US Department of Energy was desperate to find a place to store high-level radioactive waste from commercial nuclear plants. It offered tribes multimillion-dollar economic aid packages if they would agree to house spent fuel rods. Sixteen tribes in the West applied for these federal grants. The New Mexico Mescalero Apaches received $300,000 to study suitable sites and were in line to receive millions of dollars if the disposal site was actually built on their land.[32] For this tribe and others, NIMBY was a luxury they decided they could ill afford.

Other minority groups organized to fight attempts to situate dumps nearby even if the dumps would bring jobs. For example, Hispanics in Kettleman City, California, won a court judgment blocking plans for an incinerator on the site of an existing toxic waste landfill. African-American residents in Wallace, Louisiana, helped thwart plans to build a multimillion-dollar wood pulp and rayon plant on the nearby Mississippi River. However, groups of minorities and poor faced a Faustian dilemma in many cases: They had to choose between a dangerous environment with a viable local economy and a safe but economically depressed environment.

Vice President Gore announced the Clinton administration's first decisions on hazardous waste disposal. He confirmed the government would try to halt operation of the nation's most recently completed hazardous waste incinerator. The incinerator, owned by a Swiss company, Von Roll, Inc., was located on an Ohio River flood plain near a residential area and an elementary school. Although the plant was considered state of the art, it was estimated it would release thousands of pounds of mercury, heavy metals, lead, and sulfur per year into an area known for its stagnant air.

However, the plant, first approved during the Reagan administration, would generate more than 100 jobs in a town of 13,000. The issue of jobs versus pollution divided the NIMBY faction from other townspeople. The numbers of proponents and opponents in the town of East Liverpool were nearly equally divided.

---

[31] R Suro, "Pollution-Weary Minorities Try Civil Rights Tack," *The New York Times,* January 11, 1993, p. A1.

[32] "Trashing the Reservations?," *US News & World Report,* January 11, 1993, p. 24.

The environmental group Greenpeace began lobbying the Clinton administration to shut down the facility permanently. In May, 1993, the EPA unveiled its latest proposals to impose restrictions on hazardous waste incinerators. EPA Director Carol Browner said that during the next 18 months, the agency would focus on reviewing permits issued to already operating hazardous waste incinerators and would give low priority to issuing permits for new incinerators. Browner's announcement had no direct effect on the Von Roll incinerator, whose permit would be reviewed later. However, it seemed to signal the Clinton administration would be more aggressive than its predecessor in enforcing environmental laws.[33]

Recycling: Another Strategy for Reducing Waste

Recycling is a partial solution to ameliorating the waste disposal problem. Public opinion and political pressure are working against the opening of more landfills and the operation of more incinerators. Therefore, converting the waste into a reusable commodity offers some promise of reducing the absolute amount of waste. In 1988, about 18 percent of municipal waste was recycled; however, 80 percent of solid waste in municipal garbage *could* be recycled. As a solution to waste disposal, recycling has both supporters and detractors.

George C Lodge and Jeffrey F Rayport conclude that government and industry will have to work together if recycling is to succeed.[34] They note business, government, environmentalists, and ordinary citizens are all trying to do the "right thing." However, these stakeholders' combined efforts have been disappointing, because there is no coordination in matching the supply of waste for recycling and the demand for recycled output.

Different stakeholders have different agendas and sometimes work at cross-purposes. Lodge and Rayport observe that many packaged-products manufacturers would like to switch to recycled plastics but worry that the supply may not be of sufficient volume or quality. Recyclers, on the other hand, would have to make expensive capital investments to process plastic, with no clear assurance of demand stability.[35]

Lodge and Rayport recommend the EPA set up a foundation, operating on a regional and national level, to design and manage a recycling infrastructure. The foundation would carry out the following tasks:

1. Setting standards and establishing definitions for environmentally acceptable products and packaging, including recycling, recycled content, and reuse.

---

[33]K Schneider, "Gore Says Clinton Will Try to Halt Waste Incinerator," *The New York Times,* December 7, 1992, p. D9.

[34]G C Lodge and J F Rayport, "Knee-Deep and Rising: America's Recycling Crisis," *Harvard Business Review* (September–October 1991), p. 133.

[35]Ibid., p. 133.

2. Developing and promoting a national philosophy and perspective on recycling, including recognizing the need for cradle-to-grave product responsibility and championing fairness in the burdens and benefits of recycling.

3. Creating and administering "green" product certification through an ecolabeling system.

4. Establishing a standard coding system for materials to facilitate recycling.

5. Recommending packaging and product design to promote the manufacture of easily recycled products from consumer goods to automobiles.

6. Identifying and outlawing packages that are "environmentally unacceptable."

7. Instituting a national container-deposit law to promote recycling in both rural and urban areas and to raise funds for the further development of the national infrastructure.

8. Funding research projects in waste reduction.

9. Implementing incentives and penalties to stimulate recycling, such as deposit fees, tax credits, and fees on virgin materials.

10. Creating markets for recycled materials by developing procurement incentives for businesses and government agencies.

11. Designing education programs to make children more aware of the benefits of recycling and proper waste management.[36]

One major problem still confounding recycling advocates is the paucity of backward channels of distribution for most waste. Backward channels are simply reverse distribution systems in which materials flow from the user's discard pile to a reprocessor and back to a manufacturer. Backward channels work well for aluminum cans and automobile batteries. Virtually all new automobile batteries are made using recycled lead. In cases where backward channels are well established, there are likely meaningful economic motivations to recycle.

Many companies routinely recycle paper, cans, bottles, and plastic. Increasingly they are asking employees to recycle office materials. Texas Instruments, for example, recycles more than 12,000 laser printer cartridges a year, as well as packing materials such as polystyrene and polyurethane. Through recycling Miles, Inc., cut its waste by 44 percent in 1992 and planned to reach a corporate goal of 50 percent by the end of 1993.[37] Cutting waste, of course, saves money for the company.

---

[36]Ibid., p. 139.
[37]"Companies Lean on Employees to Be More Environmentally Conscious," *The Wall Street Journal,* April 27, 1993, p. A1.

In the fall of 1991, Browning-Ferris Industries (BFI) opened a new recycling plant in Pittsburgh—its 24th. Although profits from those plants have been modest, top management expects recycling to become increasingly important. BFI officials pay very close attention to market forces, carefully monitoring their customers' supply and demand needs. The company's representatives make sure customers receive recyclables that are sorted and packaged according to the customers' specifications. BFI plans to use technology to make its operations less labor intensive and is confident that its strategy is sound for the future.[38]

A Systems Approach to Waste Minimization

Every product goes through a life cycle from its creation to the end of its useful life. The steps in this cycle involve the participation of separate organizations that have little incentive, other than economic, to coordinate their efforts to minimize waste.

The problem of pollution control and decreasing access to dumping sites has engendered interest in finding ways to minimize the amount of effluence and waste we create. The Society of Environmental Toxicology and Chemistry (SETAC), founded in 1979, is a professional organization of 2,000 members. It brings together environmental scientists, engineers, academics, government officials, industry representatives, and public-interest groups to discuss issues of environmental management and develop solutions to environmental problems. SETAC members try to develop holistic procedures for studying environmental consequences associated with the cradle-to-grave life cycle of products or processes. As Exhibit 16–4 shows, SETAC has developed a life cycle assessment approach as a tool to help identify, assess, and solve the environmental concerns associated with products, processes, and activities.

At the 1990 SETAC annual meeting, participants developed the above framework. The major stages are (1) raw materials acquisition; (2) manufacturing, processing, and formulation; (3) distribution and transportation; (4) use/reuse/maintenance; (5) recycling; and (6) waste management. Each stage receives *inputs* of materials and energy and produces *outputs* of materials or energy that move to the next phase and release waste into the environment. Energy sources may include natural gas, petroleum, coal, hydroelectric power, solar energy, wind, and wood. Waste is defined as material having no beneficial use.

Companies and governments can use this assessment model to establish baselines of information about a system's overall resource requirements, energy use, and emissions. They can also identify points within the life cycle

---

[38]M Engebretson, "The Greening of BFI," *Business Ethics* (January/February 1992), pp. 16–17.

EXHIBIT 16–4

*A technical
framework for life
cycle assessment*

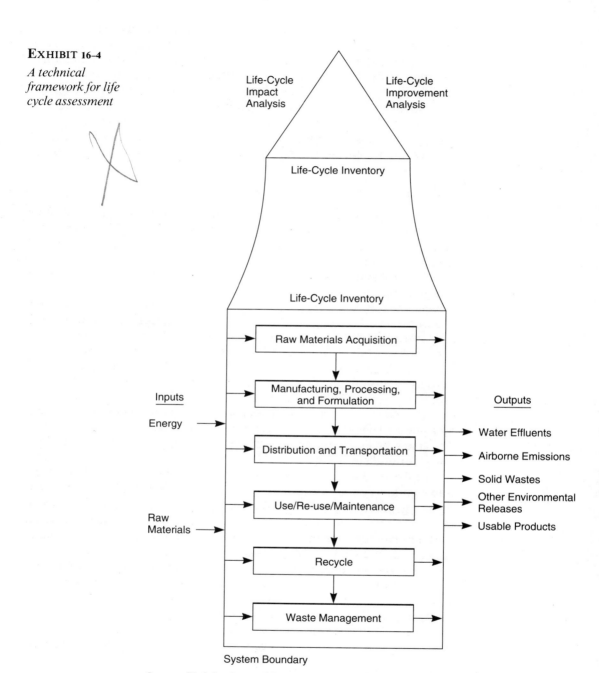

Life-Cycle
Impact
Analysis

Life-Cycle
Improvement
Analysis

Life-Cycle Inventory

Life-Cycle Inventory

Raw Materials Acquisition

Manufacturing, Processing,
and Formulation

Inputs

Outputs

Energy

Distribution and Transportation

Water Effluents

Airborne Emissions

Solid Wastes

Use/Re-use/Maintenance

Other Environmental
Releases

Raw
Materials

Usable Products

Recycle

Waste Management

System Boundary

SOURCE: *Workshop Report of the Society of Environmental Toxicology and Chemistry: A Technical
Framework For Life-Cycle Assessment* (Washington, DC: SETAC Foundation, 1991), title page.

as a whole, or within a given process, at which they can achieve the greatest reduction in resource requirements and emissions. Finally, they can compare the system inputs and outputs associated with alternative processes.[39]

Waste Management

Two key sets of laws govern the waste management industry. The Resource Conservation and Recovery Act (RCRA) is responsible for supervising disposal of 500 chemicals. The Superfund Act, which calls for the cleanup of more than 20,000 abandoned sites, provides funds to companies that specialize in decontaminating soil and water.

The EPA controls the selection of technology for cleanup treatment and can hold a company liable for years after the job is completed if it is found *post facto* to be inadequate. Waste cleanup and removal has been slow and expensive, but new technologies, partly supported by the Superfund, are beginning to make the task easier. Development of these processes created a new, multibillion-dollar waste disposal consulting and engineering industry.

Between 1986 and 1988, 16 waste management firms went public. Chemical Waste Management's profits grew from $25 million in 1985 to $115 million in 1988.[40] But by 1992, the rosy financial picture changed. The economic recession reduced the volume of waste that needed to be collected, treated, and discarded. Companies lost their enthusiasm for cleanup projects. According to the industry newsletter *Environmental Business Journal,* revenue growth slowed to 10 percent in 1990 and 2 percent in 1991. Industry experts recommended that waste management companies explore recycling as a new endeavor.

It is very difficult to forecast the impact of regulation and the clout of public opinion in the waste management industry. This point is illustrated by the strategies adopted by the medical waste disposal giants, Waste Management Inc. (WMI) and Browning-Ferris. WMI invested in incinerators to burn medical waste in anticipation that new, rigid regulations requiring burning would be passed. As it happened, regulators decided the material could be handled in a less costly way, such as sterilization in steam-cleaning autoclaves.

Environmentalists and NIMBY stakeholders opposed incineration of medical waste because emissions included heavy metals and dioxin. Some suggested that steam-cleaning autoclaves, which are safer and cheaper to operate, could be used instead. To spread its risk, Browning-Ferris had invested in both technologies. BFI reported its medical waste revenue for the

---

[39] *Workshop Report of the Society of Environmental Toxicology and Chemistry: A Technical Framework for Life-Cycle Assessment* (Washington, DC: SETAC Foundation, 1991), pp. 1–27.

[40] "The Big Haul in Toxic Waste," *Newsweek,* October 3, 1988, pp. 37, 39.

year ending September 1992 was up 27 percent from the previous year. Disappointed Waste Management executives commented that they had expected a new rash of regulation that did not occur, but wishfully declared their investment "may not be wrong, we may just be early."[41]

Until the late 1980s, environmental engineers usually sealed and buried untreated toxic waste in landfills. Nearly all experts agreed this method was risky. No matter how carefully drums and barrels are buried, they can leak. New methods destroy or detoxify the waste.

Burning.   Westinghouse Electric Corporation developed a 30-inch-long "plasma" torch that generates temperatures as high as 10,000 degrees Fahrenheit. The torch can be used to burn the waste into harmless gases. It is used most effectively on fluids such as PCBs, carbon tetrachloride, and methyl ethyl ketone, which have a low concentration of solid material.[42] Rollins Environmental Services, Inc., uses an incinerator that encloses toxic metals in a glasslike coating before they are buried in a landfill.

Biological Treatment.   Detox Industries developed specialized microbes that eat PCBs. The microbes metabolize the PCBs into water, carbon dioxide, and cell protoplasm. Once the bugs are done with their job, they either starve or are themselves eaten by other organisms. Microbes have been used for many years to treat municipal sewage, but their use in toxic waste disposal is fairly new. Researchers in universities and chemical firms are genetically engineering microbes to eat mercury, lead, and even arsenic.

When the Exxon *Valdez* spilled its oil into Prince William Sound, scientists sprayed the beaches with fertilizer, hoping the normal bacteria that lived on the beaches would be stimulated to feed on the oil residue. Within a month, the treated beaches were nearly clean and the bug population had increased a hundredfold. This kind of bioremediation is generally considered safer than burning because it leaves no residue and the bugs die once their food source is gone. The drawbacks are that the bugs usually attack only one contaminant and may not work in sites where multiple toxins are present. In addition, bacteria work more slowly than other methods and need nutrients and oxygen to survive.[43]

Separation.   Another cleanup process entails separating liquid pollutants from the soil. The contaminated soil is cooked in giant ovens that convert the liquid in the soil to gas. After the gas is filtered, the pollutant particles are buried in landfills, and the clean soil can be returned to the earth.[44]

[41]J Bailey, "How Two Garbage Giants Fought Over Medical Waste," *The Wall Street Journal,* November 17, 1992, p. B6.

[42]J Holusha, "Putting a Torch to Toxic Wastes," *The New York Times,* June 21, 1989, p. D1.

[43]R D Hof, "The Tiniest Toxic Avengers," *Business Week,* June 4, 1990, pp. 96, 98.

[44]S Gilbert, "Finding a Place for Hazardous Waste," *High Technology,* October 1988, pp. 26–30.

Alternative Fuels: Another Strategy for Reducing Waste

Generating energy is a major source of pollution. Recycling is one alternative to reducing waste and by-products of fossil fuel. Another is for companies to adopt new, nonpolluting or less polluting fuels.

Wind Power.   In the early 1980s, wind power seemed to promise a way to generate electricity without using fossil fuels and without leaving any waste by-products. In 1991, Iowa-Illinois Gas & Electric Company and Windpower Inc. teamed up to develop wind farms. The proposed joint venture planned to put wind turbines on agricultural land in Iowa. Using clusters of giant propellers, the turbines powered generators that produced electricity. This technology was a great improvement over older machines. The president of Windpower's parent company, Kenetech, Inc., predicted that the 1990s would be a transition decade for wind power and that wind power would contribute as much as 10 percent of the nation's electricity by the year 2010.[45]

Within a year, new technology made wind power even more attractive as an alternative power source. A comparison of wind-powered and oil-fired plants showed that the cost of wind turbine production from capital investment to operation and maintenance was about 5 cents per kilowatt-hour, about half the average retail price for power nationwide. A kilowatt-hour is enough electricity to light ten 100-watt bulbs for one hour. In contrast, at an oil-fired plant, the same amount of electricity costs 5 cents in fuel alone. Capital investment, operation, and maintenance expenses are all additional costs. For fossil fuel plants already in operation, the generation costs are lower. But for new operations in areas where the wind is sufficient, wind turbines may be a cheaper alternative.

The negative aspect of wind farms is that they change the landscape visually and will kill any birds that wander into the propellers.[46] In addition, since winds vary in intensity, backup is required, and technology for backup systems requires further development.

Hydroelectric Power.   The technology of hydroelectric power dates back to the mid-nineteenth century. Today about 20 percent of the electricity generated worldwide comes from hydroelectric plants. In areas with appropriate water sources, such plants are economically competitive with fossil fuel plants. However, rivers must be dammed for hydroelectric generation, and some stakeholders charge that the resulting ecosystem damage is an unacceptably high price for this kind of power.

---

[45]D Stipp, " 'Wind Farms' May Energize the Midwest," *The Wall Street Journal,* September 6, 1991, p. B1.

[46]M L Wald, "A New Era for Windmill Power," *The New York Times,* September 7, 1992, p. B1.

Solar Power.   Since the oil shortages of the 1970s, solar power has become a more popular alternative for heating homes and small businesses. However, very few utilities outside of California have integrated solar energy into their grids. At this writing, solar energy for commercial use is still considerably more expensive to generate than electricity from traditional fossil fuels like coal and oil. If new solar technologies continue to advance, projected costs for solar-powered, grid-connected systems could be cut in half by the end of the century. Within 20 years, solar thermal systems could occupy a significant niche in a portfolio of electricity-generating utilities.[47]

Thermal Energy.   Thermal energy can be tapped from several natural sources. Hot-water reservoirs lie about a mile underground in an area along the Pacific Rim called the Ring of Fire. This area, as well as the Mediterranean, are volcanically active and can be exploited for small-scale energy sources. In fact, steam from geysers already supplies much of San Francisco's electricity.

Hot dry rock mining is another geothermal option. According to scientists, under the Earth lies a gigantic furnace that holds 30 times as much energy as all the gas, oil, and coal deposits combined. A project is under way at Los Alamos National Laboratories in New Mexico to develop an electricity-generating plant. Wells are driven from the surface into the rocks, whose temperature reaches 400 degrees Fahrenheit. Under high pressure, cold water is forced through cracks in the hot rocks and then pumped back to the surface. When the plant is operating commercially, the hot water will heat butane, which will drive turbines. In the West, the cost should be competitive with those for conventional electric plants.

Recycling and use of alternative fuels will help decrease the amount of carbon dioxide and other pollutants released into the air and lower the volume of hazardous waste requiring cleaning. Despite all these efforts, we will continue to generate waste, use large quantities of fossil fuel, and have to deal with the by-products of an industrial economy. Hazardous waste disposal is, and will continue to be, a major industry in the United States and all industrialized countries.

Radioactive Waste in the United States	Many stakeholders do not realize radioactive contamination comes from a number of sources other than nuclear power plants. Weapons facilities, hospitals, and laboratories all generate huge volumes of contaminated material. There are three levels of radioactive waste: low, intermediate, and high. Each has different potencies and poses varying levels of danger to the public.

---

[47]D C White, C J Andrews, and N W Stauffer, "The New Team: Electricity Sources Without Carbon Dioxide," *Technology Review* (January 1992), pp. 43–50.

Low-Level Waste.   Workers in hospitals, nuclear plants, and other industries generate a considerable proportion of radioactive waste. Such waste contaminates clothing, tools, and cooling and cleaning water. Although its radioactivity is short-lived, its volume is enormous. In 1980, Congress passed legislation aimed at making states responsible for disposal of low-level radioactive waste generated in state.

In 1985, Congress amended the law to require that states unable to dispose of the waste would, whether they wanted to or not, have to take possession of the waste and be held liable for any damages resulting from their failure to do so. This law was due to go into effect in 1996.

State governors had a major role in crafting the 1985 law and gave it their unanimous support. They and members of Congress agreed it was unfair for Washington, Nevada, and South Carolina (which had existing dump sites) to serve as the dumping grounds for the entire nation's low-level radioactive waste.

New York State proceeded to choose potential dump sites, but the NIMBY syndrome hit residents in the targeted areas. In 1990, New York State sued the federal government, alleging that Congress had trampled on state sovereignty by putting itself in charge of issues that should have been reserved for state legislative and executive bodies.

The Supreme Court heard the case in 1992 and was sympathetic to New York's argument. Justices Sandra Day O'Connor and Anthony M Kennedy suggested that Congress could no more require the states to assume the burden of nuclear waste than it could make states legally liable for all crimes committed with handguns within their borders.[48]

In June 1992, the Supreme Court ruled in a six-to-two decision that it was unconstitutional for Congress to hold states responsible for the waste. Justice Sandra Day O'Connor, who wrote the decision, based it on the 10th Amendment, which provides that powers not expressly given to the federal government are "reserved to the states" or to "the people."[49]

By 1993, only South Carolina and Washington State accepted low-level radioactive waste. In May, New York officials announced that due to local opposition, they were putting their search for a local dump site on hold. South Carolina, which had been accepting 84 tractor-trailers full of New York waste per year for eight years, finally lost patience. South Carolina officials announced they might cancel their contract with New York, leaving 200 hospitals, nuclear power plants, research laboratories, and companies with no place to dump their by-products. As in many other states, the NIMBY syndrome left New York without a storage plan for the future and producers of waste with an uncertain future. A medical researcher at the

---

[48]L Greenhouse, "Justices Hear Attack on Waste Law," *The New York Times,* March 31, 1992, p. A17.

[49]L Greenhouse, "High Court Eases States' Obligation over Toxic Waste," *The New York Times,* June 20, 1992, p. 1.

University of Rochester noted uncertainty over disposal of radioactive isotopes may jeopardize his $6 million AIDS grant.[50]

Intermediate-Level Waste.   This material includes reactor components, resins, heavily contaminated equipment, and waste by-products. Low- and intermediate-level radioactive waste is usually buried in pits or sealed in concrete.

High-Level Waste.   Spent fuel from reactors presents the gravest problems in storage. Uranium-238, which comes from nuclear fuel and waste, has a half-life of 4.5 billion years.[51]

The accidents at Three Mile Island and Chernobyl focused the world's attention on nuclear contamination and how it could and should be handled. For most Americans, the immediate concern was whether US facilities were really safe. Despite loud and repeated assurances from the nuclear energy industry, people were reluctant to build more nuclear plants. A less dramatic but more realistic concern was how nuclear plants would deal with their waste once they were too old to be operated safely.

On average, the 15 plants closed by 1993 operated for only 12.7 years, although they were licensed for 40 years. The questions were how to dismantle old utilities and what the cost would be. The Nuclear Regulatory Commission (NRC) requires utilities with nuclear plants to put aside as much as $135 million per plant to pay for dismantling costs. A Stanford University study concluded that by the beginning of 1993, utilities should have set aside a total of $33 billion. The NRC estimated only $4 billion actually had been collected.[52]

Fort St. Vrain in Colorado was the first fully operational nuclear power plant to be taken apart in pieces. Built in the 1970s, the plant had suffered a variety of small problems that caused frequent shutdowns. After cracks developed in the reactor's steam tubes, the plant's owner, Public Service of Colorado, decided it should be decommissioned and dismantled.

This facility, which had cost $224 million to build, was small compared to many others around the nation. Yet the cost of taking it apart was estimated at $333 million, and the technology needed was not always obvious. Engineers sometimes had to create models to figure out how to take the plant apart. The utility's customers will pay for the dismantling until the year 2005.

---

[50]S Lyall, "Failing to Build a Dump, New York Faces Shutout," *The New York Times,* May 21, 1993, p. A1.

[51]"Living with Nuclear Waste," *The Economist,* January 21, 1984, pp. 72–73.

[52]R Johnson and A de Rouffignac, "Nuclear Utilities Face Immense Expenses in Dismantling Plants," *The New York Times,* January 25, 1993, p. A1.

How to dispose of nuclear spent fuel has been an issue since the end of World War II. In the early days of the nuclear age, there was little concern about safe disposal. In 1983, the Nuclear Regulatory Commission, in conducting a routine check of old records, unexpectedly found a 6.5-acre radioactive dump site in Wayne, New Jersey. Between 1948 and 1960, the Atomic Energy Commission, the predecessor of the Nuclear Regulatory Commission, had conducted atomic bomb research on the property. Left-behind radioactive sludge grew into open mounds that were exposed to rain and runoff. The research facility left nearly 2,000 tons of waste on the ground or buried in pits. Radiation eventually leached into a local stream adjacent to residential housing.[53]

Finally, in 1982, Congress set guidelines for burying radioactive waste. In the year the guidelines were passed, more than 8,000 tons of highly radioactive spent fuel had already piled up at power plants. Most of the waste was held in shallow pools initially designed to store it for only several months.

The military, which created 80 percent of high-level waste, stored its residue in huge steel tanks in Washington State, South Carolina, and Idaho. A new military waste site, to be developed at a cost of $700 million, was located under the New Mexico desert near Carlsbad. The first ventilator shafts were sunk, and excavation of storage rooms began in 1983.

Environmentalists protested any attempt to ship radioactive waste over land to the disposal facility. Politicians, responding to public antipathy to nuclear waste, exhibited the NIMBY syndrome. Governor Cecil Andrus of Idaho was so determined to keep it out of his state that in 1987 he ordered a boxcarful of radioactive waste stopped at the Idaho border and sent back to the Rocky Flats nuclear weapons plant in Colorado.

In 1988, the Department of Energy announced there were cracks in the 300-foot-long rooms of the New Mexico storage facility. Disposal of plutonium-contaminated clothing, equipment, solvents, and other waste stalled. Congress, worried about environmental safety, refused to transfer ownership of the land from the Department of the Interior to the Department of Energy.[54]

By 1993, the Department of Energy had fallen 12 years behind its deadline for opening a facility in Nevada. Utilities around the country were desperate to find storage sites for high-level waste. The Boston Edison-owned Pilgrim plant applied to the Nuclear Regulatory Commission to increase its storage capacity by two-thirds, allowing it to operate until its license expired in the year 2010. Pilgrim and the now closed Yankee Rowe plant in western Massachusetts together stored more than 400 tons of high-level nuclear

---

[53]R Hanley, "Atom Waste Found in Town in Jersey," *The New York Times,* June 8, 1983, pp. A1, B4.

[54]K Schneider, "Safety Questions Still Delay Nuclear Waste Plant," *The New York Times,* June 13, 1989, p. A23.

waste by mid-1993. On-site storage raised concerns that if cooling water were suddenly lost, the resulting fire could melt the metal casings that enclosed the uranium fuel pellets.[55]

Summary

Environmental issues present stakeholders with profound challenges and dangers. Businesses, governments, environmental groups, and individuals all have a tremendous stake in promoting clean air, water, and earth.

Since the beginning of the Industrial Revolution in the early nineteenth century, industrial and urban waste have seriously damaged the environment. The United States has taken measures to deal with some of the worst cases of air, water, and hazardous waste pollution. The Environmental Protection Agency, established by Congress, oversees programs for control of air pollution, water pollution, pesticides, radiation, and waste management. During the 1980s, the performance of the EPA fell far short of environmentalists' expectations, but the 1990s promise to be a decade of environmental activism.

The Clean Air Act of 1970 placed clean air legislation under EPA supervision. Federal air quality standards were drawn up with state participation. The initial act and subsequent amendments were helpful in reducing air pollution. President Bush submitted his administration's proposed revision in 1989, and the Clinton administration pushed forward in enforcing the Clean Air Act of 1990. Although the new act does not satisfy all stakeholders, it addresses some critical US problems such as acid rain and ozone reduction.

Clean water legislation also came under EPA oversight. Progress was slow during the Reagan years, but there were some notable successes in cleaning up harbors, rivers, and lakes. Drinking water in many communities is showing signs of antiquated and inadequate filtration. Abandoned toxic waste sites, pesticides, and industrial waste contamination threaten underground water supplies.

The EPA tracks and manages hazardous waste under the Resource Conservation and Recovery Act. Congress established a Superfund designed to clean up the worst of the nation's toxic waste dumps. The EPA is still finding sites that were abandoned years ago, and communities are trying to evaluate resulting health problems.

Waste management is now a multimillion-dollar business. Communities insisted that companies dump their by-products in someone else's "backyard." New technologies, partly funded by government, are devising ways to safely dispose of chemicals and other potentially dangerous industrial by-products.

---

[55]S Allen, "Pilgrim Asks to Increase Radioactive-Waste Storage," *The Boston Globe,* April 8, 1993, p. 35.

The most difficult and hazardous waste is radioactive waste. It comes from a variety of sources, including hospitals, laboratories, weapons plants, and commercial nuclear reactors. The United States has never developed a safe means of disposing of the tremendous volume of nuclear material it has generated. In recent years, nuclear weapons plants have been cited for decades of unsafe operation and disposal of waste products. Authorities will struggle with this problem for the foreseeable future.

Questions

1. What are the duties of the Environmental Protection Agency?
2. What are some mechanisms companies can use to reduce their pollution?
3. What are the major clean air issues for the 1990s?
4. What are the major clean water issues for the 1990s?
5. What is NIMBY? What hazardous waste issues do local communities face?
6. What are the most important sources of alternative power? How realistic is this technology commercially?

Projects

1. Contact your state environmental agency. Find out how the state and federal governments work together to reduce environmental hazards.
2. Go to your city, town, or local government offices, and find out about recycling policies in your community.
3. Contact an environmental lobbying group in your community. Attend meetings to find how it develops its agenda, solicits funding, and carries out its mission.
4. Choose a product of interest to you. Trace its life cycle according to Exhibit 16–4. Identify all sources of environmental contamination, and recommend ways to eliminate the problem.

BETA CASE 16
ENVIRONMENTAL ISSUES

Ken Braddock, Beta's vice president for ethical products, poked his head into Bill Parker's office. "Want any lunch?" he asked. "I'd like to run something by you." The two men walked to the executive dining room and found a corner table. After ordering a light lunch of cold turkey and pasta salad, Braddock leaned back in his chair. "Bill, I am really upset. As you know, we have a fairly large volume of toxic waste in our radiopharmaceutical division. We've been using Waste Disposal Associates to handle the material, and until recently we have been pretty satisfied with their prices and performance."

"Then what's your problem?" asked Parker.

"My problem is that Waste Disposal Associates has just been cited by the Michigan attorney general's office for violating state and federal laws covering disposal of chemical waste. According to my buddy in the State House, the newpapers are going to have this plastered across page one tomorrow morning."

"Okay, Ken, let's take this from the top," soothed Parker. Tell me everything that is going on."

Braddock promptly launched into a recitation of the facts as he knew them. He had been called late the previous evening by a former college classmate who was an aide to the attorney general. The aide classmate told him the following story.

Two employees of Waste Disposal Associates quit their jobs six months ago, then filed lawsuits against their former employer. They charged they had repeatedly reported dumping violations to their superiors. The superiors told them to either forget about it or cover it up. One employee had made a deposition in which he alleged that Waste Disposal had failed to file manifests (shipping documents) with the state of Michigan. If the manifests were not filed as the law required, the state could not track the waste. Apparently Waste Disposal drivers were dumping large amounts of toxic substances in landfills or burying them in unauthorized drums. The manager of one of Waste Disposal's own dumps had written to a company official a year ago, telling her the company's disposal practices were inviting disaster. So far, Waste Disposal's top managers have denied any wrongdoing, claiming they have not withheld manifests or authorized any illegal dumping.

"I know these people at Waste Disposal," sighed Braddock. "They are one of the most aggressive companies in the waste disposal business. They have disposal contracts from New York to Saudi Arabia. On the other hand, the lawsuits are coming in like bees to honey. Bill, I have no idea if waste is being dumped illegally. Even if it is, I don't know whether it is *our* waste. After all, we may not be responsible. We gave them the contract in good faith."

"Hey, Ken," Parker interrupted, "if the press finds out our waste is involved, we're going to get really bad publicity regardless of who's responsible."

"Well, what should I do?" moaned Braddock.

17. THE INTERNATIONAL ENVIRONMENT

Maintaining the environment is a global problem and one that is exacerbated as economic development progresses. Economic growth has undoubtedly improved the standard of living across much of the globe—but at a great cost to the environment.

Clean air, clean water, and toxic waste management are issues that concern every nation; they are not purely domestic concerns. Rivers, oceans, and wind currents carry one country's environmental problems across national boundaries. Many countries have environmental policies and regulations that govern their own institutions, but each nation's economic, legal, and social systems produce a different approach. In every country tension exists between the cost of environmental protection and remediation and the public's economic well-being.

This chapter examines sustainable development as an underlying concept. *Sustainable development* seeks to balance economic development and protection of the environment. Economic development is not a purely domestic issue; it is also linked to international trade policy. The General Agreement on Tariffs and Trade (GATT) promotes an antiprotectionist agenda to foster development while still protecting the environment.

Environmental issues in the European Community, Eastern Europe, and Asia elaborate on the theme of sustainable development and provide illustrations of private and governmental environmental decision making. The World Bank's exhaustive study on the environment and its relationship to international trade policy provides additional insight into this topic. The chapter also examines events leading to the Rio Earth Summit and its implications for multilateral environmental treaties.

Sustainable Development

In 1987, a United Nations Commission chaired by Norway's then Prime Minister Gro Harlem Brundtland, sponsored a conference to discuss the concept of sustainable development. Since the Brundtland conference, the concept of sustainable development has become increasingly important to the discussion of the impact of economic development on the environment.

The National Research Council's definition of sustainability cautions that "world conservation strategy should include management of the use of a resource so it can meet human demands of the present generation without decreasing opportunities for future generations."[1] The issue of the future is crucial to the concept of sustainability.

It is very difficult to predict all the consequences of even the best-intentioned actions. For example, assume a factory is built using a technology that removes a certain percentage, but not all, of its effluence. It is hard to know with certainty what the long-term trade-offs are between putting people to work so they can support their families and degradation of air quality.

The notion of sustainable development demands that regulators, policymakers, private enterprise, and other stakeholders measure economic progress as correctly as they can. Current statistics on education, infant mortality, and nutrition are all important in determining a country's gross domestic product or gross national product (both important indicators of progress). But these statistics are inadequate for assessing the costs to future generations of today's economic development. When we make economic choices in the mid-1990s, we pass on to future generations a wide range of physical, human, and natural capital that will determine their welfare and their heritage to future generations.

In making choices, we face unclear trade-offs between environmental protection and economic development. This chapter discusses the difficult issues involved in understanding these long-run trade-offs. The goal is to help us understand more fully what the consequences of domestic and foreign policy and multilateral treaties mean to future generations.

Trade Policy and the Environment

In the winter of 1992, shortly before the Earth Summit meetings in Rio de Janeiro, the secretariat of the General Agreement on Tariffs and Trade (GATT) issued a report on trade and the environment.[2] The report specifically addressed the link between agriculture and trade. Its major point was that European Community (EC) and US agricultural policies seriously hurt the environment. US programs that aim for higher yields per acre encourage increased use of chemical fertilizers and pesticides. European Community

---

[1] National Research Council, Committee on Global Change, *Research Strategies for the U.S. Global Change Research Program* (Washington, DC: National Academy Press, 1990).

[2] GATT is a 108-nation international institution whose mission is to foster trade, resolve trade disputes, and lower trade barriers such as tariffs. Members include all the major industrialized nations and many developing countries.

countries establish high tariff barriers blocking American products grown with these chemicals. GATT was concerned that protectionist groups would lobby environmentalists and persuade them to support tariff and nontariff barriers that restrict international trade.

The report specifically criticized the US decision to ban Mexican yellow fin tuna, because Mexico's fishing methods also killed dolphins. It warned governments not to take unilateral actions to export domestic environmental policies. GATT's position reflected its concern that the United States and other nations might use trade sanctions to force their concepts of sound environmental practices on other countries. The report claimed "such environmental imperialism would be a fast track to chaos and conflict."[3] GATT asserted countries should set their own policies, because each nation is different. No country should appoint itself the world's guardian of environmental imperatives. Talks on environmental issues should be multilateral and foster intergovernmental cooperation.

In general, GATT took the position that free trade was not a major contributor to environmental degradation. Expanded trade was likely to lead to greater wealth and diffusion of technology, giving nations the resources with which to protect and upgrade environmental practices.[4] The World Bank agreed with this perspective, noting that "liberalized trade fosters greater efficiency and higher productivity and may actually reduce pollution by encouraging the growth of less polluting industries and the adoption and diffusion of cleaner technologies."[5]

While the GATT and World Bank positions reflect the most prevalent view of the link between the environment and trade, some argue that polluting industries will seek to locate where environmental laws are more lax. A few even suggest developing countries will compete for foreign investment in "dirty" industries by lowering their environmental standards.

There is scant evidence for this view, however. Chile, for example, has few controls on industrial emissions and is open to foreign trade and investment. Its cheap and efficient labor force, rather than its lack of environmental regulations, draws multinational investment. Moreover, the potential liability of foreign firms that pollute is so high that most are unwilling to assume the risk.

Increasingly management of the international environment is being seen as a multilateral problem that must be addressed quickly, effectively, and multilaterally. Individual nations no longer have the luxury of putting off environmental concerns for another day or another year.

---

[3]D Dodwell, "GATT Issues Warning Against Environmental Imperialism," *Financial Times,* February 12, 1992, p. 3.

[4]Ibid.

[5]*World Development Report 1992: Development and The Environment* (Washington, DC: The World Bank, 1992), p. 67.

The Environment and the European Community

"Green" Politics

Between 1972 and the mid-1980s, the EC adopted several action plans that generated a spate of environmental directives. In 1987, the EC placed the issue of the environment near the top of its agenda, and member nations made an explicit commitment to move to "a high level of [environmental] protection."[6]

Nevertheless, it was difficult to achieve agreement among countries that varied widely in their own political structures, national interests, levels of industrial development, and economic well-being. Unlike the United States, most European governments are made up of coalitions of many large and small special-interest parties. "Green" parties representing environmental interests are now major players in European governments.

The first national Green Party was organized in Germany in the late 1970s. It was an amalgamation of left-wing, ecology-oriented groups that had little in common except their commitment to the environment. Despite a great deal of internal dissention, the German Green Party held its first Congress in January 1980. On March 22, 1983, 27 people walked through Bonn carrying a huge rubber globe and the branch of a tree dying from Black Forest pollution.

Calling themselves *die Grunen,* the Greens entered the West German national assembly building and took seats as the first new party to be elected in more than 30 years. They insisted on being seated between the conservative Christian Democrats and the left-liberal Social Democrats. They considered themselves the political voice of citizens' movements such as ecology (anti-toxic waste, radiation, air pollution, and pro-eco development), anti-nuclear energy, peace (antimissile movement, demilitarization), and feminism.

Within a short time, there were organized Green parties in all 12 European Community countries agitating for an environmentally sound EC policy. Eurocrats agreed a common environmental policy was critical to a united Europe. However, they disagreed about who should pay for the policy and how to implement and enforce it.

In October 1992, EC environment ministers met to discuss the EC Commission's green strategy for the 1990s. The ministers were concerned about how they would handle the issue of subsidiarity as applied to the environment. The Maastricht Treaty vaguely and generally defines *subsidiarity* as the concept that political authority should be exercised at the level most appropriate to the function in question and that government should supplement, not replace, action by individuals and families.[7]

---

[6]R Vernon, "The Triad as Policy Makers" (Unpublished paper, Center for Science and International Affairs, John F Kennedy School of Government, Harvard University, December 1992), pp. 24–25.

[7]The Maastricht Treaty was passed by the European Community leaders in December 1991. If voters in each of the 12 countries approved the treaty, they committed their countries to new, common economic, social, political, and monetary policies.

If subsidiarity were applied to environmental policy, each country would implement its own environmental rules. Even though countries share waterways and are greatly affected by one another's airborne pollution, national rules and regulations would prevail over common EC directives. From the Greens' perspective, it was essential that all 12 nations ratify the Maastricht Treaty to ensure a common environmental policy.

By the end of December 1992, 8 of the 12 countries had ratified the treaty. When Denmark voted against the Maastricht Treaty in June 1992, its vote was based partly on the fear that the EC would dilute Denmark's own high environmental standards. In May 1993, Denmark reversed its earlier vote and approved a modified treaty that included a common environmental policy.

Britain postponed its vote on the Maastricht Treaty. British Greens wanted measures considerably stronger than those proposed by the commission. They promoted a program that "greened" EC policies from transport to energy and pushed for the formation of a "green police force" to enforce common standards.

Karel Van Miert, environment commissioner of the EC, lobbied for a single, strong EC environmental policy. Danish ratification put to rest the issue of subsidiarity in environmental policy. There is every indication that European Community economic and environmental integration will continue and that a common environmental policy will override national interests.

Environmental Policy Implementation

Although all 12 EC member countries have their own cultures, political systems, and national agendas, the EC Commission and Council have pushed them toward a more uniform approach to the environment.[8] The 12 nations agree it is necessary to establish a single European Environmental Agency (EEA) but disagree on where it should be located and how much power it should wield. In 1992, 11 of the 12 members agreed on particulars, but France refused to support the agency unless it was located in Strasbourg with the European Parliament instead of in Brussels with most other EC offices.

Despite France's intransigence on this matter, the European Commission continued to issue environmental directives to member countries. These directives covered a variety of environmental concerns, from filtering factory smoke to muffling lawnmowers to protecting birds. By the end of

---

[8]The European Commission is one of the four major institutions of the EC. The other three institutions are the Council of Ministers, Parliament, and the Court of Justice. The commission president is Jacques Delors of France. Delors, the 17 commission members, and their staffs develop rules and regulations (directives) for member countries. The five larger nations have two representatives each, and the five smaller ones have one representative each on the commission. Each nation must vote on a Commission directive before that directive becomes a national law.

1992, the Commission reported member countries had "transposed" 85 percent of its directives into national law.

Individual national governments implemented directives as they wished. No institution existed to measure or evaluate their actions. Without an EC environmental agency to levy penalties, the EC could not enforce the rules or even find out whether they had been broken.

Some governments voluntarily spent large amounts of money to clean up water or air, even during recessionary times. They looked at their neighbors who ignored the rules and asked themselves whether they should continue to bear the cost if other members refused.

The poorer countries charged the Commission was too ambitious and imposed excessively costly rules. For example, the Commission's drinking water directives came under heavy fire. The directives mandated that every trace of lead, pesticides, nitrates, and bacteria be removed, even though health risks from tiny residual amounts of these substances were unproven. The rules also dictated that the water look clear even if its safety was not affected. The greatest costs were attached to the last "few steps towards perfection," although the benefits were not obvious.[9]

Environmental spending in the EC is huge. In 1992, the annual bill, excluding the nuclear power industry and water, was about 38 billion pounds (nearly $65 billion). Wealthy industrialized countries like Germany, Denmark, and the Netherlands had much stricter environmental standards and spent much more than did poorer countries such as Portugal, Greece, Spain, and, in some instances, Italy.

The poorer countries believed they could not finance tougher environmental measures and assumed the richer EC countries would help them with the costs. EC environmental experts agreed a successful common environmental policy would have to address costs. The northern European countries would have to decide whether they would help the southern countries and, if so, which directives were the most important.

Corporate Involvement.   Corporations inside the EC were important stakeholders in developing and implementing environmental policy. In the early 1990s, more and more companies began revealing information about their green performances. Many companies developed publications to inform stakeholders such as shareholders, employees, and local communities where they operated. Corporations in Europe did not have to comply with rules as strict as those in the United States. However, industry realized the quality of its voluntary compliance would help shape future EC laws.

Norsk Hydro's subsidiary in the United Kingdom published a comprehensive report on its environmental impact. British Airways and British

---

[9]B Maddox, "High Cost of a Cleaner Europe," *Financial Times,* November 3, 1992, p. 16.

Petroleum also produced publications about their environmental operations. In mid-1992, ICI published a frank and comprehensive environmental report listing the numbers of prosecutions for its own environmental violations worldwide. It gave data on the amount and type of waste it produced and where the waste ended up. Although Greenpeace and other environmental groups criticized the reports as too general and too vague, others asserted these and other companies were initiating a process of disclosure and cost assessment that was a very positive step toward environmental responsibility.[10]

Corporate Europe took another giant step forward in March 1993. After three years of discussion, the European Commission established a voluntary eco-management system for corporations. When the commission first drafted its proposals in 1990, it recommended mandatory eco-audits for all industrial companies larger than a specified size. That scheme was rejected, but negotiations proceeded.

The new, voluntary Eco-Management and Audit Scheme (EMA) included the establishment of corporate environmental management systems. Participating companies were required to

1. Establish environmental policies, goals, and management systems.
2. Systematically self-assess their environmental policies through site audits at time intervals no longer than three years.
3. Provide information to the public about the results of the audits.
4. Have independent verification by external auditors, who would be licensed by each nation.

All audits had to contain figures on each site's pollution emissions, waste output, consumption of raw materials, energy and water, and noise levels. They had to present overall company policy, goals and eco-management policies of the site, and the name of the accredited external auditor. In return for adhering to this process, companies could use a logo to promote their involvement as long as they did not use it on their products or promotional materials. While some critics worried that this voluntary system would be made mandatory, most companies saw the system as a positive and low-risk means of establishing green credentials, boosting their corporate image, and establishing systems the EC would eventually impose anyway.[11]

The EC is making rapid progress toward a comprehensive and uniform environmental policy. It still faces problems of who should bear the cost, what body should implement its policies, and what responsibility it has to its newly independent neighbors in Eastern Europe.

---

[10]P Knight, "The Truth But Not the Whole Truth," *Financial Times,* April 15, 1992, p. 10.

[11]A Jack, "The Green Time Bomb," *Financial Times,* March 31, 1993, p. 14.

The Environment and Eastern Europe

In 1989, the world looked in wonder at the demolition of the Berlin Wall. The Soviet Union disintegrated soon afterward, leaving the rest of its former political and economic bloc countries to establish independent governments. For the first time since the end of World War II, horrified observers were able to see the environmental cost of Soviet-led industrial policies.

Eastern Europe was a cesspool. Pollution in East Germany was so pervasive that all life was extinct in one-third of the country's waterways. Farmland was so heavily contaminated by pesticides that even hardy earthworms failed to survive. Mountain peaks were barren because acid rain had damaged 90 percent of all the trees in the country. The then West German news magazine *Der Spiegel* called East Germany "a cauldron of poison."[12] East Germany's environmental problems were duplicated all over Eastern Europe.

The Example of Poland

In 1983, the Polish government designated 27 geographic areas as "areas of economic hazard." These danger zones covered 11.3 percent of the country's land and water mass and were home to 12.9 million people. Government officials said even the best areas of the country had suffered serious environmental damage and the worst were ecological disasters.

By 1989, pollution-related losses to forests, crops, buildings, and human health had cost Poland up to 20 percent of its national income. None of Poland's waterways had drinkable water; 65 percent were loaded with salt, mercury, cyanide, and human feces. Even industries were afraid to use the water. The Vistula River was an open sewer, and 53 percent of the lakes were too polluted for industrial use.

A World Bank study found coal mines threw their untreated corrosive waste into rivers and canals. These chemicals ate right through the pipes that carried them. Coal-powered factories and utilities had no scrubbers, and very few had filters. The winds carried their airborne pollutants for miles in every direction.

Car exhausts further added to air pollution. Poland had no emissions control regulations, and car engines burned an oil-gasoline blend that emitted up to eight times more hydrocarbons and 50 percent more carbon dioxide than plain gasoline.

Fifty percent of Poland's forests were badly damaged, and another 17 percent were ravaged by sulfur dioxide and other chemical pollutants. Eighty-three percent of Poland's farmland was highly acidic. Forty-one animal species became extinct in the 1980s, and 66 percent of the remaining species were jeopardized.

---

[12]"East Germany: Cauldron of Poison," *World Press Review,* March 1990, p. 66.

Life expectancy for men who survived infancy was lower than it had been in the late 1960s. In upper Silesia, where industry was concentrated, cancer rates were 30 percent higher than normal, respiratory disease was up 47 percent, and every fourth pregnancy resulted in medical complications. The infant mortality rate was 20 per 1,000, compared to 6 per 1,000 in Sweden.[13]

By 1991, the market economy had greatly reduced the pollution level in Poland. Between the beginning of 1990 and mid-1991, the government eliminated industrial subsidies and centrally controlled energy prices. The price of gasoline was cut free to rise to world market levels. Electricity charges doubled, and the price of coal rose more than 250 percent.

As the cost of energy rose, old factories became increasingly inefficient and many quickly went out of business. With the cost of energy rising, factory and utility company managers tried to find ways to burn coal more efficiently. Instead of releasing the 4.2 million tons of sulfur gas each year, they tried to recover it and sell it for profit. In Poland's case, market incentives are cleaning up the environment more quickly than government regulation can.[14] However, environmental damage will take many years to ameliorate and cure.

The Example of the Former Soviet Union

When people discuss the former Soviet Union and the environment, they nearly always do so in the context of the 1986 Chernobyl accident. Zhores A Medvedev, author of *Nuclear Disaster in the Urals,* reported that prior to the Chernobyl explosion, there was virtually no discussion of the environment within the Soviet Union. The government withheld news of catastrophic accidents from the press and the populace. Few people challenged the view that central planning served the interests of environmental protection better than capitalism did. The Soviet nuclear industry had no competition and no responsibility to external stakeholders. It also had no incentive to use modern, safer, but more expensive technology.

Like the Chernobyl plant, most of the other nuclear plants still in operation after the Soviet breakup were unsafe. In 1991 alone, more than 270 malfunctions occurred at nuclear plants. Even today Chernobyl-type reactors furnish about one-half of Russia's nuclear power. So far, Russia has resisted pressure to shut down even the most dangerous reactors, because it has no other power source.[15]

---

[13]L Tye, "Poland Is Left Choking on Its Wastes," *The Boston Globe,* December 18, 1989, p. 1.

[14]P Fuhrman, "Breathing the Polish Air," *Forbes,* June 24, 1991, p. 40.

[15]"Preventing Chernobyl II," *Business Week,* June 8, 1992, pp. 44–51.

Western experts worry about Russia's reliance on unsafe and outdated technology. In November 1992, Russian and Western technical experts got together at a meeting sponsored by the United Nations International Atomic Energy Agency. Senior Russian officials told a watchdog group of Western experts that they will continue using Chernobyl-type plants indefinitely. The officials asserted that although the plants have problems, they have been made safer.

Western scientists remained skeptical, calling the plants' internal workings "plumbers' nightmares." Unlike Western nuclear plants, none of Russia's plants is surrounded by a container to limit contamination in case of an explosion. The chairperson of Russia's Research and Development Institute of Power Engineering, Dr. Eugene Adamov, expressed his country's tension between economic needs and safety concerns. He defended Russia's policy, saying, "Reagan and Bush set out to destroy the 'Evil Empire,' and they succeeded. Now it seems you want to destroy our economy as well . . . What we need from you is medicine for the illness, not just [for] the symptoms."[16]

Three months after the February 1993 conference, two fires and an oil leak at Chernobyl heightened fears that safety measures were lax at this and other nuclear plants. But Chernobyl provides power to Kiev, Russia, and several Eastern European countries, including Poland, the Czech Republic, Hungary, and Romania. And even if Chernobyl were completely shut down, nobody knows how to dismantle it.[17]

In the post-Chernobyl years, the Soviet public began to confront the truth about other forms of environmental degradation. Water usage was a major problem. In the 1950s, under the Soviet regime, hydroelectric dams created reservoirs that covered a total area greater than the Netherlands. As industry and agriculture used more and more water from the 1960s on, the water table fell. Salinization and dust storms destroyed topsoil and ruined vast tracts of cultivated land.

The Aral Sea, once the world's fourth largest sea, became an ecological disaster. Over the past 30 years, its area has decreased by 40 percent. Sand and dust storms blow up from the lake bed and carry debris over an area of 100,000 miles. All commercial fishing is gone.[18]

Massive amounts of DDT were used as a pesticide in the cotton fields around the sea. Infant and child mortality rates are now about 50 to 60 per 1,000 live births, more than 10 times higher than in most industrialized countries and much higher than in many developing countries.

---

[16]M W Browne, "Russians Planning to Continue Using Faulty Reactors," *The New York Times,* November 8, 1992, p. 1.

[17]L Hays, "Fires at Chernobyl Heighten Safety Concerns," *The Wall Street Journal,* February 4, 1993, p. A14.

[18]Z A Medvedev, "The Environmental Destruction of the Soviet Union," *The Ecologies* 20 (January/February 1990), pp. 24–29.

Deforestation is rampant in the former Soviet Union. Forests are disappearing at the same rate as those in Brazil. In Siberia, inefficient harvesting and erosion destroy more than 5 million acres of trees each year.[19]

In the provinces of Uzbekistan and Moldavia, chemical poisoning has left so many children mentally retarded that the school curriculum had to be simplified. Respiratory diseases afflict nearly all children and elderly people in the affected areas. As these and other provinces assessed the state of their own environments in the early 1990s, they began to realize the Soviet legacy was nothing short of a national tragedy.

Russia's environmental future is unclear. The country is beset with political problems, a dearth of foreign currency, and food shortages. The degree to which the government seems interested in environmental cleanup is in direct proportion to outside offers of money and technological assistance. Russian peasants have a long history of endurance in times of adversity. It seems likely the present regime will count on this attribute as it deals first with its economic woes.

Managing the Eastern European Cleanup

Each of the Eastern European revolutions featured strong environmental programs initiated by underground political movements already active prior to the breakup. In many instances, environmental grass-roots activism created the organizations and political bases on which broader demands for political change emerged. By 1990, Eastern European polls showed environmental issues were the public's primary concern.

All of the industrialized Eastern European countries face ideological, economic, and financial dilemmas. How should they balance growth with cleanup and jobs with pollution control? Should environmental programs endanger a quarter of a million jobs in the Polish, Hungarian, Czech, and Slovakian coal-mining and processing industries?[20] In centrally planned economies, these questions never arose. Heavy industry needed electricity. Coal mines provided the fuel for power. The state, unconcerned about pollution, subsidized production and kept workers employed.

Western Europe is taking some responsibility for an environmental cleanup in Eastern Europe. In 1990, the European Commission pledged $365 million to clean up Poland and Hungary, Denmark's parliament earmarked $75 million, and Sweden gave $20 billion.[21] Other countries, including the United States, also made donations, but these combined sums were just a tiny fraction of what will eventually be needed to restore clean air and water.

---

[19]"Toxic Wasteland," *US News & World Report,* April 13, 1992, pp. 43–51.

[20]"Cleaning Up the Fouled Workers' Paradise," *US News & World Report,* April 30, 1990, p. 27.

[21]"Eastern Europe's Big Cleanup," *Business Week,* March 19, 1990, pp. 114–15.

West Germany assumed much of the burden of East Germany's cleanup. When the two countries merged, East Germany ceased to exist, and the former East Germany became part of the EC. As an EC member, a united Germany had to make its environmental standards consistent with those of the other member nations. The former West Germany, which was responsible for some of the pollution in its eastern neighbor, put its considerable resources behind the task. West Germany had used East Germany as a dumping ground for a decade, paying the government hard currency to take its toxic waste.

Although foreign investors saw great investment potential in Eastern Europe, they were worried about having to pay for cleaning up communism's pollution. Western investors looked askance at printing plants, breweries, chemical plants, and automobile factories, wondering whether they would be held responsible for cleanup when environmental regulations were passed and enforced. A top manager in a global pharmaceutical company said, "Everyone is extremely sensitive about this subject. The first question anyone asks is not 'Show me your balance sheet,' but 'show me your environmental audit.' "[22]

Since major insurance companies will not write policies on questionable environmental investments, some Eastern European countries adopted measures that limited investor liability. The Polish government, for example, permitted Unilever to buy a company at a discount in exchange for cleaning up. Philips Lighting, an affiliate of the Dutch Philips, bought a larger number of shares than is usually allowed for a foreign company in a second company as compensation for pollution problems. The government of Poland and yet another investor set up an escrow account to fund a cleanup. Under the agreement's terms, the money would revert to the government if it was not used.[23]

In the next decade, investors, domestic companies, and governments will develop ways to foster environmentally sounder practices. Most experts agree the situation will improve, but few think the cleanup job will be cheap, easy, or quick.

The Environment and Asia

As Asian economies gathered steam in the early 1980s, pollution reached worrisome proportions. Some countries, like Singapore, were small, and their governments regulated industrial pollution and motor vehicle exhausts. Most of the others exercised little or no control over toxic emissions from factories and traffic, agricultural degradation, and filthy energy sources.

[22]M Simons, "Pollution Blights Investment, Too, in East Europe," *The New York Times,* May 13, 1992, p. A1.
[23]Ibid.

More people are hurt by environmental damage in Asia than anywhere else in the world, simply because Asian countries have such large populations. Indonesia's population alone is more than half of that in the entire EC. Asia's pollution affects nearly half the people in the entire world. To make matters potentially worse, Asia's population and cities are growing twice as fast as Europe's and North America's.

Taiwan, the Philippines, Thailand, Indonesia, Hong Kong, India, Bangladesh, and, most of all, China constitute ticking environmental time bombs. But what incentive do these countries have to defuse the bombs? One persuasive argument for change is to look at what will happen if these countries do *not* change. For everyone who breathes poisoned air, health costs grow. For every acre of land lost to erosion, people cannot eat. For each release of industrial waste into rivers, fishers lose their livelihood. Realistically, Asian environmental practices will change only when active "green" stakeholder movements force them or their authoritarian governments to impose regulations on themselves.[24]

Taiwan: An Example of Unfettered Development

Taiwan, with one the highest population densities in the world, represents one of the worst examples of environmental neglect in Asia. More than 20 million people live on a mountainous island the size of the Netherlands. Because much of the island is uninhabitable, people are crowded into areas where they can farm or manufacture. Between 1980 and 1990, the number of factories in Taiwan doubled to 90,000 and more than 10 million cars were registered.

By the early 1980s, Taiwan's industrialization had created substantial health hazards. In the capital of Taipei, car, truck, and motorcycle exhausts created so much air pollution that the city was covered in a gray haze. By 1989, one of Taipei's industrial suburbs had air pollution levels higher than those on a bad day in Los Angeles in the 1960s.

The Taiwan Bureau of Environmental Protection, established in 1982, set acceptable air pollution levels at 140 micrograms of matter per cubic meter of air. In the United States, in contrast, the EPA's acceptable standard was only 75 micrograms.[25]

Petrochemicals, leather tanneries, and pesticide plants were Taiwan's fastest-growing industries. They all used hazardous chemicals and did little or nothing to monitor their air- and waterborne wastes.

Ubiquitous water contamination led to the highest rate of hepatitis infection in the world. Ninety-nine percent of human waste was never

---

[24]"Pollution in Asia," *The Economist,* October 6, 1990, pp. 19–20.
[25]M Shao, "Newly Industrialized Taiwan's Pollution Begins to Reach Worrisome Proportions," *The Wall Street Journal,* July 15, 1983, p. A1.

treated before its disposal. Fourteen of the country's 17 rivers were badly polluted.

Early in 1990, the government began taking the environment more seriously. The Bureau of Environmental Protection announced the government and private sector would spend $40 billion to clean up the environment. New laws were passed, enforcement officers were hired, and fines were imposed. Some cynics noted Taiwan's worst polluters were going offshore to China, where regulations were virtually nonexistent. But most observers believed the "green movement" was catching hold in Taiwan.

Environmental degradation in Taiwan could be remedied. In the 1980s, Japan proved technology and national commitment could reverse environmental damage of even mammoth proportions. There was no question that the price would be high and some of the worst polluters would seek out other countries in Asia where enforcement was less rigorous.

China: A Nation in Transition

China is Asia's waking giant. This vast country of more than 1.2 billion people is rapidly industrializing. In the past, China's contribution to worldwide environmental degradation has been small compared to those of industrialized nations. But at its current rate of development, China has the potential to become one of the world's biggest polluters. The tension between economic development and environmental preservation is ongoing and unresolved. For the most part, questions about sustainable development have not been asked, much less answered.

In 1982, China's Ministry of Construction became the Ministry of Construction and Environmental Protection. It was charged with implementing new laws on environmental and marine protection. Between 1982 and 1984, the government doubled the number of environmental monitoring stations to 650 and quadrupled the number of environmental protection workers to nearly 27,000. Most of the antipollution effort was concentrated in cities with scenic tourist sites and was paid for with fines levied against offending industries.

These measures were not as impressive as they might sound. Since China was, and in many ways still is, a centrally planned economy, fines were simply allocated as costs of production and did not constitute a meaningful bottom-line penalty. Factory managers had no incentive to make environmental concerns a major issue.

In 1984, the government created the National Environmental Protection Agency. Most of its employees were minimally educated and trained. The main office in Beijing had 100 workers who analyzed pollution data but did little else. Although its 20,000 field workers had the power to shut down factories, impose heavy fines, and deny permission for construction of certain industries, in practice they rarely did so.

In fact, national policy worked against environmental protection. Rural development was the key element of the government's economic drive. More than 15 million small, local factories were built between 1978 and 1988. They raised income levels in the countryside and absorbed surplus rural labor. By 1988, these factories accounted for more than one-quarter of China's industrial output. However, they also contributed to pollution. China's National Environmental Protection Agency estimated that 40 percent of these small and mid-size factories had pollution problems.

In fact, China's overall industrial development repeated the worst mistakes of England's industrial revolution. High-sulfur coal constituted more than 70 percent of all fuel consumed in China. In the late 1980s, a visitor to Huhohot, the capital of Inner Mongolia, saw and smelled the haze of greasy coal smoke hovering over this city of several million people. In the evening, cooking stoves burned charcoal, whose fumes contributed to the smog.

Water quality was no better than air quality. Tap water was not—and still is not—drinkable in most Chinese cities and towns. Work units, factories, and villages provide huge steel containers of boiled and filtered drinking water. By 1989, 29,000 miles of waterways were so heavily polluted that they no longer sustained marine life. Industrial and domestic sewage ruined nearly one-third of China's coastal fishing.

Pesticides such as DDT, long banned in the United States, were regularly used in China until the end of the 1980s. Untreated human waste was spread on the fields as fertilizer. Effluence filtered into rivers, lakes, and canals.[26]

About 5 billion tons of topsoil were washed away each year, and 1.1 million acres of farmland were covered by the concrete of encroaching cities. Original forests disappeared so quickly that experts predict that at this rate, not one acre of natural forest will survive in the year 2000. Because of erosion and deforestation, deserts are expanding at a rate of more than 600 square miles per year and by the year 2000 will cover twice as much area as in 1949.[27]

In 1989, a small cadre of Chinese environmentalists sounded a warning about China's virtually unrestrained economic degradation. The president of the Chinese Academy of Scientists warned there could be "a deadly threat to the Chinese population if immediate action is not taken to halt pollution."[28] In 1989, only 10 percent of Chinese families owned a refrigerator loaded with CFCs. What would be the effect on the ozone layer if, as the government promised, every family in China had one by the year 2000?

Although China passed stricter environmental legislation in 1989 and 1990, enforcement remains very lax. Pollution problems are still growing.

---

[26]"It's Foggy Again," *The Economist,* May 19, 1984, p. 40.

[27]C Nickerson, "China Copies Worst Polluters," *The Boston Globe,* September 20, 1989, p. 1.

[28]Ibid, p. 1.

In 1991, acid rain caused nearly $3 billion in damage to crops, forests, and buildings across China. Factories were expected to pump increasing amounts of carbon dioxide into the air. The 1991 level of 15.5 million tons will rise to 1.4 billion tons by the year 2000 if air pollution is not controlled. In many cities, air pollution exceeds World Health Organization standards by five to six times—about seven to eight times as bad as air quality in New York City.[29]

China spends about 0.8 percent of its gross national product on improving the environment. The World Bank estimates China would have to spend 1.5 percent, or near the US level, just to control the current deterioration. It remains to be seen how China will balance its economic development with environmental controls. How long will it take and what price will be paid before China addresses sustainable development as a political, social, and economic concern?

The World Bank Perspective on Development versus the Environment

In 1992, the World Bank published the *World Development Report 1992*.[30] The study addresses four major themes through which it explores the relationship between the environment and economic development. The *Report* notes that sound economic policies can deliver environmental benefits and that government and the private sector must work together to achieve those benefits.

Since the private sector does not provide strong incentives to halt environmental degradation, the governmental role is critical. For example, when a country's government eliminates subsidies for fossil fuels and water, gives poor farmers property rights, and makes heavily polluting, state-owned companies compete, both economic efficiency and the environment benefit.

The Four Themes

Water and Sanitation.   The World Bank estimates household use of water will need to rise sixfold in the next 40 years to meet demand. As people in developing countries continue to move from the countryside to cities, urban populations will triple. Currently as much as 90 percent of the water in the least developed countries goes to irrigation, compared to 39 percent in high-income countries. Governments around the world will have to reallocate

---

[29]S WuDunn, "Chinese Suffer from Rising Pollution as Byproduct of the Industrial Boom," *The New York Times,* February 28, 1993, p. 20.

[30]Much of the following discussion is taken from the World Bank, *World Development Report 1992: Development and the Environment.*

water, an undertaking rife with profound political, economic, and social implications.

Most urban residents of developing countries want water piped into their homes, and many are willing to pay for it. Their governments, however, assume the people cannot bear the full cost. Therefore, governments have used their limited public resources to subsidize poorly constructed and unreliable systems. Residents who are poorly served must buy water from private vendors, paying up to 10 times what they would pay for efficiently piped water.

The World Bank recommends a variety of programs to service those unable to pay and provide a variety of options to those willing and able to pay. Two alternatives, privatization and franchising water supplies, have been successfully adopted in Africa and Latin America.

Emissions from Energy and Industry. Household energy use creates indoor and outdoor pollution. In Africa and South Asia, people burn wood and plant fibers inside their homes, creating indoor pollution. In China, India, and Eastern Europe, people burn soft coal, whose exhausts are major outdoor pollutants. As people turn away from these polluting fuels, they will likely switch to cleaner coal, oil, gas, or electricity for cooking and heating. Making cleaner fuels available at affordable prices will accelerate the pace of switching.

Electric power generation accounts for 30 percent of all fossil fuel consumption worldwide. A shift to clean coal or natural gas can reduce emissions of carbon monoxide and particulates by 99.9 percent. The World Bank recommends that all new power plants using coal be equipped with particulate matter trapping devices to clean emissions. Once installed, these traps must be well maintained.

Conversion to renewable energy sources such as solar energy and wind power also shows great promise. Each year, the Earth receives about 10 times as much energy from the sun as is stored in all fossil fuel. The unit costs of solar energy have fallen by 95 percent since the early 1970s. Wind power technology is improving, and unit costs can be greatly reduced.

Vehicles account for 50 percent of oil consumption in most developing countries. They produce as much as 95 percent of lead and carbon monoxide emissions. Vehicle maintenance standards in developing countries are generally low. Without major intervention, developing-country vehicle emissions could quadruple by the year 2030. Malaysia, Singapore, and Mexico are currently converting to lead-free fuel. They are using a combination of market incentives such as fuel and vehicle taxes. They are also passing regulations that mandate emission standards and require manufacturers to install catalytic converters.

Industrial pollution is fairly easy to regulate if plants are big enough and few in number. Ample technology is available to deal with emissions from industries such as cement, metallurgy, chemicals, paper, and pulp. But in much of the developing world, there are thousands of small plants whose by-products are impossible to track. Smaller industries, particularly leather tanning and gold mining, are especially dangerous, because they release toxic chemicals into water supplies.

Mexico City: An Example of Urban Pollution.   Mexico City is located high above sea level in a valley surrounded by volcanoes. Over the past 30 years, its population has exploded. In December 1989, pollution levels in Mexico City were higher than the levels that killed people on the streets of London in the 1950s. In 1991 Mexico City's population exceeded 20 million, with thousands more arriving every day.

Transport contributes about 97 percent of carbon monoxide, 66 percent of nitrogen oxide, and 48 percent of total emissions to air pollution levels in the city. A toxic cloud loaded with lead from leaded gasoline hovers above the valley. According to the World Health Organization, the lead content in the atmosphere is 40 percent above permissible levels.

The city government has been trying to devise a remedy since the mid-1980s. The government-owned gasoline company, PEMEX, tried a variety of gasoline brews to cut down on carbon monoxide emissions. One new product reduced carbon monoxide but greatly increased ozone and lead levels.

The Mexico City government also tried to reduce emissions by encouraging car owners to tune up their engines and requiring a sticker certifying the procedure had been done. This policy was a notorious failure. Entrepreneurs immediately went into the fake sticker business. Car owners could acquire phony stickers at a cost much lower than that of a tune-up.

In 1989, an obligatory program of color-coded stickers required motorists to leave their cars at home one day a week. Residents responded by buying junk cars to drive on the one day they could not drive their regular cars.

Despite the corruption and scams associated with these plans, Mexico City is making some progress. Since 1991, all new cars are required to have catalytic converters. Unleaded fuel is more widely available, and the price of leaded and unleaded gas has risen by 50 percent. Modern, clean urban public transport is growing faster than demand.[31]

Rural Environmental Challenges.   Rural people and policymakers face two major environmental challenges. The first is preventing degradation resulting from growing demands for food, fuel, fiber, and from poor management due to poverty, ignorance, and corruption. The second is preserving forests, wetlands, coastal areas, and grasslands.

---

[31]"A City Drowning in Smog," *South,* February 1991, p. 17.

In the future, most increased food production will come from higher yields on existing farmland. But more intensive cultivation will cause environmental problems such as overfertilization and overuse of pesticides that run off into the water supply.

The World Bank recommends governments adopt policies that will strengthen local research and develop credit systems to enable farmers to make long-term investments. It also suggests governments impose taxes on pesticides to reduce their use and undertake research to develop less toxic substances. Farmer education and training programs and follow-up assessments are critical.

Communal resource management is common in many developing countries. Sometimes management breaks down, resulting in overgrazed ranges, depleted woodlands, and overfished lakes and rivers. Sound communal practices can be encouraged by fostering effective leadership and legal protection. However, the World Bank warns, nationalization of communal lands is almost never a good idea.

Whether or not nationalization makes sense, government-owned and managed land is the norm in many developing countries. Governments have sponsored settlement programs on these lands, with mixed results. Countries in West Africa and the Amazon Basin have successfully allocated land to settlers, loggers, and extractive industries while continuing to protect the rights of indigenous people. However, these situations are the exception.

The impact of logging on government-owned tropical forests has been particularly destructive. In 1990, a joint report of the World Resources Institute and the United Nations found 40 million to 50 million acres of tropical forest were cleared each year for agriculture and other development. The rate of loss was nearly 50 percent higher than that reported in 1980 by the United Nations Food and Agriculture Organization.

Spokespeople for the World Resources Institute declared their estimates were probably quite conservative. In nine major tropical countries, total annual losses of forest acreage were about four times as high as estimates from the years 1981 to 1985. Brazil suffered the highest losses, between 12.5 million and 22.5 million acres a year. Myanamar (Burma) lost more than 500 times the 1980 estimate.[32]

The World Bank notes tropical forests are almost always owned by governments. Only governments have the authority to establish tropical forestry zones that constrain agricultural degradation and foster managerial practices that protect biodiversity and the ecosystem. The Bank recommends that governments provide economic incentives to discourage farmers, loggers, and squatters from using the land.

---

[32]P Shabecoff, "Loss of Tropical Forests Is Found Much Worse Than Was Thought," *The New York Times,* June 8, 1990, p. A1.

Proper logging procedures and policies, combined with more prudent use of cut timber, is essential. Tropical forests must be protected to conserve soil, prevent erosion, and establish flood control. The Tropical Timber Organization found that fewer than 1 percent of tropical forests are under sustainable management. Sophisticated assessment and selection of species and size of trees and other vegetation are necessary to preserve delicate ecosystems.

International Environmental Challenges. International agreements are most effective when they are based on reciprocity and address national interests. The major problem is that they are very difficult to enforce. Since there is no supranational body with the power to punish offenders, enforcement rests on the goodwill or moral suasion of each participant.

International Agreements on the Environment: Before Rio and Beyond

Since the early 1970s, the world population has jumped 66 percent and world economic output has doubled. During the same period, the pressures of population and industrial development have accelerated the destruction of the Earth's soil, seas, forests, and wetlands at increased rates each year. In the 1980s, it finally became clear that nations had to take common action to tackle these problems.

The early international agreements focused on reducing chemicals that diminished the ozone layer and contributed to the buildup of greenhouse gases. The "greenhouse effect" occurs when carbon dioxide and other gases, such as methane, nitrous oxide, and chlorofluorocarbons (CFCs), trap the sun's heat in the atmosphere. The atmosphere heats up like the interior of a greenhouse. Scientists disagree about the consequences of the greenhouse effect. Some say ice caps will melt, sea levels will rise, and cities will be flooded. Rain patterns will change, turning fertile farmland into dust bowls.

Recent research using mathematical models of the world's climate suggests global warming could lead to a new ice age. Canadian scholars predict the world's temperature will rise three to eight degrees Fahrenheit in the twenty-second century if people continue to pour heat-trapping gases into the atmosphere at the current rate. According to their data, the warmer seas will cause more water to evaporate, producing more moisture in the winter. Much more snow will fall in the far northern hemisphere and will stay on the ground year round, forming glaciers that eventually will move south.[33]

Some scientists scoff at all the doomsday predictions, admonishing their colleagues and telling the public not to be alarmed. They argue that we need to gather more evidence before we make any predictions or worry unnec-

---

[33]W K Stevens, "Scientists Suggest Global Warming Could Hasten the Next Ice Age," *The New York Times,* January 21, 1992, p. C4.

essarily. However, even they concede that greenhouse gases are potentially very dangerous.

The great majority of scientists are seriously concerned about the consequences of global warming. Since the early 1980s, they have urged governments to take measures to reduce emissions of gases that produce the greenhouse effect. The unresolved issue is how rigorous these measures should be.

An equally serious consequence of gas buildup is the thinning and eventual destruction of the ozone layer that protects the Earth from the sun's radiation. The major culprits in ozone destruction are CFCs used in aerosol cans, refrigerators, and other cooling devices such as air conditioners. Without the protection of the ozone layer in the atmosphere, the rate of skin cancer will rise and crop growth will suffer.

In 1985, the United States, Canada, the European Community, and 15 other countries signed the Vienna Convention on the Protection of the Ozone Layer and, in 1987, the Montreal Protocol. These agreements focused on eliminating CFCs and halons by the year 2000.

In March 1989, 124 nations held a conference in London to discuss the greenhouse effect. Top environmental officials of the European Community called for total elimination of CFCs by the end of the century. President Bush pledged the United States would comply and would phase out their use. Hungary, Trinidad and Tobago, Zambia, the Philippines, and Malaysia promised a 50 percent reduction by the year 2000.

Three months later, the US Environment Protection Program sponsored a follow-up conference in Helsinki, Finland. Developing-country attendees based their participation on economic restructuring. The poor nations urged the industrialized countries to help them find alternatives to fossil fuel. In the keynote address, President Moi of Kenya said all nations had an obligation to protect the atmosphere, but poor nations needed financial and technological help. The Western industrialized countries and Japan stopped short of establishing a special international fund but ordered a report on the possibility of an ozone conference in London in 1990.

In June 1990, representatives of 100 countries met in London to discuss ozone depletion. Ninety-three nations agreed that by the year 2000, they would halt the production of chemicals that destroy the ozone layer. This agreement went well beyond the 1987 treaty calling for a 50 percent reduction by 1998. Developing countries were given a 10-year grace period in which to comply. The agreement created a new international body with a 14-member executive committee to administer a fund to help poorer countries make the transition to new technologies.[34]

Although the United States participated in the ozone conferences and agreed to phase out CFCs, it was less agreeable when it came to reducing

---

[34]M W Browne, "93 Nations Agree to Ban Chemicals That Harm Ozone," *The New York Times,* June 30, 1990, p. A1.

carbon dioxide, the leading greenhouse gas. At the Second World Climate Conference in Geneva in October 1990, the United States, the world's largest polluter, was the only major industrialized nation to oppose specific limits on carbon dioxide emissions. An atmospheric scientist for the Environmental Defense Fund called the United States an "outlaw nation."[35]

The Bush administration, reluctant to commit the United States to a policy that it believed might interfere with economic growth, invited other nations to a 1992 Earth Summit. Held under the auspices of the United Nations, one major goal of the summit was to deal with global warming. President Bush proposed that, over the next 16 months, countries work on a treaty.

The Earth Summit, Rio de Janeiro

The international environmental agenda had taken on unprecedented dimensions. Finally, nations and their leaders recognized the seriousness of overpopulation, pollution, and the decline of natural resources. The United Nations initiative specifically addressed the conflict between economic growth and the preservation of natural resources.

Heads of state and negotiators from 170 countries agreed to meet in Rio de Janeiro in June 1992 for an "Earth Summit." No one thought this summit would result in easy answers. The summit was only the first step toward a fundamental restructuring of the industrial and social priorities of developed and industrializing countries. Agenda items were to be worked out in advance, and two treaties were to have been negotiated and prepared for signing.

If meaningful progress was to be made, industrialized countries would have to reduce their dependence on natural resources and decrease pollution. Developing countries would have to cut population growth, change farming techniques, and adopt methods of development that would conserve resources and diminish harmful by-products. The summit's goal was to achieve sustainable development.[36]

The United Nations Conference on Environment and Development (UNCED) put together an 800-page agenda that the secretary of the Rio summit called "the most comprehensive international program ever proposed on environmental protection." The agenda encompassed more than 100 initiatives to be taken before the year 2000 to cut energy use, protect ocean resources, promote sustainable agricultural practices, and control toxic waste. With considerable difficulty and contention, the participants agreed to support a declaration making the eradication of poverty a global

---

[35]D Dumanoski, "US Is Alone at Climate Talks in Resisting Curbs on Gases," *The Boston Globe,* October 29, 1990, p. 1.

[36]"Growth Vs. Environment," *Business Week,* May 11, 1992, p. 68.

goal. It also made the biggest polluters commit to cleaning up their own mess and helping poorer countries improve their standards of living in an environmentally sound way.

Summit organizers agreed active US participation was critical. Throughout the preliminary negotiations, the Bush administration repeatedly threatened to boycott the summit if participants insisted on precise goals and methods for pollution reduction. A month before the meeting, it was still unclear whether President Bush would attend. Bush assured business leaders that he would not make a "bad deal" and would sign no agreements that did not protect the US economy.[37]

Two binding treaties were to be presented to the assembled nations: the Treaty on Global Warming and the Treaty on Biodiversity.

Treaty on Global Warming.   After 10 days of talks prior to the summit, diplomats agreed on the text of a treaty to curb global warming. The Bush administration succeeded in removing limits on carbon dioxide and other greenhouse gas emissions. Environmentalists were sharply critical of US negotiators who said they would not sign any accord requiring the United States to adhere to targets and timetables.

In mid-May, President Bush announced he would attend the Earth Summit and sign the global warming treaty that "aimed" at reducing the gases that cause global warming. Vice presidential candidate Al Gore called the administration's policy one of "photo opportunities and symbols instead of real commitments."[38] The president's environmental advisers countered this charge, claiming the treaty set in motion a global process for stabilizing the concentration of gases at 1990 levels. Eventually 143 nations, including the United States, signed the draft treaty.

Treaty on Biodiversity.   Another group of negotiators worked on an equally important treaty on biodiversity and hoped to have a draft approved before the June meeting. US officials maintained the draft was unacceptable because it would force the US government to take responsibility for wildlife preservation away from individual states. The United States also opposed the provision that made nations responsible for the environmental effects of the actions of their private companies in other countries. Administration negotiators insisted that biotechnology be considered apart from biodiversity and objected to the premise that all genetically altered organisms were inherently unsafe. They did agree in principle that developing countries

---

[37]M Wines, "Bush Likely to Go to Ecology Talks," *The New York Times,* May 7, 1992, p. A1.

[38]K Schneider, "Bush Plans to Join Other Leaders at Earth Summit in Brazil in June," *The New York Times,* May 13, 1992, p. A8.

should be compensated for genetic materials such as plants with cancer-treating properties.[39]

Despite US and Japanese objections, 98 nations adopted the biodiversity treaty on preserving plant, animal, and microbial species. The biodiversity treaty required developed countries to help finance and provide expertise to industrializing countries, where most of the protected species are found. Scientists warned half the world's plant and animal species could be extinct by the year 2050 if action were not taken soon.

The Meeting.   As the Rio summit got under way, several issues had been settled:

1. Negotiators had agreed in principle that polluters should bear the cost of pollution, poverty should be eradicated, and family planning should be promoted.
2. They recognized that industrialized countries, which had created many of the problems, bore responsibility for remediation.
3. They agreed, in general, to give priority to the needs of developing countries.
4. They developed a $600 billion agenda to save the planet but did not specify from where the money would come.
5. They agreed to try to reduce carbon dioxide and other greenhouse gas emissions to 1990 levels, but did not make such reductions mandatory.
6. The United States committed $75 million to helping developing countries pay for the environmental agenda.[40]

The Rio summit was the largest meeting of national leaders in history. More than 35,000 participants took part in a conference, and 153 nations signed the treaties on global warming and biodiversity. In contrast, only 15 nations had signed the 1985 Vienna convention on limiting ozone-depleting chemicals.

Delegates approved three nonbinding documents: a statement to guide forestry practices, a declaration of principles on environmental policy, and Agenda 21, the massive blueprint for environmental action. The United States remained the only nation that publicly refused to sign the biodiversity treaty.[41]

The Aftermath of Rio.   The Rio summit left financing, timetables, and compliance mechanisms to future negotiations. The US presidential

---

[39]J Perlez, "Environmentalists Accuse U.S. of Trying to Weaken Global Treaty," *The New York Times,* May 19, 1992, p. C4.

[40]"Summit to Save The Earth," *Time,* June 1, 1992, p. 58.

[41]P Lewis, "Storm in Rio: Morning After," *The New York Times,* June 15, 1992, p. A1.

election changed administrations and the government's attitude toward environmental policy. In April 1993, President Clinton announced the United States would follow a specific timetable to reduce the threat of global warming. Specifically, he promised to sign five executive orders directing the federal government to

- Instruct federal agencies to change purchasing policies to use fewer substances harmful to the ozone layer.
- Commit the government to buy more American-made vehicles that use fuels such as natural gas, ethanol, methanol, and electric power.
- Require agencies to buy and use more recycled products.
- Require agencies to buy energy-efficient computers.
- Require federal offices that use toxic chemicals to publicly report their waste and releases.

President Clinton's announcement came only one day before scientists announced the ozone layer had dropped to record low levels over North America, Europe, and parts of Asia.

In addition to government policy on ozone depletion, President Clinton announced he would sign the biodiversity treaty. On June 4, 1993, the president kept his promise and signed the Treaty on Biodiversity. Although the treaty required approval by two-thirds of the Senate, it was expected to pass easily.[42]

International commitment to the environment resulted in a small measure of success. In June 1993, scientists at the National Oceanic and Atmospheric Administration reported that a haze of atmospheric pollution over the Arctic had declined steadily in the last decade. The haze, which peaked in the early 1980s, was a soup of sulfate particles and sulfuric acid droplets. Scientists attributed the entire problem to industrial effluence from European and Soviet smokestacks.

The improvement was due to Western European environmental controls and to coal- and oil-burning Eastern European industries' conversion to natural gas. Scientists hope their new finding means less risk that the Arctic snow and ice cover will melt.[43]

Summary

The concept of sustainable development permeates the discussion of economic development and environmental protection. Each country or region

---

[42]R L Berke, "Clinton Supports Two Major Steps for Environment," *The New York Times,* April 22, 1993, p. A1.

[43]J R Luoma, "Sharp Decline Found in Arctic Air Pollution," *The New York Times,* June 1, 1993, p. C4.

faces trade-offs and compromises in government policy in promoting environmental protection and remediation. In general, protectionism and trade barriers tend to harm sustainable development measures.

Each region faces environmental problems and develops its own measures based on unique political, social, and ideological bases. The newest industrializing nations face some of the toughest decisions about the environment. They must balance their need to raise their national economic levels against growing international pressures to ameliorate environmental problems. This chapter discussed the European Community, Eastern Europe, and Asia in this context.

The World Bank is one of the most active and influential international bodies in suggesting policy approaches for developing countries. Its 1992 report provided developing countries with major thematic proposals for sustainable development.

In recent years, nations have begun to grapple with the possibilities for international consensus on environmental issues. The Earth Summit in Rio was a major step forward in developing global policy on the environment. It remains to be seen how its treaties will be implemented, but it signaled the seriousness with which world leaders are approaching environmental issues.

Questions

1. What is sustainable development? Pick a country in West Africa. Research that country's economic situation and suggest policies for sustainable development. Take into account the social structure, government, geography, and climatic conditions.
2. South American countries are at different stages of economic development, degree of foreign investment, and natural resource potential. Compare Brazil's environmental situation to Chile's. What are the particular problems of each country?
3. What environmental concerns would you have if you were contemplating setting up a bottling plant in Russia?
4. What should US policy on participation in international environmental treaties be? Give reasons why the United States should stay out of these treaties and reasons why it should participate.

BETA CASE 17
INTERNATIONAL ENVIRONMENT

Brian Madison was struggling with a difficult investment decision. "I guess I need to bounce this idea off someone with specific experience," he mumbled to himself.

Beta was committed to developing a worldwide presence in generic drugs, many of which it produced and marketed outside the United States. The company had plants in Europe, Latin America, and Asia. Now Madison was seriously contemplating manufacturing in a plant in the Moscow suburbs. The drugs made there would be sold in Eastern European markets.

The whole issue began when the general manager of one of Russia's largest drug-manufacturing companies visited Detroit. Since the breakup of the Soviet Union, many managers of formerly state-owned companies were authorized to develop joint venture agreements with American and European partners. The joint ventures would be privately owned, profit-earning enterprises subject to minimal government supervision.

But Madison had just read the May 1993 KPMG Peat Marwick industry report on pharmaceuticals. Jonathan J Halperin, president of FYI Information Services for a Changing World, a Washington-based research organization specializing in the former USSR, urged caution. He wrote, "The regulatory structure in the CIS [Commonwealth of Independent States] is quite advanced and developed, but it falls apart when it comes to implementation. A large percentage of prescription drugs are mixed and ground by pharmacists rather than in production plants, so that maintaining quality control is difficult . . . just to get a pharmaceutical product to market in the CIS requires complex navigation through the regulatory system."

Madison was particularly worried about one specific aspect of the regulatory system: environmental controls. Since drug manufacturing requires the use of chemicals and potentially toxic compounds, would the Russian regulatory structure and process dictate the procedures for disposing of waste? If Beta entered the joint venture in a plant that had been operating for some time, would it be responsible for environmental problems created by the previous tenant?

Madison buzzed his secretary, Tom Hansen, and asked him to call Robert Mobley, the corporate attorney. "Hey, Bob, we really need to get some data on this proposal," Madison said. "Would you get your people to find out as much as you can on Russian regulation of pharmaceuticals? Also, find out what the rules are about waste disposal and other environmental issues. I have the finance department working on the financial risk, and I've contacted a firm to assess political risk. Do we know anyone who specializes in environmental risk in that part of the world?"

Mobley sighed. He knew little, if anything, about Russian environmental protection. "I guess I'm going to have to learn more than I ever thought about the international environment," he mused. "I wonder where I should start looking."

18

MULTINATIONAL CORPORATIONS

As we discussed in earlier chapters, managing social issues is fraught with difficulty even for firms that operate in only one country. When managers of multinational corporations confront social issues in multiple national environments, their tasks are compounded.

know of A *multinational corporation (MNC)* is "a parent company that controls a cluster of corporations of various nationalities."[1] Generally, if a company has three or more affiliates outside the parent, or home, country and is involved in foreign direct investment, it can be called a multinational corporation. These corporations follow multinational strategies of "building strong and resourceful national subsidiaries that [are] sensitive to local market needs and opportunities, . . . allowing them to manage their local businesses by developing or adapting products and strategies to respond to powerful localizing forces."[2]

In recent years, managers and international business scholars have made a distinction between multinational and global companies. A *global company* tries to standardize its operations across all functional areas. Global strategies aim at capitalizing on highly coordinated, scale-intensive manufacturing and R&D operations. They manufacture and export standardized products worldwide, using a standardized approach to marketing where possible. But global companies must also respond to the demands of local governments and the needs of local markets. These demands limit their ability to standardize.

Ford Motor Company is a good example. Ford is embroiled in a long-standing internal controversy regarding the design and manufacture of a single car for the world market. In 1981, Ford tried to position the Escort as its

---

[1] R Vernon, *Sovereignty at Bay* (New York: Basic Books, 1971), p. 4.
[2] C A Bartlett and S Ghoshal, *Transnational Management,* (Homewood, IL: Richard D Irwin, 1992), p. 116.

"world" car. Disputes among engineers in Europe and North America undermined that strategy. In 1985, Ford decided to take another look at making a global car and by 1987 had given Ford Europe the go-ahead to put together a team of engineering, marketing, and finance people on both sides of the Atlantic. Ford plans to position the Mondeo as its global car. Only time will tell whether this strategy will work.[3]

The key tasks of managers of global corporations are to

1. Search the world for (*a*) market opportunities, (*b*) threats from competitors, (*c*) sources of products, raw materials, and financing, and (*d*) personnel. In other words, such managers have global vision.
2. Seek to maintain a presence in key markets.
3. Look for similarities rather than differences among markets.[4]

As Exhibit 18–1 shows, multinational or global corporations must deal with stakeholders in each quadrant of the stakeholder influence map in every country in which they do business. Some of the opportunities and constraints multinationals face are similar to those of domestic firms, but some are very different and often far more complex. This is because the issues of greatest concern to stakeholders can differ across countries, as can the power of a particular stakeholder group.

This chapter discusses the origins of multinational corporations (MNCs). It examines the impact of MNCs and global companies in host countries and the issues these firms face in a shrinking world.

CASE   *Cigarettes and International Advertising*

The major tobacco companies operate worldwide. Most, like R J Reynolds (a subsidiary of RJR-Nabisco) and Philip Morris, belong to extremely large, global conglomerates that also sell a variety of other products. Despite their diversity, the portion of revenue from cigarettes sold at home and abroad is enormous. Philip Morris, for example, had revenues of $21 billion and profits of $5.6 billion from worldwide tobacco sales in 1991.

During the 1980s, the domestic and global markets for cigarettes changed markedly. By the mid-1980s, antismoking forces in industrialized countries had raised public awareness of the dangers of smoking so high that some governments passed laws to ban cigarette advertising and to restrict smoking in public places.

---

[3]R L Simison and N Templin, "Ford Is Turning Heads with $6 Billion Cost to Design 'World Car'," *The Wall Street Journal,* March 23, 1993, p. A1.

[4]D A Ball and W H McCulloch, Jr., *International Business* (Homewood, IL: BPI/Irwin, 1990), pp. 18–19.

EXHIBIT 18–1

The multinational corporation in international business

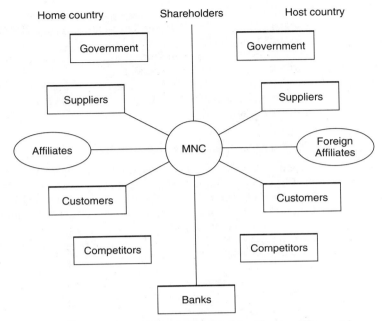

SOURCE: R Grosse and D Kujawa, *International Business: Theory and Managerial Applications* (Homewood, IL: Richard D Irwin, 1988), p. 23.

The Canadian Example

Canada was one of the first nations to pass a federal law banning cigarette advertising. The law, approved in the summer of 1988, was scheduled to go into effect in January 1989. It prohibited newspapers and magazines from carrying tobacco ads and restricted retail displays of tobacco products. It also limited tobacco companies' sponsorship of some sports activities and cultural events.

Tobacco multinationals quickly mobilized their forces in opposition. Imperial Tobacco was Canada's market leader. At the time the law was passed, Imperial, which made Player's and Du Maurier cigarettes, had a 56 percent market share. Rothmans Inc., the manufacturer of Rothmans and Benson & Hedges, was Canada's number two manufacturer. US-based Philip Morris, Inc., owned 40 percent of that company. Both Imperial and Rothmans were British owned. The number three manufacturer, RJR-Macdonald, was a unit of RJR-Nabisco, Inc.

Led by Rothmans, the three tobacco companies quickly challenged the Canadian law on grounds that it infringed on free speech.[5] No one expected a quick ruling, and the matter was expected to eventually go to Canada's Supreme Court for a final decision.

By 1991, the Canadian government's assault on smoking focused on two strategies. First, the government banned nearly all cigarette advertising and prohibited

---

[5]G Lamphier, "Cigarette Maker Files Legal Challenges to Canadian Tobacco Advertising Ban," *The Wall Street Journal,* July 21, 1988, p. 22.

smoking in all public and work sites. Second, it made cigarettes prohibitively expensive. Between 1984 and 1991, the federal tax on a pack of cigarettes jumped from 42 cents to $1.94 Canadian. Additional provincial taxes raised the price of a pack of cigarettes to $5.50 Canadian. In contrast, the US price of a pack of cigarettes in May 1991 was about $1.70, including all taxes.

In the spring of 1993, the Canadian government announced the most stringent package warning system in the world. Nearly the entire packaging surface carried health warnings.

The European Community Example

As part of its process of abolishing trade barriers and harmonizing advertising rules, the European Community (EC) began to deal with promotion of tobacco products. More than 600 billion cigarettes were sold yearly in the EC. In 1989, the European Commission proposed restricting print and poster ads. Companies would be able to present information only about tar and nicotine content. Health warnings would have to cover at least 10 percent of total ad space. In countries such as Belgium, where three official languages were spoken, the warning would have to cover 20 percent of the total package surface.

Europe's ad agencies and cigarette companies were furious. A senior executive of Philip Morris's EC headquarters in Switzerland fumed that ads were the only tool they had for competing in the cigarette market, since prices were determined by EC-imposed excise taxes.[6] The European Commission rejected the criticism, pointing out that the Commission was obligated to take health problems into account when harmonizing any advertising legislation.

Cigarette companies quickly looked for new ways to advertise their products. Philip Morris, whose sales in Western Europe were about $4 billion, worked with Formula One racing and other European sporting groups that relied on cigarette sponsors. RJR-Nabisco and Britain's BAT also tried to find alternatives.

In March 1990, the French government announced it would propose a total ban on cigarette advertising and prohibit tobacco companies from sponsoring sporting events beginning in January 1993. It also announced an increase of 15 percent in the price of cigarettes.[7] A poll at the beginning of 1992 showed French consumers overwhelmingly supported the new rules. Polls also indicated 84 percent of the French public approved of the law and 65 percent supported pressure to enforce it.[8]

Cigarette Companies' Strategy

Responding to anticigarette rhetoric and government bans on advertising, Philip Morris, R J Reynolds, BAT, Rothmans, and other tobacco firms worked furiously to develop new markets in Eastern Europe, Asia, Africa, and Latin America. In 1989, Philip Morris and its ubiquitous Marlboro brand sold more cigarettes abroad that it did at home. By 1991, Marlboro accounted for 11.6 percent of the global market. Only the state-owned Chinese monopoly, which sold its entire output domestically,

---

[6]B Toman, "EC May Chase Tobacco Symbols Like Marlboro Man into the Sunset," *The Wall Street Journal,* October 10, 1989, p. B5.

[7]"French Plan to Ban Ads for Cigarettes," *The Boston Globe,* March 29, 1990, p. 4.

[8]"Delight, Disgust, Disregard Greet French Antismoking Law," *The Boston Globe,* November 2, 1992, p. 7.

had a bigger market share. BAT, in third place, supplied 10.3 percent of the total world market.

Eastern Europe offered a huge new market. Riding high on a phenomenally successful Joe Camel advertising campaign, R J Reynolds entered a joint venture with a newly privatized factory in Russia and took over a factory in Kazakhstan. Executives expected the Russian factory to reach full capacity by mid-1993.[9]

BAT entered a joint venture agreement with the Hungarian state-owned company that supplied 45 percent of the local market. But for the time being, BAT continued to export its Pall Mall, Lucky Strike, Kent, John Player Special, and HB brands from Western Europe and the United States to its Eastern European markets.

Philip Morris and the soon to be divided Czechoslovakian government made a deal. Philip Morris agreed to pay $430 million to buy Tabak, the country's biggest cigarette company.[10] Philip Morris bought three factories in Eastern Germany in 1992, bringing production into local markets.

Asian markets also continued to grow. In 1990, the Thai government complied with US trade pressure to open its cigarette markets to US imports. By 1991, American companies controlled 80 percent of the Hong Kong cigarette market and were chipping away at the Japanese and South Korean markets that were formerly state-owned monopolies.[11]

Questions

1. Should the US government pressure developing nations to open their markets to American cigarettes?
2. How effective are advertising bans in reducing cigarette use?
3. What is the Clinton administration's stand on cigarette use and export?
4. What strategies are tobacco companies likely to adopt as antismoking campaigns continue to gather strength?
5. As advertising bans proliferate in industrialized nations, should cigarette companies be constrained from advertising in developing countries? If so, what mechanism could be used to enforce that regulation?

Common Characteristics of Multinational Corporations

MNCs of every nationality have three areas in common:

1. *Common ownership.* MNCs can be owned by a large number of shareholders, by governments, by families, or even by a single person. Any entity that owns a share in a particular MNC owns that share wherever in the world the company operates through wholly owned subsidiaries.

2. *Common resources.* Among the resources affiliates share are money, people, patents, trademarks, copyrights, and other technology. If an MNC

[9]S Erlanger, "R J Reynolds in Russia: Can Josef Camel Be Far Behind?," *The New York Times,* August 1, 1992, p. 39.
[10]R Cohen, "Philip Morris to Buy Control of Czech Cigarette Maker," *The New York Times,* May 21, 1992, p. D1.
[11]"Asia: A New Front in the War on Smoking," *Business Week,* February 25, 1991, p. 66.

needs to fund a new subsidiary in one country, it can use profits earned elsewhere. MNCs can move managers with special expertise to whatever locations most need their talents. They can—and do—hire a very large proportion of their workers outside the home country. Globally integrated firms select managers for their particular skills, not necessarily by nationality. An American global company like Coca-Cola may assign a French manager to its Singapore subsidiary or a German manager to its subsidiary in Taiwan.

3. *Common strategy.* MNCs develop strategy for all of their affiliates and allocate resources to whichever subsidiaries can use them most effectively.

Thanks to these common attributes, MNCs are strong and adaptable compared to domestic firms. Foreign subsidiaries, incorporated in the countries in which they are located, enjoy the same privileges and protection to which domestic corporations are entitled. However, their interests go far beyond those of any country's economy. Their multinationality, large size, and great strength allow MNCs to escape many of the rules and regulations that constrain smaller firms, especially purely domestic companies.

Raymond Vernon observes that MNCs "stir uneasy questions in the minds of men [and women]. Is the multinational enterprise undermining the capacity of nations to work for the welfare of their people? Is the multinational enterprise being used by a dominant power . . . as a means of penetrating and controlling the economies of other countries?"[12] These questions are not new; they have been asked since the first MNCs were formed. Later in the chapter, we will explore some issues that generate these questions.

Origins of the MNC

The international trade that preceded and fostered the creation of MNCs began in the eighteenth century. As we noted in Chapter 6, large corporations emerged by the mid-nineteenth century. A few developed the attributes of multinationals.

Singer was the first American company to have all the attributes of an MNC. In 1850, I M Singer borrowed $40 and a workshop from a friend and in 11 days designed a sewing machine. Within a year, he had taken out domestic and foreign patents and was manufacturing in the United States. In 1855, the company, then called I M Singer & Company, sold the French patent to a French merchant and helped him establish a factory. This arrangement worked out very badly; the merchant refused to pay Singer the agreed-on royalties and even sold competitors' sewing machines. Singer vowed never to sell a patent again. Instead he would develop his own overseas business.

---

[12]Vernon, *Sovereignty at Bay,* p. 5.

Singer exported machines to independent franchised agents in Europe and by 1861 had salaried representatives in Scotland and England. Soon after, the company established its own sales offices in London.

In the spring of 1867, the company's directors decided to build a factory in Glasgow, Scotland, in the hope of supplying European markets at lower cost. During the 1870s, Singer formed what would become an international business network. By 1883, the firm had 26 offices in Great Britain and others as far away as Capetown, South Africa, and Auckland, New Zealand. The company built factories in Great Britain, Austria, Canada, and the United States to serve markets all over the world.[13]

Singer Sewing Machine meets our definition of a multinational corporation. It had a common strategy in deciding where and how to organize its operations worldwide. It had a common pool of resources in finance, in management, and, most important, in patents. Singer's large size and ability to shift resources to meet competition gave the firm tremendous advantages over competitors. A substantial proportion of its workforce and sales force was non-American. Finally, Singer's shareholders "owned" the company wherever it operated. Singer was not a global corporation because it did not rationalize its production worldwide and did not seek to standardize its technology for all markets.

Several factors made early MNCs like Singer possible. First, transportation advances such as railroads and steamships enabled companies to ship resources from one subsidiary to another and to facilitate the export of finished products. Second, the completion of the transatlantic cable in 1858 and the development of Morse-coded radio signals in 1901 greatly enhanced communication capability.[14] Customers could easily tell manufacturers which aspects of the product they liked or disliked. Finally, the gold standard, used for major currencies worldwide until 1914, helped stabilize currencies and reduce risks of business failure stemming from national recessions and depressions. Outside the United States, rising incomes in the industrialized countries created new markets for products such as sewing machines, washing machines, radios, and even automobiles.

By the beginning of the twentieth century, American firms were producing farm equipment, electrical products, printing presses, and revolvers in Europe, leading one concerned observer to write of "an American invasion, not with armed men, but with manufactured goods."[15] By 1901, Westinghouse had the largest manufacturing plant in Europe. By 1914, Ford was

---

[13]M Wilkins, *The Emergence of Multinational Enterprise: American Business Abroad from the Colonial Era to 1914,* (Cambridge, MA: Harvard University Press, 1970), pp. 37–45.

[14]H Martyn, *Multinational Business Management* (Lexington, MA: D C Heath, 1970), p. 40.

[15]F A McKenzie, *The American Invaders* (New York: Grant Richards, 1902), cited in C Tugendhat, *The Multinationals* (New York: Random House, 1972), p. 16.

producing fully one-fourth of all automobiles built in England.[16] Mira Wilkins explains the dramatic impact of US expansion into Europe:

> The U.S. triumph was one of ingenuity: new products, new methods of manufacturing, and new sales and advertising techniques. Americans who made overseas commitments had something distinctive to offer foreign customers. They sought not only to cater to, but to create, foreign demand. From sewing machines to drugs to oil to insurance, aggressive and imaginative marketing gave Americans an advantage. Americans went abroad when they discovered their advantage.[17]

The early MNCs were not exclusively American, however. For instance, Bayer, the German chemical firm, expanded into New York and by 1908 was in Russia, France, and Belgium. The British-Dutch firm Lever Brothers (now Unilever) aggressively expanded into other countries prior to 1900.

British companies undertook more foreign direct investment (FDI) than firms in any other country in the early twentieth century. However, the main thrust of British investment was what Jack N Behrman called colonial investment, "where (1) mineral or other resources are developed abroad for sale into metropolitan or developed countries and/or (2) exports from the metropolitan country are developed by investments in distribution and perhaps packaging and limited processing in the importing country."[18] British investments in Australia represented the first type of colonial investment, and much of Britain's trade with India fit Behrman's second description.

American foreign direct investment soon surpassed British FDI, first in Mexico (1919), then in Canada (1922), and finally in all of Latin America (1929).[19] From 1923 to 1929, many American manufacturing-oriented companies greatly expanded foreign investment. In 1914, only 19 major companies could be identified as having both market-oriented and supply-oriented investments in foreign countries; by 1929, the list had grown to 50 companies.[20]

The number of companies engaged in foreign operations proliferated, and the extent of their investment grew. As Wilkins noted, "U.S. companies were (1) going *to more countries,* (2) building *more plants* in a particular foreign country, (3) manufacturing or mining *more end products* in a particular

[16]Tugendhat, *The Multinationals,* p. 15.

[17]Wilkins, *The Emergence of Multinational Enterprise,* p. 66.

[18]J N Behrman, "The Multinational Enterprise in 1976 and After," in *The Management of the Multinationals: Policies, Operations, and Research,* ed. S P Sethi and R H Holton (New York: The Free Press, 1974), p. 13.

[19]Wilkins, *The Emergence of Multinational Enterprise,* p. 155.

[20]M Wilkins, *The Maturing of Multinational Enterprise: American Business Abroad, 1914–1970* (Cambridge, MA: Harvard University Press, 1974), p. 142.

foreign land, (4) investing in a single alien nation in a *greater degree of integration*, and (5) *diversifying* on a worldwide basis."[21]

By 1929, manufacturing had become the leading economic sector for US foreign direct investment, and mining had declined considerably in relative terms. Petroleum became the second major engine of foreign direct investment, leading to the emergence of five major US oil companies that, along with the predecessors of British Petroleum and Royal Dutch Shell, became known as "The Seven Sisters."[22]

Companies built plants outside their home country for a variety of reasons. As US manufacturers continued to build facilities outside the United States, suppliers built foreign plants to keep those firms as customers. For example, suppliers to the automotive industry, such as tire, plate glass, and auto accessory manufacturers, followed their customers into Western Europe and Canada.[23]

Another reason companies chose to manufacture abroad was to avoid protective tariffs. William Lever, founder of Lever Brothers, explained in 1902,

> The question of erecting works in another country is dependent upon the tariff or duty. The amount of duties we pay on soaps imported into Holland and Belgium is considerable, and it only requires that these shall rise to such a point that we could afford to pay a separate staff of managers with a separate plant to make soap to enable us to see our way to erect works in those countries. When the duty exceeds the cost of separate managers and separate plants, then it will be an economy to erect works in the country that our customers can be more cheaply supplied from them.[24]

Yet another reason for direct foreign investment was to diminish host country criticism. Developing countries in particular were hostile to companies that simply took profits out. Domestic production returned at least some of the profit to the country in the form of wages and taxes.

Foreign direct investment virtually ceased during the Great Depression. US foreign direct investment grew by only 1.5 percent over the entire period from 1929 to 1940. During World War II, Western European international commerce declined even further. With Europe at war, many American companies sought to expand into Canada, Mexico, and South America. However, under the Trading with the Enemy Act of 1917 (revised in 1941),

---

[21]Ibid., p. 138.

[22]For a history of the world's major oil companies' development into MNCs, see A Sampson, *The Seven Sisters: The Great Oil Companies and the World They Shaped* (New York: Viking Press, 1975).

[23]N H Jacoby, "The Multinational Corporation," *Center Magazine* 3, no. 3 (May 1970), p. 39.

[24]Quoted in Tugendhat, *The Multinationals*, p. 10.

US companies were severely restricted in their foreign operations. For instance, a Swedish subsidiary of an American company could not sell to a Norwegian customer because to do so would aid the Nazi occupation of Norway.[25]

In 1946, the level of US foreign direct investment as related to gross national product was only 3.4 percent of GNP, the lowest point in the twentieth century. But the situation changed quickly. Between the end of World War II in 1945 and 1970, several factors contributed to US direct foreign investment growth of approximately 700 percent.[26]

First, the US government took a strong role in rebuilding the economies of Western European countries and assisting the economic development of less developed countries. Through the European Recovery Program and the North Atlantic Treaty Organization, it spent over $2.8 billion in the first five postwar years.[27]

Second, productive efforts to reduce trade barriers were made. The 1948 General Agreement on Tariffs and Trade provided a means for reducing import and export restrictions, facilitating the growth of the MNC by opening new markets to low-cost producers. Also, the formation of regional trade agreements, such as the European Economic Community (1957), European Free Trade Association (1960), Latin American Free Trade Association (1960), and Central American Common Market (1960) led to expanded regional markets for goods produced in member countries.

Regional trade agreements are notoriously difficult to sustain, and today only the European Community and the nascent North American Free Trade Agreement still have a significant impact on markets. By all assessments, the EC's influence will be even greater in the late 1990s as internal barriers among member countries continue to fall and plans for a single currency progress.

Further technological developments in transportation and communication were a third factor enabling the rapid growth of MNCs. Innovations such as the computer, the telex, and more recently the facsimile (fax) machine increased the ability of centralized management to communicate with subsidiaries and allocate resources to them to maximize results for the total company.

In the 1960s, US multinationals were joined by European and Japanese MNCs. In the 1980s, they were joined by MNCs from newly industrializing countries such as Brazil, India, and South Korea in setting up subsidiary networks around the world.[28]

---

[25]Wilkins, *The Maturing of Multinational Enterprise*, p. 50.

[26]A V Phatak, *Managing Multinational Corporations* (New York: Praeger Publishers, 1974), p. 16.

[27]Wilkins, *The Maturing of Multinational Enterprise*, p. 286.

[28]R Vernon, "Same Planet, Different Worlds" in *The Global Economy: America's Role in the Decade Ahead,* ed. W Brock and R Hormats (New York: W W Norton, 1989), p. 126.

From Multinational to Global: The 1990s

In the 40 years since World War II, several factors fostered the transformation of some multinationals into global companies that operated in every corner of the world. Table 18–1 lists the top 20 global corporations in mid-1992.

Technology

By 1990, the price of international communications had fallen, in real terms, to about one-twentieth of what it was in 1950. A long-distance traveler or shipper paid only one-quarter as much in 1990 as in 1950. With the development of containerization, the cost of transporting goods among subsidiaries or to middlepersons fell and reliability increased. American multinationals, as well as foreign MNCs and global companies, were able to scan markets everywhere, assess their potential, and achieve economies of scale in products, advertising, and packaging.

Manufacturing facilities became more flexible with the increased use of the computer and the introduction of multipurpose, numerically controlled tools. For some types of production, multinationals no longer had to seek

TABLE 18–1   The World's 20 Largest Public Corporations, June 1992

Rank 1992	Rank 1991	Company	Percentage Change from 1990
1	3	Royal Dutch/Shell (Netherlands/UK)	−34%
2	2	Exxon (US)	12
3	1	NTT (Japan)	−14
4	6	Philip Morris (US)	11
5	4	General Electric (US)	3
6	12	Wal-Mart Stores (US)	20
7	17	AT&T (US)	−81
8	15	Merck (US)	19
9	7	IBM (US)	−109
10	19	Coca-Cola (US)	17
11	16	Toyota Motor (Japan)	−2
12	20	British Telecom (UK)	38
13	23	Glaxo Holdings (UK)	13
14	18	Bristol-Myers Squibb (US)	18
15	22	Du Pont (US)	18
16	11	Sumitomo Bank (Japan)	−21
17	9	Mitsubishi Bank (Japan)	−26
18	39	Unilever (Netherlands/UK)	4
19	26	Procter & Gamble (US)	11
20	34	General Motors (US)	−151

SOURCE: *The Wall Street Journal,* September 24, 1992, p. R26.

out locations where labor costs were lowest. Companies using flexible computer-directed processes could now operate efficiently in countries with higher labor costs. For example, some South Korean and Taiwanese firms set up production in California and other West Coast states.

The 1990s heralded a new era of global networks. Two powerful modern technologies led to the development of global information-processing systems. Computers and digital (computer language) communication became the core of information technology. When linked together in networks, computers reached their full potential. Telecommunications systems, using digital technology, helped companies achieve economies of scale by eliminating barriers of time and space.

Enterprise Structure

As travel and communications facilities improved, the rate at which MNCs began to establish subsidiaries outside their home countries increased rapidly. Joint ventures and project-specific associations called *strategic alliances* also proliferated in number and complexity.

MNCs formed new strategic alliances to spread financial risk, open markets that otherwise would be closed to them, and pool technology. For example, Hanson Trust PLC's US arm, Kaiser Cement Corporation, sold a plant to Mitsubishi Mining & Cement Company. The sale marked Mitsubishi Mining's first entry into the US market.[29]

Fujitsu Ltd., a huge Japanese high-tech conglomerate that makes computers, telecommunications equipment, and semiconductors, expanded in the late 1980s. It bought substantial equity in Amdahl Corporation, an American maker of IBM-compatible mainframes, and in Britain's biggest computer company, International Computers Ltd. By 1991, these two companies had contributed more than $2 billion to Fujitsu's overseas revenues. Fujitsu plans to continue forming strategic alliances worldwide, leaving managerial decisions to its overseas partners.[30]

Open Borders

Cooperation among the members of the European Community and the signing of the North American Free Trade Agreement (NAFTA) went beyond purely economic issues. During the 1990s and into the next century, international cooperation will extend to environmental, political, and social issues.

The European Commission continues to draw up guidelines for environmental standards, social policy, and labor relations. The EC is

---

[29]P Sebastian, "Hanson's Kaiser to Sell U.S. Plant to Japanese Firm," *The Wall Street Journal,* February 9, 1988, p. 6.

[30]B R Schlender, "How Fujitsu Will Tackle the Giants," *Fortune,* July 1, 1991, pp. 78–82.

contending with the emergence of right-wing political and social factions, immigrant flight from the former Soviet bloc, and the costs associated with cleaning up Eastern European factories. The NAFTA negotiations also have taken on social issues. Soon after the 1992 US presidential election, the Clinton administration's trade representative, Mickey Kantor, pressed Mexico for higher environmental standards, child labor laws, and minimum-wage rules. Any serious trade agreement cannot and will not ignore social issues.

Very little progress has been made in restarting the stalemated negotiations of the General Agreement on Tariffs and Trade (GATT). Since its beginning in 1947, the 108-member GATT has been a worldwide force for tariff reduction and the lowering of trade barriers. Since the Clinton administration took office, increased tensions among the United States, the EC, and other trading partners have diminished the chances for a successful conclusion.

Issues such as antidumping pacts on steel and other products created friction among members. (*Dumping* is defined as selling abroad at prices lower than those charged in the home country or other markets.) Many countries have applied antidumping legislation to incoming goods. For example, in the summer of 1992, Hewlett-Packard Company sold medical equipment to an Israeli hospital. A local Israeli company protested, accusing Hewlett-Packard of "dumping" its products at unfairly low prices to render the Israeli company noncompetitive. Philip Morris Company ran afoul of EC antidumping measures when it exported food to the EC. In retaliation, the EC raised tariffs on Philip Morris's and other US companies' foodstuffs.[31]

In January 1993, the United States imposed steel tariffs on six EC steelmakers and six other countries, including Brazil, South Korea, Mexico, Sweden, Austria, and New Zealand. In addition to the tariffs, the United States levied antidumping penalties on some of these countries. The US move came just 10 days after the EC itself imposed duties of between 11 and 30 percent on steel exporters from Croatia, the Czech and Slovak republics, Hungary, and Poland.

The heating up of trade rhetoric and the imposition of retaliatory tariff and nontariff barriers threatened open borders. Some trade experts predicted the NAFTA agreement was in serious trouble and the GATT would not be signed anytime soon. They noted that tariff increases and the retaliatory responses they engender ultimately hurt consumers and hindered economic development. The passage of NAFTA through Congress in November 1993 provided some badly needed impetus to trade discussions.

Developing-country multinationals are relative newcomers to global competition. They have some cause for concern. As industrialized countries

---

[31]R Keatley, "Antidumping Laws Keep Out Goods That Pacts Would Ordinarily Let in," *The Wall Street Journal,* February 26, 1993, p. A11.

form huge trading blocs, outsiders may have less opportunity to penetrate the protectionist barriers these blocs may erect. Developing-country multinationals are most at risk, since developed-country MNCs already have established subsidiaries within the blocs and enjoy the privileges of local firms.

Ideology and the MNC

The growth and expansion of multinationals has generated an ideological debate between industrialized countries, which are home to most MNCs, and industrializing-country hosts. To host countries, multinationals are associated with industrialization. They perceive that the multinationals bring jobs, higher levels of technology, and more sophisticated products. They also note that multinationals bring pollution, corruption, and trivial, unnecessary consumer goods. Raymond Vernon observes that because of its size and power, "the multinational enterprise has come to be seen as the embodiment of almost anything disconcerting about modern industrial society . . ."[32]

John Kenneth Galbraith argues that multinationals attract criticism because they are so powerful.[33] We enumerated the sources of MNC power earlier in the chapter, but there is an additional component of power that goes beyond size and money: the fact that multinationals can escape many of the laws and regulations that apply to domestic enterprises by shifting their activities to another country. A graphic example is the MNC's ability to use transfer pricing to shift profits among subsidiaries to get the best tax advantages. As the case at the beginning of the chapter points out, another strategy is to sell products banned in one country in another country with less stringent regulations. Developing countries argue MNCs do nothing to alleviate the severe and persistent problem of external debt that cripples their economies.

NAFTA and the Maquiladores: An Example of MNC Controversy

The Birth of the Maquiladora.   In 1966, the Mexican and US governments signed an agreement allowing in-bond manufacturing plants along the Mexican–United States border. The concept did not really catch on until the Reagan administration took office in the early 1980s. The Mexican government permits the plants in these areas to import American-made parts and processed materials, which are then assembled and packaged using Mexican labor. As long as the finished products are subsequently exported, the

---

[32]R Vernon, *Storm Over the Multinationals* (Cambridge, MA: Harvard University Press, 1977), p. 19.
[33]J K Galbraith, "The Defense of the Multinational Company," *Harvard Business Review* 56 (March–April 1978), p. 84.

Mexican plants do not pay import duties on the parts. The US government, in return, does not charge American companies import duty on the finished product beyond the value added by the Mexican operations.

Since the maquiladora system began, many Japanese and increasing numbers of Korean and Taiwanese firms have also established operations in Mexico. Their manufacturing firms inside the United States get access to cheap Mexican labor and avoid the transportation costs, tariffs, and nontariff barriers they would encounter if they did their assembly elsewhere.

The subject of maquiladores and their problems and opportunities engendered fierce controversy in the early 1990s as discussions about the creation of the North American Free Trade Agreement progressed.

History of NAFTA.   To understand the conflict over maquiladores, we must review the circumstances leading to the development of the North American Free Trade Agreement (NAFTA). In March 1990, the United States and Mexico agreed to negotiate a free trade pact that effectively would create a unified North American market. Shortly thereafter, Canada joined the discussions. Experts agreed this pact would have enormous implications for all three countries. The United States would benefit from access to Mexico's cheap labor, while Mexico would reap the benefits of US investment, expertise, and technology. Canada would also get some benefits in the form of cheap labor, but its advantages were much less predictable.

All agreed the negotiations would be difficult but pointed to the growing US-Mexican trade statistics as an indicator of potential benefits. Between 1988 and 1989, US exports to Mexico rose 21 percent. US imports from Mexico rose 17 percent in the same period, making Mexico the United States' fourth largest trading partner.[34]

Not everyone relished the prospect of the huge market the pact would create. Groups of US farmers and food processors argued that Mexico would become the "salad bowl" for the rest of North America. Between 1985 and 1991, US imports of Mexican food more than doubled. By 1991, Mexico was supplying one-quarter of all fruits and vegetables imported into the United States.

Many food-processing operations moved south of the border. Multinationals like Kraft, Campbell, and Pillsbury Company set up Mexican operations. Pillsbury decided to move some of its Green Giant frozen vegetable operations to Mexico. Instead of paying workers $9 an hour in California, the company paid $5 to $8 per day in Irapuato, Guanajuato. In addition to low wages, Mexico's low land prices and lax environmental laws made prospects even brighter for American companies.[35]

[34]P Truell, "U.S. and Mexico Agree to Seek Free-Trade Pact," *The Wall Street Journal,* March 27, 1990, p. A3.

[35]"Mexico: The Salad Bowl of North America?," *Business Week,* February 25, 1991, p. 70.

Most of the US and Canadian opponents of NAFTA pointed to the potential for lost jobs and environmental hazards. They were also concerned about illegal immigration from maquiladores along the border. However, the Bush administration was involved with election-year politics. President Bush pushed the negotiations along swiftly, and on August 13, 1992, the United States, Canada, and Mexico agreed to terms that would create a regional trading bloc of 370 million people producing $6 trillion worth of goods and services each year. However, without the approval of the legislative bodies of all three participants, the pact would not take effect by the January 1, 1994, deadline.

Within days, the Democrats charged the bill would not adequately address issues such as environmental controls, worker protection, and incentives to American manufacturers to remain in the United States. Candidate Clinton declared, "We must sign a pro-growth, pro-jobs treaty with Mexico that does not sell out our workers or our environment."[36]

A broad coalition of manufacturers, farmers, and environmentalists descended on Washington. Despite the strong support of multinational corporations, such as Caterpillar Inc., Eastman Kodak, and Pfizer, and organizations that included the US Chamber of Commerce and the National Foreign Trade Council, passage seemed far from assured.[37]

The International Trade Commission's report in February 1993 concluded NAFTA would be only a small boon to the US economy. Although it would boost exports to Mexico, it would create fewer than 100,000 jobs in the United States by 1995. Other projections showed American companies would also lose 170,000 jobs to Mexico in the same period. While the border states would benefit, the Midwest, South, and West could suffer. Critics pointed to flaws in the study, noting it omitted the impact of exchange rates and potential devaluations of the peso on trade flows.

Trade representative Mickey Kantor sounded an ominous note when he said the United States would walk away from negotiations if environmental and labor issues could not be resolved satisfactorily. With Canadian Prime Minister Mulroney having resigned and Mexican President Salinas's term due to expire in 1994, Canadian and Mexican political problems also threatened to undermine the agreement.

Ethical Issues and NAFTA.   NAFTA raised three major ethical issues that were very difficult to resolve:

- What do businesses owe workers whose jobs are lost either at home or in other countries? Are lost jobs acceptable to a society? How can

---

[36]K Bradsher, "Gephardt Leads Charge Against Free-Trade Pact," *The New York Times,* July 28, 1992, p. D7.

[37]"How Many Broom-Makers Does It Take to Kill a Trade Pact?," *Business Week,* July 20, 1992, p. 29.

companies value different wage and benefit packages in various cultures? How should the tax burden be figured in? What compromises should companies that contemplate moving make?

· What do businesses owe the world in terms of environmental protection? Are there absolute standards (beyond those mandated legally) regarding worker safety and environmental protection to which companies should adhere? Should more stringent US or Canadian standards be adopted by all Mexican firms? If standards are written into the agreement, how should they be enforced?

· What do businesses owe their international communities? Should MNCs be responsible for developing infrastructure if they move across the border? Should they be responsible for workers' housing and sanitation? Should MNCs adopt measures to ameliorate the effects of poverty beyond those mandated in the agreement?[38]

Codes of Conduct

As we have observed, very few of a home country's laws cover the activities of that country's subsidiaries abroad. The first major attempt to regulate direct investment was made in 1929 by the League of Nations. The Great Depression quickly dampened interest, and the issue was dropped.

Since World War II, international organizations have met with little success in their attempts to implement international codes of conduct for MNCs. The few codes that exist cover all sorts of issues from investment decisions to health and safety and environmental standards. Most of them try to minimize the negative effects of industrialized-nation MNCs on developing countries. Three major international organizations have drawn up, or are in the process of formulating, codes of conduct for MNCs. These are described in the following section.

International Codes of Conduct

International Chamber of Commerce (ICC). The ICC's goals are to promote international trade and the free market. In 1972, the ICC issued the first voluntary code, which made a set of nonobligatory recommendations to the MNCs and their home and host countries. The code urged MNCs to provide host countries with operating plans and information about their activities. In addition, the ICC recommended that MNCs hire local labor and take on local partners in joint venture arrangements. It urged host countries to allow repatriation of profits, offer loans, and let the MNCs operate without unreasonable restrictions.

---

[38]M Kaeter, "NAFTA: Economic Boon or Ethical Boondoggle?," *Business Ethics* (March/April 1993), pp. 22–25.

Organization for Economic Cooperation and Development (OECD).   The OECD is a Paris-based group representing government, industry, and union interests in the industrialized countries. In 1976, it established voluntary guidelines covering financing, taxation, disclosure of information, competition, transfer of technology, and industrial relations. Under its guidelines, MNCs are supposed to follow the laws and regulations of the member countries, and nations are supposed to treat MNCs as though they were national companies.[39]

United Nations Code for MNCs.   The UN code, unlike the ICC and OECD codes, focuses on the problems of developing countries. Progress on this code has been painfully slow, and the code remains to be completed. The code promises to go further than the other two in dealing with human rights issues. It prohibits multinationals from doing business in South Africa and makes recommendations for consumer and environmental protection. In addition, it encourages MNCs to shift ownership to host-country nationals and promote heavy local involvement in decision making.[40]

A Domestic Code of Conduct for MNCs: The Japanese Example

In April 1991, the Keidanren, Japan's Federation of Economic Organizations, adopted a Global Environmental Charter to guide its corporate members. The basic philosophy behind the charter was that a company is closely bound up with the global environment as well as with the community in which it operates. Most of the large firms that belong to this organization are multinational or global companies. The Keidanren listed 11 guidelines for Japanese corporations to follow:

1. General management policies such as protecting the environment and ecosystems, making sure products are environmentally sound, and protecting worker health and safety.
2. Corporation organization systems such as developing internal systems to handle environmental issues. Implementing internal control systems to make sure that regulations are being carried out.
3. Concern for the environment includes all company activities, including site assessment. It ensures that product research design and development lessen environmental burdens. Companies are

---

[39]R Grosse and D Kujawa, *International Business* (Homewood, IL: Richard D Irwin, Inc., 1991), p. 461.
[40]F Debout, "Regulating the Multinational Corporations: A Rising Challenge" Northeastern University, Boston, MA, (Unpublished paper, 1987).

required to heed all national and local laws for environmental protection and even to set additional standards if necessary.

4. Technology development means that companies should try to develop innovative technology to conserve resources and protect the environment.

5. Technology transfer includes seeking the appropriate means for domestic and overseas transfer of technology consistent with environmental measures.

6. Emergency measures require Japanese corporations to use all their technology to remedy any environmental accident and, in case of a major disaster, to provide assistance even when they are not responsible.

7. Public relations and education entail the development of environmental educational programs for all stakeholders, including employees.

8. Community relations means that companies and their employees should actively participate in community environmental programs.

9. Overseas operations should come under the same guidelines of protecting the environment at home.

10. Contributions to public policies demand that companies share with others information gained from their experience. They should also propose rational systems to administrative authorities for formulation of environmental policies.

11. Response to global problems encourages companies to cooperate in scientific research on causes and effects of global environmental problems.[41]

International codes cannot—and do not—compel multinationals to behave according to the codes' recommendations. Nevertheless, many corporations have voluntarily adopted codes or procedures intended to guide their operations at home and abroad. Chapter 5 on ethics identifies some critical ethical issues multinational companies face.

In its code of conduct, General Dynamics devotes a separate section to overseas activities. This code observes that "special care must be taken to identify and accommodate the differences between international markets and those in the United States." It goes on to say, "a company operating on a global scale will inevitably encounter laws which vary widely from those

---

[41]Keidanren, "An Environmental Charter for the Business World," *Economic Eye* (Winter 1991), pp. 23–25.

of its own country. These laws may . . . conflict with one another . . . [General Dynamics'] policy is to comply with all laws which apply in the countries where [it does] business."[42]

Dow Corning Corporation developed an approach to ensure worldwide compliance with its code of conduct. Once a year, a Business Conduct Committee (BCC) audits the firm's 20 sales and plant sites across Europe, Asia, and Latin American. A typical issue the BCC might examine is how a plant in Brazil deals with local environmental regulatory authorities.[43]

Codes for guiding corporate behavior abroad are common among US multinationals and are becoming almost universal. They promote a uniform standard of behavior and make a declaration of good intent to the host countries in which their subsidiaries are located. Less common are serious attempts to monitor and enforce the codes. When companies have local personnel heading subsidiaries or have host country governments as partners, they generally find it more difficult to impose home country standards on personnel practices. Local standards of behavior take precedence, especially in developing countries.

Caterpillar Tractor's code, for example, states that the company intends to "select and place employees on the basis of qualifications for the work to be performed—without discrimination in terms of race, religion, national origin, color, sex, or handicap unrelated to the task at hand."[44] Obviously there are circumstances in which this statement, which is based on the US Civil Rights Act of 1964, that are unenforceable. In some countries, certain religions cannot work together peaceably and women cannot work with men. Still other countries do not encourage, or even allow, people with disabilities to participate in the workforce.

Problems can also occur when multinationals include statements about the environment. On the one hand, the statement demonstrates corporate concern for the well-being of the host country and sets a corporationwide standard of behavior. On the other hand, it may be legally or culturally impossible to live up to industrialized-country standards in a developing-country environment. Regardless of the difficulties of devising and complying with global codes, such codes prescribe a basic standard of behavior across nations. They also signal the seriousness with which MNCs regard their host countries' needs.

Even with codes and standards of behavior, MNCs find some issues difficult to manage. Host country and home country expectations and requirements cannot always be reconciled or resolved. Stakeholder groups in home and host countries may have conflicting or even irreconcilable demands.

---

[42]"General Dynamics Standards of Business Ethics and Conduct," August 1985.

[43]*Business International,* December 7, 1987, pp. 386–87.

[44]Caterpilllar Tractor Company, "A Code of Worldwide Business Ethics," in F D Sturdivant and L M Robinson, *The Corporate Social Challenge,* rev. ed. (Homewood, IL: Richard D Irwin, 1981), p. 443.

Managing MNC–Stakeholder Conflict

Thomas N Gladwin and Ingo Walter note that MNCs are "open systems that survive to the extent that they are effective in management of external demands, particularly of those interest groups [stakeholders] upon which they depend for a continuing flow of resources and support."[45] MNCs, they point out, face overlapping jurisdictions, host country nationalism, physical distance from headquarters, conflicting ethical systems, and differing social objectives. Although the individual issues they must manage are almost endless, the issues fall into the broad categories listed in Exhibit 18–2.

A discussion of all the issues with which an MNC must deal would occupy an entire book. In this section, we will examine some issues that present MNCs with challenging problems, fascinating opportunities, and frustrating constraints.

Managing the Legal System: Whose Laws Prevail?

No global legal system covers the operations of multinational corporations. Multinational corporations must conform to the legal systems in each country in which they are located. In many cases, countries sign bilateral treaties guaranteeing to honor each other's legal system and treat the subsidiaries of multinationals as though they were local firms. This system tries to ensure that MNCs will be treated fairly and equitably in one another's countries and will have legal redress in local courts.

The US legal and regulatory structure covers domestic and foreign-owned corporations located in the United States. But, except for some specific issues, the US law does not extend beyond US borders. However, Congress decreed US corporations should be covered by a few specific laws, regardless of where they operate and irrespective of local law. This extension of one country's law to its corporations outside its borders is called *transnational reach.* The laws and regulations described in the following sections affect US corporations and their subsidiaries wherever they operate.

Antitrust Legislation.   The Sherman Antitrust Act covers all US corporations wherever they operate and all foreign-owned corporations located on US soil. As we discussed in Chapter 8, restrictive business practices have been illegal in the United States for nearly a century. US courts determined that when multinationals take anticompetitive actions outside the United States, those actions affect US competitiveness. Therefore, the courts prohibit US multinationals from engaging in price fixing, production limiting, market allocation, or any other actions that limit competitiveness if those actions "substantially affect" US business. The Reagan and Bush administrations relaxed their enforcement of antitrust laws, but the Clinton administration seems to be taking a firmer line.

---

[45]T N Gladwin and I Walter, *Multinationals Under Fire: Lessons in the Management of Conflict* (New York: John Wiley & Sons, 1980), p. 5.

Exhibit 18–2

Stakeholder issues for MNCs

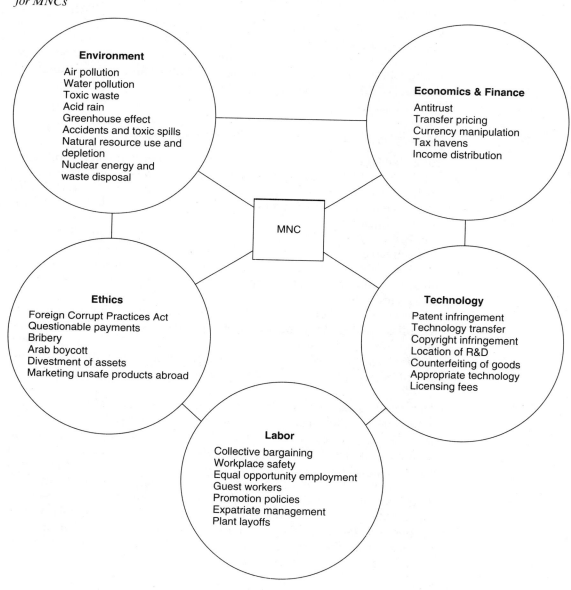

Environment

Air pollution
Water pollution
Toxic waste
Acid rain
Greenhouse effect
Accidents and toxic spills
Natural resource use and depletion
Nuclear energy and waste disposal

Economics & Finance

Antitrust
Transfer pricing
Currency manipulation
Tax havens
Income distribution

MNC

Ethics

Foreign Corrupt Practices Act
Questionable payments
Bribery
Arab boycott
Divestment of assets
Marketing unsafe products abroad

Technology

Patent infringement
Technology transfer
Copyright infringement
Location of R&D
Counterfeiting of goods
Appropriate technology
Licensing fees

Labor

Collective bargaining
Workplace safety
Equal opportunity employment
Guest workers
Promotion policies
Expatriate management
Plant layoffs

The Organization for Economic Cooperation and Development (OECD) is a 24-member group of the most highly industrialized nations. Its "Guidelines for Multinational Enterprises" establishes a voluntary set of principles for MNE operations, including guidelines on competitive behavior.

The European Community put its antitrust policy in the hands of the EC Commission when it forged the Treaty of Rome in 1957. The idea was to keep the issues out of the hands of national politicians. The Treaty of Rome gave the Commission the authority to crack down on price fixing, cartels, and other anticompetitive practices undertaken by companies operating across EC national borders. These rules apply to US, Japanese, and any other country's multinationals if those firms are incorporated within the EC.[46]

Foreign Corrupt Practices Act.   In 1977, Congress passed The Foreign Corrupt Practices Act (FCPA) in response to disclosures of questionable and illegal payments made to foreign officials by some US companies. Many of these payments were made by foreign sales representatives of US firms. More than 400 US corporations, including American Airlines, AT&T, Colgate-Palmolive, Exxon, Firestone, Gulf, ITT, Lockheed, and Textron, have admitted having made kickbacks, bribes, and other payoffs. Some of these companies and others falsified and manipulated company records to hide their activities.

The FCPA explicitly prohibited payments made to foreign officials to secure business. The five activities prohibited by the act were

1. the use of an instrumentality of interstate commerce (such as the telephone or the mails) in furtherance of
2. a payment, or even an offer to pay, "anything of value," directly or indirectly,
3. to any foreign official with discretionary authority or to any foreign political party or foreign political candidate,
4. if the purpose of the payment is the "corrupt" one of getting the recipient to act (or to refrain from acting),
5. in such a way as to assist the company in obtaining or retaining business for or with or directing business to any person.[47]

Accounting provisions were added to the antibribery prohibition to allow the Securities and Exchange Commission to monitor corporate expenditures. These provisions "require each issuer to make and keep accurate records, books, and accounts, which, in *reasonable* detail, accurately and fairly reflect the transactions and dispositions of the assets of the firm."[48]

---

[46]"The EC's Competition Policy," *The Economist,* March 14, 1992, p. 82.

[47]H Baruch, "Foreign Corrupt Practices Act," *Harvard Business Review* (January–February 1979), pp. 33–34.

[48]O R Gray, "The Foreign and Corrupt Practices Act: Revisited and Amended," *Business and Society* (Spring 1990), pp. 11–17.

Throughout the 1980s, the Reagan and Bush administrations repeatedly initiated legislation to amend and water down the FCPA. They and many businesspeople complained the law hurt US firms. Critics noted payoffs and donations were a way of life in much of the world. Since Japanese and many European countries did not prohibit their companies from following local customs, US firms were at a competitive disadvantage.

In 1988, one section of Reagan's Omnibus Trade and Competitiveness Act amended the FCPA. The amendment received little notice even though it was the first substantive change in the act since 1977. The amendment defined *reasonable detail* as the "level of detail and assurance as would satisfy prudent officials in the conduct of their affairs." A parent corporation was required to use reasonable influence to convince a foreign subsidiary to comply with the FCPA. If the US parent was in a minority joint venture position, it was required to demonstrate good-faith efforts in accounting practices.

The amendment limited future criminal liability to intentional actions to circumvent the law or falsify the firm's books. No criminal liability would be imposed for failing to comply with the FCPA's accounting provisions unless a person knowingly circumvented established internal procedures.

The amendment specifically prohibited payment to foreign officials for expediting or securing routine matters such as obtaining documents, processing papers, or securing phone, electric, or water services. At the same time, the amendment increased civil and criminal penalties. It increased criminal penalties from $1 million to $2 million for companies and $10,000 to $100,000 for individuals. Maximum imprisonment remained at five years. A civil penalty of $10,000 was established, and companies were prohibited from making payments for their executives.[49]

Overall, the FCPA has substantially influenced US companies doing business abroad. It remains to be seen how Clinton's Justice Department will pursue suspected violators.

Antiboycott Law.   In 1978, Congress passed a law making it illegal for American companies to participate in the Arab boycott of Israel. Arab countries began the boycott in 1955, when they blacklisted people and companies doing business with Israel. The principal participants were Saudi Arabia, Syria, Bahrain, Iraq, Jordan, Kuwait, Lebanon, Qatar, and the United Arab Emirates.

The law specifically prohibits American companies from furnishing information about past, present, or future business relationships with boycotted countries or blacklisted people. The exceptions to the law allow companies to comply with the boycotting country's requirements as to where the products originated and where they will eventually go and with that country's visa requirements. In other words, a US company *is* allowed to state

---

[49]Ibid.

that its products *are* entirely made of French, American, or Japanese raw materials and are wholly made in the United States, Japan, or anywhere else. Under the law, no American company is permitted to declare its products are not of Israeli origin even if the Arab country asks for that guarantee.

Over the years, many American companies have paid fines for breaking this law. Some have preferred to pay the relatively modest fines rather than suffer business losses. However, when federal investigators probed dealings between Baxter International and the Syrian government, the media drew public attention to the Anti-Boycott Law and its ramifications.

In December 1992, *The Wall Street Journal* reported that federal authorities believed Baxter International had agreed to ship millions of dollars of underpriced hospital supplies to Syria as a bribe to get off the Arab blacklist of companies doing business with Israel. Baxter was also charged with paying more than $1 million to various parties in the Middle East for architectural, engineering, and construction plans. A federal grand jury had been convened two years earlier to determine whether Baxter broke the law in getting off the blacklist in 1989. Although there had been many civil actions against US companies that violated the law, this was the first time a criminal inquiry took place.[50]

The focus of the investigation, G Marshall Abbey, was Baxter's general counsel and senior vice president. The investigation showed Baxter once agreed to build an intravenous fluid plant for Syria. After Jewish groups protested, Baxter changed its mind. In 1988, Baxter sold its intravenous plant in Ashdod, Israel, but it denied it sold the Israeli plant to get off the blacklist.

In March 1993, Baxter became the first US company to plead guilty to a felony charge of violating the US Anti-Boycott Law. It also became clear the details of the case would never have been known unless an angry former investigator for the US Department of Commerce had not blown the whistle. The investigator was told by his boss not to pursue the matter, but he persisted and eventually gathered evidence that a Baxter Middle Eastern unit and G Marshall Abbey had given the Arab boycott authorities more than 330 items of information in violation of the law.

Baxter International and Abbey agreed to pay the US government $6.6 million in civil and criminal fines. Abbey, who was not charged criminally, agreed to pay a civil fine of $101,000. Baxter was also prohibited from doing business in Syria and Saudi Arabia for two years.[51]

Within hours after the settlement, Baxter executives began conferring with security analysts and Jewish leaders in the United States. The company vowed it wanted to do more business in Israel and even offered to donate money to the Simon Wiesenthal Center in Los Angeles. For the time being,

---

[50]T M Burton, "Baxter Made Cut-Rate Deal with Syria to Escape Blacklist, U.S. Probe Finds," *The Wall Street Journal,* December 22, 1992, p. A3.

[51]T M Burton, "How Baxter Got Off the Arab Blacklist, and How It Got Nailed," *The Wall Street Journal,* March 26, 1993, p. A1.

it was unclear which Baxter executives would stay and whether some would eventually become a public relations liability and be fired.[52]

National Security Law.   This law states that US firms, their foreign subsidiaries, or foreign firms that are licensees of US technology cannot sell a product to a country if the US government has determined that the sale would affect national security. This law also covers the sale of US corporations or businesses to foreign companies. When a prospective buyer is a foreign government, the deal comes under particularly tough scrutiny.

The investigatory body that oversees foreign purchases of US companies is the Committee on Foreign Investment (CFIUS). CFIUS has representatives from the US treasury, defense, commerce, state, and justice departments. It also includes representatives of the Office of Management and Budget, the president's Council of Economic Advisers, and the US trade representative's office.

CFIUS examines prospective foreign takeovers of US firms to determine whether there is "credible evidence" that a purchaser "could threaten to impair the national security." If it does not find a problem, the deal can go through within 30 days. If it wants to take a closer look, it has 45 days to advise the White House on whether to approve the sale. The president can unilaterally stop any deal that he thinks will threaten national security.[53]

The US government tries to walk a line that encourages foreign investment while safeguarding national security. In October 1992, President Bush signed legislation requiring the president to explain to Congress whenever the president decides *not* to stop a sale. The legislation also prevents companies controlled by foreign governments from buying certain defense contractors until CFIUS explicitly approves them.

In fact, the issue of national security raises some very tricky problems. In 1993, more than 98 percent of the electronic packaging business, 80 percent of the inner workings of US-made computers, and 75 percent of the robotics markets were owned by foreign companies. How would CFIUS rule if a foreign company wanted to purchase the only remaining US manufacturer of a critical computer chip? Even if the chip had no direct defense application, could the sale be considered a national security risk?

Managing Labor: The Issue of Guest Workers

Europe.   The breakup of the Soviet Union and the former Eastern bloc nations spawned a flood of refugees to Western Europe. The industrialized countries of Western Europe feared the economic and social consequences of unrestrained immigration. Western European governments worried that

---

[52]T M Burton, "Baxter Seeks to Soften Fallout from Guilty Plea in Boycott Case," *The Wall Street Journal,* March 29, 1993, p. B1.

[53]R Wartzman, "Foreign Moves to Buy U.S. Defense Firms Face Higher Hurdles," *The Wall Street Journal,* November 2, 1992, p. A1.

immigrants were willing to work under less favorable conditions and for much lower wages than their local counterparts. These governments were also concerned that the exodus from newly freed nations would drain the workforce needed to rebuild those countries' domestic economies. Underlying these economic issues was the largely unspoken concern that immigration would exacerbate ethnic, religious, and racial tensions.

Eastern European workers were not the only immigrants into Western Europe. Before the breakups, factories in the newly liberated countries were filled with workers from Vietnam, Cuba, Pakistan, Sri Lanka, and Africa. Rather than go back to their own countries, some sought asylum in the West.

By 1992, more than one-half million foreign workers were laboring in the EC. Many were working for the companies involved in building Frankfurt's new airport and Euro Disney near Paris. Most of those workers and others on construction projects had no legal rights. They had no health benefits, received their meager wages in cash, and lived in substandard housing. Their employers did not pay taxes on their wages, thereby receiving tax breaks not enjoyed by companies that obeyed the law.

Investigators found that in 1991, 90 percent of German construction companies used illegal Eastern European workers. The companies refused to take responsibility for their workers. They and other large companies all over Europe asserted that subcontractors, over whom they had no control, dictated who worked and who did not.

By 1992, Western European government officials began to realize their worst fears. Racial and religious tolerance eroded as the economic burden of 17 million immigrants strained social services and economic opportunity. This huge influx came at the same time multinationals such as Daimler-Benz, Volkswagen, and BMW cut back production in Europe.[54]

Japan.   Even Japan, one of the most homogeneous countries in the world, attracts guest workers. In 1986, about 30,000 non-Japanese workers were employed in Japanese and foreign firms in Japan. When oil prices fell and construction work was cut back in the Middle East, workers from Pakistan and Bangladesh arrived on student visas, claiming they wanted to learn to speak Japanese. After the Olympics building boom in Seoul, Korea, waned and travel restrictions were lifted in South Korea, more than 600,000 Koreans arrived in Japan to look for work. They were joined by Thai and Filipina women who took hostess jobs in Japan, often working for gangsters in brothels, restaurants, and laundries.[55]

Some large Japanese MNCs hired guest workers, particularly if those workers had skills that were in short supply in Japan. In December 1989, the Justice Ministry revised Japan's immigration law, making it easier for

[54]A McCormick and K Moran, " 'Them,' " *Fortune,* July 13, 1992, pp. 96–98.
[55]"No Way to Treat a Guest," *The Economist,* June 2, 1990, p. 36.

foreign scientists, engineers, and other professionals to work in Japan. At the same time, the ministry tightened the rules on unskilled illegal immigrants, levying heavy fines and jail sentences on those caught after June 1.

By 1990, nearly 200,000 illegal unskilled workers were in Japan. A study conducted by a group of respected university professors found these workers could not alleviate Japan's acute labor shortage. Moreover, they concluded, the high cost of providing housing, training, and other social services outweighed any benefits the workers might provide. In fact, guest workers could even have an adverse impact on wages and working conditions of native Japanese. Since most sent their wages home, they did not contribute to Japan's economic development.[56]

In 1993, the plant closings and layoffs that had troubled the United States and Europe over the previous several years hit Japan. Even the largest companies, including Nippon Telegraph and Telephone, announced cutbacks. Although few outright layoffs occurred, it became clear Japan was entering difficult economic times. Would the Japanese show the same antipathy toward guest workers that Western Europeans had? Would Japanese politicians express some of the reservations about Latin American and Caribbean immigration that US members of Congress, mayors, and local representatives had communicated?

Protecting Intellectual Property

The stakeholder issue of intellectual property rights infringement is one of the gravest problems for MNCs. There is very little in the way of worldwide protection for intellectual property rights such as patents, copyrights, trademarks, and technological know-how. Sovereign nations and their own legal systems decide what protection they will give to the intellectual property rights of foreign companies that operate within their borders. Much of the protection for American businesses operating abroad lies in the support of the US government and the pressure it can bring to bear on host governments rather than on the force of law.

In 1986, the Reagan administration proposed new legislation to protect American trademarks, copyrights, and patents. Commerce secretary Malcolm Baldrige observed, "People are dancing all over the world to US [pirated] tapes—fast dancing and slow dancing."[57] He estimated the new legislation would (1) strengthen present laws against imports that infringe on US copyrights and patents, (2) make it easier for American companies to seek judgments under US trade laws, (3) ease antitrust restrictions on companies that work together to license certain technology, and (4) permit

---

[56]I Rodger, "Japan's Dim View of Guest Workers," *Financial Times,* January 25, 1991, p. 6.

[57]"White House Files Bills to Crack Down on Trademark Thefts," *The Boston Globe,* April 8, 1986, p. 53.

denial of trade preferences for nations that condone counterfeiting or pirating of US products.

Wherever possible, US courts continued to strengthen protection for American companies through the late 1980s. For example, in 1986 a federal judge ruled that US copyright laws extended to the internal design of computer chips. This decision came in a copyright infringement battle between Intel and Japan's NEC Corporation. The practical effect of the ruling was to strengthen US companies' position as the leading makers of microprocessors.[58]

But the computer industry was only one of many industries that needed protection from foreign competitors. The International Trade Commission (ITC) estimated that foreign competitors unfairly copied or stole US intellectual property, costing US companies between $43 billion and $61 billion in worldwide sales.

American companies responding to an ITC questionnaire cited Taiwan as the most frequent offender. Mexico came next, then South Korea and Brazil.[59] Thailand and Indonesia were also accused of being flagrant violators, especially of computer software copyrights and pharmaceutical patents. Some trade bodies even asserted that developing-country governments supported infringement because they could earn revenue through sales taxes on the exports of counterfeit goods.[60]

In 1987, the US government, on behalf of American corporations, increased pressure on Asian violators. For example, US trade officials threatened Thailand with the removal of preferential trade privileges that allowed some Thai goods into the United States duty free. Thailand's copyright and trademark laws protected only the works of its own citizens and those who were signatories to the Berne Copyright Convention, an intellectual property union that pledges reciprocal rights to its member states. Although the United States was not a signatory, US officials argued that Thailand was obligated to extend protection to Americans according to bilateral treaties. Under enormous American pressure, the Thai government moved to amend its copyright law to guarantee protection to US companies operating in Thailand.[61]

By the end of 1992, four years after the US Congress passed tough legislation against foreign counterfeiting, American companies still complained they were losing billions of dollars because of inadequate protection of intellectual property. A coalition of more than 100 of the largest US

---

[58]B R Schlender, "Copyright Ruling on Chips Called Boost for U.S. Producers Against Competitors," *The Wall Street Journal,* September 24, 1987, p. 7.

[59]"U.S. Losing Billions on Foreign Theft," *The Washington Post,* February 28, 1988, p. 84.

[60]P T Bangsberg, "Asians Act to Tighten Copyright Protection," *Journal of Commerce,* June 23, 1987, p. A1.

[61]N B Williams, Jr., "Asian Product Piracy Focus Shifts to Thailand," *The Boston Globe,* March 20, 1988, p. A9.

exporters urged the government to more closely monitor international agreements and fight the pirates. "Special 301" became one of the government's weapons in this battle.

Special 301, a section of the 1988 trade law, directs the US trade representative to openly identify those countries that fail to protect intellectual property rights. It was used in 1991 when India refused to protect US pharmaceutical and chemical patents. Carla Hills, then the trade representative, slashed $60 million worth of Indian products from the duty-free preference program for developing countries. Faced with penalties, most countries agreed to negotiate and give in to US pressure.[62]

Some notable progress, such as China's agreement to join the Berne Copyright Convention, has been made. However, the US level of frustration remains high. Unless a multinational agreement to protect intellectual property is included in the final GATT agreement, it is unlikely that US, Japanese, or European multinationals will be able to sufficiently protect their intellectual property against pirating by developing countries.

Summary

Multinational corporations have commonly shared ownership, resources, and strategy across countries. Their large size and power enable multinationals to circumvent many of the rules that constrain purely domestic organizations. Although some MNCs existed in the first half of the nineteenth century, it took the development of transportation and communication facilities and currency stability to enable companies to spread internationally. Companies engaged in direct foreign investment to avoid tariffs and diminish host countries' criticism that they were exploitative.

After World War II, reduced trade barriers and technological developments helped multinationals flourish. Enterprises changed in structure as they formed strategic alliances with other multinationals. In the 1980s, newly opened borders within the European Community and between the United States and Canada offered new opportunities, but also potential new barriers to trade. As industrializing host countries sought ways to exercise their autonomy, they urged international organizations to develop codes of conduct for the MNCs that operated inside their borders.

Multinational corporations face several major stakeholder issues. The legal environment for multinationals varies from country to country. The problems of guest workers and other labor issues are particularly important in the 1990s as Eastern European political blocs continue to crumble and Japan enters a recession. Intellectual property rights are still subject to violation, and counterfeit products flood world markets. Within each category

---

[62]N Dunne, "Idea Pirates 'Dodging Rules,' " *Financial Times,* December 3, 1992, p. 5.

are many issues and participants. In the absence of a comprehensive code of international law, governments will continue to intervene on behalf of their countries' corporations. Until such law becomes reality, multinationals will continue to operate in an uncertain political, legal, and economic environment—and one that varies from country to country.

Questions

1. What are the common characteristics of MNCs?
2. What environmental forces fostered the growth and proliferation of MNCs?
3. Discuss the evolution of codes of international conduct for MNCs.

Projects

1. Call or write to the United Nations to find out about the latest movement toward worldwide codes of conduct for MNCs.
2. Write a three-page paper more fully discussing each of the four US laws that cover American corporations wherever they operate.

BETA CASE 18
MULTINATIONALS

Brian Madison was not happy. He was worried about the renewed outcry over pharmaceutical companies' profits. In fact, President Clinton had just called the profits "shocking." For more than a year, a variety of stakeholders had criticized the industry for excessively high profits and taking advantage of unfair tax breaks.

Madison remembered the uproar in May 1992, when *The Wall Street Journal* and *The New York Times* carried stories about the Puerto Rican tax situation. The newspapers had analyzed a just released General Accounting Office (GAO) report suggesting that a 16-year-old tax provision provided a bonanza in profits for the US drug industry. The report was quick to point out that the pharmaceutical industry was already the top profit-making business in the United States.

Beta had opened its manufacturing plant in Puerto Rico in the spring of 1980. One primary reason for the Puerto Rican investment was the tax break provided by section 936 of the Internal Revenue Code. This provision, enacted in 1976, exempted US corporations' income earned in Puerto Rico from US income tax.

In May 1992, *The New York Times* reported that during the 1980s, 22 American drugmakers received $8.5 billion in federal tax credits. These tax credits were designed to increase employment in Puerto Rico. Indeed, the *Times* conceded, many people *were* put to work; Beta alone employed more than 700 people in Puerto Rico. Madison's calculations showed that for each worker hired, more than 4.7 other jobs were created on the island. The GAO report had omitted any mention of these jobs, which were indirectly supported by the pharmaceutical industry's spending.

Surely, Madison concluded, no one could deny employees contributed to the local economy by spending their wages and paying local taxes. In all, Beta's capital expenditures and investments had totaled more than $162 million in Puerto Rico since 1980.

The GAO report charged that in 1987, the last year for which it had data, US drug companies paid an average of $26,512 to their Puerto Rican workers and received an average of $70,788 in tax credits for each employee. That meant that for every dollar paid in wages to Puerto Rican workers during the year,

companies received an average of $2.67 in tax benefits.[63]

But this was another year and another president. Bill Clinton's Congress might be far more amenable to a revision of the tax code. In addition, public opinion seemed to be swinging toward some sort of control on drug company profits wherever the companies operated.

---

[63]M Freudenheim, "Tax Credits of $8.5 Billion Received by 22 Drug Makers," *The New York Times,* May 15, 1992, p. D3; H Stout, "Drug Firms Get Tax Break Exceeding $70,000 for Each Worker in Puerto Rico," *The Wall Street Journal,* May 15, 1992, p. A4.

MANAGEMENT'S CHALLENGE FOR THE REST OF THE 1990s

The last decade of the twentieth century may be the most exciting, uncertain, and potentially rewarding period in corporate history. The regulatory and legal climates are changing as President Clinton appoints new people to government agencies and the courts. Unanticipated national and international events have created an unstable and often unpredictable economic climate. Proliferating technological advances have added to the uncertainties, but they have also presented a panoply of opportunities.

Beta Pharmaceuticals, like other large companies, faces numerous decisions; some have to be made immediately, others can be deferred. Beta has encountered opportunities and problems and has experienced accomplishments and failures. As Beta assesses its performance at its annual June board of directors meeting, it might be any large American company struggling to take stock of itself and respond to the myriad economic and social pressures it encounters each day.

Beta had some good years in the early 1990s. Sales and profits were up. Research and development efforts were on schedule, although some glitches occurred. Brian Madison realized there was no getting around the fact that the recent past had been tranquil compared to the uncertainties Beta would face in the next several years.

The election of Bill Clinton in 1992 created new economic, social, and political environments. The technological environment presented challenges and opportunities more rapidly than companies could respond.

The administration's economic recovery package and health care reform bill created tremendous uncertainties domestically. It was still unclear what impact international events would have on American companies. The North American Free Trade Agreement might present major opportunities for Beta and other companies to manufacture and market in Mexico. Burgeoning Asian markets were also promising. Of course, the social issues attendant to overseas operations often differed greatly from those at home, and potential problems, such as hazardous waste disposal and workplace conditions, would have to be resolved.

Waiting for the last participants to straggle into the meeting, Brian Madison wondered whether the company could have done a better job of social issues management. He recalled how enthusiastic he and Joan McCarthy had been about implementing the social issues agenda. The public affairs department had taken its charge seriously. It had compiled several position papers and made recommendations to management on a variety of subjects. The department now had a sophisticated, complex computer program for stakeholder analysis and issue tracking. Madison and McCarthy met regularly to discuss each stakeholder priority and to try to anticipate new issues before they became problems.

But, Madison thought, no matter how well you plan, unexpected crises occur. Just look at the new problem Sam Powell's biotech division was facing with those radical animal rights people. The division was getting some fascinating and potentially lucrative results despite ups and downs in the early 1990s.

The FDA had refused to approve the division's major new drug, a bioengineered version of a protein the body uses to fight infection. The FDA faulted the division on its data collection, asserting the data did not show a clear reduction in deaths among the patients who took the drug. Sam Powell, while disappointed with the FDA's decision, was determined to continue data collection and gain the agency's approval.

Powell and his staff were really excited about their new initiatives in animal bioengineering. The US Patent and Trademark Office, which had imposed a five-year moratorium on approvals of animal-testing patents, resumed issuing the patents. Beta's scientists were particularly interested in producing genetically engineered mice that developed AIDS. The mice would help them and other scientists better understand the effects of anti-AIDS drugs on humans.

Powell and his people were stunned by the wave of stakeholder intervention they encountered. As soon as animal rights advocates got wind of Beta's plans, they began picketing company headquarters. They held signs accusing Beta of inflicting pain and suffering on laboratory animals and chanted slogans about Beta being a "killing factory." Employees were accosted, plied with literature, and accused of developing an army of small animals genetically programmed to suffer. A few activists tried to get into headquarters, and one actually punched a guard before the police intervened. Now picketers were kept away from the building's entrance, but they continued to hand out leaflets, chant, and verbally abuse employees.

Although Brian Madison was thoroughly annoyed with the activists' tactics, he acknowledged that ethical issues were involved here. In his own view, *people* with AIDS took precedence over mice with AIDS. He could not imagine how Beta or any other pharmaceutical company could operate without performing tests on animals. Beta's policy dictating humane treatment of animals was one of the most stringent in the industry. But, Madison privately admitted, if he were not involved in the industry, he might have a different outlook. In any case, Beta would have to deal with this whole area of animal testing very soon.

Finally, everyone was seated around the large walnut table. Madison welcomed them and moved quickly through the agenda. He had deliberately saved many of the social issues for last. He knew some problems defied quick and easy solutions. Others involved ethical judgments that were sure to be controversial.

At least Beta had appointed two new outside directors. One, a senior pastor with one of Detroit's largest African-American churches, was a bright, articulate man who brought a valuable perspective to meetings despite his tendency to preach rather than discuss. The other was an executive from a company that supplied some of Beta's chemical products. His expertise and breadth of knowledge had been highly beneficial to the company.

Beta had also resolved the issue of document retention. After talking to other drug company executives, Madison had concluded there would be more danger to the company if documents were destroyed than if they were kept. History aside, if Beta were involved in future litigation, dumping documents might appear to constitute a cover-up.

Madison looked down the table at Joan McCarthy and asked her to bring members up to date on issues her department had handled. He himself would have to address other items when she was finished.

McCarthy turned to her notes. "Gentlemen," she began, "the first issue is our advertising policy." Hearing the word *gentlemen,* Madison looked around. He suddenly realized McCarthy was one of only three women in the room; the other two were secretaries. Hiring women was certainly one area in which the company had not progressed, he thought. McCarthy reviewed Beta's previous advertising policy and enumerated the new guidelines the company had adopted.

McCarthy went on to discuss Beta's relationship with political action committees (PACs), noting the issue had been assigned to a policymaking committee. Discussion had been contentious and difficult. Nevertheless, the committee had reached a tenuous consensus, and a subcommittee was now drafting a document that would go to top management.

After covering a few other topics, McCarthy broached an ongoing concern: "Our next item is our policy toward women."

John West, vice president for human resources, interrupted, "Joan, I think that falls under my jurisdiction. As a matter of policy, we are making every effort to add qualified women in all positions. If President Clinton can appoint as many women as he has to high government posts, we ought to be able to bring more women into top management positions."

"I agree," Madison chimed in. "Last year, we committed ourselves to bringing women into these jobs. Obviously we have not made a sufficient recruiting effort, and maybe we have fostered a climate in which women don't have sufficient upward mobility. This issue isn't going to be put aside for another year. John, you and Joan will convene a task force by next month. We are going to systematically examine our policies and implementation record in hiring, promotion, and support for women.

"And while we are at it, we are also going to look at how well we have done with minorities. Demographics are changing, and our workforce has to reflect these trends. By this time next year, we are going to have a plan in place that everyone in this company understands. We are going to attract the most qualified and best-trained people in the industry. It seems highly unlikely to me that all those candidates are white males." At the other end of the table, the director sitting next to the pastor heard a soft, "Amen."

For the next two hours, the board and top managers discussed a variety of matters from the Beltane controversy and the E-Targa issue to tax breaks in Puerto Rico. Brian Madison could not shake off his uneasiness about this portion of the meeting. When it came to social issues, the company tended to either avoid decision making or react to situations only when they reached crisis proportions.

Despite Madison's personal commitment to planning, formulating, and implementing social issues strategy, Beta had accomplished much less than he had hoped. What could he, his top managers, and the board of directors do to ensure that issues were addressed in a rational, organized way? How could Beta more effectively anticipate issues before they became crises? How could the company convey to middle managers its commitment to the process? Even more important, what policies and management mechanisms could Beta develop to ensure that middle managers were committed to social issues policies and rewarded for their implementation?

INDEX